eBook and Digital Learning Tools

for

International Relations

Third Edition

ERIC B. SHIRAEV
VLADISLAV M. ZUBOK

Carefully scratch off the silver coating with a coin to see your personal redemption code.

05480619-FX4E-BV8E

This code can be used only once and cannot be shared!

If the code has been scratched off when you receive it, the code may not be valid. Once the code has been scratched off, this access card cannot be returned to the publisher. You may buy access at **www.oup.com/he/shiraev-zubok3e**.

The code on this card is valid for 2 years from the date of first purchase. Complete terms and conditions are available at **https://oup-arc.com**.

Access length: 6 months from redemption of the code.

OXFORD
UNIVERSITY PRESS

Directions to access your
eBook and Digital Learning Tools

VIA THE OUP SITE

Visit **www.oup.com/he/shiraev-zubok3e**

↓

Select the edition you are using and the student resources for that edition.

↓

Click the link to upgrade your access to the student resources.

↓

Follow the on-screen instructions.

↓

Enter your personal redemption code when prompted on the checkout screen.

VIA YOUR SCHOOL'S LEARNING MANAGEMENT SYSTEM

Log in to your instructor's course.

↓

When you click a link to a protected resource, you will be prompted to register for access.

↓

Follow the on-screen instructions.

↓

Enter your personal redemption code when prompted on the checkout screen.

For assistance with code redemption or registration, please contact customer support at **arc.support@oup.com**.

INTERNATIONAL RELATIONS

INTERNATIONAL RELATIONS

THIRD EDITION

ERIC B. SHIRAEV
GEORGE MASON UNIVERSITY

VLADISLAV M. ZUBOK
LONDON SCHOOL OF ECONOMICS

NEW YORK   OXFORD
OXFORD UNIVERSITY PRESS

Oxford University Press is a department of the University of Oxford.
It furthers the University's objective of excellence in research, scholarship,
and education by publishing worldwide. Oxford is a registered trademark of
Oxford University Press in the UK and certain other countries.

Published in the United States of America by Oxford University Press
198 Madison Avenue, New York, NY 10016, United States of America.

For titles covered by Section 112 of the US Higher Education
Opportunity Act, please visit www.oup.com/us/he for the latest
information about pricing and alternate formats.

Library of Congress Cataloging-in-Publication Data

Names: Shiraev, Eric, 1960- author.
Title: International relations / Eric B. Shiraev, George Mason University,
    Vladislav M. Zubok, London School of Economics.
Description: Third Edition. | New York : Oxford University Press, [2019] |
    Previous edition: 2016. | Includes bibliographical references and index.
Identifiers: LCCN 2019006860| ISBN 9780190648527 (paperback : alk. paper) |
    ISBN 9780190648589 (loose leaf) | ISBN 9780190648534 (paperback,
    instructor edition : alk. paper) | ISBN 9780190648541 (ebook, epub)
Subjects: LCSH: International relations.
Classification: LCC JZ1242 .S555 2019 | DDC 327—dc23 LC record available at
https://lccn.loc.gov/2019006860

9 8 7 6 5 4 3 2 1

Printed by LSC Communications, United States of America

Brief Contents

Contents

CHAPTER

3 Realism and Liberalism 78

CHAPTER

4 Alternative Views 116

Preface

Students today have unprecedented access to global political information. Statistics, video clips, tweets, maps, eyewitness reports, scholarly articles, and biographies—all are just a click away. Yet many students struggle with contextualizing and evaluating what they encounter. They lack the background to even begin studying international relations.

We have designed this book as an accessible guide to help every student understand the essentials of this dynamic and vital field. Students should leave the course with a more engaged attitude and a more analytical mindset—attributes that will serve them well for the rest of their lives. This third edition of *International Relations* offers a **clear learning framework** as well as a wide variety of **engaging pedagogical tools**. We introduce key concepts, actors, and issues; summarize major international events and developments; systematically present contending theories and approaches; and consider real-world applications of theory. Students will come away not only with a broad and deep understanding of key information and concepts but with the ability to **think critically and communicate more effectively**. In approaching the complexities of global issues, our goal is to foster an open mind and a willingness to take on new perspectives.

What's New in This Edition?

Responding to feedback from both instructors and students, we have made several significant updates in this edition of *International Relations*:

- A new chapter on the evolution of global politics (Chapter 2) provides essential historical context in one place for ease of reference.
- Realism and liberalism are now covered in a single chapter (Chapter 3) to more efficiently and effectively compare and contrast these two major theories.
- Chapter 1 includes a new discussion of both globalization and anti-globalization.
- A heavily revised Chapter 8 focuses on asymmetric threats, covering evolving forms of terrorism, cyberwarfare, and insurgency.
- New tables outline applications at different levels of analysis.

Throughout, we have incorporated discussions of both historical and contemporary developments, including the Syrian Civil War, the Russian-Ukrainian conflict, trade tensions between the United States and China, chronic instability in the Middle East and North Africa, and Brexit.

A Clear and Consistent Learning Framework

The chapters are organized by learning objectives so that students know what to expect. After the foundational Part I, each chapter presents material in the following order:

1. **Ideas.** We begin by covering basic concepts and definitions, key facts and developments, and major international problems related to the chapter's theme.
2. **Arguments.** Next, we present the main frameworks and approaches used to analyze these facts, events, and problems. We include a wealth of conceptual discussions, including major alternatives to realism and liberalism.
3. **Contexts and Applications.** After presenting key concepts, actors, issues, and theories, we show students how to apply a variety of approaches at individual, state, and global levels of analysis.

Each chapter closes with an extended Case Study that focuses on real-life ramifications and poses new questions. Chapter Reviews then revisit the learning objectives to help students structure what they are learning.

A Critical-Thinking Approach

We introduce the critical-thinking approach in Chapter 1 and carry it through every chapter. Rather than merely presenting facts and theories of international relations, we show students how to explain and evaluate them critically:

- **Debate**, **History Lab**, and **Case Study** sidebars all engage students in a dialogue and include questions to prompt in-class discussions and activities.
- **Check Your Knowledge** questions at the end of each main section not only help students track their progress but encourage deeper reflection.
- **Chapter Reviews** incorporate higher-level questions to help students achieve each learning objective.

This approach helps students extract more valuable, complex information from a collection of facts. In addition, it teaches them to be informed skeptics.

We know from experience that students need substantial context to fully understand contemporary issues and to apply analytical frameworks. In our new chapter on history as well as in abundant examples throughout the book (e.g., in History Lab sidebars), we give students the background to make connections. We examine parallels between past and present while considering the limits of historical analogies. This carefully integrated context not only gives students a way to frame information but also helps correct misconceptions.

An Emphasis on Engagement

International Relations engages students with the content through a robust set of pedagogical tools:

- **Learning Objectives** focus students on the key information to look for in each chapter.
- **History Lab** boxes present current or historical events and issues and contain Critical-Thinking questions that can easily be used for class discussions or written assignments.
- **Debate** boxes prompt students to consider their own views on a controversial question (What's Your View?).
- Icons point to relevant videos, simulations, readings, or links available at **www.oup.com/he/shiraev-zubok3e**.
- **Check Your Knowledge** questions appear toward throughout, checking student comprehension at key points.
- **Key Terms** are boldfaced, listed at the end of each chapter, and defined both in the margin and in the glossary at the back of the text.
- The extended analytical **Case Studies** at the end of every chapter feature in-depth explorations of noteworthy developments from the past several decades (such as the Cuban Missile Crisis, "misperceptions and realities" in the War on Terror, and "celebrity interventions" in humanitarian issues).
- In the **Chapter Reviews**, we map out the key concepts by learning objective and associate them with critical thinking questions.
- An online appendix on international relations (IR) careers provides descriptions of the major career categories as well as resources for finding positions in the field of IR.

Teaching and Learning Support

Oxford University Press offers instructors and students a comprehensive teaching and learning package of support materials for adopters of *International Relations*, Third Edition.

Ancillary Resource Center

The Ancillary Resource Center (ARC) at **www.oup.com/he/shiraev-zubok3e** is a convenient single destination for resources to accompany this book. Accessed online through individual user accounts, the ARC provides instructors with up-to-date ancillaries while guaranteeing the security of grade-significant resources. In addition, it allows OUP to keep instructors informed when new content becomes available. Register for access and create your individual user account by clicking on the Instructor's Resource link at **www.oup.com/he/ shiraev-zubok3e**.

The ARC for *International Relations* contains a variety of materials to aid in teaching:

- **Instructor's Resource Manual with Test Item File**—The Instructor's Resource Manual includes chapter objectives, detailed chapter outlines, lecture suggestions and activities, discussion questions, video resources, and Web resources. The Test Item File includes more than eight hundred test questions selected and approved by the authors, including multiple-choice, short-answer, and essay questions.
- **Computerized Test Bank**—Instructors can create and edit questions within the Computerized Test Bank, create randomized quizzes and tests with an easy-to-use drag-and-drop tool, publish quizzes and tests to online courses, and print quizzes and tests for paper-based assessments.
- **PowerPoint-Based Slides**—Each chapter's slide set includes a succinct chapter outline and incorporates relevant chapter graphics.

Course Cartridges

For qualified adopters, OUP will supply the teaching resources in course cartridges designed to work with your preferred Online Learning Platform. Please contact your Oxford University Press sales representative at (800) 280-0280.

Ebook

This text is also available as an ebook, which can be read on any browser-enabled computer or mobile device and comes with the ability to transfer individual chapters or the entire book offline.

Digital Learning Tools

International Relations comes with an extensive array of digital learning tools to ensure your students get the most out of your course. Several assignment types help teach core concepts, promote data literacy, and simulate real-world political challenges. Activities are optimized for mobile and include auto-graded assessments to immediately show students their results. Within a range of supported learning management systems, results can be recorded to gradebooks. Access to these activities is free with the purchase of a new print or electronic textbook. These and additional study tools are available at **www.oup.com/he/shiraev-zubok3e**, through links embedded in the enhanced ebook, and within course cartridges. The activities are described below.

Interactive Activities: Several simulations allow students to take the perspective of decision makers. Designed to be assigned as homework, these activities take approximately 5 to 20 minutes to complete. They conclude with assessments, and results can be automatically recorded in an interoperable LMS gradebook. Contact your local Oxford University Press sales representative for more information. Topics include:

Stopping an Epidemic
Building the USS Relief
Intervening in Bhutan
Preventing World War
Keeping the Peace in Gineau-Bissau
Negotiating with China
Negotiating the Lisbon Protocol
Free Trade
Climate Change

Video Activities: Links to relevant, timely videos show students the real-world applications of what they are studying. Each video includes a brief assessment to make the connection between course content and contemporary global issues. Topics include:

Kinds of Bias That Shape Your Worldview
In Praise of Conflict
How China Is (and Isn't) Fighting Pollution and Climate Change
How Nationalism and Globalism Can Coexist
The Rise of Isolationism
A Feminine Response to Iceland's Financial Crash
Why Nations Should Pursue Soft Power
The Need for Hackers to Prevent Cyberwarfare
The Intricate Economics of Terrorism
Keynesian Theory
Terrorism as a Failed Brand
Inside the Mind of a Former Radical Jihadist
The Case for Optimism on Climate Change
100 Solutions to Reverse Global Warming

Additional Online Study Tools: Many additional online study tools are available at www.oup.com/he/shiraev-zubok3e for students' self-paced learning and assessment. For each chapter, these include interactive flashcards, chapter review PowerPoint slides, key terms quizzes, chapter quizzes, chapter exams, short answer essay tests, videos, web activities, and web links.

Learning Management System integration: OUP offers the ability to integrate OUP content into currently supported versions of Canvas, D2L, or Blackboard. Contact your local rep or visit oup-arc.com/integration for more information.

Packaging Options

Adopters of *International Relations* can package **ANY** Oxford University Press book with the text for a 20 percent savings off the total package price. See our many trade and scholarly offerings at **www.oup.com**, then contact your local OUP sales representative to request a package ISBN. **In addition, the following items can be packaged with the text for free:**

- *Oxford Pocket World Atlas*, **sixth edition**—This full-color atlas is a handy reference for international relations students.
- *Very Short Introduction* **Series**—These very brief texts offer succinct introductions to a variety of topics. Titles include *Terrorism*, second edition, by Charles Townshend, *Globalization*, third edition, by Manfred Steger, and *Global Warming*, second edition, by Mark Maslin, among others.
- *The Student Research and Writing Guide for Political Science*—This brief guide provides students with the information and tools necessary to conduct research and write a research paper. The guide explains how to get started writing a research paper, describes the parts of a research paper, and presents the citation formats found in academic writing.
- *Current Debates in International Relations*—This volume presents forty-nine readings drawn from major scholarly journals, magazines, and newspapers including *Foreign Affairs, Foreign Policy, International Relations,* and *The Wall Street Journal*. It provides a broad selection of articles—both classical/theoretical and practical/applied—and steers students through major international issues, offering contending yet complementary approaches.

Acknowledgments

Invaluable contributions, help, and support for this book came from many individuals. We are grateful for the insightful feedback and critical advice of colleagues and reviewers, the thorough efforts of research assistants, and the patience and understanding of family members. We also take this opportunity to acknowledge the tremendous support we received at virtually every stage of this project's development from the team at Oxford University Press. Executive Editor Jennifer Carpenter championed this project from the start; editorial assistant Patrick Keefe saw to the details; the Development Editorial team under Thom Holmes provided constant support and good ideas before and during the writing stage; and Senior Production Editor William Murray guided the book through production. Thank you for your care and professionalism.

Special thanks to William Wohlforth from Dartmouth University; Mark Pollack, Richard Immerman, and Petra Goedde from Temple University; Mark Kramer and Mary Sarotte from USC; Norman Naimark, David Holloway, and Mikhail Bernstam from Stanford University; Thomas Blanton from the

National Security Archive; William Taubman from Amherst College; Odd Arne Westad and Mike Cox from the London School of Economics; John Ikenberry from Princeton University; Ted Hopf from the National University of Singapore; David Sears from UCLA; James Sidanius from Harvard University; David Levy from Pepperdine University; Bob Dudley, Colin Dueck, Eric McGlinchey, and Ming Wan from George Mason University; Cheryl Koopman from Stanford University; Philip Tetlock from the University of Pennsylvania; Christian Ostermann, Robert Litwak, and Blair Ruble from the Woodrow Wilson Center; Andrew Kuchins from the Center for Strategic and International Studies; Alan Whittaker from the National Defense University; and Scott Keeter from the Pew Research Center for inspiring us early and throughout our careers.

We received constant help, critical advice, and validation from our colleagues and friends in the United States and around the world. We express our gratitude to John Haber, Mark Katz, Dimitri Simes, Paul Saunders, Henry Hale, James Goldgeier, Eric John, Peter Mandaville, Jason Smart, Richard Sobel, Henry Nau, Martijn Icks, Stanislav Eremeev, Konstantin Khudoley, and Vitaly Kozyrev. A word of appreciation to Olga Chernyshev, Elena Vitenberg, Michael Zubok, John and Judy Ehle, Dmitry Shiraev, Dennis Shiraev, and Nicole Shiraev. We can never thank them enough.

We also thank the reviewers commissioned by Oxford University Press for this third edition:

Emily Acevedo, California State University, Los Angeles
Michael Allison, University of Scranton
Thomas Lefebvre, Trinity College

Theresa Schroeder, Radford University
Daniel C. Tirone, Louisiana State University
Robert Weiner, University of Massachusetts, Boston

We continue to be grateful to the reviewers of the first and second editions as well for their insightful and valuable comments.
Second edition reviewers:

Richard Aidoo, Coastal Carolina University
Juliann Emmons Allison, University of California–Riverside
Leslie Baker, Mississippi State University
Teh-Kuang Chang, Ball State University
David Claborn, Olivet Nazarene University
Mariam Dekanozishvili, Coastal Carolina University
Laura Dodge, George Mason University

Sean Ehrlich, Florida State University
Vaidyanatha Gundlupet, University of Texas at San Antonio
Marcus Holmes, College of William & Mary
Mir Zohair Husain, University of South Alabama
Colin D. Pearce, Clemson University
Marc Schwerdt, Lipscomb University
Daniel Tirone, Louisiana State University

First edition reviewers:

Victor Asal, State University of New York at Albany

Abdalla Battah, Minnesota State University, Mankato

Dylan Bennett, University of Wisconsin–Washington County Austin Carson, Ohio State University

Suheir Daoud, Coastal Carolina University

José de Arimatéia da Cruz, Armstrong Atlantic State University

Daniel Friedheim, Drexel University

Nathan Gonzalez, California State University, Long Beach

Gregory Granger, Northwestern State University of Louisiana

Eric A. Heinze, University of Oklahoma

Marcus Holmes, Fordham University Lisa Kissopoulos, University of Cincinnati Clermont College

Tobias Lanz, University Of South Carolina–Columbia Jeffrey Lewis, Cleveland State University

Patrice McMahon, University of Nebraska–Lincoln

Andrea Neal-Malji, University of Kentucky

James Rae, California State University–Sacramento

Christopher J. Saladino, Virginia Commonwealth University

We would be remiss if we did not express a word of gratitude to the administration, faculty, staff, and students at our academic institutions where we have consistently been provided with an abundance of encouragement, assistance, and validation.

Maps of the World

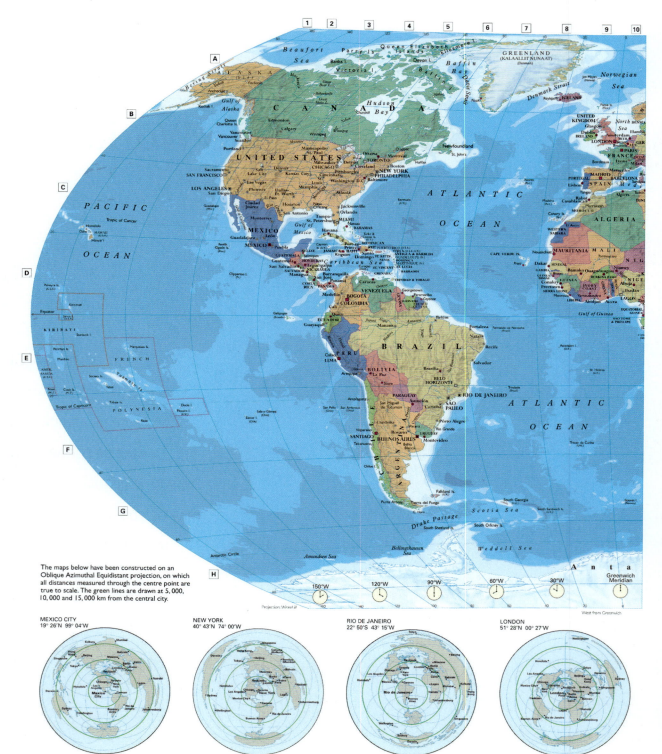

The maps below have been constructed on an Oblique Azimuthal Equidistant projection, on which all distances measured through the centre point are true to scale. The green lines are drawn at 5,000, 10,000 and 15,000 km from the central city.

MEXICO CITY
19° 26'N 99° 04'W

NEW YORK
40° 43'N 74° 00'W

RIO DE JANEIRO
22° 50'S 43° 15'W

LONDON
51° 28'N 00° 27'W

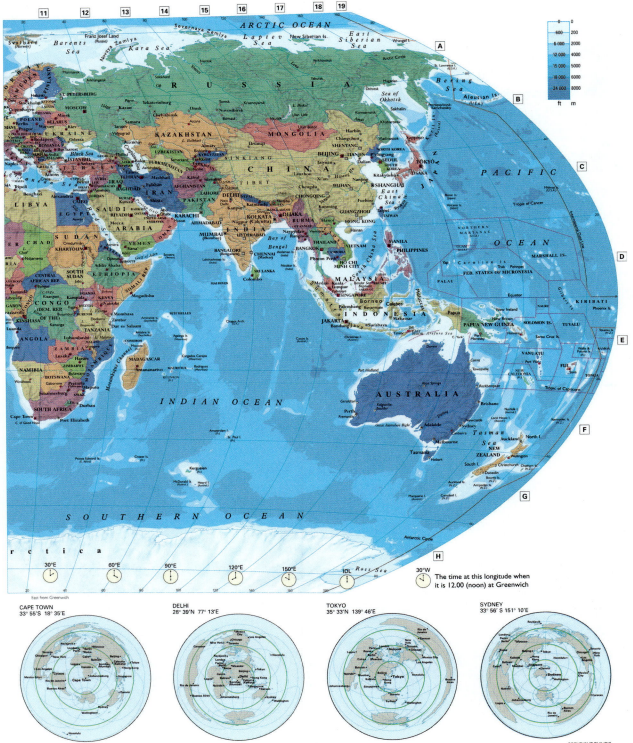

| 11 | 12 | 13 | 14 | 15 | 16 | 17 | 18 | 19 |

ARCTIC OCEAN

Franz Josef Land
(Russia)
Severnaya Zemlya
New Siberian Is.
Svalbard
(Norway)
Barents Sea
Novaya Zemlya
Kara Sea
Laptev Sea
East Siberian Sea
Wrangel I.

A

NORWAY
SWEDEN
Murmansk
Salekhard
Norilsk
Vorkuta
Arctic Circle
St. Lawrence I. (U.S.A.)
Bering Sea
Aleutian Is. (U.S.A.)

B

Helsinki
St. PETERSBURG
Arkhangelsk
R U S S I A
Yakutsk
Sea of Okhotsk
Magadan
Petropavlovsk-Kamchatskiy

Stockholm
Perm
Yekaterinburg
Tomsk
Krasnoyarsk
Komsomolsk
Sakhalin
Khabarovsk

ESTONIA
MOSCOW
Kazan
Chelyabinsk
Omsk
Novosibirsk
L. Baikal
Ulan Ude
Irkutsk

POLAND
Minsk
BELARUS
Kiev
Samara
Saratov
Volgograd
KAZAKHSTAN
Astana
Barnaul
Vladivostok
Sapporo

Prague
Berlin
UKRAINE
Odessa
Astrakhan
L. Balkhash
Almaty
MONGOLIA
Ulan Bator
Harbin
Changchun
NORTH KOREA
Pyongyang
TOKYO
OSAKA
Kitakyushu

AUSTRIA
HUNGARY
ROMANIA
Black Sea
GEORGIA
Tbilisi
UZBEKISTAN
KYRGYZSTAN
Urumqi
BEIJING
TIANJIN
SEOUL
SOUTH KOREA
Dalian

PACIFIC

C

Naples
GREECE
ISTANBUL
TURKEY
Izmir
ARMENIA
Baku
TURKMENISTAN
Ashkhabad
Dushanbe
SINKIANG
Lanzhou
Xi'an
Nanjing
SHANGHAI
East China Sea

Benghazi
Alexandria
CYPRUS
SYRIA
Damascus
Beirut
Baghdad
TEHRAN
Mashhad
AFGHANISTAN
TIBET
Chengdu
CHONGQING
WUHAN
Fuzhou
Taipei
TAIWAN

LIBYA
CAIRO
ISRAEL
JORDAN
IRAN
Isfahan
PAKISTAN
DELHI
Kathmandu
BHUTAN
DHAKA
Kunming
GUANGZHOU
HONG KONG
Hainan

EGYPT
SAUDI
RIYADH
KUWAIT
Shiraz
UNITED ARAB
EMIRATES
KARACHI
AHMADABAD
Kanpur
BANGLADESH
BURMA
MANILA
NORTHERN MARIANA IS. (U.S.A.)

O C E A N

D

CHAD
KHARTOUM
ARABIA
YEMEN
Mecca
OMAN
Muscat
MUMBAI (Bombay)
Nagpur
KOLKATA (Calcutta)
Rangoon
THAILAND
BANGKOK
VIETNAM
CAMBODIA
PHILIPPINES
Yap
PALAU
Caroline Is.
Truk
Ponpei
FED. STATES OF MICRONESIA
MARSHALL IS.

SUDAN
Sana'
Gulf of Aden
Socotra (Yemen)
BANGALORE (Bengaluru)
HYDERABAD
CHENNAI (Madras)
Andaman Is. (India)
Nicobar Is.
HO CHI MINH CITY
MALAYSIA
Medan
Kuala Lumpur
BRUNEI
INDONESIA
Equator
NAURU
KIRIBATI

CENTRAL AFRICAN REP.
ETHIOPIA
SOMALI REP.
Mogadishu
MALDIVES
Colombo
SRI LANKA
SINGAPORE
Palembang
Borneo
Celebes
PAPUA NEW GUINEA
New Ireland
TUVALU

E

CONGO
UGANDA
KENYA
Nairobi
SEYCHELLES
Chagos Arch.
JAKARTA
Bandung
Java
Surabaya
Makassar
Papua
New Britain
Port Moresby
SOLOMON IS.
Santa Cruz Is.

KINSHASA
TANZANIA
Dar es Salaam
Zanzibar
Mombasa
COMOROS
Agalega Is. (Mauritius)
Cocos Is. (Austr.)
Christmas I. (Austr.)
Timor
Arafura Sea
C. York
Darwin
Cairns
VANUATU
Port Vila
Wallis & Futuna Is. (Fr.)
SAMOA

ANGOLA
ZAMBIA
Lubumbashi
L. Malawi
MADAGASCAR
Antananarivo
MAURITIUS
RÉUNION (Fr.)
Rodrigues (Mauritius)
Port Hedland
AUSTRALIA
Townsville
Rockhampton
NEW CALEDONIA
FIJI
Suva
TONGA

NAMIBIA
BOTSWANA
Bulawayo
ZIMBABWE
Harare
Cargados Carajos (Maur.)
Alice Springs
Brisbane
Norfolk I. (Austr.)
Lord Howe I. (Austr.)
Tropic of Capricorn

F

Windhoek
SOUTH AFRICA
Pretoria
Johannesburg
SWAZ.
Maputo
Durban
Amsterdam I. (Fr.)
St. Paul I. (Fr.)
Geraldton
Kalgoorlie-Boulder
Perth
Fremantle
Adelaide
Great Australian Bight
Newcastle
Canberra
SYDNEY
Auckland
North I.
Kermadec Is. (N.Z.)

INDIAN OCEAN
Cape Town
C. of Good Hope
Port Elizabeth
Prince Edward Is. (S. Africa)
Crozet Is. (Fr.)
Kerguelen (Fr.)
Tasman Sea
Melbourne
Hobart
Tasmania
NEW ZEALAND
Wellington
South I.
Christchurch
Dunedin
Chatham Is. (N.Z.)
Bounty Is. (N.Z.)
Antipodes Is. (N.Z.)

G

r c t i c a
McDonald Is. (Austr.)
Heard I. (Austr.)
Macquarie I. (Austr.)
Campbell I. (N.Z.)
Auckland Is. (N.Z.)

SOUTHERN OCEAN

Antarctic Circle

H

30°E   60°E   90°E   120°E   150°E   IDL   Ross Sea   30°W

East from Greenwich

The time at this longitude when it is 12.00 (noon) at Greenwich

0	0
600	200
3 000	2000
12 000	4000
15 000	5000
18 000	6000
24 000	8000
ft	m

CAPE TOWN
33° 55'S 18° 35'E

DELHI
28° 39'N 77° 13'E

TOKYO
35° 33'N 139° 46'E

SYDNEY
33° 56'S 151° 10'E

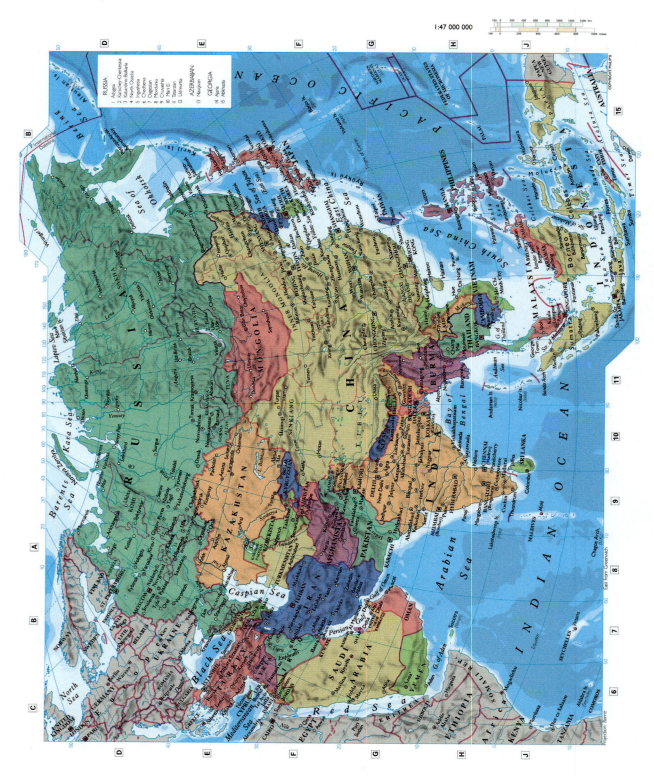

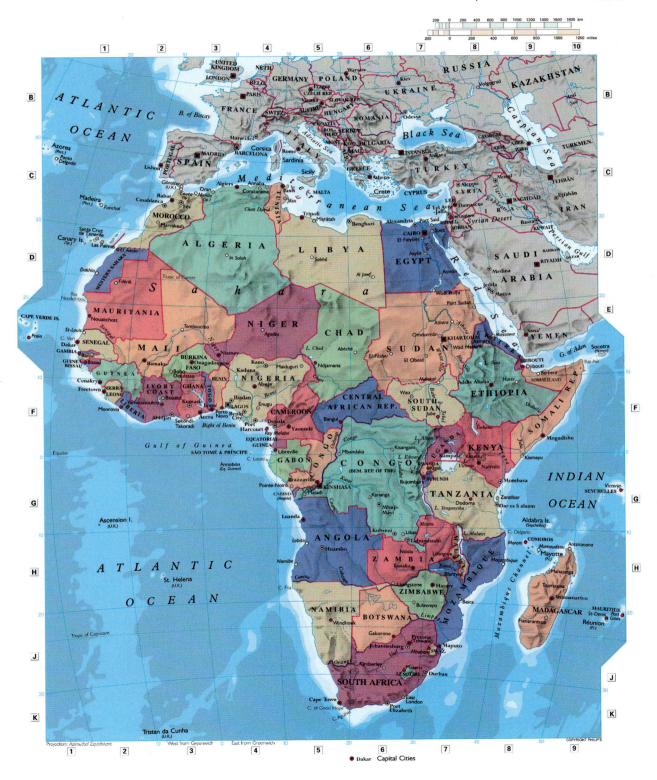

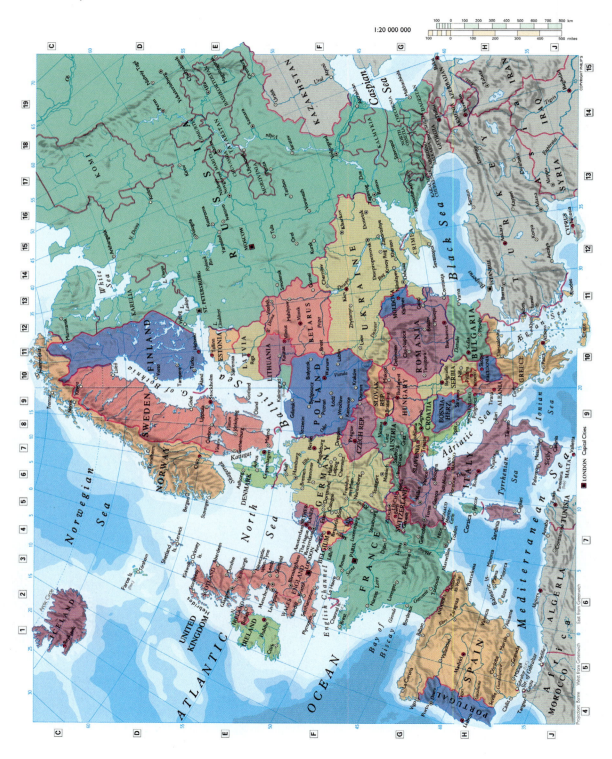

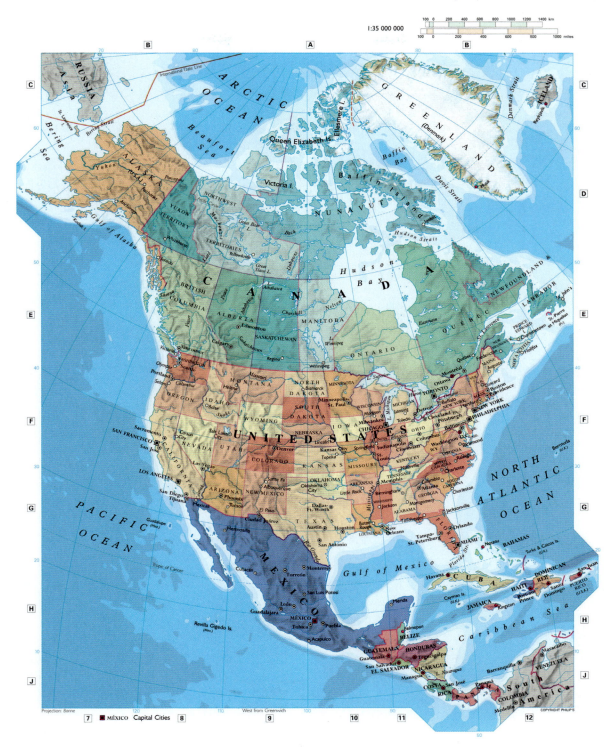

1:35 000 000

Projection: Lambert's Azimuthal Equal Area

■ LIMA   Capital Cities

COPYRIGHT PHILIP'S

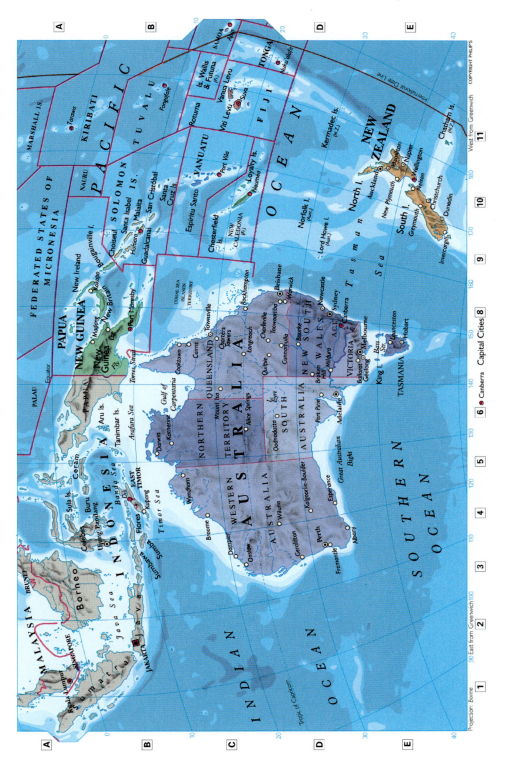

Introducing International Relations

> *It is possible to live in peace.*

— MAHATMA
GANDHI (1869–1948)

The global political world changes fast. Consider these examples from recent history:

- Brexit, the United Kingdom's withdrawal from the European Union (EU) in 2019 and later. How will this development affect the stability and future of the EU?
- Devastating civil wars in Syria and Yemen. What do ongoing instability and bloodshed in the Middle East mean for international peace?
- Rising tensions between the United States and Russia. Is the West adequately prepared to confront evolving security challenges such as cyberattacks and interferences with national elections?

In this introduction to international relations, we respect history as a key source of knowledge while thinking critically about contemporary events. Because the world is dynamic and complex, we discuss a broad range of ideas and arguments in approaching questions of vital importance. For instance, which international challenges should take priority as we face environmental, nuclear, economic, and terrorist threats? We will see that international relations involves not only states, such as the United States and China, but also international actors such as the EU, whose critical roles are constantly changing. Studying international relations is urgent and vital in a world facing matters of war, pollution, poverty, human rights violations, and injustice. All these problems require not only critical understanding but also educated solutions.

Previous page: U.S. border wall at Tijuana, Mexico. Why do sovereign states need to protect their borders? Do you or don't you personally believe in a possibility of a borderless world and why?

We invite you to join us in considering questions of global politics across time, cultures, borders, and disciplines, not as a passive reader but an active explorer. The better you understand the world, the better you can navigate it. Welcome to the study of international relations.

Learning Objectives

1.1 Key Concepts in International Relations

How do countries and nonstate global entities interact? What causes instability and war? How does global politics affect your life? **International relations (IR)** is the study of interactions among the world's governments and nonstate actors, including international organizations, multinational corporations, and individuals participating in global politics. These interactions take many forms. They may be territorial disputes, negotiations about migration, trade agreements, economic sanctions, charitable activities, court decisions affecting another country, or international aid deliveries following a natural disaster. A subfield of political science, international relations is partly about ideas, arguments, and theories. It is also an applied field because it seeks to understand the realities of today's world and to suggest solutions to the world's many problems.

international relations (IR) The study of interactions among states, as well as the international activities of nonstate organizations.

Facets of IR: Security, Law, and Political Economy

Even an abridged list of topics within international relations can quickly become long, but several remain at its core year after year. We can group these into three main areas: (1) international security, (2) international law, and (3) international political economy.

1. **International security** refers to issues that governments and non-state actors face in striving for mutual safety at the global level. Countries try to secure their borders, maintain armed forces, and make

international security Issues that governments and nonstate actors face in striving for mutual safety at the global level.

deals with other countries to reduce outside threats and respond to aggressions. Diplomats, nongovernmental groups, social media, journalists, and private individuals can influence security-related problems. One of the most important issues in global politics is that of war and peace. In today's world, many countries and nonstate actors try to avoid the use of military force and act through diplomacy. Others use surreptitious tactics such as spreading misinformation and conducting cyberespionage or cyberattacks. At the same time, however, military confrontations continue. Stop for a moment and identify at least two significant military conflicts today. Where are they? Who is fighting? Why are they fighting? Ask your professor to discuss them in class.

international law Mutually agreed rules and norms for international interactions among governments, institutions, organizations, and individuals.

2. **International law**, the second main area of study, is about mutually agreed formal rules and norms for international interactions among governments, institutions, organizations, and individuals. Why do you need to show your passport when you cross the border to visit Canada? Could you become a citizen of two, three, or even more countries? If you are a foreign tourist in France, can you be charged with jaywalking in Paris? We will learn that international law is effective only as long as countries recognize and follow it; there is no supreme power above countries to enforce it.

international political economy (IPE) The interactions of politics and economics in an international context.

3. The study of **international political economy** focuses on economic relations and how global, regional, and local markets affect individual countries and the international system. Countries buy and sell their natural resources and manufactured products, offer and accept financial assistance, and support or block certain economic transactions with other countries. For example, check the labels on your clothes to see where they were manufactured. Why do your clothes cost what they do? International agreements can reduce trade barriers and help countries buy less expensive products and services from other countries. These actions can have domestic implications, however: at companies that can't compete with the lower prices, jobs are at stake.

The field of IR differs from comparative politics, which focuses on comparing political entities and systems rather than on how they interact. These disciplines sometimes overlap, however, and IR has become increasingly multidisciplinary. An IR specialist nowadays should know the basics of fields such as government, economics, history, sociology, cultural studies, psychology, and military studies, to name a few. For instance, if you study contemporary diplomacy and wars in the Middle East, you have to know the history of the Persian and Ottoman empires and the Arab caliphates (areas under Islamic rule). You must have an understanding of the different strands of Islam and the importance of cultural identity. You have to examine the historic role of the West and other countries in the region. You need to learn the history and politics of Israel and Saudi Arabia, just as an example. You also need to learn about the growing role of women in the region's affairs. And you have to be

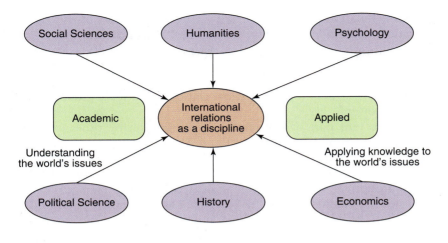

FIGURE 1-1
The increasingly multidisciplinary field of international relations.

familiar with the political economy of oil and natural gas. In brief, IR scholars and decision makers must gather and analyze data and ideas from many fields. (See Figure 1-1.)

States and Sovereignty

State sovereignty is a central concept in the study of international relations. A **state** is commonly defined as a governed entity with a settled population occupying a permanent area with recognized borders. We will use the terms *state* and *country* interchangeably in this text. **Sovereignty** refers to independent authority over a territory. In the context of international relations, states (countries) are sovereign when they have no authority above them that mandates what they do within their territory, such as collecting taxes. India and Pakistan, for example, became sovereign states in 1947, following colonial rule by the United Kingdom.

As history shows, territorial and religious disputes frequently cause international military confrontations. Sovereignty is not only about territory but about the allegiance of the people living within it. As a concept, sovereignty emerged in Europe in 1648, when a handful of Christian kingdoms and principalities forged an agreement after many years of warfare. The goal was twofold: (1) to keep the Roman Catholic Church from dictating the religious identity of their population, and (2) to keep coexisting states from interfering in each other's domestic affairs.

Several factors underpin state sovereignty, including international treaties and states' economic and military capacities; sovereignty is thus stronger in some states than in others. Colonial legacies have also played an important role. For instance, the official state boundaries of many African countries emerged as a result of colonization by Western powers within the last two hundred years. These boundaries largely ignored the ethnic and tribal

state A governed entity with a settled population occupying a permanent area with recognized borders.

sovereignty The supremacy of authority exercised by a state over its population and its territory.

divisions that had existed for centuries. Western politicians, mostly from Britain, France, Belgium, Portugal, Germany, and Italy, guided cartographers and ethnographers in drawing the borders of new countries—often with a pencil and a ruler. Some African governments, such as the Central African Republic and Somalia, are currently facing significant challenges related to control of their territory, battling numerous tribal warlords and rebel groups that challenge state power.

An important part of sovereignty is recognition by other states. Consider the case of Somaliland and Puntland. They declared independence from Somalia in the 1990s, but most other countries do not consider them independent. And in an example that has serious implications for international security, groups of Islamic fundamentalist rebels operating in Syria and Iraq proclaimed the Islamic State of Iraq and the Levant (known as ISIS) in 2013. Other countries did not recognize ISIS and condemned its rampant violence. Beginning in 2014, the United States, Russia, and other countries have sent armed forces to combat and defeat ISIS.

internal affairs A state's domestic matters or policies in which other states or organizations are not involved.

According to the definition of sovereignty, a state can consider what happens within its borders' **internal affairs** as strictly domestic matters or policies in which other states or organizations are not involved. For example, internal affairs can include border control, army building, currency printing, tax collection, and legislation. In Chapter 6, we will discuss countries' jurisdiction, or their official right to make legal decisions and judgments within their territories. States can limit their own sovereignty, however, by delegating authority to international organizations (such as the United Nations) or by complying with international treaties. Most members of the European Union voluntarily gave up their currencies (such as marks, franks, liras, and pesos) to establish one common currency, the euro, in 1999. In international relations, the concept of sovereignty is essential, and there are many instances in which it is limited by other states or taken away forcefully. The ultimate violation of sovereignty is occupation by foreign powers.

Nations and Nation-States

nation (1) A group of people who have established sovereignty over a territory and set up internationally recognized borders. (2) A large social group sharing common cultural, religious, and linguistic features and distinguishing itself from other large social groups.

The terms *state, country,* and *nation* are often used interchangeably but are not truly synonyms. In most cases in this book, we use *state or country* because *nation* has several meanings. We can think of a nation as a legal term or as a collective identity. In legal terms, a **nation** is a group of people who have established sovereignty over a territory and set up internationally recognized borders. About two hundred states in existence today (and the number is always changing) consider themselves nations, recognized—and this is very important—by a majority of other states. A nation may also refer to a large social group sharing common cultural, religious, and linguistic features and distinguishing itself from other large groups. It is common to say the "Finnish nation," referring to people who live on the territory of Finland, speak the Finnish language, and have ancestors of Finnish origin. The meaning of a phrase such as "British nation," however, is more complicated, as the British population is extremely diverse. If a distinct cultural or ethnic group forms

History Lab Alsace-Lorraine

Between 1871 and 1945, France and Germany battled for control of a territory known as Alsace-Lorraine (see Map 1-1). People who live in this border region today are ethnic Germans but also speak French, and the territory now belongs to France. Following the Franco-Prussian War (1870–1871), the newly formed German Reich annexed (took over) Alsace-Lorraine. In 1919, however, after Germany's defeat in World War I, France reclaimed its sovereignty over the territory. Not for long. When Germany attacked and occupied France in 1940, the residents of the region became citizens of Hitler's Third Reich. Only in 1945, when the British-American troops defeated the Nazis, did Alsace-Lorraine again become part of France.

After these many years of violent disputes, Strasbourg, the principal city in this region, became the official seat of the European Parliament in 1999. There, representatives from France, Germany, and other member states meet to discuss and resolve common issues.

CRITICAL THINKING

Labs are useful for gathering facts, testing hypotheses, and discussing research results. "History Labs" look in depth at key historical developments, posing questions about what happened and why. Using the case of Alsace-Lorraine, an area that was contested for decades between France and Germany, we can explain the conflicts between India and Pakistan, Armenia and Azerbaijan, China and Japan, Argentina and the United Kingdom, Israel and Syria, Russia and Ukraine, Moldova and Russia, to name a few. Why do people fight over territories? ❶ What factors other than control of resources can contribute to territorial conflicts? Consider issues such as security concerns, pride, or ethnic identity. ❷ How is it that the territorial dispute in Alsace-Lorraine was finally resolved, yet scores of disputes in other places continue to cause international tensions? What lessons can we draw from this conflict?

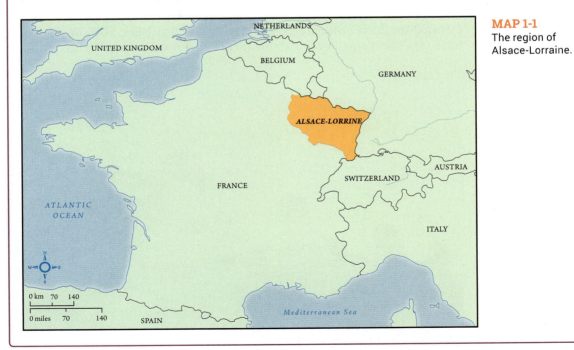

MAP 1-1
The region of Alsace-Lorraine.

nation-state A sovereign state formed by a distinct cultural or ethnic group.

separatism The advocacy of or attempt to establish a separate nation within another sovereign state.

a sovereign state, it is frequently called a **nation-state**. (We will return to the discussion of nation-state and nationalism in Chapter 4.)

Ethnic minorities' claims for nationhood pose a constant challenge to many sovereign states. Moreover, some scholars claim that nations can be constructed even before they acquire a physical space and gain sovereignty over it. **Separatism** is advocacy of or attempts to establish a separate state within an existing sovereign state. States almost always resist separatism, seeing it as a grave threat to state sovereignty. In 2017 and later, many people in the autonomous Spanish province of Catalonia, which has its own language (Basque), demanded national independence. The Spanish government, however, refused to recognize Catalonia as an independent state. In another example, Kurdish nationalists in Turkey and Iraq often speak of the *Kurdish nation*, although there is no Kurdistan as a sovereign state with internationally recognized borders. Turkey, in fact, has gone so far as to outlaw the pursuit of Kurdish national identity. A final contemporary example is China's struggle against national separatism in its predominantly Muslim area Xinjiang. What other examples could you add to this list?

Globalization and Anti-Globalization

globalization The growing interdependence of countries and their economies, the growing importance of international exchanges of goods and ideas, and increased openness to innovation.

Two opposing tendencies are present in today's international developments. **Globalization** refers to the growing irrelevance of state borders, the importance of international exchanges of goods, services, and ideas, and increased openness to innovation. It is a major shift in politics, communications, trade, and the economy at large. Cellular phones designed in Finland and manufactured in China now ring in African towns and villages. Millions of people have jobs and bring home a stable income because factories create products

Turkey has outlawed the pursuit of Kurdish national statehood. Why don't some large ethnic groups, such as the Kurdish people, have a sovereign state?

for sale in other countries. Communications, travel, and international commerce have eliminated many political, legal, ideological, and cultural barriers. Optimists believe that through globalization the world will abandon old prejudices. Such a world is destined to become more dynamic, flexible, and tolerant than ever before (Bhagwati 2004). Mutual openness and trust are the most reliable foundations for a stable and prosperous world (Ikenberry 2011a).

There is, however, resistance to globalization as an ideal. **Anti-globalization** is an array of international movements that see globalization as aggravating old problems and creating new ones. One of the most obvious problems is the growing contrast between wealthy and poor regions—often labeled the global North and the global South. Advocates of anti-globalization offer a variety of responses, ranging from a more active role for the state in economic affairs to religious fundamentalism. Countries like China and Russia have taken practical steps to restrict the access of their citizens to the global Internet. Furthermore, some scholars argue that major institutions and global trade agreements have often harmed poor countries instead of helping them (Stiglitz, 2017). Some believe that globalization helps primarily powerful international monopolies, corrupt governments, and bureaucracies. Others maintain that people even in wealthy countries lose jobs because of globalization: unemployment occurs when corporations transfer their production to other places where labor is cheap (Held 2007).

anti-globalization
Resistance to globalization, or an active return to traditional communities, customs, and religion.

Check Your Knowledge

1. Define and explain state sovereignty.

2. Give two interpretations of the term *nation*.

3. What is separatism? Is separatism always dangerous for international peace? Why or why not?

4. Compare and contrast globalization and anti-globalization. Could there be, in your view, a policy protecting from the negative impacts of globalization and anti-globalization?

1.2 Key Actors in International Relations

The most important actors in international relations are those entities that have both the resources and the means to implement their decisions in the international arena. Such decisions are typically based on specific interests, such as political, economic, and ideological concerns. The actors also have the will and the means to influence other key international actors. Although, ultimately, there are individuals who make decisions, the study of international relations commonly refers to institutions and organizations as key actors, including governments, intergovernmental, and nongovernmental organizations.

State Government and Foreign Policy

Citizens today cannot gather in a city square to vote directly on international trade agreements or foreign wars. (Of course in free societies people can petition before governments and openly demonstrate to have their voices heard). Instead, they have representatives who possess the authority to deal

state government An institution with the authority to formulate and enforce its decisions within a country's borders.

foreign policy A complex system of actions involving official decisions or communications related to other nation-states, international institutions, or international developments in general.

diplomacy The practice of managing international relations by means of negotiations.

with international affairs. These officials are either elected or appointed to represent a **state government** (which we may also call a *national government* or simply a *government*)—an institution with the authority to formulate and enforce its decisions within a country's borders.

State governments conduct **foreign policy**—actions involving official decisions and communications, public or secret—with other state governments, nongovernmental organizations, corporations, international institutions, and individual decision makers. Ministries of foreign affairs usually implement a country's foreign policy via embassies or other official offices in foreign countries. The content of foreign policy ranges from peace treaties to threats of force; from trade agreements to trade sanctions; and from scientific, technical, and cultural exchange programs to visa and immigration policies (We will discuss foreign policy in Chapter 2 and in many other places in the book.)

Diplomacy is the practice of managing international relations by means of negotiations. State governments usually prefer diplomatic means of interaction, but violence or the threat of it frequently backs diplomatic moves. In cases where formal diplomatic relations do not exist between two states, informal channels of communication may involve third parties, special emissaries, and even personal contacts. For example, for many years Iran and the United States did not have official diplomatic relations. Mediators included Pakistan, Turkey, and international organizations. In 2015, Tehran and Washington signed a landmark treaty, together with Russia, China, France, the United Kingdom, and Germany, that placed limits on Iran's nuclear programs (Magri and Perteghnella 2015). However, this treaty has been frequently criticized by the Trump administration, until finally, in 2018, the United States pulled out of this agreement. You can check the status of this treaty or a new set of negotiations today.

In today's democratic states (such as the United Kingdom, the United States, or India), all three branches of government—*executive*, *legislative*, and *judicial*—commonly participate in foreign policy:

- Within the *executive branch*, government structures dealing with international relations include a ministry or department of foreign affairs. (In the United Kingdom, it is called the Foreign Office; in the United States, it is the State Department; in India, it is the Ministry of External Affairs.)
- The *legislative branch* passes laws about the direction and handling of foreign policy. In democratic countries, parliaments commonly ratify (or approve) international agreements signed by state executive leaders. In the United States, every international treaty signed by the president must be "advised and consented to" by a two-thirds vote in the Senate. Congress also allocates money to conduct foreign policy according to the federal budget. Congress may also instantly stop financing policies or specific actions related to foreign policy.
- The *judicial branch* is involved in foreign policy in several ways. For example, courts can make assessments about the applicability of certain international laws or agreements on the territory of the state. The courts also decide on claims submitted by foreign countries including businesses and

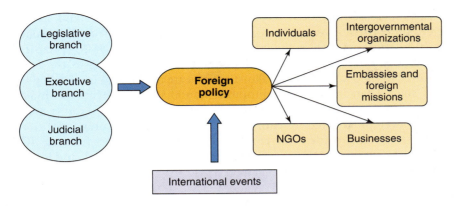

FIGURE 1-2 How foreign policy works in democratic states.

private individuals. (In Chapter 6, we will discuss international law in more detail.)

In some countries, such as the United States and France, the executives have significantly more influence on foreign policy than in other countries, such as the United Kingdom and the Netherlands. Differences between foreign policy executed by democratic and nondemocratic governments are also important, as we will discuss later in the book. Figure 1-2 gives an overview of how foreign policy works in democratic states. Crafting foreign policy is a complex process based on traditions, competition, alliances and treaties, domestic groups of interests, public opinion, and the impact of the media.

Intergovernmental Organizations

Besides sovereign states, **intergovernmental organizations (IGOs)** are another major player in international relations. These are associations of several nation-states or nongovernmental organizations established for the purpose of international cooperation. The most prominent example is the *United Nations (UN)*, which was formed in 1945 to increase the collective responsibility of its member states, keep peace through a voluntary collective effort, and serve as an authoritative mediator in international conflicts. (In Chapters 3 and 6, we will discuss its role in depth.)

Other IGOs are created for a combination of strategic economic, security, and political purposes. We will see later how the *North Atlantic Treaty Organization* (NATO) led a military action in Bosnia in the 1990s, in Afghanistan after 2001, and against the Libyan government in 2011. We will also describe and explain the role of the Shanghai Cooperation Organisation in shaping security policies in Eurasia and globally. Still other IGOs pursue primarily economic goals; the Organization of Petroleum Exporting Countries (OPEC), for example, sets standards for how much oil member states should produce and sell on the global market. Of course, the economic and political goals of IGOs are often interconnected and interfere with one another. OPEC's power to set global prices, for example, is severely limited by strategic, political, economic, and other differences among its members.

intergovernmental organization (IGO) Association of several nation-states or nongovernmental organizations for the purpose of international cooperation.

IGOs increase the global accountability of individual states and, to some degree, limit their sovereignty. States receiving loans from international financial institutions such as the *International Monetary Fund (IMF)* (Chapter 7) must modify their financial and economic policies according to the Fund's standards. In theory, international institutions are not created to dictate policy to any state. Their mission is to promote mutual security, create a climate of trust, monitor international treaties, and encourage financial stability and economic development. Yet, in reality IGOs can be dependent on powerful, rich countries, which provide a big share of these organizations' funding. IGOs can suffer from internal discord and from bureaucratic, political, and ideological biases, as we will discuss in Chapter 3.

Nongovernmental Organizations

In recent years, a growing set of nongovernmental actors have played an increasingly important role in the foreign policy of many countries. **Nongovernmental organizations (NGOs)** are public or private interest groups attempting to influence foreign policy, raise international concerns about a domestic problem or domestic concerns about a global issue, and offer help in the solution of these problems. The NGOs we will study deal mostly with international issues. (There are also NGOs dealing with domestic problems.) NGOs today support nuclear disarmament and environmental protection; relief programs in poor regions; and the distribution of medicine, educational services, and other forms of international assistance and cooperation. NGOs are usually the product of individual volunteer efforts or civic movements. Some of them may receive government support in the form of grants.

nongovernmental organization (NGO) Public or private group unaffiliated formally with a government and attempting to influence foreign policy, to raise international concerns about a domestic problem or domestic concerns about a global issue, and to offer solutions.

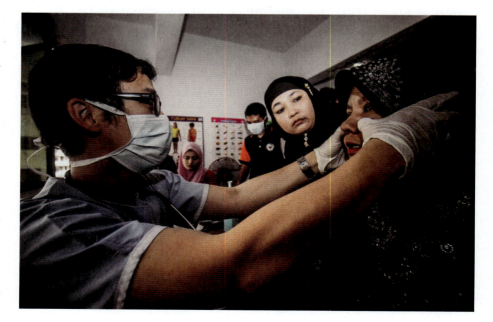

What kinds of solutions can NGOs offer?

The role of NGOs today is increasing for at least three reasons. First, in many democracies, NGOs help hold government bureaucracies and political appointees accountable to the public. In turn, democratic standards can support the missions of NGOs. For instance, the U.S. Freedom of Information Act (FOIA), which the U.S. Congress voted to strengthen in the 1970s, led a group of investigative journalists to establish the National Security Archive in 1985. This public group does not receive government funding and calls on the U.S. government to declassify and release foreign policy-related information. Recently, the National Security Archive released transcripts of more than twenty interviews the FBI conducted with the former Iraqi president Saddam Hussein following his capture by U.S. troops in 2003. Many other document collections have been published in print or electronically.

A second reason for the prominence of NGOs is the growing attention to humanitarian problems. These problems include health, safety, and security concerns, as well as *human rights*, the most fundamental moral principles or standards of human life (a topic we will examine in detail in Chapter 10). Even the most powerful government organizations cannot pay sufficient attention to every pressing global problem. After the end of the Cold War in the early 1990s, for example, hundreds of NGOs provided desperately needed assistance in African countries. NGOs raised funds to address the spread of AIDS, small arms and violence, corruption, and the collapse of health services in developing countries. While governments are often selective in their reaction to violations of human rights and political freedoms, many NGOs prioritize these issues and quickly bring them to the media's attention.

Finally, NGOs have benefited from new communication trends and information technology. Social media gives NGO activists and individuals more visibility in an era when an increasing proportion of the world's population—including two-thirds of American adults (Pew Research Center 2017)—receives news through such channels. Via online platforms, NGOs can also raise funds, solicit volunteers, and organize complex projects without relying on governmental bureaucracies or big news organizations.

The NSA maintains a large repository of declassified U.S. documents.

Check Your Knowledge

1. What is the role of diplomacy in foreign policy?

2. What is the difference between NGOs and IGOs as international organizations?

3. Are you aware of NGOs in your area? What do they do? Many NGOs recruit their new employees through internship. Do your local NGOs offer internships?

1.3 Facing Global Challenges

Studying IR will provide you with essential analytical tools to explain and help address global problems. You will be better prepared to influence discussions about your country's foreign policy, and you will begin to see ways to build a more prosperous and stable world. Before we continue, stop for a moment and list five or six of the most significant challenges and issues the world is facing today. What can be done to address them, and what role can you play individually? Here we will mention just a few critical issues as a starting point. We will revisit these and many other interconnected challenges in the following chapters.

Violence, War, and Weapons of Mass Destruction

Conflict and violence—internal as well as international—are both major sources and consequences of instability. Violent conflicts take human lives, inflict suffering, disrupt international trade, damage the environment, and require substantial material resources. Instability, in turn, serves as a source of new conflicts and wars.

Each war has its own origin, history, and consequences. Nevertheless, violent conflicts often stem from similar causes. Military dictatorships conducting brutal policies against their own population are likely to act violently against neighboring states. Unstable or failing governments often turn to radical and violent measures to defend themselves. Unsettled ethnic conflicts frequently threaten international peace. Small radical groups, which may not be directly affiliated with any country, can also cause violence and international instability. They may try to achieve their political goals by violence or threats of hostility against authorities or the civilian population. International terrorism has emerged as a threat to stability and a serious international problem as well, as we will see in Chapter 8. In this chapter, we also will examine several new sources of aggression and conflict, including new technologies and the rapidly evolving forms of cyberwarfare.

What can be done to reduce violence and instability? No single or short-term policy will prevent or end violent conflicts, but scholars have put forward at least two views on potential strategies. On the one hand, some argue that powerful countries have no viable option except to maintain international stability through economic sanctions and military involvement. On the other hand, force may breed more violence because the causes of instability are deeper than they may seem: they are often not only political but also economic, social, and psychological. Regardless, the international community, as many believe, has an urgent responsibility to reduce poverty, address injustice, and invest in education. We look in depth at security and instability in Chapters 5 and 8, and we address international threats, violence, and injustice throughout this book.

weapons of mass destruction (WMD) Nuclear, chemical, and biological weapons that can quickly and indiscriminately kill tens of millions of people.

Nuclear, chemical, and biological weapons—known as **weapons of mass destruction (WMD)**—can quickly and indiscriminately kill tens of millions of people. The fate of our planet rests at the fingertips of a few government officials with access to nuclear arsenals. This is not an exaggeration: if even a fraction of the existing nuclear weapons were to be used, human life as we know it would end.

Nuclear proliferation is the spread of nuclear weapons, materials, information, and technologies. Only a few countries openly possess nuclear weapons, including the United States, Russia, China, France, the United Kingdom, India, Pakistan, and North Korea. Israel, as many experts believe, has nuclear weapons without declaring them, and South Africa had them but later destroyed them. The only two nuclear weapons that have been used in the course of history were the atomic bombs the United States detonated over the

Japanese cities of Hiroshima and Nagasaki in 1945. The Soviet Union tested its first atomic bomb in 1949, and a nuclear race ensued between the Russians and the Americans, lasting until the end of the 1980s. In the early 1990s, after the collapse of the Soviet Union, the United States helped to remove nuclear weapons from newly independent countries, including Kazakhstan and Ukraine, which have been parts of the Soviet Union (Hoffman 2010). In recent years, an international concern has grown to prevent North Korea from developing its nuclear capabilities (Fleitz, 2018).

nuclear proliferation The spread of nuclear weapons, material, information, and technologies to create nuclear weapons.

Chemical weapons are toxic materials that can cause death, serious injury, or temporary incapacitation. These can be delivered via devices such as bombs, capsules, and sprays. Biological weapons include biological toxins or infectious agents (such as bacteria, viruses, and fungi), which can be used to kill or incapacitate one or several targeted individuals or an entire population of a large area. Biological and chemical weapons can be used in various ways for strategic and tactical purposes, including intimidation and threats. Several international agreements prohibit production, storage, and use of chemical and biological weapons. For example, the Chemical Weapons Convention (CWC) is a multilateral treaty that bans all chemical weapons and mandates their destruction within a specified period. The Biological Weapons Convention prohibits the development, production, and stockpiling of biological and toxin weapons. However, there is a concern that some countries,

U.S. President Donald Trump met with North Korean leader Kim Jong-un in June 2018. How might the goals of political summits vary culturally and individually?

such as Russia and Syria, are continuing to produce them or have failed to destroy their arsenals.

How should the world address the danger of WMD, nuclear proliferation, and chemical or biological warfare? Two strategies exist. Most governments these days support the idea that the nuclear countries should gradually reduce their nuclear arsenals and that no new countries should acquire these weapons. Others prefer universal nuclear disarmament, which would mean that every nuclear state gives up its nuclear weapons once and for all. Which strategy do you find more practical? How can further proliferation of nuclear weapons be stopped if some countries want to develop them? How can countries stop the development of new nuclear missiles? We will consider these questions and related arguments in Chapter 5.

Environmental Problems

▷

How China Is and Isn't
Fighting Pollution and
Climate Change

Environmental problems caused by human activities threaten health and well-being. Many factors play a role, including industrial and agricultural development, the rapid growth of urban areas, and increased consumption. We can group environmental problems into two broad categories: *contamination* and *depletion*. Contamination refers to pollution of the air, water, and soil. Depletion refers to diminishing resources, such as forests and fresh water. In response to these dual concerns, many governments have taken measures such as opening national parks to limit tourism and commercial construction and restricting the use of land and water.

Who or what will keep contamination and depletion in check? Some solutions can stem from government regulations, scientific publications, public awareness, and the initiatives of NGOs and international institutions. Corporations and individuals alike bear responsibility. There is no universal agreement, however, on how to address international environmental problems such as ocean pollution or global climate change. For instance, have you heard of the Great Pacific Garbage Patch? It is a huge area of exceptionally high concentrations of debris, plastics, and chemical sludge trapped in the ocean by the currents. What measures can we take to address such a problem? How should we clean up this garbage patch, and how can we prevent new contamination?

Strict rules for manufacturing and agriculture can be effective, though they have limitations—and they must be put in place to begin with. Political gridlock can impede progress on environmental initiatives. Some countries, such as China and India, argue that their priority is not protecting the environment but alleviating poverty. They see it as the responsibility of developed countries in the West to address environmental challenges. How do we keep our environment safe while also ensuring economic development? There are no easy answers. International relations as a discipline teaches us that every decision about the environment is a trade-off. In Chapter 9, we will discuss how to evaluate the gains and losses.

Extreme Poverty

Over two centuries ago, British scholar Thomas Robert Malthus predicted that food supplies could not keep up with a growing population. Such a shortage, he warned, would result in wars and violence. Today our planet has enough resources to supply every human being with food, water, and basic medical care. In the 1950s and 1960s, spectacular progress in agriculture, often called the *green revolution*, seemed to remove the danger of mass famine. Why then do extreme poverty and famine persist in some parts of the world, especially in South Asia, sub-Saharan Africa, East Asia, and the Pacific?

According to the United Nations, nearly 800 million people live on less than $1.90 per day. More than 600 million people do not have access to running water. Preventable infectious diseases continue to kill hundreds of thousands of people, predominantly children, every year. In 2017, there were an estimated 216 million cases of malaria worldwide. More than 435,000 people died from this disease (WHO 2017).

Can most countries drastically reduce poverty? Some scholars argue for the benefits of *market economies*, like those in Japan, the United States, and most Western countries. In this model, companies produce as much as they can, people purchase the goods they need, and prices rise or fall with relatively little government planning or regulation. Almost every prosperous country in today's world has implemented market principles in their economies. Critics argue, however, that the market, if left to itself, creates huge income disparity and keeps millions in poverty. Other critics of the market economy instead suggest a sustained global effort based on the redistribution of wealth through massive investment in poor countries. Would you support a global tax—for instance, 1 percent of your annual income—to help the world's poor? If not, why? If yes, who should manage these funds? We will discuss the global economy and development in Chapters 4 and 7 and poverty in Chapter 10.

Environmental and economic problems are often interconnected. The Brazilian Amazon, home to 60 percent of the world's rain forest (which produces 20 percent of the earth's oxygen), is threatened by rapid development. Is it possible to move people out of poverty while preserving the environment?

Violation of Basic Rights

Governments face increasing international pressure to protect their citizens against injustice, systematic violence, unlawful seizure of property, and physical abuse. Billions of people, however, lack access to adequate legal resources and judicial protections. In many parts of the world, property rights and civil rights are guaranteed only to small groups of people who are political or business elites. Personal connections consistently outrank the law.

Historically, some governments committed widespread rights violations in the name of ideologies such as Communism, fascism, and Nazism, or because of ethnic, racial, and religious bias. Today, the governments of countries such as China, North Korea, and Iran do not hesitate to imprison people for political dissent. Many governments conceal violations of human rights behind arguments of culture, traditions, or values. In some African and Asian countries, women but not men are brutally punished for adultery.

Poverty is closely related to rights violations as both a cause and an effect. Human traffickers earn billions of dollars through force and fraud, and their victims number in the tens of millions (U.S. Department of State 2018). Many victims of rights violations are children, who endure untold physical and sexual exploitation: hundreds of thousands are traded as slaves, are forced into drug trades, or become child soldiers. Myriad other rights violations, often stemming from conditions of extreme hardship, include denying religious freedom or access to education.

The world is far from agreeing, however, on what rights should be considered universal. Do you think a universal constitution could clearly spell out the most general, basic rights of people regardless of their nationality, culture, or religion? If you agree, which rights should be universal and which international agency could enforce them? Chapters 6 and 10 explore such debates related to international law, traditions, and human rights.

Overpopulation and Migration

Overpopulation—unsustainable population growth—presents significant challenges. The world's population is more than 7.3 billion now and is projected to grow to 8 billion by 2025. Overpopulation in combination with poverty threatens the minimal conditions necessary to sustain a reasonable quality of life. It can lead to serious health, environmental, and social problems, including rampant crime. Even as birthrates have been declining in the United States and in most parts of Europe, Latin America, the Middle East, and Asia (World Bank 2018), life expectancy has been steadily increasing, posing financial troubles for many countries' social welfare programs (Sheiner 2018). Declining birthrates affect the traditional structure of the family and put additional pressures on governmental welfare programs.

Global migration is the movement of populations across state borders in search of better living conditions and jobs. In 2013, according to the United Nations, over 232 million people, or 3.2 percent of the world's population, were international migrants—an increase of 57 million since 2000 (United Nations Information Service 2013). In 2016, the number rose to 244 million (Pew Research Center 2016). Many people migrate legally, often for economic or social reasons, and voluntarily become citizens of other countries. In 2018, nearly 50 million people living in the United States were born in other countries (Pew Research Center 2018a). At the same time, however, more than 65 million people have recently been subjected to involuntary migration: they are forced to move from their homes and often must cross international borders for fear of their lives (Hill 2018). When they arrive in a new country, many of them continue to face significant challenges. Receiving migrants often causes resistance and polarizes domestic politics in many developed countries.

How do you think wealthy countries should assist other countries that struggle with overpopulation and poverty problems? Do you believe that states should negotiate with each other and then agree on quotas for immigration? Or perhaps you think that people should move across borders without restrictions? We will discuss the full range of these problems in Chapters 7 and 10.

A Path to Peace and Economic Improvement

International relations as a discipline does not focus solely on threats and problems. One of the most important reasons we study international relations is to design policies toward building a stable, healthy, and prosperous world. Success stories are an important part of informed opinion, and international relations offers many examples of conflict resolution and sound political management. We will study such examples in every chapter; here we mention just two.

In 1992, the Czech and Slovak leaders of Czechoslovakia reached an agreement to split the country and establish two independent states. In the past, partitions of one country into two had primarily led to war and destruction. But this case was a dramatic example of a peaceful separation. After the partition, both countries joined the European Union, and today they remain close economic and political partners. What can we learn from this peaceful separation? Could other countries deal with ethnic separatist movements in a peaceful and civilized way, without resorting to violence? We explore these questions in Chapters 3 and 8.

A second example is China's recent economic success. In one generation, China evolved from an isolated and poor country into one of the world's biggest economies. In the 1990s, the government abandoned revolutionary slogans and encouraged entrepreneurship. Hundreds of millions of people have moved out of poverty and formed the middle class, and China has become an assertive player in international affairs. Yet can it be a fair player? What can other countries learn from China's economic model? In Chapters 4 and 7, we will explore these questions in more detail.

Important political decisions lie ahead, with our future at stake. We will be returning to these and many other problems in every chapter. In the concluding section of the book, we will revisit them once more, as we ask you to consider what solutions your generation may find.

▷

In Praise of Conflict

Check Your Knowledge

1. What is nuclear proliferation?

2. What are the main sources of regional and global instability?

3. What proportion of the world's population does not have access to running water?

4. Are global birth rates declining, increasing, or remaining steady?

1.4 Studying International Relations

The study of international relations includes three basic kinds of investigation: *informational*, *interpretive*, and *critical*. In informational investigation, we gather facts to describe events and developments. In interpretive investigation, we analyze the facts to explain why events take place. In this stage, we rely on concepts or schemes to organize and interpret what we know. (In Chapter 3, we will present some of the most important approaches, theories, and tools for studying international relations and applying the findings.) The third type of investigation is critical thinking, in which we look critically at the facts and their interpretations.

Gathering Information

Policy makers, their advisers, journalists, NGO activists, and researchers all rely on information about international relations. How do we gather unbiased, factual information?

GOVERNMENTAL AND NONGOVERNMENTAL REPORTS

Governments and nongovernmental organizations alike release periodic publications about the economy, defense, commerce, tourism, employment, education, consumer spending, and other developments. For example, in the United States, the Federal Reserve—the central banking system—submits a semiannual economic report to Congress. Nonprofit organizations also provide information that can affect policy. One example is the Center for Global Development in Washington, D.C. (www.cgdev.org), which publishes evidence-based analyses of how the policies and practices of developed countries affect people in the developing world.

How do we judge the reliability and accuracy of a report? We have to consider three factors. The first is the *self-interest* of the organization publishing it. Even statistical publications can distort data or omit relevant facts for political or other purposes. A second factor is the *professional prestige* of the institution providing a report. The accuracy of past publications contributes to this reputation. The third factor is *competition* from other sources of information. Statistical reports should be obtained from—and crosschecked against—several sources. A competitive environment, when facts can be tested and discussed openly (compared to the one when information is censored), should positively affect the quality and type of information presented. Still the rapid rise of social networks created a paradox: unprecedented capacities for exchanging information among billions of people create opportunities for spreading inaccurate or purposefully misleading reports. In addition, some stories shared via social media have not been properly researched or fact-checked. Be aware of this when you search online for information, and rely only on credible sources.

In developing democracies or nondemocratic countries, the quality of government reports is often in doubt because it is difficult to confirm their accuracy. Some nondemocratic governments deliberately distort statistics on issues such as the spread of HIV, the use of illegal drugs, and violence against women. In democratic countries, in contrast, citizens, political groups, the media, and NGOs can easily challenge their governments if important data are omitted. Government offices often have statutory obligations to release complete and accurate reports.

EYEWITNESS SOURCES

Eyewitness reports provide documentation of events by those who observed them directly. For example, journalists can often enter a foreign country or a zone of conflict to conduct interviews and take pictures, and then make that information available to the world. (Not without risk, however; in many parts of the world, journalists face imprisonment or persecution and can even be killed for doing their job.) Representatives of NGOs can sometimes visit places where formally accredited journalists or diplomats are prohibited. Thanks to such reports, the world learned about violence in Chile in the 1970s; ethnic cleansing in Bosnia in the 1990s; human trafficking in contemporary Southeast Asia; corruption and suppression of opposition in Russia; and serious violations of human rights in Syria, Somalia, and many other countries.

eyewitness report
Documentation of an event by someone who observed it directly.

Despite the valuable information such reports provide, an important caution is that eyewitness accounts can be unreliable or biased. Research shows that even when witnesses try to describe facts truthfully, they can inevitably put their spin on what they saw and remembered. People tend to see their in-group members more positively than out-group members (Carpenter and Krendl 2018). In addition, some eyewitness accounts are intentionally biased. Political memoirs, for example, while providing details previously unavailable, may be written primarily to show off achievements.

OFFICIAL COMMUNICATIONS

Official documents are often the best available sources on how states interact with each other. A *communiqué*, which is an official report about an international meeting, regularly provides clear and unambiguous information about the intentions, expectations, and actions of two or more states. Correspondence between state leaders is often helpful in understanding policy strategies. Letters exchanged between the U.S. president Franklin Roosevelt and the Soviet leader Joseph Stalin during World War II reveal avoidance of ideological disagreements for the sake of defeating Germany (Zubok 2009).

Speeches and press conferences of political leaders are valuable sources of information. They articulate domestic political goals, such as public mobilization. Winston Churchill, for example, delivered one of his most famous speeches in Fulton, Missouri, on March 5, 1946. He hoped to convince the United States to be in alliance with Great Britain to contain the Soviet Union's power. U.S. presidents usually articulate their foreign policy objectives every year in an annual report known as the State of the Union. They also set priorities in their press conferences or other official statements.

Social media has become a new channel for policy-related statements.

Social media is a relatively new channel for policy-related statements. U.S. President Donald Trump has been a major user of Twitter among heads of state. What could a content analysis tell us about his tweets? You might consider the tone, the countries or foreign leaders mentioned, and the actions suggested. Other countries' leaders, such as French President Emmanuel Macron, didn't tweet much. According to Politico, in 2017 President Trump and Pope Francis had about 40 million followers each on Twitter, which was fewer than President Obama had when he was in the presidential office (Politico, 2017). How could the statements of world leaders—and the channels used for these messages—affect international relations, in your view? Do these direct appeals to the public help or hurt a country's foreign policy goals?

Secrecy is often necessary in certain diplomatic negotiations. Most government documents remain classified for years: states are interested in keeping their secrets away from the public. Sometimes journalists and researchers use the FOIA to declassify secret documents by the United States government just a year or two after they were created. Some classified documents can be leaked to the press. The controversial group WikiLeaks in 2010 released to the Internet tens of thousands of stolen classified documents related to international communications among governments. As a result, many American diplomats and their colleagues in other countries were compromised. The U.S. government argued that this was a criminal act. Later, in September 2017, WikiLeaks released documents showing how a small Russian company helped government agencies there collect data on Russian cell phone users. In 2018, it became known that a private Western group called Cambridge Analytica had collected the information of fifty million Facebook users. This information was allegedly used to influence U.S. elections and the British referendum on Brexit. These and other cases pose an important moral and legal dilemma. Should journalists and researchers use only legally obtained documents? Why or why not?

INTELLIGENCE

intelligence
Information about the interests, intentions, capabilities, and actions of foreign countries, including government officials, political parties, the functioning of their economies, the activities of nongovernmental organizations, and the behavior of private individuals.

Leaders and diplomats rely on both open and covert sources of **intelligence**—any information about the interests, intentions, capabilities, and actions of foreign countries. This type of information can concern government officials, political parties, the functioning of economies, the activities of NGOs, or the behavior of private individuals. The U.S. federal law known as FISA (the Foreign Intelligence Surveillance Act) establishes legal rules for the physical and electronic surveillance and collection of intelligence information. However, are these rules always followed? In the 2013 scandal involving former U.S.

History Lab | Facts and Lies: The Katyn Massacre

Sometimes governments or individuals spread deliberate lies and fabricate documents. By creating fake information, political forces hope to manipulate public opinion, gather sympathy and support, justify their actions, or receive political and material gains.

We learn from history that politicians have often lied to their people about significant international developments. Consider the case of the Katyn massacre. In 1940, Soviet authorities secretly ordered the execution of more than 22,000 Polish officers during Soviet occupation of Polish territory. The Nazis discovered the mass graves in 1943 and began to use them as a propaganda tool in hopes of splitting up the anti-Nazi coalition of the Soviet Union, Great Britain, and the United States. Stalin's government resorted to denial, accusing the Nazis of committing the murders. The Western Allies of the Soviet Union, willing to keep strategic relations with Moscow, accepted the Soviet government's version. The Allies then downplayed an international medical commission's reports suggesting that the murders were committed by the Soviet secret police (Zaslavsky 2004). During the Nuremberg trials in 1945 and 1946, the former Allied powers falsely ascribed the Katyn massacre to the Nazi regime. Only in 2010 did the Russian government openly acknowledge committing the murders, calling the tragedy a "military crime."

CRITICAL THINKING

❶ In 2018, the governments of Iran and Russia accused Western governments of lying about the chemical attacks against civilians in Syria. Western governments, in turn, accused Iran and Russia of a cover-up. How have changes in communication technology affected opportunities for leaders to spread misinformation about their policies and other countries' actions? ❷ Find out more about political leaders making misleading statements about international events and foreign policy. Why did they do this? What factors may reduce or increase a leader's incentive to mislead the domestic and international community? ❸ For the sake of argument, are there instances when a leader would be justified in misleading the public about some international developments? First support and then critically discuss your case.

---

intelligence employee Edward Snowden, the public learned that governments had access to the private communications of hundreds of millions of people. This revelation raised important legal questions related to intelligence gathering in today's global world. New technologies often make the line between private data and intelligence information blurry. Private companies and governments can have access to an individual's ideological affiliations, political preferences, volunteer activities, and voting history. Could this information be used to affect public opinion in foreign countries on certain issues or even sway elections?

Not all intelligence influences a state government's decision making. Three main criteria affect the usability of intelligence. First, the information should have particular relevance for security and foreign policy; second, the information should come from a reliable source and be checked against other sources; and third, political leaders must trust and accept the information. Timely access to intelligence information across government departments is also important. For decades, bureaucratic rules often delayed the effective use of intelligence information by the Central Intelligence Agency (CIA; a major

Why do governments and private companies gather information about you? Where do we draw the line between national security and individual privacy—and who draws it?

intelligence-gathering organization of the federal U.S. government). Changes that began in 2015 were aimed at removing such barriers and providing better communications among CIA divisions responsible for information gathering and intelligence analysis.

Another complicating factor is the sheer number of intelligence signals, none of which are conclusive enough alone. In the United States, United Kingdom, Russia, and China, several intelligence services report to different government agencies. They may be in competition with each other and are not always well coordinated. Many so-called intelligence failures are shown in retrospect to be leadership's failure to recognize foreign threats (Goodman 2008). For instance, the U.S. government overlooked the impending attacks on the World Trade Center and the Pentagon in 2001, despite intelligence signals that indicated a possible criminal use of civilian aircraft by foreign nationals (Wright 2006).

SURVEYS

survey Investigative method in which groups of people answer questions on a certain topic.

In **surveys,** groups of people answer questions on a certain topic. In the United States, for example, surveys are used to calculate presidential approval ratings, which are important indicators of popular support for U.S. foreign policy. Although public opinion does not set foreign policy directly, it does constrain it. Presidents and other decision makers are unlikely to go against overwhelming public opinion. History shows that to avoid an electoral defeat, a democratic government has to generate public support for its foreign actions and international programs (Shiraev and Sobel 2006).

Two types of surveys are the most valuable for study of international relations: *opinion polls* and *expert surveys*. Opinion polls gather information, usually on a national sample, about attitudes related to other countries, international events, or their own country's foreign policy. Expert surveys reflect professional opinions about a country, a country's foreign policy, or an international problem. For example, NGO Freedom House in Washington, D.C., publishes annual reports on the degree of democratic freedoms in most countries. Based on experts' evaluations, the *Freedom in the World* survey provides an annual evaluation of the state of global freedom. These ratings determine whether a country is later classified as free, partly free, or not free. To some, these ratings are an accurate measure of individual freedoms. To some critics, the numbers are too subjective and biased. Transparency International (TI) is another NGO that uses surveys. To create its Corruption Perceptions Index, TI compiles surveys that ask international entrepreneurs and business analysts to express their perceptions of a country's level of corruption (see Table 1-1).

Focus groups are another survey method used intensively in foreign policy planning, conflict resolution, or academic research. A typical **focus group** contains from seven to ten experts who discuss a particular situation and express their opinion about issues raised by the group's moderators. They are often given the opportunity to analyze issues in an informal atmosphere, relatively unconstrained by their government, military rank, or academic position.

focus group A survey method involving small discussion groups used intensively in foreign policy planning, conflict resolution analysis, and academic research.

CONTENT ANALYSIS

One tool for examining information is **content analysis**—a research method that systematically organizes and summarizes both *manifest* content (what was actually said or written) and the *latent* content (the analysis of meaning) in speeches, interviews, television or radio programs, letters, newspaper articles, blogs, and other reports. For example, specialists have found that the more ideologically driven a U.S. president's speech is, the less sophisticated are the explanations of foreign policy (Tetlock 2011).

content analysis A research method that systematically organizes and summarizes both what was actually said or written and its hidden meanings (the manifest and latent content).

EXPERIMENTAL METHODS

The study of international relations can also rely—surprising as it may sound—on experiments. In **experiments** (often called *laboratory experiments*

experiment A research method that puts participants in controlled testing conditions. By varying these conditions, researchers can examine the behavior or responses of participants.

TABLE 1-1 Corruption Perceptions Index, Selected Ranks and Countries, 2017 (Updated June 2018)

Rank	Country
Top 7 (least corrupt)	New Zealand, Denmark, Finland, Norway, Switzerland, Norway, Singapore
16–19	Austria, Belgium, the United States, Ireland
51–54	South Korea, Grenada, Namibia, Italy
85 (shared by several)	Argentina, Benin, Kosovo, Kuwait, Solomon Islands, Swaziland
Bottom 7 (most corrupt)	Libya, Sudan, Yemen, Afghanistan, Syria, South Sudan, Somalia

The lower the rank of a country, the less corrupt the country is perceived to be.

DEBATE > THE CORRUPTION PERCEPTIONS INDEX

The Corruption Perceptions Index, based on several surveys from IGOs, NGOs, and research firms, ranks countries according to their perceived level of corruption. It is important because politicians and businesspeople often consider it when making decisions about international agreements or investments.

The Index is not without its biases, however (Cobham 2013). Corruption exists in every country and is very difficult to measure directly. It is based mainly on experts' perceptions, which a score of factors can influence—many unrelated to corruption. For example, a number of critical media reports, a few failed interactions as a result of cultural misunderstandings, or even bad experiences at an airport can potentially affect how a traveling diplomat or businessperson views a country.

WHAT'S YOUR VIEW?

❶ Do you think the Corruption Perceptions Index should be used as a serious indicator? Why or why not? ❷ What are some practical applications of the Corruption Perceptions Index? Suggest ways to improve the Index's validity.

Transparency International publishes the Corruption Perceptions Index.

or *simulations*), scholars put participants in controlled conditions as in a game. By varying these conditions, the researchers can examine behavior and learn about strategies, stereotypes, perceptions, thinking errors, and habits (Kydd 2005). Certainly, nobody stages a small war to find out how countries would behave under extreme circumstances. Yet scholars have reconstructed "real-life" situations for decades.

One early contribution of experimental methods was related to group decision making, such as within a government team or the president's cabinet. It was shown, for instance, that when people make decisions in groups, they often become less critical of proposals initiated by the leader. This phenomenon is *groupthink*—the tendency of groups to make rushed or illogical decisions because of an emotional but false sense of unity and support for the leader (Janis and Mann 1977). In Chapter 4 we will return to this phenomenon as it relates to IR.

Experiments can be used for educational goals to study conflict analysis and resolution. Participants in experimental situations play different roles and make decisions representing conflicting sides, such as is the case for Israeli and Palestinian authorities, Russian and Ukrainian officials, or the leaders of Iran, Syria, and the United States. The resulting discussions can be used for educational purposes. In scientific experiments, such decisions are carefully recorded and analyzed.

Analyzing Information

analysis Breaking down a complex whole into smaller parts to understand its essential features and their relationships.

Knowledge of international affairs takes more than observation. **Analysis** is breaking something complex into smaller parts to understand their essential features and relations. This process is difficult enough in general, but it can be especially daunting in IR. What makes countries' leaders change their foreign policy course? Are there specific policies that are likely to prevent war? Will the world benefit from having a strong global government elected by all world citizens? These and scores of other questions cannot be answered without looking into broader ideas about how international relations works.

THE IMPORTANCE OF THEORY AND ITS APPLICATIONS

A **theory** is a general concept applied to facts for the sake of analysis or explanation. Generally, theory is based on assumptions that have to be supported or disproved by facts and observations (evidence). You can think of it as a lens through which we can view a situation in a structured way. For example, there is a theory (we will return to it in Chapter 3) suggesting that developed democratic countries tend not to wage war against one another. This theory produces many new questions, such as whether building stable democracies globally would eventually lead to global peace. Theorizing about international relations requires strong *empirical* (observation-based) knowledge combined with a measure of creativity and imagination.

> **theory** A general concept or scheme applied to facts for the sake of analysis or explanation.

Many foreign policy debates ultimately rest on competing theoretical visions. The dominant theories in the last half a century were realism and liberalism. More recently, an approach known as constructivism began to win support among those who study international relations. There are other alternative theoretical approaches, including Marxism, feminism, and world-systems theory (Walt 2005a). Different theories present different rules for the analysis of international relations. It is becoming increasingly common these days to take into consideration several theoretical perspectives. In Chapter 3, we consider the main theories describing international relations, their commonalities, and their differences.

APPLICATIONS AT THREE LEVELS OF ANALYSIS

Theories in international relations must be applied and tested. In this book, we will analyze how different theories determine the way people look at the major issues in international relations, ranging from war and terrorism to the environment and human rights. We will discover how difficult and tricky it is at times to apply theories to infinitely rich realities. Theories may bring different conclusions as we apply them to different contexts.

> **levels of analysis** Categories that allow an observer to use different degrees of generalization and complexity while analyzing international relations.

In this book, we consistently apply theories to three **levels of analysis**—categories that allow an observer to use different degrees of generalization and complexity while analyzing international relations (Table 1-2). The first level refers to decisions by individual actors, such as presidents, prime ministers, and other officials, that is, formal and informal leaders. Somebody has to make a decision, sign a treaty, stop a conflict, and initiate a policy. We will apply knowledge of international relations to see how and why leaders make those decisions. The second level is policies of countries, involving complex political institutions, ideologies, political parties, customs, and traditions. The third level is the dynamics of a complex and interconnected global system of international relations as a whole.

> **critical thinking** A strategy for examining, evaluating, and understanding international relations on the basis of reasoning and valid evidence.

Thinking Critically

Critical thinking is an active and systematic strategy for understanding international relations on the basis of sound reasoning and evidence (Levy 2009).

TABLE 1-2 Levels of Analysis

Level	Description	Example
Individual	Focuses primarily on the role of political leaders and the effects of their decisions.	In January 1950, Kim Il-sung, the ambitious and nationalistic Communist leader of North Korea, successfully lobbied Soviet leader Joseph Stalin to support his attack on South Korea.
State	Focuses on domestic political, economic, and social factors.	Many foreign policy actions are designed to satisfy potential voters. In the United States, domestic lobby groups are another domestic factor that can affect foreign policy.
Global	Focuses on the complex interaction of global factors and contexts; considers the effects of globalization.	Booming manufacturing and industrial production leads to increases in water and air pollution.

It is not simply criticizing, disapproving, and passing skeptical judgments on your government or international developments. It is a set of skills that you can master. It is a process of inquiry, based on the important virtues of *curiosity*, *doubt*, and *intellectual honesty*. Curiosity helps you "dig below the surface," to distinguish facts from opinions. Doubt keeps us from being satisfied with overly simple explanations. And intellectual honesty helps in recognizing and addressing bias in our own opinions.

DISTINGUISHING FACTS FROM OPINIONS

Scientific knowledge is the systematic observation, measurement, and evaluation of facts. This knowledge is rooted in procedures designed to provide reliable and verifiable evidence. The study of international relations is not a "hard science." The behavior of states, NGOs, and international organizations is difficult to describe in terms of mathematical formulas and controlled experiments. We still, however, can learn to separate facts from opinions. Facts are verifiable events and developments. Opinions are speculations or intuitions about how and why such developments may or may not have taken place.

One of the most dramatic episodes in international relations was the Cuban Missile Crisis in 1962. The U.S. representative to the United Nations, Adlai Stevenson, presented photographs of Soviet nuclear missiles in Cuba taken by an American spy plane. Stevenson presented facts: the Soviet missiles had been placed on the island a few weeks earlier. Years later, in 2003, U.S. Secretary of State Colin Powell similarly sought to persuade a skeptical United Nations to authorize the American invasion of Iraq. He presented pictures of Iraqi facilities that allegedly produced WMD. However, these facilities have not been found, and most experts today are certain that the U.S. administration did not have evidence of factories producing nuclear weapons in Iraq. At best, it acted on convictions and lacked the facts.

Distinguishing facts from opinions can be complicated. Some facts are deliberately hidden or distorted by state authorities or interest groups. Other facts are in dispute for many years. For example, Armenia and Turkey for many years now have remained in disagreement on the nature and scale of the mass death of Armenians at the hands of the Turks in 1915. The Armenian position is that the Turkish state orchestrated the killings and that 1.5 million died. Turkey insists that the deaths were war casualties and that the numbers were much smaller. The disagreement about the facts has caused many years of tensions between Armenia and Turkey (Akçam 2007).

When we seek information online, we must be especially cautious: Many seemingly reliable stories present opinions disguised as facts. Even more often, facts are presented in a selective, one-sided way. As a case in point, Americans have become more polarized and partisan over the past ten years. In the beginning of the 2000s, 49 percent of Americans had mixed, bipartisan views of politics; by 2017, this number was down to 38 percent. Studies and public opinion research (Kiley 2017) show that people tend to embrace the facts they like and the events they approve of but ignore information that appears to challenge their views.

Our desire to be objective is often constrained by the limits of language. Most articles we read are *framed* so that contradictory and confusing information becomes simple. Often, facts that challenge the article's view are omitted. Framing in the mass media works with remarkable effectiveness (Graber and Dunaway 2014; Ward 1999).

We also attach convenient verbal labels to the subjects we discuss. Labels such as *hawks, warmongers, aggressors, victims, doves, defeatists, hardliners,* and *softies,* to name just a few, frequently appear in the media. How accurately do these terms describe specific behaviors and particular events? International relations provides many examples showing that decision makers, like most people, often assume things when it is convenient to do so.

Separating facts from opinions should help you navigate the sea of information related to world events. It can start with looking for new and more reliable sources of facts. You can take the following steps:

1. Whenever possible, try to establish as many facts as possible related to the issue you are studying.
2. Check your sources for their reliability. Some supposed facts may also be more plausible on the surface than others.
3. If there is a disagreement about the facts, try to find out why the differences exist. What are the interests and motivations behind these differences? The more facts you obtain, the more accurate your analysis will be.

LOOKING FOR MULTIPLE CAUSES

Virtually any international event has many underlying reasons or causes. As critical thinkers studying international relations, we need to consider a wide range of possible influences and factors, all of which could be involved to varying degrees in the shaping of international events. (See Figure 1-3.)

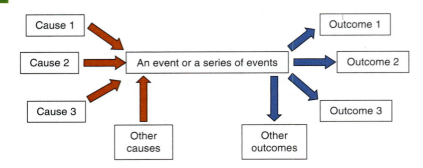

FIGURE 1–3 Multiple causes and outcomes of events.

As a historic example of multiple causes, many Americans tend to explain the collapse of Communism in Eastern Europe and the Soviet Union by Ronald Reagan's unrelenting military and economic pressure. Although this pressure was real, the Soviet Union's demise was caused by several factors, including disillusionment with Communist ideology, a growing economic and financial crisis, and the disastrous domestic policies of Soviet leadership.

As another, more contemporary example, look at the global decline in fertility rates—the average number of children a woman has. Why is this decline taking place? Is it just a reflection of increasing living standards in countries like India and Brazil? Or are women in countries like Turkey and Iran gaining more power within the family to decide how many children they have? Or maybe more women choose career over family, as some do in South Korea and Japan? An answer should look for the many factors influencing fertility rates, including cultural practices, economic development, women's education, and government policies. (We will return to this topic in Chapters 4 and 10.)

BEING AWARE OF BIAS

How Bias Shapes Your Worldview

We have to keep in mind that our opinions, as well as the opinions of people around us, may be inaccurate. Every interpretation of the facts is made from someone's point of view. And people tend to avoid information that challenges their assumptions and gravitate to information that supports their views (Graber 2010). Nobel Prize–winning studies show that people tend to bring emotional biases to simple logical judgments (Kahneman and Tversky 1972). When it comes to international relations, it is easy to support leaders we like and to oppose the policies of those we dislike. (Think of the Democrat–Republican divide in the United States, which is deepening, as we noted earlier.) Our personal attachments, interests, preferences, and values have a tremendous impact on the facts we gather and on the judgments we make about international events. Ask your classmates which periodicals they read the most. Opinion polls show that people's party affiliations are correlated with their choices of the news sources they prefer to check (Kiley 2017; Pew Research Center 2010). There are no completely unbiased newspapers or television networks. Be self-critical for a moment and answer these questions: Which printed and online publications do you like the most? To get world news, do you prefer to watch CNN or Fox News? How do your choices correspond with your views of international relations?

Bias is often caused by different experiences and life circumstances. Personal emotions can deepen misunderstandings and disagreements by causing us to refuse to learn new facts and accept new information. **Parochialism**, a worldview limited to the small piece of land on which we live or to a particular group we belong, necessarily narrows the experiences we can have. It is a powerful roadblock in the study and practice of international relations.

An emphasis on critical thinking will help you as a student of international relations. You will learn to retrieve verifiable knowledge from apparently endless fountains of information, from media reports to statistical data banks. You will also learn to be an informed skeptic and decision maker.

parochialism A worldview limited to the small piece of land on which we live or to the narrow experience we have.

Check Your Knowledge

1. What is a theory in IR, and how can it be applied in foreign policy?
2. Explain the method of content analysis.
3. What are three essential components of critical thinking?

CASE STUDY

Can Democracy Be Exported?

Background

During a class discussion, we asked, "Can democracy be exported from one country to another?" Several students immediately said no, citing recent headlines. Other students disagreed. They turned to the examples of Japan and Germany more than sixty years ago. The governments of these two countries—both military dictatorships and both sworn enemies of the United States—had lost World War II, and the occupying powers established new political systems. Eventually, after years of transition, Japan and Germany became prosperous democracies and the United States' allies. In fact, a military occupation resulted in a peaceful democratic transition. "Democracy can be exported," these students concluded.

Whose arguments were more compelling? Which history lab provides more compelling facts? To have a productive discussion, it is often important to ask more specific, detailed questions that will require the use of supporting facts. We suggested these follow-up questions:

- Why was democracy successful in Germany and Japan, and why has it failed so far in Afghanistan and Iraq?
- What is the difference between the international situation and political conditions in Germany and Japan in the 1940s and in Afghanistan and Iraq today?
- Should the foreign policy of the United States today favor or hinder the "export of democracy"?

To address these questions, we decided to review some basic facts from the past and then critically compare them with more recent developments. Our assessments and predictions should have practical applications: They will help us in making more informed judgments about democracy, military conflicts, international conditions, and the future of foreign policy.

Analysis

Unlike Germany and Japan, Iraq and Afghanistan did not fight in a major war against the United States and its allies. Neither country signed a capitulation agreement. Most people in Iraq and Afghanistan saw the U.S. military presence as illegitimate. Almost immediately, too, an organized armed opposition to foreign occupation emerged.

Further in contrast to Japan and Germany in the 1940s, Iraq and Afghanistan are culturally diverse communities with multiple ethnic, tribal, and religious groups. In Japan and Germany, the foreign occupational force successfully imposed its authority in provinces. In Iraq, and even more so in Afghanistan, local warlords, not the central government, established their power in many places (Crawford and Miscik 2010).

What, in summary, were the differences between the occupations of Germany and Japan, on one hand, and the occupations of Iraq and Afghanistan on the other? What were the differences in the United States' policies in these cases? What were the international context and international factors that affected the outcome?

History of Modern Institutions and Democratic Governance

In the twentieth century, before World War II, both Germany and Japan had experience with modern bureaucratic and civil institutions and (in Germany's case) a constitutional democracy. Afghanistan and Iraq had very little experience with modern institutions, not to mention democratic governance.

International Economic Context

Before the occupation, Germany already was the most industrialized country in Europe, with advanced education and science. Japan held the same distinction in Asia. Both countries had educated professional classes. The United States helped German and Japanese exports and pulled these countries' economies into the U.S.-led international trade system. By contrast, Iraq and especially Afghanistan did not have advanced economies or sizable professional classes. Iraqi oil can stimulate the country's economy. Afghanistan, however, does not have easily accessible natural resources.

International Relations and Domestic Context

In Germany and Japan, there were no significant forces capable of or willing to organize an armed resistance against the occupying powers. In fact, political groups, which collaborated with the occupation authorities, mobilized people to accept change and to build democratic institutions. This was in part a reaction in Germany and Japan to the crushing military defeat and the dismantling of the older political system. The presence of the Soviet Union in eastern parts of Germany and near Japan created a clear choice for the Germans and the Japanese: to accept America's influence or to fall under the Soviet influence. They made up their minds in favor of Western models. In Afghanistan and Iraq, domestic and foreign opposition to the occupation worked to dismantle democratic reforms.

International Legitimacy of Occupation

Any foreign occupation may be viewed as illegitimate. A long occupation further erodes the legitimacy of local authorities. In Germany and Japan, the occupation had international legitimacy—most countries considered it necessary to occupy and reform the two countries that had been aggressors and caused significant destruction in Europe and Asia. Also, the United States was using the perceived threat of the Soviet Union to prolong the occupation. In Iraq and Afghanistan, there was no such significant foreign threat. The population in these countries commonly viewed the governments in Baghdad and Kabul as "American puppets."

International Support

Both occupation and institution building require lasting domestic and international support. In the 1940s, the vast majority of Americans, according to Gallup polls, supported the war and the occupation of Japan and Germany. They gave their troops full support at home. American allies, such as Great Britain, France, and South Korea, welcomed for their own reasons the presence of the American forces in Germany and Japan. In contrast, the engagements in Afghanistan and particularly in Iraq divided the nation, created divisions among U.S. allies, and caused significant criticism globally. (See Table 1-3.)

We have briefly compared the conditions in four countries and linked them to the ability to conduct democratic reforms while under military occupation. As you can see, we have found ourselves drawing on history, political science, economics, sociology, psychology, and other disciplines as well. You may add your own assessments and use new facts to support them.

Case Study Questions

1. Consider the following position. *Some foreign governments should be helped to govern only after they first establish order and stability; then they can be assisted with efforts in building democratic institutions.* Do you support it? Why or why not?
2. Discuss why in some countries, such as in South Korea, there was no major violent resistance against foreign powers.
3. In 2014, Russia annexed the Crimean Peninsula—a territory of Ukraine, a sovereign state. Research and discuss why the people of

TABLE 1-3 Building Democracy under Occupation: The Cases of Four Countries

Developments	Japan	Germany	Afghanistan	Iraq
Declaration of War by the United States	Declared	Declared	Not declared	Not declared
Military Occupation	By the United States	By the United States and allies	By the United States and allies	By the United States and allies
Ethnic Composition of the Occupied Countries	Relatively homogeneous	Relatively homogeneous	Ethnically and religiously diverse	Ethnically and religiously diverse
Infrastructure of the Occupied Territory	Relatively developed	Developed	Almost absent; difficult to administer	Underdeveloped; difficult to administer
Perception of Foreign Occupation	Perceived as a result of their own military defeat	Perceived as a result of their own military defeat	Perceived as foreign aggression and invasion	Perceived as foreign aggression and invasion
Experience with Democracy	Modest experience before the 1930s	Experience before 1933	Almost absent	Almost absent
Economic Factors	Developed economy	Developed economy	Underdeveloped economy	Underdeveloped economy
Accountability of New Officials	High	High	Low	Low
Political Mobilization Against the Occupation	None	None	Significant and persistent	Significant and persistent
Foreign Support of the Occupation	Strong	Strong	Mixed	Mixed

Crimea did not resist the annexation. What was the reaction of the international community outside of Russia to the annexation? What international actions would you personally suggest to resolve the Crimea problem?

4. Visit the websites for Gallup and Pew Research to find out how many Americans now consider the United States' involvement in Iraq and Afghanistan a mistake. How many Americans supported and opposed the U.S. military actions back in 2003 compared to the most recent numbers? Should public opinion influence the president's decision making and foreign policy, especially in regards to war? Why or why not?

Introducing International Relations

1.1 Define the scope, aims, and key concepts of international relations as a discipline.

International relations focuses on interactions among the world's governments and nonstate actors. Key concepts include security; international political economy; international law; sovereignty, nations, and states; and globalization and anti-globalization.

Q: Can a nation-state not be sovereign? When might this happen? Look for specific examples.

1.2 Identify the major actors in international relations and the main areas in which they interact.

Key actors include state governments, IGOs as associations of several states, and NGOs as public or private interest groups.

Q: What factors explain the increasingly important role of NGOs today?

Q: What are the strengths and limitations of NGOs as international actors?

1.3 Examine major challenges and problems the world is facing today.

Global challenges include instability, violence, and war; nuclear proliferation; environmental problems; poverty; human rights violations; economic challenges; and population challenges.

Q: What types of policies or strategies might help reduce global instability and violence?

Q: What actors or measures could help counteract the environmental challenges of contamination and depletion?

1.4 Describe the methodology of gathering, analyzing, and thinking critically about information in international relations.

Methods of gathering information include open sources such as reports, speeches, and statements; intelligence; surveys; and experiments. To analyze information, we use theories of international relations, which must be connected to practice. We can apply theories at three levels of analysis: individual, state, and global. Thinking critically involves recognizing that opinions are different from facts, that events have multiple causes, and that bias distorts information.

Q: Why are experimental methods useful in IR? What are their limitations?

Q: When and why can government intelligence information be biased?

KEY TERMS

analysis 26
anti-globalization 9
content analysis 25
critical thinking 27
diplomacy 10
experiment 25
eyewitness report 21
focus group 25
foreign policy 10
globalization 8
intelligence 22
intergovernmental
   organization (IGO) 11

internal affairs 6
international law 4
international political
   economy 4
international relations (IR) 3
international security 3
levels of analysis 27
nation 6
nation-state 8
nongovernmental
   organization (NGO) 12
nuclear proliferation 15
parochialism 31

separatism 9
sovereignty 5
state 5
state government 10
survey 24
theory 27
weapons of mass destruction
   (WMD) 14

The Evolution of International Relations

> *We can learn from history, but we can also deceive ourselves when we selectively take evidence from the past to justify what we have already made up our minds to do.*

> —MARGARET MACMILLAN, HISTORIAN

History provides us with a rich base for understanding how international politics can succeed or fail. In a sense, it is a laboratory in which many experiments have already been conducted. Ignoring history may doom us to repeat the mistakes of the past, from trade wars to broken alliances, to deadly regional, and even to global conflicts. International institutions, conditions of peace, attitudes of tolerance, and models of international cooperation should not be taken for granted. History offers not only context but critical lessons in the study of international relations.

In this chapter, we begin by examining the origins and development of the international system, which happened in the territories that became Europe. We go on to explore the effects of the First and Second World Wars on the evolution of global politics. Finally, we consider the Cold War and significant post–Cold War developments. Note that the major developments we cover are far more complex than they may at first appear. Every major international situation you hear about today—from border disputes to ethnic and religious conflicts, terrorism, and even cyberattacks—has deep historical roots.

Previous page: The Peace Memorial in Hiroshima, Japan, commemorates those who were killed when the United States dropped the atomic bomb on August 6, 1945. Why in your view do we have to study events of the past, such as this one? Why can't we just ignore history and focus on the events of the day instead?

2.1 Explain the origins of the international system, noting key developments following the Peace of Westphalia.

2.2 Discuss how the major trends of nineteenth-century European affairs affected twentieth-century world history.

2.3 Recognize how the First World War set the stage for the Second World War.

2.4 Describe the effects of the Second World War on the modern international system.

2.5 Analyze the Cold War's origins, its key events, and the factors that brought about its end.

2.6 Outline key trends in the international developments of the post–Cold War era.

Learning Objectives

2.1 The Origins of the Modern International System

Something unique began happening in Europe between about 1450 and 1650. A novel and complex system of international relations was emerging, one that had never existed before in any part of the world. It was based on the concept of sovereignty—independent authority over a territory (as discussed in Chapter 1).

The Peace of Westphalia

The emergence of a new system did not happen overnight. Nor did it occur peacefully. It began with one of the deadliest conflicts in early modern history: the Thirty Years' War (1618–1648), a culmination of a religious power

Peace of Westphalia A series of peace treaties signed in 1648 in the Westphalian (German) cities of Osnabrück and Münster to end the Thirty Years' War, a religious conflict between Catholic and Protestant powers.

struggle between Roman Catholics and Protestants. In 1648, exhausted by war, European powers signed a series of treaties known as the **Peace of Westphalia**, which formally recognized the sovereignty of foreign states. (See Figure 2-1.)

As a result of this revolutionary principle of sovereignty, Protestant and Catholic rulers gained independence from Rome. They could now determine what religion would be practiced in their countries. In addition, Protestants now had, at least in theory, the right to practice their faith in Catholic countries, and vice versa. The Peace of Westphalia was thus a critical development in the transition from religious to secular rule. The resulting international system of European states lasted for more than two centuries. This system did not prevent wars in Europe, but it established permanent rules that helped limit the scope of many conflicts.

Military Growth and the Rise of Capitalism

Between the sixteenth and eighteenth centuries, European armies grew more professional, increasing their firepower, discipline, and military skills. European states developed military capacities that surpassed those of other states, including the Ottoman Empire. The establishment of permanent national militaries in Europe added to centralized control by sovereign states over their borders and population.

Military conflicts became mostly a business between sovereign rulers, a way to sort out territorial uncertainties and disputed possessions. Along with the growth of permanent national militaries came commonly accepted rules of behavior, and states turned to diplomacy to win allies. All wars now would end with well-defined treaties, many of which were honored later. The set of major players kept changing, however. The traditional powers were England, France, Spain, Austria, and Sweden. Early in the 1700s, Prussia and Russia entered into the European system.

Meanwhile, the capitalist economic system began to take hold, in which private owners controlled state trade and industry for profit. The Scottish economist Adam Smith (1723–1790) promoted the idea that capitalism, based on international trade rather than conquest, leads to state power and wealth. The countries of Europe, however, continued to compete for territory. The exponential growth of national militaries continued. Both the rise of capitalism and the growth of militarism would define the development of the international system during the nineteenth century. The new technology and resources generated by capitalism enabled the rise of modern military machines and new mechanized warfare.

Check Your Knowledge

1. What did the Peace of Westphalia establish?

2. What other key developments marked the beginning of modern international relations?

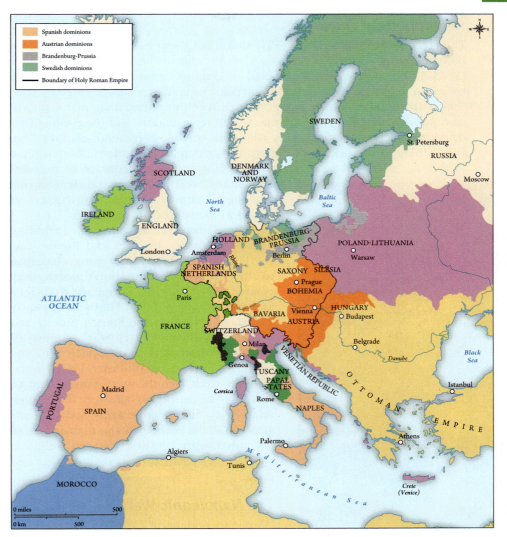

MAP 2-1
Europe in 1648.

2.2 Revolution, Industrialization, and Conquest in Nineteenth-Century Europe

The nineteenth century was a period marked by revolutions and by rapid economic and technological changes. European power came to dominate the world. Despite moments of stability and peace, militarism and the potential for new types of conflict grew both within and outside of Europe.

Revolutionary Thinking

republic A state in which supreme power belongs to the people and their elected representatives.

legitimacy The right to rule accepted by the people and other states.

The French Revolution (1789–1799) shook the Westphalian system to its core by repudiating all royal sovereigns. On the heels of the American Revolution (1773–1785), it proclaimed the goal of creating a new kind of sovereignty based on democracy and national interests. Instead of a Europe ruled by families with so-called divine rights, French revolutionaries imagined a system of **republics**, or states ruled by the elected representatives of the people. This development was influenced by the work of the seventeenth-century English thinker John Locke, who set out the principles of modern liberalism for democratic forms of governance. According to Locke's concept of political **legitimacy**, which explores the right to rule and the acceptance of authority, true power rests with those who are governed.

The European monarchies, including England, Austria, Prussia, and Russia, saw the French Revolution as a grave challenge to their preferred international order. They created several antirevolutionary coalitions and sent troops to defeat France in the early 1800s. In response, the French proclaimed a "national revolutionary war" against all European monarchs and appealed to the people of Europe for solidarity. The national military draft (requiring all young men to serve in the military) allowed the French republic to field a large army, led by energetic generals. France, in the first decade of the nineteenth century, invaded Belgium, southern German lands, Switzerland, and Italy.

Napoleon Bonaparte (1769–1821) first envisioned Europe as a confederation of states. He changed his view to build a French Empire that would dominate the European continent for years.

The Napoleonic Wars

Napoleon Bonaparte (1769–1821), a French military leader who crowned himself emperor in 1804, channeled the enormous energy of the revolution in a new direction. He transformed the vision of a republican Europe, a confederation of nation-states, into a vision of a French Empire dominating Europe. Napoleon's main objective was to create what he called the "Napoleonic system" across all of Europe, so that the continent would abide by the rules of trade established in Paris.

From 1805 to 1812, Napoleon defeated and occupied Austria, Prussia, and Spain, and almost united the entire continental Europe under his power. Napoleon violated the principles of Westphalian sovereignty: he abolished the Holy Roman Empire, which had encompassed vast territories in Central Europe since the Middle Ages, and he humiliated the Pope. Yet later, he turned to restoring some of the old structures of the European international system, as he thought they would help sustain his new empire. He kept some of the kingdoms of Europe intact. After eliminating old dynasties, he made his relatives kings and princes (Broers 2014).

For all his liberal promises and reforms, Napoleon ruled his empire in Europe by force, not by consent. His main enemy became England, which had seized all of France's colonies in America and Asia. He began a continental blockade of England in 1806, banning English goods from Europe.

Napoleon suffered critical military setbacks, however, when he attempted to control Spain and Russia. In 1812, he invaded Russia and took Moscow. The Russian emperor, Alexander I, refused to recognize Napoleon's victory. For Russia, the war became a matter of national survival. Attrition, cold, disease, and starvation eventually forced Napoleon to retreat from Russia, and he ultimately lost almost his entire Grand Army. Emboldened by Napoleon's defeat in Russia, peoples in German states and Austria revolted. The allied armies of Russia, Austria, and Prussia entered Paris in 1814, forcing Napoleon to abdicate. Napoleon's final defeat came at Waterloo, Belgium, at the hands of British and Prussian armies in 1815 (Lieven 2011). The Napoleonic Empire was no more.

Reestablishing Stability: The Concert of Europe

In Europe, 1815–1914 was a period of shifting alliances among the great powers. This group of countries was known as the *Concert of Europe* and included Austria, France, the United Kingdom (encompassing England, Wales, Scotland, and Ireland as of 1801), Prussia, and Russia. Their common goal in this era was to restore the Westphalian international system. But in the absence of a conductor, each country remained fearful that another European power could threaten its vital interests.

THE CONGRESS OF VIENNA

At the Congress of Vienna (1815), a series of meetings to reestablish stability in Europe, the sovereign rulers of the Concert of Europe attempted to demonstrate the viability of the old system. The continent had fundamentally changed, however. Sovereignty as a principle had taken hold, yet the old notion of legitimacy of such sovereignty changed. The previously incontestable "divine" right of monarchs to rule was increasingly rejected, and the idea that true power rested in the people took shape. The French Revolution paved the way for European countries to transform into nation-states: countries with uniformly educated citizens who shared a language and a culture.

Great Britain conducted a form of diplomacy known as *brilliant isolation* (MacMillan 2013). This tactic meant that London changed its allies according to its interests, sometimes pitting the continental European powers against one another to prevent the dominance of a single power. The British foreign policy

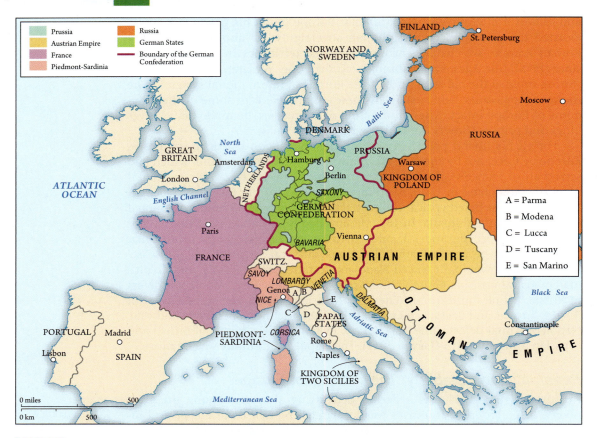

MAP 2-2 Europe in 1815, after the fall of Napoleon's empire.

was concerned with Russia, a vast land empire that in the nineteenth century included Finland and most of Poland, and reached across Siberia to China. Russia continued to expand vigorously to the south, confronting the Ottoman Empire and Iran. In London, the Russian expansion triggered *Russophobia*: a prejudiced view and fear of Russia as a country. British diplomats and statesmen were convinced that the Russian armies would threaten British control over the Mediterranean Sea and in India. This logic pushed Great Britain to support the Ottoman Empire in a military conflict with Russia that erupted in 1853.

THE CRIMEAN WAR

In the Crimean War (1853–1856), Great Britain together with France, the Italians, and the Turks fought against Russia. The cause of the conflict was the resistance of European states to Russia's ambition to dominate the Ottoman Empire. The British navy bombarded Russian ports and naval bases, and brought French and Turkish troops to Crimea, where they laid siege to Sebastopol, the main base of the Russian navy in the Black Sea. Russia, lacking railroads and modern industries, lost the war and had to sign a humiliating treaty; it could no longer maintain a navy in the Black Sea. The Crimean War ended Russia's dominance in the Concert of Europe, halted the country's ambitions to expand, and forced it to modernize.

Industrialization

The century between the Congress of Vienna and World War I (1815–1914) was also a period of remarkable technological and industrial development. These rapid changes began in England in the 1830s, then spread to France, Germany, other European countries, and the United States. **Industrialization**—wide-scale development of mechanization and industries following technological advancement—meant power. Within a century, steel cruisers had replaced sailboats in navies. Rifles, machine guns, and mobile artillery replaced old-fashioned muskets. Military capabilities transformed entirely with the invention of aircraft, submarines, radio-electronic equipment, and other weapons and technologies. Modern countries now held absolute power over the rest of the world.

industrialization Development of industries based on mechanical technology and serial mass production.

Colonialism and Imperialism before 1870

Industrialization stimulated and enabled the further growth of European colonial empires, which had rapidly expanded after Christopher Columbus and Vasco de Gama's explorations in the fifteenth century. Among European powers, a new practice emerged: **colonialism**, the occupation of lands overseas and dominating indigenous people to promote trade and extract wealth. First Spain and Portugal, and then the United Kingdom and France, engaged in this practice. Colonialism is linked to the broader idea of **imperialism**, the doctrine that gaining control over more territory is essential to a country's wealth, security, and greatness.

colonialism The practice of occupying lands overseas and dominating indigenous people to promote trade and extract wealth.

Motivations for these policies ranged from economic to religious to political. Colonialism and imperialism profoundly changed European economies, political thinking, and identities, as well as the fate of colonized people around the world. Europeans began to think of themselves as "a superior race," destined to dominate and "civilize" other peoples in the Americas, Africa, and Asia. In the United States, European settlers and their descendants decimated the Native American population. Instead of exploiting them, as they did with African slaves, they eliminated them or enclosed them in reservations.

imperialism The doctrine that gaining control over more territory is essential to a country's wealth, security, and greatness.

European companies fueled a massive slave trade from Africa to North America, as well as to Central and South America. The main agent of British colonial policy in India was the British East India Company, a private trade organization chartered by Queen Elizabeth I in 1600. During the first century of its existence, it competed with the Dutch East India Company, leading to several military conflicts. By the end of the eighteenth century, the British East India Company had taken over some French colonies and had begun to colonize India, reaching deals with regional rulers. The Company behaved as a private arm of the British government. In the early nineteenth century, the Company began trading with China and developed a very lucrative opium business, which was legal at that time.

When China attempted to bring the opium trade under state control, war broke out with Great Britain. China lost the First Opium War (1839–1842), owing largely to its inability to compete with the powerful British navy, and was forced to cede the island of Hong Kong to the British. In addition, British citizens living in China became exempt from China's laws (Westad, 2012). This "unequal treaty," as it became known among the Chinese, was only the first of what would be many infringements on Chinese sovereignty.

The Rise of Nationalism

nationalism
Individual and collective identification with a country or a nation, and its language, culture, and history; often tied to the belief that an ethnic group has the right to form an independent state.

Two important ideas affected the international system during the era of industrialization and imperial conquest. The first was *liberalism*—a political philosophy or worldview founded on ideas of liberty and equality. (We will discuss liberalism in depth in Chapter 3.) Another crucial development was the rise of **nationalism**, individual or collective identification with a country or a nation. Sovereignty is related to nationalism through the idea that power belongs to the people who live in a certain territory and who share a certain identity, language, and culture. (We will discuss nationalism again in depth in Chapter 4.)

THE REVOLUTIONS OF 1848

In 1848, a series of revolutions shook several European capitals and other major cities. The common people revolted against monarchies in France, Prussian and German lands, Italy, and the Austrian Empire. These uprisings took place under the banners of liberalism and nationalism, marking an important turning point. Although most of these revolts ended in military defeat, the ideology of nationalism continued to win new supporters. From that time on, the idea of creating or preserving a "nation-state" became a dominating theme of most European conflicts.

Liberalism and nationalism posed new challenges for Europe's *polyethnic empires*—regions inhabited by various peoples speaking different languages. In the 1848 revolution in the Austrian Empire, the nationalist elites of Vienna, Prague, and Budapest declared independence, attempting to form separate nation-states. With skillful diplomacy and military support from other countries, above all Russia, the Austrian Empire survived. In 1866, however, Austrian Emperor Franz-Joseph offered a great compromise to the Hungarians, forming a dual empire: Austria-Hungary.

THE FRANCO-PRUSSIAN WAR AND GERMAN UNIFICATION

While liberalism and nationalism weakened the Austrian Empire, they helped create a new state called the Reich of German People, or simply Germany. Beginning in the 1860s, the Kingdom of Prussia, ably led by Count Otto von Bismarck (1815-1898), pushed to unify most of the German principalities and lands that had remained decentralized for centuries. France, fearful of the potential for German unification, declared war, while other great powers, such as Great Britain and Russia, watched from the sidelines (Kennedy, 2017). The Franco-Prussian War (1870–1871), which France lost, resulted in a unified Germany and marked the end of French dominance in western and central

Europe. The creation of a unified Germany went in parallel to the creation of a unified Italy in 1871

Those events, particularly the creation of Germany, had a lasting impact on the course of international relations. A large, modern nation-state, rather than a conglomeration of small and weak principalities, now dominated the continent. Supported by the top German universities, science and technology flourished. The economy and military grew, surpassing those of Great Britain and France. Fearing increasing German power, Great Britain turned to alliances with France (1904) and with Russia (1907). The century-old British fears of Russian expansion were put aside; the new threat in London's view was the German Reich. Not only could Germany one day dominate continental Europe, it could also build a navy that would threaten British supremacy at sea and its vast colonial empire (Kennedy 1987).

A New Global System in the Age of Imperialism (1870–1914)

At the end of the nineteenth century, the United States and Japan, both with modern industries and advanced militaries, joined the international system as new influential players. The European concert thus began to evolve into a global system. Historians call this period (roughly 1870–1914) the age of imperialism, when European states had maximum global power and vast colonies.

France and Great Britain built the strategic Suez Canal in 1869, linking the Mediterranean and the Indian oceans in what is now Egypt. France began building, and the United States finished, the Panama Canal (1914), which greatly shortened the trade routes between the Atlantic and Pacific oceans. Great powers, especially the British and French, competed with each other to colonize as many overseas territories as they could. In Asia, the British colonized all of India, Burma (modern-day Myanmar), and Malaysia; the French colonized Indo-China. Only the Kingdom of Siam (Thailand) retained independence. The Dutch controlled Indonesia. In 1904–1905, Russia and Japan clashed in northern China and Korea over territorial ambitions. (See Figure 2-2.) Japan emerged victorious in what was called the Russo-Japanese War, marking the first time in centuries when an Asian country had defeated a European empire. The United States stepped in to mediate a peace treaty between the two enemies.

The great European powers scrambled for colonial control in Africa between 1881 and 1914. Great Britain, France, Portugal, Belgium, Germany, and Italy occupied almost the entire continent. The European powers claimed they wanted to eradicate slavery in Africa and bring its people to civilization. European thinkers, such as Houston S. Chamberlain (1855–1927), came up with racist theories that rationalized colonization. The famous English poet Rudyard Kipling composed a poem praising "the white man's burden" to civilize other "races."

In 1884, German Chancellor Bismarck convened a conference of all European powers in Berlin, which recognized the territories occupied by those powers in Africa as their effective possessions. The Berlin conference was Germany's attempt to play the role of peacemaker and to regulate the rivalry

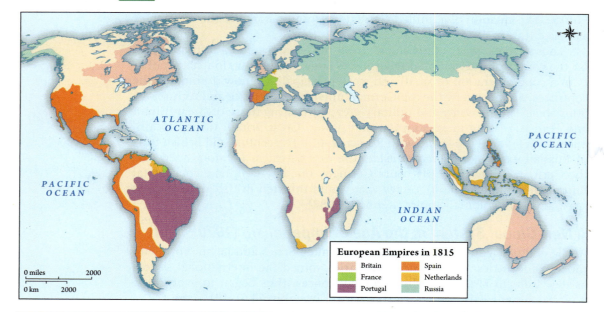

European Empires in 1815

Britain	Spain
France	Netherlands
Portugal	Russia

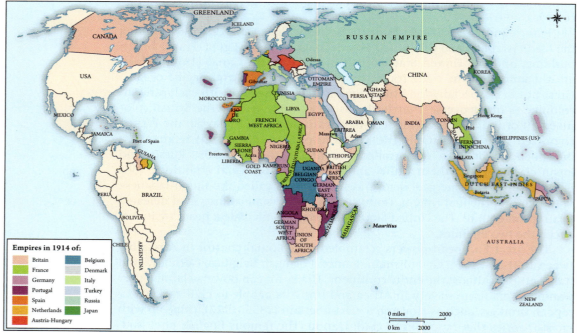

Empires in 1914 of:

Britain	Belgium
France	Denmark
Germany	Italy
Portugal	Turkey
Spain	Russia
Netherlands	Japan
Austria-Hungary	

MAP 2-3. Europe's global reach. Almost every country in the world was under European control at some point in its history.

among the great powers. Further, it signaled Germany's colonial and imperial ambitions.

Nationalism in all European countries, but especially in Germany and France, helped fuel the fear of one another's growing power. Nationalism and militarism led to massive propaganda campaigns in the media, schools, and many areas of public life. The *balance of power*, or the complex power dynamics among European countries, was precarious and unstable (we will explore this concept in more detail in Chapter 3). No European country's borders and power were absolute and unchallenged.

Check Your Knowledge

1. What was the greatest objective of the Napoleonic System?
2. What did the Congress of Vienna decide?
3. Define and compare colonialism and imperialism.
4. How did the unification of Germany affect European relations?

2.3 The Great War (1914–1918) and the Flawed Peace

The unstable balance of power in Europe could have endured for some time, but it was a conflict on the periphery of the great empires that pushed them into a deadly conflict. In 1914, a small conflict in the Balkans spiraled out of control and ignited a global confrontation. (See Figure 2-4.) When a Serbian terrorist in the Bosnian city of Sarajevo assassinated Austrian Archduke Franz-Ferdinand, a complex diplomatic crisis ensued. Austrian-Hungary blamed Serbia for the assassination, issued an ultimatum, and then declared war. Germany backed Austria-Hungary. Russia showed solidarity with Serbia, another Slavic Orthodox country, and declared mobilization of its military forces. At this point, the German leadership and the military considered the war inevitable and simultaneously declared war on Russia and France. One historian argued that this chain reaction of events could have been prevented. The European powers, he wrote, "sleep-walked" into the war (Clark 2012). What became known as the Great War (and later called World War I) lasted until 1918, taking the lives of more than 40 million people. The old international system had collapsed (MacMillan 2013).

The Great War involved two major European alliance systems: Germany and Austria-Hungary as the Central Powers on the one side; and the Allied Powers of Russia, France, and Great Britain on the other. British India, Canada, and Australia entered the conflict as well. The Ottoman Empire (Turkey) entered the war against Russia on the side of the Central Powers. The war gained a global momentum that made it extremely difficult for any participant in the international system to remain neutral.

The expectations of a short and victorious war proved wrong. Neither coalition of great powers could prevail. The war brought financial instability, created huge debts for all participants (who borrowed money from the United States), and forced governments to ration food and other resources (especially

MAP 2-4 Europe in 1914, at the outset of World War I.

in Germany). The frontlines of the war crossed France and Belgium, northern Italy and Austria-Hungary, Bulgaria and Romania, eastern Turkey, and vast expanses of Russia. Military actions also took place in the Middle East and even in Africa. Naval warfare increasingly disrupted global trade. The British navy blockaded Germany, and German submarines retaliated by sinking British and other Allied ships.

The Collapse of Russia, Germany, and Austria-Hungary

Two developments tilted the course of the war in 1917. First, the Russian Revolution overthrew the Tsarist autocracy; Russia stayed in the war for most of the year before plunging into anarchy. The German leadership backed a new Communist government in Moscow, led by the revolutionaries Vladimir Lenin (1870–1924) and Leon Trotsky (1879–1940). Immediately after Russia's collapse, Germany seized huge areas of the former Tsarist Empire, including Polish lands, the Baltics, and Ukraine. The Turkish and German forces advanced eastward as far the Caspian Sea. New Russian leaders signed a humiliating peace with Germany and its allies in March 1918, accepting all their territorial conquests. Yet the Russian Revolution cleared the road for the second development: the United States' entry in April 1917 on the side of the Allied Powers. Germany's aggressive submarine warfare in the Atlantic threatened American trade and contributed to the United States' decision to intervene.

The resources of the German Reich were overstretched. In November 1918, the political leadership in Germany signed an armistice agreement with the Allies. What followed was the collapse of Germany as a nation-state, a collapse that was even more sudden and surprising than that of the Russian Empire in 1917. German allies signed separate armistices. The Austrian-Hungarian Empire imploded; new nation-states, such as Hungary and Czechoslovakia, declared independence.

The collapse of Russia, Germany, and Austria-Hungary defined the military and political outcome of the First World War. The United States, Great Britain, and France were clear victors, yet they inherited many prewar challenges. The greatest challenge was Russia, where the Communist Party (the Bolsheviks) seized power in November 1917. The Bolsheviks rejected Western liberalism and nationalism, demanded the abolition of capitalism and the end to colonial empires, and called for a global revolution of workers and peasants. This was an ideology of total rejection of the old world order, including the Westphalian principle of sovereignty. Bolshevism became the foundation of a new state called the Union of Soviet Socialist Republics (USSR, or the Soviet Union). The Communists set up the Communist International (Comintern) in Moscow, which advocated for world revolution and the destruction of colonial empires. The Soviet state, however, confronted severe security problems inherited from the collapsed empire. The tandem ideas of global revolution and territorial security would define Soviet foreign policy for decades to come.

The League of Nations and the Interwar Years

Meanwhile, the victorious powers vowed to transform the armistice into a lasting peace. U.S. President Woodrow Wilson, who brought his country into the war, proclaimed his *Fourteen Points*, promising a new international order of justice and freedom (we will discuss these further in Chapter 3). Wilson promised American support for national self-determination. He touted the **League of Nations**, an international organization that could protect smaller countries from aggression and steer the world toward cooperation and peace. Wilson spoke against imperialism: he urged European great powers to free their colonies. Wilson advocated for free trade, which he argued could provide international stability, resolve conflicts, and reduce the likelihood of war. These principles created what one historian called "a Wilsonian moment" in international relations: the expectations that the postwar world would indeed be more stable and peaceful (MacMillan 2003; Manela 2009).

U.S. President Woodrow Wilson on his League of Nations tour in 1919.

The League of Nations was established at the Paris Peace Conference (January 1919–January 1920). The League was the first global organization aimed at prevention, mediation, and peaceful resolution of interstate conflicts, support of basic human rights, disarmament, and economic cooperation. The peace conference, however, turned out to be a bitter disappointment for advocates of a fair and stable international order. The leaders and public opinion in Britain and France refused to apply the Wilsonian principles to Germany. And instead of playing a global role following the ideas of President Wilson, the United States did not join the League of Nations.

The Treaty of Versailles (signed in the Palace of Versailles, near Paris, in June 1919) brought a formal end to the Great War in Europe. The Treaty obligated Germany to pay reparations to Britain, France, and other countries; reduced the German army to the minimum; and banned Germany from maintaining a navy and an air force. It also returned disputed territories such as Alsace-Lorraine to France and declared all German conquests in the East null and void. The British navy continued the blockade of Germany until it signed the treaty. Hungary and Bulgaria, treated as Germany's allies, were also defeated and diminished. The new Austria was small and weak. By the 1920s, Europe was much poorer, more nationalistic, and less stable than it had been before the war.

The First World War brought the Ottoman Empire to its end and for decades destabilized the Middle East and North Africa. Meanwhile, European imperialism and colonialism advanced. The French established control over the territories of today's Lebanon and Syria; the British took Iraq, Transjordan, and Palestine. The United Kingdom became the dominant power in the Middle East, controlling the Suez Canal and the oil resources. India remained a British colony, and the Indian independence movement led by Mahatma Gandhi (1883–1944) was suppressed by 1922. In Africa, the colonial empires stayed intact: the United Kingdom and France divided German colonies among themselves.

The United Kingdom, France, and the Netherlands also kept their vast colonial empires in Asia. Japan took the Pacific islands that had formerly been under German control. The biggest changes took place in China, where the traditional empire had ended. A new Chinese nationalist movement emerged, inspired by the 1917 Russian Revolution and Communism (Westad 2012).

Check Your Knowledge

1. Which empires had collapsed by the end of World War I?
2. What was the formal purpose of the League of Nations?

2.4 The Second World War

At the end of the First World War, Germany was disarmed and humiliated. The task of imposing the punitive Versailles Treaty on the defeated Germany fell to France. In 1923–1925, France occupied the Rhineland, the most industrialized area of Germany, to ensure that Germany paid its reparations. France also formed alliances with Poland, Czechoslovakia, and Romania to help keep Germany in check.

Germany was suffering from hyperinflation: market prices for major consumer products could often double within days. In response, the Americans and British stepped in with the Dawes Plan (1924), giving the German government an international loan to stabilize its finances and invest in industry. The United Kingdom also persuaded France to end the occupation of German lands and end Germany's status as a pariah country. Germany was invited to join the League of Nations (Steiner 2013; Sharp 2009).

Instability continued, however. Millions of Europeans no longer trusted the old elites; the young—especially in Germany—felt betrayed by their elites and were eager to seek justice and revisit the results of the Great War. Meanwhile, war veterans brought home a culture of militarism and violence. Industrial workers supported the ideas of Bolshevism, and several Communist-inspired uprisings broke out in Germany and Hungary. Everywhere in Europe, except for the United Kingdom, democratic parties lost the support of their voters. Radical Communist parties formed after 1919 continued to grow, especially in Germany, France, and Italy.

fascism A form of extreme nationalism characterized by rejection of individual and political freedoms, by open racism and bigotry, and by state control of industry, finance, and commerce.

The Rise of Fascism

A new political force, aside from Communism, was **fascism,** a form of extreme nationalism characterized by rejection of individual and political freedoms, by open racism and bigotry, and by state control of industry, finance, and commerce. This system of government first came to power in Italy in 1922, when the king and the old elites, intimidated by the Communist threat, ceded power to Benito Mussolini (1883–1945).

Mussolini, the new Italian leader, was a spectacular manipulator and demagogue: rather than presenting rational arguments, he appealed to the desires and prejudices of ordinary people. He loved publicity. He knew what to say to workers, war veterans, and those struggling financially, and he made a nationalist promise to create a Great Italy. Fascists chose dictatorship over liberal democracy and replaced the elites who had dominated Italy before the Great War. Mussolini wanted to build an economy based on state-run corporations, subservient to the fascist state and to his personal will. Mussolini rejected the Paris peace settlement of 1919: In his logic, Italy fought on the side of the Allies but did not receive any new territories or colonies.

Nationalists in several European countries emulated Mussolini's fascism, especially

Fascist leaders Adolf Hitler (left) and Benito Mussolini in 1941.

in Germany, where Adolf Hitler (1889–1945) became the leader of the Nazi movement. Hitler preached racism, extreme German nationalism, and anti-Semitism. He promised the dissolution of the humiliating Versailles Treaty of 1919 (Knox, 2007).

The Aftermath of Economic Crisis

The collapse of the U.S. stock market in 1929 initiated a chain of developments that undid the economic foundations of international stability and peace. The United States and Great Britain attempted to stem the financial and economic collapse. At the same time, however, the great powers chose the policy of protecting their own currency and economies. International trade and finance contracted rapidly. The Great Depression—a severe worldwide economic crisis—lasted through the 1930s. Capitalism seemed broken beyond repair (Boyce 2002).

In Germany, the economic crisis boosted Nazism. When old German elites had asked Hitler to form a government in 1933, he and his party seized total control, proclaiming the Third Reich of the German people. The Nazis resorted to violence and provocations, banned all other political parties, and put big business under the government's control. Hitler renounced the 1919 Versailles Treaty and pulled out of the League of Nations. He claimed he wanted justice for Germany. In reality, however, Germany's domestic and foreign policies were directed toward revising the international order and preparing for a war of conquest and domination in Europe (Kershaw 2000).

The Return to Militarism

Fascists in Italy and the Nazis in Germany launched programs of rearmament, which were conducted both openly and secretly. In Italy, Mussolini pushed for an ambitious naval program, openly challenging British supremacy in the Mediterranean. In 1935, he ignored the League of Nations and sent Italian troops to conquer Ethiopia; the United Kingdom and France did not stop him.

appeasement A foreign policy of concessions to an aggressive power in hopes of avoiding conflict.

Historians argue whether Hitler's aggressive tactics in particular could have been prevented. What happened was that the Western powers, above all Britain, chose **appeasement**, a foreign policy of concessions to an aggressive power in hopes of avoiding conflict. The British goal was first to avoid another war against Germany and later to create time for rearmament. This lack of resistance emboldened Hitler. France did not want to oppose Germany alone. In 1936, Hitler moved German troops into the Rhineland, which had been demilitarized according to the Versailles Treaty. British and French leaders did not stop him. In March 1938, Hitler annexed Austria, making it part of the German Reich. In September 1938, at a meeting with Hitler in Munich, the British leader Neville Chamberlain (1869–1940) accepted Hitler's demands to annex the Sudetenland, the borderlands of Czechoslovakia, populated mostly by ethnic Germans. France acquiesced, thus breaking its security pledge to one of its key allies in Europe. The Munic meeting became a sad symbol of appeasement of Nazism. The appeasing governments believed that Hitler would stop his aggressive behavior once his demands were met. In reality, Hitler proceeded unchecked. In March 1939, Germany occupied the rest of Czechoslovakia (Lukes and Goldstein 1999).

Until this point, the Soviet leader Joseph Stalin had both built up military power and conducted diplomacy to contain the rising German threat. After 1933, the Soviets joined the League of Nations and supported the principle of "collective security" in Europe against fascism and Nazism. Yet neither Western powers nor their allies, above all Poland, wanted to enter into security alliances with the Soviet Union's Communist regime. In 1939, Stalin shocked the Western powers when he made a rapid turnabout and signed a Treaty of Non-Aggression with Nazi Germany. The two dictatorships agreed to divide Poland, as well as other countries of Eastern Europe, into German and Soviet spheres of interests. Stalin believed he had thwarted Western designs (real or imagined) to pit Germany against the Soviet Union. Hitler, meanwhile, felt he was at last free to launch his war of European conquest.

Simulation:
Preventing
World War

A World Again at War

On September 1, 1939, Germany launched an attack on Poland, starting World War II. On September 17, Soviet troops occupied the eastern parts of Poland and annexed them, according to a secret agreement with Germany. Hitler expected that the United Kingdom would remain neutral. Yet reluctantly, British and French leaders kept their promises to protect Poland in case of aggression and declared war on Germany. Still, they did not attack Germany, fearing the destructive impact of modern warfare, especially German air bombing. This inaction left the initiative in Hitler's hands.

Germany defeated and occupied western parts of Poland. In April–May 1940, Hitler launched a *Blitzkrieg* ("lightning war") in the West: Germany crushed the resistance and occupied Denmark, Norway, the Netherlands, and Belgium, and then finally struck against France. After six weeks of mobile air and tank warfare, France collapsed as a military power and a state. The British forces were surrounded at Dunkirk, France, and only Hitler's error and the British spirit prevented the *Wehrmacht* (the German armed forces) from annihilating them. Hitler signed an armistice with the provisional French leadership in which Paris and northern France remained under German occupation and the southern region became a pro-German puppet regime headquartered in Vichy (a city in central France). In the spring of 1941, Germany, in alliance with fascist Italy (called "the Axis powers" as of 1936), attacked and occupied Yugoslavia and Greece. Hitler was building the new empire he had envisioned in Europe (Mazower 2000).

East Asia was also plunging into a major conflict. Japanese elites embraced militarism and a nationalist form of imperialism, directed primarily against China. In 1931–1932, the Japanese military invaded Manchuria, the large northeastern part of the historical Chinese Empire. Japanese nationalist propaganda trumpeted the concept of the *Greater East Asia Co-Prosperity Sphere*, in which Japan would bring modernization to the rest of Asia. In reality, Japan was on a collision course with the Soviet Union for control of territory.

During the Second Sino-Japanese war, which lasted eight years, China suffered terrible defeats and civilian losses. The legacy of the war negatively affected Chinese–Japanese relations for many years.

In 1937, the Second Sino-Japanese War (between China and Japan) erupted; it would last until 1945. China suffered terrible defeats and civilian losses (most notably in 1937 in the Nanking Massacre), but even so Japan could not force its enemy to capitulate. The Soviet Union, fearful of Japanese aggression, became the main backer of China. Japan feared Soviet Communism and kept a large army on the Soviet and Mongolian borders. The longer the war lasted, the more it pushed Japan into international isolation (Best 2003; Westad 2012).

In September 1940, the Japanese leadership signed a military pact with Germany but in April 1941, signed a nonaggression pact with the Soviet Union. Japan now focused on the challenges south of its borders and in the Pacific. Tensions grew between Japan and the United States. In July 1941, the U.S. Administration under President Franklin D. Roosevelt (1882–1945) imposed an oil embargo on Japan, demanding that Japanese troops be withdrawn from China. This move triggered Japan's attack on the United States at Pearl Harbor in December 1941, as well as its conquest of British, French, and Dutch colonies in Southeast Asia (Best 2003).

Turning the Tide

In Europe, Hitler's dream was to see the German Empire expanding to the East, to eliminate the Soviet Union, and to colonize the Slavic people. The German dictator admired the British Empire and initially sought to make peace with it. At the same time, he despised the United States. His megalomaniac ideas contributed to strategic blunders, affecting the course of international history. On June 22, 1941, Hitler broke the pact with Stalin and attacked the Soviet Union. Within a few months, the German army approached Moscow.

The Soviets suffered heavy casualties but pushed back, as the German army became stranded during the harsh winter.

Another major blunder followed for Hitler. In December 1941, after Japan and the United States went to war, Hitler declared war on the United States. The war turned truly global. On one side were the Axis powers: Germany, Italy, Japan, and their satellites (Hungary, Romania, and Vichy France). On the other side were the Allies: the United Kingdom and the British Empire, the United States, Canada, the Soviet Union, and several others. The United States waged naval warfare against Japan in the Pacific, turning the tide in 1942. Meanwhile, German forces were defeated first by the British in Northern Africa in late 1942 and then crucially at Stalingrad by the Soviets in early 1943.

Hitler's intention was to eliminate Slavic national elites and to turn parts of Europe, especially Ukraine, into a German colony. In 1941–1942, the German forces killed millions of Jews in Eastern Europe; this mass annihilation set the stage for the Holocaust, the deliberate extermination of six million Jews from all territories under German control. More millions died from famine or were terrorized in Poland, Yugoslavia, and Greece, and later in Italy and the Netherlands (Mazower 2008).

In 1943–1944, the tide of war decisively turned in favor of the Allies both in Europe and in the Pacific. The U.S. military joined the British in North Africa, landed in Sicily, and began to liberate Italy. In Italy, the king and elites arrested Mussolini in July 1943, and Italy attempted to surrender to the Allies. Germany had to send its troops to occupy the peninsula, but the unraveling of the Axis powers had begun. In June 1944, the Allied forces landed in Normandy and liberated France and Belgium. By the end of 1944, the Soviet army had dealt several major defeats to the German forces and had pushed them out of the Soviet Union. In the Pacific, the Japanese troops still advanced in China, but the U.S. navy retook many Pacific islands and the Philippines.

The United States continued to use its enormous financial, industrial, and technological resources to help Great Britain and the Soviet Union against Germany and its allies. Roosevelt, Stalin, and British Prime Minister Winston Churchill (1874–1965) met at Tehran, in Iran (1943), and later at Yalta, in the Soviet Union (1945), to discuss common war aims, military strategy, and political plans. Most importantly, "the Big Three" leaders agreed that they would never sign a separate peace with Germany and would conduct the war jointly until the unconditional surrender and destruction of the Third Reich (Kimball 1997; Pechatnov 2006). The alliance of the United States, the United Kingdom, and the Soviet Union was very effective. Still this wartime cooperation contained the seeds of future problems.

The 1945 Yalta Conference among Winston Churchill, Franklin Roosevelt, and Joseph Stalin laid important foundations for the future world order.

History Lab — The United Nations Security Council

In 1945, the United States, the Soviet Union, and the United Kingdom, the victors of World War II, created a global international organization called the United Nations. Together with their war allies China and France, they proposed a governing body of the United Nations—the Security Council. These five states became permanent members of this council, with the right to veto any decision voted by all other members of the United Nations. Other countries also joined the Security Council for two-year terms on a rotating basis, yet they have no veto power.

CRITICAL THINKING

❶ Do you believe the "big five" should eventually lose their permanent status and veto power? Why or why not? ❷ Should other countries be given permanent membership on the Security Council? Why or why not? If so, which specific countries would you recommend, and why? ❸ Imagine the Security Council were dissolved. How might global affairs be affected as a result? Discuss several scenarios.

The End of World War II

In the winter–spring of 1945, the Allies encircled Germany, advancing from the West, the East, and the South. On April 30, Hitler committed suicide, and on May 8, the Third Reich surrendered. The collapse of Germany revealed the enormity of postwar reconstruction. The scope of human and economic catastrophe was much greater than the devastation after World War I. In the Soviet Union, where the most brutal warfare took place, a staggering twenty-seven million perished from war-related causes. In the rest of Europe, over ten million died (military and civilians). Many European cities and much of the continent's infrastructure were in ruins.

On the Pacific front, American planes dropped two atomic bombs on the Japanese cities of Hiroshima and Nagasaki on August 6 and 9, 1945, killing tens of thousands of civilians. On August 9, Stalin fulfilled his promise to the United States to join the war in East Asia: the Soviet army attacked the Japanese forces in the Far East, in violation of the Soviet-Japanese nonaggression pact. Japan's surrender followed shortly thereafter. The Chinese government signed the Sino-Soviet treaty of friendship and alliance on August 14, 1945, accepting Stalin's demands. The outline of a new East Asia was created, as often before, by war or force, more so than by treaties (Pechatnov 2012; Hasegawa 2005).

Nazism and fascism left a profound political impact on Europe and the world. World War II altogether took the lives of more than sixty million people globally. Restoration of the prewar status quo was impossible. A new era of international relations was to come.

Check Your Knowledge

1. Which major political factors influenced international relations in the 1930s?

2. Explain the policy of appeasement.

3. What was the *Greater East Asia Co-Prosperity Sphere*?

4. Which countries represented the Allied nations, and which were Axis powers?

2.5 The Cold War

The alliance of the victorious powers of World War II (the Soviet Union, the United States, and the United Kingdom) did not last long. Instead of solid peace and international cooperation came the **Cold War** (1947–1991), a state of hostility between the West—led by the United States—and the Soviet Union. It was characterized by threats, hostile propaganda, economic sanctions, an arms race, and other preparations for total war. The conflict began in Europe and divided the continent but stopped short of open warfare. The Cold War then became global and contributed to wars and other military conflicts in Asia, Africa, and Latin America. This global confrontation lasted for over four decades.

Cold War
(1947–1991) A period of global confrontation primarily between the Soviet Union and the United States, characterized by the division of Europe into hostile blocs, intense military buildup, and military conflicts in the rest of the world.

The Origins of the Cold War

Many factors contributed to the Cold War. Traditionally, research into its origins has focused on the effects of Communism, Soviet insecurity, Russian despotism, and Stalin's paranoia (Mastny 1979). More recent research has highlighted several other factors, including the rise of the United States as a global power, American insecurity, the impact of the Second World War on Europe, and the rise of nationalism and anticolonialism in Asia (Westad 2017; Zubok 2007).

The vacuum of leadership in Europe after World War II allowed two superpowers to emerge: the United States and the Soviet Union. Would they cooperate or would they become rivals? Roosevelt died in April 1945 and was succeeded by Harry Truman. The last meeting of the Big Three (in July–August 1945) was held in Potsdam, Germany, territory occupied by the Soviet army. At this meeting, Stalin, Churchill, and Truman confirmed the old agreements: the Allies would jointly occupy Germany, which was divided into four sectors (the United Kingdom gave part of its zone to France). (See Figure 2-4.)

The momentum behind U.S.-Soviet cooperation, however, was fading fast. Truman and his advisers thought the Soviet Union should accept American terms for a postwar international order. The predominance of American power in 1945 was obvious: during the war, the U.S. economy had almost doubled, and over half of global industrial production was now in the United States. The country controlled two-thirds of the world's monetary wealth, and new international financial institutions had legitimized the U.S. dollar as a global currency. Washington thus held a powerful influence over the economy and politics of other countries. Finally, the United States had become the first and only atomic power.

American power and assertiveness alarmed Stalin. The Soviet dictator felt his country was entitled to a "security belt" of states with pro-Soviet regimes. Freely elected governments in Eastern Europe, Stalin suspected, would be pro-American, pro-British, and anti-Soviet. He began to build pro-Soviet regimes in Eastern Europe using coercion and manipulation (Zubok 2007).

Stalin's actions in turn alarmed the Americans and the British. The Soviets looted their zones of occupation in East Germany and Manchuria and closed them to international trade. The British warned the U.S. government that the Soviets could threaten trade routes in the Mediterranean Sea and between

containment A
policy of preventing
a hostile country's
expansion or
influence; in the Cold
War, this referred
to exclusion of the
Soviet Union from the
U.S.-led international
order.

Europe and the Middle East. The British government, in a flashback to the Crimean War of the nineteenth century, encouraged the United States to form a common front against what they saw as "Russian ambitions." (Kent 2005).

CONTAINMENT POLICY AND PRACTICE

In 1946–1948, U.S. foreign policy was rapidly reoriented from Soviet inclusion to **containment**: a policy of excluding Stalin's empire from the U.S.-led international order. This reorientation reflected a profound change in American international behavior. Until this moment, the mainstay of American foreign policy had been the 1823 Monroe Doctrine. Under this policy, the United States was the guarantor of security in the Western Hemisphere and avoided commitments in the rest of the world. This was one of the reasons "the Wilsonian moment" did not last after 1919. The geographic protection of two oceans had allowed the United States to choose between isolation and intervention, according to American interests. However, the World War II development of long-range bombers and the atomic bomb ended geographic security. The United States was motivated to build a permanent superior military force and engage in preemptive policies against future aggression, above all in Europe.

The Truman Doctrine and the Marshall Plan.   The Democratic Truman Administration, with Republican support, initiated a series of policies that implemented containment in practice. These included the Truman Doctrine (1947) to protect Turkey and Greece and the Marshall Plan of financial assistance to European countries, including Germany (1947–1951). Stalin boycotted the Marshall Plan, which, in theory, had applied to all of Europe. He also forced European countries under Soviet domination to follow this boycott. In February 1948, a coup in Czechoslovakia marked the beginning of what would be four decades of Communist rule in Eastern Europe. All of these events only confirmed the American perceptions of a new threat. The Soviet Union, a former ally against Hitler, became an ideal enemy in the American imagination: a huge empire with a *totalitarian* regime, alien to basic American values. The United States saw itself as the only country that could not only save the world but also remake Europe in the American way. This ideological campaign went hand in hand with the construction of the U.S.-led international order (Foglesong 2007).

The Soviet Blockade of Berlin.   The core element of the Cold War in Europe was the divided Germany. The United States wanted to build up capitalist and democratic West Germany and incorporate it into the new European order. In contrast, Stalin wanted to keep his zone of occupation and incorporate it into the Soviet-dominated eastern part of Europe. In 1947 the United States and Britain united their zones of occupation in Germany and began to reconstruct them, ignoring the Soviets.

In response, in 1948 the Soviet Union imposed a blockade on the Western zones of Berlin, where the American, British, and French military were stationed in accordance with the 1945 Potsdam agreements. With the blockade, the Soviet leader hoped to force the Western powers out of Berlin, but the

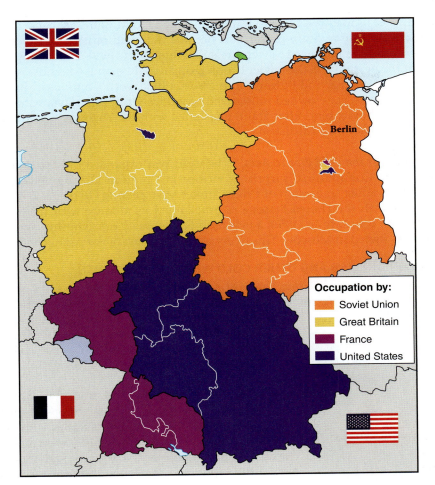

Occupation by:
- Soviet Union
- Great Britain
- France
- United States

MAP 2-5
The four occupation zones of Germany, 1945–1949.

Western allies organized a successful airlift to supply the city. In 1949, Stalin had to lift the blockade without reaching his goal. Germany became two new states: the Federal Republic of Germany, a protectorate of Western powers, and the German Democratic Republic, a satellite of the Soviet Union. These two states did not recognize each other until the 1970s and would stay divided until 1990 (Eisenberg 1996; Naimark 1996).

The Formation of NATO.   Stalin's aggressive moves helped the U.S. leaders advance the policies of support and alliance with the countries of Western Europe, which had already participated in the Marshall Plan (Hogan 1987). On April 4, 1949, at a conference in Washington, D.C., the foreign ministers of twelve countries joined the North Atlantic Treaty Organization, known as NATO. It originally consisted of Belgium, Britain, Canada, Denmark, France, Iceland, Italy, Luxembourg, the Netherlands, Norway, Portugal, and the United States. This treaty (under Article 5) obligated the United States—for the first time in its history—to go to war if any member of the alliance came under attack. American military power thus became the main protector of Western Europe against a perceived Soviet threat (Trachtenberg 1999). On the opposite side of the new divide, the Soviet Union reorganized Poland, Czechoslovakia, Hungary, Romania, and Bulgaria into a Soviet bloc, with Communist parties in power, and a state-owned militarized economy. Only Yugoslavia remained outside the Soviet bloc, after Stalin quarrelled with the Yugoslav Communist leadership (Naimark 2010).

Expansion of the Cold War to Asia.   The Cold War expanded to East Asia following the Communists' surprising victory in China in October 1949. The new Communist leadership of China, under Mao Zedong (1893-1976), broke relations with the United States and proclaimed its alliance with the Soviet Union. On February 14, 1950, a new Sino-Soviet treaty of friendship and alliance was signed in Moscow. This treaty meant the start of the Asian Cold War.

THE KOREAN WAR AND OTHER COLD WAR DEVELOPMENTS

The Cold War first became "hot" in Asia, when North Korea, using mostly Soviet aid and arms, under Communist leader Kim Il-sung (1912–1994), attacked South Korea in June 1950. As in many other cases in history, a local conflict drew in great powers. What ensued was the conflict known as the Korean War (1950–1953).

The Korean War.   In 1945, Korea was divided between Soviet and American troops along the 38th parallel. In 1949, those troops withdrew, leaving in place two antagonistic governments, one pro-American, the other pro-Soviet. Kim Il-sung wanted to destroy the rival regime in the south and unify the entire country. Stalin sanctioned the North Korean attack, mistakenly believing it would be a quick operation. Instead, the United States entered the war and obtained UN resolutions to defend South Korea and restore peace. The resolutions formed a unified military command under American leadership. Inexplicably, the Soviet Union boycotted the UN session and did not use its veto power to block the resolutions. This was the first time since 1945 the UN had played such a prominent role in war. American diplomatic victory was followed by a military victory: U.S. troops destroyed the North Korean army and moved to occupy North Korea (Stueck 2010).

In China, Mao Zedong decided to send the Chinese army to defend North Korea and stop

Kim Il-sung during the Korean War in 1952 with the first North Korean female woman pilot.

American forces, but without formally declaring war on the United States. What had looked like a sure defeat for Stalin and his satellite suddenly turned into a strategic gain. The Chinese intervention in October–November 1950 reversed the course of the Korean War. It also consolidated the Sino-Soviet alliance.

The Korean War consolidated NATO as well. The events on the Korean peninsula signaled to European states that the threat of a new war was real. The United States increased its military presence in Europe. Washington began to focus on nuclear weapons as a means to defend its European allies against the Soviet Union. Security concerns influenced economic strategies. West Germany, France, and other European countries to the west of the Soviet bloc began to take steps toward effecting a closer economic and political integration (Trachtenberg 1999; Hitchcock 2010).

The Growth of Two Superpowers.   In the 1950s, the Cold War reached its peak and became the primary factor shaping international relations in Europe and Asia. Instead of an old world order, where several great powers competed and chose alliances, the Cold War created two centers of power, or *poles*: one in Washington and the other in Moscow. In this global confrontation, there was almost no room for neutrality; states had to choose one side or the other and could not easily change their alliances. Stalin's death in March 1953 made the global situation less stable. The Soviet leaders were torn between the desire to ease tensions and the fear of being forced into unacceptable concessions (Zubok 2007).

Yet the United States was not ready for any comprehensive agreement with the Kremlin. The Republican Administration under President Eisenhower (who took office in January 1953) pursued a policy of global containment of Communism and pushed U.S. allies to share the burden. With this policy in mind, Americans created anti-Soviet and anti-Chinese blocs from the Middle East to Asia and the Pacific. American and British intelligence staged a coup in Iran (1953) to bring Iran into the Western orbit (Milani 2011). Central America also felt the Cold War. The United States overthrew the pro-socialist government in Guatemala (1954), under the pretext of protecting the Western Hemisphere from Communism. Washington continued testing thermonuclear weapons to demonstrate the United States' military superiority over the Soviet Union (Trachtenberg 1999).

A Nuclear Arms Race.   The United States publicly declared that any form of Communist aggression in Europe or Asia would trigger retaliation by American nuclear forces. After two world wars, a third world war, now with nuclear weapons, appeared plausible. Both American and Soviet leaders, however, began to realize that a nuclear conflict could mean the end of civilization. In 1955, the Soviet and American leadership met in Geneva, Switzerland, for the first time since 1945 and held talks on reducing the danger of a surprise attack. The United States, however, still refused to consider treaties with the Kremlin that could regulate the rivalry. Such treaties, American leadership believed, could undermine the precarious alliances in the West. And Soviet leadership, acting with more confidence, refused to make any concessions to the West.

The Soviet Union tested its own thermonuclear weapons in 1953 and 1955. In October 1957, the Soviets launched the first intercontinental ballistic missile, carrying *Sputnik,* an artificial satellite. The Kremlin now had the technical capacity to deliver a nuclear warhead to the Western Hemisphere. This threat heightened American insecurity and added yet more fuel to the arms race.

The Berlin Wall. The new Soviet leader, Nikita Khrushchev, became known for his erratic foreign policy. He demanded in 1958 and again in 1961 that Western armed forces leave West Berlin, where they had been stationed since 1945. A serious crisis accompanied by ultimatums and threats followed. In the end, Khrushchev chose to erect the wall around West Berlin in 1961. The Americans did not react because their rights in West Berlin were not violated. U.S. President John F. Kennedy, however, went to West Berlin in 1963, offering assurances that West Berlin would remain a part of the West. For many years, until 1989, the wall would separate West Berlin from Communist East Germany, a symbol of the Cold War (Harrison 2000; Fursenko and Naftali 2006).

JFK in Berlin, 1963

The Cuban Missile Crisis. Soviet and Western behavior during the Berlin crisis came to be called **brinkmanship**: a strategy of approaching the brink of an open conflict with the expectation that the enemy would "blink" first, make concessions, or back off. This international environment manifested itself in the most infamous and dangerous crisis of the Cold War, the Cuban Missile Crisis (October–November 1962), when the Soviet Union and the United States came to the brink of a direct military clash. Cool heads, secret communications, and several lucky breaks prevented nuclear war. We will turn to this crisis in detail in Chapter 4.

brinkmanship A strategy of approaching the brink of an open conflict with the expectation that the enemy would "blink" first, bargain, or back off.

DEBATE > TO BE OR NOT TO BE PREDICTABLE?

Cold War historians in Russia, the United Kingdom, and the United States tend to agree that Soviet leader Nikita Khrushchev's foreign policy was unpredictable and his actions were often erratic. He repeatedly issued threats to the West, yet on other occasions he promised peace. He made many provocative and even belligerent statements that later were retracted. He made many risky diplomatic decisions. Some argue, however, that Khrushchev's unpredictable behavior helped the Soviet Union keep the West in a state of constant uncertainty. Global war did not break out under his leadership. Khrushchev was able to reach out to the United States and maintained a dialogue with the West.

WHAT'S YOUR VIEW?

❶ Is a leader's unpredictable foreign policy a strength or a liability? Could it be a combination of the two? Discuss, using examples from today's foreign policy decisions. ❷ Is it strategically beneficial for a political leader to be unpredictable so that the opponents are left guessing what his or her next move would be? Or are stability and predictability more valuable strategies in diplomacy? ❸ What comparisons could you potentially make between Khrushchev and U.S. President Donald Trump, and why?

DECOLONIZATION AND THE VIETNAM WAR

Another major factor that changed the world at the time was **decolonization**, which began after World War II and regained momentum in the 1950s in the Middle East, in Southeast Asia, and later in Africa. Geographers and journalists created the term the *Third World* to designate the huge areas of the world outside the West (the First World) and the Soviet bloc (the Second World). The breakthrough in decolonization came in 1955, when the former colonies of India, Pakistan, Indonesia, and others convened at a conference in Bandung, Indonesia. Twenty-nine countries from Asia and Africa, including China, sent delegations to this conference. The participants—representing nearly half of the world's population—declared they would stay out of the Cold War, observing the principles of nonintervention in other countries' affairs.

Washington opposed the existence of colonial empires in theory, but in practice, the Cold War politics compelled the United States to back the European colonial powers. Washington needed military bases overseas and feared that a quick dissolution of colonial empires could weaken their European allies and help the Communists gain power globally. Such a development would give the Soviet Union access to strategic resources and materials in the Third World, including oil and uranium, and would threaten American military bases. Finally, Washington hoped that former colonies would choose American over Soviet models of development. The West's concerns were real. Moscow also globalized its foreign policy, offering assistance and development advice to any anti-Western government, including Egypt, Syria, Burma, India, and Indonesia. The Soviets aimed to undermine the system of alliances the United States had created in Asia—and they were in part successful.

The Suez Crisis. The first major confrontation involving a developing country and the colonial powers was the Suez crisis of 1956. When Egypt nationalized the Suez Canal, which belonged to Britain and France, the British and French forces, helped by Israel (a new state created in 1948 after the British colonial authorities withdrew from Palestine), attacked Egypt. Both the Soviet Union and the United States denounced this action as an act of aggression. Washington, not wanting to antagonize the Arabs, forced Britain and France to stop the war. The Suez crisis humiliated Britain and France, shook NATO to its core, and accelerated decolonization (Westad 2017).

The Vietnam War. Decolonization began to change the nature of the Cold War. Many new leaders appeared in Asia and Latin America, ranging from recent law school graduates to guerillas, who for years had fought against colonial powers in the jungles. Many of them were Marxists and admired the Soviet Union and China. In 1954, the Communist forces in Vietnam defeated France as a colonial power. For the United States, this meant that all of Indo-China, including Laos, Cambodia, and Thailand, could become Communist. U.S. policy makers feared a domino effect, in which Communist influence would spread from country to country, and the U.S.-dominated "free world" could collapse like a falling row of dominos.

decolonization
Process by which colonies in Asia and Africa become independent of the European masters.

Captured Viet Cong guerrilla fighters, 1965. With the support of the North Vietnamese army, the Viet Cong fought against South Vietnam (late 1950s–1975) and the United States (early 1960s–1973).

In 1954, the Americans reached a compromise with the Soviet Union and China: Vietnam was temporarily divided across the 17th parallel: Communists were in control to the North and the French to the South. The United States soon replaced the French and began to support an anti-Communist government of South Vietnam. In the early 1960s, the government of North Vietnam decided to unify the country by force and began a guerrilla war against South Vietnam and its American sponsors. They acted without Soviet or Chinese consent. The United States in response poured money, resources, and military advisers into South Vietnam. During the Vietnam War (1955–1975), the United States bombed Vietnamese cities in the North and the jungles where guerrillas could hide. Scholars agree that it was a war the Americans could not win, despite their vast economic and military superiority (Logevall 2014; Westad 2017).

THE RISE AND FALL OF DÉTENTE

détente The period of relative relaxation of international tensions during the Cold War from late 1962 to the mid-1970s.

The word *détente* in French means "relaxation of tensions"; this is the term given for the period from the end of the Cuban Missile Crisis in 1962 until 1975. Brinkmanship and nuclear threats were replaced by negotiations and diplomatic summits. People in both Western and Eastern blocs had grown tired of living in an atmosphere of tension and fear. Numerous international treaties were signed during the détente period. Some of them, like the 1975 Helsinki Final Act, remain important today. At the same time, these summits and treaties failed to bring the Cold War to an end in the 1970s.

Four factors in particular contributed to the failure of détente diplomacy. First, the U.S. leadership failed to achieve a graceful exit from Vietnam.

The North Vietnamese leaders, despite Soviet and Chinese pressure, continued their fight to complete victory. This victory emboldened other Marxist guerrillas in Africa to fight against the West, and so again, the Soviet and American interests clashed in the Third World (we will discuss the war in Angola in Chapter 5). Second, the Soviets—now under the leadership of Leonid Brezhnev—believed that the Soviet military buildup made Washington more agreeable (Zubok 2007). This was a grand illusion. An eminent historian of the Cold War concluded that the Americans "were simply not willing to tolerate that the United States could have an equal in international affairs, in the 1970s or ever" (Westad 2017, p. 500). Third, European leaders also became disillusioned with détente. The main focus of Soviet-American relations at that time was negotiations to limit strategic forces on both sides. Yet no treaty could alone stop the arms race. Europeans wanted instead more trade, consumerism, and more civil rights for both Western and Eastern parts of Europe (Foot 2010; Moyne 2012). Finally, decolonization and volatility in the Third World further complicated détente politics throughout the 1970s.

THE CONTINUATION OF THE COLD WAR IN ASIA AND THE MIDDLE EAST

China was an obvious enemy of the Soviet-Western détente. In the 1970s, China resurfaced in international affairs following the Chinese Cultural Revolution (1966–1976), a period of political and economic turmoil.

Chinese Modernization. Nixon's visit to Beijing in 1972 returned China to the forefront of world affairs. After Mao's death in 1976, the Chinese leadership under Deng Xiaoping (1904-1997) set a new course of modernization for China. China's economic relations with Japan began to expand rapidly. In 1979, Deng suggested that China could become a strategic American partner, containing Soviet ambitions in Asia, in exchange for American assistance in Chinese modernization. In the early 1980s, the United States began to assist China to build up its power against the Soviet Union (Westad 2017).

The Iranian Revolution. In Iran, a major event developed that would affect international relations for years to come: the Iranian Revolution of 1978–1979. For many years, Shah Mohammad Reza Pahlavi (1919–1980) was one of the most important American allies in the Middle East and South Asia. Mismanagement and corruption contributed to the demise of his regime, however (Milani 2011). The fall of the Shah meant the United States was losing the Cold War in the region. The Iranian Revolution followed a script that almost all experts of the Cold War had failed to envision. Led by the charismatic Ayatollah Ruhollah Khomeini (1902–1989), Iranian Islamic leaders proclaimed the United States the *Great Satan* and took hostages at the U.S. embassy in Tehran. They also arrested and killed thousands of Communists and Soviet sympathizers.

The Afghan Revolution and Soviet Intervention. The Iranian events resonated in neighboring Afghanistan, which had remained neutral for most of the Cold War. In 1974–1978, a series of palace coups brought to power the revolutionary military and leftist intellectuals. They pushed for land reform, equal rights for women, and compulsory education for children. However, Afghanistan quickly became a hotbed for radical Islamists, who viewed the secular regime in Kabul and its Soviet backers as their mortal enemies. In December 1979, after a long hesitation, the Soviet government decided to introduce Soviet troops into Afghanistan "to protect the revolution." The Soviet forces killed the brutal leader of Afghanistan, who was suspected of disloyalty, and installed a puppet government. The United States interpreted this action as Soviet aggression and a threat to the oil-rich Gulf (Kalinovsky 2011). Ronald Reagan (1911–2004) became the U.S. president in 1981 and vowed to continue waging the Cold War until victory.

THE END OF THE COLD WAR

In 1985, Reagan had a negotiating partner in the Kremlin. Mikhail Gorbachev (b. 1931) belonged to the young generation of Soviet leaders and wanted to end the era of confrontation. Ideologically a committed Communist, Gorbachev belonged to a generation of educated Soviet people who were open to new ideas, including liberal and social democratic views. He wanted to reform the country and faced a choice: a steep new race against the West and its allies in Asia or cooperation with them. Gorbachev chose the latter. The superpowers' summits in Geneva (1985), Reykjavik (1986), and Washington (1987) initially focused on the limitations and reductions of nuclear weapons. Both leaders agreed that nuclear war should never be fought and could not be won. Gradually, Gorbachev's agenda broadened, as he began to change the Soviet economic and political systems and accepted Western norms of human rights. In December 1988, Gorbachev declared at the United Nations that force should never be used in international relations. This was a remarkably idealistic goal: even Wilson's Principles and the Atlantic Charter did not exclude the use of force (Wilson 2014; Taubman 2017).

Why did the Cold War come to an end? We will explore this question further in the Case Study at the end of Chapter 5. For now, we will briefly touch on several factors. Gorbachev wanted much more than another détente; he proposed gradually dismantling the two blocs and making the Soviet Union join the former enemy—the West—to construct a new peaceful international order. In 1988–1989, the Soviet Union withdrew from Afghanistan, reduced its troop levels in East Asia, and normalized its relationship with China. In 1989, a series of popular movements ended the Communist regimes in Poland, Hungary, East Germany, Czechoslovakia, Bulgaria, and Romania. On November 9, 1989, after weeks of mass protests in East Germany, the Berlin Wall fell. West Germany proclaimed a plan for unification with East Germany (Levesque 1997; Maier 1997; Nevers 2003). Gorbachev made these changes possible and did not resist them. The economic bloc that tied these countries to the Soviet Union collapsed, and the military bloc was formally dissolved in July 1991.

By contrast, American global power grew rapidly during the 1980s, buoyed by continuing globalization and the technological revolution. Computers, robotics, and smart weaponry changed economies, communications,

People from East and West Berlin climb on the Berlin Wall at the Brandenburg Gate, November 9, 1989, marking the symbolic end of the Cold War.

and the nature of warfare, and the United States was at the vanguard of all these processes. Western Europe embraced geographic and political integration: the United Kingdom, Denmark, and Ireland joined the European Economic Community (EEC) in 1973; the countries of Southern Europe joined in the 1980s. In 1987, EEC members agreed on the Single European Act, which would create a common market where capital, goods, and people could move freely within Europe. In a few years, this act would become the foundation for the European Union, a more integrated Western Europe with a common currency and common governing and legislating institutions. Soon the integration process was extended to Eastern European countries as well.

The collapse of the Soviet bloc in Europe in 1989 provided the United States with a unique opportunity to build a new international order according to Western, primarily American, norms. The Republican Administration of U.S. President George H. W. Bush (1924-2018) pushed for German unification on Western terms, as a member of NATO. Gorbachev consented. In October 1990, the Soviet Union, the United States, the United Kingdom, and France signed the treaty of final settlement, and Germany's unification was complete. Germany acknowledged its post–1945 borders and vowed not to develop weapons of mass destruction (Bozo, Roedder, and Sarotte 2017).

In November 1990, in Paris, the NATO countries, the Eastern European countries, and the Soviet Union agreed to reduce their military forces in Europe. Most of the European states, the United States, Canada, and the Soviet Union signed this "Charter for a New Europe," based on democratic norms and the observation of human rights, and the rights of countries to join or not alliances in the way they want. The United States, NATO, and the EEC were the architects of the new order.

Gorbachev's bold vision and diplomacy were undermined by the rapid disintegration of the Soviet Union. His domestic economic reforms were misguided and failing, and the policies of political liberalization inspired national republics, some of which had been incorporated in the Soviet Union by force, to claim sovereignty and independence. In August–December 1991, the Soviet Union dissolved into fifteen independent states; the largest of them, the Russian Federation, accepted the international legal responsibilities and rights of the disappeared superpower, including the permanent seat at the United Nations Security Council.

The Cold War ended suddenly and momentously, followed immediately by the disappearance of the second pole of the old international system. This rapid change created a lasting legacy of economic, political, and legal problems for Eastern Europe and the post-Soviet space. Yugoslavia also collapsed along ethnic lines into a brutal war in 1991. The place of former Soviet allies, from Poland to Bulgaria, in the new Europe was unclear. Even less clear was the place of the Russian Federation, Ukraine, and other post-Soviet states. Would they be included or excluded in the new world order? In the United States, the end of the Cold War became conflated with the demise of Communism and the collapse of the Soviet Union; this was interpreted as validation and triumph of U.S.-led institutions and American principles. Most importantly, the United States remained the only superpower, and most of the world looked to Washington for money, ideas, and decisions on how to manage international affairs (Ikenberry 2010).

Check Your Knowledge

1. Explain the meaning of the term *Cold War*.

2. What is containment? Give an example from contemporary international relations.

3. Explain brinksmanship, suggesting examples from contemporary politics.

4. Explain the domino effect.

5. Define and explain détente, suggesting several reasons why it failed.

6. What was Gorbachev's role in ending the Cold War?

2.6 The Post–Cold War Era

After the Cold War ended, globalization continued in many spheres. The Internet changed how the world communicated. Political news, as well as information about science, technology, culture, and consumer goods, became instantaneously available in any place with electricity and connectivity.

The new international order, built on liberal norms of cooperation, was not without challenges, however. First came the ongoing instability of the Middle East and the expanding threat of terrorism. Other major developments included the rise of China and the resurrection of Russian power. As the main stakeholders in the global order, the United States and the European Union faced a host of new political crises.

Changing Transnational Norms

A major test of the post–Cold War world came in August 1990, when Iraq invaded Kuwait, a small neighboring country. In response, U.S. troops, aided by other NATO military forces, initiated the Gulf War (1990-1991) and defeated the Iraqi dictator Saddam Hussein. This short war demonstrated the absolute superiority of the American military and the role of the United States as an indispensable force of justice. Gorbachev backed the UN resolution to remove Iraqi troops from Kuwait but tried to prevent the war. The collapsing Soviet Union, however, was no longer an obstacle to Washington's designs.

One major development of this era was the increasingly important role of nonstate actors on the global stage (Iriye 2002). In addition to NGOs, organizations of regional cooperation gained prominence, as did transnational communities and trade organizations. The International Monetary Fund (IMF) and the World Bank remained important in influencing and often defining the economic policies of developing countries and the new states in the former Soviet space. Members of the European Community demonstrated the most remarkable degree of transnational integration in the world, signing the Treaty on European Union in Maastricht, Netherlands, in 1992. For the first time in history, sovereign states had agreed to delegate crucial elements of their sovereignty to a supranational government.

Many scholars of international relations wrote about the epochal transformation of the very nature of politics, including international politics. Instead of sovereign states, these scholars argued, transnational communities were becoming primary actors, forming relationships based on common democratic values. Instead of going to war over disputes and territories, states increasingly sought institutions of international arbitration. Abiding by the new transnational norms became the only way of achieving not only economic prosperity, but international security as well (Wendt 2003).

The Twenty-First Century

Any complacency with the liberal world order was shattered after the terrorist attacks in the United States on September 11, 2001, during the presidency of George W. Bush. In response, the United States proclaimed a "global war on terrorism." This declaration manifested itself as a set of economic, political, and military actions aimed at destroying Al-Qaeda, the organization that had perpetrated the attacks. Many states around the world joined the campaign against international terrorism. The United States and its NATO allies, with the cooperation and assistance of other countries, including Russia, occupied Afghanistan, the main base for Al-Qaeda operations (2001).

Two years later, the United States attacked Iraq, a move the White House rationalized by pointing to the threat of terrorism and potential WMD. The occupation would last until 2011. In contrast to the Gulf War, U.S. military operations against Iraq in 2003 were controversial from the start. Not only Russia, but also Germany and France, key U.S. allies in Europe, opposed the decision to invade. Although the invasion succeeded in toppling Hussein's regime, the collapse of the old dictatorship produced a civil war that caused hundreds of thousands of casualties among civilians. The Middle East became even less stable than before, as the chaos in Iraq helped spawn new terrorist organizations, such as the Islamic State. Afghanistan also became an unstable American protectorate, as the defeated Taliban militants came back, and the United States and its NATO allies had failed to build a stable statehood there.

In North Africa, the Arab Spring of 2011 sparked hope, but quickly gave way to instability. The fall of dictatorships in several Arab countries, including Tunisia, Egypt, Libya, and Syria, contributed to a breeding ground for radical terrorism. In Syria, the dictator Bashar al Assad's efforts to remain in power led to an ongoing, multi-sided armed conflict (the Syrian Civil War, 2011–present) that has claimed hundreds of thousands of lives. Refugees have fled to Europe in search of safety. With Russia's help, Assad reasserted his control.

In the eastern parts of Europe, the U.S. and EU strategy of integration yielded impressive results. In 1999–2008, all countries from the former Soviet bloc became members or candidate members of NATO and joined the EU; three former Soviet republics, Estonia, Latvia, and Lithuania, did the same. This success, however, came at a cost: the failure to find a framework for cooperation and integration with Russia, a large state that succeeded the Soviet Union (Goldgeier and McFaul 1999).

Leaders in Moscow witnessed the failure of Gorbachev's vision of "Europe from the Atlantic to the Urals." They increasingly viewed the NATO expansion and the post–Cold War global order as stacked against Russia's interests. They viewed American domination as the root of this problem. Particularly after the American occupation of Iraq in 2003, anti-Americanism spread in Russia. The Kremlin began to abandon liberal policies and instead applied authoritarian methods of governance. Under Russian president Vladimir Putin (b.1952), the domestic trend toward authoritarianism and his suspicion of NATO's continuing expansion fueled an increasing tension with the United States and its allies (Shiraev and Zubok 2000; Savranskaya and Blanton 2018).

Frustrated with Russia's newly defiant behavior, many in the United States demanded a tougher course on Putin. In 2009–2010, the Administration under U.S. President Barack Obama attempted to return to partnership. This policy failed, however, and after 2011 Washington and Moscow were on a collision course. Prompted by the political turmoil in Ukraine in 2014, where the United States, the EU, and Russian interests were in conflict, Putin annexed Crimea (as we will discuss further in Chapter 5). This made the shift from cooperation to confrontation irreversible (Sakwa 2016).

Meanwhile, the global position of the United States weakened. The U.S. financial crisis in 2008 turned into a most serious global recession since the 1970s; it affected U.S. allies the rest of the world. The protracted occupations of Iraq and Afghanistan undermined the tolerance of the American public for active international engagement. Despite the progress of European integration, it was clear that Europe would not become a powerful political actor, and its economic power did not grow as fast as that of Asian countries. In East Asia, China demonstrated economic growth and development that eclipsed any previous examples in world history, including the economic rise of Great Britain, Germany, and the United States.

China became more interlinked with the West economically and financially but, contrary to Western liberal expectations, did not transform toward liberal democracy. After the Soviet collapse, the Chinese leadership did everything to retain full political control, distancing itself further from Western norms and values, including human rights. During the last decade, especially under the leadership of Xi Jinping (b.1953) China began to invest globally, attempting to rival the United States for global predominance, and shrinking the influence of Western liberal organizations, such as the IMF and World Bank.

In the second decade of the twenty-first century, many elements of the post–Cold War appeared to be in disarray. The Russian militant actions in Ukraine in 2014–2015 shattered the illusion that wars in Europe had been eradicated. The EU had been buffeted by a series of crises, including Greek insolvency (2010–2012), stemming from the global financial crisis of 2008, the decision of the United Kingdom to leave the EU ("Brexit," 2016–2019), and the political volatility of other members, such as Hungary and Italy. The election of Donald Trump (b.1946) as U.S. president in 2016 reflected the discontent of many Americans with the domestic and international status quo. President Trump undertook actions that broke with the policies of maintaining relations with NATO, the EU, and other traditional friends. Trade barriers and tariffs challenged the free-market policies of the past and created a threat of trade wars, above all with China. How might the structures of the international order continue to evolve?

Check Your Knowledge

1. After the end of the Cold War, in what ways did non-state actors become more important?

2. What factors contributed to global instability in the first two decades of the twenty-first century?

CASE STUDY

The What-Ifs of History

What if George Washington had struck a deal in the 1770s to allow the Thirteen Colonies to remain in the British Empire? How profoundly would such a deal have affected international politics? If Stalin had accepted economic assistance from the United States in the 1940s, would the Cold War have taken place? Would the United States have gone to war in Afghanistan and Iraq if Al Gore had won the U.S. presidency in 2000?

Some political scientists construct thought experiments to imagine alternative historical outcomes that might potentially have occurred (Carr 1961; Tetlock et al. 2005). They use *counterfactual* analysis, which involves thinking through why events happened and how they might have happened differently or not at all. The aim is to learn from both what happened and what could have happened. To keep thinking about causality in history, consider the following alternative scenarios as examples:

- Imagine that U.S. President Woodrow Wilson (in office 1913–1921) would have convinced the Republican Senate Majority Leader Henry Cabot Lodge to ratify the 1919 Paris Accord. The United States would have thus joined the League of Nations. Could this potentially have prevented World War II? Why or why not?
- Could U.S. President Lyndon B. Johnson (in office 1963–1968) have deescalated the war in Vietnam in the mid-1960s? After he was elected in 1964, he wanted to negotiate with the Vietnamese "anytime, anywhere," but he did not do this. What if he had?

Analysis

If we want to learn from history—alternative or actual—we should accept that international relations are too complex to be entirely changed by a single decision of a single individual (Gelb and Betts 1979). More than who the president or prime minister is, what matters are ideologies, institutions, and international context. By this logic, for instance, the identities of the U.S. and Soviet leaders in the 1940s may not have been as significant as the mutually antagonistic ideologies of the emerging superpowers. On the other hand, individual decisions can have massive significance in the course of history. Consider U.S. President Harry S. Truman's decision to use atomic weapons against Japan in 1945. What factors led to that decision? What would have happened if the United States had not bombed Japan? A similar set of decisions produced the Korean War in 1950. What if Joseph Stalin had not supported Kim Il-sung? What if Mao Zedong had not sent troops to North Korea?

Not all political scientists and historians support counterfactual explorations. The argument against this line of thinking is that mainstream historical research should not be speculative. Advocates point out, however, that most of our history lessons contain counterfactual assumptions. For example, textbooks often claim that U.S. President John F. Kennedy's decisive actions during the 1962 Cuban Missile Crisis prevented nuclear war.

Note that it can be difficult to separate the individual strengths and weaknesses of world leaders from underlying contexts and circumstances. After all, individuals do not make decisions in a vacuum. Counterfactual history is about exploring useful "what if" scenarios. By addressing the question "What could have happened?" we can give more careful and critical attention to the question "What happened?" Most importantly, "what if" scenarios can help us anticipate the possibilities of tomorrow.

Case Study Questions

1. Suppose Hillary Clinton had won the 2016 U.S. presidential election instead of Donald Trump. How and why might U.S. foreign policy have been different as a result? For example, how might the state of affairs have changed between the United States and North Korea?

2. Suppose the United States and its Western allies reached a deal with the militants in Syria, Iraq, and Afghanistan (including, for the sake of the argument, the Taliban and al-Qaeda). What kind of international situation might develop in the Middle East and Central Asia as a result?

TIMELINE: SELECTED KEY EVENTS IN INTERNATIONAL RELATIONS

1648	Peace of Westphalia
1765–1783	American Revolution
1789–1799	French Revolution
1803–1815	Napoleonic Wars
1815	Congress of Vienna
1839–1842	First Opium War
1848	Year of Revolution in Europe
1870–1871	Franco-Prussian War
1914–1918	World War I and the end of the Austro-Hungarian, Russian, German, and Ottoman empires
1917	Russian Revolution
1939–1945	World War II
1947–1990	Cold War
1950–1953	Korean War
1955–1975	Vietnam War
1990-1991	Gulf War; Dissolution of the Soviet Union
1992-1993	Establishment of the European Union
2001	September 11 Terrorist Attacks
2001–present	Afghanistan War
2003–2011	Iraq War
2008	Global Financial Crisis
2011–present	Syrian Civil War
2017–2019	Brexit

The Evolution of International Relations

2.1 Explain the origins of the international system, noting key developments following the Peace of Westphalia.

The Peace of Westphalia (1648) formally recognized the sovereignty of foreign states, legitimizing a state's right to determine its own religion and policies. Over the next two centuries, capitalism began to take hold alongside the rise of permanent national militaries.

Q: How did both the rise of capitalism and the growth of militarism change warfare?

2.2 Discuss how the major trends of nineteenth-century European affairs affected twentieth-century world history.

The nineteenth century saw rapid economic and technological development as well as a number of watershed revolutions. Key policies included nationalism, imperialism, and colonialism. Militarism developed alongside the potential for a large-scale conflict both within and outside of Europe.

Q: How did industrialization transform military capabilities?

Q: How did the rise of nationalism affect imperial conquest?

2.3 Recognize how the First World War set the stage for the Second World War.

The collapse of Russia, Germany, Austria-Hungary, and the Ottoman Empire defined the military and political outcome of the First World War. The Treaty of Versailles (1919) was extremely punitive toward Germany, leaving it vulnerable economically and politically. By the 1920s, Europe was much poorer, more nationalistic, and less stable than it had been before the war.

Q: Why did diplomatic efforts after World War I fail to create stability in Europe?

2.4 Describe the effects of the Second World War on the modern international system.

Nazism and fascism left a profound political impact on Europe and the world. The scale of destruction and human tragedy inspired a renewed search for a stable international order. The redistribution of power following the war, however, paved the way for the Cold War.

Q: What were the turning points in the downfall of the Axis powers?

Q: What institutions were designed to create a stable world order?

2.5 Analyze the Cold War's origins, its key events, and the factors that brought about its end.

The vacuum in Europe after World War II allowed two superpowers to emerge: the United States and the Soviet Union. Early in the Cold War, key events included the Truman Doctrine and the Marshall Plan (1947), the Soviet blockade of Berlin (1948–1949), and the formation of NATO (1949). Related military conflicts included the Korean War (1950–1953) and the Vietnam War (1955–1975). The Cuban Missile Crisis of 1962 brought the world to the brink of nuclear war. Gobachev's reforms beginning in 1985 helped end the Cold War while also contributing to the dismantling of the Soviet Union.

Q: Why did détente diplomacy fail?

Q: How did developments in China affect the Cold War?

2.6 Outline key trends in the international developments of the post–Cold War Era.

Ongoing instability in the Middle East and the global increase in terrorism threatened the international order following the Cold War. Other major developments included the rise of China and the resurrection of Russian power.

Q: How did U.S. foreign policy evolve after the Cold War?

Q: How did the rise of China after the Cold War affect the international order?

KEY TERMS

appeasement 54
brinkmanship 64
Cold War 59
colonialism 45
containment 60

decolonization 65
détente 66
fascism 53
imperialism 45
industrialization 45

legitimacy 42
nationalism 46
Peace of Westphalia 40
republic 42

CHAPTER 3

Realism and Liberalism

> *The sad duty of politics is to establish justice in a sinful world.*
>
> —REINHOLD NIEBUHR

In his classic science fiction novel *1984* (published in 1948), George Orwell described a world divided among three rival empires. Locked in a balance-of-power system, the empires form and break alliances and yet are permanently at war against one another. Governments repress the population by controlling information, rewriting history, preying on fears, and mobilizing against nebulous enemies.

Orwell's dystopia was a grim satire of international relations in the late 1940s. Only a few years earlier, the United States and Great Britain had been allied with the Soviet Union against Hitler's Germany. By 1948, however, they were in a Cold War against their former ally. Orwell's novel reflected the fear of a vicious cycle of chaos and violence.

Instead of leading to another world war, however, the Cold War ended in a manner that inspired hope for a better world order. In 1987, Mikhail Gorbachev, the Communist leader of the Soviet Union, published the book *Perestroika: New Thinking for Our Country and the World*. It was a call to world leaders to reject the use of force in foreign policy and to put aside ideological differences in the name of economic and cultural cooperation. During momentous changes in Germany and Eastern Europe in 1989, Gorbachev refrained from using force.

On the one hand, Orwell's gloomy predictions appeared outdated and wrong. Yet on the other, global peace never truly came. Numerous deadly conflicts and wars broke out in the years that followed, and new conflicts continue to emerge. Is peace possible after all?

Chinese President Xi Jinping walks with Russian President Vladimir Putin during a welcoming ceremony in Beijing in 2018. Do you believe that countries can maintain international stability and peace today without turning to violence or using threats of violence?

These examples illustrate the debate between the two dominant ways of understanding international relations: realism versus liberalism. Continuing warfare speaks to the views of *realism*, which holds that power is the key issue in international politics. By contrast, the ideals of Gorbachev's *Perestroika* represent *liberalism*, which emphasizes that by overcoming power games, an international community can be created.

This chapter describes the main principles and applications of realism and liberalism, as well as how their proponents have responded to one another. In the concluding section, we discuss the impact of these debates on our world and our thinking.

Learning Objectives

3.1 Describe the key principles of realism, and explain how they evolved over time.

3.2 Discuss the meaning of states' power, polarity, and interests in realist theory.

3.3 Explain why and how liberalism dismisses the principles of power politics.

3.4 Discuss the liberal ideas of soft power and international institutions.

3.5 Distinguish different approaches and traditions within realism and liberalism.

3.6 Critically apply realism and liberalism to international relations on the levels of individual decisions, specific policies of states, and global developments.

anarchy Applied to realism, the lack of any executive power above individual states capable of regulating their behavior.

realism A school of international relations that focuses on power, security and state interests.

3.1 Realism

One way of thinking about international relations is as a game of chess. Players consider strategies for attacking and defending, deceiving, positioning, and holding ground. In chess, no supreme authority tells the players how to move their pieces.

In the context of world politics, this situation is called **anarchy**: it is not total chaos, as one may think, but a world government is absent. **Realism** is an approach to international relations that focuses on states (sovereign countries) and their interests, balance of power, and the structure of international relations. According to realism, only states can be players in international relations.

They defend their interests, protect their resources, create alliances, react to outside threats, and impose their will on others (Walt 1987).

The key argument of international realism is that *sovereign* states react to the situation of global anarchy by relying on their own resources. As the argument goes, the main goal of states is *power*, the ability or potential to influence other actors. Because anarchy cannot be eliminated in world politics, there is never enough power for any country. Sovereign states thus bargain with one another, pursue a mutual balancing of interests, build coalitions, and develop policies to implement their own decisions. We will discuss power further in this chapter but will begin with an overview of realism's historical and intellectual roots.

The Roots of Realism

Realism as a concept has a long history. In the fifth century BCE, military leader and historian Thucydides wrote in his *History of the Peloponnesian War* that in Greece, which was divided among many independent states and statelets, "The strong do what they will and the weak suffer what they must." Two thousand years later, as independent cities and principalities constantly squabbled on the Italian peninsula, philosopher Niccolò Machiavelli wrote in *The Prince* (1532) that it is not enough when others like and respect a state; it is better when they fear its power.

Beginning in the middle of the seventeenth century, Europe became a chessboard for balance-of-power games. As we discussed in Chapter 2, the Peace of Westphalia in 1648 marked a vital agreement on the principle of sovereignty. The English thinker Thomas Hobbes witnessed the Westphalian peace from Paris, where he wrote his landmark philosophical book, *Leviathan*. He pessimistically observed that mankind was driven by "a perpetual and restless desire of power that ceases only in death."

The Rise and Influence of Realpolitik

Following the Peace of Westphalia, the European power struggle continued for two centuries as European monarchies transformed into nation-states. The set of players changed, but all of them, including Great Britain, France, Russia, Austria-Hungary, Germany, Italy, and many smaller states, honed the realist skills of balancing power and changing alliances. In the 1820s–1840s, Austrian statesman Klemens von Metternich (1773–1859) skillfully placed the Austrian Empire in the center of European politics. In the 1860s, Prussian Chancellor Otto von Bismarck executed a power play, combining short, victorious wars with brilliant diplomatic balancing. Under Bismarck's leadership, Prussia ended Austria's hegemony (dominance) and unified a multitude of smaller German states into the mighty German Empire in 1871. Metternich's and Bismarck's maneuvers became known as **realpolitik**, a system of politics or principles based on the realities of power rather than moral or ideological considerations.

The two world wars and the Cold War shaped an entire generation of realist thinkers. Even in the United States, where realpolitik was unpopular,

realpolitik A system of politics or principles based on realities of power rather than moral or ideological considerations.

The Congress of Berlin, by Anton von Werner. This 1878 meeting led by German chancellor Otto von Bismarck marked the peak of an international system based on a balance of power among several of the most influential European states.

Read more about the practitioners of modern American realism.

realism became a dominant approach after World War II. In his 1948 work *Power among Nations*, German-born American thinker Hans J. Morgenthau identified international anarchy as the main problem causing all sovereign states to seek more power. At the same time, like Hobbes, he believed the related essential problem was power-hungry human nature. For him, power and state survival, rather than moral principles and liberal ideals, were the most important underlying principles of politics. Morgenthau saw all other factors, from geography to customs, as relevant only as long as they affected state power. He warned that any governmental attempts to challenge these fundamentals in the international arena would lead to failure (Morgenthau, 1948/2006). In American diplomacy, George Kennan, Paul Nitze, and Walter Lippmann, among others, argued that maximizing American power should be the foundation of U.S. strategy in the Cold War. The argument centered on how much military power the United States needed to keep its predominance in the world.

Neorealism

As the Cold War continued, scholars of international relations began to challenge Morgenthau's version of realism. New generations of scholars (among them Kenneth Waltz, George Quester, Robert Gilpin, Stephen Van Evera, and Jack Snyder) shifted the focus of analysis. Their versions, known as **neorealism** (or **structural realism**), focused on the structure of the **international system**—the global configuration of all great powers and other sovereign states—as the main factor in international relations. According to the neorealists' argument, beginning with the prominent book *Theory of International Politics* (Waltz 1979/2010), the founding principle of the international political

neorealism (structural realism) The theory that each state seeks a secure place in the international system according to the distribution of power.

international system Checks and balances among states as they exercise their power to promote their interests.

system is anarchy. Neorealists saw states' essential goal as seeking more security rather than as accumulating power.

In fact, the neorealists moved completely away from the idea of power-hungry human nature (Waltz 2001). According to this view, the structure of the international system defines the behavior of nation-states; human choices and individual instincts only reflect this important reality. By this thinking, which values security over power, sovereign states would: (1) prefer the balancing of power to violence and war; (2) prefer defensive actions over offensive ones; and (3) seek to preserve the existing international system rather than challenge it.

Neorealists have a slightly more optimistic view than classical realists on the likelihood of peace (Walt 1998). Still, neorealists argue that concerns about state security are paramount in international relations. Countries continue to consider all other countries as potential enemies, and international treaties cannot fully substitute power (Mearsheimer 2003).

Check Your Knowledge

1. What is power from the realist perspective?

2. According to realists, what defines the international system?

3.2 Realist Arguments about Power and Sovereignty

What is power, and how does it affect international relations? From the realist perspective, **power** is a state's ability to protect its own security and impose its will on other states and actors. It takes military, economic, political, and other forms. A state's power depends on a multitude of factors, including size and population, geographic location, economic infrastructure and finances, and even historical lessons the state learns from the past.

power A state's ability to protect its own security and impose its will on other states and actors.

For realists, power defines national interests (see Figure 3-1). Morgenthau famously postulated that national leaders conduct foreign policy "in terms of interest defined as power." It means that more powerful countries have a broader scale of interests than less powerful countries. Realists argue that complete equality between any two nation-states is impossible. Neorealists modified the discussion of interests. National interests, Waltz argued, are defined not only by power, but even more by the state's place in the existing configuration of international system. Neorealists do not argue that weak states are doomed to become subservient to big powers. Rather, they can choose with which stronger country they can ally. From the neorealist perspective, even small states have room to bargain and have reasonable opportunity to improve their international situation.

Power Distribution

Realism contends that power is unevenly distributed in the world according to a hierarchy. Some states' overwhelming power relative to the power of other

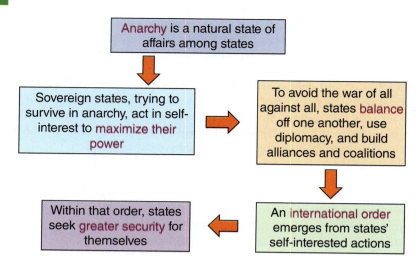

FIGURE 3-1 The logic of realism.

states has at times culminated in hegemony (domination) by a great power or powers, as we discussed in Chapter 2.

For many centuries, states reacted to international anarchy by constantly striving for a best possible *balance of power* with other states (Chapter 2). The bigger and stronger states offer protection to smaller and weaker states in exchange for political and economic concessions. Balancing strategies run the gamut from peaceful to violent and can result in regional or even global war. Sovereign states build alliances to shift the balance of power in their favor, and they may put constraints on other states that attempt to do the same.

According to the realist approach, the type of power distribution defines the *international system*, or the configuration of units in global politics. The concept of *polarity*—an understanding of where power is centered—is essential in this view. The configuration can be **unipolar** (one center of power), **bipolar** (two centers of power), or **multipolar** (multiple centers of power). The most prominent example of a multipolar order is the power balance in Europe from 1815 to 1914. This is the best-known example of a multipolar order because it was based on multiple centers of power or influence. Throughout most of this period, the United Kingdom was in the center of the international system and had the largest colonial empire; yet, it had to balance its power among other countries, including the United States, Russia, Germany, France, and Japan. The global power balance from 1945 to the mid-1980s was bipolar; it was dominated by the United States and the Soviet Union, although a number of countries (China, India, and others, including several oil-producing countries) had sought to erode this bipolarity. After 1991, when the Soviet Union broke-up into many states, the international system became unipolar because no coalition of powers could seriously challenge the military might of the United States.

unipolar A world organization based on only one center of power or influence.

bipolar A type of world organization based on two centers of power or influence.

multipolar A world with multiple centers of power or influence.

Sovereignty in Realist Thinking

Does a sovereign state have the right to do anything it pleases on its territory? As you recall from Chapter 2, sovereignty reflects states' capacity to control their territories and implement their own laws.

In 1823, U.S. President James Monroe outlined a set of unilateral principles of American foreign policy in the Western Hemisphere. In what is now known as the *Monroe Doctrine*, the United States declared it had no interest in European conflicts. At the same time, it stated that the United States would resist any attempt of a European power to intervene in the Western Hemisphere. Such attempts would be considered dangerous to the peace and safety of the United States (Monroe 1823/2015).

Cuban dictator Fidel Castro in 1967. In an example of a small ally influencing a big power, Castro was able to obtain Soviet support for Cuba's military engagement in the wars in Angola in 1975 and the Horn of Africa in 1977. Can any American ally today influence the policies of the United States in a similar way, and if so, how?

During the second half of the twentieth century, the concept of unlimited and unchallenged state sovereignty came under increasing criticism. Many such questions arose following government-sponsored mass killings of civilians in Turkey, Germany, Japan, the Soviet Union, and other states. As the world reacted to the aftermath of these atrocities, several international efforts attempted to impose standards of international behavior that would limit the rights of state governments within their territories. These efforts included, among others, the UN Human Rights Charter of 1945, the Nuremberg Trials of Nazi leaders in 1946, and the Helsinki Final Act of 1975.

Realists argue that the most powerful states have more capacity to exercise their sovereignty (see Figure 3-1). For instance, after the Cold War, the United States could choose to violate the sovereignty of states it perceived as dangerous. At the same time, the United States opposed any international agreements it viewed as encroaching on American sovereignty. One such agreement is the 1997 Kyoto Protocol on global climate control policies, which the U.S. Congress declined to ratify (officially agree to) in 2001. More recently, the United States unilaterally withdrew from several treaties, including the Antiballistic Missile Treaty (2002), the Paris Agreement (2017) to combat climate change, and the Intermediate-Range Nuclear Forces treaty (2019).

Smaller states do not have such freedom of choice. Still, despite their weaknesses, these states have a number of means to protect their sovereignty. One of the most important is bargaining, or negotiating deals with stronger powers. Smaller countries, despite limiting their sovereignty to accommodate bigger powers, often bargain successfully to receive economic and political benefits. For example, East Germany was completely dependent on Soviet military and economic support, and yet it influenced the Moscow leadership to build the Berlin Wall in 1961 (Harrison 2000). In another example, Cuba coerced the Soviets into accepting direct Cuban military engagement in the wars in Angola in 1975 and the Horn of Africa in 1977.

Read about the War in Angola and the Cuban strategies.

The Security Dilemma

A state's drive to build more efficient national security through accumulating power (such as by designing and building new weapons) generates additional insecurity for other participants in the international order. As realists see it, this is a key paradox in the dynamics of international power: the more secure one state feels, the less secure others are.

security dilemma A realist concept in which even states with purely defensive intentions may end up in an arms race.

In what is known as the **security dilemma**, even a state with purely defensive intentions may end up in an arms race. Imagine that state A declares its major goal is peace and acts to fortify its borders. The government of state A sees this as a purely defensive measure. State B, however, sees this in a different way: why is A fortifying itself if it desires peace? State B then decides to build up its army to be able to destroy A's fortifications. Thus, these dynamics lead to the exact opposite outcome that state A had wanted to achieve.

This hypothetical scenario may seem simplistic, but modern history is replete with similar cases. Germany's decision to develop its own security and build a modern fleet of dreadnought battleships between 1900 and 1907 presented a security threat to the United Kingdom, which then joined in an anti-German alliance with France and Russia. As a result, Germany became surrounded by a superior coalition of enemies, and some of its leaders regarded a preemptive war as the only response to growing insecurity. In another example, during the 1970s, the Soviet leadership continued to build its strategic forces without regard to reactions from other states. Consequently, in the next decade, most of the great powers considered the Soviet Union a main threat to their security and to the international order in general.

Iran's army displays a missile during a 2018 parade in front of the portraits of supreme leader Ayatollah Ali Khamenei, right, and the late revolutionary founder Ayatollah Khomeini. If one country's military grows stronger, how do other countries react?

If a state perceives a weakness in an existing international order, it may challenge the power distribution by generating aggressive policies. Such a state (sometimes called a *rogue state*) may disregard the rights and sovereignty of other countries, while exhibiting belligerent, expansionist, and dangerous behavior in the international arena. For example, Iraq in the 1980s acted aggressively by annexing Kuwait in 1990. Numerous conditions contribute to the predatory behavior of some states (Wendt, 1992). Such actions dramatically shift the balance of power, causing other states to panic.

Rapid shifts of power produce various reactions. States form alliances with others against the prevailing threat. This was, for instance, the reaction of most states in Western and Northern Europe to the rapid growth of Soviet power after 1945; they formed NATO and sought an alliance with the United States and the United Kingdom. Similarly, American envoys in the 1950s persuaded the royal rulers of Saudi Arabia and Jordan that secular nationalist Egypt was a growing threat, and urged them to form a counteralliance against this country.

Nation-states also can **bandwagon**, or make an alliance with the powers that otherwise could threaten their security. Weaker countries may easily gravitate, or move closer politically and militarily, to a greater power or to the existing coalitions of states in direct proximity to them. For instance, Italy, Hungary, Romania, and Bulgaria allied with Nazi Germany in 1938–1941, in response to Germany's growing power. The decision to bandwagon becomes likely when a state is small or does not have useful allies; the decision is based on the hope that the threatening power will moderate its aggressive intentions (Walt, 1987).

bandwagon Making an alliance with powers that could otherwise threaten a nation-state's security.

DEBATE > WILL THE GLOBAL POWER STRUGGLE EVER END?

Realism is an evolving concept. Consider, for example, whether the United States should continue to strive for a unipolar order or support moving to a multipolar world. One group of experts argues that international stability and peace depend on many states acting together. For instance, in *Ethical Realism*, Anatol Lieven and John Hulsman (2006) write that the United States cannot act alone in a global world: it will quickly exhaust its resources and fail. America should therefore continue to play a leadership role but act more cautiously, pay greater respect to other states, and use the strengths of its allies.

Critics of ethical realism maintain that power still determines the international order and that most other states are incapable of making a difference (Joffe 2009). This means that the United States is bound to be the leader for some time, whether other states want it or not. Moreover, as soon as the United States gives up its domination, the world will fall into chaos.

WHAT'S YOUR VIEW?

❶ Imagine defending the view that the global power struggle should and will eventually end. As a starting point, you might argue that the most powerful countries, including the United States, should become less "selfish". If big powers start considering other countries' interests, the world will face significantly fewer conflicts. Look at the current policies of President Trump. In what direction do they lead? ❷ Now imagine defending the view that the power struggle will never end because states will exploit the weaknesses of other states. According to this thinking, as soon as the United States shows signs of weakness, other states will assume leadership roles and start a new round of power struggles. ❸ Which of these positions do you find more compelling, and why?

Offensive and Defensive Realism

The ultimate use of power is war. Carl von Clausewitz (1780–1831), a prominent Prussian military thinker, coined the motto that war is a continuation of policy by "other means." For Clausewitz, war and its ultimate expression, "a pitched battle," is necessary to validate the state power, just as cash is necessary to validate a business transaction. In Morgenthau's interpretation (remember, he is regarded as a classical realist), wars are inevitable.

When structural realism became a prominent theoretical concept, students of international relations disagreed over the question of when sovereign states are likely to go to war. Security, they argued, is the main goal of sovereign states, and generally most countries prefer to keep the existing international system rather than attack it. This means that wars are not inevitable. So why do some countries still go to war, despite the risks and the lessons of the past? Some neo-realists (such as Kenneth Waltz, Stephen Van Evera, and Jack Snyder) maintain that state leaders consider war only as an ultimate, final resource. Contemporary **defensive realism** argues that the cost and destruction caused by war outweigh any military or economic gains that war could produce.

defensive realism The view that the cost and destruction caused by war outweigh any potential gains.

Other scholars (such as Tandall Schweller, Peter Liberman, and John Mearsheimer) suggest that stronger states tend to maximize their power and that there is nothing wrong with this tendency. As the thinking goes, the most powerful state in an international system is expected to be the most secure. **Offensive realism** holds that some countries ignore cost-benefit calculations and choose violence and aggression, given the anarchic nature of the international system. Napoleon's France, Hitler's Germany, or Hussein's Iraq saw the benefits of offensive policies as great, and the risk of doing nothing as even greater. Hitler, in an infamous example, was prepared to gamble on the existence of his country to build "a thousand-year Reich" that would dominate the world. To preserve stability and security in the international system, great powers must act in time against such states (Kaplan 2006; Sobel and Shiraev 2003 (see Table 3-1).

offensive realism The view that some countries choose violence and aggression because of the anarchic nature of the international system.

TABLE 3-1 Neorealist Arguments about War

Neorealist Views	Main Assumptions
Defensive Realists	Wars are preventable. State leaders, in most occasions, recognize that the costs and risk of military-driven expansions outweigh the benefits of gains. Therefore, war is most often rejected out of pragmatic calculations.
Offensive Realists	Some states, ignoring cost-benefit calculations, choose to become rogue states and to exercise aggressive, belligerent policies against their neighbors. Therefore, state leaders should not expect moderation from aggressive states. Force is a legitimate means to overwhelm the aggressors.

Both offensive realists and defensive realists seek supportive evidence in history. In some cases, the strongest states have started wars to prevent undesirable shifts of power that were perceived as security threats. In 1914, the German General Staff reasoned that Germany had the best chance to defeat Russia and France then, not five or ten years later, when Russia would have built more railroads, reformed its armed forces, and become virtually invincible. Thus, the defensive logic of the German military led to offensive conclusions.

After 1945, the existence of nuclear weapons made the costs of war between nuclear states prohibitively high. As a result, the confrontation between the United States and the Soviet Union remained a Cold War, and most of the military conflicts became **proxy wars**— superpowers helped smaller states fight for independence or sovereignty but did not participate directly. During proxy wars, great powers clashed vicariously by supporting their fighting clients. The involvement and intervention of other states into local wars or military conflicts depend, as realists argue, on the structure of international relations, and on states' perceptions of their security interests.

proxy wars A war instigated by a major power that does not itself become involved.

Read more about proxy wars.

Nonmilitary Responses in Realism

It is misleading to understand the realist approach as exclusively pro-military or pro-war. Realists try to explain why wars occur frequently; however, they value peaceful means for conducting foreign affairs. Realists understand that war is always extreme and that power can be implemented in other forms. Nonmilitary actions include a wide range of measures and policies.

Economic incentives or direct **economic aid** (money one state grants to another) is an example of nonmilitary responses conducted with the help of diplomacy. In 1948, the U.S. Congress approved the first $5 billion of a special aid package to European countries devastated by the long war. Eighty percent of the Marshall Plan that the United States provided for Europe in 1947–1952 was distributed as grants to the existing political, economic, and cultural institutions. The plan helped European governments restore economic and political stability and form a Western bloc against the Soviet Union. At the end of the twentieth century, both positive economic incentives and **economic sanctions** (financially and commercially penalizing measures) were frequently used. In 1956 the United States used economic sanctions to force the United Kingdom to stop its aggressive actions in Suez. Sanctions have recently become more frequent and invasive means of conducting foreign policy, particularly for the United States and the European Union with regard to Iran, Russia, North Korea, and other states who are perceived to destabilize the international system. With globalization of finances and new capacities to transfer and monitor money around the world, such sanctions can be highly damaging and even threaten state sovereignty.

economic aid Money one state or organizations connected to this state grant to another, often as a non-coercive instrument of foreign policy.

economic sanctions The deliberate, government-driven withdrawal, or threat of withdrawal, of customary trade and financial relations in an effort to change another country's policies.

Check Your Knowledge

1. What is anarchy in the context of international relations?

2. What is neorealism, and how is it different from classical realism?

3. Why can't states be equal according to realism?

4. What are some similarities and differences between offensive realism and defensive realism?

5. Explain proxy wars, and give examples.

Diplomacy, as you remember from Chapter 1, is the art and practice of conducting negotiations between states. It can frequently be chosen as a form of pressure on national governments and coalitions. Diplomacy can be coercive, meaning that it can be based on significant pressure or forceful persuasion of one state by another and must involve the threat of limited use of force. To illustrate, the anti-secession law China adopted in 2005 in relation to Taiwan suggests a peaceful means of unification with a reluctant neighbor. However, the law also provides a legal foundation for more forceful action designed to some degree to intimidate Taiwan. Diplomacy can also be used as a form of *quid pro quo* (this for that) bargaining. In 2004, for instance, Libya agreed to stop its nuclear program in exchange for Western investments and recognition.

3.3 Liberalism

Liberalism A school of thought based on the mitigation of power politics, the need for international cooperation, distribution of shared interests, and the role of nonstate actors in shaping state preferencesand policy choices.

Not to be confused with the liberal political stance, **liberalism** is an approach to international relations based on the mitigation of power politics, the need for international cooperation, the distribution of shared interests, and the role of nonstate actors in shaping state preferences and policy choices. Liberalism opposes realist explanations, which emphasize cost-benefit analysis and state security interests. International liberalism is based on three fundamental and interconnected principles (**Figure 3.2**):

1. It recognizes the realities of uneven power distribution but rejects power politics as the inevitable outcome of international relations. It questions explanations based on *zero-sum* outcomes of security interests, in which one country's gain would necessarily mean another country's loss.

2. It sees international organizations and nonstate actors as shaping international preferences and state policy choices.
3. It emphasizes international cooperation and mutual benefits.

International liberalism did not appear overnight. Its ideas have been tested by history, and its supporters have seen their convictions validated at some points and challenged at others.

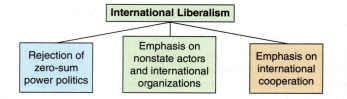

FIGURE 3-2 Fundamental Principles of Liberalism

The Roots of Liberalism

The liberal approach to international relations has deep intellectual and philosophical roots. All major religions—including Hinduism, Judaism, Buddhism, Christianity, and Islam—hold out the promise of perpetual peace. But the most significant boost to internationalist ideas came from Europe during the eighteenth century. There, the idea of "political liberalism" emerged, directed against the inherited privileges of nobility and the role of the established church. According to political theories developed by John Locke (1632–1704) in England, Voltaire (1694–1778) in France, and others, political freedoms could transform politics. To put it simply, a monarch would always fight other monarchs. Free and enlightened individuals, however, would have no reason to clash. They would prefer mutually beneficial trade and business.

In his 1795 essay *Perpetual Peace*, Immanuel Kant argued that the road to a stable international system demands a contract among states, which he called *a league of peace*. His ideas provided key concepts for contemporary liberal perspectives on international relations. Do these perspectives remain relevant today?

The German philosopher Immanuel Kant (1724–1804), in *Perpetual Peace* (1795), argued for just such a stable international system. In this system, a federation of independent republics would share mutual responsibilities, respect for the rule of law, and joint economic interests. Without the constraints of the law, states would behave like "savage people" in the wilderness. But the road to civilization demands a contract among states, which Kant called *a league of peace*. Like the police in a community, this league should be governed by law to secure freedom and peace.

Kant's ideas provided key concepts for contemporary liberal perspectives of international relations. Scholars often summarize the ideas of Kant as the *Kantian Triangle*. It consists of *republican constitutions* (today we call it democracy), a *commercial spirit* of trade (economic interdependence), and *international law* (including the activities of international institutions that promote it) (Russett and Oneal 2001). This triangle describes the three major brands of liberalism: legal, economic, and institutional.

In the eighteenth and nineteenth centuries, European scholars came to believe that human beings and states alike are capable of reason, self-restraint, and cooperation—the foundations of stability. These ideas are rooted in rich philosophical and cultural traditions. In particular, *humanism* maintains that moral norms (e.g., do unto others as you would have them do unto you) and the pursuit of mutually beneficial interests can bring about prosperity and peace. The nineteenth and early twentieth century produced classic thinkers of international liberal thought, such as John Stuart Mill (1806–1873) and Giuseppe Mazzini (1805–1872). British writer Norman Angell, in *Great Illusion* (1910), became the classic author of economic liberalism. Wars, he wrote, disrupt economic order. The territorial gains achieved by war cannot compensate for much greater losses in business and international trade. International trade would gradually lead to prosperity for an ever-growing number of countries and peoples. Other liberal thinkers warned that war would remain common as long as old political elites pursued power politics. Joseph Schumpeter, an economist from Austria-Hungary, wrote in *Sociology of Imperialism* (1919) that military aristocracies were the main agents of territorial expansionism and international violence. Yet the ever-greater prominence of the *bourgeoisie* (or entrepreneurs and the middle class) would lead to the decline of this class and the likelihood of wars.

Read about Kant's *Perpetual Peace* (1795).

DEBATE > ARE HUMANS INHERENTLY SELFISH AND VIOLENT?

Not all European intellectuals were captivated by the belief in an individual's propensity for peace and reason. Warfare was often associated with manhood as a component of a noble character. Even Immanuel Kant wrote that "a prolonged peace favors the predominance of a mere commercial spirit, and with it a debasing self-interest, cowardice, and effeminacy, and tends to degrade the character of the nation." (Kant, The Critique of Judgment, 1790) In the nineteenth and early twentieth centuries, people were intrigued by the ideas of influential philosophers such as Friedrich Nietzsche (1844–1900) and psychoanalyst Sigmund Freud (1856–1939). Nietzsche believed that only the strong and the power-driven rule the world. Freud argued that irrational forces dominate human behaviour, and, after the devastation of World War I, he grew extremely skeptical about the ability of humans to preserve peace. Aggression, he believed, is embedded in the human *psyche*, and social institutions are often incapable of stopping hostility and violence.

WHAT'S YOUR VIEW?

This is a centuries-old debate about human nature: If left to their own devices, are humans likely to choose peace and cooperation over egotism and rivalry, or will violence prevail? Let's look at this discussion from a different angle. Discuss conditions, both domestic and international, under which you think people are likely to choose cooperation over rivalry. Also, discuss conditions that in your view are likely to cause violence. To support your arguments, pick an ongoing international conflict to see if the conditions you have suggested are present there.

The ideas of Kant, Angell, and Schumpeter remained popular among liberal internationalists. In an open, democratic system, state leaders respond to peaceful, law-abiding citizens who are involved in economic exchanges (Doyle 1986). Thus, a democratic system of government was itself crucial to preventing international violence. Would this assumption prove correct?

World War II and the Grand Alliance against the Axis powers led to the revival of all three strands of liberalism: institutional, economic, and legal. The creation of the United Nations, the Bretton-Woods financial international institutions, the Marshall Plan, and other initiatives linked institutional and economic liberalism together. The United Nations acted in 1946 to urge the Soviet Union to observe its international obligation to withdraw Soviet troops from Iran. The United Nations Universal Declaration of Human Rights (1948), approved by both democratic and nondemocratic countries, was an important precedent: an international organization set the common norms and definitions that transcended, at least in theory, the old definition of state sovereignty created by the Peace of Westphalia.

The Cold War, with its obsession with security and its nuclear crises, privileged the agenda of realism. But the agenda of liberal internationalism continued to expand and diversify, especially after the 1960s. Scholars turned to study the ability of international institutions to promote cooperation among countries. Others began to regard multinational corporations, wrongly as it turned out, as players that might soon substitute for sovereign states (Haas 1964; Kindleberger 1970; Vernon 1971). In *The Anarchical Society*, Australian scholar Hedley Bull argued that sovereign states do not live in complete anarchy.

They always tend to develop a "civilized" international society, with shared rules and norms. Bull showed that countries, despite a frequent lack of trust, strive to develop and observe common regulations and institutions (Bull 1977).

Neoliberalism

The *Kantian Triangle*, as we discussed earlier, produced three influential strands of liberal theorizing: institutional, economic, and legal. The institutional strand influenced the development of **neoliberalism**, or **neoliberal institutionalism**, which argues that state interests remain critical in international relations, yet in the context of complex interdependence among states. As the thinking goes, sovereign states prefer cooperation to power politics and do not seek short-term advantages if international institutions promise them lasting security (Keohane and Nye 1989, p 20).

neoliberalism The theory that state interests, while critical in international relations, are realized in the context of interdependence among states.

Complex interdependence has three main features:

- First, states interact through multiple channels, including informal ties and economic, financial, and cultural contacts.
- Second, security is not always the prime agenda of state-to-state interactions. Different issues become important at different times, such as trade and currency regulations, human rights concerns, and the economic assistance of wealthy countries to poor ones.
- And third, military force is typically not used by countries against other countries.

Neoliberalism is quite different from classical liberalism. Instead of humanistic principles, such as rationality and moral values, neoliberalism emphasizes the role of international structures. The discussion breaks down as follows:

- Neorealists claim that sovereign states support the international system and seek relative gains according to the structure of this system. These relative gains, neorealists argue, can include better terms of economic treaties, bigger share and voice in international institutions, and more security for less money invested in military alliances.
- Neoliberals, by contrast, believe that sovereign states under certain political and economic conditions receive absolute gains from building international and transnational institutions. In other words, even for the wealthiest and strongest powers, such as the United States, it is absolutely advantageous to be part of international trade agreements with many smaller countries, because such agreements create a greater volume of trade and larger profits. Some liberal theorists even argue that the international system has already been gradually transformed into a global community (Iriye 2002). Complex interdependence and a growing number of international institutions and organizations have been transforming world politics into a model of global governance based on cooperative values. In Chapters 5, 6, and 7, we will discuss how the liberal logic of absolute gains and global community has affected specific security, economic, and other policies around the world.

The end of the Cold War brought new converts and arguments for neoliberal concepts. Soviet leader Gorbachev called for the rapid reduction of tensions between the United States and the Soviet Union. Scores of experts, from journalists to state officials, discussed possibilities for a world order based on freedom of choice. Some liberal critics even declared that the principles of neorealism could not be applied to developed democracies. According to these critics, states are not just billiard balls on a table, but complex units consisting of individuals and voluntary groups. In a democratic country, individual citizens and groups elect their governments. In their foreign policy, these governments reflect the interests and preferences of many domestic actors. This strand of liberalism views states as institutions that are serving the needs of individuals and groups. Accordingly, states, like people, are capable of goodwill, self-restraint, and cooperation (Moravcsik 1997).

Check Your Knowledge

1. What are the fundamental principles of liberalism?
2. How does neoliberalism differ from classical liberalism?

3.4 Liberal Arguments

Diplomacy manages international politics through negotiations. Sovereign states establish embassies in other states and keep channels of communication open to them. Although these channels can be used for espionage, misinformation, and intimidation, diplomacy helps promote trust, avoid violent confrontations, prevent the use of force, and reduce the potential loss of property and human lives. Liberalism argues that diplomacy can be effective in these ways as long as state leaders act honestly, express goodwill, and aim for nonviolent solutions.

Harold Nicolson, a British historian and diplomat, published *The Evolution of Diplomatic Method* in 1954. Diplomatic rules, procedures, and techniques of

Syrian refugees cross the border between Lebanon and Syria, as millions have been displaced. What can the international community do to prevent such a crisis in the future?

History Lab — Diplomatic Efforts in an India–Pakistan Conflict

In December 2001, in the wake of a terrorist attack on India's parliament for which India blamed a Pakistan-based Islamic terrorist group, India and Pakistan amassed over a million troops on the Indo-Pakistani border. These countries had gone to war several times before, most recently in 1971. Now they threatened each other with nuclear missiles. The entire international community joined urgent efforts to avoid imminent violence. After weeks of relentless diplomatic talks, the standoff eased and reciprocal concessions began. Pakistan's leaders promised to stop cross-border infiltrations of civilian combatants into India-controlled Kashmir. India, in exchange, withdrew its navy from the North Arabian Sea and lifted the flyover ban imposed on Pakistani commercial jets. India also agreed to upgrade diplomatic ties with Islamabad.

Indo-Pakistani relations remain tense and difficult, but international diplomacy proved its efficacy in easing military threats.

CRITICAL THINKING

❶ Why did diplomacy work in this particular conflict but fail in others, such as during the conflict between the United States and Iraq in 2003? Compare these two conflicts by paying attention to (a) the willingness of the involved governments to communicate with each other and (b) the ability of the international community to influence the conflicting sides. ❷ Can you think of other, more contemporary conflicts in which diplomatic efforts led to a peaceful resolution? Which international and domestic conditions contributed to this diplomatic success?

negotiations changed over time, he wrote. And they continue changing. Conducted in secrecy for centuries, diplomacy has become more accessible to scrutiny. Diplomacy has also become increasingly multinational and even global. During the Cold War, the United States and the Soviet Union agreed that diplomatic talks were preferable to accusations and standoffs. Historically, diplomacy has played an increasingly important role in maintaining peace and stability (Jonsson and Langhorne 2004).

Liberalism and neoliberalism should not be understood as an outright rejection of power politics. All versions of liberalism accept the primacy of sovereign states and their right to use force to protect their interests (Sharp 2009). Moreover, liberal concepts do not ignore the reality of war. As we saw in Chapter 2, the Bush administration used liberal justifications to wage a war in Iraq in 2003. The Obama Administration, backed by liberal rhetoric, used military force to destroy the Gaddafi regime in Libya in 2011 and nearly took similar action against Assad's regime in Syria in 2013. The disagreement between realists and liberal internationalists centers on when and how to use force in international relations. New generations of diplomats, politicians, and scholars change the tone and scope of this debate.

Realists view diplomacy as an instrument of adaptation to the changing distribution of power in the international order. Liberals have a more proactive agenda for diplomacy: They view it as a tool for entities cooperating as complexly interdependent states and maintaining international norms.

The liberal view of diplomacy includes more international actors than realism. Not only great powers, but smaller states, the United Nations, and other international organizations and NGOs become important diplomatic actors. Liberals point out that European countries, including such small countries as the Netherlands, played a crucial role in making human rights a basic concern for European diplomacy in the 1970s—while the United States and the Soviet Union still played power games. In 1975, the Conference on Security and Cooperation in Europe signed the Helsinki Final Act. This document bound the thirty-five states that signed it, including the United States and the Soviet Union, to respect and protect humanitarian concerns and human rights, such as the right to receive information, exchange ideas, or unify families across the state borders. It was a triumph of liberal internationalism (Thomas 2001; Morgan, 2018).

Democratic Peace Theory

democratic peace theory The theory that democracies are not likely to fight one another.

Scholars have further advanced Kant's thesis on "perpetual peace." Scholars of political science and international relations Michael Doyle, Bruce Russett, and James Lee Ray propose what is known as the **democratic peace theory**. It suggests that, although democratic states can go to war against nondemocratic ones, democracies do not fight one another. Most twentieth-century wars took place between nondemocratic countries or between democracies and authoritarian regimes. There is hardly a single case in which democratic countries governed by stable political institutions went to war against each other. Why? Democratic peace theory gives three reasons:

- **First, the institutions of representative democracy discourage going to war against other democracies.** These institutions include parliaments, a free press, pluralist public organizations, and public opinion. They hold political elites accountable and make it difficult for them to plot aggressive strategies, especially against other democratic countries (Owen 2005).
- **Second, because of shared values and norms of behavior, democratic states regard each other as partners rather than enemies.** Democratic states, unlike autocracies, develop a culture of compromise and negotiation. Consensus building at home translates into tolerance abroad. Mutual concessions help democracies address disagreements between themselves and to resolve conflicts peacefully. These norms become accepted by foreign policy elites and leaders, which makes wars less likely (Maoz and Russett 1993).
- **Third, economic interdependence makes war unacceptable for economic reasons.** (As we saw earlier in this chapter, Norman Angell made the same point in 1910.) Many theorists and practitioners agree that peace and the prosperity of democratic states depend on free markets and international trade. Therefore, state leaders and business groups regard military conflicts as ruinous because they damage a complex economic and financial infrastructure (Oneal and Russett 1997; Gartzke 2007).

Democratic peace theory has made the biggest contribution to studies of international relations in recent decades. Many embraced it and recommended using it to guide foreign policy. Critics, however, argued that this theory was incomplete and if used in practice could lead to dangerous consequences. We will return to this controversy later in this chapter.

Soft Power

In the 1980s, Joseph S. Nye (b. 1937) argued that power can be either *hard* or *soft*. Hard power involves coercing other states by using military force or economic means. **Soft power**, by contrast, is about cooperation, not coercion, and emphasizes shared economic and social success (Nye 1990). This type of power stems from many factors, including attractive ideals and values and, more broadly, an influential culture and way of life. It includes media that reports credible information instead of propaganda; foreign policy that benefits international peace and stability; and a culture that is inclusive and not based on racism and rabid nationalism. Soft power is not about material reality and wealth, but one can argue that these things flow from it, particularly from culture and values. In this way, soft power can be more effective than hard power. It wins hearts and minds without winning wars. It produces voluntary allies, not reluctant satellites (Nye 2004).

soft power A state's ability to influence other states by good example and by economic and social success.

Soft power is volatile and fluid; it is difficult to calculate. It operates largely through *perceptions*. (See Figure 3-2.) State actions or policies can increase or diminish it (Gause 2005; Mitzen 2005). American soft power has ebbed and flowed. The Vietnam War, the occupation of Iraq in 2003, and the global financial crisis of 2008 all significantly weakened it. America's technology, sports, universities, international aid, the opportunities the country offers to immigrants (more than one million are naturalized every year)—among other reasons—add to its soft power. A country's international image is based on many factors, including the leadership figure. According to several surveys, President Trump and many of his key policies have been unpopular around the globe during the first two years of his presidency, and ratings for the United States have accordingly declined in many nations. Yet America still received a high rating for its living standards, culture, and civil liberties (Pew Research Center 2017a).

Soft power applies not only to states; IGOs, NGOs, and individuals can serve as models, too. As supporters of liberal internationalism hope, they demonstrate the advantages of liberal ideas over power politics. At the same time, it is incorrect to consider concepts of soft power as tools of liberalism and hard power as the only instrument of realism. Supporters of realpolitik and

Demonstrating soft power at work, Rondae Hollis-Jefferson of the Brooklyn Nets, second from left, with colleagues helps build a house near Johannesburg, South Africa, in 2017. As part of the NBA Africa Game, and Habitat for Humanity South Africa, 200 volunteers from the NBA help build 10 homes.

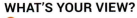

DEBATE > WHICH COUNTRY HAS THE MOST SOFT POWER?

Some countries may gain soft power and squander it later. Some countries have been very successful at developing technologies, education, science, or trade. Others have provided excellent social conditions for their citizens. Still others are known for order, efficiency, and low crime rates.

WHAT'S YOUR VIEW?

❶ Which countries today have effective soft power, and why?
❷ Is the soft power of the United States increasing or decreasing? What about the soft power of China? Defend your position.

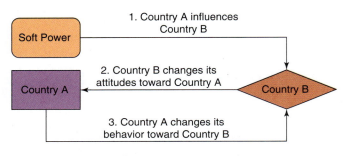

FIGURE 3-3 The effects of soft power. Sources: Nye, 2002, 2004.

liberalism may use both of these powers in combination (Nye 2004).

It is not correct to attribute soft power only to liberal democratic norms. Stalin and Hitler also had soft power in the eyes of millions of their followers and used this power with devastating effect. During the early phases of the Cold War, the Soviet Union had soft power as well. (See Figure 3-3.) Communist models were popular in Asia, Africa, and Latin America, especially in countries struggling for independence from European colonial rule (Westad 2007; Nye 2011).

In the late 1940s, a devastated Europe, including Germany, viewed the United States as a magnanimous nation. With the Marshall Plan, as we saw in Chapter 2, the United States put the values of international peace and prosperity above narrow interests (Gaddis 2006). A democratic, nonhierarchical society, the United States proclaims that all people are "created equal." Many Europeans longed to see American ideals applied in their warravaged societies. American movies, music, products (such as Coca-Cola), cars, and fashion all won millions of hearts worldwide. Even in the Soviet Union in the 1960s, some young men and women admired the American lifestyle and culture.

There is an ongoing debate about China's soft power. During the last decade, this Communist country invested billions into the economies of developing countries of Africa, and Latin America. People in Africa welcome the Chinese economic expansion because they bring jobs and build roads and airports. Chinese businesses do not ask questions about democracy and human rights, but they often do more for economic and social development than the United States has done in the past. Does it mean that China has acquired soft power over the countries where it has done its business? Some believe the answer is yes. The Chinese model of development has pulled millions out of poverty, built modern infrastructure, and created a real alternative to Western development models. Critics, however, say that China does not have soft power, only the power of money. Very few countries, they maintain, want to copy the Chinese Communist regime, which has been turning more authoritarian and restrictive in many respects, including with regard to providing access to the Internet, persecution for religious beliefs, and political rights.

Unilateralism and Multilateralism

Until the Second World War, the United States often practiced what the press and politicians called isolationism. That is, U.S. statesmen wanted to maintain freedom of choice in a world dominated by other great powers, which practiced cynical realpolitik. In practical terms, the United States practiced **unilateralism**, relying on its own resources rather than on international organizations and alliances with other states. Unfortunately, this approach, adopted in the 1930s, contributed to favorable conditions for aggressive actions by Japan and Germany.

In contrast to unilateralism, **multilateralism** involves coordinating foreign policy with allies, as well as participating in international organizations, coalitions, and blocs. Following the Second World War, the United States adopted a multilateral approach, seeking cooperation with other states in the name of common security and global well-being. This approach helped the United States to remain an effective leader of the Western bloc and contain the Soviet Union. International organizations can play an important role in legitimizing multilateral liberal policies. For example, during the Gulf War of 1990-1991, the United Nations passed a resolution that denounced Iraq's occupation of Kuwait. This move gave the United States international legitimacy in creating a coalition of 39 countries. The U.S. military, helped by the money and some forces from the coalition members liberated Kuwait.

In contrast, in 2003 the United States occupied Iraq without the resolution of the United Nations and against the will of American allies, such as France and Germany. Critics of this occupation argued that this action represented an American return to unilateralism, which threatened to split the Western alliance and complicated the task of conflict resolutions in the Middle East. We will return to unilateralism and multilateralism in Chapter 4.

unilateralism
Reliance on a state's own resources rather than support from others; acting alone in foreign policy.

multilateralism An approach to international relations supporting states, international organizations, and nongovernmental organizations in concert.

Check Your Knowledge

1. According to democratic peace theory, what are three reasons stable democratic countries do not fight one another?

2. What is soft power? Give an example.

3. How is liberalism different from neoliberalism in international relations?

4. What are some similarities between realism and liberalism?

History Lab   How Much Does Public Opinion Affect Foreign Policy?

In democratic societies, does public opinion matter in foreign policy? Realists give public opinion a limited role: realpolitik is not supposed to be bound by public opinion. By contrast, liberal internationalist policy can depend largely on public support (Kagan 2004). Historical facts suggest that although public opinion (systematic scientific polling on foreign policy began about eighty years ago) does not necessarily direct foreign policy, politicians often seek favorable opinion polls to support their foreign policy strategies. For example, the U.S. policy of containment of the Soviet Union, with its strong liberal multilateral component, depended on public backing and agreement between the Republican and Democratic parties (Nacos, Shapiro, and Isernia 2000).

After you examine Table 3-2, you will see that most of the time, the American public was supportive of Washington's military actions abroad, especially if they were short-term and caused few casualties. At the same time, you can see that when the people were against using America's military power abroad (like in Rwanda in 1994), the government was reluctant to act too. During the last twenty years, particularly after the Western military intervention in Afghanistan and Iraq, the American and western European public has grown wary of the use of force abroad, and no longer support military actions, even when they are proposed for the sake of liberal internationalism. There is no longer a domestic consensus in the West for "good" wars waged for humanitarian purposes.

But can political leaders influence public opinion in a desirable, pro-government, way? Studies show that leaders can shape public opinion only to an extent. An important element of public opinion is the *policy climate*, which is the prevailing sentiment among policy makers and other influential individuals. Policy climate is difficult to measure. It includes beliefs about what the government, international organizations, and nongovernment groups should do on the international level—particularly when faced with international conflict or security threats. Opinion leaders air their views in public debates, speeches, policy statements, televised interviews, printed publications, and the Internet (Sobel 2001; Page and Shapiro 1988). Certain foreign-policy decisions, especially the ones related to military interventions can often prevail only within a favorable policy climate.

Overall, studies of U.S. public opinion show an interesting picture of opinion–policy relations that can be summarized as shown in Table 3-3.

CRITICAL THINKING

❶ What factors can affect people's views of a particular country (unfriendly) and a particular international conflict? ❷ How can public opinion related to foreign policy be manipulated via the media and social networks? Can foreign governments be engaged in such manipulation? ❸ Do you think a democratic country, such as the United States or Canada, should always have a national referendum about the country's military engagement in a foreign military conflict? Explain your reasons.

The trend toward isolationism

TABLE 3-2 Public Opinion and U.S. Use of Force Abroad

Countries, Dates	Polls	General Approval (percent)	General Disapproval (percent)	Outcome
The war against Japan, 1941	December 1941; NORC; personal, 1,283;	82	12	War
The Korean War 1950	December 1950; NORC, Personal, 1,252	55	36	War
The Korean War 1953	June 1953; NORC, Personal, 1,285	38	51	End of the war
The Vietnam War 1967	August 1967; Gallup, 1,525	60	32	War
The Vietnam War 1972	June 1972; Gallup, 1,535	35	64	End of the war
Military involvement in Angola, 1976	January 1976; Yankelovich, Skelly & White, 951	21	59	No ground troops
Military actions in Ethiopia, 1978	April 1978; Harris, 1,529	13	71	No ground troops
Military intervention in Grenada, 1983	October 1983; ABS/WP, 1,505	71	22	Occupation
Invasion and arrest of president of Panama, 1990	January 1990; HTRC, 1,510	72	18	Invasion
Military involvement in Rwanda in 1994	June 1994; CBS, 978	28	61	Non-involvement
Air strikes against Yugoslavia, 1999 (U.S. and NATO)	April 1999; CBS, 878	59	29	Strikes
Military actions against terrorist groups in Afghanistan, 2001	October 2001; Gallup, 2,042	89	5	War
Military actions against Iraq Spring 2003	Various polls, spring 2003	60–70	20–25	War
Participation in an international military action in Darfur 2007	CNN/ORC poll, October 2007	61	32	No U.S. direct military action

TABLE 3-2 (*Continued*)

Countries, Dates	Polls	General Approval (percent)	General Disapproval (percent)	Outcome
Military actions against Libya Spring 2011	**Gallup, March 27, 2011**	47	37	Strikes
2017 Military action against Syria	**CBS poll, April 2017 1,006**	57	36	Strikes

Abbreviations: NORC: National Opinion Research Center; HTRC: Hart-Teeter Research Companies

Source: Shiraev and Sobel 2006, 2019.

TABLE 3-3 The Impact of Public Opinion on Foreign Policy

The impact of public opinion on foreign policy is likely to increase if:	
(1)	A national election is scheduled in the near future and opposition is strong: incumbent officials need public support for reelection.
(2)	Support for or opposition to a certain foreign policy-related issue is overwhelming and consistent: officials may argue that they have a "mandate."
(3)	Majority opinion agrees with decision makers: officials are likely to use polls as justification for their action or inaction.
The impact of public opinion on foreign policy is likely to weaken if:	
(1)	No national election is scheduled in the near future and the political opposition is relatively weak.
(2)	Support or opposition is weak or inconsistent: officials may argue that the public is uncertain or divided.
(3)	Majority opinion disagrees with decision makers: officials are likely to ignore or downplay the polls.

Sources: Rosenau 1961; Holsti 1992; Sobel and Shiraev 2003; Yankelovich 2005.

3.5 Comparing Realism and Liberalism

What are the main points of comparison between the realist and liberal approaches? Table 3-4 summarizes these comparisons from three angles.

First, realism focuses on sovereign states, whereas liberalism focuses more on international institutions. Many realist thinkers have gradually acknowledged the strength of IGOs and NGOs but believe that no international institution can change states' drive to balance power among themselves (Mersheimer 1994-95). To liberal thinkers, the growth of IGOs and NGOs has led to reduced emphasis on states as actors.

Second, according to realist views, a gain in power by one state may be in the context of a *zero-sum game*: when one side wins, the other loses. Therefore, states should watch one another's *relative* gains. Neorealists argue that states strive to maximize their security but not necessarily their power; this necessitates compromises and cooperation (Schweller 1997). Liberal institutionalism, as we discussed earlier, focuses on *absolute* gains in security, achieved through the cooperation of states in building an international order. International organizations, open markets, and diplomacy should help avoid zero-sum games and maximize the interests of all countries involved.

And third, realists believe that war cannot be eliminated and avoided because military force, or the threat of it, is the most effective means of power balancing. Liberalism accepts the use of force for liberal goals but does not regard an interstate conflict as a necessary element of international order.

Both traditions, despite significant differences and disagreements between their followers, may seek and establish common ground related to international conflict, cooperation, and international organizations. On the following pages, you will see how realist and liberal principles are applied in specific international contexts.

Check Your Knowledge

1. Summarize the primary differences between realism and liberalism.

2. Where might realism and liberalism overlap?

TABLE 3-4 Realist and Liberal Views of International Relations Compared

Issue	The Realist Tradition	The Liberal Tradition
International actors	Sovereign states are the principal actors in international relations, yet the role of IGOs and NGOs can be acknowledged.	States are important but not the only actors in international affairs. International institutions and nonstate actors gain greater importance.
International order	Order and stability are achieved through relative gains, by power balancing among states, and by mutual fear of a major war; this does not completely exclude compromises and cooperation.	Security and stability are achieved through absolute gains by all participants in the international order, through interdependence and by goodwill, mutual trust, and compromise.
Use of force	Military force and threat of force are the most efficient means of power balancing.	Military force is used to restrain the aggressor and only after international diplomacy fails.

3.6 Critical Applications of Realism and Liberalism

Even a brief description of rival approaches to international relations reveals that none of them provides all answers for all cases. During the Cold War, the realist view was predominant. Realism failed, however, to take many new factors and developments into account, such as the peaceful and sudden collapse of the Soviet Union at the end of the Cold War. The United States was left as the only great power, and yet it could not create a stable international order. It is unclear now whether the United States can remain the world's leader for long. What kinds of realist policies will we see in the future?

About twenty years ago, liberal approaches came to the forefront. Most recently, however, liberalism has run into unexpected challenges. On one hand, the trends toward economic integration, free trade, and financial integration reduced states' willingness to fight each other. Yet on the other, the same trends laid the foundations for global financial shocks. If liberal norms and institutions are to become the core of the international order, how do we address problems such as international terrorism?

Realism Applied

How successful has realism been in interpreting international relations? What are the strengths and weaknesses of this approach? We will examine these questions at three levels: individual, state, and global.

REALISM AT THE INDIVIDUAL LEVEL

Hans Morgenthau (1948), the best-known classical realist, wrote about the roles of morality, intuition, and emotion in the leader's actions. Neorealists, however, no longer believe that individuals have that important an impact on power politics. Rather, they maintain, the course of international relations is shaped mostly by the international structure. Kenneth Waltz, the founder of neorealism, describes in *Man, the State, and War* (1958) three levels of analysis (he calls them "three images"): individual state leaders, state politics, and the international system. Waltz writes that aggressive leaders such as Hitler could unleash wars, but he suggests that only the structure of the international system explained why the United Kingdom, France, and the United States did not initially act to stop Hitler. Other neorealist authors argue that Gorbachev, for all his extraordinary initiatives, also could not escape the structural realities. It was not necessarily the weakening Soviet Union, but rather the winning United States that reshaped the international system according to its interests (Wohlforth 2003; Sarotte 2009).

REALISM AT THE STATE LEVEL

While insisting on the importance of economic and military policies, realists in the past were often reluctant to consider other domestic political factors. Realists generally believed that states, democratic or not, tend to disregard ideological and political differences with other states if it suits their security interests.

For years, despite its consistent claim of support for freedom and democracy, the United States supported a wide range of dictatorships and nondemocratic regimes in Latin America, Africa, and Asia.

Domestic politics, however, plays a big role in international relations. Robert Putnam (1988) argues that a country's foreign policy is conducted on at least two levels: the domestic and the international. At home, domestic groups pursue their interests by pressuring the government to adopt favorable policies. Politicians respond to those groups' pressures. At the international level, governments play a balancing act between domestic interest groups and foreign policy goals. Leaders of sovereign states have to act simultaneously on both levels, much as a game played on two chessboards. (That is why this model is called *two-level game theory*.)

Domestic lobbies and social movements play a significant role in the foreign policy of democratic states. Interest groups could be representatives of the military, corporations seeking defense contracts, the national security elite, foreign policy experts, or lobbying groups (Wittkopf & McCormick 2004). In peacetime, and in the absence of immediate foreign threats, democratic states find it more difficult to conduct power politics. Any initiative in international relations requires **bureaucratic bargaining**—compromises with bureaucracies and lobbies, which often pursue different agendas (Marrar 2008). A ruling political party, for example, may make concessions to the opposition party on domestic policy in exchange for support on foreign policy—a process known as **log rolling** (Laver 1979). During the early stages of the Cold War, many U.S. congressmen and senators supported the containment of Communist threats, but only if new military bases would go to their constituents. These bases created jobs, brought additional revenues, and satisfied many voters.

bureaucratic bargaining The process by which lobbies, political groups and institutions express their interests and make trade-offs and compromises.

REALISM AT THE GLOBAL LEVEL

The realist view of international relations had its greatest influence during the Cold War. The Soviet Union and the United States seemed to be in a permanent struggle for predominance and security, with other, smaller powers adapting to the bipolar international system. Yet the Cold War is long over. How well does the realist view of international relations explain the complexity of today's world?

Neorealists today remain skeptical regarding liberal claims of a global community and global governance based on cooperation values. Instead, they remain convinced that countries will pay attention to their security and are unlikely to maintain peaceful and mutually profitable cooperation without a consolidating force, such as the United States, that keeps global and regional developments in check (Betts 2011). As neorealists believe, power politics is not obsolete, and the time for power balancing has not passed. The traditional problem of domination in the international system did not disappear. The presidency of Donald Trump revived the realist discussion about the United States' leading role in international affairs. The political disarray and weakening of American leadership, some argue, have created opportunities for China, Russia, Iran, and other powers to fill the vacuum in the international system.

log rolling A concession made by one party to the other party on domestic issues in exchange for their support on foreign policy.

What If NATO Did Not Exist?

NATO is an alliance that emerged in 1948–1949 out of uncertainty about Soviet intentions and fears of another war in Europe. Critics say that, in response to NATO, the Soviets created a militarized Warsaw Pact. The standoff between the two military alliances kept Europe divided for decades.

British statesman Lord Hastings Ismay, the first general secretary of NATO, is credited with saying that NATO was created to "keep the Soviet Union out, the Americans in, and the Germans down." From a realist perspective, this means that deterrence of the Soviet threat was only one side of the coin; the other side was to provide Western Europe with an effective system of collective defense. An attack on one member of NATO means an attack on all, which in turn means, at least on paper, that the security of NATO members is indivisible. Two old enemies, Germany and France, were locked into the same organization of collective defense. Also, most crucially, this organization brought American forces into Europe on a permanent basis. In effect, realists argue, it was American military superiority that solved the question of Western European security in the period between 1949 and 1989 (Trachtenberg 1999).

Let's imagine, however, that NATO had never been created. Would Europe have been more secure, united, and stable? That is highly improbable. Without NATO and an American security umbrella, France and other countries would have remained wary and insecure about Germany and its power. Great Britain might have returned to its traditional policy of balancing some European countries against others. Even if Europe had avoided the clean divide between the two blocs, it would have returned to the instability and insecurity that had existed between two world wars. Also, as historians of European integration argue, without NATO, European integration would have been a much more difficult project, troubled by security concerns and rivalries (Ludlow 2010).

These considerations explain in part why NATO was not disbanded after the end of the Cold War and the collapse of the Soviet Union. Instead, NATO expanded eastward, in order to extend the same system of security to Eastern European countries. Some scholars consider it a major miscalculation, an attempt to apply a good recipe from one historical era to another era after most historical conditions had changed. They consider NATO's expansion as the main reason of current tensions with Russia. The defenders of NATO's expansion, however, recall Ismay's words and point out that Russia and Germany still have to be contained and that Americans should therefore continue to be the protectors of Europe. Would you agree?

Others argue, however, that Japan and India, China's old-time regional rivals, oppose any rapid and forceful shifts in the balance of power in China's favor. India has moved to balance China by strengthening its ties with the United States. Russia has too many problems with its neighbors and, besides, cannot build a full alliance with China because the political and economic interests of these two countries are too different (Pant 2011).

Liberalism Applied

How well have liberal ideas stood the test of reality? We will examine liberal assumptions in light of decisions by individual leaders, state policies, and the global context.

LIBERALISM AT THE INDIVIDUAL LEVEL

In an attention-grabbing piece published in *Foreign Affairs* in 2006, biologist Robert Sapolsky argued that humans are not naturally aggressive. Human choices, he states, are the product of rational calculation and social context. Rational choices by state leaders should therefore help avoid violence (Sapolsky 2006).

The advocates of liberalism like this argument. But if people are by nature inclined to peaceful behavior, why do countries so often engage in conflicts and wars? One potential answer is that individual state leaders have different weaknesses and strengths in the face of domestic politics and interest groups. Weak political leaders, as liberals argue, often yield to domestic pressures to start war. In July 1914, German Kaiser Wilhelm II and Russian Tsar Nicholas II became hostages of domestic factors, and military mobilization became their only option. Both empires suffered defeat and collapse. In the 1931–1941 period, another weak leader, Emperor Hirohito, succumbed to pressures from Japanese militarism, generals and admirals, who saw a historic opportunity to build an empire that would dominate the Far East. After four more years of barbaric war, the Japanese Empire surrendered.

The implementation of liberal principles in international relations requires domestic consensus, political strength, and courage. President Woodrow Wilson failed to convince the opposition at home when he pushed for U.S. participation in the League of Nations in 1919–1921. Franklin Roosevelt was stronger and more skillful than Wilson and succeeded in priming American public opinion for supporting the United Nations and other pillars of institutional liberalism in 1941–1945. In West Germany (when Germany was divided), Chancellor Willy Brandt (1913–1992) pushed for engagement and collaboration with European Communist states in 1969–1971, believing that cooperation would work better than conflict. The peaceful reunification of Germany and the end of the Cold War vindicated Brandt and his choices.

LIBERALISM AT THE STATE LEVEL

Domestic politics strongly influences foreign policy. Political outcomes in turn depend on the type of government, the nature of policy institutions, the frequency of elections, and the design and ownership of the media. All these affect state leaders' international priorities.

German Chancellor Willy Brandt kneels before the monument to the Jews killed by the Nazis.

Democratic peace theory, introduced earlier in this chapter, assumes that democratic states are unlikely to engage in war against one another (Christison 2002; Jervis 2002). Jack Snyder and Edward Mansfield looked at countries that are not fully democratic but only *in transition* to democracy. These countries might actually be *more* prone to war compared to stable but authoritarian regimes. Why? Democracy allows political groups to compete openly. If democratic institutions are immature and unstable, some of these groups may use nationalist, populist, and demagogic slogans and agendas to devastating effect (Mansfield and Snyder 2007; Snyder 2000). In Africa, the Middle East, and Central Asia, efforts to replace autocracies with democratic institutions can generate instability and war (Gause 2005). In Pakistan's history, some periods of democratic rule were followed by long periods of military dictatorship. It is unclear which governments of Pakistan—authoritarian or democratic—were less confrontational against India.

During the Cold War, the United States acted against weak democratic regimes in Guatemala (1954), Brazil (1961, 1964), and Chile (1973) (Rosato, 2003). In these cases, the United States feared that those countries could fall into the Soviet orbit; this fear points to the role of balance of power, the argument that is made from the realist agenda. Critics of democratic peace theory also argue that war often finds support of public opinion in democratic countries (Chan 1997). Perhaps democracies in the recent past have had other reasons for not going to war against each other (Layne 1994). For instance, the Soviet Union provided a common enemy, and the United States was too powerful to be challenged. Therefore, it was an easy choice for smaller democracies to form the U.S.-led military and political bloc against the Soviet Union. This allowed them to resolve their differences peacefully.

LIBERALISM AT THE GLOBAL LEVEL

The global level is the most important context for liberalism, as well as for realism. Globalization, or the growing interdependence of countries and their economies, brings not only opportunities but also new challenges for liberal approaches to international relations. Economic liberalism must find better answers to the problem of how to face a growing threat of instability of global financial markets. A financial panic among banks and their patrons may lead to a flight of capital from one or many states, resulting in the disappearance of billions of dollars, the end of investments, unfinished construction, and massive unemployment. Only big countries or countries with great financial resources can resist the volatility of financial markets. Among them, most prominently, are the United States, the European Union, China, and Germany.

Institutional liberals supported NATO and EU expansion in the 1990s, and they continued their support when both institutions experienced difficulties in recent years. Still, they have to prove that global governance would work, say in the absence of the American leadership. Some argue that without the United States' military power and political will, NATO is likely to withdraw from Afghanistan and may even fall apart.

Optimists remain undaunted, however. Most scholars of liberalism continue to use *game theory* and collect enormous amounts of historical data to demonstrate that, given a choice between cooperation and noncooperation, sovereign states rationally prefer to cooperate. In the classic *prisoner's dilemma* situation, for example, two players' outcomes depend on the simultaneous choice each one makes. Some political scientists use formal exercises that test the behavior of decision makers, such as state leaders, who must predict and react to the decisions of other state leaders. Their work compares the likelihood of decisions that favor cooperation against the likelihood of selfish decisions. We will return to this subject in the next chapter when we discuss the political psychology of world leaders.

Liberal scholars argue that the world's interdependence diminishes the ability of powerful states to act unilaterally, which reduces the chance of military conflict. Globalization stands for interconnectedness and, therefore, for multiple interests. The complexity of and urgency of global problems may also support liberal ideas. International projects in the twenty-first century increasingly require the shared economic and financial resources of many states. Even the United States, the world's biggest economic and military power today, cannot police the world. The role of international and nongovernment organizations will increase simply because there are no alternatives.

As we have seen, democratic peace theory still has to be tested on a global scale. In today's world, states that try to borrow from Western democracy often fail, in the face of corrupt bureaucracies, inertia, fierce opposition, and political, ethnic, and religious violence. Russia, Ukraine, Colombia, Pakistan, and many other countries have all had difficulty building democratic institutions. Sadly, weak democratic states may have to resort to violence internally and externally. Does this mean that illiberal nondemocratic regimes, such as those in Singapore and China, are better partners for international relations than Pakistan where democracy is weak? Does it mean that the new democratizing Egypt is a less reliable partner for regional stability than the old Egypt of military dictatorship?

The next decades may provide some answers. Princeton University's Robert Keohane believes that most important remedies to domestic conflicts and violence are land reform, environmental cleanup, better education, and health care. These policies can best promote stability and prosperity. The military will still have a role to play. However, international organizations, economic support, and international cooperation can strengthen civilian public sectors and address ethnic and social problems (Keohane 2005). Although very few would probably argue against better education and health care, a key challenge is to find sufficient resources to accomplish these ambitious projects.

Some ideas of liberal internationalism may sound quite revolutionary. In 1994, Gidon Gottlieb offered the concept of "states plus nations": ethnic groups, he explained, should receive the special legal and political status of a nation. A world of traditional states, in his view, would evolve into a

Check Your Knowledge

1. Explain log rolling as a feature of bureaucratic bargaining.

2. Why do neorealists remain skeptical regarding liberal claims of "global community"?

3. Why would neorealists favor nuclear disarmament?

4. How does public opinion affect foreign policy?

system of many nations, not necessarily with physical borders. Citizenship in a nation could be granted to people living in separate states, such as people of Chinese descent in Europe, Asia, and America. They would still pay taxes and serve in the military where they live. However, nationality would be matter of cultural heritage, not the "motherland," and territorial conflicts would decrease. The massive migrations that continue to take place in the twenty-first century should put Gottlieb's proposal to the test.

In the next chapter, we will turn to a variety of approaches that in many ways challenge realism and liberalism.

CASE STUDY

The European Union as a Liberal Empire

Background

The European Union is the greatest liberal experiment in world history. Twenty-eight European countries within several years willingly transferred a great part of their sovereignty to the transnational institutions of a broader European government. At the core of this experiment was the determination of a group of European politicians and diplomats to prevent another war in Europe. Above all, they sought to address the historic rivalry between France and Germany, not via power games and alliances, but through economic cooperation and rapprochement. NATO helped the architects of this cooperation because it resolved the problem of security from external threats (Ludlow 2010).

In 1951, the European Coal and Steel Community (ECSC) placed the power to make decisions about the coal and steel industries, located in France and West Germany, in the hands of an independent organization. Jean Monnet, an advocate of European integration, served as its first president. The Marshall Plan, which also helped to promote European economic and financial cooperation, favored a united European economic and trade market. With American consent, in 1957, European leaders signed the Treaties of Rome, creating the European Atomic Energy Community (EURATOM) and the European Economic Community (EEC). Member states removed trade barriers between one another, forming a free-trade zone called informally the *Common*

Market (Haas, 1958). In 1967, the European Parliament was established. Common economic policies were followed by common financial policies.

The European project survived the end of the U.S. gold standard in 1971 and the political troubles of the late 1960s–early 1970s, as well as the tensions brought on by France's expensive domestic agricultural subsidies and the economic recession stemming from the sharp rise of oil prices in 1974. Despite all of these negative occurrences, the Common Market strategy paid off. Western European states linked the value of their national currencies (the "European currency snake") to the dollar. Innovations and investments helped economies to adapt to expensive energy. And in 1973, the EEC expanded, with Denmark, Ireland, and (after years of reluctance) the United Kingdom joining; Greece, Portugal, and Spain followed during the 1980s.

The advocates of greater European integration decided to accelerate their plans at the end of the Cold War. In 1987, France and West Germany, as well as other members of the EEC, agreed on the Single European Act, to create a common space for capital and labor and a political union. In 1989–1990, the last obstacle to the union—the agreement on common European currency—was resolved (Bozo, 2009). In 1992, just months after the Soviet Union's collapse, European leaders signed the Maastricht Treaty (named after a city in the Netherlands) that put European integration on a fast track. The European Community became the European Union (EU). Many countries, EU members, signed in 1995 a treaty in the town of Schengen, Luxemburg, abolishing border checks between them. People from these countries now could travel around the Schengen zone without obtaining visas in their passports, In January 1999, Germany, France, Italy, and other eight member-states of EU introduced the euro, a common currency.

The EU acquired full-scale executive, legislative, and judicial institutions: the Council of the European Union, the European Commission (both in Brussels, Belgium), and the European Court of Justice (in Luxembourg). Strasbourg (France) is the official seat of the European Parliament. Luxembourg hosts the Secretariat of the European Parliament, although many sessions and committee meetings are held in Brussels. The EU as a "superstate" has a flag, an anthem, a central bank, a supreme court, a parliament, a president of the European Commission, developing armed forces, a sizeable bureaucracy, and a huge budget. By 2004, Austria, Finland, Sweden, Poland, the Czech and Slovak Republics, Hungary, the Baltic States, Slovenia, Cyprus, and Malta had joined the Union. Bulgaria and Romania became members in 2007. With the Treaty of Lisbon that year, the EU attempted to set up a coordinated security and foreign policy. Still, the main decision-making bodies of the EU are legislative ones (Parliament and Council). There is no strong pan-European executive.

After some good years, the structural problems of the EU came to the surface. The financial crisis of 2008–2013 revealed major problems in the EU design, particularly its lack of functionality at the time of economic strains. The acute financial problems in Greece, Italy, Ireland, and Portugal sharpened the discussion of the future of the European Union. There is a powerful argument that a single European currency makes any effective responses

People's March for Brexit Vote, London, UK, 2018.

to economic or financial crises more difficult to implement. The future of the European Union depends on collective action to resolve these financial and economic problems. In 2010–2012, member states created the European Financial Stability Facility to preserve the financial stability of the union. They agreed on serious financial measures to avoid a deep crisis and required the governments of Greece, Spain, and Italy to take serious austerity measures to reduce their national debt. The search for coordinated policies continues.

Analysis

Let's compare the arguments of liberal institutionalism and its critics:

- **Integration or protectionism?** The European Union was created to defend four economic freedoms: the free flow of capital, labor, products, and services. Supporters of early unification argued that integration in one functional area would almost necessarily lead to integration in others (Haas, 1958). European states managed to combine economic growth with generous support of social programs. Governments invested heavily in education, health care, employment, and the environment. Europe seemed to be a continent characterized by long-lasting peace and stability. To many, the liberal ideas have shown their effectiveness.

  Critics today point out instead that the crisis is pushing European states toward nationalism and protectionism. History shows that sovereign states tend to protect their own economies against cheap foreign products, services, and labor. Today, Greece, Italy, and Spain suffer very high unemployment among its young population, and free labor migration in the EU contributes to this problem. There is growing opposition to immigration, particularly from Eastern Europe and the regions to the south of Europe. The freedom of labor movement created strong resistance from the labor unions in France and Italy. Recently, a number of European countries began to cut their spending on education and other social programs. Critics also argue that Germany, the most successful economy of the EU, became a donor of less successful European economies and a "dictator" promoting monetary discipline and neglecting unemployment and social protection.

Case Study Questions

- **Euro-bureaucracy or national decision making?** Liberal supporters of the EU insist that the progressive decline of sovereignty of European states was a good thing. It makes rivalries and wars in Europe impossible. There is no way back, liberals argue—only forward—to a more efficient Europe, capable of dealing with financial and social problems of all its member states. The EU, supporters suggest, should further expand the mechanisms of "collective rule" in Brussels: work on criminal law, taxation, and standards in social policy—including unemployment benefits, pension plans, funding for education, and a few more issues. The Union should also have a central office in charge of EU foreign affairs and a small but viable military force.

Critics disagree. They believe that further erosion of state sovereignty is harmful because it transfers sovereignty to bureaucrats in the central government and moves it farther away from voters. Local authorities and communities can no longer decide what is right for *them*. Critics in particular focus on the sprawling Euro-bureaucracy. There are too many offices, institutions, rules, and regulations in Brussels. Still, other critics think that new institutions are actually useless because they cannot substitute for sovereign states. Take, for example, the EU office of foreign affairs. Will it have real power to make decisions, or will it become a new expensive institution? Many argue that all attempts to create a European military are impractical.

Opponents also predict that if the financial crisis continues or reemerges, Europe will be essentially split between successful states, such as Germany, and the states in debt, most of which are in the southern part of the continent. They say that future battles in Europe will be about nationalist ideas and national identity.

- **Is the European Union in danger, or is it only in transition?**

Some observers have warned that populist, nationalist regimes will take over in much of Europe and thus weaken democracy. The British referendum of June 2016 unexpectedly gave the majority to those who wanted the United Kingdom to leave the European Union. In March 2017, the British government formally invoked Article 50 of the Maastricht Treaty; it meant that the UK will have to leave the EU at the end of 2019. At the point of writing, the outcome of "Brexit" remains undecided. This process, however, split and polarized British politics, and inspired other nationalist political parties, the Popular Front in France and the Alternative for Germany, to argue that European states should take back their sovereignty, stop immigration, deal with unemployment, and boost social programs.

Euro-skeptics predict more troubles ahead, and a major conflict between nationalists and EU principles and policies. Liberal Euro-optimists are sticking to their principles, however. They are confident that the European project has no good alternatives, is reformable, and will be successful. It has survived difficulties in the past. Liberals also argue that a common "European identity" is widely shared by young and successful professional classes, and it is crucial for the future of the European project. The outcome of "Brexit" on the future of EU, whever it will be, should be watched attentively.

Realism and Liberalism

3.1   Describe the key principles of realism, and explain how they evolved over time.

Realism is a school of international relations that focuses on security, state interests, and the constant balancing of power. States attempt to ensure that others do not become significantly stronger. In the mid-nineteenth century, realpolitik emerged, focusing on practical realities of power rather than moral or ideological considerations. During the Cold War, neorealist scholars emphasized the structure of the international system.

Q: What are the realist and neorealist views of states' responses to anarchy, the absence of a global government?

3.2   Discuss the meaning of states' power, polarity, and interests in realist theory.

States constantly gain or lose power, affecting the international order. According to the realist approach, the design of the international order is determined largely by polarity, the distribution of power among states. A state's geographic location, history, ideology, political regime, or economic conditions can affect its interests and thus its power politics.

Q: How and why do great powers emerge?

3.3   Explain why and how liberalism dismisses the principles of power politics.

Liberalism rejects power politics and instead emphasizes international cooperation and mutual benefits. It further emphasizes the importance of international organizations and nonstate actors in shaping state preferences and policy.

Q: Explain the principles of liberalism in thirty seconds, giving at least one example of liberal principles applied to foreign policy.

3.4 Discuss the liberal ideas of soft power and international institutions.

The premises of liberalism include the power of diplomacy, democratic peace theory, and soft power to encourage cooperation and engagement. Liberalism promotes the idea that states can solve problems by acting together. To achieve this outcome, states need to engage in effective cooperation that cannot be achieved without international institutions. Cooperation, in turn, will reduce confrontation. However, liberal principles must be tested in action.

Q: What are some examples of soft power?

3.5 Distinguish different approaches and traditions within realism and liberalism.

According to realpolitik, states need a strong economy and military, efficient diplomacy, and few international commitments. Neorealism emphasizes power structure and order. According to neoliberalism, state interests are realized in the context of interdependence.

Q: Compare and contrast realism and liberalism.

3.6 Critically apply realism and liberalism to international relations on the levels of individual decisions, specific policies of states, and global developments.

Realists tend to ignore individual factors. At the state level, realism explores how domestic forces affect foreign policy. Realists argue in favor of consolidating force to keep developments in check. According to liberalism, the choices of political leaders affect outcomes of war and peace; ideas, interests, and institutions influence states' foreign policies; and domestic and international opinion shape foreign policy.

Q: Give an example of realpolitik in the United States' foreign policy.

Q: How does liberalism explain individual foreign policy decisions? Give examples.

KEY TERMS

anarchy 79
bandwagon 86
bipolar 83
bureaucratic bargaining 104
defensive realism 87
democratic peace theory 95
economic aid 88
economic sanctions 88
international system 81

liberalism 89
log rolling 104
multilateralism 98
multipolar 83
neoliberalism 92
neorealism (structural realism) 81
offensive realism 87
power 82

proxy wars 88
realism 79
realpolitik 80
security dilemma 85
soft power 96
unipolar 83
unilateralism 98

Alternative Views

> *It's much, much better to talk to one another than about one another.*
>
> ANGELA MERKEL,
> GERMAN
> CHANCELLOR

From 2013 to 2015, a militant fundamentalist group called the Islamic State of Iraq and Syria (ISIS) rapidly expanded to control a significant territory of western Iraq and eastern Syria. The UN declared ISIS a terrorist group, and a global coalition was formed in 2014 to prevent the movement's continued deadly violence and expansion. In 2015, Russia moved its armed forces to Syria and began a bombing campaign there, partly in response to the Syrian government's request for help combating ISIS and other oppositional forces. The United States and an international coalition moved in as well, using air strikes against ISIS. As a result of fierce local and international involvement, by 2018 ISIS no longer controlled a sizable territory, and its fighters had suffered heavy casualties. Yet many of them did not surrender.

From the beginning, ISIS leaders chose not to cooperate or negotiate with the international community; they did not practice realpolitik to bargain for their own survival. If they hoped to create a viable state, what motivated their seemingly self-destructive decisions? Why did they choose confrontation over survival of their self-proclaimed state? Time and time again we encounter similar examples from history. Neither Saddam Hussein's regime in Iraq in 2003 nor the Taliban government in Afghanistan in 2001 chose negotiations or bargaining to preserve their regimes from collapsing. What were their reasons? Neither realism nor liberalism could address this question in a satisfactory way.

This chapter will explore alternative approaches that go beyond the two major theories in explaining international politics. We will consider how perceptions, social norms, inequalities, conflicting economic interests, gender, race, identities, and psychological factors shape the behavior of leaders, states, and nonstate global actors.

A Syrian soldier in 2018, following a victory against ISIS fighters, who were driven by their belief in a possibility of an Islamic state. Why have many people turned to destruction and died for the sake of certain beliefs and ideas?

Learning Objectives

4.1 Describe the necessity of interpretations beyond realism and liberalism.

4.2 Explain what the constructivist view brings to the study of international relations and foreign policy.

4.3 Discuss how Marxism, postcolonial studies, and feminism approach international relations.

4.4 Describe how political culture and identity factors can affect international politics.

4.5 Discuss psychological factors influencing foreign policy and individual decisions.

4.6 Apply alternative approaches to interpreting the behavior of leaders, states, and global nonstate actors.

4.1 Why Alternative Interpretations?

What can alternative views offer that realism and liberalism do not? Proponents of realism and liberalism explain international relations as the sophisticated and *rational* actions of states and organizations—actions that are supposed to maximize utility. But how rational are the choices of international actors? How often do specific interests, ideological biases, or misperceptions become the driving forces behind political decisions? This chapter presents approaches to international relations that go beyond realism and liberalism to explore the causes, patterns, and outcomes of international relations:

- *Constructivism*, a relatively new approach to international relations, argues that states develop their interests and notions of security according to diverse social norms and historical experiences. It posits that power, anarchy, and security have different meanings for different global actors at different times. For example, Israel may see Iran's nuclear program as a serious threat, whereas Russia may see it as peaceful and thus acceptable. Like individuals, states can exaggerate external threats, underestimate dangers, or even completely overlook them. During the past twenty years, constructivism became a third major theoretical approach to international relations, challenging and (to some degree) advancing both realism and liberalism.

- Other alternative approaches focus on *conflict and inequality* as defining factors in international relations. For example, Marxism explores how the capitalist motivation for profit explains the actions of countries' ruling elites. Meanwhile, postcolonial and feminist theories consider the significant effects of inequality. These approaches call for serious changes in the current international system; they are critical toward Western models of development and modernization.

- Another approach, close to constructivism, focuses on *culture* and *identities*, including the ways people and institutions perceive themselves and others. Religious values, ethnic pride, nationalism, democratic norms of behavior—all can shape countries' foreign policy priorities. These factors sometimes affect the political will to use or not to use force.

- Finally, *political psychology* focuses on decision makers, the contexts in which they make decisions, and how they react to opportunities and crises. This field explores the complex mechanisms of political behavior—including political leaders' individual life experiences, emotions, biases, misperceptions, rationality, and irrationality.

> **Check Your Knowledge**
>
> 1. What do alternative views offer that realism and liberalism do not?
>
> 2. What are some common themes among alternative approaches?

4.2 Constructivism

The decisions of global actors depend on circumstances. Advocates of **constructivism** argue that fundamental elements such as power, anarchy, state interests, security, and sovereignty change over time and in consideration of context. States interpret, or *construct*, the facts available to them. In other words, these interpretations are not directly and necessarily rooted in human perception or instantly influenced by the coverage of world events on social media. They do not appear quickly as the result of leaders' rational or irrational decisions; they tend to evolve gradually as societies, governments, ideologies, and the world evolve (Wendt 1992).

constructivism An approach to international relations that considers state actions and policies in light of how societies and institutions interpret, or *construct*, information.

Realists, as you will remember, assume that, in a condition of anarchy, states act to protect their vital interests by building up their power and measuring it against other states. Liberal internationalists insist that the development of international trade, institutions, and international law can modify vital interests and encourage states to cooperate. Notice that both realists and liberals assume that states have interests. Constructivists join this discussion by raising a critical question: *Where do state interests come from?* Who defines which interests are to be respected as vital, legitimate, and essential—and which can be disregarded? To answer, constructivists emphasize the importance of social norms, perceptions, and rules in defining such interests (Wendt 1999; Checkel 1998).

To reemphasize: constructivism does not contend that foreign policy decisions just spring from the imagination of influential actors. Rather, these decisions are rooted in *collective* principles, as meanings are *socially and histori-cally constructed*. Such principles can remain relatively stable or predictable in cases where a country's government, ideologies, and political systems punish or disapprove of dissent on major political issues. For example, Iranian cit-izens who openly criticize their country's foreign policy put themselves at risk. In democratic societies, by contrast, people and institutions often loudly disagree on their country's foreign policy. The American public dis-agrees substantially with international relations experts on what constitutes the country's greatest threat (Pew Research Center 2018b). Such debates have complex and indirect effects on foreign policy in democratic states (Tomz and Weeks 2013).

Socially Constructed Meanings

Socially constructed meanings have governed political decisions since ancient times. In the fifth century BCE, the Athenian historian Thucydides described how fear and honor, in addition to self-interest, provoked Greek cities to go to war. Constructivists would agree with much of what Thucydides wrote. Fear, of course, is a major factor in realism as well (e.g., realists consider fear of in-ternational anarchy). Yet the realist approach does not explain why a coun-try's military power evokes intense fear of neighbors in one situation but not in another. For instance, Russia today has a much greater nuclear arsenal than the Soviet Union did during the 1950s. And yet then, in the early stages of the Cold War, however, Washington and Moscow assumed that a potential nu-clear conflict was real. Both sides based their specific policies on their mutual fears of a sudden nuclear attack. Today, the United States and Russia—despite the difficulties in their relations and despite many new deadly nuclear weap-ons being developed—interact on the assumption that nuclear weapons must never be used.

Reactions motivated by fear can have long-lasting effects on international interactions and state interests. In addition, fear adds an element of irrational-ity to human decisions. Consider how the sudden Japanese attack against the United States in 1941 transformed American foreign policy for decades. To this day, the **Pearl Harbor syndrome**—the focus of individual attitudes and state policies on avoiding sudden and devastating attacks—affects American foreign policy. After Pearl Harbor, Washington sought to maintain a position of absolute military superiority and often acted preemptively if it perceived a security threat from abroad (Zubok 2007).

Pearl Harbor syndrome Individual attitudes and state policies focused on avoiding sudden and devastating attacks.

From the viewpoint of constructivism, Thucydides' "honor" is also a social category that shapes international behavior. It is a state's search for re-spect, international credibility, prestige, and reputation. "Honor" can also be given a warped interpretation. In early 2003, Saddam Hussein, then in power in Iraq, refused to cooperate with the United Nations and the United States, fearing exposure of his weaknesses (Woods, Palkki, and Stout 2011). Hussein also wanted to maintain his image in the Arab world as an uncompromising fighter against Western powers (Primakov 2009). As Thucydides might have argued in ancient Greece, Hussein's defiance in the face of American power stemmed from a warped sense of honor.

Pearl Harbor under attack, December 7, 1941. This event shaped American perceptions of national security for decades afterward. What milestone events have shaped your perception of international security and international politics?

Three Types of International Environments

Perceptions of how states should act—if these perceptions are shared by other states—translate into actions and shape a particular international environment:

- States may view the international environment as a gigantic battlefield, for example, in which individual states compete as enemies for power and resources, using all means necessary to win (Wendt 1992). This view of competing states recalls the violent and anarchic society described by English philosopher Thomas Hobbes (1588–1679) and is thus called the *Hobbesian model*.

- Other states may perceive their environment differently. To them, states are not necessarily enemies. Instead, they interact as reasonable opponents: they observe the rules of the game and try to compromise with one another to balance their interests. This view is the *Lockean model* and has its roots in the philosophy of English Enlightenment thinker John Locke (1632–1704).

- Finally, some states may see the world as driven by fundamental norms of ethics, based on recognition of the rights of others and a genuine desire to preserve international peace. This is the *Kantian model*, named after German philosopher Immanuel Kant (1724–1804). (See Table 4-1.)

At pivotal moments in history, especially at the end of major wars, dominant states and their leaders have to decide on the principles of a new postwar

TABLE 4-1 Key Assumptions by Type of International Environment

Type of Environment	Key Assumptions	Example
Hobbesian (after Thomas Hobbes)	• States are enemies and rivals. • States engage in power politics. • Political conflicts have zero-sum outcomes. • Self-interest and security are states' primary interests.	Stalin did not believe in a lasting cooperation between the Soviet Union and the capitalist powers; instead he believed in reliance on one's own power and aimed for Soviet domination.
Lockean (after John Locke)	• States are competitors that can be reasoned with. • Force and compromise are used in combination. • Mutual restraint is a norm of behavior. • International treaties build security.	Churchill believed that power balancing would contain any rivalry. He was prepared to divide the post-World War II world into separate spheres of influence, maintaining a strong British Empire.
Kantian (after Immanuel Kant)	• States are partners. • Cooperation is the main mechanism of international relations. • Nonviolence is a norm of behavior. • Collective security is the ultimate goal of all states.	FDR believed in building lasting institutional foundations for postwar peace and global partnership.

Sources: Wendt 1992, 1999; Zubok 2007.

international environment. For instance, U.S., British, and Soviet leaders met in Yalta in 1945, a few months before the end of World War II. The three leaders could not agree on a common vision for the postwar world. As a result, fears grew, and the global confrontation known as the Cold War began (Plokhy 2010).

Historical Lessons

States draw different lessons from international relations and may have very different understandings of what constitutes a fair game. Why did Canada and Cuba choose and sustain different policies toward the United States, for example? Canada, a former British colony, was for a long time in confrontation with the United States, and yet achieved an equal relationship with Washington on the basis of common values and mutual trade. Cuba, a former Spanish colony, fell under the United States' economic domination and was run by U.S.-backed dictators until 1959. Fidel Castro (1926–2016) and a group of young revolutionaries overthrew a pro-U.S. dictator (Fulgencio Batista), rejected Washington's domination, and allied with the distant Soviet Union. They adopted the Communist ideology and were eager to provide bases in Cuba for Soviet nuclear missiles that targeted the United States. After the collapse of the Soviet Union, Cuban foreign policy arguably became more pragmatic, but tensions with the United States continued to define the relations between the two countries. The United States under President Obama began to dismantle the sanctions against Cuba, but in 2017, the Trump administration suspended this process.

For constructivists, history clearly shapes the international environment. If diplomacy does not bring justice in response to suffering, or if the world leaves an aggressor unpunished, then a Hobbesian environment is likely to take shape. In contrast, if states interact efficiently for a long time, support international institutions such as the United Nations, and make room for nongovernmental organizations, then a status quo can emerge based on trust, bringing humanity closer to the Lockean or even the Kantian ideal (Wendt 1992). Similar logic guided the United States and the European Union's member states in their responses to Russia's 2014 annexation of Crimea from Ukraine. The Western countries imposed a series of economic sanctions on Russia, but their end goal was not simply to feel good about their actions. Rather, they hoped to make Russia change its behavior, so that the European order, based on Kantian values, could be sustained in Eastern Europe (Blinken 2015).

Check Your Knowledge

1. Describe three main factors in foreign policy decision making according to the constructivist view.

2. Constructivism suggests that fear affects the behavior of states. Suggest examples in which countries have underestimated or overestimated threats against them.

3. Explain key differences between the historical experiences of Canada and Cuba. Pick another country and discuss how its experiences have affected its foreign policy today. Suggested cases: Germany, Japan, China, South Korea, or Russia.

4.3 Marxism, Postcolonial Studies, and Feminism

conflict theories Approaches that emphasize economic, social, and political inequality as a source of contradictions and tensions among social groups.

Conflict theories emphasize economic, social, and political inequality as primary sources of conflict and international tension. Here we focus on Marxism, postcolonial studies, and feminism to highlight the roles of social classes, ruling elites, males, and other dominant groups in shaping foreign policy and global affairs. Dominant groups or entire states impose their will on less powerful groups or states, creating an unequal international order to serve their interests. In doing so, they generate conflicts, violence, and wars. Reducing tensions both domestically and internationally will undoubtedly require liberation from this order and from inequality.

Marxism (and Leninism)

Marxism A social, political, and economic theory that interprets international relations as a struggle between states representing ruling elites interested in control over territories, people, and resources.

Marxism interprets international relations as a struggle between states representing ruling elites interested in control over territories, people, and resources. It was one of the most influential schools of social, political, and economic thought during the twentieth century. The German philosopher and political theorist Karl Marx (1818–1883) regarded human history as driven by the struggle between social classes—the *haves* and the *have-nots*. Marxism views a state as an instrument of the dominant classes or groups, such as the aristocracy or capitalists, to oppress and exploit other classes, such as peasants or workers. The state conducts its foreign policy according to the interests of the ruling classes, which are to maximize their power and wealth at the expense of other social classes and other states. To Marxists, only a revolution of industrial workers, the *proletariat*, can save humanity from the eternal cycle of oppression and injustice. Marxists propose to do so by establishing **Communism**—a classless political and social order of equals ideally free from oppressive governments (Marx and Engels 1848/2011).

Communism
A classless political and social order that is ideally free from oppressive government.

Vladimir Lenin (1870–1924), who led Russia from 1917 to 1924, adapted Marxism to explain developments in the early twentieth century. According to Lenin, capitalism concentrates wealth in the hands of a few banks and industrial corporations. This imbalance, in turn, produces unbridled **capitalist imperialism**, a global struggle among international corporations and banks for territories and resources. According to Lenin, sovereign states participating in this struggle are just obedient "executive committees" of powerful corporations and banks expressing the interests of super-wealthy elites. In search of new markets and resources, Lenin argued, just a handful of capitalist European and North American countries colonized Africa and Asia in the nineteenth century and kept Latin America in a state of dependency. Lenin called for a world revolution, a violent takeover of power and resources, as the only way to save humanity from imperialism and war (Lenin 1916/1996).

capitalist imperialism (Lenin's theory of)
A global struggle among international corporations and banks for territories and resources.

Throughout the twentieth century, Communist revolutionaries justified violence as long as it was aimed against capitalism or the revolutionaries' opponents. Communist states included the Soviet Union, the People's Republic of China, parts of Eastern and Central Europe, Vietnam, Cuba, and North Korea. Marxism-Leninism promotes *distributive justice*, according to which the contemporary world's distribution of resources and power is fundamentally unfair and therefore should be changed by any means, including local violence and civil war. Marxism-Leninism rejects liberal values, political democracy, pluralism, and individualism in the same way it rejects private property and the free-market economy. Capitalism here is viewed as a source of exploitation and inequality. Political democracy is ridiculed as a façade to deceive the oppressed and the poor, to divide them, and to rule over them (Ziegler 1981).

After World War II, many Communist parties in Western Europe distanced themselves from Leninist views. They turned instead to social-democratic models in which all social classes can share wealth and power. Several Communist parties in Asia, such as those in China, Laos, and Cambodia, chose different models of Marxism to follow. Lenin's theory of imperialism, however, remained particularly popular among the champions of anti-elitism, anti-capitalism, decolonization, and national liberation.

Neo-Marxism And Dependency Theory

Some scholars, beginning in the 1990s, declared that traditional Marxism (which was developed a century ago) was no longer an appealing alternative to capitalism. Marxists' endorsement of violence and their persistent inability to deliver economic prosperity—in the countries where they have been in

Communist Party of India-Marxist (CPI-M) supporters participate in a rally during a strike in Kolkata, India, in 2019. The strike was called against the government's alleged antiworker policies and unilateral labor reforms.

power—contributed to Marxism's steady decline after the mid-1990s. Arguments for a new, reformed Marxism proposed that it could justify resistance to capitalism's inequalities but discourage violence and authoritarianism (Vattimo and Zabala 2014).

In the 1960s and 1970s, some Western thinkers turned to **neo-Marxism** to argue that world capitalism should not be destroyed but rather reformed through science and smart progressive policies. In Asia, Africa, and Latin America, neo-Marxists reacted against *liberal modernization*, which advised states to follow the American market-based model of economic and social development. This model generated economic growth but also rapidly contributed to social inequality (see Chapter 7).

Argentinean scholar Raúl Prebisch (1901–1986) argued that the structures of international relations—and trade in particular—make it impossible for countries to grow out of poverty. The free market keeps poor states dependent on rich states, while supplying the latter with cheap labor and raw materials. Only by building its own industries and "substituting" for foreign goods by producing its own can a state emerge from dependency. These views became the foundation of **dependency theory**, which holds that resources and power generally flow from poor states to wealthy states.

American sociologist Immanuel Wallerstein (b. 1930) formulated a related view known as *world-systems theory*. He used a Marxist concept, *hegemony*, which claims that a few industrial countries have an advantage in world affairs, whereas other states are kept behind (Wallerstein 1979). World-systems theory divides the world into a **core**, consisting of the developed states that exercise their hegemonic power, and the **periphery**, including former colonies and underdeveloped

dependency theory The view that the world economic order is based on the flow of resources and power from a "periphery" of poor states to a "core" of wealthy states.

core Economically developed states that exercise their hegemonic power.

periphery Former colonies, and underdeveloped, chronically poor states.

and chronically poor states. The core states, located mainly in North America and Western Europe, impose free-market rules on the poor states to keep the periphery in permanent poverty and dependence (Gereffi and Korzeniewicz 1993).

The interests of the core and the periphery are in conflict. The core states share an interest in maintaining the established economic order while eliminating challenges from the periphery. The Soviet Union and China in the twentieth century challenged the capitalist core. Yet the Soviets and Chinese could not reshape the global economic, financial, and trade systems. In the end, China and the Soviet Union (shortly before its collapse) decided to become part of a world system dominated by the United States, Western Europe, and Japan (Goldfrank 2000). The financial global crisis that started in 2008 brought fresh attention to the issue of economic inequality. Radicals (those who focus on bringing about sweeping changes in social institutions and laws by abrupt and often forceful means) supported by the *antiglobalist movement* claimed that globalization, praised by liberal theoreticians in the early 2000s, in reality benefited only rich countries. A new round of development studies included discussions of how the wealthy countries can help those who lag behind economically (Wallerstein 2004; Arrighi 1994; Arrighi and Lu Zhang 2011).

In the 2000s, several Latin American countries, including Venezuela, Bolivia, Ecuador, and Nicaragua, turned to "softer" models of Marxism in domestic policies. These policies were aimed at bringing about more economic justice, participatory democracy, and welfare programs. To emphasize the shift, this period was labeled *Pink Tide* (symbolically, "pink" is lighter than "red," which has been historically associated with Marxism-Leninism). These policies, however, led to budgetary overspending and, after the sharp drop of oil prices in 2014, brought several leftist governments down. However, the applicability of even "softer" Marxist recipes for mitigating the inequality of wealth and power in the world, as well as inside each country, remains an open question.

In an era of economic growth and diminishing poverty, the influence of neo-Marxism is likely to diminish. If social and economic inequality grows, however, some new derivative of Marxism is likely to come back and win the allegiance of millions around the world. We will return to these discussions in Chapter 7.

Postcolonial Studies

postcolonial studies
The critique of Western domination in postcolonial Africa, Asia, and Latin America.

Using the assumptions of Marxism-Leninism, **postcolonial studies** critique Western domination in postcolonial Africa, Asia, and Latin America (collectively known as the global South; see Chapter 7). The postcolonial view criticizes the self-ascribed racial and cultural superiority of the Western world over the non-Western world. Proponents of this view cite the policies of Europe and North America as the main source of global problems. According to this approach, European imperialism and racism have shaped the very language of international relations, which divides the world into "us" against "them" (Said 1994; Spivak 1999). Advocates of postcolonial studies argue that the West retains its dominance over the rest of the world through cultural and informational means and that state military agendas and international corporations perpetuate colonialist policies (Huggan, 2016; Gregory 2004). Western thinkers and journalists define the West as a norm and depict attempts to overthrow Western domination as counterproductive and irrational (Said 1979; Fanon 2005). Further, this approach contends that the Cold War was mainly waged in Africa, Latin America, and Asia, preventing the development of these regions and causing the suffering of non-Western peoples after the Cold War was over (Huggan 2016; Chakrabarty 2007; Westad 2007).

Feminism

Other conflict approaches focus not on social classes and wealth, but on social divisions such as gender and race. Again, social and political injustice are seen as a source of conflict in international relations.

Feminism is the view that women do not have equal rights and opportunities to those of men and that massive and global changes are needed to achieve social justice. Feminist scholars have produced a wealth of works linking gender inequality to international relations. They argue that most existing approaches to international relations contain the gender bias of the male-dominated world and thus these theories must be revised (Dicker 2016; Hirschman 2010).

First, feminists say, men created legal and cultural rules, religions, government institutions, and policies that systematically discriminate against women—directly and indirectly—and satisfy men's political interests and personal needs. Global studies show that women in the past fifteen years filled slightly more than 20 percent of parliamentary seats worldwide—and fewer than 15 percent of ministerial-level positions (IPU, 2018; Hunt 2007). Women hold less than 11 percent of board seats on Fortune 500 companies, which are the largest U.S. companies. Globally, women hold only 17 percent of corporate board seats (Catalist, 2018). Outside Western countries, women seldom play a significant role in policy-making in defense, security, or diplomacy. Feminism argues that the task is therefore to change policies to give women institutional support to represent their interests in the policy-making process globally (Waylen 2010). (See Tables 4-2 and 4-3.)

feminism Critical approach arguing that men's political domination and their oppression of women shape international relations.

TABLE 4-2 Percentages of Women in Lower or Single Houses of Parliaments, Selected Countries, 2017

Rwanda	Bolivia	S.Africa	U.K.	China	U.S.A.	Russia	Brazil	Iran	Kuwait
61	53	42	32	24	20	16	11	6	3

Source: Inter-Parliamentary Union 2018

TABLE 4-3 Percentages of Women on Corporate Boards, Selected Countries, 2017

Norway	France	Sweden	Canada	U.S.A.	India	Taiwan	S.Korea	Japan
46.7	34	33.6	21.6	19.9	8.6	4.5	4.1	3.5

Source: Catalist, 2018.

Second, feminists say, defense and security policies for the most part reflect a traditional masculine culture rooted in the centuries-long customs that accepts war and violence rather than consensus and peace (McBee, 2018; Cohn 1987). For centuries, women's views of politics and conflict as well as their preferences for nonviolent conflict resolution were not taken into consideration. In fact, studies show that women as a group tend to differ from men in their leadership style and understanding of security (Ayman and Korabik 2010). If women occupied more positions of power and if feminine qualities and attitudes rather than masculine ones were more valued, many feminists conclude, we all would live in a much more peaceful world (Dicker 2016; Hunt 2007).

Third, there is a strong correlation between violence against women and violence in foreign policy. Countries that tolerate inequality between men and women and accept aggression against women are more prone to use force abroad as well (Patterson 2006). Domestic gender inequality influences a state's choices between violence and cooperation, peace and war, even in democracies (Caprioli and Boyer 2001). In sum, feminist scholars argue, women should have the freedom and opportunities to make their own choices in everyday life and politics alike (Snyder-Hall 2010).

Feminist scholars disagree among themselves. Some of them propose more radical solutions to change the predominance of patriarchal system of values in the world. They dismiss more moderate feminist scholars who argue that liberal values and the increased number of women in the positions of power would erode the male-values domination (Ferree 2012).

Researchers and advocates of feminism have directed attention to serious international issues—including modern sex slavery, the trafficking of women and children across borders, rape and other forms of sexual violence, the lack of protection for women and children in war zones, and AIDS (Buzan and Hansen 2009, 212).

Check Your Knowledge

1. What are the key points of Lenin's theory of capitalist imperialism? Discuss whether these points are applicable today.

2. Why did neo-Marxist scholars react against *liberal modernization*?

3. Explain the core and the periphery in Wallerstein's arguments.

4. Why are postcolonial studies discussed as a conflict approach?

5. How does masculine culture relate to international relations? Suggest an example of a policy or decision rooted in a masculine culture.

4.4 Political Culture and Identity Factors

The discussion of feminism brings us to the study of political culture and identity factors. How do values, beliefs, attitudes, and affiliations make a difference in global affairs?

Political Culture

culture A set of values, behaviors, and symbols shared by a group of people and communicated from one generation to the next.

Culture is a set of values and symbols shared by a large group of people, expressed in behavior and communicated from one generation to the next

(Shiraev and Levy 2017). **Political culture** is the predominant kind of attitude and behavior of a community or country toward political authority and politics in general. It is rooted in local customs and cultural beliefs. Political culture is not a consensus or uniformity on political issues; people still tend to disagree on almost everything. According to a global survey, three out of four people around the world say their country is divided and even more divided than it was ten years ago (BBC Global Survey, 2018). Rather, political culture is a dominant perception concerning the rights and obligations of citizens—and the rules and practices of political participation.

Applied to international relations, studies of political culture suggest at least two main points, one domestic and the other international. First, a country's foreign policy is rooted in its domestic political culture. If most people in a country (think of Afghanistan, for example) distrust any foreign power to make decisions on their behalf, this attitude will play a major role in this country's policy. Second, different countries' political cultures affect the relationships between such cultures and the abilities of their governments to influence policies. In the West, it is often important in diplomatic negotiations to make a legal agreement or understanding that is politically binding. In many Asian cultures, establishing trust or opening a dialogue between two governments (think, for example, about North Korea and the United States) often appears more important in negotiations than making a formal deal (Gordon 2018; Zartman 2018).

Comparative politics teaches us about at least three types of political culture (Almond and Verba 1963). In the traditional or *parochial* political culture, citizens are only remotely aware of the presence of the central government. Most of them make local decisions regardless of state policies because people are unaware of what is happening in their country's capital. In the *authoritarian* political culture, people obey the government in most areas of their lives. If they do not, they are punished for dissent. They have little opportunity for feedback, disagreement, or activist participation in politics. In the *participatory* or democratic culture, the government can remain powerful, but citizens have the right to influence politics, elect their leaders, organize associations, and express their opposition. In democratic countries, participatory political culture is part of people's everyday life. The governments of these countries base their policies toward one another on shared principles and avoid confrontation and war with each other (see the arguments about democratic peace in Chapter 3). Also, mixed types of political cultures exist, especially when countries undergo political transition (Levitsky and Way 2010). Notice that governments can come and go overnight, yet political cultures tend to last. (See Table 4-4.)

In the United States and France, as examples, the elements of participatory democracy are strong, whereas the elements of parochial or authoritarian culture are relatively minor. In contrast, in Afghanistan and Iraq, parochial culture has dominated for centuries, and participatory culture had little opportunity to develop (though it is now developing). This is one of the reasons why Western attempts to impose far-reaching political reforms in these countries during the period of occupation after 2001–2003 were unsuccessful. This does not mean that participatory political culture is impossible in some countries: you hear these pessimistic arguments quite often and from various sources. The point is that the dominant political culture can be an obstacle to political and social reforms.

political culture
A set of values and norms essential to the functioning of international and national political institutions, including the attitudes of states toward each other and individual citizens.

TABLE 4-4 Types of Political Culture

Parochial	People are only remotely aware of the government; they do not form a political community.
Authoritarian	People obey the government, act like subjects, and have little impact on its policies.
Participatory or Democratic	People act like citizens, have the right to influence politics, elect their leaders, organize associations, and express their opposition.
Mixed or Hybrid	Elements of two or three types of political cultures coexist or transition from one type to another.

Differences in political cultures are not of course the only factors affecting bilateral relations. Countries like Russia and Saudi Arabia show elements of all three political cultures, but authoritarian culture prevails. And yet Saudi Arabia and the United States remain strategic partners. With Russia, however, several Washington administrations in the 2000s failed to develop stable relations, and tensions between the two countries continued for most of the twenty-first century.

Authoritarian states control the means of education and communication to spread information that is politically useful; they often use censorship to limit access to information that they think can hurt them. Authoritarian states can mobilize masses against other states, to distract them from domestic problems, using fear of other countries and the slogans of national solidarity to mobilize public support. Authoritarian political culture combined with economic nationalism can destabilize the entire international order (Fukuyama 2011, 2018).

With a monopoly on most information, authoritarian governments can control the process of political mobilization. In the twenty-first century, the Internet, mobile devices, and social networks have eroded technological barriers and geographic distance. The popular protests in Tunisia and Egypt in 2011, in Ukraine in 2014, and in Iran in 2017–2018 are examples of how modern means of communication could destabilize and even destroy authoritarian states. These realities have caused authorities in China, Russia, and elsewhere to censor their communication networks and limit the free flow of information. Afraid to lose power, these authorities tend to control information to filter or even generate news that is favorable to them.

Identity Factors

identity The characteristics by which a person is recognizable as a member of a cultural group, such as a nation, an ethnic group, or a religion.

Identity refers to how people see themselves as members of national, ethnic, religious, gender, or political groups. Common identity comes from shared history, culture, and language—and can generate passions in state-to-state relations that economic self-interest cannot. Nationalist and religious passions can be particularly destabilizing and even dangerous (Fukuyama 2018). During the war in Vietnam, American leaders spoke of winning "hearts and minds"—and this is often more difficult than winning a military conflict. Successful foreign policy is impossible without attractive cultural symbols—the "soft power" we discussed in Chapter 3.

IDENTITIES AND CIVILIZATIONS

Identities are certainly broader than political cultures. Let's turn to the familiar example of Canada and Cuba. Can identity factors help us to understand the difference between their relations with the United States? Canada and the United States share common identity roots in the British Empire and in Anglo-Saxon traditions. Cuba has roots in the Spanish Empire, Catholicism, and the Caribbean culture. Do you think these factors played a role when the Castro government launched its anti-American policies and convinced its people of the threat of imperialism coming from the North?

Political scientist Samuel Huntington (1993) argued that cultural factors and identities were fundamental to human behavior and can be more important than political, military, and economic interests in international affairs. He was writing at the time when the Cold War was over and the world was seemingly turning to a new era of cooperation, peace, and disappearing borders. Huntington turned to a subject that to many political scientists was a rather "uncomfortable subject and argued that cultural identity matters in politics. Moreover, he stated that cultural identity would be a source of future international conflicts. He believed that countries could share common identities and form a "civilization" rooted in centuries of collective experiences and practices. The liberal-democratic political culture, Huntington argued, is a product of Western civilization based on the classical legacy of Greece and Rome, Catholicism and Protestantism, European languages, the separation between religion and state, the rule of law, social pluralism, civil society, traditions of representative rule, and individualism. Other civilizations are based on values and experiences associated with Islam, Buddhism, Hinduism, the Eastern Orthodox faith, and other religions and traditions. Whereas in Western Christian countries politics has become separated from religion, in Islamic countries a unity of religion and politics is often emphasized. Huntington believed that non-Western civilizations would resist the expansion of democracy associated with Western political culture. Like tectonic plates in geology, civilizations will experience friction along their fault lines, thus giving rise to conflicts, especially in Eurasia where Christian and Muslim cultures coexist geographically (Rose 2013).

Huntington and other scholars argue that the major conflicts in world politics are not necessary between states but rather between "civilizations" unified by cultural values. Iran and Saudi Arabia are rivals, in this view, not only because of their competition for leadership in the region but rather because of a deep-seated animosity between Persian (mostly Shia) and Arab (mostly Sunni) civilizations. Similarly, Western countries have treated Russia with great suspicion, not just because of its actions and policies but because Europe views Russia as an alien, unpredictable, and dangerous civilization (Huntington 1993; Neumann 1996; Shiraev and Khudoley 2019).

RACE AND ETHNIC CONFLICT

Theories of **racial and ethnic prejudice** maintain that world politics remains rooted in the superiority of some racial, national, cultural, or ethnic groups over others. Racial and ethnic prejudices affect international relations in at least two general ways. First, political leaders interpret the world in racial or cultural

A boy holds his stepsister in Nyamata, Rwanda, in 2004, ten years after the civil war that left him orphaned. The world's most powerful countries were late to respond to the extreme ethnic violence that took the lives of hundreds of thousands of Rwandan people. The consequences of that war are still felt today.

terms; and second, dominant states primarily pursue the interests of white majorities.

We have already mentioned that post-colonial studies focus on how racism shapes international relations. Indeed, during the nineteenth and most of the twentieth centuries, theories of racial superiority, such as social Darwinism, justified European domination, slavery, and colonialism. Later anthropological and cultural studies rejected these ideas, emphasizing multiculturalism and equality.

Postcolonial studies, too, may point to sources of racial and ethnic conflict. In this view, Western powers have long represented a white culture of colonialism and racism. This leads to a double standard in their foreign policy. For example, the major powers took almost no action to stop the conflicts involving black Africans in Biafra in the 1960s and in Rwanda in 1994. Many Western leaders continue to doubt African countries' capabilities of self-governance, which often results in the West's lack of trust in and commitment to Africa (Gates 1998; Moyo 2018).

NATIONALISM, TRIBALISM, XENOPHOBIA, AND FUNDAMENTALISM

Identity-related attitudes affect politics especially when people express solidarity with social groups to which they belong in opposition to "others." There are at least four kinds of such attitudes: nationalism, tribalism, xenophobia, and fundamentalism. They have direct and indirect impacts on diplomacy and global affairs.

nationalism
Individual and collective identification with a country or a nation. Nationalism also can become the belief in a nation's special role. Often, it is the belief that an ethnic group has the right to form an independent state.

Nationalism has many definitions, but generally it is an individual and collective form of identity with a country or a nation. Members of an ethnic group may never see one another and yet view themselves as a unified group, particularly when threatened (Anderson 2005). Nationalism is often the belief that an ethnic group has the right to form an independent state. It can serve simultaneously as a consolidating and a dividing force (Muller 2008). Before 1948, Jews and Arabs in Palestine lived together under the British administration. When the British withdrew, the Jews in Palestine formed an independent state of Israel supported by the Soviet Union, the United States, and several Western countries. The neighboring Arab leaders went to war against Israel and lost. This led to the flight of the Palestinian Arabs from their lands and the formation of two sharply distinct national groups, Israeli Jews and Palestinian Arabs, which have remained in conflict for years (Smith 2016; Fromkin 2009). In the 1990s, the collapse of Yugoslavia led to the spark of nationalism, a violent conflict that took the lives of more than thirteen thousand people, an international military intervention, and the emergence of several new independent countries in Europe (Sobel and Shiraev 2003). Populist nationalism was on the rise in Europe after 2016, as demonstrated by the Brexit referendum in the United Kingdom, the strengthening of populism in Italy, the rise of nationalist authoritarian governments in Poland and Hungary, and the appearance of a strong nationalist parties in Germany, the Netherlands, and Austria.

National identity can coexist peacefully alongside other beliefs and patriotisms. The forms of nationalism, however, can become divisive and violent (Theiss-Morse 2009). One such form of nationalist hatred is *chauvinism*, an exaggerated belief in national superiority. Even more radical is neo-Nazism, a dangerous combination of anti-Semitism, militarism, and racism. National identity is a powerful factor in political mobilization during conflicts and wars. People will put aside their political differences to stand shoulder to shoulder as citizens against another state. Political parties mend their differences to defend their country against a foreign threat. In its virulent, active form, nationalism can be an effective substitute for a participatory political culture, especially in authoritarian states. Despite their serious disapproval of the authoritarian leader Slobodan Milošević, the Serbian political opposition moved to his side during NATO's bombing campaign against Serbia in 1999. The Russian government since 2006 has continued to use the nationalist "card" to mobilize public opinion against the West (Shiraev and Khudoley 2019). And so did the Iranian authorities, claiming the dangers coming from the West as the reason to unite all the people around the government (Rasmussen 2018).

Both nationalism and **tribalism** may be associated with **xenophobia**, which is a deep-seated fear and hatred of foreign countries and foreigners. In Afghanistan, for example, resentment of any foreign military presence has a long history (Hopkirk 2004). Xenophobia exists in democracies as well.

tribalism A way of thinking and a movement identifying itself not with nation-states, but rather with a religious or ethnic group.

xenophobia Fear and contempt of foreign countries and foreigners, helping politicians and regimes to mobilize public opinion, defeat political opposition, win elections, neutralize critics, or justify war.

Members of French far right party Front National (National Rally), with their leaders Marine le Pen and Jordan Bardella, pose during a campaign meeting in Paris in 2019. The party takes a nationalist, anti-immigration stance.

DEBATE > WHAT DOES IT MEAN TO BE A *PATRIOT* OR A *NATIONALIST*?

The labels "nationalist" and "patriot" are often confusing. Scholars for years debated the many meanings of these terms (Fonte 2017; Kosterman and Feshbach 1989). Moreover, the terms *nationalist*, *patriot*, *patriotic*, or *unpatriotic* are often deliberately misused to boost one's popularity and scorn political opponents. Just what does it mean to be a Korean, Mexican, or American patriot? In public discourse, as research shows, being a "patriot" has always been more suitable than being a "nationalist." Some, however, consider "nationalism" and "patriotism" dangerous elements associated with people's obedience to authority.

WHAT'S YOUR VIEW?

Imagine that the president of the United States together with Congress have decided to send a significant number of military personnel to fight in an overseas conflict. Opinion polls show that the majority of Americans are in favor of this military action. Which of the following opinions would you consider most *patriotic*, and why? **A** I support this decision because I love my country and believe we must support our president and our Congress in times of crisis regardless of what public opinion reveals. **B** I support this decision because I love my country and because the majority of Americans are in favor it. **C** I oppose this decision because I love my country and do not want it to fight a foreign war.

Check Your Knowledge

1. Explain *parochial*, *authoritarian*, and *participatory* political cultures.

2. Why is a country's political culture relevant to international relations? Give examples.

3. How does identity (ethnic, religious, political, etc.) affect people's views and actions related to foreign policy and international relations? Give examples.

4. According to Huntington, what are the roots of the liberal-democratic political culture?

5. How does nationalism influence international relations? Give examples of positive and negative influences.

6. Define xenophobia. Suggest the ways in which xenophobia can affect a country's foreign policy.

7. Explain political fundamentalism.

One example is a fear of immigrants. A 2011 study found that in the European Union, almost 50 percent believed that immigrants "are taking employment opportunities from the local population" (Eurobarometer 2011).

Fundamentalism is a form of identity rooted in religious beliefs. Fundamentalists advocate a return to the past—often an imagined past, before modern influences came to undermine traditional values. To them, openness, globalization, and democracy threaten local cultures and their status. *Private* fundamentalism can be found among devout believers of Islam, Christianity, Judaism, and other religions. It has little impact on international politics. *Political* fundamentalism, in contrast, advocates its vision of how its government should function and the foreign policy it should conduct (Husain 2005). ISIS is an example of Islamic fundamentalism that has profoundly changed international relations. We will further examine fundamentalist beliefs and their impact on international relations in Chapter 8.

4.5 Political Psychology

Political psychology studies the interactions between political and psychological factors in individual and group behavior. Political psychologists use the behavioral and cognitive sciences to gather and analyze information about world leaders and their policies (Houghton 2008). Most of their data comes from politicians themselves—their statements, interviews, press conferences, speeches, memoirs, and documented decisions. Other research data come from history labs (where scientists analyze historical decisions), opinion polls, and experimental studies. Political psychology is not just a theoretical study. In the United States, political psychologists find employment in the fields of intelligence analysis, risk assessment, national security, and foreign policy.

How do individual psychological factors affect international relations? Every time the United States elects a new president, political strategists around the world start guessing. What are the views of the new president? Will there be a new foreign policy direction in Washington? Politicians (and not only U.S. presidents, of course), in theory, should make decisions and conduct policies on behalf of countries and international organizations. Yet political leaders can be proactive or passive, vindictive or forgiving, cooperative or confrontational, rely on ideology or on intuition, and turn to advisers or act alone. The election of Donald Trump as president in 2016 has especially enhanced the interest in psychological factors affecting politics and foreign policy (Wolff 2018; Kurtz 2018). Trump's seemingly unpredictable style of action sparked enthusiastic praise from his supporters and serious concerns from his opponents. Yet, can unpredictable behavior be rational, logical? Political psychologists study rationality in international relations.

Rational Decision Making

According to the **rational model** in political psychology, leaders try to maximize the positive outcomes and minimize the negative consequences of their decisions. In other words, they tend to act, for the most part, rationally. If two leaders act logically, then mutual trust based on interpersonal contact becomes crucial, so that state leaders will act openly and sincerely, try to narrow their differences, and arrive at a mutually acceptable solution. This process involves concessions, goodwill gestures, proposals, retractions, and compromises (Cholett and Goldgeier 1962/2002; Barner-Barry and Rosenwein 1985). In the difficult 1990 negotiations over the reunification of Germany, for example, decision makers were able to find reasonable compromises. The Soviet leader Mikhail Gorbachev agreed to withdraw troops from East Germany in exchange for West German financial assistance to the Soviet Union and pledges not to expand NATO eastward beyond Germany (Sarotte 2009). The problem is that some leaders prefer to take quick actions without much reflection, whereas others prefer to be more careful. U.S. president Barack Obama, as many observers noted, generally erred on the side of caution, recognizing the high costs of quick and hasty decisions in foreign policy. Many assessments of Obama's foreign policy use the words like "academic," "cautious,"

fundamentalism
A point of view or social movement distinguished by rigid adherence to principles rooted in tradition (typically religious tradition) and often by intolerance of individual rights and secularism.

political psychology
The study of the interactions between political and psychological factors in individual and group behavior.

rational model In political psychology, the view that politicians act, for the most part, logically, to maximize positive outcomes and to minimize negative outcomes.

and "indecisive" (Osnos 2014). President Trump, as experts argue, came to power with the bold slogan referring to "putting America first," yet showed a propensity for theatrical exaggeration, hasty decisions, and risk taking (Haas 2018). Political leaders are not destined to fall into two simplistic categories of "the risk takers" and "the cautious." Tendencies for risk aversion and risk taking can certainly coexist in one person.

The fast-growing volume and complexity of information is a serious challenge to any decision maker. Too much information can be just as great a barrier to clear and accurate decision making that too little information can be (Nye 2002). How can a leader take in an overwhelming amount of information before making policy decisions? The U.S. president begins the workday by reading a document called the President's Daily Brief (PDB), a procedure created during the Cold War. Reducing complex and voluminous evaluations to a short PDB provides much-needed simplicity. However, it also risks the loss of regional and local contexts or of crucial details.

Approaches based on rational models also maintain that if we, as observers, had full access to information, we could explain international relations as a bargaining process. We could take stock of the potential gains and losses of the participating sides. The problem, however, is that political leaders are guided not only by pragmatic calculations. They can have personal biases, emotions, aspirations, and ambitions that affect their policies as well.

Biased Decision Making

Decisions in international relations are too ambiguous and complex to explain by rational models alone (Hart 1991). Human thinking is not completely rational, even in the most important decisions, when people believe they act logically (Steinbruner 1974; Cutler 1981). Political psychologists assume that leaders often make biased decisions caused by emotions, misperceptions, and the pressure of deadlines. Leaders may not always search for the best decision and may settle on the first acceptable or convenient alternative. Others may be stubborn—afraid of appearing weak or unwilling to lose credibility. As Professor Jerrold Post, a former CIA analyst, wrote in a memorandum to Congress in 1990 describing Saddam Hussein of Iraq, "Saddam's worldview is narrow and distorted, and he has scant experience out of the Arab world" (Post 1990). Saddam presented himself as the only Arab leader to champion the Palestinian cause. He saw himself as a revolutionary, as a martyr. If need be, he was prepared to go down heroically. Neither negotiation nor surrender fit his image of what the actions of a great leader should be.

ANALOGIES IN DECISION MAKING

analogy The comparison of a new situation to a familiar one. Analogies may provide quick answers in place of a lengthier discussion.

Decisions can also be biased by a reliance on **analogy**. Comparing new situations to familiar ones can provide quick answers. As we have seen, analogies in policy-making may reflect both rationality and bias (Jervis 1976; Cholett and Goldgeier 2008). After World War I, most European statesmen feared that any international crisis would lead to war. Constrained by this frightening analogy, British and French leaders signed a deal with Hitler in Munich in 1938, allowing him to dismember Czechoslovakia. In time, their action became the basis of an analogy, too. President Lyndon Johnson and his advisers evoked the "Munich analogy" in sending U.S. troops to defend South Vietnam. The argument was that anything less would be appeasing Ho Chi Minh just as Britain and France had appeased Hitler (Khong 1992). The Munich analogy was used again in 1991, when Iraq occupied Kuwait. President George H. W. Bush compared Saddam to Hitler to justify a U.S. invasion. Negotiations with the Iraqi dictatorship, he believed, would endanger regional and world peace. Western leaders also were reluctant to negotiate with the regime in Syria for the fear of appeasement.

PROSPECT THEORY

One of the most remarkable contributions to our understanding of decision making comes from experimental studies. **Prospect theory** (for which one of its developers, Daniel Kahneman, won the Nobel Prize in 2002) states that even when people are acting in a seemingly rational way, they use various cognitive shortcuts (heuristics) and thus consistently miscalculate their chances of success and failure (Kahneman and Tversky 1979). Emotions and misperceptions, too, affect how politicians evaluate the international situation and make decisions (Larson 1985; 1997). Prospect theory has offered significant applications for the study of diplomatic, military, and national security decisions. For example, Russia's decision to take over Crimea in 2014 has had devastating consequences for international relations. Why did Moscow act this way? Political psychologists suggest that a complex set of psychological factors and, possibly, cognitive errors have had a big impact on Putin's decisions to make this risky decision (Forsberg and Pursiainen 2017).

prospect theory
Theory stating that people consistently use cognitive shortcuts and thus miscalculate their chances of success and failure.

CONSISTENCY, RESISTANCE, AND ACCESSIBILITY BIASES

What kind of heuristics and biases affect the decision-making process? We will illustrate by mentioning just three biases. In **consistency bias**, new information is more likely to be accepted if it accords with an individual's prevailing opinions. Political leaders, as political biographies show, often like to receive the information that is consistent with their (the leaders) views (Caro 2012). Similarly, in **resistance bias**, people tend to stick to their decisions even when new evidence challenges their assumptions (Levy 2009; Heider 1959). Therefore, scores of political leaders (willingly or not) surround themselves with advisers who mostly confirm what the leaders already believe in or want to hear. Finally, **accessibility bias** occurs when people pick not the best option but one that is easily available and easily understood.

What do these biases mean for international relations? Biases tend to steer politicians more often toward hawkish, violent choices than to nonviolent, reconciliatory strategies (Kahneman and Renshon 2007). They too often exaggerate the evil intentions of their adversaries and underestimate peaceful initiatives. Leaders also tend to be uncritical of their own actions and reluctant to compromise. Former president George W. Bush might have displayed consistency and resistance bias when the United States started two wars, in Afghanistan in 2001 and Iraq in 2003. Bush's initial self-confidence led him to reject views critical of his foreign policy (Woodward 2007; Renshon 2009).

consistency bias In cognitive theories, the rule that the human mind operates so as to keep beliefs, opinions, and ideas consistent.

resistance bias In cognitive theories, the rule that leaders resist changing their ideas about international relations.

accessibility bias In cognitive theories, the rule that a leader tends to pick the option that is most easily available.

The Obama administration with its cautious approach to foreign policy can be viewed as a reaction to the previous period of interventionism under President Bush. Obama's personal cognitive bias formulated as "do not do stupid [shit] stuff" in foreign policy was expressed in several of his exchanges with the press (Rothkoff, 2014). The Trump Administration entered the White House with a clear desire to revise Obama's policies. Trump's style of foreign policy demonstrates a lack of consistency with the previous administrations, as well as a resistance to the attempts of foreign policy elites to define his course (Brands 2018).

GROUP PRESSURE

group pressure In political psychology, the ability of other people to alter individual decisions.

Another source of bias in foreign policy decisions is **group pressure**: the ability of other people to alter individual decisions. In a phenomenon called *group inhibition*, influential others can delay, alter, or prevent a leader's decision. Conversely, in *group facilitation*, political experts and advisers can encourage decision makers to act decisively and sometimes recklessly. Nationalistic and xenophobic ideas facilitated by the inner circles of advisers that surround leaders can influence foreign policy in significant ways (Chua 2018). Sometimes experts fail to contradict the erroneous perceptions of policy makers, who may have already decided on a course of action. The George W. Bush administration, critics say, pressed the CIA to report that Iraq was on the verge of producing nuclear arms (Goodman 2008). We will return to the group pressure phenomenon in the Case Study in this chapter.

PSYCHOLOGICAL FACTORS

Finally, biased decisions could be caused by a leader's own psychological problems as a result of substantial stress, strong emotional commitment to an issue, or psychological illness. As examples, experts turn to U.S. presidents Franklin Roosevelt and Richard Nixon, the shah of Iran Reza Pahlavi, or former Libyan leader Muammar Gaddafi (Robins and Post 1995; Milani 2011; Caro 2012).

Life Experiences

political socialization The study of how individuals acquire their political knowledge and beliefs.

Can we understand foreign policy decisions better by studying how decision making develops? **Political socialization** examines how individuals—including political leaders— acquire and change their political beliefs during their lifespan (Sears, Huddy, and Jervis 2003). Two types of studies of political socialization can be useful for international relations. One is the study of generational changes in people's political beliefs, including views on foreign policy. For example, before the Vietnam War, U.S. citizens gave U.S. foreign policy bipartisan support (Hilsman 1959). Since the late 1960s, however, the American public has tended to have dissimilar views on foreign policy actions (Shiraev and Sobel 2006). Many factors affect people's views of international events. Why is it important to know about public opinion in the study of foreign policy? In democracies, leaders are aware of and try to influence public opinion. As we learned in Chapter 3, when leaders lack public support, they may change policy.

The second type of study in political socialization examines how leaders develop their views of politics and the world (Murray 1943; Erikson 1969). Views of political leaders tend to evolve (Gott 2011). President Jimmy Carter, for example, underwent difficult personal transformations before he embraced the importance of defending human rights as a cornerstone of his presidential foreign policy (Glad 2009). The views of presidents Bush, Obama, and Trump were evolving too.

Studies in political psychology suggest that political leaders tend to form their core political beliefs and ambitions relatively early in life (Jost and Sidanius 2004). Many sources indicate that entire political careers are often shaped by the desire for recognition, achievement, search for approval, and redemption (Volkan and Itzkowitz 1984; Renshon 2011). Other individuals do not have any extraordinary personality traits appearing early in life and yet develop and reveal them in the right place at the right time during adulthood (Schultz 2005).

As you can see, there are parallels between political psychology and constructivism in that both describe how political leaders construct and interpret information related to politics and foreign policy. Political scientists mostly emphasize the power of political institutions. Political psychologists, however, attempt to look inside the human mind through empirical research and experiments.

> ## Check Your Knowledge
>
> 1. Why don't rational models fully explain international political behavior?
>
> 2. What are consistency, resistance, and accessibility biases in decision making? Suggest examples.
>
> 3. What do political socialization studies add to our understanding of foreign policy?

4.6 Critical Applications of Alternative Views

How well do constructivist, Marxist, postcolonial, feminist, identity theories, and political psychology approaches hold up in practice? To judge, we have to apply them critically to actual cases and contexts in international relations. Constructivist views and political psychology share a similar concern for how countries' leaders make decisions. Rich empirical data show the importance of the individual's character in shaping political choices (Sears et al. 2003). Conflict theories focus on injustice as a driving force behind political decisions. What do these studies reveal at each level of analysis? (See Table 4-5.)

Alternative Views at the Individual Level

Marxists argued for a long time that once oppressive social classes were defeated, equality and justice would win. Yet in Cuba under Fidel Castro the regime became even more oppressive than before, relying on the arrest and execution of opponents. Iran after 1979 became even more repressive and corrupt (Milani 2011). The Marxist arguments proved false in these cases because they failed to account for the importance of individual factors.

TABLE 4-5 Applications of Alternative Approaches at Three Levels of Analysis

Level of Analysis	Application
Individual	Political leaders' choices matter in international relations. Formative cultural experiences, education, and personal lessons all have an impact on a leader's foreign policy decisions. Individual factors are complex, however, and are interconnected with evolving cultural identities.
State	Collective experiences and institutional biases help define national interests. Conflict theories emphasize that multiple political forces compete for domestic power and resources. Democratic political cultures encourage competing ideas and limit war; authoritarian political cultures limit freedom and encourage international conflict. Prejudice and bias affect foreign policy.
Global	Ethnic and religious identities remain strong factors in global politics. Globalization affects identities, however. Marxist warnings about a growing global conflict between the rich and the poor highlight the need for policies to reduce inequities.

VISIONARIES VERSUS FANATICS

Individual qualities matter in world politics. Mikhail Gorbachev, the last leader of the Soviet Union, fundamentally changed international relations in 1988 with the idea that the United States, Canada, other NATO countries, and a reformed Soviet Union share similar values, including worldwide peace. Gorbachev called for nuclear disarmament and the renunciation of the use of force in international relations (Rey 2004). At the time, many realists dismissed Gorbachev's vision as unworkable, but his ideas proved a catalyst for the peaceful overthrow of Communism in Eastern and Central Europe.

Gorbachev's *visionary* ideas were rooted in his individual character. First, he became convinced that the West was no longer an enemy. Second, he turned to the West not only because of growing Soviet economic difficulties but also because he believed in Western economic and social models. Culturally, Gorbachev was a *Westernizer*, in stark contrast with previous and contemporary leaders in Moscow (Rey 2004; Zubok 2007; Zubok 2014). A shift in values and perceptions in Moscow, as constructivists would argue, changed Russia's foreign policy in the 2000s (Shiraev and Khudoley 2019).

Adolf Hitler, by contrast, was a *fanatic* who challenged the entire international system. His beliefs and values in the 1930s and 1940s were xenophobic, anti-Semitic, and anti-elitist. He envisioned Germany's global domination and was obsessed with the elimination of all Jewish people. He hoped to restore an Aryan culture based on its mythic roots. Many Germans, disillusioned with liberal democracy and hoping that a strong state would solve their problems, followed him (Kershaw 2000). Whereas Gorbachev was a visionary member of a transnational community based on Western values, Hitler was a dangerous fanatic promoting war, racism, and anti-Semitism. Both cases suggest that, in certain political moments, a single person's cultural values and identity can change the course of history.

In reality, visionaries and fanatics are few and far between. Most political leaders remain pragmatic because they are dealing with domestic and international events based on practical calculations rather than value considerations. To most of them, avoiding crises and winning the next election are more important goals than adhering to a set of ideological beliefs. In your view, who can be called a dangerous fanatic in today's international system? Political psychology is best suited to study the context of individual decisions and to answer this question. Some leaders are driven by irrational motives. Illness can diminish an individual's ability to reason. So can extreme circumstances. Alexander George pioneered the study of leadership under stress or crisis. He suggested that a leader's psychological problems or idiosyncrasies could disrupt strategic decision making (George 1969). Mohammad Reza Shah of Iran (1919–1980) suffered serious medical and psychological problems that could have contributed to the fall of the government of Iran in 1979 (Milani, 2011; Robins and Post, 1995). There is evidence that Soviet leader Leonid Brezhnev's addiction to medication, for example, could have contributed to the fateful decision to send Soviet troops to Afghanistan in December 1979 (Zubok 2007).

INDIVIDUAL INSTABILITY AND IRRATIONALITY

How do individual instability and irrationality affect global politics? Many countries lack legal mechanisms for replacing a sick or unstable leader. Authoritarian regimes tend to conceal the sickness of leaders out of fear of domestic instability. Cuban authorities did not reveal Fidel Castro's declining health until he passed authority to his brother Raúl in 2007. North Korea similarly refused to discuss the health of its leader, Kim Jong-il, before he passed away in 2011. Even in a more transparent, democratic society, a leader's personal problems may affect foreign policy. The rise and evolution of terrorism also point to the importance of discussing irrationality in decision making. We return to this discussion in Chapter 8.

THE EFFECTS OF LIFE EXPERIENCES

The evidence regarding the impact of early experiences on political leaders' decisions remains inconclusive. Did Castro's early beliefs about Cuba–U.S. relations shape his revolutionary policy for thirty years? Did Gorbachev's early experience of World War II make him averse to the use of violence when he became the Soviet leader? How did Obama's biracial background teach him about tolerance and caution? How did Trump's youth and career in real estate business affect his leadership during his presidency? Although early life events surely affect decisions, we have little reliable and verifiable evidence connecting a leader's formative experiences with specific actions (Immelman 2017; Post 2008; Kowert 1996). The political preferences of Castro, Gorbachev, Obama, and Trump may be better explained by many other factors that shaped their identities later in their lives. Biographical and psychological studies of political leaders, military commanders, and diplomats can be incomplete, selective, and sometimes misleading. Nevertheless, they frequently provide important information about foreign leaders' behavior, their habits and weaknesses, as well as potential threats. This information should be given careful consideration by intelligence and international security decision makers. (See Table 4-6.)

TABLE 4-6 Political Psychology: The Influence of Personal History on U.S. Presidents' Politics

President	Upbringing and Political Style
Richard Nixon	Nixon tended to feel lonely and anxious as a child. He turned to politics to compensate for personal insecurities. As president, he avoided big gatherings and the media and preferred solitude and closed-door deals, which led to success in some of his realpolitik designs in foreign policy; they also led to the Watergate scandal and his resignation.
Jimmy Carter	From his youth, Carter highly valued ethics and was committed to avoiding violence. These attitudes motivated him to constantly seek justice and put human rights at the center of his foreign policy. His idealism and often his moralistic approach to politics led to several diplomatic successes but also to serious mistakes.
Ronald Reagan	Raised in a lower-class family, Reagan worked his way up and made use of his excellent communication skills. He acquired strong conservative beliefs later in life and considered Communism to be a source of global problems. Labeled a "warmonger" and political "dinosaur" by his opponents, he was able to remain a stoic anti-Communist, a value that contributed to the successful end of the Cold War.
George H. W. Bush	With his strong Christian beliefs, combined with several tragic events in his personal life, Bush put moral values at the center of his politics. He preferred conservative values, moderation, and common sense in his international decisions. He decided not to humiliate the Soviet Union at the end of the Cold War but chose violence to resist Iraq in 1990–1991.
Bill Clinton	Growing up having a step-father (but not a biological one who had died before Bill was born) he future president developed a profound ambition to distinguish himself. He was often brilliant in domestic politics, articulate and persuasive in his decisions, cautious (in Rwanda and Somalia), tough and committed to collective action (in Bosnia) in foreign policy but reckless in his personal life.
George W. Bush	Coming from a powerful upper-class family, Bush grew up in a privileged environment with financial security but faced severe personal problems. He overcame alcoholism by turning to religion and work and thus developed a sense of self-righteousness. As president, he saw the War on Terror as a global and spiritual struggle between good and evil.
Barack Obama	As a biracial child growing up in Hawaii and Indonesia, Obama developed a respect for the world's diversity. His mother's death from cancer made him determined to show his compassion toward people's suffering. Obama became an overachiever and learned to navigate the American political system, often preferring compromise and persuasion to confrontation. His cautious approach to foreign policy (especially in Syria) drew both praise and criticisms worldwide.
Donald Trump	Raised in a wealthy family in New York, Trump was ambitious and achievement-oriented from a young age. He has repeatedly demonstrated a strong desire to be the center of attention and to exercise his personal control. He tends to be outgoing, bold, competitive, self-assured, and nacissistic. His fight against complacency in domestic and international affairs has drawn overwhelming support as well as fierce, almost unprecedented, criticisms from the public in the United States and globally.

Sources: Reeves (2001); Post (2005b); Glad (2009); Renshon (2004, 2011); Takiff (2010); Immelman (2017); Gingrich (2017); Wolff (2018).

WOMEN VERSUS MEN AS LEADERS

What about the feminist idea that women would do better than men if they occupied positions of power? Women in power have not always engaged in peaceful policies. They often cannot eradicate corruption either. U.S. secretaries of state Madeleine Albright in the 1990s and Condoleezza Rice and Hillary Clinton in 2001 to 2013 did not steer foreign policy decisively on the path of peace. Albright and Rice had to justify military campaigns in Kosovo, Afghanistan, and Iraq. Clinton did not challenge Barack Obama's military actions in Libya and constant use of unmanned planes to kill militants in Pakistan and Afghanistan. Feminist scholars argue back that, in order to succeed, women must adapt to the political and cultural environments created by men. Women, they state, compared with male leaders, are likely to possess a more conciliatory approach to foreign policy (Schein 2002). Yet women may not have the immediate economic and political resources to reduce corruption and violence. They also have to work in a predominantly male atmosphere. Could you suggest other reasons why women in top leadership positions have often not been able to achieve peace and address injustices? Alternative views can enrich our understanding of how state politics and institutions affect a country's international behavior. Most national leaders face a host of institutional and political forces that constrain their freedom of action and influence foreign policy.

A feminine response to Iceland's financial crash

Alternative Views at the State Level

Beyond individual decision making, foreign policy is also a result of **bureaucratic bargaining**. This is the process by which political groups and government institutions fight for their interests and make compromises. We already looked at "log rolling" from the realist perspective in Chapter 3. The constructivist approach suggests many more ways through which a country's bureaucracy can influence and bias foreign policy. Certain theories become popular and influential among a country's political elites. During the Cold War, for example, the *domino theory* became common wisdom among the political elites in the United States: According to the theory, the loss of a single country to Communism in Asia or Latin America would trigger a chain reaction, and soon all neighboring countries would fall into Communist hands. After the end of the Cold War, democratic peace theory (Chapter 3) became nearly as influential in Washington's top institutions.

bureaucratic bargaining The process by which political groups and institutions express their interests and make trade-offs and compromises.

Constructivism also helps in understanding how cognitive factors shape international behavior in authoritarian states. In the 1950s, U.S. analysts hoped to predict how the political beliefs of members of the Soviet Politburo would translate into foreign policy. **Cognitive maps**, or diagrams of information processing and decision making, were used (sometimes unsuccessfully, to be frank) to predict Soviet decisions. However, studies show that cognitive maps can explain political choices. Take, for example, a choice made in Afghanistan by the Taliban, a political movement based on revolutionary Islamist ideology (Husain 2005). The core of the Taliban's cognitive map is spiritual solidarity

cognitive map Model of information-processing and decision-making.

with Muslims fighting for a caliphate, a regional religious commonwealth. It was therefore inconceivable that the Taliban leadership would cede to U.S. pressure to hand over another Muslim, Osama bin Laden, after the attacks of September 11, 2001. In those circumstances, the Taliban leaders chose war. Similarly, cognitive maps of ISIS leaders embraced martyrdom—a dramatic display of suicidal ideas to obtain sympathy and admiration, and to recruit new followers. In 2015–2017, ISIS leaders in Syria used suicide killings as a key method of their military operation (Winter 2017). (See Figure 4-1.)

Studies show that in democracies, the decision-making process is more open to inquiry, scrutiny, criticism, and free discussion, compared to authoritarian systems. Authoritarianism is rooted in secrecy. Political opposition and concerned groups can draw attention to foreign policy issues and can serve as a restraining force on governmental decisions, especially those related to foreign aid or the use of military force abroad (Sobel 2001; Nacos, Shapiro, and Isernia 2000). Historically, leaders of democratic states should therefore tend to seek broad political support for their decisions.

In authoritarian regimes, decisions are made in relative secrecy. The authoritarian leader secures support among a small inner circle of reliable supporters and imposes decisions on the rest of the political elites. Individual leaders should therefore play a more significant role in foreign policy than in democratic political contexts. (See Table 4–7.)

In reality, the differences are less clear. Officials in democratic countries, too, may shield valuable information from public scrutiny (Goodman 2008). Since the 1940s, sensitive information important to U.S. decision making has been disseminated to a narrow circle of people on a "need-to-know" basis. Political pressure of "higher" offices exists in every society. Yet it will be intellectually dishonest to argue that democratic and authoritarian political cultures are no different in terms of their transparency. It is all a matter of degree and historical perspective.

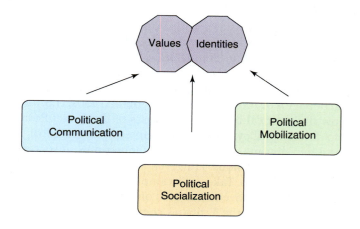

FIGURE 4-1 Factors affecting political values and identities.

TABLE 4-7 Decision Making in Authoritarian and Democratic Contexts

	Authoritarian Context	Democratic Context
Political Environment	Decisions are made in political isolation and are not seriously scrutinized or influenced by other political forces.	Group decision making is scrutinized and critically appraised by the media, political opposition, and public opinion.
Type of Political Support	The authoritarian leader secures support from a small inner circle of reliable supporters, secret police, and the military. The leader imposes decisions on the rest of the political elites.	Democratic leaders tend to seek broad political support for their decisions from government, the media, political parties, and public opinion.
Situational Factors	An individual leader's choices play a crucial role in decision making.	Policy mistakes by an individual leader are likely to be prevented or corrected by other political actors, including individuals and institutions.

History Lab   Two-Level Games

Political scientist Robert Putnam (1988) offers an aid to testing constructivist assumptions. His **two-level game** model suggests that leaders make foreign policy with one eye on international factors (the first level) and the other eye on domestic developments (the second level). State leaders operate on both levels. Domestic forces affecting policy decisions include legislative institutions, lobbying groups, political opposition, media, and often the military. The impact of these institutions depends on the country's constitution and democratic traditions. Democratic leaders have to think about reelection even in the midst of an international crisis. Most famously, Winston Churchill and George H. W. Bush led their countries in military victories in Germany and Iraq but lost elections, in 1945 and 1992, respectively.

The conflict between Israel and the Arab states provides an incredibly complex example of a two-level game. Israel cannot make too many concessions to the Palestinians without antagonizing a big part of the electorate. Among the Palestinians, the groups and leaders that support negotiations with Israel often face domestic backlash as well. At the same time, supporters of a tough approach on both sides risk losing broad popular support (Mahler 2004).

CRITICAL THINKING

1 Domestic politics can affect foreign policy either positively or negatively. What could you suggest as some potentially positive impacts of two-level games? **2** According to the Treaty Clause of the U.S. Constitution, international agreements signed by presidents must be confirmed by a "super majority" (two-thirds) of the Senate. Would you argue for or against an amendment to change the required supermajority to a simple majority? If adopted, would this amendment, in your view, reduce or increase the impact of domestic politics on foreign policy?

two-level game
A model in which states react to both domestic and international politics.

Strategic plans remain classified for decades, and foreign policy errors are rarely subject to independent investigation. The United States used secret diplomacy and covert operations against the Communist powers for years. Similar strategies are pursued today against international terrorist organizations.

Collective experiences may either help in democratic transitions—as we saw in the examples of Germany and Japan after World War II—or become obstacles to national reintegration. Although Germany has been a single state since 1990, citizens from former Communist East Germany continued for some years to harbor resentment toward fellow citizens and politicians from the western part of the country. People in North and South Korea are still sharply divided by ideology and politics. Residents of Taiwan, although they may share a similar language with their counterparts in China, have vastly different collective experiences and attitudes than those who live in the People's Republic of China.

Collective experiences of the very same events naturally differ from country to country. Europe in the twentieth century lost tens of millions of lives in wars and suffered massive devastation. For the United States, despite heavy casualties, these conflicts were for the most part foreign wars, and the country emerged in 1945 as the strongest and wealthiest in the world. As a result, many Europeans take a much more cautious attitude toward the use of military force than Americans do (Costigliola 2000). This could have contributed to the divisions that emerged within NATO after the United States invaded Iraq. (See Table 4–8.)

TABLE 4–8 Collective Experiences and Foreign Policy: Comparative Cases

Country	Example
United States	The Great Depression shaped the identity of millions and helped the U.S. government abandon isolationism during and after World War II. The Vietnam War had a profound impact on the foreign policy views of the 1960s generation. The war in Iraq divided the entire generation of Americans in the early 2000s.
Soviet Union	Memories of the Nazi invasion and the Great Patriotic War against Germany (1941–1945) provided widespread popular support for the Soviet regime. Soviet leaders and the majority of citizens believed that they had the right to occupy Eastern Europe after World War II and to defend themselves against Western imperialism. The legacy of the Great Patriotic War helped the Russian government to sustain the patriotic and nationalist idea for years.
Cuba	U.S. attempts to overthrow Castro's government in the early 1960s rallied millions of Cubans to its support. Their collective memories were shaped by images of heroic struggle against the United States. These memories continue to divide the Cubans.
North Vietnam	First China, next France, and then Japan colonized Vietnam. Communists exploited this experience to win power in the 1950s and later to direct anticolonial sentiment against the United States. Yet in the twenty-first century, the new generation of Vietnamese people began t see the United States as a partner, not a historic foe.

Most Vietnamese these days do not consider the United States an enemy. U.S.-Vietnam bilateral trade reached nearly $52 billion in 2016. Indeed, Vietnam has become America's fastest growing export market. U.S. investment in Vietnam has grown to nearly $10 billion. More than thirteen thousand Vietnamese exchange students attended U.S. colleges several years ago (Gang 2011). Their number has increased to more than twenty-two thousand (U.S. Department of State 2018a). In contrast, after the American occupation of Iraq and Afghanistan, more people in Muslim countries began to view the United States as hostile (Pew Research Center 2015).

Alternative Views at the Global Level

How can feminist ideas be assessed globally? More countries now promote women to positions of power. France, for example, requires that large companies will raise their proportion of female directors to 40 percent by 2020. In Spain, public and large private companies were required by law to reach that same goal in 2015. Norway introduced a similar requirement more than a decade ago (Beck 2011). Although few women are yet heads of state, more and more women, particularly young professionals from Western societies, are involved in nongovernmental organizations. Political psychologists say that women, as a group, on average adapt better to intercultural communication, display greater tolerance, and work better in groups than men (Shiraev & Levy 2017). Increasingly, educated and well-trained women are successfully managing grassroots networking, humanitarian aid, and fundraising. This influx of women in NGOs may, in turn, signal monumental changes to come in the whole of international relations (Hunt 2007).

Does the capitalist "core" serves the interests of just a few wealthy states? The facts are inconclusive so far. The old core, dominated by Washington, may be giving way to a new core in Asia. In China, the state has retained a firm grip on finances, accumulated multibillion-dollar reserves of Western currency, begun new economic transformations, and achieved impressive growth (Arrighi 2010). The new rich, like those in China—who have criticized global inequality for decades—have appeared, but global poverty persists. Global poverty remains a global challenge. We will return to this paradox in Chapter 7.

Globalization causes social, cultural, and ideological changes as well as political and economic ones. In response, some political elites have turned to *hybrid* political cultures, based on elements of authoritarian and traditional culture, and many authoritarian states practice some form of democracy (Krauthammer 2008). Some leaders prefer emphasizing local and regional values and contrast them with the liberal values of the West. In the 1990s, Singapore's leader, Lee Kuan Yew, spoke eloquently about Asian values. By advocating a form of capitalism based on Confucian values and strong authoritarian power, he sought to compete more effectively with the West (Mahbubani 2002). Russian leaders proposed what they called *sovereign democracy* to defend authoritarian forms of governance combined with some democratic principles (Shiraev 2013). After the Cold War, authoritarian

competitive authoritarianism A hybrid political culture with a competitive electoral system in which a single leader or party dominates. The government uses state power to defeat opposition and mobilize public opinion.

countries switched to **competitive authoritarianism**—a strategy for preserving legitimacy and power (Levitsky and Way 2010). Under competitive authoritarianism, elections are regularly held, but a single leader or party dominates. The government uses police, courts, and tax agencies to harass the opposition, control the media, abuse state resources, and manipulate electoral results.

Economic liberalization does not necessarily cause democratization. Germany, Japan, and South Korea did abandon authoritarianism and turn to democracy in the twentieth century, but the lessons of these success stories may not apply universally. Today Venezuela, Kenya, China, and Russia all combine free-market economies with authoritarian policies. Many countries in fact use nationalism to argue against democracy on Western terms.

The "export" of democracy to other countries usually fails when there are no local conditions or actors to support it (McFaul 2009). Still, supporters of democracy should not become discouraged. Democracy has many faces and can adapt to many local conditions. And the outcome may not resemble the American, Canadian, or French models.

Samuel Huntington believed that "civilizations" based on different religious, cultural, and political foundations are unlikely to cooperate. He warned, as you will remember, that future conflicts would happen, not between nation-states divided by interests, but between civilizations divided by values (Huntington 1993). The developments of the twenty-first century have neither confirmed nor contradicted this prediction so far.

On the one hand, critics find the idea of the "clash" a bit exaggerated. China ("Confucian civilization" in Huntington's typology) does not want to clash with anyone; its leadership speaks instead of peace and economic cooperation. Most Asian and Latin American leaders discuss global cooperation instead of competition with the West.

On the other hand, pessimists point to the strength of Islamist parties in Egypt; the rise of violent, religion-inspired fundamentalism; and the continuing clashes in Syria, Iraq, Yemen, Somalia, Nigeria, and Sudan. They predict that Islamic fundamentalism, despite its several setbacks, and anti-Western attitudes will flourish.

Check Your Knowledge

1. Who are visionaries and fanatics in international relations?

2. Explain the Munich analogy, offering two contemporary examples.

3. Describe how socialization studies explain decision making in international relations.

4. Why is it important to monitor the psychological health of leaders?

5. What is bureaucratic bargaining in foreign policy? Suggest an example.

6. What are cognitive maps, and how do they help analyze a country's policies?

7. What are the two levels in Robert Putnam's theory? In what ways can foreign policy affect domestic policy?

The Cuban Missile Crisis

Background

The Cuban Missile Crisis was one of the most dramatic events of the twentieth century. It also could have been the most tragic, leading the world to a nuclear war. Which lessons from the Cuban Missile Crisis could we apply today?

In 1962, the Soviet leadership decided to place a number of nuclear missiles in Cuban territory. The missiles, if launched, could have reached most major cities in the United States. (See Map 4-1.) The Soviets moved the missiles surreptitiously and denied their actions in the United Nations. President John F. Kennedy issued an ultimatum to the Soviet premier Nikita Khrushchev, demanding a stop to the missiles' deployment. Kennedy ordered a naval blockade of Cuba to prevent the Soviet vessels carrying the missiles from entering the area. Khrushchev promised retaliation. The world was on the brink of a major confrontation between Moscow and Washington: a nuclear war seemed inevitable. Fortunately, both leaders found a way to resolve the conflict. How did they do this? What led to the conflict?

In *Essence of Decision* (1971), Graham Allison argues that bureaucratic politics provides the best explanation of the decision-making process during the Cuban Missile Crisis. For years, Allison's book remained a standard text for applying rational models of decision making to crisis management in international relations. In the 1999 edition, based on new access to Soviet, Cuban, and American archives, the authors argued that both leaders acted rationally to pursue pragmatic goals: Khrushchev sought to improve Russia's position within the balance of power, and Kennedy sought to restore the international status quo without provoking a war. Ultimately, the United States' overwhelming military superiority helped Kennedy to settle the crisis (Allison and Zelikow 1999). (See Figure 4-2.)

The Cuban Missile Crisis

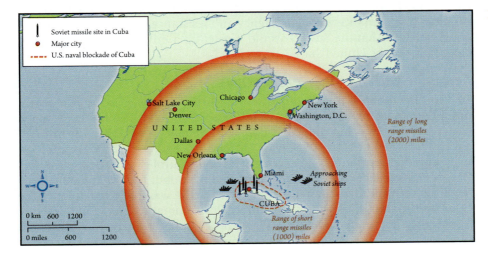

MAP 4-1 Range of missiles' penetration in the Cuban Missile Crisis.

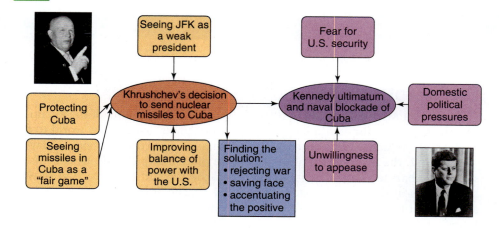

FIGURE 4-2
Perceptions and motivations of Khrushchev and Kennedy in the Cuban Missile Crisis.

Analysis

Constructivist View

What if we step aside from the traditional rational model and look at the Cuban Missile Crisis through a constructivist lens? If seen from this angle, Khrushchev's main motivation changed: It was first to shift the balance of power in the Soviets' favor, but later to defend Cuba from an American invasion. In 1961, the United States had trained Cuban nationals to invade Cuba, and the CIA had made plans to assassinate Castro. U.S. policy makers failed to understand that their provocative actions might have triggered Khrushchev's fears of a possible full-scale U.S. invasion of the island. For the Soviet leader, who boasted of the inevitability of a global Communist victory, a successful U.S. invasion of Cuba and the defeat of Castro would have been an unacceptable blow to his prestige and to the position of the Soviet Union in the world. Policy makers in Washington could not imagine that the Soviet Union would care so much about Cuba and would dare send missiles and troops across the Atlantic. In accordance with consistency and resistance bias, the American analysts believed that the Soviets would not set up a military base within such close range of the United States.

Feminist and Marxist Perspectives

To a conflict theorist, both Kennedy's and Khrushchev's decisions were essentially human—and, as feminists would add, also male. The leaders stepped back from the abyss but only after they had brought the world to the brink of a war. And what if Castro, instead of Khrushchev, had been the main decision maker on the Communist side? What if he had control over nuclear weapons? Castro was a recent convert to Marxism-Leninism, but he was arguably more revolutionary minded than Khrushchev—Castro was prepared to sacrifice Cuba on the altar of the world revolution. Postcolonial studies might describe him as reacting to the white male Western world. Fortunately, Khrushchev in this case proved more pragmatic than fanatic and revolutionary.

Political Psychology Perspective

The rational model assumes that Khrushchev, like Kennedy, would have acted logically in weighing cost-benefit options. The Soviet leader might have wanted, for example, to improve the strategic position of the Soviet Union with respect to the United States. Yet this interpretation is incomplete. It fails to reflect Khrushchev's personal insecurities caused by his policy failures. He was unable to force Western powers out of West Berlin from 1958 to 1961. Chinese Communists criticized him for ideological mistakes, and his reform of the Soviet economy failed to produce the expected results. Khrushchev was therefore desperate to gamble for success in Cuba. He considered himself a clever decision maker, and his prestige depended on the outcome of this missile venture (Blight, Allyn, and Welch 1993; Taubman 2004).

New evidence from archives also reveals that Khrushchev relied on erroneous assumptions about the United States' decision making. He evaluated Kennedy in a biased way, viewing the president from the vantage point of his own life, shaped in the trenches of World War II. For Khrushchev, Kennedy was a spoiled "rich kid" from New England, a toy in the hands of hardliners, and a pushover when it came to international affairs.

Kennedy and his advisers likewise knew very little about the top leadership and decision making in the Soviet Union. Washington received contradictory messages from Khrushchev: some of them quite belligerent and cocky, some more conciliatory. Kennedy was lucky to have an adviser, Llewellyn

On October 16, 1962, President John F. Kennedy announced that the United States had established a "quarantine" of Cuba, after discovering Soviet nuclear missiles there. The president promised that his country would deliver "a full retaliatory response upon the Soviet Union" if the Soviets attacked the United States.

(Tommy) Thompson, who had just served as the U.S. ambassador in Moscow. Thompson met Khrushchev many times and interpreted his decisions not just in accord with the rational model but with knowledge of Khrushchev as a person. In the end, Thompson was convinced that Khrushchev was bluffing and recommended that Kennedy suggest a way for Khrushchev to save face—the secret trade of Soviet missiles in Cuba for U.S. missiles in Turkey. Thompson was right. As it turned out, Khrushchev never contemplated using the nuclear weapons and tried to reduce the chances of accidental miscalculation. He even ordered his commanders to keep the nuclear warheads in storage facilities.

Political Psychology Perspective

As veterans of World War II, Kennedy and Khrushchev shared a crucial formative experience. For all their differences as individuals, in the domestic pressures they faced, and in their ideologies and biases, the U.S. and Soviet leaders shared a common fear—the fear of unleashing a world war with nuclear weapons. This fear dominated the influence of analogies. Kennedy rejected the Munich analogy, which would have suggested he appease the Soviets. The last thing Khrushchev wanted was to provoke the United States, as the Japanese did at Pearl Harbor in 1941, into a full-scale war. For Khrushchev, nuclear weapons in Cuba were just a means of deterring U.S. aggression against Cuba.

We cannot guarantee that a dangerous crisis of similar proportions will never occur again. Yet we can reduce the potentially deadly consequences of any international crisis if we learn lessons from history. The main lesson of the Cuban Missile Crisis is that rational decision making is very difficult under extreme stress, with a fluid situation and time constraints. In such conditions, politicians may turn to their emotions and biases. Another lesson is the need to avoid a dangerous chain reaction of decisions that could drive opponents to make dangerous decisions.

Case Study Questions

Consider one of the following scenarios. If you were president, how would you deescalate and resolve the crisis?

1. China attempts to take Taiwan militarily.
2. Iran directly threatens Israel.
3. India and Pakistan, both nuclear powers, plunge into war over Kashmir.
4. Russia makes the decision to build a big military base in Central America.

Remember, in your decisions you should take into consideration the impact of misperceptions, brush off the arguments of your most hawkish advisers, and add your knowledge of history—all to find a solution short of war.

CHAPTER 4
REVIEW   Alternative Theories

4.1 Describe the necessity of interpretations beyond realism and liberalism.

International relations are influenced by a great number of factors beyond those highlighted in realism and liberalism. Alternative approaches broadly consider how international actors define their interests, and why they might choose one policy over another.

Q: What are the key limitations of realism and liberalism in understanding international relations?

4.2 Explain what the constructivist view brings to the study of international relations and foreign policy.

Constructivism emphasizes social norms and the historical experiences of states and social groups. It does not necessarily challenge mainstream theories of international relations. Rather, it provides valuable information, based on social and political sciences, about how and why states develop policies and interests. In this view:
• State interests are constructed through interpretation of facts.
• States create their international environment.
• Countries draw different lessons from history.

Q: Why are the lessons of history important for constructivists? Why do decision makers often overlook these lessons?

4.3 Discuss how Marxism, postcolonial studies, and feminism approach international relations.

Conflict theories pay attention to different forms of inequality and discrimination. They claim that state interests are defined by ruling elites trying to secure power.

Q: Why have dependency and Marxist theories regained popularity in recent years?

4.4 Describe how political culture and identity factors can affect international politics.

Cultural and identity theories turn to values and perceptions. Political culture and identity are shaped by collective experience, religion, ethnicity, and other group and individual experiences. Nationalism, tribalism, xenophobia, and fundamentalism add to the complexity of global affairs.

Q: How can political culture and identity factors affect interpretations of international events? Suggest examples.

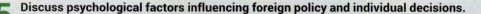

4.5 Discuss psychological factors influencing foreign policy and individual decisions.

Political psychology focuses on inner mechanisms of political behavior. Policy decisions are not necessarily rational, and both individual and group factors affect foreign policy.

Q: Using the ideas of constructivism and political psychology, identify at least three of the most dangerous political leaders in today's world. Give examples to support your argument.

4.6 Apply alternative approaches to interpreting the behavior of leaders, states, and global nonstate actors.

- Leaders' choices can be rational or biased, affected by both immediate and life experiences.
- Domestic bureaucracy, political competition, democratic contexts, and access to information affect foreign policy decisions.
- Global developments affect state interests and policies, which in turn affect the world.

Q: What are some examples of two-level games in foreign policy?

KEY TERMS

International Security

РЕСПУБЛИКА КРЫМ

> *Eternal vigilance is the price of liberty.*
>
> —DEMOSTHENES
> (384–322 BCE)

For decades following the Cold War, Europeans became accustomed to overall peace and security on their continent. It came as a shock in 2014 when Russia annexed Crimea, a beautiful peninsula that was part of the sovereign Ukrainian state. Russian President Vladimir Putin offered several reasons for this move. He claimed that Russia wanted to protect Ukraine's Russian-speaking population in Crimea against the nationalists, who took power in Kiev following a violent coup in 2014. He voiced fears that Ukraine would become an ally of NATO and that Russia would lose its Crimean naval base. He also criticized the United States; in his view, it was supporting Ukrainian nationalists and was nudging Ukraine to associate with the EU and join NATO, thus ignoring Russia's security concerns.

The United States, the EU, and the majority of UN members considered the Russian annexation of Crimea a gross violation of international norms. The NATO countries sent military equipment and troops to the Baltic countries and Poland to reassure them. In addition, the United States and the EU imposed economic and financial sanctions on Russia. The Trump Administration sent anti-tank weapons to arm Ukrainians against Russian attacks. Russia, however, continued to support separatist regions in southeastern Ukraine and introduced retaliatory sanctions against Western countries. The danger of large-scale war in Eastern Europe passed, but the Russian-Ukrainian conflict remains a frozen conflict for years to come.

War and related fears of insecurity remain the foremost issues in international relations. How do countries define and build their security strategies? Why do these plans often lead to new threats and even wars? Is global security achievable, and, if so,

Previous page: Russian Defense Minister Sergei Shoigu (left) and President Vladimir Putin lead a meeting with top brass in Moscow in 2014, with a map in the background showing Crimea. Russia's takeover of Crimea ended a time of stable liberal order in Europe. For the sake of international security, should Russia be accommodated or should more political and economic pressure be used against Russia?

by what means? In this chapter, we introduce security challenges, explore the types of policies in response, and consider a range of approaches and applications.

> **5.1** Describe the scope of national and international security.
>
> **5.2** Explain variations in security policies.
>
> **5.3** Discuss security from realist, liberal, constructivist, and alternative perspectives.
>
> **5.4** Critically apply international security at each level of analysis.

Learning Objectives

5.1 Security Principles

Sovereign states act to protect their autonomy and territorial integrity from domestic and foreign threats. Some act alone, relying on their economic might and armed forces, but most seek help from foreign states and international organizations and prefer negotiations and compromise over military engagement. Twenty-first century **security policies** are supported by expensive bureaucratic and military machines and influenced by political parties, media, and lobbying groups.

National and International Security

National security has traditionally been understood as the protection of sovereignty, territorial integrity, and interests. Maintaining the state's armed forces, obtaining and modernizing weapons, keeping aircraft and battleships, training specialists, and developing mass-mobilization plans are all essential components and require a vast government infrastructure (Sarkesian, Williams, and Cimbala 2007). National security used to be treated as distinct from domestic security, which is commonly associated with fighting criminal activities and is handled by the police. However, some countries also use their military to address domestic security concerns and to enforce the law. For example, the Turkish army continues to combat groups fighting to create an independent Kurdistan on the state's territory. Russia uses its military and massive internal security forces to keep Chechnya and Ingushetia, its southern ethnic provinces, under control. These days, security also increasingly involves the use of information in cyberspace, which we will discuss in Chapter 8.

International security—mutual security issues involving more than one state—is a natural occurrence in the era of globalization. Security is *bilateral* when it involves two states and *multilateral* when it involves more than two. NATO is the best-known multilateral security organization. Another is the Shanghai Cooperation Organization, formed by Kazakhstan, China,

security policy
Principles of international behavior to advance a state's fundamental interests and ensure national security.

national security
A state's need to protect its sovereignty, territorial integrity, and vital interests.

international security
Mutual security issues involving two or more states.

TABLE 5-1 Examples of International Security Pacts

International Security Pact	Year Established	Description	Major Goal(s)
The Treaty of Friendship, Cooperation and Mutual Assistance (Warsaw Pact)	1955	Organized by the Soviet Union, this pact involved Communist states in Eastern Europe.	Keep Soviet military presence in Central Europe against NATO.
The Organization of American States (OAS)	Late 1940s	Initiated by the United States, it includes the countries of North, Central, and South America.	Security of the American continents; common action on the part of those states in the event of aggression.
The Association of Southeast Asian Nations (ASEAN)	1967	Includes countries located in Southeast Asia: Indonesia, Malaysia, the Philippines, Singapore, Thailand, Brunei, Myanmar, Cambodia, Laos, and Vietnam.	Contain Communism and have mutual protection.
Central Treaty Organization (CENTO)	1955 (dissolved in 1979)	Included Iran, Iraq, Pakistan, Turkey, and the United Kingdom.	Containment of the Soviet Union.
The Shanghai Cooperation Organization	1996	Includes Kazakhstan, China, Kyrgyzstan, Russia, Tajikistan, India, Pakistan, and Uzbekistan.	Keep separatism in check; confront terrorism; balance U.S. power in the region.

The wreckage of a car near a military checkpoint in Mogadishu, Somalia, in 2018. In failing states, deadly incidents such as car bombings both reflect and create instability.

Kyrgyzstan, Russia, and Tajikistan in 1996 with the Treaty on Deepening Military Trust in Border Regions. This group, which currently includes eight member states and three observers, later agreed to reduce their military forces in those areas. Table 5-1 provides a sample of international security pacts.

Threats to international security come from many directions and sources. Historically, they have primarily taken the form of direct intimidation and hostile actions of countries, leading to wars. Such wars still happen, as the Ukrainian–Russian situation demonstrates. Other threats come from failing states and nonstate actors, such as the Taliban and the Islamic State (ISIS), which we discussed in the previous chapter.

Failing states (often called fragile states) are those in which governments are incapable of exercising their major functions. Because these countries cannot control territory or impose law and order, violence and lawlessness spread, terrorist groups operate freely, civil wars arise, and the population suffers massively. Syria, Libya, Somalia, Chad, Sudan, and the Central African Republic are currently considered failing states.

failing state A state in which the government is incapable of exercising its major functions, defending borders, or making key decisions.

Conflict and War

Studying conflict and war is essential to our understanding of national and international security. A **conflict** is any antagonism between states, IGOs, or NGOs over territory and resources or over differences in values and perceptions of security. Conflict typically reflects the inability of a state or an international organization to achieve its goals because of other actors' resistance or unwillingness. Conflicts remain nonviolent if conflicting sides use no force to resolve them. India and Pakistan were created by the British partition plan in the Indian Independence Act. The partition did not work out peacefully, and the two states engaged in a bloody two-year war. In 1965, India and Pakistan went to war again over the area of Kashmir. In 1971, India supported the separatism of Bangladesh, then a part of Pakistan, and this resulted in yet another war. In 1974, India tested its first nuclear device (called "Smiling Buddah"); Pakistan became a nuclear state in 1998. Since then, the two countries have come several times to the brink of conflict; some believe that the possession of these weapons deterred both sides from military hostilities (White-Spunner 2017; Dixit 2002).

conflict An actual or perceived antagonism between states, international organizations, or nongovernment organizations.

Violent conflicts involve the use of force. Their ultimate form is **war**, an organized violent confrontation between states or other social and political entities, such as ethnic or religious groups. Victory is achieved by superior force, not by diplomatic negotiations or legal rulings. Such discussions resume only after hostilities end in an armistice. If one side surrenders, it is forced to accept conditions imposed by the victors.

war An organized violent confrontation between states or other social and political entities, such as ethnic or religious groups.

At the same time, wars do not exclude political bargaining. Prominent Prussian military officer and thinker Karl von Clausewitz (1780–1831) called war "a continuation of policy by other means," He meant that states use wars to protect their strategic interests and to reduce or eliminate domestic and international threats. During the Cold War (and especially recently), the divide between war and nonviolent conflict became less evident. After the end of the Cold War, international actors increasingly began to practice forms of hostilities that were different from direct military actions by the armed forces. In most recent times, especially in the era of the Internet, such hostilities are involving a country's cyberattacks, deliberate disinformation via media, and meddling with elections, often on a limited scale, to pursue this country's political goals. We will turn to these evolving security issues in Chapter 8.

War is a most extreme strategy in security policies. If chosen, it affects a broad range of international issues and, ultimately, the behavior of other states and international organizations. Security policies in democracies are born out of continuous debates among political elites, security officials, military experts, and the media. Authoritarian leaders often have a more direct, individual impact.

U.S. Marines participate in an ongoing U.S.-Thai joint military exercise in Thailand in 2018.

Types of War

offensive war A war launched as a means of occupying a territory or achieving a larger strategic or operational objective.

defensive war A war in which at least one side is mainly intending to defend itself.

preventive war A war launched by a state to protect itself when it believes that other states might threaten it in the future.

preemptive war A war launched to destroy the potential threat of an enemy when an attack is believed to be imminent.

Wars can be classified by goals, means, and motives behind them. Some states launch an **offensive war** as a means of occupying a territory or achieving a larger strategic or operational objective. An example is Germany's invasion of Poland on September 1, 1939, which began World War II. From Poland's perspective, however, the war was a **defensive war**. Labeling a war offensive or defensive is important for several reasons. One reason is international legitimacy, which affects the official reaction of other states to the war. Offensive actions typically lead to criticism, international condemnation, or forceful resistance, whereas defensive wars evoke sympathy and support. It is common for countries to camouflage their offensive actions as defensive (Fabre and Lazar 2014; Levy 1984), as examples in previous chapters illustrate.

By their motives, war can be preventive and preemptive. Some states start **preventive wars** to protect themselves if they believe that other states might threaten them in the future. In 1904, Japan's rulers acted on this logic to declare war on Russia because they believed it was necessary to "knock out" or weaken Russia before it secured new territories and became stronger in East Asia. There are also **preemptive wars**, which are launched to destroy the potential threat of an enemy when an attack is believed to be imminent (Beres 2008). In 1967, Israel was convinced that Egypt, Syria, and Jordan were mobilizing to attack it; the government thus launched a preemptive, surprise air attack against these Arab states. In 1999, NATO considered the bombing of Serbia a preemptive operation to stop the army's imminent attack against ethnic Albanians living in Kosovo. As you can imagine, some disagreed with

History Lab | War in Angola

An international conflict in Angola in 1975 started as a prolonged civil war among three rival political factions: the National Front for the Liberation of Angola (FNLA), the Peoples' Movement for the Liberation of Angola (MPLA), and the National Front for the Total Independence of Angola (UNITA). The incident rapidly began to attract the attention of other states out of concern for their security interests. Neighboring Zaire provided support for the FNLA, while Cuba provided the MPLA with weapons, military advisers, and soldiers. The Soviet Union and the United States did not get involved directly in the hostilities but backed their clients with financial and military support. The Soviets supported MPLA and Cubans, whereas the United States funneled aid to FNLA. Americans also encouraged South Africa to fight in Angola on behalf of UNITA. Thus, a conflict grew into a regional war.

It was also a classic proxy war between the two great powers (See Chapter 3). The Soviet Union and the United States were not directly involved in the Angolan war, but both claimed that it was important to their strategic security interests. For almost thirty years after foreign troops left Angola, other countries continued to fuel the civil war through illegal arms sales to the feuding sides. The MPLA proved victorious in 2002, by which time more than five hundred thousand people had died.

CRITICAL THINKING

❶ Discuss whether a proxy war may be justified by a country's security interests. Consider this case: For many years the United States used the Colombian military to fight the powerful local forces involved in cocaine trafficking to the United States and globally. ❷ If you were the leader of a state, under what specific circumstances would you approve and manage a proxy war? ❸ Consider a regional conflict (ask your professor to help choose) in which thousands of people were systematically slaughtered and the regional security was threatened. Would you approve of a proxy war to stop the unfolding war? Explain your reasoning.

these motives and explanations and considered the measures as acts of aggression. The idea of preventive and preemptive wars remains highly controversial, a subject to which we will return later.

In terms of their scope and consequences, wars can be *local*, *regional*, or *global*. Local wars typically involve two states, but a civil war need not engage other neighboring states. However, local wars are likely to draw in other countries and become regional wars. Other countries can be in close geographic proximity, or they even can be distance powers, especially in today's world. Take, for example, the conflict in Syria, which began several years ago and drew several countries into the war. It is therefore difficult to make clear distinctions between a local and regional war.

Syrian troops and pro-government gunmen in 2017. The crisis in Syria began locally but has drawn many global actors, including the United States and Russia.

Some local or regional conflicts or wars grow into *world wars*, with global consequences. World War I was triggered by Austria-Hungary declaring war on Serbia in 1914; in response, Russia declared mobilization, and Germany declared war on Russia and France. As previously mentioned, World War II began when Germany attacked Poland in 1939, leading Britain and France—allied with Poland—to declare war against Germany.

Wars, conflicts, and security threats in general can be *asymmetrical* or *symmetrical*. An asymmetrical conflict does not involve regular armies but small groups of combatants who try to avoid open fighting (Fearon and Laitin 2003). An example is **guerrilla warfare**—political violence by identifiable, irregular combat units, usually to seize political power, win autonomy, or found new states. *Gangsters* and *pirates* also practice violence, but their goal is financial, not political (Boot 2009). Guerrilla wars create significant security problems for states because they require special military strategies. The United States responded to guerrilla warfare by North Vietnam asymmetrically, by massive bombing of this country; yet this approach failed to win the war in Vietnam (1964–1975). The Soviet military practiced the same asymmetrical approach in Afghanistan against the local guerrillas (1979–1988), yet ultimately had to withdraw from Afghanistan without achieving victory.

Over the last two centuries, states prepared their armed forces to fight in symmetrical conflicts, in which an attack by one state is likely to cause a comparable response from the other. A classic example of a symmetrical security conflict is the Cold War between the United States and the Soviet Union. This war can also be seen as a transition period from frequent and open hostilities to more complex types when both sides cannot rapidly destroy each other but instead maintain mutual rivalry while engaging in diplomatic bargaining. The United States and the Soviet Union maintained diplomatic relations, signed many treaties, and even developed trade and economic relations with each other. At the same time, they were waging proxy wars against each other in Korea, Vietnam, Ethiopia, Angola (see History Lab: War in Angola), and other places.

After the Cold War ended, conflicts often included international terrorism and new, hybrid forms. Their impact on international security and on international relations will be considered at length in Chapter 8.

In the past, states commonly engaged in *predatory wars* for treasures, raw materials, trade routes, territories, and human beings as a workforce. Colonial expansion in the nineteenth and twentieth centuries—conducted by European powers such as France, Britain, Belgium, Italy, and Russia in Africa and Eurasia—is an example. More recently, Iraq occupied Kuwait in 1990 to gain possession of its vast oil resources and infrastructure. Other wars, called *retaliatory wars*, are waged by a state to weaken or punish another. China attacked Vietnam in 1979 to punish Hanoi for the occupation of Cambodia and removal of the Communist regime there. There are also *ethnic* and *religious wars* caused by conflicts between various groups struggling for their beliefs, rights, territories, and independence (Soeters 2005). For example, the conflict in Nagorny Karabakh between Armenia and Azerbaijan (open hostilities started in 1988) and the wars of Yugoslavia (1991–1999) have had ethnic

guerrilla warfare Political violence by identifiable, irregular combat units, usually to seize state power, win autonomy, or found new states.

Read about Operation Desert Storm (1990).

characteristics. An example of religious war was the Iran-Iraq War (1980–1988) between two predominantly Muslim states, where Iran claimed it was fighting for the Shia faith against the Sunni state.

The difference between most types of war, such as offensive and retaliatory or preventive and preemptive, is often unclear. Twelve countries formed a coalition to perform air strikes against the ISIS guerrillas in Iraq and Syria, but their motives varied greatly. Furthermore, many types of war overlap. For example, a war can be offensive, local, and preventive at the same time. As we will see in this and other chapters (especially Chapter 6), countries initiate their policies and wage war based on how they see and interpret international conflicts. The definitions and perceptions we have discussed allow governments to justify their military actions or use restraint. Under most circumstances, however, states try to avoid wars because they are risky and deadly and can lead to significant losses, defeat, and even destruction of a state. With this caution in mind, states usually design security policies that can help them achieve their goals short of war.

> ## Check Your Knowledge
>
> 1. The Fund for Peace regularly posts the Fragile State Index at www.fundforpeace.org/global. Which countries are in the "very high alert" category? Which countries are "most improved"? Describe the situation of a country in the former group and how one in the latter improved its status.
>
> 2. Explain the difference between national and international security. In which ways do these fields interact? Use the United States (or any other country) as an example.
>
> 3. Explain bilateral and multilateral security.

5.2 Security Policies

In nineteenth- and early twentieth-century Europe, many international actors tried to combine rationality and morality to develop an international system of rules and regulations for warfare and to ban the use of certain arms. (We will turn to the concept of "just war" in Chapter 6.) During both world wars, however, states turned to the "total war" strategy to achieve unconditional defeat of the enemy. This concept is generally rejected today. Moreover, states, IGOs, and NGOs develop policies to limit weapons of mass destruction (WMD)—nuclear, chemical, and biological. In 1968, the leading nuclear powers signed the Non-Proliferation Treaty (NPT) with the goal of stopping the dissemination of nuclear weapons. Seven years later, the Biological Weapons Convention banned the development and possession of these WMD. A similar convention for chemical weapons took effect in 1997. Over the last decades, however, *conventional weapons* and computer technologies have been drastically upgraded so that they can also cause large-scale destruction.

Countries' failure to choose the right strategy may have serious consequences. During the Cold War, the United States often responded asymmetrically to the Soviet security threat, by trying to achieve the position of absolute superiority. The United States, because of its wealth and the size of its economy, could afford this approach. The Soviet Union tried to respond

TABLE 5-2 Types of War and Strategies	
Intentions and Policies	Offensive, Defensive, Preventive, Preemptive, Symmetrical, Asymmetrical, Mixed
Purposes	Predatory, Retaliatory, Political, Mixed
Strategies	Conventional; Nonconventional, with Weapons of Mass Destruction; Symmetrical and Asymmetrical; Mixed
Scope and Consequences	Local, Regional, Global, Mixed

symmetrically to the American threat and achieved power parity with Washington in terms of the number of nuclear weapons. Yet the Soviet economy, much smaller and weaker, could build such immense military power only at the expense of the people's needs, which undermined the Soviet Union (Gaddis 2006; Zubok 2007). The variety of state responses to foreign threats only begins with symmetry–asymmetry considerations (see Table 5-2).

Unilateral versus Multilateral Foreign Policy

Security policies can also be based on unilateralism or multilateralism. The state that adopts a **unilateral** policy relies primarily on its own resources (Kane 2006). In contrast, states adopting a **multilateral** policy coordinate their efforts with other states or international organizations. Sometimes security policy can be a combination of both: In 2003, the United States unilaterally decided to start a war against Iraq and acted against the resolution of the UN. However, American diplomacy hastened to create "the coalition of the willing," including the United Kingdom, Poland, Denmark, and Australia, who backed these actions and even sent troops to Iraq.

Isolationism

Isolationism is a policy of avoiding military interventions abroad, and also nonparticipation in international alliances, organizations, and collective security efforts. Usually, only a big power can afford an isolationist stand. The United Kingdom practiced a policy of "brilliant isolation" during the nineteenth century; it joined coalitions with other countries only to fight Napoleon, the Russian Empire, and the rising power of Germany. Isolationism largely governed U.S. policy until World War I and remains a strong current in public opinion. Under President Obama, more than 50 percent of Americans said that their country should "mind its own business" instead of being a leader of global liberal order (Pew Research Center 2014a).

Public opinion leads democratic countries to choose isolationism and nonalliance even when this policy hurts their security interests (see Figure 5-1). After World War I, strong public reluctance in the United Kingdom and the United States to get involved in new military conflicts produced a powerful

multilateralism
Coordination of foreign policy with allies; participation in international coalitions, blocs, and international organizations.

isolationism A policy of nonintervention, and also nonparticipation in international alliances, organizations, and collective security efforts.

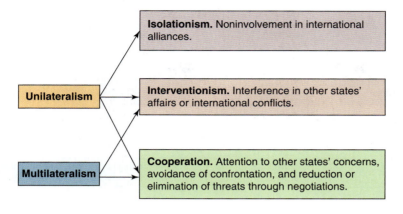

isolationism; this stand of great powers allowed Nazi Germany and fascist Italy to seize control over much of the European continent (Jonas 1969).

Interventionism

Interventionism is a policy of interference in other states' affairs and conflicts without regard for their consent. Interventionism can be driven by very different motives and has led to opposite consequences. During the eighteenth and nineteenth centuries, Britain, France, Russia, Germany, and the United States intervened around the world. The goal of their interventions was to expand their colonial empires, strengthen their influence there, and prevent other powers from gaining advantage over others. Such interventionism led to conflicts and wars, for instance, the Opium Wars between the United Kingdom and China (1839–1842, 1856–1860), the Russo-Japanese War (1904–1905), and the U.S.-Spanish War (1898) (O'Brien and Clesse 2002). After 1895, Japan became the first modern Asian power to act in the same interventionist way in China and the Pacific. Japan's interventionism was a cause of its war with the United States.

After the Cold War, the motives of interventionism changed considerably: the United States, as the leader of the democratic West, began to use military interventions abroad with humanitarian aims: to stop ethnic violence and prevent authoritarian regimes from using indiscriminate force against their population. This was practiced first in the NATO intervention in the former Yugoslavia (1995–1999), and then in Libya (2011). The benefits and consequences of this new type of interventionism are widely discussed and often disputed, as we will discuss further in Chapter 10.

interventionism A policy of interference in other states' affairs or international conflicts without regard for their consent.

Cooperation

Small states like Switzerland, Sweden, or Austria choose neutrality but cannot afford to be isolationist or interventionist; they are interested in collective security efforts. Some of them prefer a consistent policy of **cooperation**, which addresses other states' security concerns (Newman, Thakur, and Tirman 2006). Geography determines these preferences to a large degree. In the 1950s, the small democratic state of Finland, neighbor to the Soviet Union, chose a policy

cooperation A foreign policy that addresses other states' concerns for their security

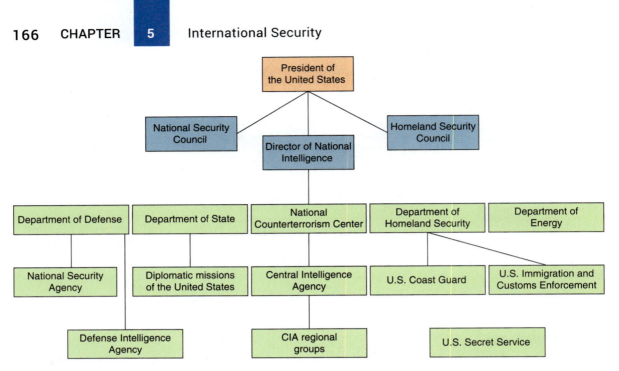

FIGURE 5-2 Major U.S. actors and agencies involved in national security.

(see Figure 5-2).

Check Your Knowledge

1. Explain the differences and similarities between predatory and retaliatory wars.

2. Explain proxy war and give an example.

3. Can a country's isolationist policy be interventionist at the same time? Explain your reasoning and provide examples.

of nonalignment and cooperation across the dividing lines of the Cold War. Finland considered the decision a reasonable bargain, while the Soviet Union saw it as a way to declare its peaceful intentions toward other European states.

Security policies typically involve a complex combination of foreign, defense, and domestic policies. In most countries, the head of state or government (president or prime minister) directs security policies with the help of a complex bureaucracy. In Washington, the National Security Council (NSC) is part of the Executive Office of the President of the United States. The president also directs the activities of other government departments, organizations, and agencies dealing with national security (see Figure 5-2).

5.3 Realist, Liberal, and Alternative Approaches to Security

For centuries, states' security policies were secret. Monarchs and politicians defined national interest as political sovereignty and territorial integrity. As soon as the national interest was protected, the state could pursue other

Types of security clearance—and who can apply for it in the United States.

interests through foreign policy. This view of security is generally supported by realists, who identify one of the goals of security policies as a favorable international balance of power.

Supporters of international liberalism believe that realist considerations lead to actions that undermine national and international security. Rather than relying on force and power structures, they seek a greater role for international and nongovernment organizations. Public opinion is also important but only if it can be expressed freely. Western Europe has shown the world that democratic states can build a stable peace based on security communities.

Why do some state leaders choose military actions while others seek peaceful solutions? In part, these attitudes are socially constructed. Values, fears, and misconceptions guide policy makers through the maze of international and domestic politics and a constantly changing world. Security policies are also collective and institutional responses to both domestic and international factors. Public opinion and NGOs play an increasingly important role in national security issues. Globalization and anti-globalization both bring changes to the lives of billions of people. Planned and unintended consequences of global processes are likely to bring new challenges to international security.

Realist Approaches to Security

According to realism, security is the main and exclusive responsibility of states, which always try to maximize their power and tend to act according to their interests in assessing threats and their own defensive capabilities. States usually observe international treaties only as long as these agreements do not conflict with state security and interests. When the international situation changes, states may abrogate such commitments in the name of security. In this perspective, the core element of every state's security is power and the ability to use it.

Geography is frequently the subject of security concerns and policies. Oceans, rivers, and mountains can act as natural security barriers. For many years Japan, Britain, and the United States thought of the seas as protection from foreign intrusions, whereas Belgium, Poland, China, and Russia were more vulnerable. States are frequently involved in conflicts regarding the protection of international trade routes, such as the Strait of Gibraltar between Europe and Africa, the Suez Canal in Egypt between Africa and Asia, and the Dardanelles in Turkey between Europe and Asia.

According to realism, security also depends on the quantity and quality of the armed forces and their mobility. History shows us numerous examples to illustrate this point. The centerpiece of British security policy from the seventeenth through the twentieth centuries was the powerful Royal Navy. The acquisition of nuclear weapons in 1945 gave the United States absolute military superiority until the Soviet Union tested its atomic weapon four years later. Countries that pursue nuclear weapons today, including North Korea and Iran, think of them as a security guarantee. The concept of *revolution in military affairs*—based on debates about the vital necessity of using modern technology in warfare and security—became a prevalent outlook on the future of war (Adamsky 2010; see Table 5-3).

TABLE 5-3 Examples of Realist Arguments Related to Security

Elements of Power	Example
Quantity of weaponry and military forces	The central goal of British security policy from the seventeenth through the twentieth centuries was ensuring that the Royal Navy was larger and more advanced than the largest navies of the other great powers.
Quality of weaponry	Development of fast-moving motorized military units and new military tactics helped Nazi Germany achieve quick victories during the first three years of World War II. Today, computer and other technologies give the United States superiority over other countries.
Presence of armed forces abroad	During the Cold War, the Soviet Union and the United States kept their armies in Central Europe. The United States continues to keep its armed forces in military bases around the world.

Smaller states lacking economic and military clout have less room for unilateral diplomacy than larger states do (Waltz 1958/2001). Thus, they often try to receive security guarantees from more powerful states and organizations. Poland, Hungary, and the Czech Republic joined NATO in 1999 for a host of reasons, above all fear of Russia (Goldgeier 1999). Vietnam and the Philippines rely increasingly on the United States to secure their interests in the South China Sea. The United States and its European allies assist Saudi Arabia militarily because they consider it a stabilizing factor in an extremely unstable region (Friedrich 2011).

International security is a dynamic process. When individual states use force or act against existing treaties and international organizations, it affects the stability of the entire international system. Foreign powers' use of force in the Middle East and North Africa for the past fifteen years has destabilized the region. If North Korea and Iran develop nuclear weapons, the regional balance of power will destabilize and the risk of war will increase. Political scientist John Mearsheimer argued that Russia's takeover of Crimea was a reaction to NATO's attempts at expansion to the East and at removal of Ukraine from Russia's sphere of influence. Russia acted as any state would in the logic of realism—to build up its own security (Mearsheimer 2014). Critics counter, however, that the annexation only added to regional destabilization and insecurity, and perhaps in the end may cause Russia to lose more than it gained.

security dilemma
A situation in which one state's efforts to improve its security cause insecurity in others.

The Security Dilemma

The situation in which one country's efforts to improve its security causes insecurity in others is known as the **security dilemma**. One state, for example, may decide to improve its security by strengthening its defensive capabilities. A neighboring state might see its security as diminished and retaliate in kind.

The security dilemma helps us understand why a disruption of the power balance or a change in the structure of the international system increases international tensions (Booth and Wheeler 2007). During the Cold War, the United States built up its naval and air bases nearest the Soviet Union to contain the spread of Communism to Europe and Asia. The Soviet Union kept a huge army in Central Europe ready to invade Western Europe in the event of an attack. Western countries, scared by the Soviet buildup, asked the United States to deploy nuclear missiles on their territory. The international system was bipolar at that time (as you will remember from Chapter 3), which made this arms race very difficult to stop. China's military buildup can be driven by the country's security concerns, yet most other states see these developments as a threat to their own security (Thu 2018).

Nuclear Deterrence

The security dilemma helps explain the policy of **nuclear deterrence**—maintaining nuclear weapons as a means of deterring others from nuclear attack. In the 1960s, top politicians in the United States began to realize that attempts to achieve superiority in nuclear weapons did not guarantee security and could cause a global calamity. The country therefore adopted a security strategy of **mutual assured destruction (informally referred as MAD)**: If two countries each have enough nuclear weapons to destroy the other, neither will use them. Some critics of this approach urged the construction of an antimissile defense instead of an unlimited arms race. Others believed that nuclear weapons should be abolished altogether.

After the Cuban Missile Crisis in October–November 1962, the United States and the Soviet Union reached a tacit agreement that they could destroy each other. This agreement did not stop the arms race, and so Washington and Moscow began to negotiate rules for arms control. New nuclear weaponry and the bipolar structure of international relations revived the security dilemma until 1987, when Mikhail Gorbachev and Ronald Reagan put a halt to the vicious circle of fears and armaments (Leffler 2007).

The Domino Theory

A practical application of realist principles to security is the **domino theory**. In this concept, the international system resembles a row of dominos standing on end: If one falls, the rest will follow. In the 1950s, President Dwight Eisenhower argued that Communist takeover in even a small country could initiate this effect and would be a major threat to international security (Boot 2007).

One of the most compelling reasons for U.S. involvement in the Vietnam War was fear of a domino-like fall of anti-Communist governments throughout Southeast Asia and beyond (McNamara 1996). These concerns were reasonable, yet exaggerated, as no massive Communist takeover ever occurred. However, anxiety regarding the domino effect continued to affect decision makers. The West supported Iraq in the war against Iran in the 1980s from fear that Islamic fundamentalists would take over in Asia and the Middle East. The United States tries to make sure that no European NATO countries will fall under Russia's political control (Baumgartner and Jozwiak 2017).

nuclear deterrence
The strategy of maintaining nuclear weapons, not to use, but to deter others from launching a nuclear attack.

mutual assured destruction (MAD)
The U.S. doctrine that, if two nuclear states have the capacity to destroy each other, neither will use its nuclear weapons.

Learn more about MAD.

domino theory
The concept that presents countries as a row of dominos, wherein if one falls, the rest will follow.

A coalition led by Saudi Arabia launched airstrikes against rebels in Yemen in 2018 to restore the former Yemeni government. The United States and Saudi Arabia alleged that the rebels receive weapons and training from Iran. According to the domino theory, if Iran cannot be checked in Yemen, it could interfere in the Shiite-majority Bahrain and elsewhere on the Arabian Peninsula.

security regime An arrangement in which a powerful country protects other states in exchange for their cooperation.

Security Regimes

The domino effect can be avoided through multilateralism. In a **security regime**, powerful countries protect other states in exchange for their cooperation with the protector (Jervis 1982). NATO emerged as a security regime in which the United States provided a nuclear "umbrella" protecting Western Europe from the Soviet Union. Responding to insecurity in Eastern Europe after 2014, the United States, the United Kingdom, and Germany deployed small military units and set up military bases in Poland, Romania, and Estonia. In this way, NATO responded to domino-effect insecurity in Eastern Europe by raising the level of military partnership and cooperation; hypothetically, a Russian attack now would inevitably lead to casualties among the Western military.

Less formally, the United States became the security regime guarantor for Saudi Arabia, Kuwait, and the United Arab Emirates (the wealthiest Arab states) against Iraq and, later, Iran (Fouskas 2003) and threats from ISIS insurgents.

Liberal Approaches to Security

Supporters of international liberalism recognize the states' primary role in security policies but also point to the increasing role of international organizations and nonstate actors. They believe that the power of states and security regimes is no longer the only key to peace in today's world.

In the liberal view, neither economic nor military power alone can bring lasting security, and military threats are seldom the best choice of action. Instead, the necessity and the desire for mutually acceptable outcomes and the complexity of international problems give countries the incentive to cooperate (Bull 1977, 1988; Ikenberry 2011a).

The previous section demonstrated that realists assume that states have two choices: increase their power or align with some states against the others (Herrmann and Lebow 2004). Liberals maintain that states have other options, such as negotiated settlements to avoid war and the creation of new institutions and norms of international cooperation. They argue that war happens when the sides in the bargaining process face too much uncertainty, cannot avoid the temptation to use force against each other, or cannot agree on how to divide the contested resources (Fearon 1995). As realists insist, a country with massive military power has more security options than a weaker state. However, military strength does not singlehandedly guarantee security: a country also needs trustworthy allies, domestic political stability, and national unity. During the American

Revolution, the Americans' alliance with France compensated in part for their military weaknesses. French political disunity in the late 1930s allowed Germany to crush France and its allies quickly in 1940. These examples show the importance of domestic factors in foreign and security policy (Walt 1991).

According to the liberal view, security policies in democratic societies should be part of the democratic process; they should be transparent and accountable whenever possible. Furthermore, the decision-making process should be more open to discussion. Strategic security decisions that affect the lives of millions should not be left to a small group of security professionals but should also include representative institutions, the media, and nongovernment organizations (Stoddard 2006).

LIBERAL INTERVENTIONISM

In principle, liberals believe that military force should be used only when diplomatic and nonviolent means are exhausted. However, liberals do not totally reject war, as they tend to approve of using force for liberal goals, such as to promote democracy or to defend large groups of people from death or acute suffering. **Liberal interventionism** accepts violence only if all diplomatic and nonviolent means are exhausted. This also means that a coalition of states and IGOs can act preventively against a predator state when international security is at stake and all diplomatic options have been fruitless. In recent years, a new controversial doctrine, based on the liberal tenet "responsibility to protect," has gained strength. This doctrine says that, when a policy of certain state governments causes mass suffering of people on their territories, other countries bear responsibility to intervene and even use military force against such governments. We will return to liberal interventionism and the responsibility to protect in Chapter 10.

liberal interventionism An approach to international relations that accepts violence to achieve liberal goals only if all diplomatic and nonviolent means are exhausted.

IGOs (INTERGOVERNMENTAL ORGANIZATIONS) AND THE SECURITY COMMUNITY

Liberals argue that the current interdependence of economic, political, and environmental issues makes a traditional balance of power, maintained by sovereign states, obsolete. In 1918 and 1919, U.S. President Woodrow Wilson's Fourteen Points called for **collective security** in which one country's security becomes the concern of all who provide a collective response to threats. This arrangement was supposed to replace a shaky balance of power in Europe, but implementing it proved difficult. As you remember, the League of Nations could not prevent or stop multiple military conflicts (Adler and Barnett 1998).

collective security An arrangement in which the security of one country becomes the concern of others as well.

International organizations such as the UN or international communities such as the EU may seem like a way to ensure collective security, but they are not designed to develop detailed security policies or to prevent military conflicts. The five permanent members of the UN Security Council have the power to support or block any policy initiated by other UN members. The UN Secretary General, whose authority and resources come from the most powerful members such as the United States, is only a mediator among member states. The EU, a seemingly influential IGO, has a vast bureaucratic structure with a substantial budget, but it does not have authority to develop a joint collective security or military policies, including collective diplomacy. Liberal scholars admit these limitations, yet they insist that benefits overshadow the difficulties. For example, the UN and EU generate greater legitimacy for their decisions because they are transparent and collective (Tavares 2009). We will return to this topic in Chapter 6.

security community
A group of countries united by mutual security interests, arrangements, and common liberal values.

An alternative to the security regime is the **security community,** which is based not on force, fear, and secret agreements but on mutual interests, voluntary cooperation, and open discussion. The idea of a security community rests in part on the sharing of rational and moral anticipations and dispositions of self-restraint in using force (Adler 2008; Deutsch, Burrell, and Kann 1957). Security communities emerged relatively recently as governments, political leaders, and other influential groups agreed on joint action and nonviolent conduct to maintain security and avoid war. Western Europe is a good example of a security community, as is North America.

Alternative Approaches to Security

In the constructivist view, countries act according to historical experience, identities, perceptions, and social norms. Canada, for example, has no concerns about U.S. military superiority because the two countries remain at peace and have not forcefully intervened into each other's affairs for over a century. In contrast, countries such as Latvia, Estonia, and Lithuania harbor security fears toward Russia because of its recent policies and, as the Soviet Union, it forcibly annexed. They remained part of the Soviet Union for fifty years.

PERCEPTIONS, IDENTITIES, AND BELIEFS

A security policy, such as a state's *propensity to use force*, is inseparable from perceptions (or misperceptions). Countries may see each other as friend, distant partner, isolationist, outcast, or enemy. For example, North Korea's development and testing of nuclear weapons alarms South Korea, Japan, and others because the country has acted erratically and belligerently in the past.

Security policies depend on how a country's political establishment sees that state's responses to security threats. The policy of containment (see Chapter 2), formulated by U.S. State Department official George Kennan in 1946–1947, was especially influential. Kennan believed that Communism would eventually collapse under the weight of its contradictions. In contrast, his colleague Paul Nitze believed that the United States needed significant peacetime rearmament to fight the Soviet threat (Thompson 2009). The competition between these two views lasted for many years.

An even more important factor in security policies is a state's international *identity*—the perceived role it plays in a regional or global community. Cuba's identity for years since the revolution in 1959 was linked to international Communism and the defeat of capitalism; for this reason, its security strategies for years remained interventionist on the global scale. Havana allied itself with Moscow militarily and economically. The Chinese identity also includes a belief in China's centrality in the world, drawing from both the imperial and Communist past. China prefers not to be part of any security alliances and does not make any binding security commitments (Westad 2017). The United States views itself as a beacon of freedom and democracy, which sometimes results in its unilateral intervention into other states but more fundamentally in its building of cooperation with other democratic states and allies.

Security identities can be shaped by painful memories: Afghanistan's identity is linked to the constant attempts of foreign powers, such as the United Kingdom in the mid-nineteenth century, to control its territory. Iran's identity was shaped by its religious rulers, but also by its memories of the country's domination by the United Kingdom, Russia, and the United States. Yet security identities change: after 1945, Germany developed a completely new international identity as an advocate of liberal causes, human rights, and international cooperation. Japan also altered its identity—if we look at its policies and public opinion—from imperialist and aggressive to peacefully democratic and cooperative (Hashimoto 2015).

If countries overcome the record of mutual resentment, they eliminate a source of the security dilemma. France and Germany have a long history of mutual violence and mistrust. After World War II, however, they began to engage in economic and political integration that led to a united European market and ended the states' long-entrenched view of each other as a threat (see Chapter 3). Different developments occurred in the relationship between India and Pakistan after their creation in 1947; for decades, each country saw the other as hostile, and its security policies reflected these attitudes.

Iranian students climb over the wall of the U.S. embassy in Tehran during the Iranian Revolution, November 4, 1979. The students went on to hold fifty-two of the embassy staff as hostages for 444 days. The U.S.-Iranian conflict affected American security policies in the Middle East and central Asia for many years.

A crucial feature of a country's security policies is its definition of security. Some countries may describe the term only in military terms, while others include economic and environmental security as well (Buzan and Hansen 2009). We will discuss environmental security in Chapter 9.

MILITARISM AND PACIFISM

militarism A tendency to rely on military force in response to foreign threats.

Militarism is an approach to international security that glorifies war, conquest, domination, and weapons: it puts a premium on the use of military force in response to most foreign threats, and it is often rooted in the sense of pride for one's country and aggressive nationalism. This perspective can be manipulated by politicians and governments to boost their ratings, mobilize action, or seek new funding. **Pacifism**, in contrast, is a principled opposition to war and a belief that international disputes should be settled by nonviolent means. This social attitude glorifies restraint, mutual concessions, respect, and peace (Zinn 2002). Militarism and pacifism reflect the never-ending argument between *hawks*, who want and tend to use force, and *doves*, who reject violence in foreign policy. Use these labels with caution, though, for they are emotionally charged and thus can be inaccurate.

pacifism A principled opposition to war and a belief that international disputes should be settled by arbitration and other nonviolent means.

Public attitudes shift constantly between militarism and pacifism. International events contribute to such changes (Hanson 2001). The many U.S. casualties during the war in Vietnam caused an increase in domestic political dissent and protests in the United States in the late 1960s and early 1970s. The term **Vietnam syndrome** refers to a general unwillingness to engage in foreign conflicts because of the perceived negative impact of the previous war. This syndrome influenced the dovish attitudes of many decision makers for years. Today, the elites of most countries include both hawks and doves. For example, the usually hawkish politicians of Israel's Likud Party must contend with the more dovish Labor Party leaders. These attitudes evolve and may change with new threats on the horizon.

Vietnam syndrome The general unwillingness to engage in foreign conflicts because of the perceived negative impact of the previous war.

States maintain international security to protect key interests of the dominant social groups. Marxism, feminism, and other conflict theories have long criticized international security policies, claiming that they are state-centric, dominated by special interests, and gender-biased.

PEACE PSYCHOLOGY

peace psychology The study of the ideological and psychological causes of war in order to develop educational programs and advocacy to reduce the threat.

Many political psychologists (see Chapter 3) suggest that international security is achievable primarily through openness, education, and goodwill. They developed **peace psychology**, which tries to understand the ideological and psychological causes of war and find practical applications of their findings (Christie 2012; MacNair 2003). Their goal is to develop educational programs to reduce the threat of violence. This approach made important contributions to U.S.-Soviet relations during the Cold War and to the relaxation of international tensions in the 1980s (Greening 1986). For example, peace psychologists organized face-to-face meetings among officials, students, teachers, and other professionals in the United States and the Soviet Union to promote trust. These days, peace psychologists focus on the psychological causes of security threats and individual and group factors of conflict resolution.

DEBATE > "AMERICANS ARE FROM MARS, EUROPEANS FROM VENUS"

When it comes to foreign policy, the United States and Europe are miles apart. Robert Kagan (2004b) expresses this idea in his bestseller *Of Paradise and Power: America and Europe in the New World Order*. Kagan echoes other experts who argue that governments have a propensity to consistently conduct either "hawkish" or "dovish" foreign policy based on their historical experience. For years, Western Europe has enjoyed security guarantees from the United States, allowing for cutbacks in their defense spending. The two sides also see the world somewhat differently, define security differently, and also perceive their threats differently. These outlooks have created divergent values related to national and international security. As a result, Europeans tend to miss the point that military strength provides for security (they act as if they are from Venus, the Roman goddess of love), while Americans (who act as if they are from Mars, the god of action and war) often fail to appreciate the idea that lasting security requires more than force.

WHAT'S YOUR VIEW?

❶ Do you agree that Western European countries such as France or Germany have adopted dovish attitudes and policies that involve consensus-seeking, compromises, reconciliatory rhetoric, and noninterventionism? Why or why not? ❷ Do you agree that the United States has embraced mostly hawkish policies fueled by constant vigilance, tough rhetoric, search for domination, and interventionist security policies? Why or why not? ❸ Do you think that European and American views of security are merging because both sides are learning from each other's experiences? Explain your reasoning.

Sources: Kagan 2004a, 2004b, 2012.

MARXISM

In the Marxist view, security policies reflect the interests of the ruling economic and political elites. To protect their wealth and power, they wage war, create international organizations, sign international treaties, and pursue their own interventionist or isolationist strategies. Marxists compare international security to an old colonial system of domination.

In the Soviet Union, Marxist-Leninist ideology reinforced Soviet expansionist policies (Shlapentokh, Shiraev, and Carroll 2008). After World War II, feeling insecure from being surrounded by non-Communist states, the Soviet Union expanded its ideological vision of security by creating a security belt of Communist regimes; after the 1950s, it began to help radical anti-Western regimes around the world (Zubok 2007). It also imposed tight security controls within its borders. For example, the government restricted people from traveling abroad. The tight control of people's movements helped the state to impose its ideology and propaganda on the population. Practically every newspaper or magazine published in the West was not allowed in the Soviet Union. The idea behind these and many similar restrictions was that the population was not supposed to know that living standards in Western countries were much higher than those in the USSR. In that way, the government could maintain loyalty of its people.

Marxists currently avoid the state-centered analysis of security and shift the discussion toward global aspects. They claim that international politics reflects, above all, the interests of wealthy, well-organized groups. Corporate media and global financial institutions support these interests; they are embedded in countries' educational systems. Marxists challenge neoliberalism and the entire capitalist world order for generating an increasing economic disparity and insecurity for the vast majority of people. Unemployment, forced migration, consistent financial troubles, and the erosion of the middle class are viewed as today's most significant security problems related to capitalism (Pitts, 2017; Davis 2011).

WOMEN AND SECURITY

Traditionally, feminism has argued that their principles could be added to international relations. The key problem for some feminists was that few women were involved in shaping military and security policy. The past two decades have brought serious changes to this issue, as more women have become decision makers in these areas (Catalist 2018; True 2009). But, as we argued in Chapter 4, other feminists see beyond the ratio between men and women in positions of power—they want to change the entire system of patriarchal views and practices in politics. Feminism, not unlike Marxism, seeks to reframe the way we all understand security.

Feminist challenges to established views, norms, and values of security emerged in the 1960s on the campuses of North American and Western European universities. Part of these challenges involved the government monopoly on security issues. Feminists were particularly wary of realism because it defined national and international security in terms of state

German Defense Minister Ursula von der Leyen, the first woman in the country's history to hold this position, greets German helicopter pilots in Mazar-i-Sharif, Afghanistan, in 2014. Historically, very few women have served as defense ministers, even in advanced democracies.

sovereignty and domination—two key values associated with masculinity. During the 1980s and later, feminists argued that the male-dominated narrative of force and war should be replaced with other narratives, including individual safety, interdependence, agreement, and shared power (Reardon 1985; Enloe 2000, 2007; Wibben 2011). They also called for security policies to be "gender mainstreamed." In other words, patriarchal views of conflict and war as a "natural" way by which sovereign states protect themselves from threats must be questioned and rejected (Stiehm 2009).

When the Cold War ended, feminists shifted the discussion from *national* security to *global* security, focusing on the problems of violence, gender and racial discrimination, and environmental degradation. They also argued that there was a lack of understanding of security as the absence of war. There should be *positive peace*, they stated, with guarantees of basic social and economic rights to all (Hirschman 2010; Tickner 1992). No discussion of security today can be complete without "gendering" or analyzing every major element of traditional approaches and issues from the feminist perspective (Sjoberg 2009).

> **Check Your Knowledge**
>
> 1. Explain the security dilemma.
> 2. Describe the differences between security regimes and security communities.
> 3. Explain liberal interventionism.
> 4. Outline major alternative approaches to security.

5.4 Critical Applications: Levels of Analysis

Evaluating security risks and seeking adequate responses must take place at several levels. These different stages help in understanding the complexity of defining and building international security.

Individual Decisions

Most states give their leader authority in the areas of national security and international relations. Therefore, a leader's views of security and their individual preferences and decisions tend to have a big impact. During the Cold War, the U.S. president accumulated extraordinary power to decide on issues of national security. Congress even granted the White House discretion to start wars, such as in Vietnam, without congressional authorization. As a result, almost every president since 1945 has significantly altered national security strategy (National Security Strategy 2017; Gaddis 1982). The trend continued after the Cold War ended, when Clinton conducted a major reevaluation of global threats. Whereas George W. Bush brought his own vision of security threats, focusing on international terrorism and the necessity to fight the rogue regimes of Iraq and Afghanistan, Obama moved to more cautious strategies based on Washington's international commitments. Trump made the "putting America first" principle the foundation for effective U.S. leadership in the world, including preservation of peace through strength and advancement of American influence (National Security Strategy, 2017).

Countries with strong political leadership change security strategies because of their leaders' will and political skills. Margaret Thatcher, the United Kingdom's prime minister from 1979 to 1990, was one of such leaders. She pursued stronger security ties with Washington and greater military spending compared to her predecessors. In countries with strong executive power, such as France or the Philippines, new leaders also tend to amend old ones or even introduce new security agendas. French President Emmanuel Macron began his term in 2017 with relentless attempts to enhance France's global role as well as its global image. President of the Philippines Rodrigo Duterte after his election in 2016 criticized a longstanding military alliance between his country and the United States (see Table 5-4 for other examples).

TABLE 5-4 Views of National Security: Selected U.S. Presidents and Soviet/Russian Leaders, 1945–2019

U.S. President	U.S. Views of National Security	Soviet/Russian Leader	Russian Views of National Security
Harry Truman (1945–1953)	Economic and military aid to governments that could be victims of Soviet expansion.	Joseph Stalin (1945–1953)	Creation of a "security belt" consisting of the countries where Communist regimes are imposed.
Richard Nixon (1969–1974)	Complex agreements with the Soviet Union and China, delegation of responsibilities to regional allies.	Leonid Brezhnev (1964–1982)	Military buildup, accompanied by arms control agreements and the creation of the European security system, combining NATO and the Soviet Union.
Ronald Reagan (1981–1989)	Military buildup to apply pressure on the Soviet Union; support of anti-Communist forces in the Third World; pursuit of nuclear disarmament.	Mikhail Gorbachev (1985–1991)	Rejection of Stalin's and Brezhnev's policies for adoption of a defensive military doctrine; the Soviet Union should join the "common European home" of economic and political cooperation; pursuit of nuclear disarmament.
Bill Clinton (1993–2001)	Enlargement of NATO; peacekeeping missions abroad but without casualties.	Boris Yeltsin (1991–1999)	Alliance with Western democracies; integration of Russia into the international system as a great power.
George W. Bush (2001–2009)	Unilateralist preemptive wars against "global terror"; further enlargement of NATO and promotion of democratic transitions.	Vladimir Putin (2000–2008)	Defense of territorial integrity; main security threat is the expansion of NATO and domestic terrorism.

TABLE 5-4 *(Continued)*

U.S. President	U.S. Views of National Security	Soviet/Russian Leader	Russian Views of National Security
Barack Obama (2009–2017)	Act in accordance with international law and in close cooperation with other states.	Dmitry Medvedev (2008–12); Vladimir Putin (2012–)	Protecting authoritarian rule at home and around the world. Confronting the West in a wide range of international issues.
Donald Trump (2017–)	Unilaterally defend U.S. strategic interests and strike deals from a position of strength.	Vladimir Putin (2000–2008, 2012–)	Defense of territorial integrity; main security threat is the expansion of NATO and domestic terrorism.

Historically, most top security officials have been men. While some may think that female leaders are more pacifist than men, examples prove otherwise. There were some male leaders who disliked using force: Jimmy Carter and Barak Obama in the United States, Gorbachev in the Soviet Union, and practically all leaders of small and neutral countries of Europe. At the same time, some prominent female leaders did not hesitate to use force. Golda Meir in Israel, Indira Gandhi in India, and Margaret Thatcher in the United Kingdom were more prone to use force than some of the male politicians who surrounded them. During their respective time as U.S. Secretary of State, Madeleine Albright, Condoleezza Rice, and Hillary Clinton all made many decisions related to America's use of force abroad and acted very decisively.

Some leaders are prone to belligerency in foreign affairs. Constructivists rightly suggest that there are generational and cultural changes in countries' top leadership and that leaders of most developed countries increasingly tend to use cooperation instead of confrontation. However, there are rogue regimes with unpredictable individuals at their helm, and the appearance of such leaders in any powerful country remains a possibility. Realists and liberals correctly believe that sudden changes in international security have dangerous consequences.

State policies' constitutional or other legal restrictions on waging war exist in several countries. However, leaders of authoritarian countries, such as Iran or North Korea, are better able to implement their individual decisions than democratic leaders (Goemans, Gleditsch, and Chiozza 2009; Debs and Goemans 2010). For this reason, we will focus on such limits in democratic countries.

Along with the constitutional checks on democracies using force in foreign policy, factors such as political opposition, public opinion, interest groups, NGOs, and the media limit individual choices. The country's historic experiences and current economic condition, domestic political competition, and the views of other countries also affect the security policies of states and international organizations.

graduated reciprocation in tension reduction (GRIT) Small goodwill steps by one or more sides in an international conflict that help to build trust and reduce international tensions.

During the Cold War, advocates of nuclear disarmament argued for an exit from the cycle of mutual insecurity. Frustrated by the superpowers' inability to guarantee international security, they believed that real policy change could begin with small, incremental steps. Such goodwill gestures would include student exchanges, trade deals, and joint projects and interviews. An American psychologist, Charles Osgood, developed the **graduated reciprocation in tension-reduction (GRIT)** model in the 1960s, and Soviet leader Mikhail Gorbachev relied on it when he transformed the security doctrine of the Soviet Union between 1987 and 1989. The result was the end of the Cold War.

WHAT'S YOUR VIEW?

❶ If GRIT was so successful in some cases, why don't political leaders use it to settle today's international conflicts? ❷ Which of the following points of view would you defend, and why?

a. This strategy should and eventually will work. International tensions cannot be resolved by force or domination.

b. This strategy does not work. Peace should be imposed: International tensions must be reduced first by military or political means. Only then can symbolic acts and goodwill gestures be effective.

State Policies

In democratic countries, national security is the subject of public debate, and political pressures exert considerable influence (Nacos et al. 2000). When international tensions arise or a war appears imminent, however, people tend to "rally around the flag." Experts call it *rage militaire*— euphoric expectations of a confrontation and a quick victory. Knowing about this effect, some political leaders may engage in a *diversionary war*, which should distract from a domestic problem and strengthen the government's position (Sobek 2008). Yet the military fervor is usually temporary. After the Vietnam War, most Americans stopped supporting long war and military commitments overseas and developed very low tolerance for casualties (Shiraev and Sobel 2006 2019). Public support for the wars in Iraq and Afghanistan eroded after the public's initial support earlier in the 2000s (see Table 5-5).

There are cycles in public opinion, which are related to generational experience. Beginning in the 1960s, most Americans saw Cuba negatively and supported tough economic and other restrictive policies toward the Cuban government. In the past ten years or so, public opinions about this country began to shift to a more positive and more cooperative tone in terms of U.S. foreign policy. However, in the last two years, Americans' opinions about Cuba have become sharply partisan (Gallup 2016).

According to recent opinion polls and electoral results, people on the left are more likely to oppose military confrontations, in accord with liberal views of international relations. Those on the right are more likely to be nationalistic and pro-military, in accord with the realist perspective. These views are reflected in popular perceptions of the major political parties: Studies show that, in the United States, Democrats are often seen as dovish and Republicans as

TABLE 5-5 Public Reaction to State Conflicts

Country	Period	Descriptions of Public Reaction
United Kingdom	mid-1850s	Fear of Russia was rampant among decision makers and the educated public, who viewed Russia as a danger to British colonies. The two countries fought between 1853 and 1856.
China	1965–1969	The Chinese Communist Party launched a massive propaganda campaign, blaming the Soviet Union for selling out Socialist values. The campaign fueled a wave of anti-Soviet sentiment in China and led to bloody skirmishes on the Sino-Soviet border in 1969.
Iran	1979	Western pressure and economic sanctions against Iran have fueled and sustained anti-Western sentiment among a significant portion of the population. An anti-American sentiment remains strong on the official level, but no longer in public opinion.
The United States	2001–	The initial public support of the military interventions in Afghanistan in 2001 and Iraq in 2003 gradually weakened, with the majority of Americans considering both as mistakes.
Russia	2014–	Russia began to regard NATO as an adversary in the late 1990s. When Russia's forceful actions in Ukraine triggered Western condemnation and action, the vast majority of the public overwhelmingly supported the Russian leadership, which denied that it had acted aggressively.

hawkish (Dueck 2010). These perceptions often tend to be inaccurate (Narizny 2003; Reeves 2001), as both parties often choose security policies based on specific interests rather than on ideology.

Take, for example, **lobbying**, an activity by individuals, groups, and corporations to influence public officials in support of or in opposition to some legislation or policies or in opposition to others. Its methods include mail and social network campaigns, voter mobilization through political rallies, political campaign funding, and op-ed pieces. History shows that lobbies represented different approaches to security. Some business groups in the past pushed for American economic and military expansion. Quakers and other groups promoted negotiations with Soviet leaders to prevent nuclear war, while people from Eastern Europe and Catholic organizations were anti-Soviet and supported huge federal spending to maintain U.S. military superiority. A powerful pro-Israeli lobby emerged between 1967 and 1973 and used strategic security goals to justify U.S. support for Israel for years to come (Mearsheimer and Walt 2007).

In 1960, Eisenhower for the first time spoke of the "military-industrial complex" that had come to dominate the country's security policies (Eisenhower 1960). Advocates of conflict theories agree with this statement and argue that lobbying helps the ruling classes, the wealthy, and the most politically

lobbying Activities with the goal of influencing public officials in support of or in opposition to legislation or policies.

Rep. Elise Stefanik has been the U.S. Representative for New York's 21st congressional district since 2015. First elected at the age of thirty, she was the youngest woman ever elected to Congress at that time. She was appointed vice chairwoman of the House Armed Services Committee's Subcommittee on Readiness.

geopolitics The theory and practice of using geography to achieve political power or seek security.

connected determine security policy. After 9/11, a new, powerful bureaucracy emerged. Homeland security as a policy now combines domestic and national security tasks. Its impact on foreign policy decision making clearly represents a dominant factor in security policies over the past two decades.

Global Factors

For centuries, sovereign states struggled for territorial and geographic advantage. Many of them used **geopolitics**—the theory and practice of using geography and territorial gains—to achieve political power or seek security. Geographical position gave some countries clear benefits in security matters, while others remained vulnerable. Geopolitics played a crucial role in the rise and fall of the great world powers (Morris 2010). The concept teaches that such shifts may lead to new trade wars and increased global military competition. On the other hand, new bilateral and international agreements, international organizations, and the necessity of global interconnectedness could put most of these concerns to rest.

A substantial change took place after the Cold War ended. Irregular wars (conflicts involving guerrillas instead of regular military) proliferated in the second half of the twentieth century, thus threatening global security. In the 1990s, wars moved away from Asia and Latin America toward Eurasia, the Middle East, and sub-Saharan Africa. This shift was caused by not only some domestic political and economic factors but also a massive dissolution of political regimes in these regions (Kalyvas and Balcellis 2010, 423). International terrorism altered the face of irregular warfare. Terrorism, especially the new forms of cyberterrorism, do not respect geographical boundaries (see Chapter 8). Small nuclear weapons can now be delivered to cities in a suitcase, and nuclear proliferation is an acute security issue.

Territorial integrity and sovereignty remain important matters affecting global security. A country's breakup or the interference of neighboring countries can create regional instability, especially in multiethnic zones with weak governments. These days, ethnic and religious violence in West Africa and the Middle East may become the most significant threats to regional and global security for years. We saw these developments in Syria in 2011, when civil war between al-Assad's government and opposition groups broke out. Four years later, Russia intervened, thus causing a massive wave of Syrian refugees to flee to Europe and the most significant migration crisis in Europe since World War II.

Some multilateral steps toward regional security have been taken, such as the Central America Regional Security Initiative (CARSI 2015). This collective effort of governments, law-enforcement agencies, and NGOs aims to prevent the spread of illicit drugs, the corruption and violence associated with them, and other global threats. It attempts to reduce the flow of narcotics, arms, weapons, and bulk cash generated by drug sales and to confront gangs and criminal organizations. If these types of efforts make a difference, they will demonstrate the importance of international organizations and coordinated security policies.

Another aspect of security involves globalization. With the increasing interconnectedness of economies and policies, factors such as inflation, unemployment, poverty, social unrest, ethnic wars, and mass migration have implications for national and international security. The essence of international relations becomes not just about state and regional politics but about energy resources as well.

Historically, the struggle for access to energy resources contributed to serious international conflicts, as both economically successful and growing economies are likely to protect their domestic and even foreign energy resources. Any disruption in the production of oil has severe consequences. For example, the Arab oil embargo against the West in the 1970s contributed to a widespread recession (Bryce 2009). For the United States, dependence on foreign oil has been a security challenge for decades (Guérot 2010), and both Democratic and Republican administrations tried to reduce U.S. dependency. In 2018, U.S. oil imports from foreign countries were between 16 and 17 percent of overall petroleum consumption, the lowest numbers in fifty years. Energy self-sufficiency is likely to be a major strategic goal of future administrations and of many other countries. In terms of strategic relations in the twenty-first century, new political alliances are likely to emerge. Former ideological and political allies (like NATO members) may turn away from their partners and gravitate toward energy-rich nations (like Russia), thus weakening strategic security regimes. Such energy alliances could easily be perceived as threats to the security of other states.

Many developing countries need an uninterrupted supply of oil and natural gas, at the lowest possible price, and they are likely to make substantial investments in their militaries to protect it. The Chinese economy needs an uninterrupted supply of oil and natural gas, at the lowest possible price, and China makes substantial investments in its militaries to protect it. China's economic growth could contribute to global tension in other ways as well: Its massive exports could undermine other countries' economies and key manufacturing industries, weakening their job markets and creating economic problems (Economy and Levi 2014; Peerenboom 2008). The competing principles of realpolitik and cooperation will be tested once again.

Check Your Knowledge

1. What are the relative roles of public opinion and lobbies in security policies?

2. Explain GRIT. What are the strengths and weaknesses of GRIT in your view? How can its strength be applied to today's international relations? Which country could you chose to apply the GRIT principles? Explain the applications.

3. What is the "military-industrial complex"?

4. Explain geopolitics and give examples.

5. What is the Central America Regional Security Initiative?

6. What role do energy resources play in international security?

7. Why has oil become a global security issue?

Ending the Cold War

Background

Why did the Cold War, a global conflict that lasted for decades, end so suddenly and without significant violence? The peaceful transformation of the security landscape and the entire international system in 1988–1991 took most experts by surprise (see Chapter 2). *Triumphalists*, mostly American conservatives, were quick to claim a U.S. victory, an expected result of the military buildup and constant pressure against the Soviet Union. By creating a military deadlock for the USSR in Afghanistan, supporting Solidarity (an anti-Communist, anti-Soviet movement) in Poland, building advanced military systems, encouraging Saudi Arabia to reduce oil prices (the main source of Soviet finances), and taking a belligerent stand in the war of ideas, the United States undercut the Soviet Union's power bases, undermined its self-confidence, and forced it to surrender.

Analysis

Declassified documents and interviews show that the triumphalist thesis is simplistic. Soviet archives reveal that the key to the security transformation was Gorbachev's desire for domestic reforms and his refusal to see the world

U.S. President Ronald Reagan and Soviet General Secretary Mikhail Gorbachev meet in 1986.

through the prism of the security dilemma. The Soviet leader acted from the position of growing weakness (the Soviet economy and finances were in disarray), but he also wanted to build an international community in Europe and Asia that would include NATO countries. He spearheaded a new image of a just, secure world and a path to achieve it—what he called the "new thinking." Liberals in the West proclaimed Gorbachev their champion. They acknowledged that he shared many ideas, including the GRIT model, with the neoliberal domestic and transnational intellectual communities (English 2000; Evangelista 1999). By applying these ideas to international relations, Gorbachev succeeded in breaking the deadlock of the security dilemma. Many across Europe and the world applauded the Soviet leader when, at the United Nations in 1988, he declared international security as "one and indivisible" and rejected the use of force in international relations.

One can also reassess the role of U.S. President Ronald Reagan in the light of liberal theories. Although the administration initially did not trust Gorbachev's intentions, Reagan recognized that the Soviet threat was disappearing and seized the opportunity to build a new framework of agreements and cooperation. The emerging mutual trust between the two leaders helped to break the cycle of insecurity. They proceeded despite the resistance of powerful national forces, including the most belligerent members of the military on both sides and government officials with hostile attitudes toward the other country (Chernyaev 2000; Leffler 2007).

Realists and neorealists began to search for more sophisticated explanations of the end of the Cold War. They argued that the Soviet Union's uncertain role in the new structures of international relations and its weakening stand in the global balance of power affected the behavior of its leaders. A younger generation, including Gorbachev and foreign minister Eduard Shevardnadze, realized that the USSR had to avoid a new round of the arms race that it could not win. Because the Soviets could not prevail over the West, they decided to join it (Wohlforth 2003). Gorbachev's new perception of common security emerged as an alternative to confrontational policies seen as dangerous, expensive, and counterproductive (Herrmann and Lebow 2004).

Constructivist assessments help explain the Soviets' and Americans' evolving ideas on security. Gorbachev, unlike the older generation of his state's leaders, no longer identified himself with a Soviet military superpower. In contrast, he viewed nuclear weapons as ensuring security against foreign threats. Nor was he obsessed with memories of World War II that had left Soviet elites deeply insecure when it came to the West. His personal aversion to the use of force and his preference for nonmilitary means to respond to security challenges were almost pacifist. In the end, he not only accepted that a unified Germany would become an anchor of peace and prosperity in Europe, but he also based his strategy on integrating the reformed Soviet Union into a "common European home"—the term used to describe a new structure for security and economic integration that included North America (Rey 2008; Zubok 2014).

Liberals, neorealists, and constructivists agree that a peaceful resolution like this one does not come about exclusively from military pressure.

As Gorbachev's perspective demonstrates, it takes rethinking national security after traditional approaches end in crisis or deadlock. The colossal military power of the Soviet Union was undermined by a corrosion of ideology and political will (Lévesque 1997 252). Influential Soviet elites became convinced that Western models based on political freedoms, private entrepreneurship, and consumerism had more to offer. "Ordinary" people also began to think differently. They were no longer prepared to shed blood for a cause they did not believe in and an empire they did not benefit from. In the end, ideas and values transformed international security.

Advocates of alternative approaches to international relations draw different lessons from this war's peaceful end. Marxists argue that the Soviet Union was never a truly Socialist country (Shlapentokh et al. 2008). Thus, Gorbachev and Soviet elites simply shifted from one mode of domination and insecurity to another neoliberal model based on global capitalist exploitation, inequality, and insecurity. Feminist critics argue that the narrative should not revolve around the actions and thoughts of just a few male leaders. Moreover, the global outcomes of 1989 were more conservative than revolutionary: Instead of building a new order that would include the post-Soviet space, Western statespeople preserved and expanded NATO, perpetuating the same old security agenda (Sarotte 2009).

Making conclusions about the end of the Cold War is not easy. It stands as a unique case—the meltdown of a major power. Yet it has generated rich and valuable discussions that reopen and reassess the tenets of national and international security today.

Case Study Questions

1. The relations between Russia and the West have recently deteriorated. What lessons could you draw from history? Suggest a path to improve these relations today. What should be done, in your view?

2. What lessons from the end of the Cold War can apply to the United States' relations with Iran?

3. Based on lessons from history, what would you do to prevent a new Cold War, between the United States and China, for example?

4. Which international conditions or factors from the end of the Cold War exist today, and which do not?

CHAPTER 5
REVIEW   International Security

5.1   Describe the scope of national and international security.

National security is concerned with the protection of sovereignty, territorial integrity, and national interests. International security refers to mutual security issues involving more than one state.

Q: Why do failing states pose a risk to international security? Give a recent example.

Q: How are the lines between local, regional, and global wars blurring? Give an example from the twentieth or twenty-first century.

5.2   Explain variation in security policies.

When developing security strategies, countries must decide between symmetrical or asymmetrical responses; unilateral or multilateral policies; and isolationism, interventionism, or cooperation.

Q: What conditions can lead a country to pursue a policy of interventionism, isolationism, or cooperation? Give an example of each.

5.3   Discuss security from realist, liberal, constructivist, and alternative perspectives.

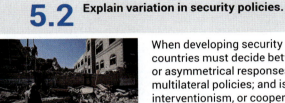

Realist policies assume the security dilemma and emphasize nuclear deterrence, belief in the domino effect, and security regimes. Liberalism has led to the creation of international organizations and security communities. According to constructivism, security policies depend on a country's current political establishment, as well as its international identity, historical experience, and social norms. Public attitudes shift constantly between militarism and pacifism. Alternative perspectives include peace psychology, Marxism, and feminism.

Q: Why would a security regime result from a realist view of international security?

Q: How does liberal interventionism differ from domino theory?

Q: What are the critical similarities between Marxism and feminism? How are they, as a whole, different from liberalism?

5.4 Consider critical applications of international security at each level of analysis.

The varying views of individual leaders have equally diverse impacts on security agendas. In democratic countries, political opposition, public opinion, and lobbying place checks on national security agendas. Globalization, anti-globalization, and asymmetric threats have profound effects on international security.

Q: Compare and contrast the individual foreign policies of American presidents since the Cold War.

Q: How do globalization and anti-globalization affect conflict over energy resources?

Q: For the sake of international security, should states have equal access to energy resources? Is this equal access achievable? Why or why not?

KEY TERMS

International Law and International Organizations

> *Insofar as international law is observed, it provides us with stability and order and with a means of predicting the behavior of those with whom we have reciprocal legal obligations.*
>
> — J. WILLIAM FULBRIGHT (1905–1995)

In 2001, Israel began building a security barrier to separate it from Palestinian territories. This wall is 440 miles (708 km) long and, in some sections, 330 feet (100 m) wide; it consists of an electric fence, a ditch up to 13 feet (4 m) deep, a two-lane asphalt patrol road (the "trace strip") built parallel to the fence with sand to detect footprints, and barbed wire. To cross the fenced area, people need a permit issued by Israeli authorities.

The Palestinian government has long considered the West Bank barrier illegal and has repeatedly asked the Israeli government to abandon it. In 2003, the UN International Court of Justice decided by a majority vote that the wall was "contrary to international law." It obliged Israel to cease construction without delay, repeal all associated laws, and make reparation for all damage caused by the construction. Other countries were advised not to assist Israel in advancing the project, and the UN Security Council was asked to consider further action.

Instead of halting construction, however, Israel completed most of the barrier. The government justified the fence as a security measure against terrorist attacks and pointed out that the court decision was advisory, not mandatory. Legal scholars in Israel wrote that a sovereign state might construct a temporary security barrier in an occupied territory. The Israeli Supreme Court ruled that the wall was legal, though it ordered that 140 acres (0.5 sq km) be returned to the Palestinians.

Which side's legal arguments are stronger? Should the governments of sovereign states obey the decisions of international

Previous page: Young Palestinians are at the security barrier of an Israeli army post in 2018. Under what conditions and when will this security barrier become unnecessary and dismantled, in your point of view?

organizations, including courts? Under what circumstances do countries have the right to disagree? These types of questions are critical in today's world. This chapter deals with the principles and consequences of international law and its role in international relations (ICJ 2004. Israel High Court Ruling 2005).

6.1 Explain the nature, principles, and sources of international law.

6.2 Describe the evolution of international law and international organizations.

6.3 Outline the principal differences among various views and approaches to international law.

6.4 Critically apply key principles of international law to individual decisions, state policies, and global developments.

Learning Objectives

In general terms, a *law* is a rule either prescribed or recognized as binding. **International law** is a set of principles, rules, and agreements that regulate the behavior of states and other international actors. In theory, states and international organizations should agree on a wide range of general rules and then enforce them properly. In reality, it is a daunting mission.

international law Principles, rules, and regulations concerning the interactions between countries and other institutions and organizations in international relations.

6.1 International Law and the Role of International Organizations

There is no formal document of worldwide legal principles and no global constitution, supreme court, or law-enforcement agency. Thus, international legal regulations are effective only as long as key actors recognize and follow them. As we have seen, Israel rejected international law when it refused to halt construction of a security barrier. Is it really necessary, then, or even practical, to have international law? The answer is *yes*, for the following reasons: the need for a secure international environment, the need for conflict resolution, and the need to coordinate domestic laws in a global world.

Sovereign states, organizations, businesses, and people need a secure environment rather than lawlessness (Bull 1977). States and international organizations set rules and establish sanctions against violations of such laws. Take maritime piracy, which disrupts maritime communication, inhibits trade, and endangers lives. A substantial increase in this crime near Somalia and the Horn of Africa about a decade ago created a collective international

Read several cases about the interaction between countries' legal systems.

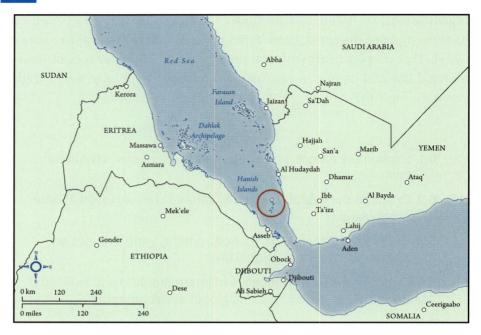

MAP 6-1

The previously disputed Hanish Islands belong to Yemen now, thanks to international arbitration.

response to uphold and enforce international anti-piracy laws (Boot 2009). As a result of an international agreement and subsequent action, the piracy in that region and the damage that it brought to international navigation reduced dramatically (Yanofsky 2013).

Although international actors constantly engage in disputes, they realize that force alone or threats of force are not the most efficient way to resolve them. Internationally observed rules help countries to resolve border issues and property rights so that agreements are kept without involving violence (Linklater 2009). During the 1990s, Yemen and Eritrea disputed control of the Hanish Islands in the Red Sea, and violence was about to erupt (see Map 6-1). In 1998, the Permanent Court of Arbitration (PCA), located in The Hague and one of the oldest institutions for dispute resolution, determined that the archipelago belonged to Yemen. Eritrea accepted this legal decision, and violence was avoided. In 2015, the PCA decided on a dispute between the United Kingdom and the Republic of Mauritius regarding several islands in the Indian Ocean and the legitimacy of the legal restrictions established by London in the area around them (the United Kingdom government wanted to create a Marine Protected Area). The decision was in favor of Mauritius.

States have different constitutional, administrative, criminal, contract, family, and property laws. Think of divorce and custody disputes, trademark and contract violations, financial obligations, copyright infringements, and compensations for faulty products or services. Numerous practical problems and disagreements between countries naturally emerged, especially in an era of global trade and travel (Keohane 2005). When supporters of

In Thailand in 2018, A U.S. military team and British cave experts were among those who assisted when twelve boys and their soccer coach were trapped in a flooded cave for five days. Joint international action was vital to the rescue.

anti-globalization pushed back, even more legal problems began to emerge. International law is therefore essential in regulating the relationships among private citizens living in different countries, between private citizens and foreign governments or nongovernment organizations, and among international organizations. International law should also be applied to fight transnational organized crime, including extortion, drug and human trafficking, kidnapping, and money laundering.

Principles of International Law

International law applies only within its **jurisdiction**, which defines how far the law can reach within a determined area of responsibility. This area can encompass two, several, or all countries (Kahler and Lake 2003). For example, the EU restricts certain food products from being imported into its countries. Switzerland, as an example, may ignore these restrictions and allow these products (unless there is an international agreement) because the EU has no jurisdiction over Switzerland. Anti-maritime piracy laws have universal jurisdiction because states agree that these rules apply everywhere. Under U.S. law, piracy committed anywhere on the high seas against a U.S. vessel carries a sentence of life in prison, regardless of the nationality of the pirates or the victims.

Sovereign states and international organizations are subject to international law. Both are also engaged in diplomacy. Diplomats have established a number of common rules and expectations that guide their official communications. Rules of *diplomatic protocol* are based on centuries of tradition and suggest how these activities should be performed. Protocol is a set of

jurisdiction The right and authority to make decisions and apply justice within a determined area of responsibility.

international courtesy rules and ceremonies, which states choose to follow assuming that others will (or are likely to) reciprocate. The U.S. Department of State (2013) issues a *Protocol of the Modern Diplomat* for professionals serving overseas or working with foreign representatives at home.

Sources of International Law

Where do the legal principles and rules regulating international relations come from? The **sources of international law** include treaties, customs, general principles, and the actions of courts and other international organizations (see Table 6-1). **International treaties** (also called *agreements, charters, pacts, covenants*, and *conventions*) are formal, written commitments between international actors that often suggest sanctions if those assurances are violated or ignored.

Every year, the United States reaches more than a hundred agreements with foreign states. You can easily see them when you search using the key words "treaties and agreements" at the State Department site. However, a state or organization usually can cancel, or *abrogate*, a treaty—especially if it has term limits. In 2002, the United States abrogated the Anti-Ballistic Missile Treaty, formed with the Soviet Union in 1972, so that it could build an anti-missile defense. In October 2018, President Trump decided that Washington would withdraw from the 1987 Intermediate-Range Nuclear Forces Treaty. The United States also withdrew from the Paris Agreement, a landmark treaty to curb carbon emissions, in 2017 and, a year later, from the 2015 "Iran nuclear deal framework," an international agreement reached by seven countries. The reasons behind abrogation are not simple because a host of political, ideological, economic, and security factors affect them. In democracy, such reasons must be openly discussed. They also can be reversed.

TABLE 6-1 Sources of International Law

Source	Example
International Treaties (Formal, Written Commitments)	Brazil and the United States reached a 2018 agreement on the peaceful uses of outer space.
International Customary Law (Based on Past Practices)	Diplomatic representatives and their families are generally free from criminal persecution and civil liability in countries where they work and live.
General Principles of Law	An international agreement is supposed to be honored; a sovereign state has the right to control the use of resources within its territory; a sovereign state has the right to either recognize or not recognize another country.
Resolutions (Formal Texts) of International Organizations or Judgments by International Courts	The UN, the International Court of Justice, NATO, and the European Parliament of the EU pass resolutions: strong recommendations on security, economic, humanitarian, or environmental policy.

A second source of international law is international **customary law, which** derives from the past practices of sovereign states, such as their general consistency in obedience to the rule or their acceptance of it. International actors simply come to see these actions as normal and reasonable under particular circumstances. For example, every sovereign state with access to the sea is expected to claim jurisdiction over its territorial waters (Gangale 2009), or visiting foreign heads of state expect to have immunity when they travel to foreign countries. Non-refoulement, another principle referring to customary law, states that an asylum seeker should have the right to freedom from expulsion from a territory in which he or she seeks refuge. (We will return to this subject in Chapter 10.)

A third source is **general principles of law**, which are common, cross-cultural principles of morality and common sense. For instance, legal decisions should be made based on *equity*—the need to be balanced and impartial. States have the right of self-defense, but their actions should be proportional to the **aggression**. If states, organizations, and businesses damage the environment of other states, they should compensate. In 2010, a British Petroleum drilling rig leaked massive amounts of oil into the Gulf of Mexico. The company immediately offered compensation to the people and organizations affected by the disaster and, overall, paid tens of billions of dollars in legal fines and cleanup costs (estimates vary).

The judgments of international organizations, along with works by legal scholars and political analysts, are yet another source of international law. After Israel named Jerusalem its capital in 1980, the UN Security Council issued Resolution 478, declaring that the country had violated international law. Partly because of this resolution, almost all foreign embassies remain in Tel Aviv. In 2017, the Trump Administration announced that it would move the U.S. embassy to Jerusalem, which caused serious international criticisms. Although some countries followed suit or announced their move in the future, most kept their embassies in Tel Aviv.

customary law Law derived from the past practices of sovereign states in the absence of repeated objections from other states.

general principles of law Cross-cultural principles of morality and common sense.

aggression An attack by a state aiming at retribution, expansion, or conquest.

Check Your Knowledge

1. Explain three arguments in support of international law. Create your own example to justify the importance of international law.

2. Explain the jurisdiction principle. Give two examples that relate to you and your country.

3. Name four sources of international law. Would you consider the "eye for an eye" principle (the custom of retaliation) part of customary law? Why or why not?

6.2 Development of International Law

The meaning of international law has been evolving over centuries (Evans 2014). An early model reflected in international laws today is in the law of nations called *Jus Gentium*, a codification of Roman law compiled during the rule of the Byzantine emperor Justinian I (482–565). The law of nations was based on natural law—rules that reflect universal interests such as honoring treaties between states. Eleven centuries later, the Dutch diplomat and jurist Hugo Grotius (1583–1645) further connected international law to natural law. In

On the Law of War and Peace (1625), he argued that wars between sovereign countries could be justifiable but only under particular circumstances. Like individuals, sovereign countries have the right to self-defense. But even in a state of war, countries should abide by certain rules. An example of natural law could be universal legal opposition to international hijacking, which is the forceful seizure of a vehicle, ship, or aircraft and its forcible diversion to a new destination against the will of its crew and passengers.

As discussed in Chapter 2, the Peace of Westphalia established an early foundation of international law in 1648. The acquisition of new lands also required justification. During the period of colonial expansion, European rulers often used the legal term *terra nullius* ("land belonging to no one") to claim territories, such as Australia, as their lawful possessions (Lindkvist 2007). Much later, this term was applied to Antarctica, the moon, the outer planets, and the deep seabed.

Laws of the Sea

The laws of the sea are among the oldest in international law. Over the ages, states involved in overseas commerce had to deal with competition, the safety of shipments, and financial disputes and needed the freedom to travel by sea and to trade with other countries. Rules thus became a necessity to minimize preventable losses. These laws are based on agreements, practical needs, and legal scholarship. Grotius (1609) formulated one central principle, **freedom of the seas, which asserts that a** state's sovereignty ends at the edge of its territorial waters. The term, **international waters** (high seas or, in Latin, *mare liberum*) thus has emerged, indicating oceans, seas, and waters outside national jurisdiction—at a certain distance from shores—that are open to all countries. Although not every state accepted these principles at first, they eventually relented, and these rules survived for centuries. Today, outside of states' territorial waters, countries and individuals have the right to navigate, conduct scientific research, use aircraft, and even lay cable or pipelines.

In the second half of the twentieth century, many new agreements were reached to regulate international navigation and sea borders. These arrangements also control exploration of the ocean surface and its seabed and protect its flora and fauna. After the 1970s, countries began to claim and enforce legal rights over the exploration and use of marine resources within their *exclusive economic zone (EEZ)*, which stretches to 200 nautical miles (370 km) from the relevant country's coast.

Laws of War

In the eighteenth and nineteenth centuries, a consensus emerged among ruling elites of various countries on the need to regulate war and to minimize its increasingly deadly consequences. The philosophical and moral tradition of **just war** had existed for centuries. Since ancient times, the supporters of this tradition claimed that war was unjustifiable simply out of moral principles. However, if war is declared, it should be conducted according to a set of ethical rules. Influenced by the just war tradition, Tsar Nicholas II of Russia and his foreign minister proposed assembling an unprecedented international

freedom of the seas The principle that countries have the right to travel by sea to other countries and to trade with them; each state's sovereignty ends with its territorial waters.

international waters oceans, seas, and waters outside national jurisdiction, known as high seas or, in Latin, *mare liberum*.

just war A philosophical concept claiming that war is unjustifiable out of moral principles. However, if war breaks out, it should be conducted according to ethical rules.

conference in The Hague to discuss how to make all wars illegal. The First Hague Conference, held in 1899, involved representatives from twenty-six states, including high-level delegations from the United States and Japan. The Second Hague Conference, proposed by U.S. President Theodore Roosevelt, was convened in 1907, with forty-four states present.

The participating countries at the second conference agreed that war must be the last resort in settling international disputes and that the right to declare it should be limited. Violence during war should also be restricted. Poisoned gases, for example, were banned because they caused great suffering to soldiers and civilians. Conference documents recognized the rights of prisoners of war and outlaw use of the enemy's flag and military uniform for deception. Pillaging, bombarding towns not defended by the military, punishing civilians, and refusing to care for wounded enemy soldiers were all deemed illegal (see Figure 6-1).

The Hague Conferences outlined the **laws of war**—common principles that states should follow in an armed conflict. For example, a state should make a *declaration of war* when it initiates hostilities against another state. A state at war has *belligerent rights*, such as the right to visit and search merchant ships, seize cargo of the enemy, or attack and destroy military forces and equipment of the enemy. States at war also expect to have their soldiers and officers treated in accordance with the decisions of the Hague Conferences, regardless of who started the conflict or who has the moral right to use violence. A suspension of hostilities was called, according to the laws of war, **armistice**. A country's formal surrender should stop all military actions, but the victors could impose the conditions of peace, as happened at the end of both world wars.

Conference participants acknowledged that a state could choose **neutrality** by rejecting any formal military or political alliance as well as foreign military bases on its territory. The neutrality concept is recognized today. Several states are currently neutral, including Costa Rica, Austria, Finland, Sweden, and Switzerland. They are obliged to remain neutral in conflicts involving other countries and to ensure that their territory is not used by other countries to stage aggression or to engage in hostile actions, such as spying.

Read more about classic laws of the sea.

laws of war Common principles that states should follow in an armed conflict.

neutrality Rejection of any formal military or political alliance.

Countries agree that the right to declare war should be limited

If war is chosen, violence should be limited

Certain cruel arms should be prohibited

Prisoners of war and the injured have rights

Civilians should not be targeted

Pillaging is outlawed

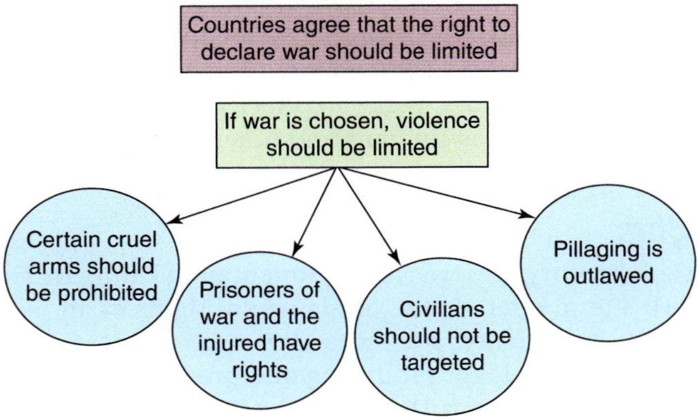

FIGURE 6-1 Major decisions of the Second Hague Conference (1907).

The Hague Conferences seemed to signal a new era in international relations. Yet for all their declarations, they failed to create an institution or mechanism that could issue effective legal actions against a country-aggressor. For one thing, talks reached an impasse over the issue of appointing international judges. Every delegation wanted to see a representative of its state appointed, and bigger states wanted a bigger share of votes. Many countries, mostly for domestic political reasons, failed to ratify the Hague resolutions or attached serious amendments, making the resolutions ineffective.

By the twentieth century, international law was increasingly understood as a corpus of rules determined by sovereign states (Evans 2014). At that time, formal accords between two or among several countries began to play a major role in international affairs. The individuals involved in developing such accords had good intentions, as we saw in the case of the Hague Conferences; however, they were unable to stop wars and atrocities. The League of Nations, created after World War I, did not protect against aggressive wars (see Chapter 3). The founding of the United Nations in 1945, to replace the defunct League of Nations, was a critical improvement, but its resolutions are also nonbinding and often remain on paper. The search for a more efficient and viable system of international law continues, as well as the debates about how to enforce this law.

Humanitarian Issues

Declaring limits on the use of war was an important step in the development of international law. Concerns about the fate of both combatants and civilians in wars grew: Who could protect people from excessive violence and harm (Abrams 1957)? There was a growing agreement that all human beings, regardless of their nationality or creed, have basic rights that international law must protect.

In 1863, Swiss citizen Jean Henri Dunant (1828–1910) founded the International Committee of the Red Cross (ICRC) to help all wounded soldiers on the battlefield. (For his work, he became the first winner of the Nobel Peace Prize.) The Red Cross was instrumental in the first Geneva Convention for the Amelioration of the Condition of the Wounded in Armed Forces in the Field, signed in August 1864 by fourteen states, on the humane treatment of captured and wounded soldiers. The International Federation of the Red Cross and Red Crescent Societies was formed in 1919, and the 1864 Geneva Convention was the precursor of three more agreements signed in Geneva in 1906, 1929, and 1949. Together, these accords legalized the rights of the captured and wounded, as well as civilians and other noncombatants (Borch and Solis 2010).

Read more about the Geneva Conventions.

Human Rights

human rights
Fundamental rights with which all people are endowed, regardless of their race, nationality, sex, ethnicity, religion, or social status.

In the twentieth century, a powerful argument about **human rights** gained prominence. This term refers to the fundamental rights of all people, regardless of their race, nationality, sex, ethnicity, religion, or social status. The UN became a major vehicle for producing and promoting international legal norms in this area. In 1948, the UN General Assembly adopted the Universal

Declaration of Human Rights. At the time when racism was widespread and segregation common, when colonial empires and dictatorships still controlled more than one-half of the world, the Declaration proclaimed in Article I: "All human beings are born free and equal in dignity and rights. They are endowed with reason and conscience and should act towards one another in a spirit of brotherhood." The Covenant on Civil and Political Rights and the Covenant on Economic, Social, and Cultural Rights, adopted in 1966, came into force in 1976. A year earlier, the Conference on Security and Cooperation in Europe, which included the United States and the Soviet Union, signed the Helsinki Final Act. This document—which was a triumph of liberal internationalism—bound the twenty-five participating states to respect and protect humanitarian and human rights, such as the right to receive information, exchange ideas, or unify families across the state borders (Thomas 2001).

The evolution of attitudes toward human rights is a remarkable success of international law. The Geneva Conventions of 1948 and 1949 have become widely recognized treaties. The former defined **genocide** as the deliberate extermination or prosecution of national, racial, ethnic, and religious groups, whether in war or in peacetime. These and other humanitarian agreements aim at limiting suffering and death during military conflicts. They protect prisoners of war and civilian noncombatants against indiscriminate violence. They also assume that states, even nondemocratic ones, must respond to the international community if authorities engage in *crimes against humanity*, including arbitrary arrests for political reasons, systematic torture, rape, or the deliberate killing or injury of civilians. We will examine policies related to human rights in Chapter 10.

genocide The deliberate extermination or prosecution of racial, ethnic, religious, or social groups, whether in war or in peacetime.

Early International Legal Institutions

The Hague Conferences established the aforementioned PCA (known as the Hague Tribunal and the oldest legal institution for international dispute resolution) to make binding decisions on disputes between cooperating states, IGOs, and private parties. The idea of international arbitration was very popular in the United States in the early twentieth century; for example, President Theodore Roosevelt asked the court to settle a disagreement the United States had with Mexico. Although most of the cases it adjudicates involve boundaries between countries, some decisions involve international business disputes. In 2014, the court awarded $50 billion to shareholders of the Russian oil company Yukos, which had been seized by the Russian government. In 2016, it ruled in favor of the Philippines in a legal case regarding China's claim to control the disputed waters of the South China Sea. However, Russia and China refused to accept the court's decision. Other countries accept such legal decisions, like in the case of the 2006 territorial dispute between Barbados on the one hand and Trinidad and Tobago on the other.

In the nineteenth and early twentieth centuries, other international organizations were established to promote cooperation in technology, communication, and law enforcement. Among them were the International Telegraph Union (1865), the International Telecommunication Union (1865), and the Universal Postal Union (1874). The countries joining the Universal Postal Union

Ecuadorian police officers inspect a bird of prey. Interpol reported in spring 2018 that a giant operation against illegal trade in wildlife and timber resulted in millions of dollars-worth of seizures and the identification of fourteen hundred suspects across the world.

pledged to cooperate in setting prices and standards for delivering domestic and international mail. The International Criminal Police Commission, founded in 1923 in Austria following consultations with law enforcement professionals from several countries, was not a global police force. Nonetheless, *Interpol* (as the organization is called today, with headquarters in Lyon, France) has eased cross-border police cooperation to prevent and combat international crime. Both the Universal Postal Union and the International Telecommunication Union are now UN agencies, and Interpol has become one of the largest international organizations.

From the League of Nations to the United Nations

The League of Nations officially came into existence in January 1920. It was the first global organization, born out of practical calculations and idealist thinking. Its structure included the Council (its top executive body, with both permanent and nonpermanent members); the Assembly (which included all representatives); and the Secretariat (playing supporting and administrative functions). Autonomous but closely connected groups were the Permanent Court of International Justice and the International Labour Organization. The League also operated several committees and commissions on health, refugees, slavery, and other issues (Henig 2010). It had some success in taking care of refugees fleeing wars and revolutions, settling some international disputes, and fighting slavery. Unfortunately, the League's inability to stop several wars in Africa, Europe, and the Pacific undermined its authority; during World War II, the organization was replaced by the UN.

The term *United Nations* was coined by U.S. President Franklin D. Roosevelt. On January 1, 1942, representatives of twenty-six states signed the Declaration of the United Nations and pledged to continue fighting together against Nazi Germany, fascist Italy, and imperial Japan (Schlesinger 2003). Three years later, representatives of fifty countries met in San Francisco to draw up the UN Charter, which they signed on June 26, 1945; the organization officially came into existence on October 24. The UN Charter proclaimed the following goals and principles:

1. To maintain international peace and security [and] to take effective collective measures for the prevention and removal of threats to the peace, and for the suppression of acts of aggression;
2. To develop friendly relations among nations based on respect for the principle of equal rights and self-determination of peoples, and to take other appropriate measures to strengthen universal peace;

3. To achieve international co-operation in solving international problems of an economic, social, cultural, or humanitarian character, and in promoting and encouraging respect for human rights and for fundamental freedoms for all without distinction as to race, sex, language, or religion; and

4. To be a centre for harmonizing the actions of nations in the attainment of these common ends.

Membership in the UN was open to all states that accepted the charter. The first session of the General Assembly of the United Nations convened in March 1946 in London, with representatives of fifty-one states. Since 1952, the UN has been headquartered in New York City.

From the start, the UN's charter, decisions, agencies, and affiliated international organizations have been an important source of international law. Although the UN does not have legislative power to enact binding rules of international law and cannot force countries to change their domestic laws, its recommendations have been crucial to the development of international principles of human rights and their defense. It created the International Court of Justice (ICJ), located in The Hague, to resolve legal disagreements submitted by states. The court's role is "to settle legal disputes submitted to it by States and to give advisory opinions on legal questions deferred to it by authorized United Nations organs and specialized agencies."

Read more about the ICJ.

Check Your Knowledge

1. Explain the *freedom of the seas* principle of international relations.

2. What are crimes against humanity?

3. Why did the League of Nations fail?

4. What is the International Court of Justice?

6.3 Approaches to International Law

Historically and currently, there has been no shortage of discussions about international law, its functions and institutions, and, most importantly, its effectiveness. Here we examine some of the most important discussions and arguments.

The Realist View of International Law

The realist approach to international law makes several interconnected assumptions. First, sovereign states by definition have no higher authority over them—not even international law. Second, international law can regulate relations among states, but it should not undermine a sovereign country's core interests, including security. Finally, without proper enforcement, international law is simply ineffective (Morgenthau 1948/2006). Because this task cannot be granted to a global organization, individual countries and their coalitions should remain the guarantors of global security (see Figure 6-2).

The realist approach does not advocate lawlessness. It argues that the anarchical nature of today's global international system makes international law

FIGURE 6-2
The realist view of international law.

important but also difficult to implement. To be effective, international law should be considered in the context of each assumption.

SOVEREIGNTY

Imagine that the UN passes a resolution outlawing the death penalty in all countries. Do the sovereign states that recognize capital punishment have to follow this international law? Many countries are likely to dismiss this possibility because the UN has neither jurisdiction nor power to enforce such a resolution. Each state is bound only by those rules of international law to which it has consented (Vattel 1758/2001). For example, the United States has not signed the 1997 Mine Ban Treaty that aimed to eliminate anti-personnel land mines globally (neither have China, Russia, India, and several other states). Although the treaty was signed by more than 160 countries, the argument of both Democrat and Republican administrations has been that land mines are essential to protect U.S. soldiers in places such as the zone between North and South Korea.

In cases of aggression, the victim state is not obligated to consult with international law about how to respond. It has the right to defend itself and to seek help from others. Nor is a state required to protect other states unless a defense agreement exists. For example, the United States must defend Japan against aggression because of agreements these two countries have signed. In this case, international law becomes effective.

STATE INTEREST

Governments typically reject any international law that may undermine their interests or impose undesirable legal, financial, or other obligations. As previously mentioned, the United States pulled out of the Paris Agreement due to President Trump's claims that it is a pernicious threat to the American economy and sovereignty (Shear 2017). Realists believe that states have the right to choose their own policies toward international organizations, including the UN. The main provisions of certain international laws are ambiguous; they leave room for states to interpret them in a way that avoids conflict with opposition at home or from other states (Morgenthau 1978). Governments, as a rule, condemn violations of international law in a highly selective manner. When such breaches do not affect a country's national interest, they are routinely ignored. After the attacks of 9/11, the United States removed sanctions on high-tech exports to Pakistan. The same sanctions were also removed from India to avoid objection from Pakistan (Sathasivam 2005). In this example, we see how politics influenced international law. Back in the1990s, the development of nuclear weapons by Pakistan and India brought international condemnation and economic sanctions from many countries, including the United States. In 2001, the United States needed the help of Pakistan in dealing with terrorist groups in neighboring Afghanistan. Removing the sanctions from Pakistan alone would have angered India. Thus, the decision was made to remove the sanctions from both countries.

LAW ENFORCEMENT

International law can be enforced under certain conditions. One is the **international mandate**, legal permission to administer a territory or enforce international law. In the 1920s, France and Great Britain, the two most powerful members of the League of Nations at the time, established such mandates to rule over a vast area of the former Ottoman Empire. France took control of what is now Lebanon and Syria; and the United Kingdom took control of Iraq, Palestine, Israel, and Jordan. Under the assumption that the people of those

international mandate Legal permission to administer a territory or enforce international law.

History Lab | U.S. Involvement with the International Criminal Court

The International Criminal Court (ICC)—the first permanent international world court—was established in The Hague in 2002 to try individuals accused of war crimes, crimes against humanity, genocide, and aggression. The Clinton Administration signed the agreement to join the court in 2000 but, assuming it would not pass, did not submit it for Senate ratification. Under George W. Bush, the country cooperated in appropriate cases without joining officially. Obama's government established a working relationship with the Court but only as an observer, and it is highly unlikely that the Trump White House will change the course.

The 2002 *American Service Members' Protection Act* (ASPA) limited U.S. government support and assistance to the ICC because, according to this legislation, it does not sufficiently protect the constitutional rights of U.S. citizens working and serving abroad (Elsea 2006). The act also prohibits, with several exceptions, U.S. military aid to countries that are party to the ICC. Supporters of this policy argue that the court's jurisdiction could violate Americans' constitutional rights, including protection from double jeopardy, trial by a jury of one's peers, and confrontation of one's accuser. Critics maintain that the United States upholds double standards on international behavior: It advocates international criminal justice for others but refuses to subject its own officials and citizens to the same rules.

CRITICAL THINKING

❶ Should there be a uniform, global standard of justice that every country must follow? Why or why not? ❷ How would you, as president, reconcile the court's jurisdiction (the applicability of its decisions in other countries) with the Constitution of the United States? ❸ Is a compromise between the two possible? If so, what would it look like?

territories were not yet fully ready to govern themselves, the French and British governments declared the legal right to administrative advice and assistance. This system survived World War II, but almost all mandated territories have since become sovereign states.

These days, the UN issues international mandates for numerous reasons. Among them are peacekeeping operations, disarmament and demobilization of ex-combatants, assistance in the conduct of elections, support for the restoration and extension of state authority, and promotion of social and economic recovery and development (UN Peacekeeping 2018).

The Liberal View of International Law

The liberal tradition challenges realpolitik and focuses on the advantages and opportunities provided by international law. It makes three main arguments, and we'll look at each in turn. First, states, like individuals, are capable of managing their relations based on shared principles. Second, international institutions can play a bigger legal role in international affairs by applying the principles of extraterritoriality and supranationalism. Last but not least, a state's claims of a legal right to wage war should be limited, as well as a state's sovereignty to commit atrocities against its people (see Figure 6-3).

REASON AND SHARED PRINCIPLES

Liberalism argues that international law is not an artificial creation of lawyers and politicians; it addresses our common and compatible needs that cement the fabric of international relations. Interdependence, mutual consent, and legal obligations are the products of common reason backed by common law (Gruber 2000). For instance, the laws that regulate our lives do not rely on coercion alone. Most people observe domestic criminal laws not only because they are afraid of jails or expect retribution from their neighbors but also because they accept the law out of a sense of social duty, shared rules, and moral principles. Some citizens commit illegal acts and, if caught and convicted, pay penalties. Yet, in general, even laws that carry little threat of sanction for their violation are observed.

Simulation: UN Peacekeeping Mission

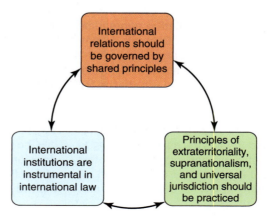

FIGURE 6-3
The liberal view of international law.

For similar reasons, states and international organizations tend to observe international law. Like domestic common law, international customary law is supported by daily, habitual, and voluntary transactions. International finance, trade, and commerce all work because they are based on rules without which the global economy could not function—especially given the growing complexity of global interdependence. International law thus becomes an increasingly practical alternative to local laws, which are enforceable only within a limited territory.

EXTRATERRITORIALITY AND SUPRANATIONALISM

If sovereign states exercise supreme authority within their territories, what legal argument can be made in support of international law? The liberal view invokes the principle of **extraterritoriality**, or exemption from the jurisdiction of local law. In the past, some foreign residents of certain areas were free from the authority of local courts. Merchants from Genoa and Venice who traveled to Istanbul were exempted by the Ottoman rulers from following the *Sharia*, or Islamic law. Similarly, many Americans lived in China back in the nineteenth and early twentieth centuries under a combination of U.S., European, and local ordinances (Scully 2001). Today, extraterritoriality applies to heads of states, diplomatic missions, and foreign military bases.

extraterritoriality
Exemption from the jurisdiction of local law.

Supporters of the liberal view further argue that, with the advancement of international organizations, ever-increasing travel, international commerce, and electronic communications, territoriality becomes increasingly difficult to enforce. The sheer necessities of our daily interactions will encourage states and businesses to turn to extraterritoriality.

Liberal theorists understand that lack of enforcement is a major weakness of international law. Therefore, they turn to **supranationalism**—the delegation of authority from sovereign states to international institutions or organizations. Supranationalism does not mean that states give up their sovereignty once and for all; they merely delegate some of it to an international institution that assumes the role of a supranational power (Close 2000). Such an institution can regulate international relations based on shared principles, which can be expanded or amended as needed. A **supranational organization** is a type of multistate political union to which member states willingly delegate some of their power and sovereignty. The EU is one of the most successful supranational organizations in history (Mak 2008). Several regional organizations—such as the African Union, the Caribbean Community, and the Cooperation Council for the Arab States of the Gulf—have the legal potential to become supranational organizations or a similar type of integrated institution.

supranationalism
The delegation of a degree of authority from sovereign states to international institutions or organizations.

supranational organization A type of multistate political union, in which member states willingly delegate some of their power and sovereignty.

The concept of supranationalism finds enthusiastic support and draws emotional criticisms. Critics have complained for some time that too many NGOs and IGOs, which are staffed by unelected officials, remain slow, expensive, and inefficient (Queenan 2013; Kissinger 2001). Moreover, supporters of conflict theory, including feminist scholars, mention that many NGOs promote an agenda set mostly by the educated upper class from Western countries. Lack of accountability of unelected professionals has always been a problem (Wapner 2002).

DEBATE > WHY CAN'T WE OUTLAW WAR?

Could the UN pass an international law to ban wars? Realists use history to argue that such a law would be ineffective unless it was enforced. In 1928, the Pact of Paris (or the Kellogg-Briand Pact) was signed by fifteen nations, including Canada, France, Germany, the United Kingdom, India, Japan, South Africa, and the United States. The agreement stated that war should be abolished forever as a means of resolving international conflicts; yet it remained without proper enforcement.

The U.S. Senate ratified the Pact but made it clear that the country would not be compelled to use force against others that violated it. In other words, Washington promised not to punish future aggressors; thus, aggressive wars could continue (Oppenheim 2008). After the treaty went into effect on July 24, 1929, the following occurred: Japan invaded Manchuria (1931), China (1937), and the United States (1941); Italy invaded Ethiopia (1935); Germany invaded Poland (1939) and Denmark, Norway, Belgium, the Netherlands, Luxembourg, and France and attacked Great Britain (1940); and the Soviet Union invaded Finland (1939). International law enforcement became, under the critical eye of realists, a serious problem (Hathaway and Shapiro, 2017).

Liberal theorists argue that, despite noticeable weaknesses, international law still "glues together" universal principles of international politics, provides agreements to ban wars, and articulates mutually shared interests. They note that fewer states have gone to war after 1945. Most countries, including former aggressors like Germany and Japan, began to regard war as illegitimate action and put serious legal restrictions on their armed forces and the action of their governments overseas. In the past seventy years, only a handful of states have annexed and held the territory of another sovereign state (Hathaway and Shapiro, 2017).

WHAT'S YOUR VIEW?

Let's assume that most UN countries, including the United States, China, and Russia agree to legally ban wars between states. Based on what you have read, argue in favor of one of these positions: **Ⓐ** The global legal ban on war not only is possible, but it will also be successfully implemented. Suggest several conditions under which this law would be effective. For example, which country or organization could be capable of enforcing this law and how? **Ⓑ** The global legal ban on war is only possible if the world agrees on a global government that has the means to enforce international law. Discuss whether such a government is possible, when, and under what conditions.

Read about earlier legal attempts to outlaw war.

universal jurisdiction
The principle that the perpetrators of certain crimes cannot escape justice by moving to another country and invoking its sovereign immunity.

Realism provides a strong argument against supranationalism: To be effective, a law must always be enforced. Unfortunately, in many cases, IGOs and NGOs rely on goodwill and the expectation that legal norms will be followed. Consider global nuclear policies, for example. The Nonproliferation Treaty has slowed the spread of nuclear weapons, but the UN has not stopped North Korean and Iranian nuclear programs (Pelligrini 2010).

UNIVERSAL JURISDICTION

The previously discussed arguments about human rights advanced the idea that international law allows interference with the affairs of states engaged in massive and systematic human rights violations. Liberalism presented the concept of **universal jurisdiction**: government officials and political leaders—even individuals with diplomatic immunity—who perpetrate heinous crimes against their own people should not escape justice when they leave their countries. Universal jurisdiction justifies their arrest and extradition. Although a country's government is typically not liable for crimes committed in its name, individuals such as politicians or military commanders who commit certain acts can be held personally liable. In the past, a similar concept, *hostes humani generis* ("enemies of the human race"), was applied to pirates, hijackers, or hostage takers operating outside any state's jurisdiction. In recent times, former Chilean dictator Augusto Pinochet, former head of Yugoslavia Slobodan Milošević, and former president of Sudan Omar al-Bashir have been legally charged for human rights violations they committed in their countries. We look at their cases and others at the end of this chapter, and we return more broadly to humanitarian issues in Chapter 10.

Critics of universal jurisdiction are skeptical that, without proper debate, judicial procedures will be ineffective in international politics. Of course, acts of genocide or other blatant human rights violations should not be left unpunished, but only when they are proven and carefully investigated. Otherwise, legal decisions may be motivated by politics or ideology. In other cases, some individuals and organizations may simply misinterpret international law because they are acting out of their own interests. Yet to others international law serves as a source to make some powerful people accountable for their actions (O'Sullivan 2017; Agier 2010). Moreover, some legal decisions or initiatives can be simply impractical.

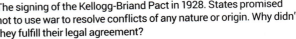

The signing of the Kellogg-Briand Pact in 1928. States promised not to use war to resolve conflicts of any nature or origin. Why didn't they fulfill their legal agreement?

Ousted Sudanese President Omar al-Bashir became the first sitting president to be indicted by the ICC. In 2009, he was charged with directing a campaign of mass killing, rape, and pillage against civilians in Darfur, Sudan.

THE LEGALITY OF WAR

Liberalism refers to the principles of just war as a means to limit violence in international affairs. These tenets state that, first, only sovereign states and legitimate authorities may pursue their strategic goals through war. Second, war is justified only when it is based on the principle of proportionality in the use of force and only against military objectives. Third, even states at war should respect humanitarian concerns for honesty and mercy (Lauterpacht 1933/2011). Liberalism also argues that wars could be significantly limited if sovereign states turned to international law principles to justify war. Countries may start wars in self-defense, but they may not use aggression, to which international law gives special attention.

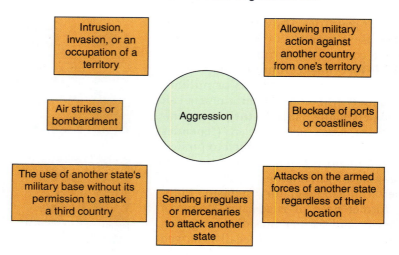

FIGURE 6-4
Aggression as defined by the UN.

There is little realistic possibility to rule out war once and for all. For example, states may use violence as their last resort or if they are under attack. Force is justified to restrain an aggressor or to stop systematic and deliberate violence, especially against ethnic or religious groups. Compelling legal arguments, however, are needed to sanction any military intervention. The Charter of the United Nations (Chapter VII) suggests three conditions necessary for the use of military force: threats to peace, breaches of the peace, or acts of aggression. In 1974, a UN special committee named seven offenses in this last category (see Figure 6-4). Military actions sanctioned by the UN are not considered aggressive acts.

Alternative Views of International Law

Supporters of other approaches to international law share some assumptions with the realist and liberal traditions. However, they pay most attention to specific factors and contexts in which international law functions.

IDEOLOGY AND LAW

States have their own expectations and create their own norms when it comes to international law. Revolutionary governments or radical movements usually reject the existing norms; their key goal is to change the system, not to uphold it. The leaders of the French Revolution (1789–1799) denounced the Westphalian *balance-of-power* system and sought to liberate Europe from royal tyranny in the name of universal rights. After the Russian Revolution in 1917, the Bolshevik government canceled all international treaties that the Russian Empire had signed.

Ideology and values are other important factors; driven by values, states can reject or embrace international agreements and organizations. For example, NATO members developed a common understanding of international law, based on respect for national sovereignty and plurality of opinions of what aggression is. This ideology cemented the alliance for many years (Schmidt 2001). Advocates of NATO insist that it has a greater goal than common defense: it supports a community of legal norms, based on shared values.

Constructivists also argue that the common values of social improvement and the desire to eliminate hunger and diseases and to stop genocide could serve as a foundation for an efficient international legal system. The challenge is to agree on such goals and their implementation.

PERCEPTIONS OF INTERNATIONAL LAW

A key argument of constructivism is that international law is based not only on shared values but also perceptions. Here constructivists turn to political psychology to interpret these factors (Reus-Smit 2009). For example, the UN gives a general definition of aggression, but leaders may interpret the term according to their own interests. Leaders often claim to initiate hostile actions as an act of self-defense, thereby hoping to avoid sanctions against them.

NATO's war in Kosovo (1998–1999)—in which a group of countries challenged Serbia's right to retain the former Yugoslavia's territories—illustrates the importance of perceptions in international law. In the eyes of Serbia, NATO countries were attacking its sovereignty within its legitimate borders. The public opinion and governments of most NATO members viewed the situation differently and rejected Serbia's explanations. They accused Serbia of aggression against the Albanians, who were the ethnic majority in Kosovo, and demanded that the Serbian army stay out of this region. When opposition from Russia and China prevented the UN Security Council from passing a resolution to approve international sanctions or military action against Serbia, NATO bombed it.

To justify the war, Washington claimed that Serbian officials had initiated a terror campaign against ethnic Albanians, and western air strikes were the only option to stop genocide (Ramet 2005). Serbia, Russia, and China sharply disagreed and claimed that subjective accusations of genocide should not have allowed international law to trample laws of sovereign states without a proper due process. In Russia's opinion, NATO fabricated a legal precedent: any groups of states could justify their aggression by humanitarian reasons.

What was the most important outcome of this conflict? Kosovo declared itself an independent state (protected by NATO troops) in 2008. Albanian forces drove thousands of ethnic Serbians out of the state. More than 110 countries, including the United States and Canada, had recognized Kosovo's independence by 2019. Yet scores of countries, among

South Ossetian separatist fighters rest during the Russian-Georgian War of 2008. Russia supported ethnic separatists and defeated Georgia, which wanted to rout them. This war raised serious tensions in the relations between Russia and NATO. Although international humanitarian law made significant progress, powerful states and groups pay only selective attention to violations.

them Russia, China, India, Iran, Iraq, Israel, Brazil and Argentina, did not recognize the new state. These events form just one dramatic example of different interpretations of and disputes over international law and universal jurisdiction.

Russian authorities explicitly used the Kosovo case as a legal precedent to justify war against neighboring Georgia in 2008. They claimed that they were protecting an endangered ethnic region of South Ossetia from Georgia's armed forces; later, they recognized South Ossetia and Abkhazia, another ethnic enclave of Georgia, as two sovereign territories. The United States and other NATO countries denounced this behavior as a violation of Georgia's sovereignty and argued that the two cases were different. The vast majority of countries did not recognize South Ossetia and Abkhazia as sovereign states.

CONFLICT THEORIES AND INTERNATIONAL LAW

Is international law a convenient instrument serving the interests of powerful social groups? Marxists contend that governments, corporations, banks, and

---

DEBATE > FROM KOSOVO TO THE RUSSIAN-UKRAINIAN CONFLICT

On February 21, 2014, Ukrainian president Viktor Yanukovych fled the capital city, Kiev, in the aftermath of violent unrest. Suddenly, the opposition was in power in Ukraine. A few days later, Russian armed units—they were without insignias, yet it was a generally accepted view that they were Russian troops—swiftly occupied strategic locations across Ukraine's Crimean Peninsula (Crimea), including airports, television stations, and the parliament buildings. A referendum on whether to join Russia was quickly held on March 16, and the voting results supported seceding. Two days later, Russian president Vladimir Putin signed a law making Crimea and the city of Sevastopol, a naval base located on the peninsula, part of the Russian Federation. The West denounced this move as an annexation of the territory of a sovereign country. To the West, this was a fundamental violation of international law, of treaties that Russia had signed with Ukraine, and of the Budapest memorandum of 1994, in which the United States, the United Kingdom, France, and Russia pledged to respect Ukraine's territorial integrity.

WHAT'S YOUR VIEW?

Russia insists that the unification of Crimea with Russia was perfectly legal and should not be called "annexation," which is the forcible takeover of another country's territory. Russia also insists that it was the will of the people that provided the legal foundation for the unification. Moreover, Russians compared the case of Crimea with the case of Kosovo, in which the people voted to secede from Yugoslavia. The West had supported this decision. Moscow also argued that after Yanukovych's flight from Kiev, there was not a legitimate government in Ukraine, so Russia was protecting the Russian-speaking minorities in Crimea against possible violence.

Most Western leaders, IGOs, NGOs, and independent observers disagreed. They declared the referendum invalid because of Russia's military pressure and because the referendum violated Ukraine's constitution. A wide range of international sanctions against Russia followed.

❶ As a lawyer, argue the case on behalf of Russia and on behalf of the United States, which opposes Moscow's position. ❷ As an independent legal observer, which position do you think appears stronger from the perspective of international law? Why? ❸ Which arguments not mentioned here could both sides use to strengthen their arguments? ❹ Could you suggest a legal compromise? Discuss its applicability today.

even big international organizations create legal rules that benefit mostly the rich (Miéville 2006). The entire international legal system is designed to maintain the economic and political superiority of a few West European and North American states at the expense of the rest of the world. For example, with the exception of China, all permanent members of the UN Security Council are nuclear states of Europe and North America.

Others insist that, deliberately or not, international law is consistently used to promote the interests of the privileged countries of Europe, North America, and Japan. The big powers support international law as long as it does not threaten the status quo or their superiority (Blanchard 1996). These states generally reject any attempt to give countries in South and Southeast Asia, Africa, and Latin America more influence. They are unwilling, for example, to reform the UN and other international organizations, and they often abuse the principle of universal jurisdiction to justify acts against less powerful states. In 1984, the ICJ ruled that the United States violated international law by waging an armed rebellion against the Nicaraguan government and by mining the country's harbors. Washington used its veto power in the UN Security Council to block the enforcement of this decision (Schulte 2005).

From the feminist perspective, gender relations are an integral part of international politics and international law (True 2009). Historically, the latter was based on an exclusively masculine perspective focusing on power, the use of force, and ultimately war. Women's expectations and values were commonly excluded, or their importance was diminished, in early legal agreements among states. In the past century, some progress was made in promoting legal foundations for gender equality, civil rights, and humanitarian issues. The law specifically protects women as victims of violence during ethnic and social conflicts. However, international law does not go far enough in protecting the rights of women globally. Segregation, sex exploitation, slavery, and systematic abuse continue. In many countries, women are routinely denied the same legal protection that men receive. Often these violations are explained as cultural traditions, and the extraterritoriality principle of international law is ignored (Chappel 2008). Feminist scholars underline the importance of extraterritoriality in support of *care ethics* in international relations, which focuses on everyone's responsibility for the suffering of human beings and, to a lesser degree, for all issues related to state sovereignty and power.

Read "South Ossetia is not Kosovo" (The *Economist*)

Check Your Knowledge

1. How can the principle of universal jurisdiction be applied to you personally? Under what conditions?

2. Why has the United States not joined the ICC?

3. Have there been any legal attempts to ban war globally? If so, name one.

4. Explain universal jurisdiction. Give one example.

5. Why are perceptions of international law important in international relations?

6. What were the most significant outcomes of the Kosovo conflict in relation to international law?

7. What other contemporary examples—comparable to the Kosovo case—could you suggest to discuss? Suggest these topics to your professor.

8. What is care ethics in international relations? In which cases does the international community fail in relation to care ethics?

6.4 Applications of International Law

Passionate critics of international law often suggest that it is too complicated and impossible to implement. Enthusiastic supporters of it counter that in today's world, international law is the most effective solution to problems big and small. Whose arguments appear stronger? Let's consider practical applications of international law.

Individual Choices

It takes individual leaders to initiate, interpret, and enforce international law. They often see, from their personal view, the ways to apply international law to their countries' foreign policy. In the past, neither realism nor liberalism paid enough attention to the role of individuals. Constructivism provides important insights here.

autocratic rulers Leaders who use unrestrained power and who follow international and domestic law only if it suits them.

The political authority that leaders exercise at home often shapes their attitudes about international law, treaties, and bilateral agreements. **Autocratic rulers**, who claim unrestrained power, typically follow international and domestic law only when it suits them. They often refer to their country's mission (the way they define it), religion, or ideology to justify their foreign policy. Mobutu Sese Seko, the ruler of Zaire (today part of the Congo) from 1965 to 1997, declared that "democracy is not for Africa." He also rejected democratic principles of government at home, allowed his associates to violate business agreements with foreign companies, illegally redistributed the resources of foreign companies, and imprisoned opponents without a trial (Wrong 2002). Modern autocratic rulers, like those in Russia or China in the second decade of our century, tend to adjust their behavior to current political conditions. These leaders use various seemingly democratic mechanisms to enhance their grip on power. They allow certain freedoms in their countries, such as in selected business and trade areas, yet restrict others, such as in civil liberties. They remain in absolute control of their foreign policy.

tyrant A ruler who uses unlimited power to oppress the people in his or her country or its foreign possessions.

An extreme form of autocratic ruler is a **tyrant**—another word for a dictator. Like Hitler and Stalin, tyrants are not constrained by laws, not even the ones they impose. They use unlimited power to oppress the people of their own country or its foreign possessions (Wallechinsky 2006). These examples suggest a major weakness of international law: Many autocratic rulers in the past simply ignored international agreements and global conventions, especially when it came to political freedoms and human rights (Burt 2010).

democratic leaders Leaders who treat the letter and spirit of the law as the core of their domestic and, in most circumstances, foreign policy.

Democratic leaders, by contrast, tend to pursue their policies within the framework of domestic and international law. Their behavior thus provides support for democratic peace theory and the liberal approach to international relations. However, contemporary developments in many countries present a significant challenge to this view. Some authoritarian leaders, as we mentioned earlier, by claiming that they support free elections, allow only limited civic freedoms in their countries. Other leaders make a travesty of elections and democratic procedures at home, creating a "hybrid" regime that combines democratic legitimacy with authoritarian practices. In their foreign policy, they are likely to treat international law arbitrarily, according to little more than immediate interests (Singh 2010). Some leaders may use authoritarian means domestically but respect international law, as happened in Egypt in 2013, when the military dismissed the country's elected president.

State Policies

Realists argue, most often correctly, that states treat international law in the context of domestic politics, policy, and security strategies. For example, South Africa, Israel, India, and Pakistan refused to sign a nonproliferation treaty, and North Korea withdrew from it, mostly because it would have placed legal restrictions on their development of nuclear weapons. In another case,

North Korean leader Kim Jong-un remains the single most important decision maker in North Korea. He has the power to interpret international law any way he pleases.

Article 2(4) of the UN Charter tells all states to refrain from using force that violates the territorial integrity or political independence of another country. Two exceptions exist: the UN Security Council's authorization and self-defense. However, the last seventy years show that democratic governments did not necessarily follow this clause but turned to Article 1, which allows the prevention and removal of threats to the peace (Loyola 2010). In other words, countries often choose legal uncertainties and contradictions to justify their policies, including war.

Governments also tend to put their domestic political interests first. For example, the U.S. president or secretary of state may not enter into Congress-binding obligations to other nations. The legislature's constitutional powers cannot be given away to other government branches, and Congress may or may not ratify a treaty. Since the Jay Treaty (named after Chief Justice John Jay) of 1795, a treaty requires a two-thirds vote in the U.S. Senate. The legal rules are a bit easier for trade deals; *executive agreements* need only a majority vote in both houses of Congress. Sometimes, when opposition in the legislature is strong, the executive branch does not want to engage in a political battle. The Clinton Administration did not push for ratification of the 1997 Kyoto Protocol to fight global gas emissions. In 2015, Obama refrained from sending Congress the Trans-Pacific Partnership (TPP)—a massive trade pact involving Australia, Brunei, Canada, Chile, Japan, Malaysia, Mexico, New Zealand, Peru, Singapore, the United States, and Vietnam. In 2017, President Trump withdrew the United States' signature from the agreement. But even after Congress ratifies an international treaty, the legislature can legally render it partially ineffective by not allocating funds or by attaching restrictions on how funds are to be used (Grimmett 1999).

Presidents may also reconsider their position on international law under pressure from Congress or constituencies. In 1993, President Clinton pledged to link trade to China's policies toward human rights, in compliance with the

Consult The *Economist*'s current Democracy Index.

U.S. Trade Act. However, he turned away from his pledge as opposition grew, thanks to growing profits from trade and investments and increasing consumer reliance on inexpensive goods manufactured in China. Similarly, ideas about revisiting the country's trade agreements with the Pacific area countries and with Europe also found domestic opposition because, as critics claim, such revisions can hurt long-term American interests: some new deals may preserve some local jobs but can push domestic consumer prices up.

Conflicts can also arise between U.S. and international law. We have already reviewed Washington's reluctance (by both Democrat and Republican administrations) to fully participate in the ICC. Some U.S. federal laws may be inconsistent with international laws. For example, Section 201 of the 1974 Trade Act states that the president may impose temporary trade barriers if an increase in imports would hurt domestic industry. Such actions may violate the rules of the World Trade Organization prohibiting trade barriers. From time to time, however, because of powerful lobbies, public opinion, and the need to get the votes of manufacturing workers, presidents impose trade barriers to help certain domestic industries. For example, Presidents Bush and Obama imposed tariffs against foreign businesses on certain occasions. In 2018, President Trump announced steep tariffs on imports of washing machines and solar energy cells and panels, as well as on steel and aluminum (to safeguard American jobs in the face of cheaper foreign products). In these and other cases, international law is pushed aside to pursue domestic goals. It should take more than a few years to estimate the economic and political consequences of such policies.

At other times, conflict with U.S. law may mean that a treaty's ratification is postponed indefinitely (Moravcsik 2001). Congress did not ratify the American Convention on Human Rights, signed by President Carter in 1978, because it violated federal and state laws by placing serious restrictions on abortion rights and implementation of the death penalty. Even existing agreements may be reconsidered. For example, the Optional Protocol to the Vienna Convention on Consular Relations lets the ICJ make the final decision when citizens have been illegally detained abroad. The United States initially backed the measure as a means to protect its own citizens overseas. It successfully sued Iran for taking fifty-two hostages from the embassy in Tehran in 1979. But the United States withdrew from the accord in 2005 after some countries that had abolished capital punishment successfully complained before the ICJ that their citizens were sentenced to death in the United States. The U.S. State Department argued that international law might interfere with domestic criminal law (Jordan 2005).

Finally, some agreements are signed but later rejected for apparent irrelevance or ambiguity. The United Nations' Convention on the Elimination of All Forms of Discrimination Against Women (1981) disallows all forms of exploitation of women and girls; it also guarantees equal access to education, employment, and health care. The Senate has held hearings on this agreement several times since 1980 but failed each time to bring the treaty to a vote (Baldez 2013). Why didn't the United States ratify this treaty? Both Republican and Democratic administrations argued that U.S. law already protects against

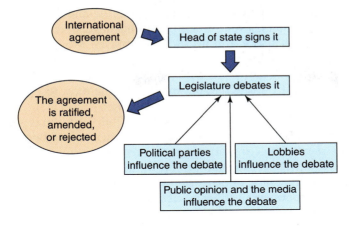

FIGURE 6-5 How domestic factors can affect international treaties. In most democratic countries, international agreements signed by executive leaders must be approved (ratified) by the legislation. Influenced by political, economic, and other interests, legislators may approve, amend, or reject treaties.

discrimination, whereas women in other countries have little or no legal protection. Empty statements without proper global enforcement are useless and often counterproductive (Kirkpatrick 2002). Signing the treaty would not have prevented many countries from violating the most basic of women's rights (see Figure 6-5).

Global Factors

How does international law apply globally? For centuries, it was instrumental in economic exchanges between states, organizations, and individuals. (We return to global economic issues in the next chapter.) International agreements have settled many territorial disputes and probably prevented many wars. The laws of war—especially those dealing with the humane treatment of civilians, captured or wounded soldiers, and nonmilitary personnel—have saved millions of lives. Today's accords protect travel, property, family rights, due process, and the well-being of many around the world. Studies show that, under the right conditions, international law is more powerful than military action in bringing stability, order, and peaceful change (Shaw 2017; Huth, Croco, and Appel 2011).

International law concerning genocide and war crimes also gained importance. The creation of the International Criminal Tribunal for the former Yugoslavia (ICTY) in 1993 in The Hague was a remarkable event. The idea came from German foreign minister Klaus Kinkel, and Resolution 827 of the UN Security Council created the institution. The court has jurisdiction over certain crimes committed in the territory of Croatia, Bosnia, and Herzegovina, which were parts of the disintegrated Yugoslav state after 1991.

The ICTY served as a model for a similar court—the International Criminal Tribunal for Rwanda (ICTR). It was created in 1994 by the UN Security Council (Resolution 955) to prosecute those responsible for the mass killings and violence during Rwanda's civil war. Because the continuing tensions in Rwanda make fair decisions based on domestic law almost impossible, it was imperative to apply international law under the watch of the ICTR.

Although critics complain about the high cost and bureaucratic inefficiency of international courts, these institutions have given many victims an opportunity to seek justice and get global publicity. Most governments and millions of people around the world support the courts' work and consider them legitimate. Carla del Ponte, a former Swiss attorney general who served as prosecutor for ICTY and ICTR, became one of the most recognized and respected lawyers in the world.

The success of international law should not hide its failures and excesses. The League of Nations was a failure. Wars and atrocities still take place. Many international laws protecting human rights remain little more than declarations. Some countries argue that human rights violations just give the West a legal excuse to intervene in other states' domestic affairs (as we will discuss in Chapter 10). Opponents of "big government" at home claim that the world does not need global legal restrictions on communications and business.

At the same time, the complexity of today's world requires greater coordination among states and international organizations. The past twenty years have shown that urgent environmental issues, global poverty, and natural disasters demand responses from across the global community. So does worldwide financial instability, as demonstrated by the global financial crisis of 2008–2011, the effects of which were felt for many years afterward. It should be imperative to hold global financial actors accountable to certain international rules. Finally, state bureaucracies remain corrupt and inefficient. These and other trends will almost certainly require strengthening and expanding international law, which also highlights the importance of NGOs and international organizations in a growing number of global issues.

Supporters of supranationalism point to the EU and **East African Community (EAC)** as successful examples of international law expansion. In 2000, Tanzania, Uganda, Burundi, Kenya, and Rwanda (South Sudan joined them in 2016) formed this economic and political union, with the goal of establishing a common market for goods, labor, and capital and one unified federation by 2023. Although a similar plan collapsed in the 1970s, steps thus far suggest that these countries are on the path to achieve their objective. Most importantly, the EAC could show that the participating countries accept binding legal rules; put aside religious, tribal, and political differences; and move toward a common strategic goal of stability, peace, and prosperity.

Not everyone is in favor of expanding international law. One serious argument is based on the view that people need transparency and accountability from their elected officials—which is difficult to expect from anonymous bureaucrats in a hypothetical "global government" (Acemoglu and Robinson 2013). Another argument against expanding international law comes from a growing number of critics of globalization. They contend that any global law would primarily benefit mostly wealthy countries and big international corporations. This criticism is supported by an increasing global gap between rich and poor countries—despite the economic progress achieved by most countries in the twenty-first century. Critics also argue that liberal laws of the Western type are frequently forced on other countries, often against their will and with counterproductive economic and political results.

Read about Carla del Ponte, a prosecutor for ICTY and ICTR.

East African Community (EAC)
An economic and political union between Tanzania, Uganda, Burundi, Kenya, South Sudan, and Rwanda.

History Lab   Rwanda and Belgium Law

A 1993 Belgian war crimes law aimed to protect civilians in time of war by relying on universal jurisdiction. This law allowed anyone to bring war crime charges to court, regardless of the country where the alleged crimes occurred or the citizenship of the accused or accuser. A local magistrate was required to investigate in order to determine whether further action was warranted.

The law was first put to use after the mass slaughter in Rwanda, a former Belgian colony. Eric Gillet, a prominent human rights lawyer, accused several Rwandans living in Belgium of war crimes. Soon cases were filed against several world leaders of the period, including Cuba's Fidel Castro, Israel's Ariel Sharon, Iraq's Saddam Hussein, the Congo's Laurent Kabila and his foreign minister, Iran's Ali Akbar Hashemi Rafsanjani, Palestine's Yasser Arafat, and America's George H.W. Bush, as well as several Guatemalan generals. Suits were also filed against international oil companies accused of connections with the military rulers of Burma. Altogether, according to the Belgian justice ministry, more than thirty complaints were on file.

Things rapidly took an absurd turn. One British citizen arrived at the Belgian embassy claiming that the BBC was trying to assassinate him. In an attempt to avoid a serious diplomatic crisis and stop frivolous suits, the Belgian government dismissed the law.

CRITICAL THINKING

Supporters claimed that this law was a brave attempt to help war crime victims facing no legal remedy or dealing with obstacles and bureaucratic delays in other courts. Critics insisted that it was an attempt to ignore state sovereignty and become a venue for ideological show trials with little legal consequence. What political and legal measures could prevent similar misuses of international legal rulings? Considering this case, would you have imposed high application fees for the plaintiffs to eliminate many frivolous lawsuits? Would you narrow down the definition of a war crime? Discuss these and other possibilities.

Some even claim that human rights violations can be used as an excuse to wage aggressive wars (Bricmont 2006; Walt 2018).

In fact, international law has been under pressure since the second decade of the twenty-first century. The idea that national governments, and only they, should figure out what is better for their citizens—in terms of their economic prosperity, and the civil and individual rights of their citizens—has gained strength. Whereas in the United States the focus of attention has been mostly on the economic gains related to international trade agreements, in countries such as Russia, China, and Iran, the argument has focused on the necessity of suppressing many political and individual freedoms. All in all, international law cannot be ordained. To be lasting, it should be accepted as just. It is up to us, the people.

Check Your Knowledge

1. How do authoritarian leaders tend to regard international law?

2. What are the two exceptions to Article 2(4) of the UN Charter? Explain why you agree or disagree with them.

3. What is the ICTY's purpose?

4. Does international law apply similarly to wealthy and poor countries? Explain your answer.

The Legacy of the Nuremberg Trials

Background

Attempts to use international law to stop genocide and limit the deadly effects of war began more than one hundred years ago. These early efforts were ineffective and frustrating from the start. The most significant change took place at the end of World War II.

During World War II, Germany, Japan, as well as their enemies targeted civilians on a scale unprecedented in modern times. *The Holocaust* (in Hebrew, *Shoah*), which was the deliberate extermination of the Jews and other groups by Germany's Nazi government, is one of the most profound cases of genocide in history. The Japanese government massacred tens of thousands of civilians in China and was responsible for widespread rape and torture in Nanking in 1937. Soviet authorities deported millions from the annexed territories in the Baltic region and Poland in 1939, along with large ethnic groups living in the Crimea and Caucasus in 1944. The German invasion of the Soviet Union that began in June 1941 quickly turned into a genocidal war, in which hundreds of thousands of people of various ethnic groups were killed. Small states in wartime Yugoslavia also practiced genocide against civilians. British and American carpet bombing of German and Japanese cities and the nuclear attacks on Hiroshima and Nagasaki in 1945 were clear violations of the Hague Conventions. The British-American massive bombing campaign aimed at causing unacceptable damage to Germany and Japan, thereby forcing unconditional surrender (Hitchcock 2008).

After several meetings, the leaders of the United States, the USSR, and the United Kingdom (the "Big Three") agreed to hold the political and military leaders of Nazi Germany and imperial Japan responsible for crimes against humanity. But how could the government of a sovereign state be put on trial? The London Charter, announced on August 8, 1945, provided the legal arguments: the German government had lost its political authority, and the Allied states had the right to establish a special court to apply the laws of war against it. This court would have jurisdiction only over crimes that took place after 1939. Legally, the Charter followed up on the decisions of the 1907 Hague Conference. It became the grounds for the Nuremberg trials against Nazi criminals in 1946, with German political leaders charged on four counts:

- *Conspiracy to wage aggressive war*—a premeditated plan to commit war crimes.
- *Crimes against peace*—wars of aggression in violation of international law.
- *War crimes*—profound violations of the laws of war, including mistreatment of prisoners of war and slave labor.
- *Crimes against humanity*—actions in concentration camps and on occupied territories in Europe.

Judges were appointed, defense lawyers hired, and witnesses called. After testimonies and deliberations, the court handed death sentences to eleven top German officials. Two others were acquitted, while the rest received long prison sentences.

Analysis

The Nuremberg tribunals had a profound and lasting influence on international law. Similar trials were held in Japan, China, Australia, the Philippines, and other countries. For example, the 1946 International Military Tribunal for the Far East (also known as the Tokyo Trials) sentenced seven former top Japanese officials responsible for genocide to death and seventeen more to lengthy prison terms. In China, thirteen separate trials were held; over 500 defendants were convicted, 149 of whom were executed. Gradually, expanded definitions of war crimes were accepted, and agreements to implement them were signed. The UN adopted the Convention on the Prevention and Punishment of the Crime of Genocide (General Assembly Resolution 260) in 1948.

Nuremberg also initiated a series of developments to establish a permanent international criminal court (which took almost fifty years) and served as a precedent for UN guidelines regarding war crimes. For example, if a country's laws do not impose penalties for war crimes, the state's head of state, officials, and citizens can be prosecuted under international law.

Critics of the Nuremberg trials introduced cautionary arguments against what it is known as *victor's justice*—a winning side's practice of applying its own rules to judge what is right or wrong. For example, during the Nuremberg trials, the Soviet Union used falsified documents to accuse the Nazis of massacring twenty thousand Polish officers in the Katyn Forest in Russia. This crime, as the Russian government acknowledged many years later, was in fact committed on Stalin's order by the Soviet secret police (Sanford 2009). The Soviets' own acts of mass killings and mass deportations were not so much as mentioned during the Nuremberg trials. Moscow literally got away with murder because it was powerful and victorious.

Realists have also been skeptical about the effectiveness of international law because it is difficult to enforce. Yet they supported the precedent created by the Nuremberg trials because these were initiated and enforced by powerful states. Realists believe that to support legal rulings, the decisive use of force is necessary to bring potential war criminals to international justice. It took NATO's massive military campaign against Yugoslavia, including the bombing of cities, to put former president Milošević on trial. And al-Bashir, even under formal indictment from the ICC, could travel outside his country because nobody used force to bring him to trial.

Advocates of liberalism and many influential NGOs have long demanded greater enforcement of international law, including the arrest and prosecution of state leaders who commit war crimes or similar acts. These demands gained momentum in the early 1990s, with support from many states and international organizations (including the UN), and practical steps followed. In less than a decade, the ICTY indicted 161 individuals and sentenced 64. One was Slobodan Milošević, the former leader of Yugoslavia, who was charged with sixty-six counts of genocide, crimes against humanity, and war crimes in Croatia, Bosnia and Herzegovina, and Kosovo between 1991 and 1999. The trial lasted four years, and Milošević died in jail in 2006. Two other defendants have died while serving their sentences.

The court also focused on atrocities committed by leaders of the paramilitary Bosnian Serbs in Bosnia—including those accused of killings, torture,

Nazi leaders on trial in Nuremberg, Germany, in 1945.

Current cases at the ICC

and running concentration camps. After many years in hiding, the commanders Radovan Karadžić, Ratko Mladić, and Goran Hadžić were extradited to the Netherlands and brought before the court. Karadžić was sentenced to forty years of imprisonment, Mladić received a life sentence, and Hadžić died before being convicted. At the same time, the ICTR, now located in Arusha, Tanzania, finished fifty trials and convicted twenty-nine persons accused of war crimes and crimes against humanity. More trials are in progress.

In 1998, 120 countries adopted the Rome Statute, the legal basis for establishing the ICC, a permanent institution that "shall have the power to exercise its jurisdiction over persons for the most serious crimes of international concern." In 2009, the ICC brought charges against the president of Sudan, Omar al-Bashir, for crimes against humanity, war crimes, and genocide. In theory, whenever al-Bashir visited another country, he could be arrested and brought to The Hague for justice. In practice, several countries (China, Nigeria, Saudi Arabia, and several others) have ignored the court's decisions. Two years later, the court brought charges against six officials from Kenya over their alleged involvement in the 2007–2008 electoral violence in that country. Some charges were later dropped, but others were sustained. In 2018, the court opened a preliminary investigation into the Venezuelan government's deadly response to anti-regime protests.

The Nuremberg trials have not only led to more than sixty years of international agreements, but they also serve as a model for trials based on the principles of extraterritoriality and universal justice. They also give hope that fundamental rights will be protected and justice will, eventually, be served.

Case Study Questions

1. What would you do to make sure that international tribunals maintain the democratic standard of protection for the individual? In democratic societies, for example, a defendant is not a criminal until he or she is convicted in a court of law.
2. Are international tribunals truly impartial? International courts, critics fear, can easily become a stage for *victor's justice*—in which a victorious country applies one set of rules to judge its own actions and another to the defeated enemy. How can the international community ensure that tribunals are not used to settle political scores?
3. Would it be beneficial to discuss, design, and enforce a new international code of laws instead of relying on legal precedents from the past? Explain your answer.

CHAPTER 6 REVIEW International Law

6.1 Explain the nature, principles, and sources of international law.

International law refers to principles, rules, and agreements that regulate the behavior of states and other international actors. Territoriality and jurisdiction principles define how far laws can reach. Treaties, customary law, general principles of law, and rulings by international organizations and courts are sources of international law.

Q: What are the main limitations of international law?

6.2 Describe the evolution of international law and international organizations.

The Treaty of Westphalia established an early foundation of international law in Europe in 1648. The laws of the sea handled competition, the safety of shipments, and financial disputes, while the laws of war dealt with common principles that states should follow in case of an armed conflict. Early international legal institutions and organizations dealt with humanitarian issues and disputes among states.

Q: Why did Nazi Germany and Imperial Japan withdraw from the League of Nations?

Q: Discuss the possible consequences if the United States were to withdraw from the UN.

6.3 Outline the principal differences among various views and approaches to international law.

The *realist view* contends that international law should not undermine a sovereign state's key interests and that, without proper enforcement, international law is ineffective.

The *liberal view* argues that interdependence, consent, and legal norms and obligations are crucial in international relations. Their evolving principles are supranationalism, universal jurisdiction, and extraterritoriality.

According to *constructivism*, historical and socioeconomic conditions, values, and identities determine countries' perceptions of international law and corresponding actions.

Conflict theory holds that international law serves the interests of dominant states and wealthy groups, at the expense of the oppressed.

Q: Compare and contrast the realist and liberal views of international law.

Q: Give arguments for and against universal jurisdiction.

Q: Suggest examples of extraterritoriality that you find useful and acceptable.

6.4 Critically apply key principles of international law to individual decisions, state policies, and global developments.

Leaders' choices strengthen or weaken international law. States treat international law in the context of domestic politics, policy, and security strategies. Most states have a strong and lasting interest in developing and maintaining international legal norms.

Q: Give a recent example of a state being penalized for abrogating international law.

Q: Explain the reasons why the U.S. government sometimes refuses to abide by international law.

KEY TERMS

aggression 195
autocratic rulers 212
customary law 195
democratic leaders 212
East African Community (EAC) 216
extraterritoriality 205
freedom of the seas 196

general principles of law 195
genocide 199
human rights 198
international law 191
international mandate 203
international treaties 194
international waters 196
jurisdiction 193

just war 196
laws of war 197
neutrality 197
sources of international law 194
supranationalism 205
tyrant 212
universal jurisdiction 206

International Political Economy and Development

> *Practical men, who believe themselves to be quite exempt from any intellectual influence, are usually the slaves of some defunct economist.*

—JOHN MAYNARD KEYNES

Even as economies began to revive in Europe after World War II, unemployment remained widespread. Citizens lacked food, fuel, and clothing. In France and Italy, the threat of Communist coups grew. Chaos and insecurity reigned from Poland to Greece.

In June 1947, U.S. Secretary of State George Marshall announced an assistance program for Europe that became known as the Marshall Plan. The following year, Congress approved the first $5 billion in aid. By 1951, the United States had spent $12.3 billion (equivalent to about $120 billion today) in sixteen countries (Hitchcock 2010).

The Marshall Plan's ultimate goal for this economic aid was to create stability and thereby prevent Communism from spreading throughout Western Europe. The program also benefited the U.S. economy, as Europeans with more money began to purchase American equipment, spare parts, technologies, and know-how, which created hundreds of thousands of U.S. jobs. Furthermore, the Plan helped resurrect European liberal democracy, which had been threatened by hunger, instability, and political radicalism. It pulled Western Europe into the U.S. financial, trade, and political orbits and initiated a host of institutions that shaped the modern West (Hitchcock 2010).

Are the lessons of the Marshall Plan still relevant? Could today's economic powers take similar action for countries in need? In the 1940s, European countries received American funding with only one condition: keep Communists away from power. Now, however, assistance from the International Monetary Fund (IMF) comes with many strings attached. For example, mandates include reducing government regulations, tightening budgets, and making financial systems transparent. Should countries

Previous page: An electric BMW i3 during the start of production in Leipzig, Germany. The i3 was the first electric car put into high-volume production by BMW. The German automobile industry benefited from the liberal system of trade after World War II. Which countries and what groups of people, in your view, did not benefit from globalization and free trade in the twenty-first century?

strictly follow such guidelines or have more freedom in decid-ing how to spend the funds? Consider the case of China, which became one of the world's top two economies without receiving massive financial assistance, but instead combined private entre-preneurship with state controls. (See the Case Study on p. 251.)

In this chapter, we discuss the economic and financial as-pects of international relations. We consider the influence of eco-nomic interests on foreign policy agendas; the impact of states and their policies on international economy, finances, and trade; the opportunities and challenges of global economic interdepen-dence; and the economic divide between the world's most and least developed countries.

7.1 Explain the major factors of international political economy.

7.2 Outline the principles of mercantilism.

7.3 Explain economic liberalism and its role in the development of the international political economy.

7.4 Describe constructivism and conflict theories in the context of international economic policies.

7.5 Explain why Marxism and conflict theories criticize the global economic structure.

7.6 Critically apply major economic views to realities of international relations at three levels of analysis.

Learning Objectives

7.1 Elements of International Political Economy

International political economy (IPE) is the study of how politics and economics interact in an international context. This subfield grew rapidly following the Cold War, which demonstrated that economic and financial policies can significantly affect global stability. Due to globalization, the financial or economic failure of one state can have profound international con-sequences, as in the global financial crisis of 2007–2008. Moreover, a powerful anti-globalization wave has now gained strength in many prosperous coun-tries. Its supporters argue that free trade and interdependency carry harmful socioeconomic consequences. This chapter will examine these claims.

international political economy (IPE) The study of how politics and economics interact in an international context.

How do state economic policies affect international relations? Which economic models have been most successful in today's global economy, and why? If economic prosperity is a crucial factor of international peace, how is it achieved? To answer these and other questions, political economists analyze such activities as production, consumption, finances, and trade.

Production and Consumption

production The process of creating goods and services with market value.

Economic **production** is the creation of goods and services with market value. For centuries, states accumulated resources and territories to enhance their power. They also controlled, funded, or regulated their productive capacities—from gold mines and oil wells to factories and trade companies. In the modern world, a state's power is measured by its **gross domestic product (GDP)**, the monetary value of the goods and services produced at a given time. (See Figure 7-1.) Although the distribution of economic and resource opportunities is not equal, many countries with few resources have implemented successful economic policies, thus boosting their GDP. Plenty of countries with vast resources, however, continue to struggle economically and financially.

gross domestic product (GDP) The total market value of all the goods and services produced within a nation's borders during a specified period.

In the twenty-first century, more production is shifting from older economic powers (the United States, Japan, and Western Europe) to emerging markets (China, India, Brazil, Malaysia, and Chile). These latter countries have substantially increased their share of global manufacturing, primarily through lower wages. Emerging markets reached nearly half of global retail sales ten years ago, and their share was growing (Woodall 2011). However, this growth has been slowing down.

consumption The selection, adoption, use, disposal, and recycling of goods and services.

A country's power is also determined by its scale of **consumption**—its selection, adoption, use, disposal, and recycling of goods and services. Consumption patterns affect *imports*, or the products and services a state purchases abroad. For example, the United States is the third largest crude oil producer in the world. However, about 50 percent of its consumed oil came from other countries for most of the 2000s. This dependency on foreign oil is in sharp decline now, thanks to innovative oil explorations on U.S. territory.

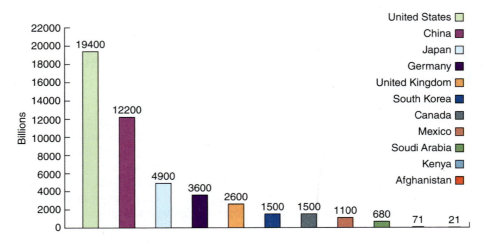

FIGURE 7-1 GDPs of Selected States, 2018 Source: World Bank 2018.

In recent years, more attention has been paid to *waste* and *pollution*—the byproducts of consumption that have become global problems. China still lags behind major developed countries in consumption, but its industries are major polluters (Economy and Levi 2014; Economy 2010b).

Finances

Historically, a state's financial resources, or *finances*, consisted of gold reserves stored in well-protected places (e.g., Fort Knox in the United States). The more gold a country had, the more power it was thought to possess. These days, finances most often mean the value of stocks and bonds traded on markets, and financial wealth is measured in paper notes or more complex indicators, tracked electronically and immediately. World finances are now so complicated that no state can manage or regulate them alone.

For centuries, states sought to control and augment their finances. Wealthy states could pay for a large military force and lend money to other states in exchange for political favors and loyalty. Great Britain dominated the world financial system in the nineteenth and early twentieth centuries, but it lost much of its wealth during World War II and dismantled its vast empire shortly after. The United States assumed the dominant financial role in the 1940s and remains the world's wealthiest nation by many standards. However, U.S. expenses have surpassed revenues over the last decade, and its dollar now somewhat depends on the financial backing of China. Meanwhile, China has been steadily accumulating U.S. treasury securities for decades and holds approximately $3 billion in U.S. currency reserves. This debt is theoretically beneficial for both countries: China gets the biggest national market for its products, and Americans enjoy the relatively low prices of Chinese goods (Seth 2018). However, domestic factors can influence a country's foreign policy, seriously affecting international trade and finances.

A currency trader watches monitors at the KEB Hana Bank's foreign exchange dealing room in Seoul, South Korea, in 2018.

currency A system of money in general use in a particular country.

National **currencies**—for example, dollars, euros, yuan, pesos, and rubles—can be converted into other currencies at an *exchange rate*. For centuries, the gold standard was the main mechanism of regulating exchange rates between currencies. National money, especially paper money, was exchanged for its corresponding value in gold, one of the world's most durable and precious metals. The gold standard ensured trade stability during the so-called first globalization of the nineteenth and early twentieth centuries, when the British pound was the world currency denominated in gold. The collapse of this system in the 1930s contributed to the formation of separate trade blocs and further reduction of world trade during the Great Depression. The **Bretton Woods system**, developed at a 1944 United Nations Monetary and Financial conference, aimed to restore the gold standard, and the U.S. dollar became fixed to the price of gold from 1945 to 1971. (In Section 7.3, we will explore the institutions created as a result of this conference.)

Bretton Woods system The financial system established in 1944 by UN policy makers to support economic liberalism.

The Nixon Administration's decision to end the gold standard in 1971 shocked international trade and many developed economies. In 1972, leading Western European countries created the so-called currency snake system, by which the fluctuation between their currencies would not exceed 2.25 percent. This system was ineffective, however; fluctuations grew in part from globalization and liberalization of financial markets. Financial speculators tinkered with the system, trading one national currency against the other, which increased volatility. In 1992, financial speculators artificially stimulated the demand on foreign currency, forcing the Bank of England to spend billions to stabilize the pound.

Now, the dollar and other national currencies fluctuate vis-à-vis each other and gold; their exchange rate depends on many factors, including GDP growth, exports and imports, and political as well as economic events. The consequences of exchange rate volatility may have significant impacts on international trade and may seriously affect all businesses and citizens. (See Table 7-1.)

TABLE 7-1 Consequences of Shifting Exchange Rates

Exchange Rate	Consequences
High	People who travel abroad are more willing to spend while traveling because they can get more for their money. However, a country's products will cost more abroad, and fewer will be exported, which could easily cause a decrease in production and a loss of jobs.
Low	People traveling abroad get less for their money and thus become less willing to spend while traveling. At the same time, exports become less expensive and thus more competitive on the global market.

Financial Globalization

The globalization of finances is a developing trend. Countries' economies are becoming more interconnected, and the movement of capital across borders is increasing. Despite the seeming openness of the financial markets, a few financial centers (London, New York, and Hong Kong) continue their domination. The positive effects of financial globalization include, for example, the ability to use credit cards overseas or easily make international transfers of funds. On the other hand, the possibilities for fraud and tax evasion have skyrocketed, and international terrorist organizations use modern financial transaction methods to finance their activities. In response to these problems, developed countries introduced new controls over transfer of money from country to country.

Countries must adapt constantly to the realities of financial globalization. Some governments have powerful financial tools, including interest rates, which banks use to lend money to private citizens and corporations. Most countries try to adjust to exchange rates, which may weaken or strengthen their economies. Some use fixed exchange rates to prevent their national currency from fluctuating against others. Over a dozen African countries have adjusted their currencies to the euro, and seven Middle Eastern states have pegged their currencies to the U.S. dollar. The goal here is partly to protect the price of the country's products from declining in foreign markets, as we discuss in the Case Study at the end of this chapter.

Trade

International trade is another volatile factor in international relations. Under most circumstances, states try to stimulate and expand their exports while depending on their imports. The difference between the two is the **balance of trade**, which is positive when exports are higher and negative when imports are higher. Before the 1970s, the United States had a positive balance of trade, but it has slipped into an ever-growing trade deficit, largely from the import of oil from the Persian Gulf and of goods from China.

balance of trade The difference between the size of a country's exports and imports.

For decades, trade imbalances created inequality in the distribution of wealth between rich and poor countries. African and most South American countries exported agricultural products and raw materials at low prices, whereas developed countries exported sophisticated products and services at high prices. As a result, poorer states owed substantial amounts of money to wealthy countries. Economic and political dependency became intertwined. In the past twenty years, the rapid growth of manufacturing in emerging markets has altered the global trade balance—consumers in Western countries owe money to China, where goods are manufactured.

The ability of states to control the movement of goods and capital has declined sharply, especially in the era of the Internet. Many corporations move their production to China, Vietnam, or Malaysia, which offer a large pool of cheap, educated, and disciplined labor. This shift affects manufacturing jobs in wealthy countries, though economists disagree on how. Some argue that losing manufacturing jobs to foreign countries should encourage people to pursue occupational training in better-paying jobs and opportunities at home (Cowen 2014). Others push for preserving domestic jobs by restricting the free flow of capital and investments.

Economic Development

development A collection of processes by which countries improve their social well-being and global economic standing.

International political economy is also concerned with **development**, a collection of processes by which countries improve their social well-being and global economic standing. Related social and economic changes include increasing per capita incomes, accumulating capital, adopting new technologies, and increasing labor skills. Five major emerging national economies are the **BRICS**: Brazil, Russia, India, China, and, more recently, South Africa. These countries have experienced rapid development in the past several decades and now meet annually at formal international summits, including the G20.

BRICS An acronym for Brazil, Russia, India, China, and South Africa, major emerging national economies.

Main Economic Actors

The world's economy and finances stem from the dynamics and trends of the global market economy and the purposeful policies and strategies of the most powerful actors, states, and IGOs. There are also multinational corporations that own or control goods and services production in several countries; among the biggest are Apple, Google, Amazon, Toyota, Microsoft, Walmart, and British Petroleum. States use their economic and financial power to influence other countries and their economic and financial policies. We already described how the United States used its exceptional economic power to introduce the Marshall Plan, which certainly affected American economic and political interests. IGOs such as the World Trade Organization (WTO) and the Transatlantic Economic Council (TEC) create international structures and

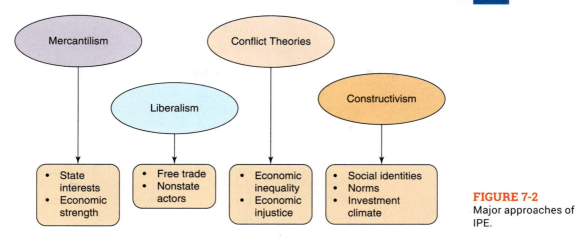

FIGURE 7-2
Major approaches of IPE.

facilitate policies of global significance. The most spectacular example so far is the set of intergovernmental agreements that created the EU (Moravcsik 1997).

Main actors' policies are also shaped by domestic politics, countries' security interests, individual choices, and various short-term factors. Last but not least, they are defined by economic theories and models. Economists and financial experts play a prominent role in countries' production, finances, and trade. To understand contemporary IPE, we must comprehend how these ideas and models occurred, developed, and are applied. (See Figure 7-2.)

Check Your Knowledge

1. What is GDP? Why do countries have different GDPs?

2. Explain the positive and negative balance of trade. How does a negative balance affect you personally?

3. Who are the major actors in IPE? What factors shape their interactions?

7.2 Principles of Mercantilism

One of the oldest economic approaches, **mercantilism** calls for the accumulation and protection of available resources under full control of a sovereign country. At the heart of this theory, which was once linked to realism, is the view that maximizing net exports is the best route to national prosperity. (See Figure 7-3.) In other words, a state must maintain a positive balance of trade. Many countries have used mercantilism along with nationalist rhetoric (O'Brien and Clesse 2002). U.S. President Donald Trump has taken this stance, claiming that previous U.S. administrations had negatively affected U.S. employment rates by allowing inexpensive foreign exports and by freely sharing technologies (Ahmed and Bick 2017).

Mercantilists assume that, globally, wealth is limited and does not grow or shrink quickly. To succeed, states should compete for territories, resources, and colonies. Their economic policies should therefore aim at accumulating natural resources and gold reserves, expanding territory, establishing exclusive trade with colonies, and receiving payments from defeated enemies.

mercantilism The economic view that emphasizes a state's accumulation of resources, capital, and trade regulation.

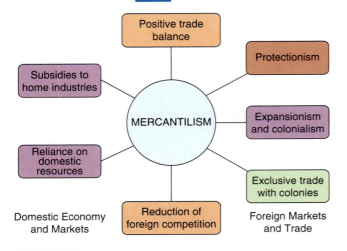

Domestic Economy
and Markets

Foreign Markets
and Trade

FIGURE 7-3
Mercantilism: A snapshot.

protectionism
Economic restrictions by a state to discourage imports and encourage domestic production, including "import substitution."

Protectionism

Mercantilism supports **protectionism**, the policy of restricting or discouraging imports and encouraging domestic production. States must make sure that most of the products and services they need are produced domestically and that natural resources—such as coal, gas, and oil—are primarily for domestic consumption. This encourages employment and limits other countries' opportunities to sell their products there. The United States practiced protectionism for most of its history and most harshly during the Great Depression. Until recently, India banned foreign supermarkets that sell products more cheaply than the country's own stores.

Another form of protectionism is **tariffs**—fees on imported goods that make them more expensive. These charges give domestic producers a chance to sell their goods, protect the domestic workforce, and perhaps reduce the negative trade balance. States may also give domestic industries direct subsidies, legislate import quotas, or negotiate with other countries to limit their exports voluntarily (Zahariadis 2008). The United States pursued the last two policies to restrict Japan's car exports in the 1970s; the better designed and more fuel-efficient vehicles threatened American

In many countries, including the United States and United Kingdom, the ideas of nationalism and mercantilism have begun to win more supporters. Was this a short-lived trend or will it continue for years?

automobile corporations. Bush, Obama, and especially Trump used tariffs to protect certain domestic markets, including steel, aluminum, and automobile tire industries. Protectionist policies are supported by strong domestic lobbies, such as wine producers in France (Mishra 2018; Haas 2012; Anderson 2005).

tariff Tax or financial charge imposed on imported goods.

Economic Sanctions

Countries may also use **economic sanctions** (the deliberate withdrawal, or threat of withdrawal, of customary trade and financial relations to pressure a government into changing its policies) against other states. The ultimate form of economic sanctions is an *embargo*, or the prohibition of trade. Usually, these policies do not last, but the United States imposed an embargo on Cuba from 1960 until 2014 and on Iran beginning in 1979. In the past, economic sanctions often preceded or followed a war. In the twentieth century, however, they were imposed as an alternative to violence. They may be used in an attempt to restrain a belligerent government, punish aggression, contain a civil war, influence policies, or simply make a political statement. In 2018, Washington imposed sanctions against Turkey over its continued detention of an American pastor, which the American government deemed illegal.

economic sanctions A state's deliberate, government-driven withdrawal, or threat of withdrawal, of customary trade and financial relations in an effort to change another country's policies.

American legislation allows economic and trade sanctions against countries that expropriate U.S. property, organize coups against elected governments, and support terrorism. Countries that violate human rights, harbor international war criminals, engage in nuclear proliferation, or fail to cooperate sufficiently with U.S. antinarcotics efforts may also become targets of economic sanctions. The Office of Foreign Assets Control of the U.S. Department of the Treasury administers and enforces economic and trade sanctions. Many of them are based on UN and other international mandates (Malloy 2015; Hufbauer and Oegg 2003).

Autarky

One of the ultimate forms of mercantilism has been **autarky**, a long-term policy of national self-sufficiency and rejection of imports, economic aid, and cooperation. Past Communist leaders favored isolationist foreign policy to reject economic cooperation or trade with capitalist countries. Albania went further: from the 1950s through the 1980s, it implemented complete economic self-reliance and stopped trading with all countries. North Korea has been doing the same for over sixty years. Their leaders assumed that a true Communist country was capable of building a prosperous economy alone. This policy has failed miserably: These states could barely provide the minimum resources for their populations.

autarky A long-term policy of national self-sufficiency and rejection of imports, economic aid, and cooperation.

Mercantilist arguments are currently making a comeback for several reasons. One is the idea that traditional economic policies could have avoided the 2008 financial crisis and subsequent global economic slowdown. Another is that many countries seek higher rates of economic growth and believe protectionist policies could guarantee it. Protectionism seems to defend against the negative effects that new challenges in technology and globalization have on labor markets. Finally, alternative models of state capitalism are evoking growing interest (Ahmed and Bick 2017). In the United States, Donald Trump appealed to

Check Your Knowledge

1. What is economic mercantilism? Which mercantilist policies benefit you personally?
2. What is protectionism? Give an example.

millions with his calls for protection of American industries and businesses. In the United Kingdom, some Tories and Labourists followed the logic of protectionism in their support of Brexit. In Russia, supporters of mercantilism backed Moscow's decisions to resist international economic sanctions (see Chapter 5), introduce countersanctions, depend less on international trade and foreign technologies, and invest in local manufacturing industries.

macroeconomics The study of the structure and performance of the entire economy, including the interrelationship among diverse sectors.

Keynesian economics The principle that national governments should conduct expansionary fiscal and monetary policies whenever necessary to ease the undesirable effects of economic recessions.

monetary policy State and financial tools to stimulate the economy, control inflation, and maintain social stability.

fiscal policy The use of government spending or revenue collection to influence the economy, push it out of recession, or create jobs.

7.3 Economic Liberalism and the Formation of IPE

Two centuries ago in the United Kingdom, a liberal alternative to mercantilism flourished. After economic liberalism failed to end the Great Depression of 1929–1939, British economic thought produced a new economic doctrine.

Keynesian Economics

British economist John M. Keynes (1883–1946) made a serious attempt to combine liberal and mercantilist concepts to create a doctrine of economic growth. A founder of **macroeconomics**, which looks at the structure and performance of the entire economy, he argued that, contrary to the assumption of free-market efficiency, governments should regulate business and especially finances (Keynes 1936/1965). According to **Keynesian economics**, states can ease a recession's undesirable effects by spending more money than their revenues allow. The idea is that an increase in business transactions and purchases will stimulate production and consumption, lowering unemployment and helping to create a prosperous middle class. Keynes's principles played a key role in understanding economic structure and performance for half of the twentieth century, when all Western economies experienced robust growth.

Following Keynes's ideas, states abandoned the gold standard and started to manipulate the money supply through interest rates—a process known as **monetary policy**. For instance, the Federal Reserve, the central banking system in the United States, can raise or lower interest rates, thus making credit more or less expensive, and open or close the flow of capital into the economy. The government can also use **fiscal policy** to influence the economy. States can raise taxes and use this money to create jobs while simultaneously fighting *inflation*, a rise in prices.

In the 1970s and 1980s, Keynesian principles came under heavy criticism from the advocates of liberal economic theories. After the global financial and economic crisis that started in 2008, discussion began about whether Keynesian policies should be revived. Some current economists support this idea, in view of unstable international markets and the decline of middle classes in some developed countries.

Economic Liberalism: The Origins

IPE is largely shaped by **economic liberalism**—the belief that international economic connections, globalization of finances, production, and labor are not only the main source of economic development but also a vital source of international cooperation, stability, and peace. Liberal economists maintain that the dynamics and structures of international trade, and globalizing markets of finances and labor, remain the key realities that shape economic developments and the distribution of power in the international system.

Economic liberalism is not a new concept. One of its founders, Scottish economist and philosopher Adam Smith (1723–1790), opposed restrictions on international trade, arguing that commerce brings prosperity and peace among nations (Smith 1776/1977). A noted follower, David Ricardo (1772–1823), believed that **free trade**—international trade left to its natural course—is the best regulator of labor and natural resources. Friedrich List (1789–1846) suggested that commercial unions among states make trade flourish and enrich all participants (List 1841/2006).

Economic liberalism gradually replaced mercantilism as a dominant trend in economic policies in the second half of the nineteenth century. However, it came under serious attack during the Great Depression and the rise of Communism, fascism, and social democracy from the 1920s to 1950s. At this time, the Keynesian approach became dominant in the United States as the rationale for the New Deal, a series of domestic programs that addressed the Depression's effects. Yet economic liberals challenged Keynes's ideas as a potentially dangerous aberration. In *The Road to Serfdom* (1944/2007), the Austrian economist Friedrich von Hayek (1899–1992) sharply criticized the idea of states regulating markets. Hayek influenced American economist Milton Friedman (1912–2006), who renounced Keynesianism as an outdated theory that did not reflect international economic dynamics (Friedman 1962/2002). He argued that the state should abandon protectionist policies and ensure that the amount of money in circulation gradually grows—an idea called *monetarism*.

Keynesian economics

economic liberalism The belief and theory that only free markets, free trade, and economic cooperation can lead to a peaceful and prosperous world.

free trade International trade left to its natural course, without tariffs, quotas, or other restrictions.

DEBATE > NATIONAL PRIDE AND FOREIGN OWNERSHIP

The Chelsea Football Club, a famous London soccer team, is currently owned by a Russian tycoon. Another Russian billionaire owns the NBA's Brooklyn Nets. China allows foreign companies to own some businesses, such as e-commerce organizations and hospitals. The German auto giant Volkswagen, however, is sheltered by law from foreign buyers.

WHAT'S YOUR VIEW?

❶ What types of businesses, if any, should be protected from foreign ownership? ❷ Suppose you are a government official who can block any ownership transfer of American companies to foreigners. From the following list, select one company to block from being sold and explain your choice.

Boeing	Microsoft
The Yankees	Google
Exxon	Whole Foods
Facebook	ESPN

Crowds greet Britain's reelected prime minister, Margaret Thatcher, in 1983. A follower of economic liberalism (like U.S. President Reagan), Thatcher pushed for economic deregulation.

comparative advantage A theory that explains why countries benefit from trading with each other instead of relying on domestic production.

Issue Navigator: Free Trade

Liberalism's main goal is free trade through international cooperation. An early argument for this goal is the principle, or law, of **comparative advantage**, which explains why countries should produce only certain goods that can be exported with profit and buy other goods on international markets. For example, Mexico and Argentina have a comparative advantage over the United States and Canada in producing oil and meat because the cost of their labor in these industries is cheaper. Therefore, Mexico and Argentina can successfully export their oil and meat, and it is profitable to increase this practice.

The principle suggests that any two countries would benefit from mutual trade because certain things are less expensive to produce in one country and sell to the other. If Britain imported corn from Argentina (which is cheaper there), it would save more labor time and resources that could focus on improving British textiles (which are in high demand in Argentina). Argentina would similarly gain from focusing on corn production while importing British textiles. In both countries, consumers would be better off because the prices of both products would be lower and their quality higher.

In the same spirit, economic liberals argue that the benefits of protecting domestic producers against foreign competitors are insignificant compared to the damage to the domestic economy as a whole: people have to pay much higher prices for domestic goods, and protected businesses have less incentive to develop, modernize, and be competitive internationally. Economic liberals also claim that economic cooperation reduces the chance of war, as businesses are likely to lobby for cooperation and international law, inducing states to choose cooperation (Oneal and Russett 1997; Rogowski 1990). (See Figure 7-4.)

International Economic Organizations

Economic liberalism, with Keynesian modifications, inspired the creation of international institutions to facilitate trade and provide financial stability worldwide, which supporters believed would lead to a more prosperous and peaceful world (Ikenberry and Grieco 2002; Keohane 2005). The Great Depression, a period characterized by high protective tariffs and the breakdown of global markets, offered strong reasons to build such institutions. Many believed that protectionism had slowed economic recovery and provoked extreme nationalism, led to a struggle for territory and resources, and ultimately contributed to World War II.

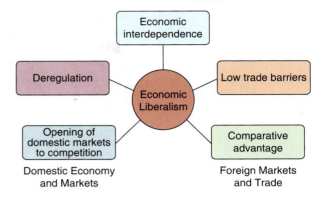

FIGURE 7-4 Economic liberalism: A snapshot.

At the Bretton Woods Conference in 1944, representatives of the United States, the United Kingdom, the Soviet Union, France, and China created the International Monetary Fund (IMF) and the International Bank of Reconstruction and Development (IBRD), which became the pillars of Western capitalism (Peet 2009). Participating states agreed to contribute parts of their gold reserves to a global "pool" to maintain the balance of payments in international trade.

THE IMF AND WORLD BANK

The IMF has quadrupled in size since its creation, to 189 members in 2019. Its goals are to maintain stable exchanges between national currencies, provide financial help to countries during financial crises, achieve macroeconomic stability, and help overcome global poverty. The International Bank for Reconstruction and Development (commonly called the World Bank) involves almost all states (except for Cuba, North Korea, and a few others) and makes loans to developing countries, especially the poorest of them, for long-term projects. Both institutions are run by an elected president, have a board of trustees, and an executive apparatus. In theory, they are governed by and accountable to all its members; however, the wealthiest donors have more votes in the governing board. The United States remains the largest shareholder, with over 17 percent of wealth and votes (Japan has 6 percent and 7 percent, and China has 6.2 percent and 4.7 percent, respectively). The headquarters of both organizations are located in Washington, D.C.; many of its leading officials are Americans or Europeans. As a result, critics complain that neither is sufficiently democratic but is an agent of interests of a handful of wealthy countries, above all the United States (Dreher and Jensen; 2007; Griffith-Jones 2001).

The IMF and World Bank provide financial help conditionally: Usually, the recipient must reform its finances according to these institutions' prescriptions, which commonly involve privatization and deregulation. It is argued that the lenders do not pay enough attention to the local conditions of recipient countries (Strand 2013). The prescriptions may also stimulate the growth of certain industries, yet cause the decline of others, thus sparking unemployment and economic disparities.

THE WTO

Other liberal international institutions include the *General Agreement on Tariffs and Trade (GATT)*, signed in 1947 in Geneva, and the *International Trade Organization (ITO)*, created the next year in Havana. ITO failed because the U.S. Senate rejected its charter: Many American politicians feared that it would become a kind of global government. However, GATT became successful during the 1960s and in 1995 was renamed the World Trade Organization (WTO); it is now a global organization including over 160 countries.

The WTO is currently the main international organization promoting economic development and growth through the removal of tariffs and the opening of national markets to international trade. It also helps enforce their agreements and resolve trade disputes (WTO 2018). It does not act as a global government or negotiate on behalf of states but provides a framework for negotiations. Using more than sixty international agreements, it insists that countries should adhere to the principles of nondiscrimination, reciprocity, and transparency in their trade policies (Hoekman and Kostecki 2010). This means that countries should have equal access to foreign markets, imported products should be treated no less favorably than domestically produced goods, and no secret deals or domestic regulations should restrict free trade.

WTO supporters hope that free trade will reduce poverty, improve standards of living, create employment, and provide new economic opportunities for billions (Park 2018; Narlikar 2005). Critics offer at least three main arguments. They believe that free trade benefits mostly rich countries while leaving underdeveloped countries to produce raw materials and supply cheap labor (discussed later in this chapter). Small countries can exercise less influence in the talks that produce new WTO rules. These rules harm small business: only big multinational corporations can thrive with free trade. Critics also stress that the organization offered no new solutions to the 2008 global financial crisis (Hopewell 2017; Cottier and Elsig 2011).

The WTO and the World Bank

Regional Trade Agreements

regional trade agreements Mutual commitments that bind several neighboring countries to pursue common economic and financial policies.

Regional trade agreements are rules and mutual commitments based on international treaties that bind countries to pursue common economic and financial policies. They usually deal with tariff reduction and elimination, but they also address transportation, communications, intellectual property, environmental standards, investments, and trade policies. In 2018, there were more than six hundred regional trade arrangements, and their number is likely to grow (WTO 2018). See Table 7-2 for examples.

Why do countries need such agreements? They gain from lower prices and seek to secure access to each other's markets and products. Many less

TABLE 7-2   Examples of Regional Trade Agreements

Regional Agreement	Main Features
European Union (EU)	The EU is the most ambitious project in economic and political integration, with a population of 500 million and a GDP of $17 trillion. It has a common currency and central banking system (the euro and the European Central Bank, respectively) and has taken steps to develop a common foreign and security policy. (See Chapter 3.)
Southern Common Market (MERCOSUR)	Comprising Argentina, Paraguay, Uruguay, and Brazil (and Venezuela from 2012 to 2016), MERCOSUR promotes the movement of goods, people, and currency among these countries, representing a total population of approximately 300 million.
Asia-Pacific Economic Cooperation (APEC)	This group of twenty-one Pacific Rim countries, including the United States, meets regularly to improve economic and political ties among member states. The group has working committees on a wide range of issues, from communications to fisheries.

developed countries need economic security and pursue trade agreements with developed states. Wealthy countries seek cheaper products and services and expect new consumers' markets to grow (Park 2018; Whalley 1997).

7.4 Constructivism and IPE

Constructivism posits that material resources and economic policies are often seen through the prism of collective values and socially constructed priorities (Reus-Smit 2009). The goals and structure of economic policies change from country to country depending on social, political, and cultural conditions (Evans 1998). Ideologies, religion, and traditional customs are also involved. For instance, free trade may be viewed as positive or negative, depending on a country's perceived role in the world market (Copeland 1996).

Using constructivist ideas, one can see the Marshall Plan as not only an economic policy but also a way to promote beliefs in free markets and free trade—as opposed to mercantilism or Communism. The Marshall Plan fostered cooperation, mutual acceptance, and the willingness of European states to become what we commonly call "the West." Governments, influential elites, lobbies, and societies at large construct economic interests and policies. This may partially explain why some countries practice protectionism more often than others or use a fixed exchange rate rather than flexibility.

Check Your Knowledge

1. According to Keynesian principles, what stimulates economic growth?

2. Explain the comparative advantage principle.

3. What is the main idea of economic liberalism?

4. What is the main goal of key international economic organizations?

5. Explain the three main arguments of WTO critics.

Nationalism and Economic Politics

national purpose In the constructivist view, a major economic goal that political and business elites want to achieve for their country.

According to constructivism, **national purpose**—a country's major economic goal or vision—can shape economic and financial policies in powerful ways. This vision is closely tied to national identity and can be stronger than the logic of rational economic benefits (Abdelal 2001). Take the example of some post-Soviet countries—such as Estonia, Latvia, and Lithuania—turning rapidly away from Russia, despite their historic economic interdependence. Belarus and Kazakhstan, by contrast, cooperated with Moscow, as doing so did not conflict with their national purpose.

Economic nationalism is often linked to mercantilism, which emphasizes the urgent importance of the domestic market. It can also be connected with liberal economic policies, however, especially when a government sees free trade with other countries as a key source of wealth.

Countries constantly redefine their national purpose and economic interests. Seeking a stronger role in world affairs in the 1990s, India turned away from longstanding protectionist policies. Instead, it began to embrace international cooperation and interdependence, allowed foreign investments, and promoted economic openness (Alamgir 2008). According to constructivism, these massive economic reforms were strongly influenced by policy makers' perception of what India should be—a competitive, educated, and efficient nation—especially in comparison with China (Smith 2013). According to the Communist Party of China's long-term strategy, China wants to use free trade and open markets to achieve total technological independence by 2025. Theoretically, the government could set a national goal to stop purchasing foreign technologies and totally rely on its own (Mishra, 2018). Is this a liberal pathway to mercantilism?

A protester lies in the street during an anti-corruption demonstration in downtown Nairobi, Kenya, in 2018.

Economic Climate

States, regions, and the global community develop an **economic climate**, or set of values, norms, and practices that can encourage or discourage investments. According to economic liberalism, manufacturers, sellers, and consumers act within the rules of supply and demand. In reality, constructivists say, scores of other factors affect their behavior.

An unfriendly business climate lacks a legal foundation, custom, and trust. If many influential states see a country's policies negatively, they are unlikely to invest there. The lack of tradition in this area severely limits the functioning of Iran's market economy, for example, which affects its participation in international economic activities. Authoritarianism, corruption, and criminalization of economic life in Russia create a bad climate for international investments. In the most extreme cases, producers stop trading openly and prefer transactions in cash only. Conversely, in established democracies with market economies backed by strong legal systems, foreign investments increase, and producers supply goods without advance payments.

A favorable economic climate means lower cost to business. Places perceived as corrupt, as a rule, lose international investors. Political events, conflicts, and international sanctions all affect a country's economic climate. Therefore, a country's foreign economic policies become inseparable from its domestic social policy and how it is perceived by others.

economic climate A set of values, norms, and practices that can encourage or discourage economic investments.

Transparency International's annual survey on world corruption

Check Your Knowledge

1. What is the main idea of constructivism?

2. What is economic climate? How does it affect investments?

7.5 Marxism and Conflict Theories: Radical Criticisms of IPE

As discussed in Chapter 4, conflict theories maintain that the world's economic structure unfairly benefits dominant social classes and groups (e.g., the wealthy, males, and whites). Such an economic order, according to this approach, should be replaced by a new and fairer one through revolution or reforms.

Marxist Views

Marxists argue that, despite a wide range of democratic changes in the past century, the gap between a few rich countries and the rest of the world remains profound. International corporations and banks, not the state governments, are the true holders of global power because of their financial resources. States serve the interests of the ruling billionaire class using diplomacy, international agreements, and international law to manage international relations, which in effect should lead to higher profits. Free-trade agreements are designed to enrich the international ruling class and give nothing to the middle class, workers, or peasants.

What do Marxists suggest? Their old recipes, urging violent revolutions and nationalizations of large banks and big corporations, lost their credibility

dependency theory The belief that the world economic order is based on the flow of resources from a "periphery" of poor states to a "core" of wealthy states.

South (global) In dependency theory, predominantly agricultural countries that depend on the rich and technology-driven (global) North.

North (global) In dependency theory, predominantly rich and technology-driven countries that benefit from the raw materials and cheap labor of the (global) South.

after many failed attempts. Failures in the Soviet Union, Cuba, North Korea, and other Communist countries disenchanted many Marxist sympathizers. Although they cannot offer a viable alternative to global capitalism, they support the antiglobalist movement that demands high taxes on the rich and rigorous social control over banks and corporations.

Economic Dependency

Dependency theory began in the research of an Argentine economist, Raúl Prebisch (1901–1986), and a German economist, Hans Singer (1910–2006). In their view, technology-driven developed nations, called the *core*, receive more benefits from international trade than technology-deprived developing countries, called the *periphery*. They showed that the latter benefit significantly from improvements in technology. Moreover, periphery countries cannot catch up under the conditions of free trade (Prebisch 1989; Singer 1999). Core countries' wealth is almost constantly increasing, whereas the periphery's is flat or decreasing.

Supporters of these views maintain that the discriminatory structure of the world's economy and trade is the main cause of global inequality and chronic poverty. Elites from the periphery reap the benefits, and the rest remain in abject poverty while working for transnational corporations. Dependency theorists began to use terms such as "global North and South" and "North–South divide" to direct attention to the failures of economic realism and liberalism. The poor, agricultural nations of the **South** (so-called, although not all are in the Southern Hemisphere) are totally dependent, economically and politically, on the developed industrial **North**. The latter is the core of the capitalist system, and the former remains on the periphery. Recall from Chapter 4 that these are the main points of world-systems theory (Wallerstein 1979).

In the 1960s and 1970s, many Third World economists became influenced by dependency theory, and some of their recommendations produced visible results (e.g., the twenty-first century rise of Brazil's economic power) (Sweig 2010). Dependency theorists accept private property and acknowledge the importance of some elements of a free-market economy. Nevertheless, they believe that the rules governing markets should change and the world's economic order should be restructured (Scott 2001).

Check Your Knowledge

1. What is the main idea of the Marxist view on IPE?

2. Explain the *core* and the *periphery*.

7.6 Critical Applications

No single international economic crisis or economic "miracle"—no matter how impressive—can prove total success or failure for certain economic policies. It is important to discover why states choose particular policies and when

TABLE 7-3 Applying Economic Approaches: The Individual, State, and Global Levels

Level of Analysis	Application
Individual	According to microeconomics, individual decisions matter. Political leaders have both the power and resources to implement their vision. When financial markets are volatile, just one decision or tweet can affect domestic and international markets. News headlines, election results, and statements made by political or business leaders influence economic and financial decisions by individual investors, companies, and entire governments.
State	Each country's financial and economic cycles, economic growth, stagnations, and recessions affect international relations, particularly trade and commerce. Many domestic political and social factors guide a state's economic, trade, fiscal, and monetary policies, which in turn influence the state's international position. Political parties and domestic social climates can sway public and decision-maker attitudes about international trade deals.
Global	Global economic and political developments both influence and are influenced by state and IGO policies. A financial crisis in one country is likely to affect global financial markets. State economies tend to respond variably to global developments, however; some are deeply affected while others are not. There has not been a universal approach to eliminating global poverty. If such a theory or approach were globally accepted, each country would likely adjust it to specific cultural and political conditions.

they become effective. We must look at the individual, state, and global levels and circumstances in which these policies developed. (See Table 7-3.)

Individual Decisions

Many theories of international business and trade are tested on the level of **microeconomics**—the field that considers the behavior of consumers, companies, and industries. Here, individual decisions play a big role; the decisions of individual state and business leaders can influence international economic policies. Among the factors affecting decisions are leadership, ideology, and the economic climate.

Political leaders base their economic policies on a variety of ideas. (See Table 7-4.) They cannot afford isolation, but they still have to choose between multilateralism and unilateralism, cooperation and noncooperation, with the international system. With the increasing price of oil and oil products in the mid-2000s, some oil-producing states began to act as unilateralists. After 2006, Iran openly pushed the development of its nuclear program, stating that Western countries would not impose sanctions because they needed Iranian oil. It miscalculated, even as it understood that unilateralism could be risky.

microeconomics The field of economics that considers the behavior of individual consumers, companies, and industries.

TABLE 7-4 Economic Policies of Selected National Leaders

Name	Country	Years in Office	Economic Decisions
Kim Il-sung (1912–1994)	North Korea	1948–1994	An authoritarian Communist leader, he hoped to build a prosperous, independent state based on *Juche* (spirit of self-reliance)—a blend of autarky, extreme centralization, and nationalism. Private property was prohibited, and foreign trade was limited.
Fidel Castro (1926–2016)	Cuba	1959–2011	Castro's economic policies were based on his belief in state planning and an inevitable confrontation with capitalism. Cuba, however, had to be subsidized heavily by the Soviet Union and, after the Soviet collapse, by Venezuela.
Mohammad Reza Pahlavi (1919–1980)	Iran	1941–1979	Pahlavi remained a reliable supporter of the United States, the free-market economy, and international trade. His reforms spawned massive corruption. He was expelled during the Islamic Revolution.
Deng Xiaoping (1904–1997)	People's Republic of China	Approximately 1981–1992	After the economic and social disaster of the Cultural Revolution, Deng concluded that the Chinese economy could be restored only by a combination of state planning and market initiative. His reforms set the foundations for the "economic miracle." With significant foreign investments, China became a leading economic power that preserves, with few modifications, the old political system.
Margaret Thatcher (1925–2013)	United Kingdom	1979–1990	Thatcher began to dismantle state regulation of the economy and weakened trade unions. She also resisted the UK's integration into the European Community, fearing that its regulations would reverse her reforms.
Lech Wałęsa (b. 1943)	Poland	1990–1995	Wałęsa opposed Communist rule and led the independent trade union Solidarity against it. As president, he promoted free-market principles but hoped to avoid its excesses. He lost power in the midst of a Polish economic recession.

TABLE 7-4 (*Continued*)

Robert Mugabe (b. 1924)	Zimbabwe	1980–2017	An authoritarian ruler, Mugabe advocated a blend of anticolonialism and nationalism. His economic policies were erratic and mostly mercantilist. Under his leadership, Zimbabwe remained one of the poorest countries in Africa.
Hugo Chávez (1954–2013)	Venezuela	1999–2013	A populist, Chávez built his economic policies on a blend of Socialist ideas, anticolonial and anti-imperialist messages, and Bolivarianism (the unification of Latin America). A dependence theorist, he repeatedly tried to use his country's oil profits to finance anti-American policies.
Muammar Gaddafi (1942–2011)	Libya	1969–2011	Gaddafi's economic policy of "Islamic Socialism" established government controls of large industries but permitted small business. Most national wealth, especially oil revenues, went to him and his supporters. During his last years in power, he improved relations with Western countries, hoping to benefit even more from high oil prices. He was overthrown by a popular insurrection supported by the West.

Microeconomics can show how consumer behavior affects international markets and overall international stability. After 9/11, the world's stock markets fell drastically. Scores of investors sold their stocks and put their money in what they perceived as a more secure investment, such as cash or gold. Acting on their instincts and impulses, they created a global financial disruption that lasted for months. This cycle repeated in the fall of 2008, when the stock market plummeted. In 2010 and 2011, rumors that Greece might default on its national debt, thus threatening the euro, led people to buy state bonds and U.S. dollars.

Usually, such "stampedes" are short-lived and help speculators to gamble on the fluctuations in currency values. Indeed, the stock market showed almost unprecedented growth in 2017 but became more volatile the following year. Economists identify many factors that affect currency. The speculation conducted by governments, however, can destabilize the international financial system in the long run. Some European governments have lobbied for a tax on any currency exchange, to discourage such conjecture.

History Lab | Discoveries and Innovations

Along with financial speculators and mass reactions, scientists and engineers also affect IPE. Discoveries, innovations, and other accomplishments dramatically affect travel, trade, and the ways products and services are exchanged (Yergin and Stanislaw 1998). The steam engine made rail and ship transportation possible, safely and swiftly moving people and goods across countries, continents, and oceans. The invention of the single-wire telegraph system allowed people to instantly send messages around the world. The spread of these technologies powered a dramatic expansion of world trade and facilitated diplomatic communications.

CRITICAL THINKING

❶ Other than the Internet, what prominent innovations and discoveries of the past twenty years have had the most significant impact on international trade and commerce? ❷ Which of today's innovations will change international markets in 2025? Will Facebook, Instagram, or Twitter play a serious role in world politics and trade, or will some other social networks gain power? Explain your answers. ❸ How could current technologies help or harm international trade? Offer several scenarios.

Even without speculators, financial markets can be unpredictable. News headlines, election results, and leaders' statements affect both individual and corporate decisions. Millions of individual decisions, swayed by mass reactions, produce greater financial volatility. Government officials generally comment as little as possible about economic problems to avoid investors' panic.

State Policies

Leaders make economic decisions based partly on political obligations. In a democratic society, politics is often about promoting economic interests (Olson 1971). In addition, a country's business and financial cycles affect international relations.

RESPONSE TO RECESSIONS

Keynesian economics became the first economic model that informed policies attempting to end recessions and stimulate expansion (e.g., the policies of the New Deal). After World War II ended, many countries held modified Keynesian ideas about increased expenses and deficits. Advocates of these concepts—such as the Truman, Kennedy, and Johnson Administrations—argued that they helped reduce the business cycle's negative impacts. Some even claimed that the era of business cycles was over.

But global recessions in the 1970s and in 2008–2009 disproved those optimistic claims. After 2013, the American economy expanded again. This time, advocates of liberal monetarism argued that consistently increasing the amount of money in circulation helped overcome the recession. Critics argued that heavy state spending on social programs should be credited for the turnaround. Others paid attention to America's technological innovations and new oil- and gas-extracting technologies (such as "fracking") (Cowen 2014).

Today, state economic policies have become extremely complex and increasingly dependent on international developments.

DOMESTIC POLITICAL AND SOCIAL FACTORS

Politics are another important domestic consideration affecting a state's economic and financial policies, international trade, and overall international situation. In turn, economic factors influence politics. Some Western political groupings are likely to reject government economic regulations and support market-oriented policies. Their political opponents are more likely to support state regulations and policies that protect the domestic labor force and various social groups against perceived market dangers.

It is difficult to promote deregulation and free-market policies in countries and regions devastated by poverty, violence, social neglect, and rampant corruption. It takes time to develop infrastructure, find investors, create jobs, and create a favorable business climate. Most governments do not have the luxury of time to experiment with free-market reforms. They need to show immediate and positive results; therefore, many choose regulation.

In the United States, where labor costs are high, many manufacturing workers oppose open global competition. For two decades, the U.S. economy has been steadily losing high-paying industrial jobs due to **outsourcing**, a practice in which companies move their production facilities to countries with fewer regulations and cheaper labor (Bergsten 2005).

outsourcing The practice of moving businesses and jobs to other countries and regions where labor costs are lower.

THE ASIAN DEVELOPMENT MODEL

Domestic political and social factors affect attitudes about *surplus-oriented* and *trade deficit-tolerant* economic policies. Remember that surplus is a core objective of mercantilism. A trade deficit is generally acceptable in free-market economies. The role of surplus and state planning was crucial to the *Asian development model*, which originated in the 1950s out of cooperation between Japan's government and private businesses. The Ministry of International Trade and Industry (MITI) identified potential overseas markets and then assisted private industries with their exports. The state also helped with market information, access to foreign technology, licensing, loans and subsidies, and (when necessary) state tariffs. This relationship between government and business helped Japan turn into Asia's economic powerhouse. During the 1960s, Singapore, Hong Kong, Taiwan, and (later) South Korea adopted this model, with remarkable results. The *Four Asian Tigers*, as these countries came to be called, demonstrated an even higher and consistent growth rate than post–World War II Western European states.

For years, East Asian economies were driven by policies, inspired by comparative advantage, to ensure a massive trade surplus. As you can see, this strategy was a combination of liberal and mercantilist policies. The countries' political parties, despite a host of differences in their domestic platforms, maintained similar views about exports (which had to be stimulated) and imports (which had to be regulated and restrained). The natural limitations of such policies eventually appeared. The trade surplus pushed up labor wages and service costs. As a result, Japan's exports became more expensive compared to those from China and other countries, contributing to over a decade of slow economic growth. These limitations, however, do not necessarily call the Asian development model into question. The tigers have continued to be stable and successful during the last two decades. The so-called Tiger Cubs—Malaysia, Indonesia, Thailand, and the Philippines—follow the same model and also demonstrate steady economic growth, albeit not as impressive as the original four.

Belt and Road Initiative A development strategy proposed by the Chinese government to include a high-capacity transport infrastructure linking East Asia to Europe, as well as a range of relevant economic projects.

More importantly, China continues to promote the Asian development model. The state and state-controlled corporations have been engaged in a huge infrastructure project known as the **Belt and Road Initiative**, a government strategy to include a high-capacity transport infrastructure linking East Asia to Europe, as well as a range of adjacent economic projects. When completed, this ambitious project could create a new level of integration across several continents. Critics, however, claim that it was China's strategy to take over Europe's port and other communications facilities, a way of building the Chinese trade empire (Balding 2018)

Globalization of trade and services and liberalization of economic rules played a crucial role in Asian development. The most obvious comparative example is India, where economic growth benefited from the telecommunications developments, globalization of services, and new state policies that stimulated investments. The large population provides inexpensive labor. In 2018, India became the sixth largest economy in the world and, since 2015, has outpaced China as the fastest growing major economy in Asia.

In the twenty-first century, manufacturing boomed in Asian countries, and their share in world imports dramatically increased. Meanwhile, trade deficits reached a new high in many developed countries, especially the United States. American and Western European economies tend to tolerate deficits after several decades of economic growth, mutually beneficial trade, and Keynesian regulatory policies. For many economists and investors, however, the United States' ongoing trade deficit is a potentially dangerous development (DiMicco 2015; Levey and Brown 2005).

Global Factors

Economic policies succeed or fail depending on business cycles, conflicts, and political decisions. Despite isolationist tendencies developing in the past decade, markets remain globally interconnected. For example, the terrorist attacks of September 11, 2001, shut down not only Wall Street but financial activities globally. Fears of an escalating military conflict in the Middle East may raise oil prices in a matter of hours. Optimistic reports about U.S. employment immediately attract global investments into the economy. Economic sanctions against a country seriously affect its national currency and global financial markets.

Many important decisions affecting the global economy come from the centers of economic and financial power in the wealthiest countries of the word. Battles continue over the direction and scope of economic policies in an era of globalization. Constructivists maintain that, in times of peace and prosperity, economic liberalism gains strength. This approach often falls out of favor, however, during tough economic times. Reacting to the Great Depression and Communism, Roosevelt, Truman, and Eisenhower accepted Keynesian policies. This was a setback for free-market principles, but it guaranteed capitalism's stability for some time. Nevertheless, two main problems were on the horizon.

Keynesian economics assumes that a well-educated elite can decide what is best for national and international economies. Yet the state often carries increasingly expensive welfare programs, including pensions and unemployment benefits. The larger problems are inflation and a decline in growth, as Keynesian support for full employment requires state investments and higher taxes. The combination of high inflation and no growth in the late 1970s, called *stagflation*, led the U.S. Federal Reserve to sharply raise the interest rate to 20 percent. In response, Reagan combined some elements of Keynesianism with deregulating many industries, weakening labor unions, and lowering taxes. These measures brought an unprecedented amount of foreign capital to the United States, curbed inflation, and boosted the economy.

In the 1990s, economic liberalism reigned practically unopposed, its principles boosted by democratic peace theory (see Chapter 3). Economic liberals claimed that the spread of free-market practices contributes to the spread of democracy and ultimately lessens the probability of war (Gartzke 2007). The IMF and World Bank began to stipulate that loan recipients must implement such neoliberal economic policies as trade liberalization, direct foreign investments, state enterprise privatization, and business deregulation.

THE WASHINGTON CONSENSUS

A serious discussion continues about the direction of economic politics and the revision of the economic and political guidelines offered to developing countries (Birdsall and Fukuyama 2011). One such approach, the *Washington Consensus* (1989), has been the maximum deregulation of production and finances to jumpstart stagnant, corrupt, and inefficient economies. Although liberal economists continue to emphasize the benefits of the free market, critics argue that the rigid application of the Consensus may unintentionally destroy the middle class, bring instability, jeopardize democracy, and give excessive power to transnational corporations and export-oriented lobbies. Economic inequality is a topic of vital importance in international relations.

In the early 1990s, the failure of state-planned Communist economies provided fresh arguments for supporters of deregulation. During those years, Russia and other former Communist countries adopted capitalism. China allowed elements of a free-market economy in a society that had prohibited private property for decades. And Indian economic elites (which at times had sympathized with the Soviet model of industrialization) also moved away from state economic planning and control. Yet for many countries, liberal economic policies have failed to deliver the expected economic benefits.

OTHER STRATEGIES TO ADDRESS THE DEVELOPMENT GAP

As predicted by dependency theory, most African and Latin American countries remained suppliers of cheap resources and services to the North. The

brain drain (or human capital flight) The exodus of the most educated and skilled individuals from poor to developed countries.

brain drain continued, as the most educated and skilled individuals moved from poor to developed countries. Some critics of liberalism claimed that deregulation of capital accounts in the 1980s–1990s destabilized the global South even more: more individuals kept their money in Northern banks, creating the "flight" of capital from poorer countries (Stiglitz 2002). However, developments over the last thirty years have complicated this argument. As we have seen, China, South Korea, Singapore, and other Asian countries amassed great wealth and became important players in global financial markets, trade, and industrial production. Some states of the South, such as Brazil, South Africa, and India, began to integrate their economies into regional and global networks.

According to the World Bank, about seven hundred million people live in abject poverty (less than $1.90 a day). Some economists argue that poor countries cannot escape the "poverty trap" without substantial subsidies from the North. UN adviser Jeffrey Sachs (2005, 2015) maintains that the solution lies in large, direct, and sustainable investments to eliminate global political-economic inequality.

Conversely, economists William Easterly (2001, 2006) and Dambisa Moyo (2010) believe that foreign direct help may destroy initiative, contribute to corruption, and create a culture of dependency instead of private entrepreneurship. The poverty trap is avoidable only if the poor are given freedom and the right incentives. Democratic transparency and accountability are essential. Yet short-term thinking and ideological dogma plague developing democracies, which risk falling victim to nationalism and protectionism (Moyo, 2018).

Finally, economists Abhijit Banerjee and Esther Duflo (2011) turn to microeconomics, maintaining that both economic aid and private entrepreneurship may work only if we better understand how the poor make financial and economic decisions. Help should be delivered, but donors should know when and how it should be distributed and when local initiatives and choices should be supported. Education and access to information are critical here (see Chapter 10).

The polluted Buriganga River in Dhaka, Bangladesh. The UN estimates that more than one in six people globally do not have access to safe, fresh water.

THE PATH TO PROSPERITY

On paper, the path to global economic prosperity may look easy. Since 2016, the United States has advocated export-led expansion and tried to reduce import-based consumption. Asians and Europeans should, in theory, slow their exports and buy more from the United States, which should decrease its spending and increase interest rates to reduce consumer spending and encourage savings. However, U.S. government spending has increased dramatically. In the long run, this situation will likely threaten the position of the dollar as the world's reserve currency and further destabilize world finances.

Meanwhile, the Chinese government is reluctant to permit the yuan to rise against the dollar. These measures would make China's exports to the United States more expensive, and U.S. products would cost less in China. Such policies are difficult to implement because of China's surplus-oriented and job-generating strategies. Europe could reduce interest rates and regulations to promote investments and trim expensive social programs. However, lowering interest rates would reduce the money supply to European banks, and downgrading social programs would require serious political sacrifices that almost no political party is willing to accept.

What if global institutions (IMF, the World Bank, WTO) took control of the global economy and trade? As we have seen, such organizations have been criticized for their corporate bureaucracy and lack of transparency (Peet 2009; Blustein 2009). They are seen as acting largely on behalf of a few wealthy states (Stiglitz 2002) and neglecting the increasing importance of international trade in Asia, Latin America, and Africa. Countries vote in global organizations based on their position in the world economy, an arrangement that is evoking increasing criticism (Hoekman and Kostecki 2010; Rapkin and Strand 2006). The granting of loans is also a matter of debate, particularly the IMF's dictating how recipients should run their banking systems and economies (Woods 2007).

The classic assumptions of economic theories may need refreshing. Global trade means the erosion of state power and the increasing influence of non-state institutions and individuals, such as financial speculator, entrepreneur, philanthropist, and NGO sponsor George Soros. Studies show that global corporations can make a profit and contribute to social policies at the same time, yet governments may no longer protect their citizens economically, and corporations may choose to benefit their shareholders before making responsible economic decisions (Hartman and Werhane 2009; Madeley 2009). Around the world, people want to invest in and work for organizations with a **corporate conscience**, in which a business follows the spirit of local and international law, ethical standards, and public opinion (Reich 2017).

corporate conscience A style of corporate self-regulation and a business model that follows the spirit of local and international law, ethical standards, and public opinion.

Check Your Knowledge

1. What is outsourcing?

2. Explain the Asian development model. Why can't the United States apply this model domestically?

3. What are the differences between macroeconomics and microeconomics?

CASE STUDY

China and Liberal Globalization

China's transformation from a country ravaged by Communist experiments into an economic and financial giant is an extraordinary story. In 2010, China became the world's second largest economy, and it is now the second-largest exporting country. Its contribution to global economic growth rose from 2.6 percent in 1981 to 28 percent in 2016. Contrary to expectations, even the 2008 global crisis did not significantly affect Chinese ascendancy. Some economists argue that, if these trends continue, China may replace the United States as the primary vehicle of international economic development within the next twenty years.

Background

China's "economic miracle" is rooted in the 1978 reforms of the Communist leader Deng Xiaoping (1904–1997), who broke with party dogma by allowing small private property, retail trade, and profit-making. Chinese politicians and economies also learned from the mistakes that contributed to the Soviet Union's collapse. Unlike Gorbachev, Deng did not combine economic liberalization with a shift to democracy. Although China wasted billions of dollars to keep existing state-run industries, the Deng reforms shepherded the emergence of a new economy, privately owned and run on market principles. More surprisingly, these reforms were implemented without significant social disturbances because the party still maintained total social control. Ending state intervention into the economy and finances was never on the agenda (Mishra 2018).

Soviet leader Mikhail Gorbachev (left) shakes hands with Chinese senior leader Deng Xiaoping in 1989 in Beijing. Both leaders inspired and managed dramatic economic reforms in their countries, with radically different results.

Analysis

From the start, the Chinese economy focused on producing consumer goods for export, primarily cheap and poor-quality clothing, toys, and other goods. During the 1990s, Chinese exports became technologically advanced, using Japanese, German, and American know-how to produce electronic goods and household durables. As a result of thirty years of uninterrupted economic growth, three to four hundred million people have risen from poverty to the middle class.

China became the first big country in the global South to rapidly become an economic superpower, avoiding many of the social and economic problems that plague other developing economies. It has not faced mass unemployment or become dependent on foreign imports and loans. Instead, it has made the leading developed states, including the United States, dependent on its exports. (See Figure 7-5.)

Domestic Factors

There were several domestic factors behind China's success. First, the country has a strong authoritarian government ruled by the Communist Party; it could therefore implement long-term policies with almost no domestic challenge. The political system did not fracture and then collapse from economic decentralization like the Soviet system did; it instead adapted to market realities with remarkable resilience and muted the political consequences of income inequality (Naughton 1995). Second, China also had an almost unlimited supply of hard-working, educated labor, mostly peasants and their children. Today, it also has

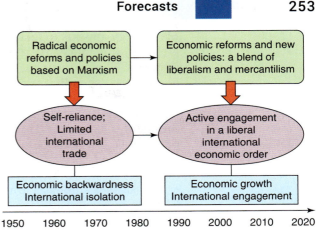

FIGURE 7-5 China's economic policies and international trade: A chronological snapshot.

one of the largest pools of skilled professionals, with many earning college degrees abroad and returning home. Third, this workforce and their incomes remain under tight state control, which maintains the *household registration system*: people must obtain a government permit to establish residence. All employees in the city must belong to *danwei* (the work unit) and receive their wages and benefits, including housing and medical coverage, from it. Party leadership established a monopoly on large capital investments through a system of state-licensed banks—above all, the Bank of China. All peasants and city dwellers must deposit their wages into these banks.

International Factors

International factors also helped China. After 1971, the United States stopped treating it as a Communist enemy and eventually considered it a strategic partner in the Cold War. This allowed China to gain access to Western technology and know-how. The China–U.S. alliance also allowed ethnic Chinese from Taiwan, Hong Kong, and Singapore to invest in the Chinese economy. This policy brought massive foreign investments to China's export-driven economy—not only from other states but from individuals and companies as well. The United States opened American markets to Chinese goods and abolished all restrictions on Chinese exports in 1994. Even more surprisingly, the United States made no systematic attempt to prevent outsourcing of American high-tech industries to China. Other Western states practiced outsourcing as well, in competition with America.

Forecasts

From a realist perspective, China may also challenge Western security. Xi Jinping had become an unchallenged leader of the party and the country;

his strategy appears to focus on using nationalism, projecting China's power globally, and squeezing the US military and trade presence out of Southeast Asia. The country has the second largest military budget in the world; its military expenditures rose to $175 billion in 2018 and continue to grow. Security experts point to China's ambitions to control the seas around it. What would the world do if China decides to take Taiwan by force? Under Presidents Obama and Trump, the United States began to take a more realist perspective, that links China's economic growth with its capacity to project its power over the world. Obama's choice had been to create a multilateral Asian-Pacific trade organization that could contain China's trade power. Trump shifted emphasis to unilateral policies: he introduced new tariffs on Chinese goods and attempts to renegotiate the terms of Sino-American trade in US favor. The Americans became much more critical of the Belt and Road Initiative and attempt to bloc the export of Chinese 5 Generation Internet connectivity, regarding it a security risk.

Liberal economists used to dismiss these arguments and focus on the benefits of Chinese economic progress, namely, lifting hundreds of millions out of poverty and offering cheap goods to the world's consumers. During the 2000s, China became the engine of economic growth elsewhere as well, investing in Africa, America, and Southern Asia (Zoellick 2012). By this logic, Chinese society will gradually evolve as a large middle class should (according to liberal theories) push for political reform. Chinese leaders believe they offer other states a new economic model to accelerate their development while preserving their independence (Mishra 2018). The turn of Xi Jinping to more authoritarianism, domestic purges, and persecution of dissent placed this liberal optimistic perspective under new scrutiny.

Constructivists view China as an unlikely global adversary of the United States because historically it has never pushed for world domination. Instead, after decades of poverty and suffering, it developed a very different national purpose—achievement and excellence—as an economic, not political, superpower. This stance may explain China's extraordinary efforts to modernize everything from airports and superhighways to high-speed trains. The government's legitimacy rests ultimately on economic improvements and growing consumption rather than ideology or political promises. For example, consumption and living standards grow every year, although per capita income is barely one quarter that of the United States.

Conversely, world-systems theorists believe that China is bent on replacing the United States as the core of the global capitalist system. These assumptions echo postcolonial studies, which expect former colonies to demand an end to Western global domination (Arrighi and Li Zhang 2011). The 2008 global financial crisis gave more credibility to such views. In a fine example of Keynesian economic policies comparable to the Marshall Plan, China's GDP grew by 8.7 percent in 2009, largely because the Bank of China provided a $587 billion stimulus package to the economy. Domestic consumption and construction soared.

Entrepreneurial spouses Richard Liu Qiangdong and Zhang Zetian are one of the richest couples in China. Will China's economic inequality result in serious social problems and regional instability?

Analysts caution against an overly rosy estimate of China's economic successes. They acknowledge that the domestic policies that may have ensured this transformation are not necessarily sustainable. Rising unemployment, underreported by the government, could be a problem. The declared war on poverty in China can also create unexpected financial, social, and demografic problems. And, as history teaches, nothing lasts forever.

Case Study Questions

1. How successful will the Chinese economic model be? How many countries will follow this example? What specific features separate China from other countries?
2. Does China have enough "soft power" to peacefully conquer people's hearts and minds globally? How can it increase this power and promote its economic policies?
3. Is it more important to have fewer individual freedoms but be economically secure or to have only some economic security but be able to exercise all individual freedoms? Explain your choice.
4. Which particular individual liberty (e.g., freedom of speech, freedom to form a party, freedom to travel) could you sacrifice for one particular economic guarantee (e.g., a full-time job, paid tuition, a pension)?

Simulation: "Negotiating with China"

CHAPTER 7
REVIEW

International Political Economy and Development

7.1   Explain the major components of international political economy.

The major components of IPE include the interaction of politics and economics in an international context; state production, consumption, finances, and trade; and economic and financial globalization.

Q: Why do governments engage in economic and financial issues?

7.2   Outline the principles of mercantilism.

Mercantilism has two primary principles: accumulating resources and protecting domestic markets.

Q: How are tariffs harmful for international trade? Can tariffs be helpful, and who would benefit from them?

7.3   Explain economic liberalism and its role in the development of the international political economy.

Classical liberalism focuses on free production, trade, and consumption. In Keynesian policies, governments should play an active role. Liberalism relies on international economic and financial institutions, as well as trade agreements.

Q: Compare and contrast mercantilism and economic liberalism.

Q: Would economic liberals support international trade sanctions and, if so, under what circumstances? Use one contemporary example.

7.4   Describe constructivism and conflict theories in the context of international economic policies.

Economic policies depend on the social, political, and cultural conditions in which these policies are implemented. Marxism argues that the world is dominated by a ruling class, which owns the major means of production. Dependency theory claims that technology-driven developed nations have been receiving more benefits from international trade.

Q: Why are the IMF and the World Bank often considered tools of the global North to dominate the global South?

Q: Which of today's domestic and international conditions are favorable for the free market policies and which are not?

7.5 Explain why Marxism and conflict theories criticize the global economic structure.

Marxists argue that global power rests with international corporations and banks, rather than with governments, exacerbating the wealth gap among countries. Further, they argue that free-trade agreements enrich only the ruling class.

Supporters of dependency theory maintain that developed states, called the *core*, receive more benefits from international trade than developing countries, called the *periphery*.

Q: What economic changes do contemporary Marxists and dependency theorists propose?

7.6 Critically apply major economic views to realities of international relations at three levels of analysis.

Political leadership affects economic choices and, in the area known as microeconomics, influences international markets.

Domestic factors affect surplus-oriented and trade deficit-tolerant economic policies. Global economic and financial cooperation has led to greater economic and political interdependence as well as new tensions and conflicts.

Q: Why is it unrealistic to fight global poverty with a single economic model?

KEY TERMS

autarky 232
balance of trade 228
Belt and Road Initiative
brain drain 247
Bretton Woods system 227
BRICS 229
comparative advantage 235
consumption 226
corporate conscience 250
currency 227
dependency theory 241
development 229

economic climate 240
economic liberalism 234
economic sanctions 232
fiscal policy 233
free trade 235
gross domestic product
  (GDP) 225
international political
  economy (IPE) 224
Keynesian economics 233
macroeconomics 233
mercantilism 230

microeconomics 242
monetary policy 233
national purpose 239
North (global) 241
outsourcing 246
production 225
protectionism 231
regional trade agreements 237
South (global) 241
tariff 232

CHAPTER

8

Terrorism and Evolving Security Challenges

On **September 11,** 2001, the radical group al-Qaeda carried out terrorist strikes against the United States. The attacks killed nearly three thousand people and destroyed the World Trade Center in New York and a portion of the Pentagon near Washington, D.C. In the aftermath, the U.S. government sent troops to occupy Afghanistan, where some of the hijackers had been trained. It took ten years to find and kill al-Qaeda founder Osama bin Laden. Radical Islamist groups continue, however, to emerge and practice mass violence. The Islamic State, al-Shabaab, and others have since appeared in the Middle East, as well as in several countries in Asia and Africa.

Another new challenge is the threat posed by the increasing number of online attacks on state and political institutions. In 2000, a disgruntled Filipino teenager created a computer virus that infected one in ten machines worldwide, causing billions of dollars in economic losses and closing down computer networks at the U.S. Department of Defense. In 2016, American intelligence obtained information about Russia's attempts to access software used in voting machines in the United States. Several government sources also revealed in 2016-2019 that Russia hacked emails of several Democratic Party organizations. These attacks resulted in the public release of thousands of stolen emails, many of which included damaging revelations about the party and its nominee, former Secretary of State Hillary Clinton.

These and other attacks have had a profound and lasting impact on both domestic and global politics. Many people in the United States have been divided for years on the issue of the Russian interference. Countries commit enormous resources

We learned about an enemy who is sophisticated, patient, disciplined, and lethal.

—FINAL REPORT OF THE NATIONAL COMMISSION ON TERRORIST ATTACKS UPON THE UNITED STATES, 2004

Light beams in place of New York City's World Trade Center, which was destroyed in the terrorist attacks of September 11, 2001. The National September 11 Memorial and Museum was opened there in 2011. Do you think our governments overestimate, underestimate, or estimate correctly the danger of future devastating terrorist attacks including cyberterrorism?

to resist and combat terrorist organizations, individual hackers, and governments that disguise their efforts and avoid open confrontation. Some analysts believe these threats can be addressed by traditional security policies. Yet others believe that terrorism, cyberwarfare, and other emerging or evolving forms of international violence require radically new security policies.

Which argument is stronger? How do these security threats affect the world? In this chapter, we explore how states, international organizations, and the entire global system deal with these challenges. We discuss contemporary threats and critically examine strategies to combat them.

Learning Objectives

8.1 Describe the logic, strategies, and methods of terrorism.

8.2 Explain emerging security challenges through the lenses of realism and liberalism.

8.3 Describe how alternative approaches view terrorism and emerging security challenges.

8.4 Apply approaches to contemporary security challenges at three levels of analysis.

terrorism Random violence conducted by nonstate actors against governments or their citizens to achieve political goals.

domestic terrorism Terrorism to achieve domestic political goals, such as dismantling a government or changing policies.

8.1 Terrorism and Counterterrorism

Terrorism is violence by nonstate individuals or groups to achieve radical political goals. It is thus a form of *political radicalism*—ideas and methods to produce rapid, dramatic change in the social or political order. Terrorism can be state sponsored in that it may receive financial, military, or logistical support from a foreign government. Yet, in essence it remains a nonstate phenomenon.

Terrorism can be viewed as domestic or international. **Domestic terrorism** pursues mostly domestic political goals such as the dismantling of a government or a change in state policies. Such actions do not necessarily present a direct danger to other states or international organizations. **International terrorism**, which is the main focus of this chapter, challenges international stability by threatening a country or region. This type of terrorism rejects international law and defies international organizations. The distinctions between the forms are imprecise; some apparently domestic acts of terrorism have regional or even global consequences.

Defining Terrorism

Using the labels *terrorism* or *terrorist* has serious consequences. The policy choices of states and international organizations often depend on how terrorism is defined. Also, violent individuals, groups, and governments typically avoid being associated with terrorism and often contest its definitions (Hoffman 1998; Sloan 2006).

LEGITIMIZATION OF MILITARY ACTIONS

Because terrorism is considered an illegal form of violence, countries may choose violent measures to deal with it. By labeling a group an international terrorist organization, a government can rationalize specific policies, just as in times of war. Note that the decision to label an act as *terrorism* or an organization as *terrorist* remains a prerogative of governments. The U.S. Department of State maintains an official list of foreign terrorist organizations, which is regularly updated.

MOBILIZATION OF INTERNATIONAL LAW

International law generally favors cooperation against terrorist groups or states accused of sponsoring terrorism. Individuals suspected of terrorist acts are subject to *extradition*, or removal from one country to the one where they committed their violent acts, to face charges. Many states cooperate with one another and extradite suspects. Yet they cooperate according to mutual agreements andowever, international law. A few years ago, for example, a British suspect named Haroon Aswat was expected to be extradited to the United States to face trial for running a terrorist training camp in America. Both governments have agreed on the extradition. However, international courts

international terrorism Terrorism that involves international groups, interaction between countries, or international organizations, often with regional or global consequences.

National Consortium for the Study of Terrorism and Responses to Terrorism

Members of a Tunisian police commando unit listen to instructions during a drill in al-Swaqa, Jordan, in 2018. The U.S.-funded center conducts counterterrorism training for law enforcement agencies from fifty-six eligible partner countries.

blocked that decision for several reasons (one of them the suspect's possible mental illness and thus his inability to defend himself in the court of law). Governments can also revoke the passports of individuals accused of terrorist activities and limit their ability to travel (Abelson 2015; Wright 2006). The need to combat international terrorism has created an unprecedented network of new bilateral and international military, economic, and intelligence sharing and financial agreements.

RATIONALIZATION OF OTHER POLICIES

Some states use swift counterterrorist measures that are questionable from the viewpoint of international law. In a historic example, after Palestinian militants assassinated Israeli athletes during the 1972 Olympic Games in Munich, the Israeli government created a special squad to scout and kill the perpetrators. The group frequently acted illegally, using almost the same violent means as the hunted terrorists. Countries may also unilaterally toughen domestic security laws, including street surveillance, passenger screening at airports, and travel restrictions for foreigners. Some view most forms of **counterterrorism** as justifiable because terrorists are "outside the law" (Klein 2005). Others disagree on legal grounds. After 9/11, many criticized the U.S. government for suspending normal juridical norms for terrorism suspects; keeping them in special prisons, such as at the Guantanamo Bay Naval Base in Cuba; and using torture to obtain information. Critics also claimed that the Patriot Act, a set of domestic counterterrorist policies signed by President George W. Bush in 2001, limited civic freedoms at home. In 2011, President Obama signed a four-year extension of three key provisions in the act. In 2015, Congress kept some parts of the law through 2019.

counterterrorism
Long-term policies and specific short-term measures to prevent and combat international and domestic terrorism.

The graves of five murdered Israeli athletes in Tel Aviv. Palestinian terrorists kidnapped and killed eleven Israeli athletes at the Munich Olympics in 1972, in a crime that shocked the world. Israel launched covert operations in retaliation.

History Lab	The *Terrorism* Label Can Be Misused

Historically, countries' policies were frequently based on how terrorism was defined. Therefore, the term was and remains subject to misuse. Some governments use the label to combat domestic opposition. Russia, Iran, Turkey, and the United States have frequently accused one another of supporting terrorism in Syria during the country's civil war. All sides rejected the accusations of others.

Governments often argue that international law does not always apply when terrorism is at stake. After 2001, U.S. authorities identified many suspected terrorists as "illegal combatants" and disregarded the protocols of the 1949 Geneva Convention Relative to the Treatment of Prisoners of War, which prohibit indefinite detention of prisoners of war. Prisoners have been kept at Guantanamo for years. This precedent caused serious domestic and international criticism of both the Bush and Obama administrations. President Trump has vowed to keep the prison functioning.

Governments and private individuals could use the *terrorism* label to settle personal scores with political or business opponents. By accusing people or groups of terrorist activities, a government can delegitimize them in the eyes of the courts and public opinion.

CRITICAL THINKING

❶ Suggest examples of the potential or actual misuse of the term *terrorism*. ❷ Search the Web for "We are not terrorists" (in quotation marks). From the results, select five cases representing different groups. What arguments do they use to separate themselves from terrorism? What do they call themselves? Why do they need to defend their image, and to whom do they appeal?

How Terrorism Works

Asking how terrorism works requires looking not only at methods, such as suicide bombings or random attacks on civilians, but also at assumptions and rationalizations.

ASSUMPTIONS AND METHODS

Terrorism is rooted in the assumption that it is practically impossible to defeat states and international coalitions in an open military battle. Governments have support from businesses, intelligence, armed forces, and law-enforcement institutions. Therefore, terrorists rely on unconventional methods to cause fear among the population of a targeted country or a group of states (Chaliand and Blin 2007). They depend on secrecy and the ability to keep their cells invisible from governments. The Internet often becomes an asset to terrorist groups because governments have little control over it (Kello 2013; Horgan 2009, 2).

Terrorist groups are often extremely difficult to infiltrate. Most are in *networks*, or loose collectives. Members of one group may not know members from others. Instead of building a formal hierarchical structure, groups tend to rely on loyalty and mutual surveillance. Their sense of collective involvement is reaffirmed by spiritual and material rewards for devotion and merciless punishments for betrayal (Miller 2013; Gunaratna 2002).

Terrorist groups use violence or threats of violence to influence governments or key decision makers. Terrorists often target civilians, including children, through random killings, bombings in public places, and attacks on shopping malls, television stations, or hotels (Nacos 2009). For example, in 2018, several ISIS gunmen stormed the Save the Children office in the Afghan city of Jalalabad, killing five people and wounding many more. This and other international aid organizations have been attacked constantly in Afghanistan in recent years, forcing many of them to curtail operations or leave (Ghazi and Mashal 2018).

Future terrorist attacks may attempt to use weapons of mass destruction (WMD). Therefore, preventing nuclear proliferation and a leak of nuclear know-how to terrorist organizations remains a priority for the international community (Howard and Forest 2008; Hoffman 2010). Terrorist organizations also are turning to cyberterrorism, which we will discuss later in this chapter.

The face of international terrorism changed irrevocably after 9/11. Previously, terrorists usually relied on **coercion and extortion**—the use of force or threats—to get what they wanted from governments, and negotiations between states and terrorists were possible (Bueno de Mesquita 2005). Bin Laden and his associates created a new brand of terrorism aimed at the moral and political defeat of the West, creating a new political order and rejecting negotiations. Technology also became a factor. In 2016, the U.S. Department of Justice charged Ardit Ferizi with cyberterrorism for hacking into a military website, stealing information on government and military personnel, and selling his "kill list" to ISIS. This was probably the first case of prosecuting a combination of terrorism and hacking (Blake 2016).

Terrorists look for publicity, or *public exposure*. By committing an act of violence, a radical group is likely to attract the attention of millions, which is important for at least two reasons. First, the group may rapidly publicize its agenda to seek sympathy (Pape 2003; Pillar 2001). Second, public exposure often helps to recruit supporters, sponsors, and new members. Copycat terrorist acts may also follow (Coleman 2004). Table 8-1 summarizes the methods of terrorism.

coercion and extortion The use of force and threats of force to compel others to comply with demands.

RAND database of worldwide terrorist incidents

Inside the mind of a former radical jihadist

THE THINKING BEHIND TERRORISM

In most cases, terrorism is portrayed as a last resort, a desperate response to an acute problem or injustice. Once the source of injustice is removed, violence will end. The Mau Mau groups in 1950s Kenya staged an uprising to overthrow British colonial rule and used terrorism to fight British forces and the local civilians collaborating with them. The British refused to negotiate and only after a costly and violent struggle suppressed the uprising. Terrorists also often argue for *collective responsibility*. They claim that civilians who die in a terrorist act pay the price for being on the side causing injustice. In his 2002 *Letter to America*, bin Laden stated that those who died in the 9/11 attacks, including Muslims, were guilty because they supported U.S. policies as taxpayers and consumers.

Finally, terrorists rationalize their acts as *retaliation*, or payback for grievances. The two perpetrators of the 2013 Boston Marathon bombing were

TABLE 8-1 Methods of Contemporary Terrorism

Methods	Examples
Attacks against civilians in public places	In 2016, three suicide bombings occurred in Belgium: two at Brussels Airport and one at a metro station in central Brussels. Thirty-two civilians and three perpetrators were killed, and more than three hundred people were injured. In Nice, a truck driver deliberately drove into the crowd on the promenade, killing eighty-six people and injuring almost five hundred. ISIS claimed responsibility for the attacks.
Attacks targeting journalists	In 2015, two gunmen—both radical Islamists—broke into the office of the satirical cartoon journal *Charlie Hebdo* in Paris and killed twelve journalists and cartoonists. Around this time, ISIS executioners in Syria murdered several Western journalists and posted the killings on the Web.
Attacks against government offices	In 2011, terrorists attacked the American diplomatic compound in Benghazi, Libya, killing U.S. Ambassador J. Christopher Stevens and U.S. Foreign Service Officer Sean Smith.
Attacks against military targets	In October 2000, two suicide bombers killed seventeen U.S. sailors and damaged the USS *Cole* in Yemen's Aden Harbor. Al-Qaeda took responsibility for the attacks.
Attacks involving hostage taking	On June 27, 1976, a plane flying from Tel Aviv to Paris was hijacked and 248 passengers were taken hostage; the plane landed in Entebbe, Uganda. The terrorists demanded the release of their fellows—mostly Palestinians—from various prisons.
Online attacks	In 2016, Russian hackers, apparently in coordination with Russian secret services, obtained access to personal and official emails of the officials of the Democratic National Committee.

reportedly venting their grievances against U.S. foreign policy in predominantly Muslim countries. After the Kenyan government cracked down against al-Shabaab, the jihadist terrorist group attacked a Kenyan college in 2015, killing 147 people. The same group operating from the neighboring Somalia has committed another deadly attack on a hotel in Kenya's capital. Twenty-one people died in this terrorist attack.

Terrorist groups pursue different goals, but most of their tactics remain consistent. There are at least five such strategies: intimidation, attrition, provocation, spoiling, and outbidding (Kydd and Walter 2006). Using intimidation and attrition, terrorists show their strength and constant willingness to

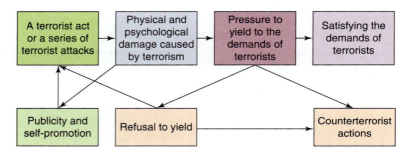

FIGURE 8-1
The process of terrorism.

destroy. With provocation, terrorists "invite" governments' overreaction and violence to keep the situation unstable. Provocations often force governments, international organizations, and individuals to respond in ways that aid the terrorists' cause. When terrorists turn to spoiling, their aim is to expose their enemies' weaknesses and inability to stop terrorism. For example, counterterrorist measures in democratic countries are often slowed down by the public debate about whether violence is the answer to violence. The outbidding strategy helps terrorists demonstrate their willingness to continuously kill, intimidate, persevere, and appear undefeatable. (See Figure 8.1.)

Terrorism: In the Name of What?

Before turning to terrorism, groups and individuals share certain goals that usually derive from *ideologies*, or comprehensive principles and beliefs. We briefly examine four major ideologies that, based on a historical analysis, inspired terrorists around the world: anarchism, radical socialism, extreme nationalism, and religious fundamentalism. (See Table 8-2.)

ANARCHISM

anarchism An ideology and movement that seeks to create a borderless, peaceful, self-governing society of free, local communes in which people generate and distribute wealth without government control.

As a political philosophy and a global movement, **anarchism** seeks to create a borderless, peaceful society of free communes in which people generate and distribute wealth without government control. There are peaceful and violent types of anarchism. Among the chief theorists of the violent school was Mikhail Bakunin (1814–1876), a Russian-born theorist who rejected any form of state, whether monarchy or liberal republic. Anarchists believe that government offices, banks, and capitalist enterprises must be destroyed and that sovereign states should be dissolved.

Anarchists have used political assassinations and other acts of destruction as a means to reach political goals. They believe that such acts will inspire people to rise up against injustice and then turn to anarchism, but that conclusion has never come to pass. While anarchism was a source of violent radicalism for many years, it has always been fragmented and poorly organized. A less dangerous, yet influential, current form of anarchism is the radical anticapitalist and anti-globalization movement.

TABLE 8-2 Tactics and Goals of Terrorism Driven by Ideology

Ideology	Tactics	Goals
Anarchism (mostly in the nineteenth and early twentieth centuries)	Acts against government officials and civilians to create panic and paralyze government and society.	Destruction of all state institutions and creation of a self-governing society of free communes.
Extreme nationalism (mostly throughout the twentieth century)	Acts against government officials and civilians of another nation to break their will; acts against other ethnic groups.	Creation of a nation-state and the eviction of other ethnic groups.
Radical socialism (mostly throughout the twentieth century)	Acts against governments to unleash a revolution of the masses or reach immediate political goals.	A new society based on the abolition of private property and the destruction of privileged groups.
Religious fundamentalism (throughout history)	Acts against those viewed as enemies of an imagined religious order.	A religious revolution and a theocracy in one country or transnational religious (theocratic) order.

EXTREME NATIONALISM

In the context of international relations, **extreme nationalism** is an ideology aimed above all at creating a nation-state. Nationalist militants have used terrorist methods for many years. In July 1914 in Sarajevo, Serbian nationalists assassinated Archduke Franz Ferdinand, heir to the Austro-Hungarian (Habsburg) throne, and his wife, Sophia, thus triggering a harsh response from Austria. The failure of European governments to resolve this crisis resulted in World War I. Nationalism-motivated terrorism was predominant throughout the twentieth century, stirring dramatic events in Northern Ireland, Palestine, Korea, Vietnam, Kenya, Algeria, Kosovo, and elsewhere. In the twenty-first century, one of the most active nationalist groups remains the Kurdistan Workers' Party (PKK). It continues its violent struggle (using tactics including terrorism) against the Turkish government to create a sovereign Kurdistan.

extreme nationalism An ideology aimed above all at creating a nation-state.

RADICAL SOCIALISM

Radical socialism seeks to destroy capitalism and liberal democracy in the name of social and economic equality (see Chapters 4 and 7). During decolonization in the 1950s and 1960s, many radical Socialist groups in Latin America and Africa used terrorism against authoritarian governments, which often relied on Western support. Abimael Guzmán, a Socialist and former university professor in Peru, formed a radical Maoist group called Shining Path (*Sendero Luminoso*) that began a bloody campaign of terror against elected officials, labor union leaders, and peasants accused of collaborating with the government (Burt 2009). Guzmán was captured in 1992 and imprisoned for life based on multiple trials in Peru.

Radical socialism An ideology that seeks to destroy capitalism and liberal democracy in the name of social and economic equality.

A youth holds a flag with the image of Abdullah Ocalan, the jailed leader of the PKK (Kurdistan Workers' Party), during the 2018 Newroz celebrations. Kurdish militants regularly clash with government forces in parts of Turkey, which considers the PKK a terrorist organization.

▷

Terrorism is a failed brand

Religious fundamentalism A set of beliefs and behaviors based on strict adherence to religious principles.

caliphate A state led by a Muslim ruler.

In the 1970s, the Red Army Faction (RAF) in West Germany and the Red Brigades (*Brigate Rosse*) in Italy targeted bankers and government officials to create instability and chaos. In 1978, Italian terrorists kidnapped and killed former prime minister Aldo Moro. Gradually, the wave of terrorism abated. Some of its leaders, including RAF's founder Ulrike Meinhof, committed suicide; others were killed or captured. Only a few Socialist groups now use terrorism as a method of struggle against capitalism.

RELIGIOUS FUNDAMENTALISM

Religious fundamentalism is a set of beliefs and behaviors based on strict adherence to religious principles. For example, radical groups inspired by Buddhism have appeared in Myanmar (Beech 2013), and a number of Islamic groups have organized terrorist acts to advance their ultimate political goal—the creation of an Islamic state. Salafism, a radical version of Islam, has inspired anti-Russian guerrillas in many regions (Hahn 2012). Al-Qaeda seeks a global Muslim state (called a **caliphate**) governed by *Sharia* law (Desai 2007). ISIS also intends to create a caliphate in Iraq, Syria, and other countries (Weiss and Hassan 2015). Jemaah Islamiyah is a Southeast Asian radical organization attempting to create an Islamic state that includes Brunei, Malaysia, Singapore, Indonesia, and the southern Philippines. The Taliban, a Sunni political movement operating primarily in Afghanistan and Pakistan, uses both terrorism and insurgency to build an Islamic state in Afghanistan. Hamas is a political movement hoping to create an independent Islamic Palestine; it is still formally committed to destroying Israel as a state. The Shiite group Hezbollah, which operates from Lebanon, also targets Israel and its supporters.

DEBATE > DO VIOLENT GROUPS CHANGE?

True or false. Think about the following statements, considering examples:

Statement 1: *Every fundamentalist or radical group supports terrorism.*
> Answer: False. Many fundamentalist groups reject violence, and most nationalist or socialist groups also categorically reject terrorist methods.

Statement 2: *Radical groups disagree about the methods they use.*
> Answer: True. It is important to distinguish any movement's moderate and nonviolent wings from its more radical wings.

Statement 3: *Violent groups don't change.*
> Answer: False. Many of them evolve, and some abandon terrorism for the sake of domestic and international legitimacy. Nationalists often shift from violence to negotiations if they see their ultimate goal, the creation of a nation-state, acknowledged by the international community.

WHAT'S YOUR VIEW?

For many years, members of Hezbollah and Hamas have pledged the destruction of the state of Israel and have found significant support among residents of Lebanon (the stronghold of Hezbollah) and the Gaza Strip (the stronghold of Hamas). Which of the following tactics would be more effective in handling these groups? Explain your choice.

1. Pursue a strategy to change their ideologies over time (through open discussions, for example) and consider every opportunity for negotiations with them.
2. Neutralize and defeat them because, although some violent groups may change, it is too risky for the region and the world to rely on this expectation of their peaceful transformation.

🔗

Hezbollah and Hamas

This brief classification does not exhaust the many principles that can motivate terrorists. Even a belief in the need to protect nature can move some individuals to violence or ecoterrorism (see Chapter 9).

Cyberwarfare and the Threat of Cyberterrorism

Military, intelligence, and scientific communities in the United States and other countries have been discussing **cyberwarfare** for years. In 2016, U.S. intelligence reported on Russia's use of cybertechniques to influence the outcome of presidential elections in 2016. The attackers included Russian secret services, hired or collaborating hackers, and the Internet whistleblowing network WikiLeaks; the main target was the headquarters of the Democratic Party's National Committee. According to American intelligence sources, Russia's president Vladimir Putin used the most sophisticated means of cyberwarfare to disrupt the electoral campaign of Hillary Clinton, the Democratic candidate, and promote the chances of her opponent, the Republican candidate Donald Trump. The Russian cyberoperations admittedly took effective advantage of the new dependence of the U.S. campaigning and electoral process on cyberspace information (Shiraev 2019).

cyberwarfare A security threat involving deliberate targeting of computers and networks of sovereign states, IGOs, and NGOs to achieve military, political, and other strategic and tactical goals.

After Trump was elected in 2016, the enraged Democrats claimed that the Kremlin aimed to disrupt democracy and accused the new president of "collusion" with Russia. During its last months in office, the Obama Administration imposed sanctions on several Russian officials. The Russian government on every occasion denied any involvement in the election. At one point, Putin—as if he was joking—attributed hacking to "patriotic Russian citizens" who were compelled to respond to the American slights against Russia. Skeptics claimed that the Russian cyber-meddling was minimal. In any case, the real or perceived Russian actions yielded disproportionate effects, exacerbating existing tensions and cleavages in U.S. politics (CNN Library, November 24, 2018). In 2017, the U.S. Congress and the Justice Department authorized independent investigation of Russian involvement in the presidential election of 2016. This was one of the major political scandals in recent history. In 2018, the Trump Administration imposed more sanctions on Russian officials deemed to be responsible for tampering with the U.S. democratic process. In 2019, the official investigation was over, which showed the absence of Trump collusion with Russia. Yet the political battles surrounding the scandal continued.

cyberweapons The variety of tools that can disrupt or destroy computer network operations.

Cyberwarfare requires the use of **cyberweapons**—the variety of tools that can disrupt or destroy computer network operations (Kello 2013). Unlike conventional military actions, cyberwarfare takes place in cyberspace, which impacts computers on a network, the Internet, and other communication systems. The ultimate goal of most cyberattacks is not only to affect the computer system but also to disrupt or destroy certain social, economic, or government functions. It is different from commercial cybercrime, which typically involves bank accounts and credit card fraud, other financial crimes, and transmission of illegal materials.

Cyberwarfare can be described along at least four dimensions. (1) There can be a state-against-state conflict in which one country targets the other's strategic computer assets. As this action can be a cause of war, however, governments may instead (2) hire companies and individuals who will attack the computer systems of the nongovernment and government structures of another state. This hybrid form of cyberwarfare provides a cover of deniability to state leaders. Cyberwarfare can also be (3) a private-to-private conflict, involving an exchange of cyber blows between nonstate entities, including NGOs and private businesses (Kello 2013). And (4) cyberattacks can be planned to unfold in the near or distant future. In 2009, Great Britain's Joint Intelligence Committee warned that Chinese-stocked components of British Telecom's phone network could be preloaded with malware or zero-day weaknesses, giving Beijing the ability to interrupt the country's power and food supplies in critical moments (Kello 2013). Nine years later, the British Defense secretary warned that Russia could launch a cyberattack against British power plans (Allegretti 2018). Neither occurred, but without access to intelligence, it is difficult to know how close the threats were to becoming reality.

As these four types show, governments, individuals, and groups can use cyberweapons to pursue their goals. A few skilled individuals can disrupt economies and the militaries of sovereign states, businesses, international organizations, and NGOs from thousands of miles away. Cyberattacks can disturb a regional or international order (Singer and Friedman 2014). Nonstate actors and individuals can play an increasingly bigger role in cyberwarfare, which can lead to dangerous, sometimes catastrophic, consequences. Moreover, some countries—notably, Russia, Iran, and China—increasingly employ potential cyberattackers to prepare and execute hostilities on behalf of their governments in secret. The United States and other Western countries prepare cyberweapons as means of deterrence (see Chapter 5).

Cyberattacks include denial-of-service (DoS) attacks, which make an organization or network resource unavailable to its users. Significant regions of Internet connectivity in such cases can be compromised. Some attacks can require replacement or reinstallation of hardware, which can take days or weeks (Greenberg 2015). Almost all cyberattacks involve the use of malware (software that interferes with computer functionality or degrades data integrity). An early incident was the seizure of secret U.S. government data by Chinese agents in 2003. Another example is the later Operation Olympic Games—a covert cyber operation (allegedly made by the United States and its allies) to affect, disrupt, and slow down Iran's nuclear facilities at Natanz (Kello 2013).

Cyberwarfare threatens every aspect of international security. A potential manifestation is **cyberterrorism**—use of the Internet by state or nonstate actors to threaten or cause significant harm. It is often a deliberate, large-scale disruption of computer networks by means of viruses, worms, phishing, and other malicious software and hardware methods and programming scripts. Threats range from significant theft of data and disruption of computer operations to the destruction of entire systems and physical equipment (Kello 2013; Gertz 2011). Cyberterrorism poses a significant threat to a country's military capabilities by threatening its logistics network, stealing its operational plans, or obstructing its ability to deliver weapons on target. Even when cyberterrorists are identified, it is difficult to retaliate against them (Lynn 2010).

Cyberterrorism Use of the Internet by state or nonstate actors to threaten or cause significant harm.

In international relations, cybersecurity consists of policies and actions to protect the operations of a state's computer system or the integrity of its data from hostile action. Cybersecurity is also a state of affairs: this term is used to describe the absence of unauthorized foreign intrusion into a country's computer systems (Kello 2013).

Artificial Intelligence and Warfare

Mechanization and computerization of warfare have long been described in sci-fi literature. The complexity and lethality of military conflicts grew together with the advancement of technology. Throughout history, military officers and other professionals remained in control of the weapons used in

Robin Li, CEO of the multinational technology company Baidu, arrives for Baidu Create 2018. The event, held in Beijing, China, was designed to promote the company's artificial intelligence (AI) resources. China has its own sovereign Internet and online search systems.

autonomous weapons Robots programmed to destroy and kill.

artificial intelligence (AI) A computer system's capability to perform tasks that normally require human cognition, emotion, and action, including complex perception, recognition, analysis, evaluation, and decision making.

artificial intelligence warfare (AIW) The use of artificial intelligence systems and devices for military applications, including attack, defense, transport, and search and rescue.

battle. During the Cold War, the superpowers' militaries turned to computers to identify, track, and navigate missiles. More recently, the same technology used in self-driving cars could let future military systems destroy targets on their own (Scharre 2017). Military robots, or **autonomous weapons**, already have the ability to carry weapons and use lethal force under the direction of a human operator. New unmanned robotic systems are already being developed, and robots will likely be given more authority to make their own decisions to destroy and kill (Arkin 2018).

Consider the development of unmanned aerial vehicles (UAVs or drones). They can perform in military settings and exercise simple and complex operations (such as surveillance of and attacks against targets) with minimal human intervention (Cummings 2017). Such devices could possibly make decisions to strike and kill if programmed to do so. Yet who will be the programmers, and what goals would they try to achieve?

Artificial intelligence (AI) is the capability of a computer system to perform tasks that normally require human cognition, emotion, and action, including complex perception, recognition, analysis, evaluation, and decision making. Essentially, AI allows a device to perceive its environment critically and maximize its chance of success at a particular goal. For example, a drone driven by AI should choose among several targets on the ground, distinguishing armed militants from civilians. Such drones will be able to recognize faces and languages spoken in their potential target areas. AI-driven technologies provide for the most optimal courses of action given the information they receive and analyze (Cummings 2017). Specialists increasingly discuss **artificial intelligence warfare (AIW)**, or

---

DEBATE > INFORMATION WARFARE

Country A wants certain politicians in Country B to lose the forthcoming election. To achieve this goal, it uses its intelligence and military to launch a series of publications into the cyberspace of Country B. These publications falsely accuse the candidates of bribery, theft, infidelity, and other forms of asocial behavior. Voters believe the stories and the candidates lose.

WHAT'S YOUR VIEW?

Is the use of information and communication technology to gain an advantage over a state—known as information warfare—a security problem? Which of the following positions do you support? Explain your answer.

❶ A country's character assassination attempts against another state's leaders are part of today's digital politics. They occur everywhere in the world, and the best defense is to ignore them.

❷ Character assassination attempts are a form of aggression. They are attacks against a state's political system and thus—like an act of physical sabotage or a terrorist act—constitute interference in its domestic affairs.

---

the use of AI systems and devices for military applications, including attack, defense, transport, and search and rescue.

8.2 Traditional Views of Evolving Security Threats

In this section, we consider contemporary, evolving security challenges through the lenses of realism and liberalism. These major theories focus on different aspects of the complex issue of terrorism.

Realism

Realism argues that a *symmetry*, or balance of forces and threats, exists in a stable world: An attack by one state could cause a response from other states, and balance is restored. A key argument in this view is that failure to respond to threats can weaken a targeted state's power and encourage further attacks. Terrorism and many forms of cyberwarfare, however, pose an **asymmetric threat** to sovereign states: in asymmetric conflicts, the relative military power and tactics differ substantially between sides (Reynolds 2012; Cordesman 2002). Because terrorists do not represent a state, it is difficult to identify the perpetrators and retaliate effectively. Further, in response to an asymmetric threat, a state does not want to escalate tension or act from a position of inferiority. A conflict initiated by means of AI also can be seen as an asymmetric threat when it is difficult to identify which

Check Your Knowledge

1. Define political radicalism. Can it be nonviolent? Why or why not?

2. How does terrorism differ from gangsterism and guerrilla warfare?

3. Explain "collective responsibility."

4. Name and explain the five key strategies of terrorism.

5. Explain the strategic goals of anarchism, radical socialism, extreme nationalism, and religious fundamentalism, especially in relation to Islamist groups.

6. Suggest ways to achieve these goals by peaceful means.

asymmetric threat
Potential use of force between actors whose power and tactics differ substantially.

government or organization is behind the attack (Cummings 2017). Terrorist groups therefore try to provoke governments to overreact or launch futile responses.

International terrorism can destabilize a balance of forces in unpredictable ways. The terrorist acts in Sarajevo in 1914 and the terrorist attacks on the United States in September 2001 are nearly a hundred years apart, yet they seem to share some similarities because of their international dynamics. (See Figure 8-2.) In both cases, nonstate groups committed acts of violence that led to war.

The large decentralization and scale of cyberspace makes new security difficult to manage from a policy perspective. Traditional security concepts such as deterrence, security regimes, or security community—discussed in Chapter 5—appear to be only marginally relevant to cybersecurity. Under these conditions, several evolving strategies are important. First, it is very important to invest in new technologies related to cybersecurity. Second, to better understand and use cybersecurity, governments should also learn about specific individuals and groups who utilize cyberweapons and their motivations behind their attacks. Students majoring in international politics and global affairs should be among the contributors to cybersecurity (Singer and Friedman 2014; Nye 2011). Third, the task of cybersecurity is often in the hands of the corporations who own and operate the majority of critical computer infrastructures; therefore, tighter cooperation between homeland security and private IT business is required.

MONITORING AND PREVENTION

Realists argue that, because states cannot effectively retaliate against terrorism in "an eye for an eye" fashion, they should instead engage in preventive measures. Many strategies for asymmetric warfare include *monitoring* and *prevention*. Intelligence gathering ranges from electronic monitoring to infiltration into terrorist organizations. These policies also include elaborate measures to prevent terrorist groups from acquiring sophisticated military technologies, including WMD. The UN's High-Level Panel on Threats, Challenges and Change stated that countries may conceivably justify the use of force, "not just reactively but preventively and before a latent threat becomes imminent" (United Nations 2004).

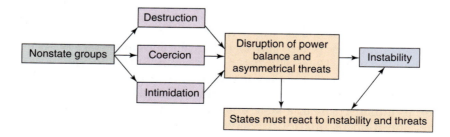

FIGURE 8-2
Asymmetric threats from the realist perspective.

PREEMPTIVE AND PUNITIVE APPROACHES

Other policies are *preemptive* and *punitive*. **Preemptive policies**, which range from the physical elimination of groups to the disruption of their financial resources, take action against terrorists before they strike. Scores of militants have been killed by drones. Such actions, as far as this argument goes, do not violate the sovereignty of other countries for two reasons: governments often secretly grant permission for such actions, and some governments, such as the government in Pakistan, Sudan, or Afghanistan, do not exercise full control over certain territories within their borders.

preemptive policies Actions against terrorists before they strike.

HOMELAND SECURITY

Another type of policy is often called *homeland security*, after the American example. The 9/11 attacks required a costly refurbishing and expansion of the U.S. government. New government structures were created to increase the control of borders and immigration, screen millions of visitors, monitor electronic communications, and investigate suspects. Governments of the EU implemented additional legal restrictions to monitor the flow of people through their borders. These policies aim at individuals and organizations suspected of helping terrorist organizations, particularly in the Middle East and Central Asia. (See Table 8-3.)

Supporters of preventive and preemptive policies suggest that reliance on international agreements is insufficient in avoiding new types of warfare such as AIW. For example, some governments (including Iraq in 1991 and Syria in 2013) violated the international ban on chemical weapons by using them against civilians. The argument is that international treaties alone won't prevent rogue regimes and terrorists from building the weapons of their choice. Most countries are likely to stop producing weapons for AIW because of the agreements their governments sign. Yet some states and

TABLE 8-3 Counterterrorist Policies: Realist Targets and Methods

Targets	Methods: Monitoring, Preemption, and Homeland Security
Camps and other facilities used for training or staging a terrorist attack	Political pressure on governments where such facilities exist; direct military strikes against camps or facilities
Financial assets of suspected terrorists	Confiscation, blocking, or control of assets used to support international terrorism
Terrorist networks and cells	Search and surveillance; operations against the existing networks; tougher immigration policies
WMDs and delivery systems	Safeguarding the sites where WMD are stored; protecting technologies to prevent their use by terrorists; ensuring nonproliferation of WMD beyond current nuclear states

terrorist groups can ignore international treaties and use or threaten to use such weapons (Scharre 2017). Therefore, only more superior weapons and preemptive actions should deter and prevent governments and individuals from using new AIW weapons.

POLICY EFFICACY

How can we measure the effectiveness of such policies? The absence of new terrorist attacks may indicate that they have worked. There are, however, both obvious and hidden side effects, including the high financial costs of counterterrorism, its impact on the economy, loss of individual freedoms, and the impact on democratic governance itself. We will address these issues later in this chapter.

In summary, realism assumes that states identify and eliminate the physical and organizational infrastructure of international terrorism. Realists also stand for punitive military operations against states that harbor terrorists and believe there should be pressure on those that financially and politically support terrorism. The combination of preventive measures and force should take the incentive from terrorist hands and eventually weaken them.

SEEING BEYOND POWER BALANCE

Most critics of the realist view claim that understanding new security threats requires examining the conditions that breed violence and political radicalism. Terrorism cannot be defeated by military means alone. There is no impenetrable shield against cyberwarfare. It takes understanding the causes of terrorism and using legal and economic means of international cooperation

Young women hold "We Love Manchester" posters after the 2017 terrorist bombing in which twenty-two people were killed after an Ariana Grande concert in Manchester, England.

to defeat violence of any kind. States are likely to succeed in protecting their security when they act together to create a better international environment and engage international institutions and nonstate actors.

Liberalism

Liberalism treats terrorism as a complex phenomenon exploiting acute social and political problems. People turn to terrorism for a reason, even if it appears to be a distorted one. Foreign occupation, chronic unemployment, the injustices of daily lives, and profound inefficiency in addressing social problems all contribute to radicalism. From the liberal point of view, policies that address these causes can isolate terrorists from those who support their activities.

CRIMINALIZING TERRORISM

In the liberal view, a democratic society should not apply one set of legal rules for its own citizens and another set for groups labeled terrorists; this concept is known as the **criminalization of terrorism**. The main point is that illegal violent actions should not cause illegal counteractions. International law can be used along with domestic laws to qualify terrorist actions as crimes and deal with them using a broad domestic and international consensus (Schultz 2004). If legal rules are not in place, they have to be set. Governments should not limit the rights of their law-abiding citizens and should draw a clear line between monitoring terrorist activities and surveilling people's daily activities. They should coordinate their policies and rely on international law against terrorist groups and their sponsors. New laws should be passed to criminalize cyberterrorism, both domestic and international. The rule of law, in the end, is the best way to confront the lawlessness that is the breeding ground of radicalism and terrorism (Samuel 2013). Figure 8-3 shows the steps in analyzing terrorism and other asymmetric threats from the liberal perspective and in choosing the appropriate counterterrorism option.

criminalization of terrorism A concept that considers terrorism a form of criminal behavior in the context of domestic and international law.

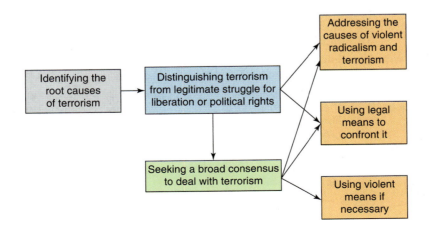

FIGURE 8-3
New security threats from the liberal perspective.

LEGAL ACTION AND EDUCATION

Liberalism does not reject military actions against asymmetric and other threats. The difference between the liberal and realist approaches is in the priorities they assign to negotiations, consensus, legal means, and the use of force. (See Table 8-4.) Supporters of the liberal view do not promise quick results from their policies but emphasize gradual improvements because social changes take time to implement.

In liberalism, any action against violent threats should be strictly legitimate. It must be conducted in accordance with international law and include, whenever possible, international cooperation. Counterterrorist measures, for example, should be a combination of negotiations, law-enforcement operations, and military actions (if necessary)—all under the guidance of local and international rules.

Such policies should legitimize counterterrorism, which should include strategic cooperation between states, international organizations, and NGOs (Cronin 2002). *Public diplomacy*, or the achievement of policy goals by engagement with local communities and elements of civil society, should become an efficient form of counterterrorism. Public diplomacy seeks to separate terrorist and other radical organizations from their popular base (Simon and Martini 2004). It thus relies on soft power (see Chapter 3) to win the "hearts and minds" of citizens and leaders alike.

Liberal principles should not be applied without considering the actual social, cultural, and geographical factors (Kaplan 2012). American experience with counterinsurgency (COIN) in Iraq and Afghanistan from 2006 to 2018 both provided confirmation for the liberal approach and revealed its limitations. Addressing the needs of the local population with efficiency, building

TABLE 8-4 Fighting International Terrorism: The Liberal Perspective

Target	Method
Violent radical groups	Deterrence by propaganda and legal policies; differentiation and marginalization of extremists; attempts to negotiate with others.
Conditions and root causes of terrorism	Improvement of the population's social and economic conditions; reduction of potential social support for radical groups.
Terrorist propaganda, justified by nationalist and other legitimate goals	International condemnation of terrorism, outlawing groups that resort to terrorist methods; support of national liberation and other legitimate causes through international organizations.
Anti-Western radicalism, especially Islamic fundamentalism	Educational campaigns; cooperation with nonextremist Islamic and other religious organizations; coordination of policies with local authorities.

local administration capacity, and respecting local customs could limit the base for recruitment of terrorism. This, however, required time and patience and tact, as well as considerable resources. Abject poverty, rampant corruption, and infiltration of foreign fighters could send the communities targeted by liberal policies back to violence.

Supporters of international law reason that, in the past, various international bans on particular weapons worked. Based on international agreements, countries stopped using poison gas on battlefields (although the Nazi government used it in concentration camps during World War II). Even existing international agreements are sufficient, if they are properly enforced, to address most military, logistical, or ethical problems associated with AIW. Among such agreements could be the UN Convention on Certain Conventional Weapons (CCW). This treaty bans incendiary weapons, mines, booby traps, blinding lasers, and weapons to injure humans through small fragments. Several Cold War agreements ban chemical and biological weapons, as well as the use of nuclear weapons in space (Scharre 2017). In short, the use of AIW can be legally limited or banned; it all depends on the countries' goodwill (McSweeney 2017).

Another argument refers to a possible interaction of law, science, and technology. Ongoing research in machine ethics is concerned with teaching machines ethical principles. In brief, AI-driven programs could eventually function in an ethically responsible fashion to limit their destructive force (Anderson and Anderson 2011). Other experts suggest the importance of a gradual evolution of conduct codes based on traditional legal and ethical principles governing weapons and warfare. In other words, international law can be a solution if states follow it (Anderson and Waxman 2013).

Others disagree. There is a powerful movement to prohibit all weapons using AI technology (BBC 2017). There are several interconnected reasons for such a ban:

- *Humanitarian reasons.* AI technologies, if they are developed and advanced, would dramatically increase the number of casualties on the battlefield and among civilians in particular. Robots are brutal, emotionless killers (Arkin 2009).
- *Strategic reasons.* Such weapons are more likely than conventional weapons to increase the element of unpredictability in warfare, which can dramatically impact both regional and global stability and increase the damage caused by the conflict.
- *Terrorism-related reasons.* AI weapons can become available to terrorists, who can use these weapons anywhere against governments and civilians to inflict maximum damage and thus to achieve their political goals.
- *Geopolitical reasons.* Because weaponry based on AI technologies requires substantial investments, few countries can afford them. This imbalance could lead to militarily advanced countries dominating over others and result in further political and economic dependency of many states that find themselves defenseless against AIW. (See Table 8-5.)

TABLE 8-5 Arguments about Artificial Intelligence Warfare

Arguments Justifying AIW	Arguments Criticizing AIW
Replacing human soldiers by robots will reduce casualties and make war less deadly.	AIW becomes an easy choice because the government will not put its own soldiers in harm's way.
Robots and AI systems will be controlled by the best technologies and safeguarding mechanisms.	Any autonomous weapon can and will malfunction; robots can run amok; and AIW can escape human control.
Robots and AI systems will be under full control of responsible and trained human beings and governments.	AIW can end up in the hands of immoral, irresponsible, or reckless governments, military commanders, or individuals.
AIW will be under the full control of governments.	Technologies and other war-related scientific discoveries can easily end up in the hands of terrorist organizations and individual terrorists.

Sources: Arkin, 2009; Open Letter, 2015.

Many leading scientists from various countries have raised their concerns regarding AIW. In a famous open letter to governments and the global community, they called for an immediate ban on the research and production of related weapons (Open Letter, 2015). The scientists claimed such weapons could be in the hands of terrorists, dictators, warlords, and others wishing to use such weapons in just a few years. Autonomous weapons can be used to assassinate people, disrupt economies, threaten nations, and kill large groups, including ethnic and religious minorities.

Check Your Knowledge

1. What is public diplomacy's possible role in combating terrorism?
2. What is the main point of the criminalization of terrorism?

8.3 Alternative Views of Evolving Security Threats

Several other approaches focus on different interpretations of terrorism and additional emerging security threats. These viewpoints include constructivism, political psychology, and conflict theories.

Constructivism

Supporters of constructivism claim that states and organizations define terrorism and conduct antiterrorist policies based on their perceptions. As perceptions change, so do policies. Counterterrorism is a product of social construction: It is based on ideological beliefs, the quality of information available to the decision makers, and the way they interpret it. Above all, constructivism attempts to understand the motivations of terrorists, their identities, and their ideas.

Violent radical groups pursue many different political goals and hold diverse creeds. Yet the choice of terrorism has three basic motives we can call the *three pillars of terrorism* (see Figure 8-4):

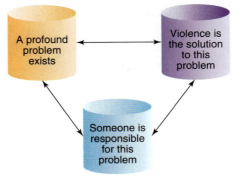

FIGURE 8-4
The constructivist view: The three pillars of terrorism.

1. *"We see a profound problem."* Terrorists generally believe that some profound injustice has occurred or is occurring. It might be a foreign occupation, ethnic or religious oppression, social and economic exploitation, imprisonment of certain individuals, or a devastating military defeat of their country.
2. *"We know who is responsible."* Terrorists see their targets as solely responsible for this injustice. They may identify the source as their own government, a foreign state, a political regime, or the international order in general. In an ethnic conflict, for example, they see one side as an innocent victim and the other as a villain. There are no gray areas.

History Lab | Northern Ireland

International attempts to deal with the sources of terrorism in Northern Ireland demonstrate the potential for, and limitations of, the liberal approach. Northern Ireland, a part of the United Kingdom, suffered for decades from a conflict between Roman Catholic and Protestant groups. While the Roman Catholics wanted to unify with the Republic of Ireland, the Protestants wanted to remain in the UK. The Irish Republican Army (IRA) and its successors used terrorist acts to attempt to remove British influence from the area. Patient negotiations, mediation from other governments, the involvement of religious and secular groups, a referendum, legal reforms, and economic assistance seemed to bear fruit. In the 1990s, the British and Irish governments, with the help of Washington, reached a series of agreements stating that Ireland could be unified only by peaceful means and only if the majority of Northern Ireland voted for

it. In 2005, the IRA promised to lay down its arms for good. Yet international agreements could not resolve the problem completely: Violent nationalist passions go beyond economic interests and legal reforms. The world and Northern Ireland do not need these passions to flare up again. [video] Terrorism in Northern Ireland

CRITICAL THINKING
❶ Discuss factors that contributed to policies to help control sectoral violence and terrorism in Northern Ireland. Consider geography, socioeconomic conditions, the efforts of other countries, the role of education, and other elements. ❷ Discuss the possibilities of applying lessons from Northern Ireland in places such as Afghanistan, Iraq, and Syria. What are the most significant obstacles to this application?

IRA terrorist volunteers at a camp near Dublin in 1966. After decades of violence, it appears that terrorism has finally been eradicated in Northern Ireland.

3. *"Violence is the solution."* Terrorists believe that only violence can direct attention to the injustice, destroy its source, force others to deal with it, and/or put an end to it. Most radical groups pay less attention to what they will do politically after the violent act is "successful" and their goal of destruction is achieved.

The Basque conflict in Spain illustrates these constructivist arguments. In the 1930s, the fascist regime of Francisco Franco (1892–1975) eradicated Basque autonomy: it banned publicly displaying the Basque flag, celebrating Basque holidays, speaking the Basque language in public places, and teaching it in schools. Even baptizing children with non-Spanish names became illegal. For the Basque people, these policies were seen as a profound injustice (pillar 1). The government was seen as solely responsible for this injustice (pillar 2). Most people resisted the policies through nonviolent means; however, several groups saw no other way but violence (pillar 3). Terrorism caused more than eight hundred deaths in the struggle for an independent Basque state.

To fight the Franco regime, several radical groups emerged, including the Basque Homeland and Freedom (ETA). In the 1960s, the ETA became a charismatic "spokesperson" for Basque nationalism (pillar 1). After a liberal republic replaced the Franco regime in 1975, the Spanish government applied liberal economic solutions to the problem of Basque separatism, including tax breaks and significant investments in the region. As a result, the Basque territories became among the most prosperous in Spain and terrorist attacks abated. But they did not end: Another violent faction emerged, replacing the

ETA militants. The new terrorists no longer benefit from the grassroots support the ETA had, but they cling to their identity as uncompromising fighters (pillar 3).

In 2010, the group declared a cease-fire but called on the Basque people to "continue in the struggle" on the path to freedom. A year later, ETA declared that the cease-fire would be permanent and that international observers might monitor it. The group also declared that it would use democratic means to achieve its political goals. In 2017, the group insisted that it had disarmed itself, yet the anxieties and even setbacks may continue for some time.

Constructivists argue that not every case of perceived injustice produces terrorism. Without a powerful ideology justifying random violence and individual sacrifice, terrorism cannot exist. The rise and fall of these ideologies should be regarded in an international context. Consider Japan and Germany after their defeat in World War II. The United States and other powers occupied both countries for years, but the Japanese and German people never resorted to terrorism.

Why not? Above all, the defeat and terrible destruction undermined any support for extreme nationalism. Also, from the viewpoint of international relations, both countries quickly became allies of the United States: Americans became their defenders against the Soviet Union and assisted their economic recovery. As a result, Germany's and Japan's identities rapidly changed–they were no longer defeated enemies but instead became part of "the free world." Both military defeat and international realignment helped to marginalize the countries' violent nationalist identities.

In contrast, at the end of the twentieth century, Middle Eastern societies became a meeting point between ideological versions of Islam (which

DEBATE > ON MORAL RELATIVISM AND TERRORISM

The West considered the attack on Israeli athletes and coaches during the 1972 Olympic Games a barbaric terrorist act. The heads of most countries condemned it, but others refused to do so. The bodies of the five Palestinians participating in the massacre were flown to Libya, where they were buried with full military honors.

In 1994, Israeli citizen Baruch Goldstein walked into a mosque in Hebron and killed twenty-nine Palestinian worshipers. Although the Israeli government condemned the massacre, Goldstein's tomb has become a place of worship for many Jews. The tombstone reads: "Here lies the saint, Dr. Baruch Kappel Goldstein; Blessed be the memory of the righteous and holy man; May the Lord avenge his blood, which devoted his soul to the Jews, Jewish religion, and Jewish land. His hands are innocent and his heart is pure. He was killed as a martyr of God."

WHAT'S YOUR VIEW?
Which of the following views would you likely support, and why?
Ⓐ Any violence is immoral, and every terrorist act is unacceptable. "Freedom fighters" become terrorists when they use terrorist methods. It does not matter which side the fighters are on.
Ⓑ Not every act of violence is immoral; there are conditions under which some forms are acceptable. In such cases, one may justify specific violent acts.

scores of Muslim scholars consider non-Islamic) and the people who looked for violent identities. The radical versions of Islam, funded by Saudi Arabia—Wahhabism and Salafism—sought to shape the identity of people in Afghanistan, Pakistan, and the Northern Caucasus from the 1980s through the 2000s. The al-Qaeda ideologues, including bin Laden, used the wars in Afghanistan and Iraq to promote an extremely violent type of Islamic identity. They argued that there was a centuries-long war between the forces of Islam and the "crusaders" from the West (i.e., the Soviets in Afghanistan in 1980–1988 and the Americans in Saudi Arabia after 1991), whom they were determined to defeat at any cost.

Marxism and Conflict Theories

Marxism and conflict theories explain most forms of terrorism as a kind of political struggle against oppressors. Classical Marxism generally supported terror against the class of capitalists, supporters of the capitalist system, and governments representing it. However, disagreements among Marxists persisted about specific policies. Lenin and the Bolsheviks (see Chapter 4) supported mass terror against "class enemies" in Russia and other countries, but not individual acts of terror. Other disagreements existed between the Soviet Union and newly formed Socialist countries, such as Cuba in the 1960s and Kampuchea (Cambodia) or Ethiopia in the 1970s. The Soviets did not endorse random killings, kidnappings, or other terrorist acts committed by radical Communist groups; however, they did not condemn them publicly and supported some of them financially. Today's Marxists do not endorse terrorism by Islamic radical groups, but they do see it as a reaction to unjust policies.

Modern conflict theorists, particularly those who regard international relations in terms of "North vs. South," may regard terrorism as an inevitable consequence of the structural inequality in the world. For them, only radical distribution of resources to the more poor regions can help to reduce terrorist activities.

> **Check Your Knowledge**
>
> 1. Name the three pillars of terrorism.
> 2. Explain the Basque conflict from the position of the three pillars.

8.4 Contexts and Applications

Realism emphasizes power politics and strength but overlooks ideology, social causes, and individual motivations involved in security threats. Liberalism pays attention to legal and social factors but often exaggerates the chances for cooperation with radical groups and rogue regimes. Constructivism helps to understand motivations and identities but often lacks practical solutions. Here we will compare the applications of different approaches to new and emerging security threats. (See Table 8.6.)

Individual Decisions

How well do theories and hypotheses work to explain the behavior of individual terrorists and terrorists groups? Law-enforcement professionals have

TABLE 8-6 Applying Knowledge of Emerging Security Threats: The Individual, State, and Global Levels

Level of Analysis	Key Issues
Individual	There is no "standard" profile of a terrorist. Individual motivations of terrorists as well as perpetrators of cyberattacks and AIW should be taken into consideration in security policies. An individual's grievances can be a factor, and this increases the role of human intelligence. Better knowledge about leaders of rogue states or terrorist groups and their inner circles is necessary.
State	Countries' domestic political and economic factors, foreign occupation, and ideological battles can inspire terrorism and other international security threats. Rogue states can choose cyberwarfare against military advanced states to achieve quick results or stir confusion and overreaction. Sharing international intelligence becomes crucial in the face of new security threats.
Global	International agreements to limit warfare and its deadliest forms should be reached because they work. Global prosperity is often an answer to political injustice, which is often a source of violence. Global international security mechanisms should be created to prevent devastating cyberattacks. Building an international, shared 5G network may be a step in the right direction.

long used behavioral profiling of criminal behavior, but attempts to create a single universal profile of the terrorist have so far been unsuccessful. Studying individuals accused of or convicted for terrorism is challenging for logistical and ethical reasons (Horgan 2011). Terrorists come from different backgrounds and are influenced by many special circumstances. What about the liberal assumption that poverty is the main source of terrorism? Studies based on statistical analyses have found a complicated correlation between a country's economic conditions and individual motivations of terrorists (Krueger 2007; Abadie 2006). Most organizers and leaders of terrorist networks never lived in poverty and even came from well-to-do families (Bernstein 2009). At the same time, their "foot soldiers" are still likely to be poor (Pape 2003).

Studies also contest a popular assumption that most terrorists are deeply disturbed. Although extreme violence such as suicide attacks seems irrational, terrorists believe that they act with complete rationality (Crenshaw 2000; 2010). An individual's decision to commit a terrorist act appears reasonable within its social context: Injustice must be eliminated (Asal and Blum 2005). Terrorists tend to believe that their actions have a deep personal and spiritual meaning. In-depth psychological studies also show that terrorists tend to express higher levels of aggression and lower degrees of understanding others' emotions than non-terrorists. A study of Colombian terrorist groups showed that those individuals were fixated on the outcomes of their actions and not on the means of achieving them, which allowed them to see harm against other human beings as permissible (Baez et al. 2017). (See Table 8-7.)

TABLE 8-7 Is There a Terrorist Profile?

Factor	Findings
Age	Rank-and-file terrorists tend to be younger individuals. Globally, younger people commit the greatest number of violent crimes of any nature.
Gender	Terrorists are mostly males, yet women join their ranks frequently and for a variety of reasons.
Occupation	There are no direct links between a person's occupation and terrorism, although unemployment is a factor.
Poverty	There is no direct correlation between a country's economic conditions and terrorism. However, poor people in areas with high levels of unemployment are more vulnerable to recruitment by radical groups.
Mental illness	No evidence exists for elevated rates of mental illness among terrorists. Partial evidence exists for depression and stress-related problems that influence an individual's search for psychological certainty, glory, and martyrdom.
Psychological insecurity	Evidence exists for low self-esteem, heightened insecurity, and elevated anger directed at other people. Terrorist groups bring sense of meaning and identity to their members.
Group pressure	Evidence exists that group pressure is a factor contributing to terrorism. Charismatic terrorist leaders tend to be manipulative and persuasive. However, some individuals disengage from such pressure.
Radical ideology	Most terrorists are radicalized in their choice of action. However, radicalization is more often a result of group pressure, not the other way around.

Sources: Reicher and Haslam, 2016; Horgan 2014, 2009; Crenshaw 2010; Sageman, 2004; Post 2004, 2008.

Theories of group influence also find empirical support. Marc Sageman (2004) examined the biographies of members of radical violent organizations, finding that they were strongly influenced by *group pressure*. Other studies show that individuals join extremist groups for the same reasons that people join gangs—to gain a sense of belonging—and only acquire extremist views later on (Horgan 2009). Refugee camps around Israel and in other parts of the world are a recruiting ground for terrorism because young people there develop an overwhelming sense of unity and a desire to fight together for a common goal. Casualties among members of these groups only contribute to greater solidarity (Post 2004).

The constructivist views of the three pillars of terrorism seem to be valid. An individual is deeply convinced that violence should be committed to address a perceived injustice. A group or organization then provides the necessary tools and means to satisfy the craving for destruction and self-sacrifice. (See Figure 8-5.)

The destruction of terrorists and their networks has been a major task of counterterrorism. But what do we know about **rehabilitation**, the process of assisting someone engaged in radical acts return to the community? Is it

rehabilitation
Helping someone who has been involved in a radical or terrorist group return to the community.

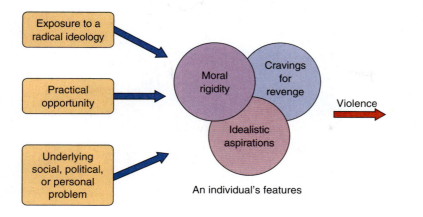

FIGURE 8.5
The inner world of a terrorist. As an individual becomes increasingly alienated from society, he or she may contemplate violent action to address the perceived injustice (Sageman, 2004).

possible to reeducate and change former radicals? The facts about the possibility of rehabilitation are encouraging yet inconclusive (Stern 2010).

State Policies

Terrorism is influenced by a variety of domestic factors. In turn, the threat of terrorism compels countries to amend their policies. We have already seen in earlier chapters how Presidents Bush and Obama were influenced by domestic politics. Let's see how the state context helps us understand the complexity of counterterrorism and terrorists' motivations.

DOMESTIC COSTS OF COUNTERTERRORISM

After 2001, the United States committed considerable resources to enhance national security. Debates continue about how much counterterrorism activities cost the American taxpayers. The Congressional Research Service estimated the cost of the global War on Terror—with operations in Iraq, Afghanistan, and other places—to be $1.7 trillion (deRugy 2015). Independent estimates, including long-term medical and other costs, pushed up the price to $3 trillion–$5 trillion (Stiglitz 2011). The War on Terror added $2.1 trillion, or more than 10 percent, to the U.S. debt (Amadeo 2017).

Discussions about the cost of security threats bring us back to the asymmetric responses to terrorism. Remember that international terrorism's main goal is to weaken the international order. Terrorists also hope to trigger excessive and costly reactions from the countries they attack. Thus, critics of U.S. counterterrorist policies claim that international terrorism will continue because of the high cost Americans pay to combat it. Terrorist acts and cyberattacks (including attempts to meddle with elections) have provoked mass anxiety and political backlash, and have caused long-term damage not only to the American budget but to the economy as well. Excessive airport security and visa scrutiny create huge delays. Critics insist that international security is important, yet the government's overreaction is damaging. Critics claim that the government should invest more in its own infrastructure, research, and education.

American troops in Afghanistan. For almost two decades now politicians have argued about how many troops, if any, should remain there.

TERRORISM AS A MEANS TO GAIN POWER

Both realist and liberal commentators rightly mention that not every radical or fundamentalist group becomes a threat to international security (Cooper 2004). A study of four hundred terrorist groups in the twentieth century found that 124 of them eventually established ties to legitimate political parties (Weinberg and Pedahzur 2003). In the past thirty years, many formerly radical political groups in Latin America have renounced violence and turned to politics. The Muslim Brotherhood, which had renounced violence, gained about one-third of the seats in Jordan's parliament; the group's moderate wing in Egypt also denounced the use of violence in 1971 (Herzog 2006). After being legalized in 2011, the Egyptian Brotherhood was victorious in parliamentary and presidential elections. The group was outlawed again in 2013 in the aftermath of the country's military coup, and its leaders were jailed and sentenced to death.

Nationalist movements can sometimes transform into terrorist groups pursuing fundamentalist agendas. In other cases, terrorist groups use instability to gain political power and form an independent state. The low-intensity conflicts fought in the North Caucasus since the 1990s transformed a secular struggle for independence from Russia into a holy war to establish an Islamist state (Saradzhyan 2010). A civil war in Syria created a power vacuum and contributed to the rise of ISIS, which violently pursued its own independent state.

DEMOCRATIC GOVERNANCE AND TERRORISM

Another issue for discussion is the effectiveness of democracies in combating terrorist threats. It may appear that authoritarian states can be more effective because they have fewer constraints than democracies in using harsh measures against terrorists. Yet history shows that such regimes cannot defeat terrorism: They just drive terrorists underground. Authoritarian states may also use the threat of terrorism as an excuse to attack the political opposition.

Chinese antiterrorist laws, for example, could facilitate future human rights abuses committed in the name of counterterrorism (Human Rights Watch 2015). The Chinese government continues to cite the threat of global terrorism to justify its crackdown on separatist forces in Xinjiang, a predominantly Muslim region, and Tibet.

Liberal democracies appear more vulnerable to terrorism than authoritarian regimes because of their openness and decentralization. Democracies often lack a political consensus on how to fight terrorism and other asymmetric threats. Critics claim that government prerogatives often undermine civil liberties. Citizens' phones are tapped, their Internet correspondence is monitored, and habeas corpus (the constitutional right to be brought before a judge) is often suspended (Ignatieff 2004). Most people agree that we need to have effective security policies without compromising democratic governance and freedoms.

In the long run, democracies tend to resist radical violence more successfully than nondemocratic regimes. Democratic means create legitimacy and help gain popular support for counterterrorism. The decline of the IRA in Northern Ireland and the defeat of the Red Brigades in Italy and the RAF in Germany showed that democratic states could overcome terrorism without compromising their democratic principles.

Emerging democracies may be most vulnerable to terrorism because they lack effective institutions and a functioning civil society. They also are likely to suffer from corruption, nepotism, and tribalism. Some members of the police, the security services, and the public may actually sympathize with terrorist causes. For instance, both democratically elected leaders and

Volunteers carry an injured child to safety after soldiers stormed a school seized by heavily armed terrorists near Chechnya in 2004. More than three hundred hostages died, including 156 children, amid explosions and machine gun fire. What caused such a high number of casualties? We can blame the terrorists, but the counterterrorism operation by the Russian government was arguably inept.

the military dictators in Pakistan have historically poor records of dealing with terrorist groups. Officials from the country's secret service (ISI) have long supported radical Islamists in Afghanistan and India. Pakistani domestic politics remain vulnerable to radical Islamism (Husain 2011; Rashid 2008).

Global Factors

Assessments of terrorism and counterterrorist policies must also take into account their global impact, which includes terrorist strategies and the effectiveness of global counterterrorism. At the same time, the global context allows us to see how international terrorism challenges or promotes international interdependence—political and economic.

THREATS TO THE GLOBAL ORDER

Is terrorism effective in disrupting the global order? The conclusions are mixed. Particularly when the demands of violent groups are specific and limited, governments tend to cooperate. Sometimes they even pay ransom money for hostages. Most of the time, however, states and international organizations refuse to negotiate with terrorist groups, which then fail to achieve their political goals. In fact, terrorism is likely to delay the solutions of international conflicts or social problems:

- The anarchist movement, even at the height of its activities in the nineteenth and early twentieth centuries, failed to destroy government institutions or establish direct democracy. To the contrary, new and powerful authoritarian states arose after World War I.
- Socialist radicalism of the 1960s and 1970s attained only limited success. A global alternative to liberal capitalism never materialized, and "red terrorism" abated.
- Terrorism has also delayed the resolution of many legitimate claims for national sovereignty, including statehood for Palestinians.

The effectiveness of international terrorism in the name of Islam deserves discussion. As we already mentioned, the damage of the 9/11 attacks was considerable and lasting. Terrorism and its threats affected the lives of hundreds of millions of people. At the same time, al-Qaeda and similar groups did not even come close to achieving their global goals. Fundamentalist Islamic movements challenged but did not overthrow the authoritarian Middle Eastern regimes targeted by al-Qaeda. Polls show that, because of the long-term destruction it caused, religiously motivated terrorism had alienated the majority of Muslims, even in the areas where it had initially won many sympathizers (Horowitz 2009). According to a global survey of attitudes in Muslim countries, 67 percent of Muslims were concerned about Islamic extremism (Pew 2013a). Although the influence of al-Qaeda and similar radical groups has been in decline all around the Islamic parts of the world (Husain 2005; Pew Research Center 2011), several new groups have emerged in the Middle East, North Africa, Nigeria, Somalia, and other countries.

Neorealists, liberals, and constructivists concur that terrorism will remain a challenge. However, the international system is generally more resilient today than it was in the past, and terrorists cannot trigger a global calamitous war, like they did in 1914. From a neorealist perspective, there is a concert of great powers to act internationally against terrorist threats, even when some may differ on specific details. Liberals correctly point to the role of the UN and its numerous institutions, as well as a host of NGOs: Terrorists may temporarily overwhelm weak or failing states, yet with the help of international cooperation—not excluding international intervention—these states no longer remain safe and lasting havens for terrorists. And some constructivists argue that, with the exception of militant Islamic fundamentalism, there is a general decline of violent ideologies around the world. We can only hope that this trend continues.

GLOBAL WAVES

As we saw earlier, anarchism motivated a wave of terrorism in the late 1800s. A second wave, inspired by anticolonialism and nationalism, began in the 1920s and lasted for several decades. The late 1960s witnessed the birth of terrorist attacks by radical Communist groups in Europe as well as Sri Lanka, Peru, and Colombia. This wave dissipated by the end of the last century, but a new wave of mainly religious terrorism had already begun in the 1980s (Rapoport 2004; Post 2005a). It spreads beyond sovereign borders, and its motives are rooted in a cultural, anti-Western sentiment (Wieviorka 2007).

The differences among these waves of terrorism are not only ideological. International terrorism since the Cold War, sometimes called *new terrorism*, has several distinct features (Crenshaw 2000; Kaplan 2012). First, terrorists have increasingly resorted to attacks on civilian populations to achieve greater carnage and more headlines. There is an increased focus on destruction; the means of terrorism has become its goal (Brandt and Sandler 2010). Second, terrorism's operations have become increasingly global. Third, terrorists more often operate in small, loosely connected groups without a centralized command. These groups are difficult to penetrate. and liquidation of one does not bring down the whole terrorist network. Terrorist leaders discourage their followers from negotiating or accepting bargains.

In addition, terrorism has embraced new technologies, including the Internet. Instead of revolvers and dynamite, terrorists can use sophisticated cyberattacks, drones, and other forms of AIW to cause maximum damage to people and infrastructures. A miniaturized nuclear device could have catastrophic consequences anywhere at any time. There are serious concerns that rogue states can develop or buy cyberweapons to use or to pass on to terrorist organizations.

Will there be another wave of terrorism? If so, where will it come from? Should we prepare for a series of nuclear attacks or anticipate a cyber assault against financial institutions and communication networks? Preventive policies may include the use of force. Yet most important, they will need coordinated policies of all responsible states and international organizations.

Former rebel leaders of the Revolutionary Armed Forces of Colombia (FARC), a radical terrorist organization, talk to police officers in their security team in 2018.

GLOBAL SECURITY POLICIES

Significant international efforts will be needed to strengthen central authority in some countries. Both realists and liberals accept the view that failing states provide a breeding ground for terrorism. Yemen, Afghanistan, Iraq, and Syria are obvious examples. Building a stronger state has become a goal of counter-terrorism policy (Boucek 2010). Another important policy is pressuring political regimes suspected of supporting international terrorism (e.g., Iran).

Part of the solution must come from within countries and regions that breed radicalism. For example, many Islamic scholars denounce the ideology of violence, which in their view has nothing to do with Islam or its basic values. Killing terrorists, as liberals argue and as the U.S. government learned in Afghanistan and Iraq, will not end the problem of radical violence because it feeds on ideologies rooted in deep social and political problems. If these problems are addressed, the threat of terrorism diminishes.

Effective policies should combine several interconnected strategies. One is the reasonable and multilateral use of force to change the perceptions of the regional or global balance of power. Another is persistent attention to social and economic problems that provide mass backing for terrorist radicals. Serious work should be done to reappraise international law and law enforcement procedures to criminalize terrorism. There must be coordinated information policies to encourage others not to glorify violence. Some of these policies may be ineffective, and tactical corrections will be necessary (Post 2005b).

Morality is also an important issue in global antiterrorism policies. Are deadly drone strikes against known terrorists acceptable if innocent people die? The New America Foundation (NAF 2012) estimated that 5 to 10 percent of all the people killed by US drones in Pakistan could be innocent bystanders, including children or hostages. There have been close to 150 civilian casualties in Yemen (NAF 2019).

Most experts writing about terrorism underline the need to understand strategies used by perpetrators of asymmetric conflicts. Guerrilla warfare, for example, is not a new form of military struggle. In twentieth-century conflicts, several political leaders gained power in their countries by launching protracted guerrilla wars. History shows that most of these movements pushed the superior, better organized, and better equipped enemy close to physical and psychological attrition. New international context may favor insurgents and complicate states' attempts to deal with guerrillas. Because mass media in democratic countries report heavily on casualties and destruction caused by insurgency's actions, public opinion in such countries may fast develop a negative view of an ongoing conflict (Boot 2013). This reaction may exhaust the will of democratic countries to engage in protracted counterinsurgencies, especially outside their own territory, and heighten the ability of insurgents to survive even after suffering grave military setbacks.

Effective counterterrorism depends on knowledge of its ultimate targets. Are we fighting against specific individuals or against the ideologies that inspire them? Will the physical elimination of a potent radical group solve the problem of terrorism? To approach these questions, see this chapter's case study on al-Qaeda. Understanding the group's past motivations and actions is crucial for building effective defense, security, and foreign policies.

Check Your Knowledge

1. Which characteristics are commonly included in the "terrorist profile"?

2. If the main goal of terrorist groups is political, why don't most of them switch to the legitimate political process?

3. Has terrorism been an effective tactic of political change? Why or why not?

4. Name and describe three waves of terrorism in history.

CASE STUDY

From Al-Qaeda to the Islamic State

Background

Al-Qaeda ("the base") is an international terrorist network rooted in an extreme Islamic doctrine that prescribes creation of a global Islamic state. An effective way to understand this organization is to look at the careers and views of its founders—above all, at Osama bin Laden (1957–2011), who was born and raised in Saudi Arabia. Although the status and wealth of his multimillionaire family provided him with many opportunities, he grew increasingly frustrated with Saudi society, particularly its move away from the fundamentalist principles of Islam (Bodansky 2001). Contemporary music, dance, entertainment, mass media, ideas of democracy, and equality between men and women all bothered him immensely (Dennis 2002).

Among those who strongly influenced bin Laden and his future al-Qaeda associates was the Egyptian fundamentalist thinker Sayyid Qutb (1906–1966), a member of the Muslim Brotherhood. After traveling in the United States, Qutb became a virulent enemy of American society and Western cultural influences; he was especially disgusted by the social equality between men and women (Qutb 1964/2007). He taught his followers about global offensive *jihad*, the right and duty to inflict violence to advance spiritual and political beliefs (Coll 2009). Qutb's teachings included the following points:

- A true and just social system can be created only on the basis of the *Sharia*, or Islamic law. Islam knows two kinds of societies, Islamic and un-Islamic, or *Jahiliya*. The latter—which is inferior and does not care for Islamic beliefs, values, laws, morals, or manners—is, according to Qutb, the contemporary world.
- A true Islamic society would have no rulers because Muslims need neither judges nor police to obey divine law. Any secular authority or legal system must be repulsive to Muslims. Any secular system—authoritarian or democratic, nationalist or Communist, the free market or a planned economy—is illegitimate unless it follows the *Sharia*.
- Muslims should use preaching and *jihad* to overthrow secular governments, even if they are ruled by Muslims. As a result, people will be free from their servitude to other men and ready to serve God.
- The present Muslim generation has laid down its spiritual arms, defeated by secularism.

Key Formative Events

The Soviet invasion of Afghanistan in 1979 gave a number of young, educated, and radical Saudis, including bin Laden, their first battlefield. They raised money and volunteered to fight against the Soviets, launching a "brotherhood" of militants. When the Soviet Union withdrew from Afghanistan in 1988, these militants considered it their historic victory over "the Satan." At this point, bin Laden met with Ayman al-Zawahiri, an Egyptian doctor who was also influenced by the ideas of Sayyid Qutb. The two formed a group, which a decade later became known as al-Qaeda. Al-Zawahiri provided ideas for its organizational structure and trained members; bin Laden supplied ideas and money. This group already aimed beyond the Soviet Union and against the "Great Satan"—the United States (Wright 2006).

Bin Laden and his associates interpreted the Gulf War of 1991, in which the U.S.-led international coalition evicted Iraqi troops from Kuwait, as another "crusade" of the West against Islam. They vowed to expel American troops from the "sacred land" of Saudi Arabia. Bin Laden also grew increasingly critical of the Saudi royal family and government, to the point of mutual hostility and had to leave the country. He moved to Sudan, where he founded a new training base for al-Qaeda militants. After 1996, the Taliban movement seized power in Kabul, and bin Laden and al-Zawahiri moved their base to Afghanistan.

Analysis

The National Commission on Terrorist Attacks upon the United States (the 9/11 Commission) aptly summarized the essence of al-Qaeda's goals and methods: "The enemy rallies broad support in the Arab and Muslim world by demanding redress of political grievances, but its hostility toward us and our values is limitless. Its purpose is to rid the world of religious and political pluralism, the plebiscite, and equal rights for women. It makes no distinction between military and civilian targets. Collateral damage is not in its lexicon" (National Commission on Terrorist Acts, 2002).

Achieving the main goal of the al-Qaeda founders—a global jihad and the creation of a global Islamic state—would mean destroying the entire global order. Nation-states would disappear, and a new, stateless, and uniform Muslim society would emerge. In the process, several regional caliphates would unify Muslims living in Europe, Africa, and Eurasia. In particular, caliphates could unify Arab states in the Middle East, North Africa, the Caucasus, Pakistan, Afghanistan, Indonesia, and Southeast Asia.

Al-Qaeda sees three main obstacles to its objectives. The most significant is Western civilization, especially its individualism, materialism, secularism, and gender equality. Followers believe that Western societies are decadent and weak; they can therefore be terrorized, undermined, and eventually overwhelmed. The second enemy is the Jews and the state of Israel. Al-Qaeda beliefs borrow heavily from the old conspiracy theories about Jewish "world dominance," including their supposed control of the world's economic and financial system. The Palestinian problem is key; to solve it, the state of Israel must be eliminated and Israel's main supporter, the United States, undermined. In speeches, bin Laden and his associates frequently referred to their enemies as "Jews and Crusaders." The third impediment is corrupt regimes in Muslim countries. Their grip on power must be weakened and their secular governments eventually abolished.

Based on these beliefs, al-Qaeda made the United States the main target of its wrath. Its leaders became convinced that, despite America's strength, the country was built on a weak secular foundation. Methods of terror could bring the entire Western civilization down. Terror attacks by suicide bombers (a tactic frequently attributed to al-Zawahiri) must strike the West and its allies repeatedly and in the most vulnerable places. "We will use your laws against you," bin Laden boasted. A weakened West would not be able to support Israel, and the global system would crumble.

Lessons

Although some reports portrayed bin Laden as a typical political player who simply despised America's policies (Hamud 2005), most viewed him as uncompromising and obsessed. Washington followed the realist logic. It concluded that talks were counterproductive, and President Obama ordered him killed on May 2, 2011, in a bold operation by U.S. Special Forces.

But the struggle against al-Qaeda-inspired terrorism continues. New leaders and organizations have emerged, including ISIS. Terrorism is too complex a social and political problem to simply go away. Much depends on the transformations in Muslim countries and on the future evolution of Islam. In some countries of the Middle East, North Africa, and elsewhere, conditions of extreme poverty and misery—alongside government corruption and injustice—have created a fertile ground for aggressive jihadism.

Case Study Questions

1. What potential developments in Muslim countries would discourage the continuation and growth of radical movements and terrorist organizations?
2. What specific foreign policy changes should the United States and the West as a whole implement to discourage radical movements and terrorist organizations?
3. How strongly do you support the view that al-Qaeda, ISIS, and other groups are largely "products" of the "clash of civilizations" (Chapter 4) and therefore not susceptible to preventive policies? Explain your answer.

CHAPTER 8 REVIEW   Terrorism and Evolving Security Challentges

8.1   Describe the logic, strategies, and methods of terrorism.

Terrorism is a form of violent political radicalism by nonstate actors.

The key strategies of terrorism are intimidation, attrition, provocation, spoiling, and outbidding.

Terrorism's main ideologies are anarchism, radical socialism, nationalism, and religious fundamentalism.

Q: How and why have the tactics of terrorism changed over time?

8.2 Explain emerging security challenges through the lenses of realism and liberalism.

The realist view states that terrorism disrupts the power balance by presenting an asymmetric threat. Liberalism argues that fighting terrorism requires understanding its causes. Liberals support the concept of criminalization of terrorism and emphasize broad international cooperation and public democracy.

Q: Explain why terrorism is an asymmetric threat.

Q: Suggest arguments for and against criminalization of terrorism.

8.3 Describe how alternative approaches view terrorism and emerging security challenges.

In constructivism, terrorism is based on beliefs, available information, and interpretations. Motives include a problem, an assigned responsibility for the problem, and absence of nonviolent choices. Conflict approaches explain terrorism as a form of political struggle against oppressors.

Q: Should terrorism diminish if the key sources of social and political injustice in the world are addressed?

8.4 Apply approaches to contemporary security challenges at three levels of analysis

There is no universal profile of a terrorist, yet most crave revenge, display moral rigidity, and have idealistic aspirations. Terrorists' motivations may change. Political leaders differ in how they understand terrorism and counterterrorism.
In the state context, terrorism is influenced by a variety of domestic factors, including its perceived cost, and may be considered a means to gain power. Democracies and non-democracies are affected by and respond to terrorism differently.
Terrorism as a method has a mixed record of accomplishing its goals, and there are several global "generations" of terrorism. Global efforts should improve counterterrorism's effectiveness.

Q: Is it possible to eradicate terrorism completely? Why or why not?

KEY TERMS

anarchism 266
artificial intelligence (AI)   272
artificial intelligence
  (AIW) 272
asymmetric threat 273
autonomous weapons 271
caliphate 268
coercion and extortion 264

counterterrorism 262
criminalization of
  terrorism 277
cyberterrorism 271
cyberwarfare 269
cyberweapons 270
domestic terrorism 260
extreme nationalism   267

international terrorism 260
preemptive policies 275
radical socialism   267
rehabilitation 286
religious fundamentalism 268
terrorism 277

Environmental Issues

> *Nature provides a free lunch, but only if we control our appetites.*
>
> —WILLIAM RUCKELSHAUS

Do your hairspray and refrigerator have anything to do with international politics? Believe it or not, they do. Scientific research has shown that chemicals known as propellants, found in aerosol products and cooling units, dangerously affect the atmosphere. In the second half of the twentieth century, hundreds of millions of people began to buy products containing these chemicals. The use of propellants has slowly depleted the protective ozone layer of the atmosphere, leading to a host of dangerous consequences such as increased incidence of skin cancer. In 1985, twenty leading industrial countries signed the Vienna Convention for the Protection of the Ozone Layer to regulate use of these chemicals in products. In 1987, forty-three countries signed the Montreal Protocol to stop production of specific chemicals or reduce them substantially.

Today's world faces overwhelming environmental challenges. In response, the international community has launched new environmental programs and initiatives. A whole new dimension of international relations has emerged. The Montreal Protocol—one of the most successful international environmental agreements to date—happened because the most powerful countries set aside their differences and agreed to act together. Yet many proposed environmental actions are vigorously contested for political and domestic economic reasons. Finding and implementing global environmental policies may be one of the greatest challenges of our century.

In this chapter, we will discuss how environmental problems and the debates around them affect international relations and policies of countries, international organizations, and nongovernmental organizations (NGOs).

The environmental organization World Wide Fund for Nature (WWF) stages an annual event called Earth Hour to raise awareness on climate change. Colombians observing the event turn off traditional lighting and instead light candles in 2018. Why is raising awareness important in environmental politics? What do you say to skeptics who insist that awareness without policies achieves very little?

Learning Objectives

9.1 Identify today's key environmental problems, major policies to address them, and the implications for international relations.

9.2 Describe similarities and differences among several approaches to environmental problems.

9.3 Evaluate international responses to environmental problems at three levels of analysis.

9.1 Environmental Problems, Disasters, and Policies

Environmental problems and policies are a relatively new subject in international relations. For many years, the consensus was that sovereign governments had full authority to deal with the land, water, air, and natural resources of their countries as they pleased. Countries reached agreements on the environment mostly to get more profits from the extraction and sale of mineral resources. Even today, states usually do not ask for permission from others to drill for oil or to burn forests on their territories. During the last few decades, however, the attitudes of international organizations and most countries toward environmental problems began to change. In part, this change is due to the realization that the world is an **ecosystem**, a biological community in which we have complex interactions with the physical environment. A *country's ecosystem*, like that of the United States, Canada, or Mexico, is part of a *regional ecosystem*, such as North America. It is also part of the *global ecosystem*—and all three are interconnected. Large-scale natural disasters, such as hurricanes, volcanic eruptions, or massive oil spills, affect the ecosystem instantly. Other changes take time to develop. Therefore, individuals, groups, and governments engage in discussions and actions to address current and potential environmental problems.

Environmental politics includes the activities of political leaders, parties, NGOs, scientific laboratories, and others to influence environmental policy. These policies address at least two major types of environmental problems: *contamination* and *depletion*. **Contamination** is any byproduct of human and nonhuman activities affecting the air, water, and soil. **Depletion** is the serious reduction of essential elements of the environment, such as loss of fresh water, clean air, forests, or entire species. As we will see in this chapter, climate change is mainly caused by one form of contamination called greenhouse gases. At the same time, even ordinary garbage can be another source of contamination. Natural processes and natural disasters may cause contamination and depletion as well. (See Figure 9-1.)

ecosystem A biological community in which life interacts in complex ways with the physical environment.

environmental politics The activities of political leaders, parties, NGOs, scientific laboratories, and others to influence environmental policy.

contamination The byproducts of human and nonhuman activities affecting air, water, and soil.

depletion The serious reduction of essential elements of an ecosystem, such as loss of forests, fresh water, or entire species.

Environmental Problems

Communities around the world face a range of
dire environmental concerns. In this section,
we look at six of the world's most pressing environmental issues, including air pollution,
ozone depletion, climate change, deforestation, loss of wildlife, and water contamination
and shortage.

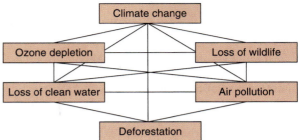

AIR POLLUTION

FIGURE 9-1 Major environmental problems.

Volcanic eruptions and forest fires have polluted
the atmosphere for centuries. Industrialization
and the growth of cities created new sources of pollution—including coal-burning
factories, massive garbage dumps, animal wastes, and open sewer systems. Smog,
an obvious form of air pollution, became unmistakable in Europe and the United
States in the nineteenth century and later appeared in big cities all over the world.
Several years ago, soot from burning was detected even in the ices of Greenland
and high in the Himalayas ("Time to Call the Sweep?" 2010).

> **acid rain** The
> accumulation of
> acids in clouds, rain,
> snow, sleet, and,
> subsequently, lakes
> and rivers owing
> to sulfur dioxide,
> nitrogen oxides, and
> other pollutants in
> the atmosphere.

In the twenty-first century, the largest sources of air pollution are power
plants using coal. Power plants produce almost a quarter of the pollution
worldwide. The second largest cause of air pollution is deforestation, or loss
of forests due mostly to human activities. Transportation (including planes,
ships, and cars), a third source, produces about 14 percent of emissions. (See
Figure 9-2.)

One of the serious consequences of air pollution
is **acid rain**, which is caused by high concentrations of
sulfur dioxide, nitrogen oxides, and other pollutants in the
atmosphere. Acid rain pollutes lakes and rivers, killing
many small life forms, damaging buildings and historic
monuments, corroding metal constructions; and affecting crops. A higher content of oxides in food is dangerous to our health.

Early negotiations regarding acid rain began in the
1970s between the United States and Canada. These
two countries signed a major treaty (often called the
Acid Rain Treaty) in 1991 to limit cross-border air pollution. Other countries signed treaties leading to automobile and factory emission controls. Because of these
efforts, the problem has somewhat diminished in urban
areas but persists in many industrial regions.

Air pollution causes many respiratory problems and
may also produce other serious long-term health consequences, especially in urban and industrial areas. The
poor, who typically lack access to health care, are the
most vulnerable to the effects.

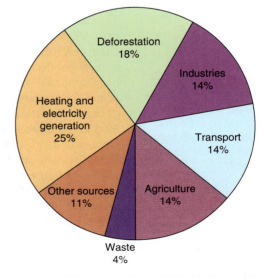

FIGURE 9-2 Sources of air pollution in the world.

History Lab   A Disappeared Sea

In the 1960s, the Soviet Union began an ambitious construction project. In order to irrigate cotton plantations and other agricultural projects, the government partially diverted two rivers that bring fresh water into the Aral Sea, a body of water shared by Kazakhstan and Uzbekistan (two Soviet republics that later became independent nations). The result was depletion, as the water supply to the Aral Sea declined significantly, and shallow streams quickly evaporated. By the 1980s, the fishing industry in the Aral Sea was in serious decline; today it is almost destroyed, being only 10 percent of its original size. By 2018, the entire eastern basin of the Aral Sea had completely dried up. It is now called the Aralkum Desert. Together with the adjacent areas, it is covered with salt and toxic substances as the result of receding water and pesticide runoff. Thousands of square miles of dry land have appeared, contributing to dust storms and damaging the environment of the region even further. The people living in the area experience a shortage of fresh water and suffer from respiratory and other health ailments.

The territory of the Aral Sea is shared by Kazakhstan and Uzbekistan. Kazakhstan is attempting to save a small portion of the northern part of the sea, which is essentially a small lake. Uzbekistan will not stop the irrigation of its cotton plantations and is more interested in searching for oil and gas on the exposed seabed. The sea is dead.

CRITICAL THINKING

❶ What lessons can we draw from this case? ❷ Who should be responsible for saving the disappearing sea? Kazakhstan and Uzbekistan, another country, an NGO, or an IGO? ❸ Suppose you served as chair of an international organization called Save the Sea, and you had significant resources at your disposal. What would you do with the sea? ❹ Is this particular environmental battle worth fighting? Why or why not?

Simulation:
Negotiating a Climate
Change Treaty

ozone depletion
Steady decline in the amount of ozone in the stratosphere, allowing the sun's damaging ultraviolet radiation to reach the earth.

Climate change
A significant and lasting alteration of global weather patterns.

OZONE DEPLETION

The ozone layer is a part of the atmosphere that protects humans and animals from the sun's deadly ultraviolet radiation. Scientists have registered a steady decline in the total amount of ozone in the earth's stratosphere—an estimated 3 percent per decade since the 1980s. This is called **ozone depletion**. Ozone "holes" have appeared over Antarctica and Australia. Research and coordinated international actions have significantly slowed the process by focusing on a major cause of ozone depletion: the chemicals that are produced naturally by marine organisms and are used in air conditioning and cooling units, as aerosol spray propellants, and for cleaning electronic equipment. No country can create a "shield" to guard its own atmosphere, which makes ozone depletion a global issue (Roan 1989). As you will remember from the introduction to this chapter, the Vienna Convention and the 1987 Montreal Protocol limited production of certain chemicals contributing to ozone depletion. Additional international agreements aim at phasing out and eliminating these chemicals entirely from industrial use.

CLIMATE CHANGE

Climate change is a significant and lasting alteration of global weather patterns (Gerrard 2007). It most often means *global warming*, or rising temperatures, but also includes the increasingly frequent abnormalities in climate conditions, such as frequent storms and devastating heat waves. It has been the most debated environmental problem of the past twenty years.

The earth's average temperatures have always fluctuated to some degree. The earth's history has included four major "ice ages" as well as warmer periods, when flora and fauna flourished. For the last thirty to forty years, however, temperatures have been steadily and rapidly rising, reaching the warmest level in twelve thousand years. According to the World Glacier Monitoring Service (see their reports online at http://www.wgms.ch), glaciers globally have lost up to 10 percent of their mass over just the last decade, and ice that for centuries blocked northern seas is retreating. The retreat of glaciers affects the availability of water for agriculture as well as for animals and plants. As the earth warmed in the last half of the twentieth century, seventeen hundred plant, animal, and insect species moved closer to the poles, at about four miles per decade (Parmesan and Yohe 2003). The World Wide Fund for Nature publishes a list of animals increasingly threatened by climate change (WWF 2018). Overall, most studies published in peer-reviewed academic journals show that the earth's temperatures are rising and that these changes are very likely due to human activities (NASA 2018). The key question is whether countries are capable of slowing down global warming. If they are, what should and can be done by each country and globally?

The debate over global climate change began more than a century ago. In 1896, a Swedish chemist and physicist, Svante Arrhenius, was one of the first to establish a connection between global temperatures and human activities. He calculated that air pollution from factories could double CO_2 levels in the atmosphere in three thousand years, warming the planet significantly. In 1938, Guy Callendar, a British engineer, also predicted a global rise in the world's temperature because of CO_2. Yet those projections were dismissed by the scientific community and essentially forgotten. Only with the start of the environmental movement in the early 1970s did attitudes begin to change. The first public hearings on global warming in the U.S. Congress took place in the mid-1970s. The policy makers, the scientific community, and ordinary citizens continue to debate climate change, its causes, and, most importantly, policies to address it.

What causes climate change? According to the widely accepted hypothesis, which finds support in many studies, climate change is caused by a combination of factors, including solar activity and variations in the Earth orbit. One of the most significant factors is the *greenhouse effect*, as the sun's radiation becomes trapped by the atmosphere, much as in a greenhouse. Instead of the glass ceiling of a greenhouse, however, this absorption results from pollutants in the atmosphere, including carbon dioxide (CO_2), methane (CH_4), and other so-called greenhouse gases. These gases affect an atmospheric layer that traps some of the sun's heat that warms the planet. The burning of fossil fuels has caused the levels of CO_2 to increase by approximately 30 percent since the eighteenth century. At present, a few industrial countries emit more CO_2 than do all developing countries together. (See Figure 9-3.)

Greenhouse emissions are the byproducts of burning to produce energy, heat homes, cook food, and make machines work. In the 1850s, the burning

Issue Navigator: Climate Change

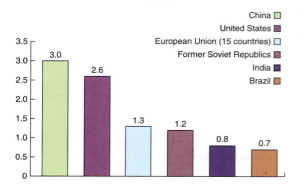

China ☐
United States ■
European Union (15 countries) ☐
Former Soviet Republics ■
India ■
Brazil ■

FIGURE 9-3 Assessment of gas emissions in 2025 (projected, if no major changes take place). Billions of tons.

▷

100 Solutions to Reverse Global Warming

of wood generated almost 90 percent of the world's energy. At the start of the twentieth century, coal produced 70 percent of the world's energy. By the 1950s, oil and coal each had about a 40 percent share. In the twenty-first century, oil still generates 40 percent of greenhouse gas emissions, followed by natural gas (25 percent), coal (25 percent), and nuclear reactions (about 5 percent) (EIA 2015; World Resources Institute 2018).

Some argue that global warming is caused by a combination of factors, including not just human activities but mostly natural processes taking place in space, on the sun, in the atmosphere, and in the oceans (Jacques 2009). Skeptics acknowledge the alarming signs of the major environmental changes but discount the scope and severity of the consequences. But even skeptics agree that any small changes in the ecosystem can have global effects. To illustrate, in the Little Ice Age of the fifteenth century, the earth's average temperature dropped by just 1°F. The Thames River in England froze, and Alpine glaciers touched villages as far south as modern Austria and Switzerland.

Although other factors may impact the temperature, the greenhouse hypothesis has received support from many authoritative scientists. Temperatures have exceeded global annual averages for almost forty consecutive years (World Resources Institute 2018). What are the consequences of climate change? The most dramatic forecasts predict a 10°F (5.5°C) climb in global temperatures during this century and a 39-inch (1 m) rise in global ocean levels due to melting ice. Even more moderate forecasts project a rise of 3 inches (8 cm). Any scenario would have catastrophic consequences for low-level inhabited territories. New Orleans, London, Amsterdam, and many other cities would have to build massive storm-surge defenses to avoid flooding. Experts also project more frequent climatic abnormalities, including heat waves, hurricanes, and typhoons, as well as severe winters in some typically warm areas. Prominent politicians have supported scientists' call for the urgency of addressing climate change.

DEFORESTATION

Deforestation The massive removal or disappearance of forests, owing to the thinning, changing, and elimination of trees, bushes, and other vegetation.

Deforestation is the massive removal or disappearance, thinning, changing, and elimination of trees, bushes, and other vegetation (Williams 2006). Fires and flooding have caused deforestation throughout history, but these losses were replenished by natural growth. Humans, too, contributed to deforestation for centuries (such as farming and logging). During the last fifty years, the destruction of forests has increased significantly, as a consequence of agriculture and construction, including some of the earth's largest forested areas—in Brazil, Equatorial Africa, and Indonesia. In Brazil, the huge Amazonian forests have been shrinking rapidly since the 1950s because of cutting and burning. Forests cover almost 30 percent of land on earth. About 1.6 billion people rely on forests for food, water, and shelter (WWF 2018a). However, over the past decade, according to the United Nations, in comparative terms, an area as large as the size of England is converted each year to other uses, mostly agriculture.

Deforestation contributes to greenhouse gas pollution, soil erosion, and **desertification**—the expansion of deserts into places previously available for agriculture. Desert expansion contributes to illness, hunger, and poverty (Johnson, Mayrand, and Paquin 2006; Rechkemmer 2004).

Desertification The expansion of deserts into places previously available for agriculture.

LOSS OF WILDLIFE

Deforestation, urban development, tourism, mining, and commercial hunting and fishing threaten animal life. Hunters illegally kill rare species of monkeys, tigers, turtles, and rhinoceros for pleasure, profit, or souvenirs. Climate change also affects animals globally, and many of them, as research has shown, cannot adapt to the changing natural conditions (Schellnhuber et al. 2006). In the last decade, more than sixteen thousand species were threatened with extinction. According to the Living Planet Index (http://www.livingplanetindex.org), populations of vertebrate species have halved in the past forty years. If the trends of past years continue, between 15 and 37 percent of species would disappear by 2050 (Thomas et al. 2004). Perhaps the largest threat is the growing indifference of the public to wildlife, conservation, and environmental issues in general. Environmental protection still draws huge support among Americans, for example, yet many people are concerned about potential costs such as losing jobs. There is an ideological and partisan divide about how Americans see environmental policies at home and abroad. In general terms, many people would love to do more to protect the environment, yet do not support environmental policies that could affect people's employment and the taxes they pay (Pew Research Center 2018).

WATER CONTAMINATION AND SHORTAGE

Chronic droughts, industrial and agricultural activity, waste, and overpopulation can all lead to water contamination and shortages. Today approximately one billion people have no permanent access to clean running water. Hundreds of millions drink unclean water directly from nearby rivers. The most troubling problems persist in India, China, and Mexico. Worldwide, agriculture is the main consumer of water, and the world's population is growing. By 2050, if trends continue, the demand for water for agriculture will double relative to 2000. Another problem comes from climate change. If the warming trend remains, more ice will melt. The disappearance of glaciers in the Tibet-Himalaya area may lead to substantial losses of river water for all neighboring countries. Because of changes in weather patterns, according to estimates, the Mediterranean region can expect a drop in precipitation of 25 to 30 percent by the middle of the century (Stern 2007).

Water pollution is another major byproduct of human activity, including sewage from towns and farms, discharges from power stations, and industrial silt. Rivers, lakes, and even seas are threatened by chemical waste. Especially dangerous are toxic heavy metals (such as mercury, lead, and cadmium) and

water pollution The byproducts of human activities that are harmful to rivers, lakes, seas, and underground water.

The International Program on the State of the Ocean (IPSO)

natural disaster A natural hazard such as an earthquake or a volcano eruption with devastating impact on the ecosystem.

oil spills. Unclean water contributes to serious illnesses in humans and kills living organisms in rivers, lakes, and oceans (Black 2011; Pearce 2007). China's rapid industrial development has dumped significant waste into major rivers, thus creating significant health hazards (Moore 2014; Economy 2010b).

Disasters and Accidents

Natural disasters, such as earthquakes or erupting volcanoes, can have devastating impacts. Yet human-made accidents, too, can have catastrophic environmental consequences. Natural disasters cannot be prevented, but their damaging consequences can be diminished through effective preparations, international assistance, and cooperation. For instance, the 2004 Indian Ocean tsunami, the most devastating in the twenty-first century, caused a significant loss of human life in many Asian countries because the affected countries had almost no early warning systems and lacked adequate preparation. The governments could not rescue many victims. Medical help was often limited. Fresh water was absent because salt water and sewage infiltrated many water reservoirs (Helm 2005). Although international forces (including the United States navy) provided prompt and effective relief efforts, the local governments were often inefficient.

In Guatemala, volunteers distribute food packages to survivors affected by the volcanic eruption in 2018.

Human-created disasters include chemical leaks, radioactive leaks, and oil spills. Among the most devastating disasters in history took place in December 1983 in the Indian city of Bhopal, where almost fifteen thousand people died and tens of thousands were injured by toxic gas leakage from a chemical refinery owned by a U.S. company, Union Carbide. At least one million people suffered serious health consequences. Union Carbide, which settled the case with the Indian government, continued to insist that the disaster was not an accident but a deliberate act of sabotage (D'Silva 2006).

The most destructive leak of radioactive materials took place at the Chernobyl nuclear plant in the former Soviet Union in 1986. Hundreds of thousands of people, even years later, continue facing serious health-related consequences. The largest series of oil spills in history took place during Iraq's takeover of Kuwait in August 1990 and the Persian Gulf War in January 1991 between the United States and Iraq. Retreating Iraqi troops destroyed Kuwait's oil rigs, setting fires and creating giant oil lakes. Between six and eight million barrels of oil spilled into the Persian Gulf. The biggest marine oil spill in history took place in the Gulf of Mexico in 2010, when an explosion in an oil platform operated by British Petroleum took the lives of eleven workers. From three to five million barrels of oil went into the water, causing serious damage to wildlife and contaminating the U.S. coastline. The economic impact was estimated at between $3 billion and $12 billion. Studies suggest that this was not just one accident associated with one oil company. Although these accidents are preventable, they may happen again and with even more devastating environmental consequences (Juhasz 2011).

Environmental Policies Today

Efforts to protect the environment include regulations and restrictions, green investment, and more comprehensive policies. Financial regulations, taxation, economic incentives, and legal directives all play a role.

RESTRICTION AND REGULATION

In 1900, the Lacey Act banned trade in wildlife, fish, and plants that have been illegally obtained, transported, or sold. This act is effective to this day. The last amendment to it in 2008 expanded its protection to additional plants and plant products and also prohibited import of illegal timber to the United States. In 1986, the International Whaling Commission banned commercial whaling. Other policies in many countries regulate legal business activities that may be environmentally harmful. To reduce deforestation, for example, nearly 40 percent of the Amazon River basin is legally protected, including approximately 25 percent in private hands. Owners must keep 80 percent of their land forested. These are examples of **conservation**—regulatory policies to protect and preserve natural resources, plant and animal species, and their habitat. Conservation is not necessarily a combination of bans and restrictions imposed by governments. Conservation is also a form of social ethics supporting recycling, care, restoration, and preservation of nature (Hambler and Canney 2013).

Conservation A policy of protecting and preserve natural resources, including plant and animal species and their habitats.

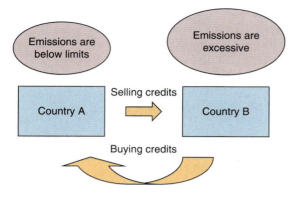

FIGURE 9-4 Emissions trading. Countries that limit their emissions can receive financial rewards. Countries that fall short of cutting their emissions pay a penalty.

Kyoto Protocol A 1997 international agreement to limit air pollution and reduce global warming.

National Centers for Environmental Information

Taxation and other financial incentives for environmental protection have gained recognition as well (ICAP 2015; Nordhaus 2008). An example is *emissions trading* to limit pollution. Here companies and countries receive "credits," giving them the right to emit a pollutant but only up to a limit. Those who cannot cut pollution that far are required to buy additional credits from others that pollute less. This mechanism creates a financial incentive to pollute less (Fusaro and James 2006). (See Figure 9-4.)

The United Nations took up a major initiative to globalize policies on climate change. In June 1992, the international meeting in Rio de Janeiro, commonly known as the Earth Summit, produced the UN Framework Convention on Climate Change (UNFCCC). The goal of this treaty was to stabilize greenhouse gas concentrations in the atmosphere. Since then, UN conferences on climate change have met periodically. A milestone was the conference in Kyoto, Japan, in 1997, when the participants signed the **Kyoto Protocol** to the UNFCCC. Most industrial countries agreed to reduce greenhouse gas emissions by an average of 6 to 8 percent below 1990 levels by 2012.

Some countries, small and big, did not participate in the Kyoto Protocol. Some stated that they would try to cut their emissions but would not participate in emission trading. Canadian officials argued some time ago that it was too expensive for Canada to contribute $7 billion per year—the price of carbon credits for this country—at a time of economic recession (van Loon 2011). The U.S. Congress during the Clinton, Bush, and Obama administrations did not ratify the Kyoto Protocol. China and India, as well as dozens of developing countries, were exempted from the treaty. A major objection was that the required emission cuts would hurt the economic situation of these countries. Without the participation of the world's biggest polluters, the UN effort seemed incomplete. Therefore, governments agreed in Doha, Qatar, to extend the Kyoto Protocol to 2020. Another global agreement was signed in 2015 in Paris. We will turn to these accords later in this chapter.

GREEN INVESTMENTS

Green investments are business ventures in which companies are involved in activities reducing contamination and depletion and introduce environmentally friendly practices. Typically but not always, green investments require governmental policies to stimulate private business. In most cases, these are investments in environmentally friendly technologies, business methods, and agricultural practices. Green investments go beyond simple restrictions. Many countries, for example, invest in reforestation to make up for lost trees and other vegetation. In China and Costa Rica, policies are being set for agriculture. The fewer trees farmers cut, the more trees farmers plant, the more money they get in form of subsidies. In the same way, **geoengineering** aims to develop technological solutions to environmental problems (Victor et al. 2009; Victor 2006). One strategy for reducing the existing accumulation of greenhouse gases involves releasing particles into the air to reflect more sunlight back into space. Another strategy includes the collection and storage of carbon gases from coal plants. Germany, for example, draws new carbon capture and storage laws (CCS) to allow companies to store CO_2 indefinitely in underground storage facilities. Regions that host such facilities receive financial compensation (German Energy

Wind-powered electricity generators have become common in many countries. Why does the United States lag behind?

Blog 2015). With most countries depending on fossil fuels for energy, particularly in the developing world, carbon capture and storage could be a viable way—if the price of it were subsidized—to reduce greenhouse emissions (PPPIRC 2018).

Wind-powered electricity generators have become common in many countries. In Denmark, 29 percent of the electricity comes from wind-powered generators. In Germany, the figure is getting closer to 20 percent. In the United States, according to the Department of Energy, it is around 6 percent. Despite an increase in the use of the wind-powered electricity since 2000, the United States lags behind many economically developed countries.

Unlike coal or oil, **renewable energy** is replaced naturally as fast as it is consumed (Kemp 2006). It draws on such alternative sources as wind, the sun, tides, and geothermal power—the natural heat within the earth. Wind-powered electricity generators, solar thermal plants, and photovoltaic power stations are examples of new technologies producing renewable energy. British Petroleum pledged to invest up to $200 million in solar power batteries (Ward and Thomas 2017). General Electric's growth strategy, called *ecomagination*, commits the company to using wind power, diesel-electric hybrid locomotives, new efficient aircraft engines and appliances, and advanced water-treatment systems. Another area of investment is *biofuels*, made from plants, vegetables, or celluloid (Brown and Brown 2012; Soetaert and Vandamme 2009). Brazil has reduced its dependence on oil and gas by producing biofuels from sugar cane. The Chinese government moved to make significant investments in wind technologies, electric cars, and electric vehicle charging stations (Shahan 2014). India has recently created National Solar Mission and is working to increase dramatically the use of the sun's energy. The government is providing up to 90 percent support for setting up solar power plants. One of the specific goals is to install twenty million solar lights around the country.

geoengineering A field aimed at developing technological solutions to environmental problems.

renewable energy A form of energy replaced naturally as fast as it is consumed.

The costs associated with this "green revolution" are still considered to be prohibitively high for many countries, especially poor ones. The International Energy Agency estimated that to reduce global oil consumption by a quarter and cut global greenhouse gas emissions in half by 2050, the world would need to invest $50 billion to $100 billion each year in clean-energy technologies, compared to about $10 billion a year spent recently (Levi et al. 2010). Even within the European Community only the most prosperous countries, such as Germany and the Netherlands, can afford to spend significant funds on renewables. Newer members of the community—Bulgaria, Romania, Poland, Latvia, Estonia, and Lithuania—have asked for assistance.

Global Environment Facility (GEF) An independent financial organization established in 1991 that provides grants to developing countries for projects that benefit the global environment and promote sustainable development.

Usually, the poorer the country is, the less inclined it is to invest in geoengineering and renewables. That places increasing pressure on wealthy countries to provide financial support through loans or grants (Shah 2014; Esty and Winston 2006). The **Global Environment Facility (GEF)**, created in 1991, provides funds for projects in six areas: climate change, biodiversity, pollution in international waters, land degradation, ozone depletion, and persistent *organic pollution* from such natural contaminants as fish and animal waste (French 1994). From the start, the GEF has supported almost two thousand environmental initiatives in countries that otherwise would not have had the financial resources. About 20 percent of the funding is distributed through nongovernmental organizations.

Without coordinated international efforts, the green revolution would be ineffective. Yet China, Japan, and the United States for many years refused the leadership role in environmental policies, citing the threat of economic slowdown. The European Union remains the most active actor in international environmental politics (see the next section).

COMPREHENSIVE POLICIES

sustainable development A comprehensive policy that meets the needs of the present without sacrificing the ability of future generations to meet their own needs. This policy is about stimulating economic growth while protecting the environment and natural resources

A more comprehensive policy is **sustainable development** that meets the needs of the present without sacrificing the ability of future generations to meet their needs. This policy is about stimulating economic growth while at the same time protecting the environment and natural resources (Blewitt 2014; Rogers, Jalal, and Boyd 2007). The idea of sustainable development emerged partly in response to a 1987 report, *Our Common Future*. Prepared by the UN-sponsored World Commission on Environment and Development, it argued that helping local economies, protecting natural resources, and ensuring social justice for all people are not contradictory but rather complementary goals. (See Figure 9-5.)

The European Union is the world's leader in designing and implementing comprehensive environmental policies. Starting in the 1970s, many environmentalist groups began to have a significant impact on Europe's political life. From the 1990s, practically all discussions of the EU's economic development focused on the environment and sustainable development.

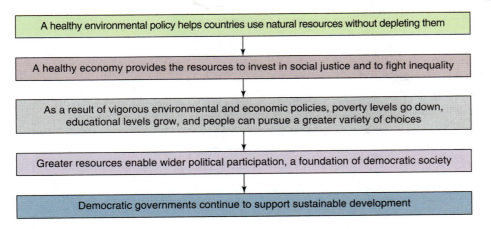

FIGURE 9-5 Main conclusions of the *Our Common Future* report.

From 2007 through 2009, the EU Climate Change program established the 20–20–20 targets (often called the *2020 Climate and Energy Package*): 20 percent of the energy consumed in Europe must come from renewable sources, and countries must reduce gas emissions by up to 20 percent by 2020. To accomplish these ambitious goals, the EU will have to impose tougher pollution restrictions, encourage low-emission vehicles, expand emissions trading, and invest in public transportation and low-energy construction. The main problem is the lack of resources to meet these targets, especially after the financial crisis and economic slowdown of the past several years. Although the supporters of the *2020 Climate and Energy Package* believed this should be a model for other countries to follow (Wurzel and Connelly 2012), skeptics also argue that, even if the 20–20–20 targets are met, their impact on climate change will be insignificant. Overall, the EU Climate Change program is an example of how countries can work together on a common strategy on energy and environmental issues. According to official data, in terms of greenhouse gas emissions, energy efficiency, and renewable energy, EU was on track to reach many of the 2020 targets (EU 2017). Although it was not possible to meet every environmental target (Mead 2018), such environmental agreements, their supporters believe, have demonstrated the importance of effective legal and political action. The process is set—you can easily check media updates—to create a new agreement targeting 2030.

Many unresolved issues remain. It is unclear how key developing countries—Brazil, India, and China—will cooperate with UNFCCC initiatives. It is also unclear how to combine comprehensive, global environmental policies with the desire of many countries for financial security, economic growth, and guaranteed employment.

Check Your Knowledge

1. What lesson did the 1985 Vienna Convention and the 1987 Montreal Protocol provide for today's governments and international organizations?

2. Which environmental problem does the Aral Sea case illustrate?

3. When and where did the largest series of oil spills in history take place?

4. Why haven't all countries switched to renewable energy?

5. What is sustainable development? Why did the 20–20–20 EU targets appear as an example of sustainable development?

POLICY IMPLEMENTATION

Environmental policies often run up against the realities of everyday life. The United States depends heavily on coal and oil; a switch to renewables is impossible without a long transitional period and huge investments. Federal and trade deficits make it extremely difficult to pay for more costly alternatives to coal and oil. In developing countries, billions of people depend on coal for heating and cooking. Sweden, despite more than a three-decade-long ban on new nuclear plants and the decision by an advisory referendum to close all nuclear plants by 2010, cannot shut down its nuclear facilities because there are no realistic and environmentally friendly replacements. Sweden has three nuclear power plants that produce about 40 percent of the country's electricity. A growing demand for energy forces the country to continue using nuclear reactors and replacing the existing ones with new reactors. Environmental policies require imagination and innovation, but there are limits. People continue to buy cars that run on gasoline—and they are becoming more efficient and less polluting, and, compared to hybrid and electric cars, they are still less expensive.

9.2 Approaches to Environmental Issues

In this section, we discuss several lenses through which we can view environmental issues.

Realist Approaches to the Environment

States have traditionally struggled for natural resources and have considered nature an asset to conquer and exploit. Experts and politicians trained in realpolitik acknowledge environmental issues but still treat them as marginal. In their view, states maintain **environmental sovereignty**—the right to use and protect their environment and natural resources. At the core of environmental sovereignty is a country's pursuit of its interests, in light of domestic politics. After the 1970s, however, many leaders began to connect the problems of depletion and contamination to national interests and security threats. It became clear that uncontrolled use of national resources and inattention to environmental problems could undermine international stability.

environmental sovereignty The right of states to use and protect their environment and natural resources.

NATIONAL INTERESTS AND SECURITY

Natural and human-created disasters are serious events affecting security and military policies, especially if they cause massive casualties and significant environmental damage. In turn, governments now accept greater responsibility than ever for dealing with the consequences. After the historic 2004 tsunami in Asia and the earthquake in Haiti in January 2010, several countries committed their military forces to the rescue operations, and U.S. naval vessels delivered humanitarian assistance. However, any deployment of foreign troops in another country, regardless of their mission, can become a source of security concerns, and international tensions can easily arise. Natural disasters in other countries can trigger immediate security concerns as well as changes in long-term environmental policies. After the Fukushima nuclear power plant was damaged by the 2011 tsunami, the coalition government in Germany—influenced in part by the events in Japan—decided to close all nuclear plants in Germany by 2022. This will require new policies and substantial investments in alternative energy sources for Germany.

This oil rig in the North Sea is one of many new ones in the Arctic region. There may be a scramble for control of this region among several countries. Will it become a major source of regional conflict?

Environmental disasters may quickly worsen existing social problems, especially in poor countries like Haiti, triggering political violence and instability. (We discuss similar cases in the next chapter.) Conversely, wars and political turmoil may have catastrophic consequences for the environment. Terrorist groups seeking to cause significant damage may focus on nuclear reactors, chemical plants, hydroelectric stations, or dams (Levi 2009). Protection of these facilities thus becomes part of a government's environmental security policies.

Depletion of natural resources is a potential cause of conflict. Realists argue that the constantly increasing demands for natural resources, clean water, and agricultural lands could become a major source of local and regional conflicts. In other words, scarcity of natural resources is an international security issue (Le Billon 2006). Israel, for example, controls most fresh water reservoirs, including underground aquifers, in the Gaza and the West Bank. While Palestinians demand full access, Israel considers water a strategic asset and uses it to put pressure on the other side. In the 1980s, Turkey began to construct hydroelectric dams using water from the Euphrates River to rotate turbines to produce electricity. These dams reduced the water flow in Syria, Iran, and Iraq, all of whom protested (Homer-Dixon 1991). The construction, however, continued. China's similar projects in Tibet caused serious concerns in India and other neighboring countries (Economy 2010b). Many observers these days call for international talks on the looming environmental crisis in the region.

▷

The Earth Is Full

THE GLOBAL COMMONS

The **global commons** includes areas that are not under any one country's sovereign control, such as the open ocean, the seabed, the atmosphere, outer space, and Antarctica. The idea of the global commons has found significant

global commons
Geographical areas not under any nation's sovereign control.

international support. However, commons have also emerged as potential sites of conflict around the world (Nonini 2007). Without international regulations, private companies or predator states could endanger the environment in the global commons and deplete its resources. And without international agreements, disputes over environmental and other policies in the global commons are likely (Grover 2006). One such area of concern is the Arctic: The polar seas began to thaw, thus allowing countries to navigate in the area during summer and explore natural resources there (Zellen 2009; Borgerson 2008). International agreements have long protected the global commons from hostile takeovers and depletion. This policy has become a strategic priority for the United States and other developed democratic states.

The 1959 Antarctic Treaty prohibits any economic exploration and military operations, including nuclear tests, on the sixth continent. No country may claim a territory in Antarctica. Additional agreements regulate research, economic, and military activities on the continent. For example, the 1991 Madrid accord bans coal mining and oil exploration in Antarctica for fifty years. In addition to these and several other agreements, international relations with respect to Antarctica is regulated by the Antarctic Treaty System. Some business activities such as tourism are allowed, as long as they are regulated and the profits are shared. In the realist view, denying privileged access to Antarctica benefits international security because it maintains the existing balance of power.

In sum, supporters of realism acknowledge the importance of environmental policies and international environmental cooperation. At the same time, realism continues to view environmental issues in the context of security interests and the balance of power.

Liberal Approaches to the Environment

Liberal models treat environmental issues as requiring a sustained and coordinated international effort. Liberal internationalism treats environmental policies as a central feature of modern-day international relations. As you will remember from earlier chapters, many liberals claim that the destructive nature of contemporary wars should make them obsolete as a policy option. Similarly, the depth and scope of today's environmental problems should change the traditional, power-driven approach to international politics. Liberals strongly believe in environmental agreements, institutions, and the involvement of nongovernment organizations (Harris 2004).

INTERNATIONAL TREATIES AND ORGANIZATIONS

The earlier example about Antarctica shows that countries can successfully figure out a common approach to the protection of an entire continent and build an effective international institution to conduct joint policies. This common approach came together with an early wave of environmental treaties negotiated in the 1970s. These treaties were mostly regional, signed by countries with shared concerns about contamination, conservation, and protection of endangered species. The Amazon Cooperation Treaty of 1978 provided guidelines to eight Latin American countries for water use, transportation, environmental research, tourism, and commercial developments in the Amazon region. In Western Europe, with the help of newly formed green parties, Environmental Action Programs (EAPs) were launched. Governments allocated funds for massive cleaning efforts in rivers and lakes. In one successful international action, countries banned chlorofluorocarbons (CFCs) in aerosol spray cans and refrigerators in response to ozone depletion.

From the very start, the most ambitious goal of environmental advocates was to develop a global policy framework under the UN umbrella. In 1973, the United Nations Environment Programme (UNEP) was founded, with its headquarters in Nairobi, Kenya. Its activities covered protection of the atmosphere and global ecosystems, promotion of environmental science and education, and an early warning and emergency response system in cases of environmental disasters. UNEP has developed guidelines and treaties on international trade in harmful chemicals, cross-border air pollution, and contamination of international waterways (UNEP 2010). In 1988, the United Nations funded the Intergovernmental Panel on Climate Change (IPCC) to evaluate the most recent science and human activities related to climate change. During the 1990s, the agenda of international environmental politics broadened. Now it included global environmental agreements. We have already discussed the 1992 UN Conference that created the UNFCCC. For the first time, a true global environmental institution was formed, with 172 countries participating. Ten years later, the Earth Summit of 2002—the World Summit on Sustainable Development—took place in South Africa.

The signing of the Kyoto Protocol in 1997 was a shining moment for global environmental politics (McGovern 2006). More than 190 countries later ratified this agreement and pledged to reduce their emissions of carbon dioxide and five other greenhouse gases. Many countries considered emissions trading. The next decade, however, was largely disappointing for environmentalists and their supporters. Powerful forces in the United States, China, Canada, and other countries began to view emerging environmental policies as a threat to their countries' economic interests. Skeptics attacked the environmental movement, warning that climate control would end in a global bureaucratic regime and huge expenditures without effect (Lomborg 2010).

Despite the global financial crisis and recession of the past decade, global environmental politics has not waned—just the contrary. In April 2009 the leaders of the United States, China, the European Union, India, Russia, and twelve other major economic powers, as well as the United Nations and Denmark, created the Major Economies Forum on Energy and Climate (MEF). The group made a strong effort to boost the UNFCCC negotiations, culminating in a December 2009 conference in Copenhagen. The Copenhagen Accord set several important goals. First, the countries pledged to keep global temperatures from increasing to more than 2°C (3.6°F) above preindustrial levels. Next, they promised to allocate up to $100 billion a year by 2020 to help developing countries deal with climate change. They also promised *transparency*: assured methods so that others could verify whether they are cutting emissions. Finally, the accord required that all but the poorest countries produce specific plans for curbing emissions (Levi 2010a).

The 2010 Cancun Agreement by 193 countries confirmed the key goals established by the Copenhagen Accord. To achieve those goals, industrialized countries would have to cut their emissions between 25 and 40 percent by 2020 compared with 1990 levels. These cuts would be voluntary and subject to international inspection. A new Green Climate Fund under UN auspices was established that would manage billions of dollars in support of climate action (Levi 2010b). In 2012, countries reached a global agreement to extend the provisions of the Kyoto Protocol until 2020. Further, a new agreement should be negotiated and reached to replace the Kyoto Protocol. However, having faced financial and economic difficulties during the past several years and witnessing oil prices rise and fall, countries remained reluctant or unable to cut their emissions when significantly faced with domestic political and economic pressures (Levi 2014).

Paris Agreement A 2015 international agreement to limit air pollution, reduce global warming emissions, mitigate adverse impact climate change, and outline international financial obligations of participating countries.

The 2015 **Paris Agreement** was an international treaty to deal with greenhouse gas emissions after 2020. The specific goal was to keep global temperature rise below 1.5–2 degrees Celsius above preindustrial levels (the time approximately two hundred years ago). The agreement also provided measures for countries to deal with the negative impacts of climate change. To reach these goals, the agreement set specific financial objectives. The agreement also set policies for greater transparency and accountability of the participating countries (UN Climate Change 2018). In 2017, President Trump, in a dramatic policy shift, stated that the United States would withdraw from the Paris climate accord. He argued that this decision was necessary to boost the nation's industry and economic independence (Stokols 2017). This decision received support from Trump backers but criticisms from most U.S. allies and partners. According to the legal rules, however, the formal notice of withdrawal cannot be submitted until 2019. The 2020 U.S. presidential elections are likely to determine the future of the agreement.

NONGOVERNMENT ORGANIZATIONS

Environmental NGOs first emerged to advocate environmental policies in areas neglected by the public or the government. Some, like Greenpeace, choose provocative and attention-grabbing strategies (see the Case Study at the end of this chapter). Others, like the Sierra Club and the National Audubon Society, focus mainly on education. The Centre for Science and Environment (CSE) is named after a successful media campaign against air pollution in large Indian cities. Partly because of this group's pressure, the government decided to use compressed natural gas as the main fuel in the capital city's buses and taxis. Still other NGOs focus on funding. The GEF, for one, provides grants to developing countries for projects that benefit the global environment and promote sustainable developments in local communities. The GEF helps countries address such problems as biodiversity, greenhouse gas emissions, pollution in international waters, land degradation, the ozone layer, and persistent organic pollutants.

NGOs, according to liberal theories, advance democratic governance and represent a wide range of interests and opinions not represented in large bureaucratic structures. They also monitor environmental policies and reveal problems that governments often overlook or ignore. NGOs educate and influence the public, launch direct actions, and enhance awareness of environmental problems.

PUBLIC AWARENESS

In a democratic society, public opinion generally affects policy making and education shapes public opinion (Hobley 2012). The more people know and care about the environment, the more supportive they are of environmental policies. Sustained educational efforts and public discussions about the environment are an essential part of the democratic process.

Global public opinion, despite fluctuations, is generally warming up to environmental issues. Global climate change was the top-rated concern in a thirty-nine-nation Pew Research Center survey in 2013: 54 percent across these surveyed countries said global climate change was a *major* threat to their country. A slightly smaller number of people mentioned international financial instability as their top concern (Pew Research Center 2013). In 2015, 64 percent of Americans said that they favored stricter limits on emissions to address climate change (Pew Research Center 2015). Specific economic circumstances, however, affect public opinion. During an economic slowdown, most Americans prioritized economic growth (54 percent) over environmental protection (36 percent; Jones 2011). The same 2015 Pew survey also revealed that Americans increasingly worry about the costs to protect the environment. In 2018, about three-quarters of Americans believed that the United States should do whatever it takes to protect the environment, compared with a quarter who believed the country had gone too far in its efforts to protect the environment. More than 55 percent of Americans named the environment as a top policy issue that the president and the Congress should tackle. Americans' views of environmental policies are strongly associated with political beliefs (Pew Research Center 2018).

ENVIRONMENTAL OFFENDERS

The World Wildlife Fund (WWF) assesses consumption habits in different countries and publishes a list of "environmental offenders." The residents of the United Arab Emirates (UAE) top the list. Each person in the UAE needs 12 hectares (30 acres) of biologically productive land and sea to sustain life—area needed to produce vegetables, fish, fruit, or rice and to absorb waste. The United States was the second-worst "offender," with a requirement of 9.6 hectares. The average global requirement, according to the WWF, is 2.2 hectares per person, but the available supply is only 1.8 hectares. What is the main point of such a list, and how effective is

The mall of the Emirates in Dubai, UAE includes an artificial mini-ski resort and is a shopping and recreational paradise. Critics say this mall consumes too much energy to entertain just a few wealthy consumers. I you were to advise the UAE government, how would you address such criticisms?

publication of the list? Could you reduce your personal consumption habits, at least for a short period of time? How? In your view, will doing so affect the environment in any measurable way?

Values and Interests

Why did international environmental politics emerge only in the last decades of the twentieth century and not earlier? Policies stem from social and political debates and reflect people's changing values and identities and new awareness of the environment.

mastery values The view that individuals may exercise control over and exploit natural resources.

harmony values The view that the environment should be preserved and cherished rather than exploited.

Mastery values encourage individuals to exercise control over nature and exploit its resources. **Harmony values** encourage a different attitude—one of preservation and care (Smith and Schwartz 1997). In the constructivist view, both harmony and mastery values affect the environmental policies of different countries and in different periods.

For centuries, mastery values dominated politics. They were behind policies of rapid industrialization and the extraction of natural resources in the twentieth century. Market competition and mass consumption reinforced mastery values in democratic societies, but these values influenced Communist countries as well. Mastery values are sometimes called modern environmental *prometheanism* (Meyer 2016)—the belief that human beings can and should master nature and remake it for the better. Harmony values, in contrast, encourage conservation and environmental protection. They are attached to concerns for the common good inherent in liberal democracy. The most important sources of values are education and science. For example, without coercion and restriction, people learn that owning a car is expensive and environmentally unfriendly. As a result, attitudes change. In Berlin, studies show, people increasingly use public transportation. In Copenhagen, close to two-thirds of people choose bicycles to do their grocery shopping. In Lyon (France), the number of cars entering the city has fallen by 20 percent compared to ten years ago. This city, as many other cities today, promotes the use of bikes and bike stations (Casson 2018). Same bike and scooter-friendly policies are being implemented in many U.S. cities such as Seattle (Washington).

International environmental policies are most effective when they adjust to local political, social, and cultural contexts and address local concerns. Environmentalism is strong in the Canadian province of Quebec, which generates eco-friendly hydroelectricity that it sells to other provinces and the United States. Elsewhere, environmental policies often run into local resistance. In Indonesia, many African countries, and Brazil, peasants oppose attempts to ban *slash-and-burn* farming—a method of farming based on cutting and burning of plants that contributes to deforestation and air pollution—because they desperately need new farmlands (Waters 2006). To stop slashing and burning, the structure of the local economies must change. New jobs for local farmers are needed, which requires significant investment. Other countries can help if they face no serious economic problems themselves. But during a recession, investments decrease. Economic booms help environmental investments.

Steady resistance to environmental policies in the United States is a more complicated case, but it too points to the connections among politics, values, and economic interests. Power companies and carmakers are not thrilled about policies limiting gas emissions because they may limit profits. The Bush, Obama, and Trump administrations allowed the use of new technologies such as hydraulic fracturing. "Fracking," as it is commonly known, sparked protests by environmental organizations and some communities mainly because of the unknown environmental consequences of this method. However, fracking several years ago has also made the United States self-sufficient in terms of oil and gas (Levi 2013).

Environmental policies are even more difficult to implement in countries exporting oil, gas, and coal. Saudi Arabia, Russia, and other oil and gas producers are genuinely interested in having other states dependent on these energy sources. A reduction in oil consumption due to environmental policies will mean a loss of profit.

Constructivism argues that changing the structure of economic incentives should go hand in hand with enhancing environmental education and awareness. However, changing values could be a more complicated task than introducing new taxes or bringing new managers.

ALTERNATIVE AND CRITICAL VIEWS

For conflict theories, economic discrimination is embedded in today's international environmental politics. **Environmental discrimination** refers to the actions and policies of the global North that sustain the contamination and depletion in the environment in the global South. Facing tough environmental policies at home, corporations continuously moved their industrial facilities to less developed countries and shipped toxic waste there for inexpensive recycling (Grossman 2007). Most climate control efforts contribute to global inequality. Rich countries can afford to slow production, cut emissions, and adopt tough conservation measures. However, as far as the argument goes, poor countries would suffer from tough new regulations, which would depress their economies. These countries were not given a chance to develop in the past because of colonialism. Environmental policies imposed by the North would have a similar effect.

Critics of imperialism and colonialism argue that, for centuries, powerful Western nations ignored environmental policies while depleting the natural resources of the rest of the world. Today, the disparity in consumption of energy between the rich North and the poor South is staggering. The United States has less than 5 percent of the global population, but it consumes almost 25 percent of the world's energy. On average, U.S. residents consume three to ten times as much energy as do people in developing countries like India and China—and thirty times as much as people in relatively poor states like Bangladesh (CIA 2018).

What are some potential solutions? There should be global *environmental justice* based on equal protection from environmental problems and a fair distribution of environmental benefits (Walker 2009). The main investment

environmental discrimination
Actions and policies of the global North that sustain the contamination and depletion of the environment in the global South.

Check Your Knowledge

1. What is environmental sovereignty? Give an example.

2. Why is depletion of natural resources a potential cause of international conflicts?

3. What are the key differences between realist and liberal views of environmental policies?

4. What is the Kyoto Protocol? What is the Paris Agreement?

5. How could public awareness affect the environmental policies of governments?

6. Compare mastery and harmony values. Can there be a compromise between these two sets of values?

7. Explain environmental discrimination and environmental justice.

in global environmental policies should come from the North (Roberts and Parks 2006). Because wealthy countries remain the main consumers of energy and the chief global polluters, they should cut their emissions first. This should allow less developed states to increase energy consumption and develop their economies. Some scholars argue that such policies will be impossible to implement unless major structural changes take place across countries. Today's environmental problems, they maintain, have their roots in the inability of the capitalist system, with its emphasis on consumption, to address the accelerating threat to life on the planet (Magdoff and Foster 2011).

9.3 Critical Applications

In this section, we look at international responses to environmental problems at three levels of analysis: individual, state, and global (Table 9.1).

Individual Decisions

In 2007, former senator and vice president Albert Gore received the Nobel Peace Prize for his global environmental advocacy. Yet former president of the Czech Republic, Vaclav Klaus, openly criticized "global warming hysteria." What makes political leaders strong defenders or entrenched skeptics of environmental policies?

Views of the environment can be understood as a continuum. (See Figure 9-6.) On the one side of this continuum is **environmentalism—** the belief in the necessity of urgent and comprehensive actions to protect the environment. Environmentalists support conservation of natural resources, push for measures against contamination, and endorse sustainable development. They believe that many environmental problems are urgent and that the earth's natural resources are limited (Cullen 2010). Commercial activities harmful to the environment should be regulated or banned. Environmentalism is associated with harmony values and a belief in growth through preservation. Environmentalism finds support among many scientists with international standing and is also rooted in *progressivism*, or the belief in deliberate social action for the sake of the common good. This social action must be ecologically sound. Environmentalists also insist that the world's environmental problems are extremely serious and that countries should do significantly more to protect the environment (Davis 2007).

Environmentalism
Belief in the necessity of urgent and comprehensive policies to protect the environment.

TABLE 9.1 Environmental Issues at Three Levels of Analysis

Level of Analysis	Application of Environmental Policies
Individual	Individual leaders' decisions and personal views affect not only domestic but international politics. A range of factors affect an individual's orientation toward attitudes such as environmentalism or environmental skepticism. These include, for example, personal experiences, education, cultural and generational norms, and political affiliations. Environmental activism, even at the individual level, can have a powerful impact on environmental policies.
State	Political factors such as party ideologies substantially affect a country's environmental policies. Across countries, some parties are environmentally "active," while others are environmentally "neutral," and electoral results accordingly affect a country's environmental policies. Political protectionists around the world argue that robust international environmental policies can hurt employment. By contrast, environmental parties (commonly called Green Parties) argue for a healthy environment, the common good, ample jobs, and a socially just system.
Global	Addressing environmental issues requires a massive, coordinated, educated, and sustained global effort. National and global environmental policies must be both effective and efficient.

At the other end of the continuum is **environmental skepticism.** Skeptics can be conservatives as well as liberal individualists who are likely to adopt mastery values and to believe that current environmental policies are too costly to be feasible and effective (Meyer 2016; Lomborg 2007, 2010a). They support conservation on a smaller scale and believe in the priority of business and market forces over government regulations (Walley and Whitehead 1994). Skeptics maintain that, although protecting the environment is important, other serious problems, including violence, diseases, and hunger, should receive more urgent care.

environmental skepticism
A questioning of environmentalism from the point of view of science or practicality.

Political leaders' education, family experiences, and other circumstances contribute to their choices. Al Gore's concern for nature was enhanced by his experience as a student, when one of his professors made him aware of rising global temperatures. Environmentalism often finds reinforcement in religious values. *Evangelical environmentalism* treats environmental problems and climate change in particular as a serious moral issue (Wilkinson 2012). Many members of all religions believe people have a spiritual duty to protect the environment (Jenkins 2008).

Scientists and politicians often disagree about the gravity of environmental problems. They also argue about which policies should be launched to deal with these problems. However, it is incorrect to portray environmental

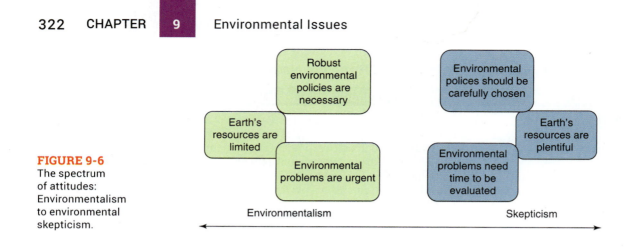

FIGURE 9-6
The spectrum of attitudes: Environmentalism to environmental skepticism.

debates as a battle between greedy, conservative, and uneducated "dinosaurs" eager to ignore environmental problems—and young, progressive, passionate, and talented activists. In fact, over the past twenty years, there has been a substantial change in environmental attitudes: government leaders are increasingly susceptible to the arguments and demands of citizens and environmental groups. CEOs of big corporations often lead massive environmental efforts and contribute substantial funds to environmental policies. Individual customs and habits change. Anyone who has lived in or traveled to Seattle (Washington) or Portland (Oregon) could have noticed how advanced and environmentally conscious their recycling polices are compared to most places in the United States. Individual leaders change their views, too. Large and small countries alike are more likely to conduct robust environmental policies because of a major shift today from mastery to harmony values among ordinary people and the governing elites. Education has sparked awareness and brought changes in the ways both regular people and politicians see the environment.

The success of international environmentalism testifies to the role of individual scientists, activists, and political leaders. In 2015, former Chinese state television reporter Chai Jing produced a documentary titled *Under the Dome* where she expressed her concern about significant pollution in China's cities. Within a few weeks, more than 100 million people, mostly in China, watched this video online, which sparked new debates about the insufficient environmental policies of the Chinese government (Tran 2015). The impact of this documentary was compared with the historic impact of *Silent Spring*. When Rachel Carson published *Silent Spring* in 1962, warning about

A photograph of Rachel Carson hangs from supports on the bridge now bearing her name in Pittsburgh, Pennsylvania. Her environmental book *Silent Spring* affected the views of millions.

DEBATE > ALARMING AND SKEPTICAL VOICES

Contemporary environmental discussions resemble the longtime debate between *cornucopians* (a term deriving from the word "cornucopia," or horn of plenty), who believed that natural resources are practically limitless, and neo-Malthusians, the followers of the nineteenth-century British scholar Thomas Robert Malthus (1766–1834), who predicted that the inevitable depletion of natural resources would generate world conflicts (Homer-Dixon 1991).

James Lovelock, a British environmental scientist, drew wide attention for his *Gaia hypothesis*, named after a Greek goddess. Lovelock believes that if nothing is done during the next fifty years, global warming will make most of the planet uninhabitable, and civilization will perish. Lovelock proposes, among other things, urgently switching to nuclear energy and building giant pipes to transfer carbon dioxide from the atmosphere to the ocean (Lovelock 2015).

Bjørn Lomborg, a Danish political scientist, calls himself a "skeptical environmentalist." In *Cool It* (2007) and other publications (Lomborg 2018) he admits that the environment is under serious stress, but more research and thinking are needed before launching multibillion-dollar projects. If the European Union adopts all the policies it wants to control noxious emissions, he says, it would cost taxpayers $250 billion, but the results would be negligible (Lomborg 2010). His organization, the Copenhagen Consensus Center, supports the idea of cost-efficient environmental policies.

WHAT'S YOUR VIEW?

This debate, like the debate between the neo-Malthusians and the cornucopians, appeals to both emotions and common sense, but it is not always based on solid research. Academics and mainstream environment experts often hesitate to support Lovelock's doomsday scenarios, and they question Lomborg's expertise. Still, the publications of both authors continue to attract great public attention.
❶ What are the weakest and strongest arguments of the neo-Malthusians and the cornucopians? ❷ Suggest several arguments that both the neo-Malthusians and the cornucopians would agree on. ❸ Propose a policy (such as an investment or conservation strategy) that could address the concerns of both the neo-Malthusians and the cornucopians.

the use of pesticides in agriculture, the book became an immediate sensation, affecting the views of millions in the United States and globally. Individuals embrace environmentalism for various reasons. Some see the problems that other people do not or don't want to see. Some, like the Canadian ecologist Bill Darnell, came to environmentalism because of their opposition to nuclear war and nuclear testing. Darnell came up with a powerful combination of words, *green* and *peace*, and cofounded one of the most famous environmental organizations, Greenpeace.

Many student radicals of the 1960s saw environmental protection as society's next frontier, and many of them later became prominent politicians. Brice Lalonde, leader of the French National Union of Students and a former minister, established Friends of the Earth. In 1981, Daniel Cohn-Bendit and Joschka Fischer, prominent European politicians and legislators, helped to write the political agenda for the Green Party in Germany. In the United States, President Jimmy Carter became a convinced environmentalist because of his experience as an engineer on a nuclear submarine and as a farmer in Georgia. In May 1977, he proposed a host of environment policies, ranging from conservation to new energy research. To set an example, Carter installed solar panels on the roof of the White House to heat some of its water boilers. At the dedication ceremony in 1979, he predicted that these panels would supply "cheap, efficient energy" twenty years later (Biello 2010).

In Europe, environmental policies have had support from conservative and liberal political leaders; in the United States, personal differences have mattered more. When Ronald Reagan came to power, many of Carter's environmental programs were discontinued. The solar panels on the White House were dismantled in 1986 and sold at auction. After Al Gore became vice president in the Clinton administration in the 1990s, he did much to revive a federal environmental agenda. When George W. Bush was in the office, he was unenthusiastic about the Kyoto Protocol and treated the UNFCCC with strong reservations. President Obama attempted to return to a more active environmental agenda after 2009 but later redirected his priorities because of the country's many other economic problems (Tumulty 2011).

State Policies

Why do political leaders in Germany and Sweden tend to enact proactive environmental policies, regardless of the political party in office? Why do China and the United States frequently appear not to do enough? Domestic politics, in addition to individual values, plays a strong role, including the impact of political institutions and political affiliations (Economy 2010b; Kamieniecki and Kraft 2007).

debt-for-nature Agreements to designate an area for environmental conservation in exchange for a reduction in the country's foreign debt.

Sometimes countries reduce their sovereignty in exchange for financial benefits. They agree, for example, on **debt-for-nature swaps**. These are international deals allowing a financially struggling state to designate an area for environmental conservation in exchange for, say, a reduction in its foreign debt. The World Wide Fund for Nature pioneered the idea of building national parks in exchange for financial incentives. In Guatemala, the $24-million debt-for-nature swap should finance conservation policies through 2021 and thus protect the tropical forest for many years. Guatemala's debt to the United States was invested in conservation efforts (Grandia 2012; ENS 2006).

The environment's place in a country's priorities depends on how that country sees its *national purpose*. For three decades, starting in the late 1940s, China defined its national purpose in terms of industrial development and rapid economic growth. Chinese Communists believed the environment must be put into the service of the revolution. Forests had to be felled, mountains leveled, and rivers reversed in their courses (Shapiro 2001). As a result, the Chinese government did not consider depletion or air and water pollution to be urgent problems. In the twenty-first century, the Chinese Communist Party changed its environmental strategies to address many rapidly emerging problems (Dutta 2005). President Xi announced a "new model of modernization" to "preserve "lucid waters and lush mountains" in China as a result of proposed massive environmental efforts. For example, the government has plans to have one in every five cars sold in China run

Members of the National Green Corps clean up plastic garbage along the Musi River in Hyderabad, India, in 2018.

on alternative fuel by 2025 (Ping 2017). To date, the results of this policy are inconclusive.

The United States has gone through policy cycles, depending on national purpose and priorities. This "seesaw" environmental history can be explained not only by individual presidents but also by the ideological polarization between the two major political parties—especially after the 1980s. The Republicans have defined national purpose primarily in terms of economic liberalism and have rejected most federal intervention. They argue that strict environmental regulations could weaken American businesses and make the United States less competitive with other countries (McGovern 2006). In contrast, the Democrats see national purpose in terms of economic regulation and robust environmental policies. They argue that green policies will create jobs and help to avoid serious future problems. There is no strong bipartisan strategy on environmental policies in Washington, and none is likely to emerge any time soon. At the same time, all the presidential administrations in the twenty-first century have agreed to support new methods of drilling for oil and gas. Such methods, in combination with several other factors, already provide for the United States' energy self-sufficiency. This also means that fossil fuels are continuing to serve as the major source of energy globally.

Democratic context can be favorable or unfavorable to environmental policies. Already in the 1970s, when the international environmental movement emerged, its opponents called it "elitist." The majority of voters may not have an adequate understanding of the scientific arguments behind environmental policies, but they immediately see that these policies are expensive. In times of economic and financial recession, the general public has a greater tendency to vote for their pockets than to listen to the warnings of environmental scientists.

In democracies, policies that require state appropriations also require support from voters. A major problem is a gap between the knowledge gathered by environmental scientists on the one hand and by the general public on the other (McCarthy 2011). And there are too many interest groups that doubt environmental studies and criticize their conclusions as either unreliable or exaggerated (Murray 2008). Also, the high cost of the proposed international environmental actions alienates many voters who fear losing their jobs or do not want to pay for these policies from their own pockets. Public opinion studies show that most people in democratic countries tend to worry about climate change and believe humans are largely responsible for it. However, people tend to be skeptical that most contemporary policies have the answers for the environmental problems. The paradox is that many people believe that such policies go too far in their restrictions while many others maintain that such policies do not go far enough (Mead 2018).

In non-democracies, environmental activism faces significant problems, including censorship and suppression. In 1995, the Nigerian military government executed "Ken" Beeson Saro-Wiwa, a prominent activist who exposed environmental abuse committed in his country by oil companies. This reminds us that environmental activities, which are protected and even encouraged in democratic countries, may be dangerous in authoritarian and corrupt states. In democracies, where the media and public opinion carry more weight, environmental policies are debated more openly than in countries run by authoritarian regimes. Highly publicized public protests and petition campaigns halted the construction of nuclear power plants in many European countries. In the 1980s, media-driven public pressure against the use of CFCs in refrigerators and aerosol sprays influenced governmental regulations and international agreements and forced companies to look for more environmentally friendly technologies. (See Figure 9-7.)

The Global Level

Environmental policies face at least three challenges at the global level: (1) the need to balance global environmental policies and local economic development; (2) the necessity for sustained and coordinated global effort by

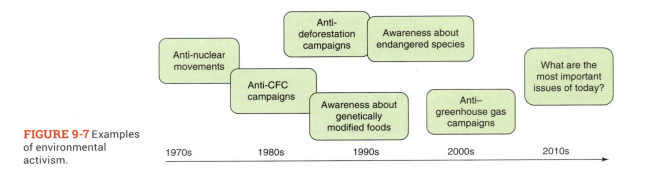

FIGURE 9-7 Examples of environmental activism.

governments and NGOs; and (3) the need for new effective strategies to deal with environmental challenges if current policies remain ineffective. All these challenges are likely to be influenced by specific political interests and ideological affiliations.

Globally, a general anti-capitalist and anti-globalist sentiment has driven some environmental activists. They believe that radical environmental policies should weaken free-market capitalism and slow down globalization, which they see as detrimental to environment. Some environmental skeptics, on the other side, have been driven by their deep resentment to progressive ideologies and environmentalism. However, many supporters of environmentalism generally argue they are not against capitalism, and they do support honest business practices. However, they are against greed and ignorance that the free market often cannot control. Supporters of capitalism tend to say that they want to protect the earth but oppose harsh regulations that halt economic growth (Mead 2018; Pielke 2010). Can environmentalism and economic interests be reconciled?

Realists point out that as long as oil and coal remain the least expensive sources of energy, countries will continue to use them. Renewables are simply too expensive. How valid are these arguments? According to the International Energy Agency, in the United States, electricity from new nuclear power plants ten years ago was 15 to 30 percent more expensive than electricity from new plants using coal. Wind power was more than twice as expensive as coal, whereas solar power cost about five times as much. In other countries, like China, a few years ago, renewables cost even more (Levi et al. 2010b). Yet in most recent years, thanks to government and private-sector investments in cleaner energy sources, their costs began to change globally. In 2015, renewable energy surpassed coal as the world's biggest source of power-generating capacity. The cost of offshore-wind energy has fallen 50 percent since 2012. Improvements in the fuel efficiency of automobiles have cut oil consumption globally. The cost of batteries in electric vehicles has fallen by 80 percent since 2008 (Energy Matters 2017).

One way to reconcile business and environmental interests is to use **socially responsible investing** (SRI), a business strategy that combines the pursuit of the social good, environmental protection, and profits—all at the same time. Today, many businesses support SRI as part of their marketing strategies. In many countries, national parks are an example of SRI. They tend to spark tourism, stimulate environmental research, and create jobs (Rodin and Brandenburg 2014; Gaston and Spicer 2004).

Green certification is another way to merge business and environmental interests. Companies that pursue responsible environmental policies receive a certificate that is supposed to make their products more attractive to consumers and thus more competitive. Logging companies, for example, are invited to apply for green certificates if they promise sustainable development. The Forest Stewardship Council, an NGO based in Germany, has drawn up rules for sustainable forestry.

How will all these programs be financed, and how will they fit into strategies for global development? Massive environmental investment in the least prosperous countries must play a major part in any international effort.

socially responsible investing (SRI) A business strategy combining the pursuit of the social good, environmental protection, and profits.

green certification The grant of certificates to companies that pursue responsible environmental policies, in order to make their products more competitive in the market.

▷

The Case for
Optimism on Climate
Change

The 2009 UN climate conference in Copenhagen pledged to set aside $30 billion a year to help the world's poorest countries deal with climate change. Rich countries also agreed, as we have seen, to allocate $100 billion per year and to direct funds from the global North to the global South to pay for emissions reduction (Levi 2010a; Levi 2010b). Many projects remain ambitious and expensive but also necessary. Desertec, an initiative backed by German firms, plans to build one hundred solar power plants and scores of wind farms in Northern Africa by 2050. If everything goes well, the project that started in 2009 should sell much of the electricity generated to Europe. In the end, consumers will pay for clean energy, and African countries will receive energy and benefit economically (Desertec 2018).

Support for new environment-friendly technologies can also take place on a global scale, and research and implementation will both benefit from multilateral efforts. Renewables and hydro sources, for example, supplied only several percent of world energy in the second decade of the 2000s, yet this share is going up. Wind power is booming in Europe and the United States thanks to private investment and government subsidies.

Enforcement of environmental policies, too, shows the need for global efforts. As realists argue, international agreements remain useless unless they are enforced. For example, the 1976 Convention on International Trade in Endangered Species (CITES) prohibited trading in rhino horn. More than 170 countries joined the treaty, including the countries most involved in horn importing—China, Japan, Vietnam, and Yemen. Unfortunately, trade simply moved onto the black market, and hunters continue to kill these rare animals.

Last, global solutions may help where government bureaucracies are slow to respond (Ebrahim 2006). After the 2004 tsunami in the Indian Ocean killed so many, UNESCO took leadership, and in 2005 an international agreement with twenty countries was reached to create the Indian Ocean Tsunami Warning System, emulating the U.S. system in the Pacific. It is hoped that such a system will be able to prevent many negative consequences of natural disasters in the future.

New environmentally friendly technologies and other innovations have difficulty moving from the research laboratory to the market. Multibillion-dollar funding itself often creates problems. Instead of pursuing long-term environmental policies, countries frequently create their own arbitrary "wish lists" of projects to be funded by international organizations (Spector 2005). The main goal is to control the money. Take, for example, water policies. The Consultative Group on International Agricultural Research showed that small, direct investments in projects designed to help regions lacking water are very effective. However, many governments insist on large investments under *their* control. This strengthens liberal claims for the importance of NGOs and independent activism in keeping pressure on decision makers.

Check Your Knowledge

1. Explain environmentalism and skepticism. Can these points of view be reconciled?

2. Discuss how the environment's place in a country's priorities depends on how that country sees its national priorities. Give examples.

3. Explain green certification.

A Greenpeace Story

Greenpeace has drawn noteworthy support from all over the world and inspired enthusiastic critics. Many admire its dramatic style of environmental activism. Others see it as dubious and self-promoting. To achieve its goals, Greenpeace often chooses confrontational and controversial methods. What, then, is the real Greenpeace, and what is its role in international environmental politics?

Background

Greenpeace traces its roots to 1971, when several young people grew increasingly frustrated over nuclear testing. Early "green peaceniks" sailed on an old fishing boat from Vancouver, Canada, to Amchitka, a small island near Alaska's west coast, with the hope of disrupting underground nuclear testing. The protesters were intercepted and the nuclear testing went on. However, many copycat groups have emerged. Such groups launched a worldwide campaign against commercial whaling and seal hunting, while other activists were turning against toxic waste and pollution.

In the late 1970s, regional groups formed Greenpeace International to oversee the goals and operations of regional organizations. Other groups chose to remain independent but to tackle similar environmental problems. Greenpeace today is a global NGO, with its headquarters in the Netherlands and offices in more than forty countries. The organization receives hundreds of millions of dollars in donations from almost three million individual supporters and grants.

Greenpeace activists use nonviolent protest to raise the level and quality of public debate about the environment. The group promotes harmony values (Greenpeace International 2015). Two of its key and interconnected methods are direct action and public education.

Activists disrupt business activities by picketing, blocking roads, jamming communications, or staging sit-ins. They also aim to raise awareness of environmental issues by sponsoring lectures, research, and educational programs. Greenpeace uses litigation and scientific research to back up its claims.

In the 1980s, it pushed for a global moratorium on radioactive waste dumping at sea. In 2003, intense lobbying efforts by Greenpeace resulted in UN sanctions on Liberia for illegal logging. In 2005, Sony Ericsson, under pressure from Greenpeace and other groups, began to phase toxic chemicals out of its products. In 2010, after years of lobbying by Greenpeace, food giant Nestlé agreed to stop purchasing palm oil, the production of which destroys Indonesian rainforests. Greenpeace's *Go Beyond Oil* campaign aims at significantly reducing, and eventually ending, the world's consumption and production of oil. Greenpeace sponsors research in the area of renewable energy.

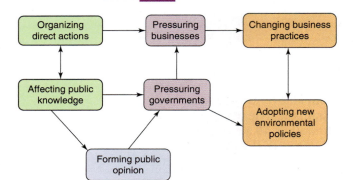

FIGURE 9-8 Methods of Greenpeace.

It also develops its own technologies, such as Greenfreeze—a refrigerator free of chemicals that contribute to ozone depletion and global warming. Greenpeace currently sponsors a global campaign to stop deliberate deforestation by 2020. Rainbow Warrior II, the organization's motor-assisted yacht, is used for protest actions as well as for research and awareness campaigns. (See Figure 9-8.)

Greenpeace has launched a campaign for the global deduction of car use and has advocated a shift toward alternative forms of transport. For Greenpeace, the world needs more electric cars. At the same time, the world needs fewer cars as more people are choosing to telecommute, riding bicycles, and using trains (Casson 2018). The key is to change people's attitudes and business practices.

Governments show different attitudes toward Greenpeace activities. Russia, for example, reacted harshly in 2013 to Greenpeace disruption of the work of an oil rig in the Russian part of the Arctic. A Russian law enforcement unit seized the Greenpeace ship *The Arctic Sunrise*, towed it to the Russian port Murmansk, and detained twenty-eight activists and two journalists on charges of "piracy" and "hooliganism." They were all released after being detained for three months.

Analysis

Critics acknowledge Greenpeace's role in environmental activism but question the significance of its efforts. Realists argue that governments are unlikely to support environmental policies that threaten their core interests. Greenpeace almost certainly exaggerated the success of its anti-nuclear campaign. The United States, the Soviet Union, and France stopped nuclear testing in the atmosphere and underground, but not necessarily and only because of pressure from environmentalists; these countries had changed their long-term strategic nuclear plans for other reasons.

Nestlé agreed not to buy palm oil from questionable sources, but these deals already accounted for less than 1 percent of the global trade of palm oil. Finally, is passing an environmental law enough? Monitoring this law's implementation is a difficult and tedious task that many environmental groups didn't focus on much in the past.

Greenpeace sometimes chooses form over substance, flashy labels over serious efforts to educate. Its promotional materials speak of "dirty energy," "deadly fuels," the "oil fuels war," "climate-destroying oil and coal companies," and "genetic pollution" (Greenpeace International 2015). Greenpeace sometimes, as critics say, chooses the wrong battles. Some activists claim that

In Hamburg, Germany, Greenpeace activists hold signs demanding clean air. In an effort to combat pollution, Hamburg banned diesel vehicles on its streets. Would you support this ban in you city today and why?

the real source of environmental problems is capitalism itself with its pursuit of profit. Yet the arguments that Greenpeace uses are protected by law. In market societies, political groups can express their opinions freely and influence politics by a wide range of lawful means. In authoritarian countries, environmental groups are ignored, their actions suppressed, and their activists jailed. This does not mean that capitalism eagerly embraces environmental values simply because this is the right thing to do. Not many people thirty years ago understood Greenpeace, its ideology, or its methods. It took a generation to attract supporters globally. Environmental policies are the product of long and difficult battles for hearts, minds, and pockets.

From the first, Greenpeace embraced the tactics of the peace campaign and civil rights movement of the 1960s, including individual acts of disobedience and appeal to moral foundations. Yet it has also evolved. Today Greenpeace relies on help from lawyers and scientists to function effectively within democracy. Online fundraising is a key to its success as well.

Greenpeace's evolution reflects broader political and cultural changes as well. It began its journey by fighting for causes that many people then opposed or misunderstood. Greenpeace's tactics in the past probably alienated many more people than they attracted. But where Greenpeace once had just a few members, it can now draw on the energy of tens of thousands of volunteers, researchers, and lawyers and a multimillion-dollar budget. Greenpeace and other groups have changed many of their tactics and targets, but they remain loyal to the goal of environmental protection.

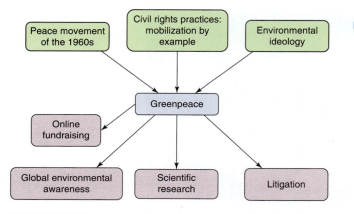

FIGURE 9-9 Greenpeace: Sources and actions.

Case Study Questions

1. Visit Greenpeace International's main website and scroll down to "Get involved" (www.greenpeace.org). Examine the list of activities and projects. Which of these do you consider the most important today, and why? Which would you support the least, and why?

2. What problem that is not addressed in this list would you want Greenpeace to focus on next? Discuss. Could you submit your ideas to Greenpeace now?

3. For many decades Greenpeace has campaigned against certain policies and decisions of big corporations. However, in the twenty-first century, Greenpeace has become a very large international corporation with an annual revenue of more than $400 million. Do you support or oppose the idea of creating an independent international NGO to monitor the activities of big nongovernment organizations? The goal of this group will be to monitor the transparency and accountability of NGOs. Do we need such a group, or should global NGOs monitor themselves? (See Figure 9-9.)

CHAPTER 9
REVIEW   Environmental Issues

9.1 Identify today's key environmental problems, major policies to address them, and the implications for international relations.

Today's environmental problems include interconnected threats to ecosystems, such as contamination and depletion, climate change, air pollution, ozone depletion, deforestation, loss of wildlife, and clean water. Environmental policies to address these problems include regulations and restrictions, green investment, economic incentives, and legal and financial directives. Countries try to balance environmental policies and economic development. Natural calamities and human-made accidents may have catastrophic environmental consequences.

Q: Using an empirical case of your choice, analyze a depletion problem that has led or might lead to an international conflict.

9.2 Describe similarities and differences among several approaches to environmental problems.

In democracies, environmental policies are debated openly.

Authoritarian governments tend to regulate environmental debates or ban them altogether.

States maintain the right to use and protect their environment and natural resources. However, it has become clear that uncontrolled use of national resources and inattention to environmental problems could undermine international stability.

The global commons approach regarding Antarctica, a geographical area not under any nation's sovereign control, showed that countries could successfully figure out a common approach to environmental protection. This approach came together with a wave of environmental treaties beginning in the 1970s and continuing up to 2020.

Q: Discuss the concept of the global commons. Give examples.

9.3 Evaluate international responses to environmental problems at three levels of analysis.

The Individual Level: Individual values, education, and leadership affect leaders' choices in their environmental policies.

The State Level: Partisan divides on environmental issues are associated with ideology and politics. In general, parties associated with progressive programs tend to support environmentalism to a greater extent. Parties supporting industrial interests oppose costly government regulations.

The Global Level: Countries try to balance environmental policies and economic development. They continue sustained global efforts and seek new strategies.

Q: Explain the different views regarding environmentalism and environmental skepticism.

KEY TERMS

Humanitarian Concerns

In May 1967, secessionists in Nigeria's southeastern provinces declared independence and the creation of a new country they called Biafra. To defeat this group, the central government blockaded the region. As food supplies and medicine failed to reach Biafra, famine and violence spread. Two to three million people died over three years, yet the rest of the world simply stood by. There was no international intervention to stop the atrocities, and the story soon disappeared from the news.

About twenty-five years later, in 1992, a violent conflict broke out in Bosnia, a territory of the former Yugoslavia. Militants representing three local ethnic groups targeted one another, and the violence spiraled. More than one hundred thousand people died on all sides as a result of massive atrocities against civilians. UN peacekeepers could not stop the violence, the scope of which had not been seen in Europe since World War II. Finally, after several years of inaction, NATO launched significant military initiatives, including airstrikes. A peace agreement was reached in 1995, and a multinational military contingent of eighty thousand occupied Bosnia. Although the operation was largely over in 1996, some troops remained there until 2004.

Why did NATO and the UN respond in Bosnia but not in Biafra? These two cases highlight a few core questions of international relations. How do international politics, a country's location, and political leadership affect how such crises are perceived and addressed? When one country faces a tragic and immense loss of life, do other states have an obligation to intervene? Should other countries and the UN be allowed to use force in a country without the express permission of its government?

Deciding on the best path in response to an international crisis involves several important considerations. International humanitarian action can have unintended consequences and

A grandmother holds her granddaughter while waiting for her husband to cross into Syria from Arsal, Lebanon, in 2018. From your informed view, what can be done—if anything—internationally to prevent such humanitarian disasters in the future?

may invite criticism from other countries. As a result, international responses tend to be selective. In 2011, the United States controversially took military action in Libya, where its NATO allies and several Arab states bombed the forces of the Muammar Gaddafi regime in support of rebels. At the same time, however, the United States and the Western allies refused to intervene in Syria, where the Assad government clashed with the opposition. And in 2015-17, Western media paid almost no attention to the humanitarian crisis in South Yemen, where the air forces of Saudi Arabia and the Arab Emirates bombed local guerillas and civilians.

This chapter covers international efforts to prevent and stop wide-scale human suffering. We will discuss constraints and limitations of these efforts, both regional and international. Assessing international experiences with humanitarian responses will spark new discussions to deepen our understanding of major challenges.

Learning Objectives

10.1 Explain major humanitarian challenges and their causes.

10.2 Discuss humanitarian policies to address these challenges.

10.3 Outline similarities and differences among key approaches to humanitarian challenges.

10.4 Examine the main components of alternative approaches to humanitarian crises.

10.5 Critically apply humanitarian policies at each level of analysis.

10.1 Humanitarian Challenges

humanitarian crisis
An incident or problem that threatens the health, safety, security, and/or well-being of many people, usually in a single geographic area.

At this very moment, millions of people are suffering from political and ethnic violence, natural disasters, persistent food shortages, acute infectious diseases, or forceful migration. These are **humanitarian crises**—incidents or continuing problems threatening the health, safety, security, and/or well-being of many, usually in a distinct geographic area. A conflict causing massive civilian deaths, like those in Biafra and Bosnia, is a humanitarian crisis. Rapidly spreading infectious diseases, acute water shortages caused by a drought, or massive hunger as a result of a flood or earthquake are other examples.

Countries, IGOs, and NGOs plan, develop, and conduct policies to deal with these crises. Humanitarian policies are based on three fundamental principles: humanity, impartiality, and independence. *Humanity* means that policies must first save lives and alleviate suffering. *Impartiality* means no preferences should be shown for any political leader, country, religion, or group. *Independence* means that humanitarian policies are not guided by participating states' open or veiled political, economic, or military objectives, such as annexing a territory or making a profit (United Nations 2006; Young 2010). (See Figure 10-1.)

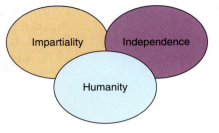

FIGURE 10-1
Three principles of humanitarian policies: Alleviate suffering first (humanity), play no favoritism (impartiality), and do not allow self-interested agendas (independence).

Humanitarian interventions are the actions of foreign powers in a humanitarian crisis, with or without the approval of a legal authority controlling the area (Roberts 2000). Besides bringing relief, these efforts also attempt to eliminate the sources of the crisis, especially human causes. Some interventions involve military force. In cases of natural catastrophes, governments usually welcome foreign aid and rescue groups. However, when political disputes or ethnic-religious strife is involved, states are much more reluctant to invite foreign countries to intervene. Countries also choose whether to participate in international humanitarian actions.

By international law, all countries have **humanitarian sovereignty**—the right to accept or reject humanitarian interventions on their territories. Article 2(7) of the UN Charter of 1945 states that "nothing . . . shall authorize the United Nations to intervene in matters which are essentially within the domestic jurisdiction of any state." Humanitarian sovereignty (a facet of state sovereignty) is an essential principle of international relations restricting interventions. However, as we shall see, it faces practical, moral, and political limitations (Weiss 2012).

Types of Humanitarian Challenges

Many humanitarian crises affect large groups of people and spread across borders. They quickly become regional and even global problems.

PANDEMICS AND INFECTIOUS DISEASES

Infectious diseases are maladies caused by biological agents such as viruses, bacteria, or parasites. Outbreaks of infectious diseases in a large population are called **epidemics**. An epidemic spreading over a continent or the world is a **pandemic**.

For centuries, our ancestors were practically defenseless against pandemics. In the 1300s, the Black Death killed almost a quarter of the European population. Around the same time, a pandemic killed millions in China, Central Asia, and India. Infectious diseases brought to America by European colonizers also caused the deaths of Native Americans five hundred years ago. Between 1918 and 1920, the Spanish flu killed fifty million to one hundred million people, including over seventeen million in India, five hundred thousand in the United States, four hundred thousand in Japan, and two hundred thousand in Great Britain.

The Ebola virus outbreak in Africa in the 1970s and again in 2014 and the cholera epidemic in Latin America and the plague in India, both in the

humanitarian intervention
Assistance with or without the use of military force to reduce the disastrous consequences of a humanitarian crisis.

humanitarian sovereignty
A country's responsibility for its own humanitarian policies and the right to accept or reject humanitarian interventions.

infectious diseases
Serious maladies caused by a biological agent such as a virus, bacterium, or parasite.

epidemic An outbreak of infectious disease in a large population.

pandemic An international epidemic that spreads across national borders.

Simulation: Stopping
an Epidemic

1990s, are just a few more recent examples of pandemics. The World Health Organization (WHO) currently recognizes more than fourteen hundred infectious diseases. Among the deadliest are lower respiratory infections, HIV/AIDS, and infections causing diarrhea, tuberculosis, malaria, and measles. These illnesses cause the death of approximately ten million people each year. Malaria alone kills an estimated four hundred thousand, mostly African children. The ray of hope is that the death rates have fallen 30 percent—due to massive prevention policies and effective treatment—since 2010 (World Health Organization 2018).

Epidemics and pandemics are undoubtedly international problems. They cause significant loss of life and trigger global disruptions. They can directly affect the functioning of governments and the preparedness of armed forces, firefighters, paramedics, and the police (Lakoff 2010; Stewart 2006). Without international cooperation, governments may overreact to a rapidly developing pandemic. As a disease spreads, death tolls rise and medication runs low; governments could close international borders and stall trade. Finally, many governments lack the resources or proper management to protect their citizens from preventable diseases. International involvement could save millions of lives (Wolfe 2011).

AIDS

Acquired immune deficiency syndrome (AIDS)—caused by the *human immunodeficiency virus* (HIV)—is a disease of the immune system characterized by increased vulnerability to infections. Although AIDS develops much more slowly than other illnesses, such as influenza, it is a pandemic. According to UNAIDS and the WHO, the total number of people infected by HIV by 2020 could be 31 million to 43 million. Nearly 36 million have died from AIDS since the start of the epidemic. Globally, only three out of four people living with HIV know they have this disease. Sub-Saharan Africa has been hit the mostt: Almost two-thirds of all individuals with HIV live there (UNAIDS 2018). Sixteen percent of new HIV infections occur in eastern and southern Africa, where around seven thousand young women aged fifteen to twenty-four become infected with HIV every week. In some countries, the rate is declining; yet it is growing in Central Asia and Eastern Europe.

AIDS is a serious global problem, but it is generally preventable and treatable with international cooperation. Wealthy countries have been able to stop the rapid spread of HIV and provide medication for the infected. Globally, deaths due to AIDS have been declining since 2007. Billions of dollars are spent on AIDS prevention and treatment

Anti-LGBT banners read "Indonesia is on LGBT emergency" and "LGBT is a contagious disease, save the young generation from LGBT people" outside the headquarters of a conservative Islamic group in Jakarta, Indonesia, in 2018. Researchers say that a climate of hatred toward gay citizens is fueling an epidemic of HIV among gay men in Indonesia.

every year in low-income countries; half the money is foreign aid. Yet, historically, people in countries without efficient health systems continue to suffer (UNAIDS 2018; "A Strategic Revolution in HIV," 2011). Poor hygiene and unsafe sex practices contribute to the problem.

CHRONIC STARVATION AND MALNUTRITION

Malnutrition is a severe medical condition resulting from constant food shortages. Chronic malnutrition leads to hunger and *starvation*, which is a severe and long-term deficiency in energy intake. Malnutrition has many causes, one of which is **famine**, or severe food scarcity. In the 1840s, a famine in Western Europe caused mass deaths and a wave of immigration to the United States, particularly from Ireland and Scotland. Throughout the twentieth century, famine continued to break out in developing countries: in India, Russia, and China in the first half of the twentieth century and in some African countries (e.g., Nigeria, Ethiopia, and Angola) in the second half.

According to the United Nations **Food and Agriculture Organization (FAO)**, six hundred million to one billion people suffer from malnutrition today. The UN World Food Programme (WFP 2018) reports that about seven hundred million people in the world do not have enough food to maintain a healthy lifestyle. In sub-Saharan Africa, at least one person in four suffers from this condition. The problem relates not only to the availability but also to the quality of food. The balanced diet largely available in industrially developed nations is out of reach for at least three billion people, who do not receive proper protein, vitamins, or minerals.

malnutrition A medical condition resulting from famine or chronic food shortages.

famine Severe food scarcity causing malnutrition, starvation, disease, and increasing mortality.

Food and Agriculture Organization (FAO) A UN agency that coordinates international efforts to overcome hunger.

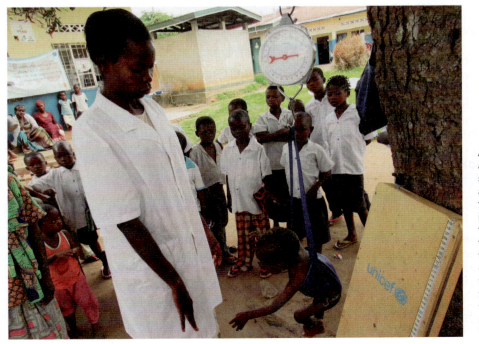

A nurse weighs a malnourished seventeen-month-old at a clinic in Congo's troubled Kasai region in 2018. The UN says three million people in the region—including four hundred thousand children—face severe food shortages due to conflict. Over thirteen million people are dependent on humanitarian aid.

ACUTE SUFFERING

The Biafran catastrophe of the 1960s is just one extreme example of acute suffering. More recently, in Syria, where multiple political factions have been fighting for years over control of the territories and resources, civilians are the easiest targets. Overall, more than five million people have been forced to leave their homes since 2012 (UNRA 2018). Those fleeing violence must spend months and years in crowded camps under constant fear of death and physical harm. Civilians in combat zones also live with the persistent threat of violence, and many develop stress-related disorders. In Syria and Yemen, two war-ridden zones of the Middle East, women and children remain the most vulnerable groups. Rape is particularly devastating because, along with physical injury, it brings long-lasting and demoralizing psychological trauma (Ritchie, Watson, and Friedman 2005; Roth and Rittner 2012). In many places, especially in countries ridden with poverty, children are often forced into slavery. According to several reliable accounts, twenty to forty million people were in slavery during the first two decades of this century (Walk Free Foundation 2018; Bales, Trodd, and Williamson 2009). Without proper and continuous international action, millions could suffer for years.

History Lab | Rwanda: A Massacre as the World Watched

Ongoing political and ethnic tensions in Rwanda grew into a civil war in 1990. The country comprises three ethnic groups—the Twa, the Hutu, and the Tutsi—of which the Hutu are in the distinct majority. After Rwanda gained independence from Belgium in 1962, a conflict between the Hutus and the Tutsis began. Dormant for decades, it degenerated into genocidal killings. Most victims were Tutsi men, women, and children pursued by Hutu militia and violent mobs. Some terrified Tutsis fled to the marshlands, where their rivals found them and killed them with machetes. In a matter of weeks, an estimated eight hundred Tutsi were brutally killed, and the surviving women were raped. Four million civilians fled to refugee camps in neighboring Burundi, Tanzania, Uganda, and Zaire.

French paratroopers were in Rwanda at the time (on a peacekeeping mandate), but they did not have the authorization to intervene. The European and the North American countries that could quickly intervene watched from a distance. Only the appeals of the neighboring African states flooded by refugees—mostly Hutus who feared revenge—triggered a delayed action from the international community. Big powers, including France, the United Kingdom, and the United States, failed to act.

CRITICAL THINKING

We often hear calls to "do something" so that the tragedies of Biafra and Rwanda do not recur. However, many political leaders decide that such incidents are not their concern.

❶ Does the world need a unified international policy to stop mass violence when it suddenly erupts? If yes, what would this policy be? If no, why not? ❷ Consider the idea of a small and well-trained international military unit whose only function is to stop violent conflicts that cause acute suffering in large groups of people. How large would the unit have to be? Which countries should contribute to it? ❸ Which country or organization should manage the unit? Suggest legal rights and responsibilities that it should have.

Causes of Humanitarian Crises

Humanitarian crises often have multiple causes, and one serious problem can lead to another. The March 2011 earthquake in Japan, the worst in a century, produced a disastrous tsunami that destroyed entire towns, killed thousands of people, and left a quarter of a million people homeless. The tsunami also damaged the Fukushima nuclear plant, causing a major radioactive threat. Although Japan is a wealthy country with an efficient government, the disaster caused devastating consequences. In less developed countries and regions, mismanagement, a lack of resources, rampant corruption, and political violence worsen humanitarian problems and delay their solution (Farmer 2012).

NATURAL DISASTERS

In the twentieth century alone, an estimated seventy million people died from natural disasters, including droughts, floods, and earthquakes. Today, economic development and technology help in dealing with severe droughts. However, earthquakes, tsunamis, hurricanes, floods, and extreme weather conditions continue to pose grave danger. In 2004, the Indian Ocean tsunami killed over 230,000 people because regional early warning systems failed or were absent. Four years later, a recordbreaking winter devastated Afghanistan: temperatures below -20°F (–30° C) caused the deaths of one thousand people and tens of thousands of farm animals. Poor communication, transportation, and sanitary conditions contributed to the disaster (Zarin 2018). Most casualties occur in less developed countries that lack state capacity, finances, and technology for preventive actions and rescue operations. Corruption and low-quality construction is another cause of loss of life. During the 2010 Haitian earthquake, 250,000 houses and commercial buildings—many of which were constructed in violation of anti-seismic standards—were destroyed. By contrast, in the Japanese earthquake of 2011, most dwellings remained intact, and only the tsunami caused significant casualties. Still, natural disasters can occur in more developed countries as well: in Puerto Rico three thousand people died when Hurricane Maria devastated this U.S. island territory in September 2017. Scores of people, including tourists, perished in deadly wildfire in a densely populated resort near Athens, Greece, in July 2018.

In the immediate aftermath of a natural disaster, most social services are absent or in short supply. Natural health hazards continue to bring devastation to millions of people, especially in remote or overpopulated regions. Some countries provide effective care, whereas others do not. Thus, international assistance plays a crucial role (Woods and Woods 2007).

MISMANAGEMENT

Indian economist Amartya Sen, winner of the 1998 Nobel Prize in economics, showed that the main cause of famine in today's world is inefficient bureaucracy. In Venezuela in 2017–2019, hunger and health problems reached the level of humanitarian crisis, after the government ruined financial stability and remained in denial of its own mistakes (Sen 1981, 2011; Naim and Toro 2018).

Weak and collapsing state structures can be a serious cause of mismanagement. When its central state collapsed in the 1990s, Somalia fell into the hands of warlords. A fragile order was preserved by brutal force or by tribal loyalties (Mohamoud 2006), but major elements of the social infrastructure disintegrated, including health care services. Multiple international sources estimate that, as a result, Somalia has one of the lowest average life expectancies in the world—only fifty-five years.

Corruption and fraud also contribute to humanitarian problems. Emergency food supplies often end up in the hands of criminals, and money meant for medication is frequently used to buy weapons. Although effective antimalarial drugs are available on the market, many Africans have limited access due to mismanagement and fraud (Webb 2014; Singer et al. 2005).

Mismanagement and its devastating consequences in failing states, just like mass killings, should be an issue on the policy agenda of governments, IGOs, and NGOs.

POLITICS

Political leaders can deliberately cause acute suffering in their country's population for their own purposes. In the twentieth century, the rulers of the Soviet Union and China caused the largest human-made famines in modern history. During the Soviet campaign of collectivizing the peasantry (1929–1932), authorities seized land, property, and livestock and forced peasants to join *collective farms*. When the farms failed to meet unrealistically high quotas for delivery of agricultural products to the state, the government seized all food. Troops blockaded many agricultural areas, particularly in the Ukraine, preventing starving peasants from fleeing to cities where food could still be found. The resulting famine killed five to seven million in the Ukraine, southern Russia, Kazakhstan, and other parts of the former Soviet Union (Martin 2001; Khlevniuk 2008). Similarly, from 1960 to 1962, Communist Chinese authorities forced peasants into agricultural labor communes and seized their crops. About thirty million people, mostly in the countryside, died from harvest failures and starvation (Jisheng 2013; Becker 1998).

MASS VIOLENCE

War or an ongoing political conflict remains the most important cause of a major humanitarian crisis. Civilians caught up in the conflict zone are typically deprived of medical care and humanitarian aid. When Sri Lanka launched a military assault on Tamil Tiger rebels in 2009, the fighting caused vast civilian casualties. People from two of India's northeastern states, Assam and Manipur, suffered from recurring ethnic and religious violence for years. Tens of thousands fled to crowded refugee camps, where malaria, measles, and other infectious diseases became widespread.

After the 2011 unrest against President al-Assad's government in Syria began, the authorities launched a lethal campaign against the rebels. They deliberately targeted the civilian population of the rebellion regions, destroyed homes and schools, and killed tens of thousands of people in the process. A bit later, the radical ISIS movement, which emerged in the midst of this civil war, on the territories without central government control, started its own campaign of brutal violence against civilians, including Kurdish Muslims and Christians. Struggling for power in the region, the Syrian government and the extremist groups provoked a massive humanitarian crisis (Stern and Berger 2015). Overall, more than 11 million Syrians—nearly half of the country's population—have been displaced (Peçanha and Wallace 2015).

In Yemen on the southern part of the Arabian Peninsula, a group of Houthi militia, named after their leader, rebelled against the government of Yemen and in 2014 seized the capital. The rulers of Saudi Arabia and UAE claimed this rebellion was a conspiracy by Iran to gain a foothold in the region. They launched a military campaign, mostly bombing raids, to restore the fallen government. During three years of war at least ten thousand people were killed, the country's infrastructure was destroyed, and three million were displaced and driven to extreme misery. Estimates are that fifty thousand children died in 2017 (Al Jazeera, March 25, 2018; Feltman 2018).

EXTREME POVERTY

About seven hundred million people worldwide live in **extreme poverty**, defined by the World Bank as living on approximately $2 per day. Several years ago, many organizations started including malnutrition, lack of access to basic education, and other criteria as important features of this condition (Payne 2013). For most of the twentieth century, the world was divided into the richer North and the poorer, underdeveloped South. Although extreme poverty is now rare in Europe, the United States, Canada, and Japan—where taxpayers support substantial welfare systems—almost 40 percent of sub-Saharan Africa is extremely poor. The rise of China dramatically improved the situation in the global South. Still, almost one-fourth of the world's poor live in India, the most populous democratic country.

Collectively, the extremely poor are also the most defenseless against disease, starvation, and physical and psychological abuse. Of all economic groups, they face the highest risk of injury or death. Poverty is a social trap, and the extremely poor are the most likely victims of a humanitarian crisis (Myers-Lipton 2015; Sachs 2005). (See Map 10-1.)

extreme poverty A profound lack of resources and the inability to access them.

OVERPOPULATION

Overpopulation is a high concentration of people within a region threatening its *subsistence*, or the minimum conditions required to sustain a reasonable quality of life. Around 1800, the world population was close to 1 billion. It grew to 1.6 billion in 1900 and to 3 billion by 1960 (United Nations Population Division 2004). It is more than 7.6 billion now and is projected to grow to 8 billion by 2025. (See Figure 10-2.)

Overpopulation can lead to serious health, environmental, and social problems, as it has in Lagos, Nigeria. The population of this industrial and commercial center has reached twenty-one million, and thousands of new job seekers arrive each month. The city became a giant agglomeration of many communities—with a prosperous middle and upper class—surrounded by sprawling slums lacking parks and other recreational areas, plumbing, and

overpopulation A high concentration of people within a region threatening its subsistence or the minimum conditions required to sustain a reasonable quality of life. It can cause serious environmental and social problems.

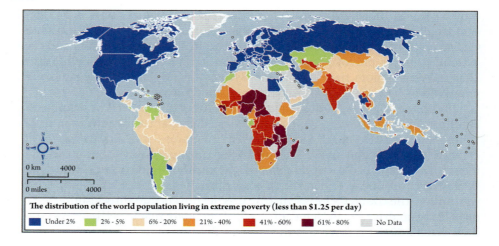

MAP 10-1
The distribution of the
world population living
in extreme poverty.
Source: The United
Nations.

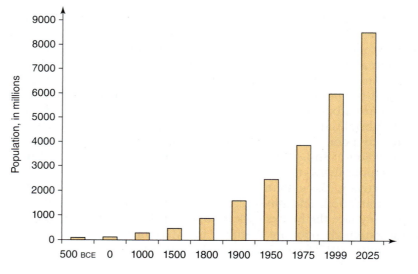

FIGURE 10-2 Global
population growth.

modern health facilities. Although the vast majority of the people have access
to electricity, running water is limited and its quality is very poor. Human
waste commonly drains into open ditches. Many overpopulated areas are also
prone to social instability, violence, and environmental problems (Angus and
Butler 2011).

A large concentration of people does not automatically lead to overpopulation, especially in economically advanced countries. New York City,
London, Sydney, Tokyo, Shanghai, Hong Kong, and Moscow are all densely
populated cities with their share of problems, but they do not fail from a lack
of resources. On the contrary, they attract greater resources and attain greater
economic success (Cohen 2005). However, issues occur where high density
and poverty coexist, as the example of Lagos suggests.

Does a high concentration of people mean poverty? Not necessarily. Monaco, a small country in Europe, has the highest population density in the world (twenty-three thousand people per square kilometer), yet its citizens are among the wealthiest anywhere. Many of them own property in Monaco but live all over the world. Furthermore, scarcely populated areas can be very poor. According to the World Bank, Cambodia has only seventy-eight people per square kilometer but an average per capita GDP of just $1,270—about one hundred thirty times less than Monaco's.

INVOLUNTARY MIGRATION

Violence, hardship, or the threat of either can also displace people within or across state borders in search of *asylum*, or a place of safety. This forced relocation is **involuntary migration**. When it comes to ethnic groups, authorities may make migration a political goal through *ethnic cleansing*—the forced removal or outright extermination of groups based on their origin and identity. Migrants fleeing from one country to another become **refugees**. They are typically willing to return to their home country, but only when the threats there diminish. International help in these cases is essential. Nearly seventy million people were displaced around the world in 2018 because of military conflict and threats to their lives, an increase from 2015 and possibly the largest number recorded since 1945 (Sommerland 2018; Peçanha and Wallace 2015).

Internally displaced persons (IDPs) are involuntary migrants who do not cross international borders. They unwillingly leave their homes or region under threats of death, starvation, or imprisonment (Phuong 2010). In the past fifteen years, there have been over forty million IDPs (UN High Commissioner for Refugees, 2018). Most of them were in Colombia, Sudan, the Democratic Republic of Congo (DRC), Iraq, Syria, and Azerbaijan. (See Table 10-1.)

Human trafficking is the illegal international trade in human beings for the purposes of exploitation. The U.S. Department of State and other organizations (Trafficking in Humans Report 2018) have estimated that twenty-five to thirty million men, women, and children are victims of trafficking. Half are minors, and more than 80 percent are girls and women. People are trafficked for sexual purposes, arranged marriages, forced labor, or illegal organ procurement. Some are ordered to beg on the streets or steal for money. Others, especially children, become soldiers. The vast majority of victims are poor and uneducated, with no means to resist injustice or cruelty.

Human trafficking is one of the fastest growing global crimes. The international criminal groups use fraud, extortion, and bribery of officials to move people across the borders (Kara 2017; Shelley 2010).

INTERCONNECTED PROBLEMS

One humanitarian challenge almost inevitably leads to another. Almost four billion people do not have access to flush toilets. Almost 2.1 billion have no access to safe, readily available water at home; for another billion, 75 percent of the water comes from nearby rivers without proper filtering. Unclean water contributes to epidemics, and hunger worsens their deadly impact (World Health Organization 2018). Unhealthy populations living in poverty

Video: The Earth is Full

involuntary migration Relocation within or across state borders due to violence, hardship, severe suffering, or a significant threat of these situations.

refugees Involuntary migrants under threat of political or religious persecution or ethnic or religious violence.

internally displaced persons (IDPs) Those who involuntarily leave their home and region under threat of death, starvation, or imprisonment.

human trafficking The illegal trade in human beings for purposes of exploitation.

Internally displaced ethnic Kachins eat at a refugee camp in Myitkyina, Myanmar, in 2018. Myanmar's army, notorious for perpetrating violence that drove seven hundred thousand Muslim ethnic Rohingyas to flee to neighboring Bangladesh, has been accused of fostering a similar humanitarian crisis in the country's north, where it battles guerrillas of the Christian Kachin minority.

are especially vulnerable. Violent conflicts in a natural disaster area add to food shortages and massive starvation. Chronic suffering also contributes to disabilities.

Let's consider an example. A middle-class individual in a developed country may live with AIDS for forty years or more, thanks to early diagnosis and treatment. In other countries, poverty and corruption shorten the lives of AIDS patients. More than two-thirds of the total infected worldwide—around thirty million people—are in Africa. Half of poor infants in Africa diagnosed with HIV die before the age of two. Overall, in the sixty-eight poor countries with the most AIDS-related childhood deaths, only 22 percent of mothers had access to treatment that prevents mother-to-child transmission of the virus (UNAIDS 2018; "A Strategic Revolution," 2011). Another issue is malnutrition; it often makes effective AIDS treatment nearly impossible because medications do not work properly in a body weakened by hunger.

The complexity of humanitarian problems not only makes international assistance imperative but also raises questions. What kind of assistance is most effective—and who should be responsible, individual states or international organizations? How far can international actors go? Should they always have consent from the affected states?

Check Your Knowledge

1. Describe a humanitarian intervention, giving an example.

2. What is a pandemic?

3. Who are the *internally displaced*?

4. What is human trafficking?

TABLE 10-1 Genocide and Forced Migration

Time and Place	Events and Consequences
1915, The Ottoman Empire	The Ottoman government, run by extreme nationalists, began to resettle 1.5 million Armenians from Anatolia to Palestine. Many of them died from starvation and brutality during this forced migration. Several groups and states consider these actions a deliberate genocide.
1922, Turkey and Greece	Millions of Greeks and Turks from the former Ottoman Empire were forced to relocate from the places where their families had lived for centuries.
1939–1949, The Soviet Union	Soviet dictator Joseph Stalin forcibly relocated about three million people from the Baltic states, Western Ukraine and Belarus, the Crimea, and Southern Caucasus into Siberia and Kazakhstan. Millions perished in the process.
1941–1945, Eastern Europe, and western parts of the Soviet Union	Nazi Germany killed twelve million civilians (among them six million Jews) and sent six million people from various parts of (mostly Eastern) Europe to Germany to work as slaves. This is universally recognized as the Holocaust or *Shoa*, the most massive deliberate act of genocide in modern history. When Germany lost the war, almost thirteen million of its citizens were forcibly relocated from eastern parts of Europe westward; some of them died.
1975–1979, Cambodia	The regime of Pol Pot and his associates killed about 1.5 million Cambodians as part of a political campaign.
1980–1989, Afghanistan	Two million Afghan refugees established temporary settlements in Pakistan and Iran during the Soviet occupation in the 1980s.
1995, Rwanda	Fearing reprisals from the ethnic Tutsis, 1.7 million ethnic Hutus fled from Rwanda into Zaire and Tanzania.
1999, Serbia	About seven hundred thousand Kosovo Albanians fearing the Serbian military crossed the Yugoslav border into Albania and Italy.
2006, Central African Republic	As a result of an ongoing political conflict, approximately 150,000 Central Africans remained internally displaced, and more than seventy thousand have fled into neighboring Chad and Cameroon.
2003–2017, Iraq	Over two million Iraqis have left their country since Operation Iraqi Freedom began in 2003. Millions more have been internally displaced due to ethnic cleansing by ISIS.
2011–2019, Syria	About three million people fled Syria to the neighboring Turkey, Lebanon, Iraq, Jordan, and other countries as a direct result of violence.
2014–2017, Ukraine	More than one million people fled from the conflict-ridden southeastern regions of Ukraine after Ukrainian forces clashed with local separatists backed by the Russian military.
2015– Yemen	A conflict launched Saudi Arabia and a coalition of Arab states to restore the fallen government of Yemen resulted in million people displaced, massive death of civilians from famine and disease.

Sources: Naimark 2002; Ramet 2005; Benvenisti, Gans, and Hanafi 2007; Hitchcock 2008; Muller 2008; Guterres 2015; UN Refugees 2018.

Pastoralist women and children displaced by drought collect water from a distribution point in Gode, in the Somali region of Ethiopia in 2018. Despite economic growth in the past decade, rural areas continue to suffer as the nation faces drought, leaving millions requiring emergency food assistance.

10.2 Humanitarian Policies

There are three types of humanitarian policies: international interventions, which may remove the immediate cause of suffering or a potential threat; relief efforts, which can help victims of a humanitarian disaster; and preventive measures, which may avert future crises. These policies frequently overlap. They can be unilateral or multilateral, depending on the involvement of states, NGOs, and IGOs, and nonmilitary or armed.

Humanitarian Intervention

Humanitarian intervention, as we discussed earlier in the chapter, is the most controversial of these policies. In **peacekeeping**, the armed forces of one or more countries cross state borders in response to genocidal violence. This intervention has two goals: to stop violence (peacemaking) and to create the conditions for lasting peace (peace building) (Bellamy and Williams 2010). The UN Security Council can authorize peacekeeping operations if all five permanent members agree. UN peacekeeping is guided by three basic principles: consent of the involved governments and groups, impartiality, and the use of force only in self-defense. The UN admits that success in peacekeeping is difficult to guarantee because such missions occur in the most difficult social and political environments. In the 2010s, there have been sixteen peacekeeping missions worldwide, including Haiti, Kosovo, Afghanistan, Timor, Mali, Liberia, South Sudan, and the DRC.

After the failure to act in Rwanda, American and European politicians argued that countries might help prevent genocide by using military force,

peacekeeping
Military or nonmilitary intervention to stop violence (peacemaking) and to create the conditions for lasting peace (peace building).

even in violation of state sovereignty. On the basis of this argument, NATO forces acted against Serbian leader Slobodan Milošević in Yugoslavia (1999) and Libyan leader Muammar Gaddafi in Libya (2011). Russia and China, both permanent members of the UN Security Council, objected. Critics claim that NATO humanitarian interventions are often based on biased or incomplete information and tend to target certain countries.

How does humanitarian intervention and peacekeeping warfare differ from aggressive warfare? First, the states involved do not plan to occupy permanently or annex another state's territory. They do not, in most cases, pursue regime change in another country or act solely on behalf of their own strategic interests. Second, humanitarian interventions aim at political forces that use deadly violence against a population or pose an immediate threat of violence. Third, such interventions require legitimacy, in the form of an international mandate such as a UN Security Council resolution (Welsh 2004). In a civil war, UN resolutions do not authorize targeting any of the feuding factions or sanction the removal of political authorities.

How can we balance respect for a country's sovereignty with the urgent need to stop a humanitarian disaster? This question is greatly debated in the theory and practice of humanitarian interventions and peacekeeping missions.

Relief Efforts

Countries struck by natural disasters normally regard immediate international relief efforts as a necessary and welcome intervention. After the 2004 tsunami destroyed coastal communities in Sri Lanka, Indonesia, and elsewhere, U.S. military personnel delivered 2.2 million pounds of emergency supplies. Twenty-five ships and ninety-four aircraft participated in the effort. After a 2005 earthquake, hundreds of relief workers arrived in Pakistan (Kashmir) with food, medical supplies, tents, and blankets. Governments welcomed the assistance and helped to distribute the supplies. In a more controversial case, Hurricane Maria struck Puerto Rico in 2017, and President Donald Trump at first balked at providing foreign assistance. Only under public pressure did he waive an old U.S. act that prohibited foreign ships from carrying goods between U.S. ports.

NGOs, private companies, and influential individuals also contribute to international humanitarian relief efforts. The American Relief Administration (ARA) shipped over four million tons of relief supplies to European countries, including Russia, after the devastation of World War I. In the 1960s, a group of young French physicians, dismayed by the world's inaction in Biafra, started Doctors Without Borders. Since 1971, this organization has delivered aid in more than seventy countries affected by armed conflict, epidemics, and disasters (Bortolotti 2006). In 2015, after Tropical Cyclone Pam devastated Vanuatu in the South Pacific, scores of NGOs sent supplies and medications. The American Red Cross immediately set up a Web page for monetary donations from individuals and organizations. In 2015–2017, several billion dollars of humanitarian assistance were delivered to Syria, Yemen, Jordan, South Sudan, and Iraq. According to one report, in 2017 a total of 6.5 billion U.S. dollars

Simulation: Building the USS Relief

came from private donors and 20.7 billion U.S. dollars from governments and EU institutions (Global Humanitarian Assistance, 2018).

Crisis Prevention

Many crises can be prevented. For example, with enough resources and political will, most infectious diseases can be controlled. Wealthy countries have practically eradicated malaria by draining and eliminating large bodies of standing water—the most common breeding grounds for the single-celled parasites that cause the illness. In countries with well-organized and well-funded health care, malaria medication is easily available. Less economically advanced countries need significant help and a coordinated global effort.

The WHO finances the development and distribution of preventive vaccines, along with educational materials. For more than sixty years, the organization has monitored influenza worldwide (Garrett 2005). Because many infectious diseases are easily spread from animals to humans, it collaborates with the FAO and the World Organisation for Animal Health (WOAH) to track disease outbreaks in animals. These groups advise governments on animal commerce, quarantines, and vaccination.

Individual countries—often acting in accord—also contribute to disease prevention. In 2006, leaders of the most economically developed nations (the G-8) announced that AIDS medication should be available to all who needed it by 2010. The Global Fund to Fight AIDS, Tuberculosis, and Malaria (GFATM) has committed over $22 billion in 150 countries to fight these three diseases.

NGOs play an increasing role in disease prevention. The Bill & Melinda Gates Foundation, founded in 2000, is the largest charitable organization in the world, attracting and distributing tens of billions of dollars in donations. The foundation conducts HIV and agricultural research, directs sanitation programs, and coordinates vaccine testing (Gates Foundation 2019; Peters et al. 2010).

Population and Migration Policies

Several humanitarian policies deal with the devastating consequences of overpopulation (Brown 2006). Some aim at improving living conditions—constructing new homes, providing access to running water, building sanitation systems, and offering health care. Others focus on sex education, teaching people about the physiology of pregnancy, childbirth, and contraceptives. They educate and empower women to play a greater role in family planning, and they teach families about their rights and responsibilities. The logic here is straightforward: As the United Nations Population Fund insists, families with few children are better off economically than families with many. The Fund also works to prevent sexually transmitted diseases, eliminate the educational gap between men and women, and reduce maternal and infant mortality.

Some countries use state-mandated policies of birth control. Facing poverty and overpopulation, China launched the **one-child policy** in 1979. Each family was permitted to have no more than one child; couples with more had

The Bill & Melinda Gates Foundation.

one-child policy
China's policy limiting the number of children that a family can have. It was in effect from 1979 to 2015.

The skyline of Shanghai, China, population twenty-three million (2011 census). The Chinese government sees overpopulation as a serious problem and uses legal means to limit births.

to pay substantial fees. Exceptions did exist: those living in rural areas or big cities, including Beijing, could have two children, as could some ethnic minorities and couples with advanced college degrees (Fong 2006).

There are many drawbacks to such birth control measures. As a result of the one-child policy, fewer people entered the labor force. Many Chinese families preferring boys over girls turned to selective abortion of female fetuses. Western critics also point to the gender bias of these policies: Families were allowed to have two children if the first child was a girl. Feminist experts view the one-child policy as a form of state violence against women's rights (Pohlman 2013). Although the policy targeted seemingly the most deep-seated values and cultural practices, China's Communist Party sustained it; opposing views were not allowed and were effectively suppressed.

With a vastly improved economy, China lifted the policy in 2015 and now allows most people to have two children. Still, China now has an estimated three to four hundred million fewer people than it could have had (the population was 1.42 billion in 2018).

ANTIPOVERTY POLICIES

Due to multiple factors—including antipoverty policies—the population below the global poverty line dropped from 36 percent in 1990 to 9 percent in 2018 (Gatesfoundation 2019). Experts use science to discuss the causes of poverty and the most effective policies to reduce it (Banerjee and Duflo 2011). Some advocate international trade and development strategies; they hope that cheap labor in poor regions will attract private investments from

DEBATE > REGULATING MIGRATION

Consider these three points:

1. Governments can sometimes restrict migration within their countries. China enforces *hukou*, a system of household registration regulating migration within the country, especially from rural to urban areas.

2. Sometimes, governments can limit their citizens' travel abroad. During the Cold War, most Communist countries did not allow their citizens to emigrate permanently and restricted even short-term travel abroad. The governments of Cuba and North Korea maintained such rules for more than fifty years (Munz 2003).

3. Almost all governments regulate and restrict immigration, which is the movement of people into a non-native country in order to settle there. Politics and economic necessities affect immigration policies (Art 2011).

WHAT'S YOUR VIEW?

States have to balance pursuing humanitarian goals with avoiding overpopulation and offering new opportunities with reducing human trafficking. There is a growing opinion that, in a world with increasingly porous borders, governments must prepare a new, globally coordinated migration policy. As you know, governments work together to address environmental problems, so why don't they cooperate on migration policy? Defend one of the following options or suggest your own.

❶ A global migration policy shall set mandatory quotas for governments of wealthy countries to accept a certain number of migrants each year. Every state will also be mandated to regulate migration within their borders to avoid overpopulation crises. Poor states will receive subsidies from a specially set global fund. ❷ A global migration policy is likely to fail because of corruption, red tape, and local politics. Instead, sovereign countries establish their migration policies and have full rights to restrict immigration and extradite illegal immigrants. Countries should coordinate such policies and make compromises from time to time, but only voluntarily.

---

wealthy countries. Others ask for greater investment in poor regions or suggest a global redistribution of wealth. Jeffrey Sachs (2005, 2015), a professor at Columbia University and an adviser to the UN, maintains that the solution is in direct and large investments into poor countries, which are locked in a "poverty trap." They cannot escape without receiving substantial help from wealthy countries. In *The End of Poverty* and other publications, Sachs argues that poverty would be completely eliminated if the rich countries invested around $200 billion to poor countries each year for twenty years.

Such direct economic assistance remains the most common policy. The United States, the United Kingdom, Germany, and France all provide direct help to dozens of countries. The FAO funds assistance projects, conducts negotiations to stimulate trade, and distributes funds to help developing countries modernize agriculture and fishing. However, many argue that direct assistance is a short-term remedy that makes people dependent on outside help and does not attack the roots of poverty. Hundreds of millions in China, India, Brazil, and Turkey have risen above the poverty level not because of

Western help but because of their economic successes. Still, market reforms can deepen inequality without eradicating poverty. A combination of economic aid and reforms and long-term investments is probably the best way to approach the issue.

The Grameen Bank, founded in Bangladesh, is an innovative approach to help the chronically poor. This bank makes small low-interest loans, called *microcredit*, to the needy without requiring *collateral*—property or valuable items that traditional banks take if a loan is not repaid (and that most loan applicants in Bangladesh don't have). How does Grameen operate without "solid" financial guarantees? It turns to communities. Every borrower must belong to a local group, which provides support and helps its members pay back their loans. Most of the bank's loans go to women, who still, compared to men, have fewer opportunities to generate an income or to obtain a commercial bank loan. In 2006, the bank and its founder, Muhammad Yunus, received the Nobel Peace Prize. Critics, however, maintain that such initiatives to elevate poverty cannot survive without tax breaks or other forms of subsidies (Sinclair 2012). The discussion continues.

REFUGEE POLICIES

States, IGOs, and NGOs provide temporary sanctuaries for refugees until they can safely return to their homes (Agier 2010, 36). Some sanctuaries, such as shelters for flood victims, are temporary. Others exist for decades, under protection from governments or international organizations, and some refugee camps become integrated into their communities. The UN High Commissioner for Refugees (UNHCR), established in 1950, coordinates international policies to protect refugees. The agency has helped tens of millions to find temporary asylum or resettle. It also has a mandate to help refugees without citizenship (UNHCR 2018).

Almost every country has its own refugee policies. In the United States and most European nations, asylum was long granted to people who were already in the country and unable or unwilling to return home because of a well-founded fear of persecution. Since the early 2000s, however, some European states have introduced admission tests, quota systems, and other legal barriers to asylum. A recent influx of Syrian refugees influenced the main political parties in Europe to demand and implement stricter refugee policies (Pai, 2018; Hainmueller and Hiscox 2007).

The crisis in the Middle East and North Africa demonstrates the complexity of the choice between action and inaction. After Gaddafi's fall in 2011, Libya plunged into a civil war and became a haven for human-smuggling rings. These groups profit from unsafely transporting tens of thousands of refugees from Syria, Libya, Iraq, and other parts of the region to EU countries. Most passengers reach Italy and Malta and then go to Germany, where they hope to be granted political asylum or work as illegal immigrants. However, thousands die in the process. The worst incident to date occurred in April 2015, when a ship carrying migrants capsized and nine hundred people died.

Check Your Knowledge

1. How does peacekeeping differ from aggressive warfare?

2. Explain the differences between peacemaking and peacekeeping.

3. What are the goals and consequences of China's one-child policy?

4. How does the Grameen Bank operate? Which lending approach did it introduce?

Italy and Malta urged EU members to start a "nonmilitary intervention" against Libya's traffickers. The UN has called the Mediterranean crisis "a tragedy of epic proportions." Not surprisingly, Germany and other European countries faced record numbers of political refugees and asylum seekers, putting pressure on national budgets (Almukhtar et al. 2015).

The Syrian civil war caused a new, unprecedented migrant crisis. More than ten million people, as a result of the war, needed substantial humanitarian assistance. About five million people fled the country, with hundreds of thousands applying for asylum in Europe. Some countries, like Germany, welcomed them. Others, including Hungary and the Czech Republic, refused most new migrants. Should the people who seek asylum remain in Europe permanently, or should their status be determined by the situation in Syria?

10.3 Traditional Approaches to Humanitarian Policies

Just like realism and liberalism differ in their approaches to international relations as a whole, so they diverge with regard to humanitarian policies. Realists argue that great power play decisive role in defining and executing these policies. Liberals believe that these policies reflect growing role of humanitarian values and international community, and testify to the growth of intenraitonal cooperation and norms.

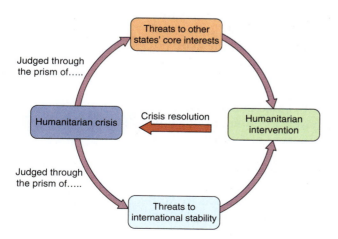

FIGURE 10-3 The realist view of humanitarian interventions.

Realist Humanitarian Policies

In the realist view, states have primary responsibility for resolving humanitarian crises within their territory. Realists do not reject humanitarian intervention as a policy option or the need for international relief efforts and preventive measures. However, they argue that states should always put their national interests first. (See Figure 10-3.)

Realists see humanitarian interventions as warranted in two cases. First, a country may intervene if a foreign humanitarian crisis directly affects its sovereignty or security (Holzgrefe and Keohane 2003). In 1971, India sent its military to East Pakistan after the latter was struck by a natural disaster and about ten million refugees moved to India.

Second, states may become involved if they cause regional destabilization. During the Biafra crisis in the 1970s, the United Kingdom helped the Nigerian government to deal with the separatists and to end its civil war. London wanted to prevent a chain of similar tribal secessions, which had the potential to destabilize fragile African states and cause economic disruption and new humanitarian catastrophes in Africa.

Realists warn that humanitarian interventions can create security dilemmas (see Chapter 5) and even contribute to instability and new wars. India's humanitarian intervention in East Pakistan led to war, producing an international crisis that drew attention from the United States, China, and the Soviet Union. India won the war, which shifted the balance of power in the region to its favor and helped establish the new state of Bangladesh in place of East Pakistan. In 1979, the Vietnamese invasion of Cambodia removed the genocidal government of Pol Pot, responsible for the deaths of hundreds of thousands of Cambodians. Yet this action also provoked China to attack Vietnam in retribution. The tension in Southeast Asia lasted a decade, until Vietnam agreed to pull out its troops.

Other actions have also drawn criticism from realists. These include NATO's military operations in Yugoslavia on the side of the Kosovo Albanians in 1999, U.S. intervention in Iraq in 2003, and NATO actions in Libya in 2011. Realists argued that humanitarian reasons alone did not justify the military force, which hurt international stability and increased insecurity of some countries. They feared an independent Kosovo could destabilize the entire Balkans and produce new humanitarian problems. In Iraq, Hussein's fall shifted the balance of power in the Persian Gulf to Iran, which was not in the interests of the West. Worst-case scenarios for Kosovo did not happen, but violence and terrorist activities continued in Iraq and Libya.

humanitarian tradition The position that human beings, regardless of their origin and social status, are morally responsible for helping those who suffer. In international relations, it means that states have a duty to protect their citizens from the consequences of natural disasters, mass violence, starvation, or infectious diseases.

Liberal Humanitarian Policies

Liberalism emphasizes not just dangers but also opportunities in humanitarian interventions. Liberals believe that preventing disasters and genocide and curbing murderous autocrats must be a priority in policies. Such plans should strengthen an international community based on law, interdependence, and peaceful cooperation. Even state sovereignty can be put aside for the sake of humanitarian principles. (See Figure 10-4.)

THE HUMANITARIAN TRADITION

The liberal approach draws on a rich intellectual and legal tradition. The **humanitarian tradition** (or *humanitarianism*) states that human beings, regardless of their origin and social status, are morally responsible for helping those who suffer (Festa 2010). Applied to

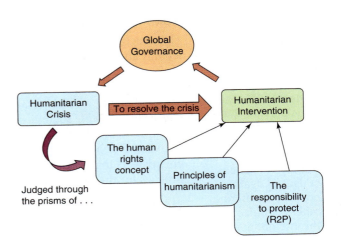

FIGURE 10-4 The liberal view of humanitarian interventions.

Bangladeshi children work in a local toy factory in Dhaka in 2018. Each adult female worker earns US$5–6 per day; every child worker earns US$2–3.

international relations, this means that states have the responsibility to protect their citizens from the consequences of natural disasters, mass violence, starvation, or infectious diseases. Humanitarianism also claims that countries have the moral right to intervene for humanitarian reasons and not just out of strategic or security considerations (Power 2002). Over the years, liberals have criticized policy that puts state interests above moral responsibility (Buchanan 2003, 2010).

HUMAN RIGHTS

The concept of human rights (discussed in Chapter 6) provides a second intellectual and legal foundation for the liberal view. The 1948 UN Universal Declaration of Human Rights states these rights broadly, and disagreements exist about their applications and specific policies. Are human rights limited to individual safety and physical integrity (Weiss 2012)? Are there additional *civil and political rights*, such as protection against discrimination and repression? Do individuals have a right to decent food, comfortable clothing, affordable housing, free health care, and high-quality education (Madigan 2007)? Different answers to these questions allow politicians to draw different humanitarian policies for their countries.

THE RESPONSIBILITY TO PROTECT

responsibility to protect (R2P) The principle that, if a sovereign country does not protect its own people from identifiable causes of death and acute suffering, other countries and the international community must take action.

The third foundation of liberal humanitarian policies is a relatively new legal concept, the **responsibility to protect (R2P)**. It states that the international community must act—and military forces may be used—if a sovereign country does not protect its own people from identifiable causes of death and acute suffering (Evans 2009). This concept appeared in scholarly publications and political discussions in the early 2000s and was embraced at the UN World Summit in 2005. Studies have shown that peacekeepers, when properly mandated and equipped, can offer protection from atrocious crimes. International interferences have already helped to prevent genocidal acts in troubled societies (Luck 2010). The use of force should be limited, however. Humanitarian intervention should be launched only in cases of large-scale loss of life or a manifest danger of it. Countries involved in humanitarian actions should use force as a last resort and only if they have reasonable prospects of succeeding (Weiss 2004, 2012). These actions also should receive support from the UN.

R2P is an evolving idea rooted in values, identity, current contexts, politics, and other factors. As the examples of the humanitarian crises in Libya, Syria, and Yemen demonstrate, this principle is applied highly selectively, primarily by Western liberal democracies, and often is contested by other states.

GLOBAL GOVERNANCE

Another relatively new concept may provide still more room for effective humanitarian policies (Rosenau, von Weizsäcker, and Petschow 2005; Hulme 2015). **Global governance** is global cooperation with little or no military power to enforce compliance. Thus, humanitarian issues should be addressed voluntarily and collectively, through a sustained international effort (Forsythe, Coate, and Weiss 2004; Keck and Sikkink 1998). This approach is based on the mutual interdependence of nations, the idea that global issues should be addressed by a collective effort, and the assumption that there is no single formula for solving all humanitarian problems. Each country has a unique history and politics. Free markets and strict government regulations each have their place. (See Table 10-2.)

Global governance is not a kind of world government that would substitute for individual countries or dictate policies on poverty, infectious diseases,

global governance The global cooperation of international actors with little or no power of enforcing compliance.

TABLE 10-2 Some Features of Global Governance

Feature	Principle
Mutual Interdependence	Humanitarian issues should be addressed collectively.
Universal jurisdiction	Global humanitarian aid, when necessary, is justified by the legal principles of extraterritoriality.
Equality among states	Equality and fairness apply, with no single international authority such as a state or a small group of states.
An increasing role for NGOs	NGOs can address some local humanitarian problems more efficiently than states can.
Pragmatism and flexibility in finding solutions	No single formula or ideology can solve all humanitarian problems. Local conditions must be considered.

or human trafficking. Global governance does not create a system of mandatory policies and practices. It uses existing structures, such as the UN or other IGOs (Rosenau 1999). Participating states have equal status when it comes to decision making, but NGOs are particularly important. The more power international law gives them, the more effective they become. *Universal jurisdiction* and *extraterritoriality* (discussed in Chapter 6) are thus essential.

10.4 Alternative Views of Humanitarian Policies

Constructivists argue that humanitarian policies depend on norms and perceptions. Humanitarian policies have played an increasing role in international relations during the past sixty years, as many societies became more open, democratic, and interconnected. A country's interests are increasingly shaped not only by fear or aspirations for power, as realists often argue, but also by concern for humanity as a whole. Democratic and wealthy countries with relatively small populations, such as Norway and Canada, became the most active in humanitarian policies. In public opinion polls, Canadians tend to see themselves as more caring, less individualistic, and less selfish than their American neighbors. These views became more pronounced after 2016, when Donald Trump was elected president (Saunders 2018; Carrière, O'Reilly and Vengroff. 2003). Russia and China are more cautious when it comes to foreign humanitarian initiatives. This attitude reflects their security interests, concern about sovereignty, and above all mistrust of Western intentions, Western media and NGOs.

DEBATE>THE UN GLOBAL COMPACT

The UN Global Compact is an initiative that urges companies, together with UN agencies and NGOs, to address humanitarian and social challenges. Participation is voluntary—business leaders join the Global Compact out of concern that traditional solutions to humanitarian problems may not work.

WHAT'S YOUR VIEW?

Many believe that, in the era of growing transparency, corporations have no alternative but to care more about their public image. Competition among businesses involves not only markets and shares but also the ability to help human lives in a positive way. Others argue that corporations ultimately are about profit, not humanitarian actions. It would be naive to expect them to adopt the features of global governance without being pressured to do so.

❶ Can a joint effort such as the UN Global Compact make a significant impact on the international system? Why or why not? ❷ Do you support the policy encouraging or mandating corporations to increasingly contribute to humanitarian policies, or would you leave humanitarian policies exclusively for governments and IGOs? Explain your answer.

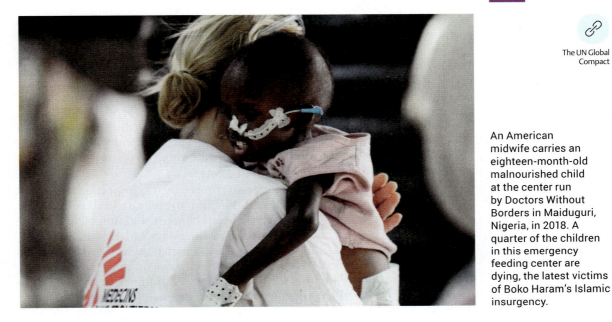

The UN Global Compact

An American midwife carries an eighteen-month-old malnourished child at the center run by Doctors Without Borders in Maiduguri, Nigeria, in 2018. A quarter of the children in this emergency feeding center are dying, the latest victims of Boko Haram's Islamic insurgency.

Perceptions, in turn, are inseparable from the international context. During the Cold War, humanitarian actions were largely subordinate to geopolitical interests—above all, the strategic interests of the United States and the Soviet Union (Weiss 2007, 31). The two superpowers also provided humanitarian assistance to build positive images of their countries (Westad 2007).

According to constructivism, a country's elites and government institutions tend to react to international events selectively, in line with their identity and therefore their interests. These groups consider the plight of people of their own race, ethnicity, or religion to be more compelling and important than the suffering of others (Finnemore 2004). During the Bosnian War, the Arab media focused on atrocities committed against Bosnian Muslims, whereas the media in Russia emphasized atrocities against the Christian Serbs, with whom most Russians share an ethnic and religious identity (Sobel and Shiraev 2003).

The evolution of societal norms helps governments and international organizations mobilize public support for humanitarian missions. So, too, hopefully, does the diminishing power of racism and xenophobia. Still, it is often difficult for political leaders to argue for massive humanitarian assistance to countries that do not evoke public sympathy.

Conflict theories maintain that inequality is the most important cause of humanitarian problems. Here, "inequality" means the lingering gaps between social groups, rich and poor, or wealthy countries and the rest of the world. Rescue operations and emergency aid are necessary, but no short-term act can address the structural issues. These theories also prescribe policies to rectify such problems. In *The Wretched of the Earth* (2005), Frantz Fanon rejected

European humanism as a model for the Third World. He argued that victims of suffering in poor countries must rise up and fight for their own security and prosperity. Others insist that the world needs global affirmative action. Wealthy nations must restructure their relations with the rest of the world. These prescriptions represent the *dependency theory* of international relations (Chapter 6).

Conflict theorists believe that Western states use humanitarian intervention not just to address suffering but also to advance their strategic imperialist interests. They argue that capitalist countries wrapped expansionist designs in humanitarian rhetoric for many years (Weiss 2007; Bass 2009). Global governance is criticized as a way for powerful institutions and countries to impose their rules and interests on the rest of the world.

Feminism notes that humanitarian problems disproportionally affect women, yet they do not receive due attention from the international community. Over the past several years, women have been the most common victims of the HIV pandemic. Women and girls are targets of mass atrocities, human trafficking, and sexual assault. Sexual violence against women has long been widespread and underreported. It was widespread during the Armenian massacre in 1915, during the partition of India in the 1940s, in armed conflicts in Latin America in the 1970s, and in African conflicts in Angola, Liberia, Sierra Leone, Rwanda, Somalia, and Sudan. Wars in East Timor, Sri Lanka, Myanmar, Bosnia, and Syria involved mass rape of civilians (Leatherman 2011). Rape is a form of intimidation and humiliation during violent conflict, and it can be a type of genocide when it is deliberately and systematically used against a particular ethnic or religious group. According to the UN, ISIS militants have stoned women and girls for alleged adultery and forced girls into marriage (Nebehay 2018).

Feminism encourages scholars and politicians to expand their traditional state-centered view of international security (see Chapter 5) and focus more on the security concerns and protection of the individual, especially women (Kuehnast, Oudraat, and Hernes 2011).

Check Your Knowledge

1. What is the UN Global Compact?

2. What solutions do alternative theories propose to address humanitarian challenges?

10.5 Critical Applications

We can apply theories of international relations to humanitarian problems only if we consider the complexity of world politics. Which theories, ideas, or assumptions provide a road map to more efficient policies? What are the proper roles of institutions, structures, and culture?

Individual Decisions

Individual motivations and decisions play an important role in humanitarian policies. Leaders may act out of conviction, ideology, or personal interest. Some are actively involved in humanitarian issues because of their deep-seated convictions. Kofi Annan (1938–2018), an influential UN diplomat from Ghana, was upset by the agency's failure to stop the Rwandan genocide.

Later, as UN secretary general (1997–2006), he became an advocate of R2P.

A leader's moral intentions and political calculations are often interconnected. Former British prime minister Tony Blair wrote that he supported the U.S. invasion of Iraq in 2003 for humanitarian reasons. At the same time, he believed that this support would also consolidate the alliance between the United States and the United Kingdom (Blair 2010).

Specific circumstances shape a leader's choice, as demonstrated by American policy. As previously mentioned, presidents have been selective about becoming involved in humanitarian crises. For example, Clinton failed to stop the genocide in Rwanda but used force to stop the ethnic cleansing in Kosovo several years later. George W. Bush rejected a humanitarian intervention in Darfur in the early 2000s because he didn't want to overcommit the United States, which was already involved in wars in Iraq and Afghanistan. Obama refused to use force against Assad in Syria because he concluded that similar intervention in Libya two years earlier had led to unforeseen negative consequences.

Former UN Secretary-General Kofi Annan.

Individual motivations can also lead politicians to hide or deny humanitarian problems in their territories, especially in countries lacking transparency. Authoritarian leaders facing little opposition at home tend to underemphasize the severity of crises in their countries. In the mid-1990s, a prolonged famine devastated North Korea, causing hundreds of thousands of deaths. The nation's leaders, however, frequently blocked desperately needed international humanitarian relief (Haggard and Noland 2009). Robert Mugabe, former president of Zimbabwe, often criticized international humanitarian efforts to help his country as imperialist ploys based on false accusations. President of Venezuela Nicholas Maduro denies that his government created an economic and humanitarian crisis and blames all of his country's problems on external forces, especially the United States. Ideology or preoccupation with their country's prestige caused several African leaders to interfere with attempts to fight the AIDS epidemics there. These leaders also accused the international community of using the AIDS crisis as a pretense to expand Western domination.

State Policies

Humanitarian policies are often inseparable from a country's domestic politics, including ideological beliefs, competition among political parties, media coverage, and lobbying efforts. A favorable political climate in a country makes humanitarian policies easier to implement. But when the substantial majority of a democratic country is not interested in a crisis, the government is under less pressure to intervene. Politicians may in fact use public opinion to justify inaction. As discussed at the beginning of this chapter, European leaders initially refrained from getting involved in the Bosnian War. In the United States, the Bush and then Clinton administrations also used negative public opinion as a reason not to intervene (Sobel 2001).

At the same time, political elites can change the policy climate. The Clinton administration helped convince Americans that the country should intervene in the former Yugoslavia, where violence had already cost one hundred thousand lives. Politicians in France, Germany, the Netherlands, and the United Kingdom also grew frustrated over their governments' inaction. NGOs and the media argued for a moral duty to launch a humanitarian military action. Finally, in 1995, a military coalition intervened.

The refugee policies of Europe's political parties reflect humanitarian principles and electoral concerns. Parties of the left traditionally support generous immigration policies, particularly for the victims of repression, and recruit heavily from immigrant communities (Sniderman, Hagendoorn, and Prior 2004). Moderate social democratic parties, with their reliance on middle- and lower-middle-class members, tend to support refugees as long as they do not threaten jobs. Parties of the political center support immigration of those with job skills, especially in the professions, but not the EU's open-door immigration policies. Right-wing parties try to limit immigration for ideological reasons. They also point to the tight job and housing markets and the need to preserve a distinct European or national identity (Mral, Krosravnik, and Wodak 2013). Libertarians generally believe in a universal right to travel and settle in the country of one's choice as long as one accepts that nation's rules and customs.

Effective humanitarian assistance requires favorable political, social, and economic conditions; the absence of violence; local customs; and low levels of corruption and fraud. Securing these criteria is challenging. In countries under authoritarian governments, such as North Korea, Syria, Afghanistan, and Somalia, humanitarian missions are much more difficult. Armed forces may stop violence, but they often contribute to protracted local conflicts and may even bring new violence (Young 2010).

Much of sub-Saharan Africa has long lacked the conditions for successful humanitarian missions. Weak and corrupt institutions, as well as some political leaders in these countries, usually support traditional customs and biases. For example, they tend to resist attempts to promote contraceptives, insisting that abstinence is the only proper AIDS prevention. As a result, many women contract HIV. Married women who are faithful to their husbands are also at risk because many men have multiple sex partners. Because people with HIV are commonly stigmatized, they frequently choose to keep their symptoms secret or refuse testing and treatment, thereby limiting their access to health care (Trinitapoli and Weinreb 2012; Patterson 2006).

Global Factors

Globalization brings new opportunities. However, it also creates new problems or deepens existing ones. Consider just a few developments—travel, migration, and climate change:

- *Global travel* creates new health risks. With international travel expanding, people can carry a dangerous infectious disease to the other side of the world before the first symptoms appear. Studies show that insects and small animals can spread disease as well (Wolfe 2011; Karesh and Cook 2005).
- *Global migration* also brings new problems and intensifies old ones. Whereas wealthier families tend to move to comfortable and less crowded places, new megacities in the developing world attract millions of migrants from poorer areas. Natural disasters and epidemics find most of their victims in such crowded places, where epidemics may spread rapidly. Globally, the poor remain the most vulnerable to health and safety threats.
- *Global climate change* (see Chapter 9) may lead to more frequent floods and droughts. Wealthy countries and regions can adjust to these changes, but others—and there will be hundreds of millions of them—will suffer unless certain preventive policies are set.

Most people in developed countries are accustomed to a stable income, a good education, medical care, and generous social benefits. Their comfortable lives may leave them more open to considering the suffering of others. The 2008 global recession and the following economic slowdown in most countries, however, may have changed that openness. To many people, a country torn apart by tribal violence may now appear more distant and their problems less significant. Others may lose their faith in the possibility of solving global problems—including humanitarian issues. The temptation to turn away is not new, and people's indifference may increase if humanitarian policies do not produce significant results. Nevertheless, calls for humanitarian action continue.

Although the principles behind humanitarian intervention (humanity, impartiality, and independence) have international recognition, many question the legitimacy of involvement without another country's consent (Chandler 2006; Rieff 2006). Realists and liberals agree on the need to enforce the rule of law and to save lives, but they insist that sovereignty can be suspended only temporarily and only as part of a sustained international effort (Keohane 2003). The need for this international enforcement is growing because the UN tends to apply R2P to humanitarian crises but has no armed forces. Thus, countries with strong militaries are likely to remain the global "enforcers." Other countries commonly reject these developments.

Another challenge to R2P is the blurring boundary between humanitarian assistance and military intervention to achieve domestic political goals (Orbinski 2009; Weiss 2004). The debate reignited in the spring of 2011, when France and Britain, supported by the Obama Administration, led the attacks against the dictatorial regime in Libya to protect the state's population from slaughter. The countries had UN Security Council authorization, yet critics, including Russia and China, argued that the military strikes violated a UN mandate prescribing neutrality in a civil war. Humanitarian interventions continue to split the international community. For example, Moscow claims that its military actions in Syria are rooted in humanitarian goals. Most NATO countries disagree, believing that expansionism is Russia's motivation.

Brian Gitta, left, and team members show the noninvasive malaria test that Gitta invented in Kampala, Uganda. Languishing with fever and frustrated by delays in diagnosing his illness, Gitta came up with a test that would not need blood samples or specialized laboratory technicians.

The level of international humanitarian response rose to a record $27 billion in 2018, $5 billion higher than in 2013 (GHA 2018). Government donors contributed three quarters of the funding, and private donors gave the rest. Is humanitarian aid effective, and how can we measure its effectiveness?

With all the praise heaped on NGOs, criticism has become increasingly audible. One issue is global coordination. A dozen large NGOs control the majority of nongovernmental humanitarian funding. Unfortunately, their efforts often duplicate one another (Agier 2010, 35). They also do not coordinate their programs effectively with the Red Cross, Red Crescent, or other UN-funded organizations.

Another problem is accountability. American and European NGOs have spent hundreds of millions of dollars on humanitarian assistance in Iraq and Afghanistan. But it is not easy to judge how much went to humanitarian aid and how much was wasted, owing to corruption and fraud. NGOs are usually audited in their countries of origin, but aid recipients are often not audited at all. Fighting factions often use financial aid to continue the violence. The BBC found that, during the 1984–1985 famine in Ethiopia, warlords posed as merchants and met with charity workers to obtain relief money, which they used to buy weapons (BBC 2010). Some warlords also manipulate donors for personal enrichment (Polman 2011). Transparent bookkeeping does not always solve the problems of corruption.

Short-term interventions alone cannot solve today's humanitarian problems. Successful term policies must be *sustainable*. What, then, are the ingredients for long-term success in a global world?

One feature is a *participatory approach*. NGOs, for example, can act as effective lobbyists for humanitarian actions. Ordinary people can contribute money and become volunteers. The Web and social media have become effective mobilization tools as well. *Transparency* is another element. Without addressing corruption, humanitarian aid programs are ineffective. Again, NGOs and other independent participants are important.

Wealth creation is also part of successful humanitarian policies. For example, the creation of a stable market economy can help combat poverty. The recent experiences of Chile, Botswana, India, and South Korea show that private enterprise can deliver essential goods, food, and services. As poverty rates go down, the middle class grows, and the quality of social services improves. The decline in fertility rates in the world's poorest regions since the 1960s is probably contributing to improving living standards.

Finally, the ingredient of *global health security* requires a serious global effort. For over a decade, some countries have been caring for the health of other nations ("International Health Regulations," 2007). For example, nations have started sharing information about new viruses and infectious diseases. *Humanitarian medicine* is a new field concerned with diseases that primarily affect the poorest countries, where the public health infrastructure is in dire condition or nonexistent. It brings medical diagnostic and pharmaceutical tools to people who otherwise wouldn't get treatment (Lakoff 2010, 60).

Effective humanitarian policies are also linked to the development of international law (Buchanan 2010) in order to legitimize efforts to fight pandemics, hunger, or the consequences of civil wars. Once again, the role of NGOs and international organizations can only increase (Ayittey 2005).

> ## Check Your Knowledge
>
> **1.** Explain the debates about R2P policy: How do supporters and opponents perceive R2P? How do they assess the consequences of humanitarian interventions?
>
> **2.** What is humanitarian medicine?
>
> **3.** What is the participatory approach to humanitarian policies?

CASE STUDY

Celebrities in Action

Background

Fridtjof Nansen (1861–1930), a Norwegian scientist and Arctic explorer, made headlines more than a century ago and many still discuss his voyages. Fewer recall that he later received the Nobel Peace Prize for his humanitarian efforts. In 1921, the League of Nations appointed Nansen as high commissioner for refugees; in this position, he helped millions of victims of World War I, the Russian Civil War, and other conflicts. He also proposed a temporary certificate giving refugees residence in countries where they were not citizens. Recognized by over fifty countries, these "Nansen passports" helped millions

Angelina Jolie, Special Envoy of the United Nations High Commissioner for Refugees (UNHCR), meets Secretary-General António Guterres at UN Headquarters in 2017 to discuss the global refugee crisis.

Celebrity activism
The involvement of famous individuals—primarily from the arts, science, sports, or entertainment—in humanitarian action.

to find new homes and survive mass violence. Nansen led the life of a celebrity while directing the world's attention to the fate of prisoners of war, refugees, and famine victims. He became one of the first world-known humanitarian activists, and his decisions had global significance.

Celebrity activism is the involvement of famous individuals—primarily from the arts, science, sports, or entertainment—in humanitarian action. In the nineteenth and early twentieth centuries, celebrities came from privileged groups, including royalty, who raised money and organized hospitals during wartime to aid their countries' soldiers. Today's stars deal with such problems as poverty, human trafficking, land mines, AIDS, hunger, and human rights. They are not from the aristocracy but are "media darlings" who can attract global attention almost instantly—far more quickly, in fact, than most politicians. When Angelina Jolie traveled to Cambodia, she reminded the world of the plight of refugees and the victims of land mines—legacies of the lethal Pol Pot regime. Her co-sponsorship of the Preventing Sexual Violence Initiative attracted a wave of sponsors and volunteers. Bono's meetings with top British and U.S. officials to discuss poverty in Africa made headlines. When singer Katy Perry visited Madagascar in 2013 to assist children with education and nutrition, scores of reporters followed, ensuring that millions would be aware of the children's problems. Thanks to Twitter, Facebook, and hundreds of blogs, celebrity activism receives ample media attention. But does it make a difference?

Analysis

Celebrities routinely donate or raise millions of dollars to schools, hospitals, refugee camps, and rehabilitation centers all over the world. In 1985, Irish singer and songwriter Bob Geldof organized Live Aid, a series of concerts in Europe and North America, to raise money for Ethiopian famine victims; he rebooted the format twenty years later for Live 8. Bono had a role in the joint decision of powerful nations to write off $40 billion of debt owed by eighteen countries, mostly in sub-Saharan Africa.

Often, celebrities are excellent fundraisers. Many of the wealthy (and not so wealthy) commonly reach for their wallets. Some are moved by the eloquent appeals of performers to sponsor international projects. Others donate for the privilege of meeting them or simply joining them in a common cause.

Celebrity activism is not only about money. Famous people also raise public awareness by helping to educate and mobilize public opinion; their name and influence make humanitarian organizations and their efforts more recognizable and, probably, more effective. When Audrey Hepburn became a goodwill ambassador for the United Nations International Children's Emergency Fund (UNICEF) in 1989, few people knew about the fund or her involvement in it. P. Diddy has contributed to the World Wildlife Fund. Ben Affleck calls for global attention to the violation of human rights in the Democratic Republic of the Congo (DRC). Many small humanitarian groups need more international attention, which famous individuals can provide instantaneously. Today's celebrity appearances can draw the instant attention of hundreds of millions. Celebrities blog or tweet to organize grassroots campaigns; many stars have relatively easy access to national political leaders and top government offices.

Several celebrities see their role as promoting awareness for specific causes. The Creative Coalition even offers training to prepare the rich and famous for public roles as social advocates. Supermodel Heather Mills and the late Princess Diana were engaged in the campaign against land mines. George Clooney and Madonna work for AIDS education; Leonardo DiCaprio has chosen environmental issues.

Critics, however, are harsh. They maintain that, despite its success, celebrity activism is not necessarily or always what it appears to be. Most celebrity activists have tens or hundreds of millions of dollars in assets. A team of "advisers" and lawyers monitors a star's every financial move and often recommends charitable donations that make sense financially. Tax incentives, especially in the United States, encourage the wealthy to contribute to humanitarian causes. Celebrities also use their humanitarian activities and the subsequent media attention to promote their products. A foreign trip can help advertise a forthcoming album or film.

Another critique is that, even if celebrities are true altruists and lower taxes or attention is not their top priority, their efforts are superficial. They often want to show the world the immediate effects of their work, but humanitarian problems require a sustained effort. It takes years to achieve real change in the struggle against poverty and disease. Many stars also lack sufficient expertise. They may believe that their opinions on social and political issues are valuable simply because *they* express them. And what if they display "celebrity activism complex"—a desire to do something important simply because it feels good? Celebrities make people listen to what they sing and say, but their actions could be misguided. For example, substantial sums of money generated by rock concerts have gone to organizations under the control of corrupt governments.

People who live in the spotlight are easy to admire or to criticize. Liberals may criticize celebrity activism for its flashy style and inattention to the deeper social causes of humanitarian problems. Others may disapprove of the rich and famous advocating controversial ideas. Yet celebrity activism may bring public attention to serious problems faster and more efficiently than governments do. Humanitarian aid provided by famous people makes a difference. Food for the starving, shelters for refugees, medications for children—they all matter. In the end, why celebrities donate their money and time is less significant than the results.

Case Study Questions

1. What are the potential benefits of reintroducing the policy of "Nansen Passports"? If the UN issued three hundred thousand of these passports, where would you send the recipients? Explain your choices.
2. What are the drawbacks of such an initiative?
3. Matt Damon made headlines by staging a mock press conference for World Toilet Day (November 19), in which he drew attention to the global sanitation and clean water problem by pledging (jokingly) not to use the bathroom for the day. Although many viewed Damon's action as a prank, some suggested that it should have made a difference. Suggest several ways that this and similar flamboyant instances of celebrity activism can be useful locally and globally.

CHAPTER 10 REVIEW   Humanitarian Concerns

10.1 Explain major humanitarian challenges and their causes.

Humanitarian crises are incidents or continuing problems threatening the health, safety, security, and/or well-being of many. Causes of such problems are mostly interconnected and can include pandemics, chronic starvation and malnutrition, environmental disasters and accidents, politics, mismanagement, neglect, mass violence, extreme poverty, overpopulation, and/or mass violence.

Q: Why is the spread of diseases an international problem?

10.2 Discuss humanitarian policies to address these challenges.

Humanitarian policies can involve intervention—the actions of foreign powers in a humanitarian crisis with or without the approval of a legal authority controlling the area. They may also address relief efforts, which provide aid to a country without violating its sovereignty, or prevention.

Q: Discuss the benefits and drawbacks of humanitarian interventions. If you were president, what three humanitarian interventions would you support, and why?

10.3 Outline similarities and differences among key approaches to humanitarian challenges.

Realists argue that a country may intervene in a foreign humanitarian crisis in two circumstances: the problem affects the state's sovereignty or security and/or the crisis causes regional destabilization.

In the liberalist view, policies are rooted in the principles of humanitarianism, responsibility to protect (R2P), and human rights. The emphasis is on international cooperation and global governance.

Q: What social and political conditions are necessary for global governance to succeed?

10.4 Examine the main components of alternative approaches to humanitarian crises.

Constructivism claims that countries build their humanitarian policies on their evolving values and perceptions and on their concern for humanity as a whole.

In conflict theories, economic and social inequality is the main cause of humanitarian problems.

Feminism argues that humanitarian problems disproportionally affect women, yet these problems do not receive due attention.

Q: What do conflict theorists argue is the root of most humanitarian crises, and what do they propose as solutions?

Q: How in your view can negative cultural stereotypes affect humanitarian policies?

10.5 Critically apply humanitarian policies at each level of analysis.

Leaders' choices are rooted in values or are affected by individual circumstances that affect humanitarian policies.

Humanitarian policies are connected to a country's domestic politics, including competition among political parties, media coverage, and lobbying efforts.

Global challenges such as migration, travel, and climate change affect humanitarian problems and policies to alleviate them.

Efficiency and sustainability of global humanitarian efforts remain key challenges.

Q: Under what circumstances, if any, should authoritarian, nondemocratic methods be used to address the most acute humanitarian problems?

KEY TERMS

Glossary

accessibility bias In cognitive theories, the rule that a leader tends to pick the option that is most easily available.

acid rain The accumulation of acids in clouds, rain, snow, sleet, and, subsequently, lakes and rivers owing to sulfur dioxide, nitrogen oxides, and other pollutants in the atmosphere.

aggression An attack by a state aiming at retribution, expansion, or conquest.

analogy The comparison of a new situation to a familiar one. Analogies may provide quick answers in place of a more lengthier discussion.

analysis Breaking down a complex whole into smaller parts to understand its essential features and their relationships.

anarchism An ideology and movement that seeks to create a borderless, peaceful, self-governing society of free, local communes in which people generate and distribute wealth without government control.

anarchy From a realist perspective, a condition of international relations that requires states to rely only on their own power.

antiglobalization Resistance to globalization, or an active return to traditional communities, customs, and religion. (See also **globalization**.)

appeasement A policy of concessions to a foreign state run by authoritarian rulers, in order to avoid a war.

asymmetrical threat The danger imposed by terrorism because a state cannot effectively retaliate and restore a balance of power.

Atlanticism The belief that the relationship between the United States and Europe is a focus of national interest.

autarky A long-term policy of national self-sufficiency and rejection of imports, economic aid, and cooperation.

autocratic rulers Leaders who use unlimited power and who follow international and domestic law only if it suits them.

balance of trade The difference between the size of a country's exports and imports.

bandwagon Making an alliance with powers that could otherwise threaten a nation-state's security.

bipolar order A type of world organization based on two centers of power or influence.

Bretton Woods institutions The international institutions created in 1944-45 to stabilize the global economy.

brinkmanship A state policy that relies on overt threats of force to extract concessions from other states.

bureaucratic bargaining The process by which political groups and institutions express their interests and make trade-offs and compromises.

caliphate A global Islamic state (one of the ultimate goals of al-Qaeda).

climate change A significant and lasting alteration of global weather. It most often means *global warming*, or the rising temperatures and increasing number of abnormal and unseasonable climatic phenomena such as devastating storms and heatwaves.

coercion and extortion The use of force and threats of force to compel others to comply with demands.

cognitive map Model of information processing and decision making.

Cold War (1946–1989) A confrontation, short of outright war, between the Soviet Union and the United States, with their respective allies on both sides.

collective security An arrangement in which the security of one country becomes the concern of others as well.

Communism A doctrine that proclaims an order based on economic equality and opposed to capitalism.

comparative advantage A theory that explains why it is beneficial for two countries to trade with each other instead of relying on their own domestic production.

competitive authoritarianism A hybrid political culture with a competitive electoral system in which a single leader or party dominates. Authoritarians use the state power to defeat opposition and mobilize public opinion.

conflict An actual or perceived antagonism between states and international or nongovernment organizations.

conflict theories Approaches that emphasize economic, social, and political inequality as a source of contradictions and tensions among social groups. Conflict theories highlight the role of social classes, ruling elites, and other dominant groups in shaping global affairs.

conservation A policy of protecting and preserving natural resources, including plant and animal species and their habitats.

consistency bias In cognitive theories, the rule that the human mind operates so as to keep beliefs, opinions, and ideas consistent.

constructivist view (or constructivism) An approach to international relations that assumes that state actions and policies are based on how leaders, bureaucracies, and societies interpret, or *construct*, information.

consumption The selection, adoption, use, disposal, and recycling of goods and services.

containment During the Cold War, Western policy to check the power and expansion of communist states.

contamination The byproducts of human and non-human activities affecting air, water, and soil.

content analysis A research method that systematically organizes and summarizes both what was actually said or written and its hidden meanings (the manifest and latent content).

cooperation A foreign policy that addresses other states' concerns for their security.

core In dependency theory, economically developed states that exercise their hegemonic power.

counterterrorism Long-term policies and specific short-term measures to prevent and combat international and domestic terrorism.

criminalization of terrorism Considering terrorism a form of criminal behavior in the context of domestic and international law.

critical thinking A strategy for examining, evaluating, and understanding international relations on the basis of reasoning and valid evidence.

culture A set of values, behaviors, and symbols shared by a group of people and communicated from one generation to the next.

currency The physical component of a country's money supply, comprising coins, paper notes, and government bonds.

customary law Law derived from the past practices of sovereign states in the absence of repeated objections from other states.

cyberterrorism Paralyzing online attacks on political, financial, and military centers.

debt-for-nature swaps Agreements to designate an area for environmental conservation in exchange for a reduction in the country's foreign debt.

decolonization The dismantling of European colonial empires, when former colonies became sovereign states.

defensive realism The view that the cost and destruction caused by war outweigh any potential gains.

deforestation The massive removal or disappearance of forests, owing to the thinning, changing, and elimination of trees, bushes, and other vegetation.

democratic leaders Leaders who treat the letter and spirit of the law as the core of their domestic policy and, in most circumstances, foreign policy.

democratic peace theory The theory that democracies are not likely to fight one another.

dependency theory The view that the world economic order is based on the flow of resources from a "periphery" of poor states to a "core" of wealthy states.

depletion The serious reduction of essential elements of an ecosystem, such as loss of forests, fresh water, or entire species.

détente The set of agreements and policies to avoid a nuclear conflict and increase cooperation between the two sides in the Cold War.

development A set of views and policies to build a modern national economy.

desertification The expansion of deserts into the places previously available for agriculture.

diplomacy The management of international relations through negotiations.

domestic terrorism Terrorism to achieve domestic political goals, such as dismantling a government or a change in policies.

domino theory An American view during the Cold War that a seizure of power by Communists in one country will produce a chain reaction of Communist takeovers in other countries allied with the West.

East African Community (EAC) An economic and political union between six countries (Tanzania, Uganda, Burundi, Kenya, South Sudan, and Rwanda).

economic climate A set of values and practices, such as the level of trust, transparency and corruption that encourages or discourages economic investments.

economic liberalism The belief and theory that only free market, free trade, and economic cooperation can lead to a peaceful and prosperous world.

economic sanctions The deliberate, government-driven withdrawal, or threat of withdrawal, of customary trade and financial relations in an effort to change another country's policies.

environmental discrimination Actions and policies of the global North that sustain the contamination and depletion of the environment in the global South.

environmental politics The activities of political leaders, parties, NGOs, scientific laboratories, and others designed to influence environmental policy.

environmental skepticism A questioning of environmentalism from the point of view of science or practicality.

environmental sovereignty The right of states to use and protect their environment and natural resources.

environmentalism Belief in the necessity of urgent and comprehensive policies to protect the environment.

epidemic An outbreak of infectious disease in a large population.

European Union A community of countries in Europe that delegated much of their sovereignty to common institutions, to promote peace and economic growth.

experiment A research method that puts participants in controlled testing conditions. By varying these conditions, researchers can examine the behavior or responses of participants.

extraterritoriality Exemption from the jurisdiction of local law.

extreme poverty A profound lack of resources and the inability to gain access to them.

eyewitness accounts Descriptions of events by individuals who observed them directly.

failing state A state in which the government is incapable of exercising its major functions, defending borders, or making key decisions.

fair trade (or trade justice) Initiatives arising from a belief that free trade alone cannot solve such lingering problems as chronic poverty, diseases, and environmental troubles.

famine Severe food scarcity causing malnutrition, starvation, disease, and increasing mortality.

fascism The doctrine and policy of a form of extreme nationalism characterized by rejection of individual and political freedoms; by open racism and bigotry; and by control of industry, finance, and commerce.

feminism Critical approach arguing that men's political domination and their oppression of women shape international relations.

fiscal policy The use of government spending or revenue collection to influence the economy, jump-start it out of recession, or create jobs.

focus group A survey method involving small discussion groups used intensively in foreign policy planning, conflict resolution analysis, and academic research.

Food and Agriculture Organization (FAO) A UN agency that coordinates international efforts to overcome hunger.

foreign policy A state's strategy in dealing with other states.

freedom of the seas The principle that countries have the right to travel by sea to, and trade with, other countries; each state's sovereignty ends with its territorial waters.

fundamentalism A point of view or social movement distinguished by rigid adherence to principles rooted in tradition (typically religious tradition) and often by intolerance of individual rights and secularism.

general principles of law Cross-cultural principles of morality and common sense.

genocide The deliberate extermination or prosecution of racial, ethnic, religious, or social groups, whether in war or in peacetime.

geopolitics The theory and practice of using geography to achieve political power or seek security.

global commons Geographical areas not under any nation's sovereign control.

global disarmament The universal and voluntary elimination by states of their offensive weapons.

Global Environment Facility (GEF) An independent financial organization established in 1991 that provides grants to developing countries for projects that benefit the global environment and promote sustainable development.

global governance The global cooperation of international actors with little or no power of enforcing compliance. This approach is based on the mutual interdependence of nations, the idea that global issues should be addressed by a collective effort, and the assumption that there is no single formula for solving all humanitarian problems.

globalization The growing interdependence of countries and their economies, the growing importance of international exchanges of goods and ideas, and increased openness to innovation.

graduated reciprocation in tension reduction (GRIT) Small goodwill steps by one or two sides in an international conflict that help to build trust and reduce international tensions.

green certification The grant of certificates to companies that pursue responsible environmental policies, in order to make their products more competitive in the market.

gross domestic product (GDP) The total market value of all the goods and services produced within the borders of a nation during a specified period

group pressure In political psychology, the ability of other people to alter individual decisions.

guerrilla warfare Political violence by identifiable, irregular combat units, usually to seize state power, win autonomy, or found new states.

harmony values The view that the environment should be preserved and cherished rather than exploited.

hegemony One state's overwhelming power in relation to other states.

human rights Fundamental rights with which all people are endowed regardless of their race, nationality, sex, ethnicity, religion, or social status.

human trafficking The illegal trade in human beings for purposes of exploitation.

humanitarian crisis An incident or problem that threatens to the health, safety, security, and wellbeing of many people, usually in a single geographic area.

humanitarian intervention Assistance with or without the use of military force to reduce the disastrous consequences of a humanitarian crisis.

humanitarian sovereignty A country's responsibility for its own humanitarian policies and the right to accept or reject humanitarian interventions.

identity The characteristics by which a person is recognizable as a member of a cultural group, such as a nation, an ethnic group, or a religion.

industrialization Creation of a large-scale modern economy based on mechanization and scientific-technological advancement.

imperialism A set of ideas and policies that promoted domination and control of powerful European countries in the rest of the world.

imperialism (Lenin's theory of) A global struggle among international corporations and banks for territories and resources.

infectious diseases Serious maladies caused by a biological agent such as a virus, bacterium, or parasite.

intelligence Information about the interests, intentions, capabilities, and actions of foreign countries, including government officials, political parties, the functioning of their economies, the activities of nongovernmental organizations, and the behavior of private individuals.

intergovernmental organizations (IGOs) Association of several nation-states or nongovernmental organizations for the purpose of international cooperation.

internal affairs Matters that individual states consider beyond the reach of international law or the influence of other states.

internally displaced persons Those who involuntarily leave their home and region under threats of death, starvation, or imprisonment.

international law Principles, rules, and regulations concerning the interactions between countries and other institutions and organizations in international relations.

international mandate Legal permission to administer a territory or enforce international law.

international political economy (IPE) The ways in which politics and economics interact in an international context.

international politics The political aspects of international relations. The emphasis on politics suggests the primary focus of these studies: power-related interests and policies.

international relations The study of interactions among states, as well as the international activities of nonstate organizations.

international security Mutual security issues involving two or more states.

international system Checks and balances among states as they exercise their power to promote their interests.

international terrorism Terrorism that involves international groups, interaction between countries, or international organizations, often with regional or global consequences.

international treaties Written agreements between nations (also called agreements, charters, pacts, covenants, and conventions).

interventionism A policy of interference in other states' affairs or international conflicts without regard for their consent.

involuntary migration Relocation within or across state borders due to violence, hardship, severe suffering, or a significant threat of these.

isolationism A policy of noninvolvement in international conflicts.

jihadism A radical political movement appealing to religious feelings and using terrorist methods to undermine sovereign states.

jurisdiction The right and authority to make decisions and apply justice.

Keynesian economics The principle that national governments should conduct expansionary fiscal and monetary policies whenever necessary to ease the undesirable effects of economic recessions.

Kyoto Protocol A 1997 international agreement to limit air pollution and reduce global warming.

laws of war Common principles that states should follow in case of an armed conflict.

League of Nations An international organization founded to promote peace (1920–1946), with headquarters in Geneva, Switzerland. Predecessor of the United Nations.

levels of analysis Categories that allow an observer to use different degrees of generalization and complexity while analyzing international relations.

liberal interventionism An approach to international relations that accepts violence only if all diplomatic and nonviolent means are exhausted.

liberalism A school of thought based on the idea that international organizations, international economic cooperation, interdependence, and democracy allow states to avoid power politics and establish a lasting peace.

lobbying Activities with the goal of influencing public officials in support of legislation or policies.

macroeconomics The field of economics that considers the behavior of individual consumers, companies, and industries.

malnutrition A medical condition resulting from famine or chronic food shortages.

Maastricht Treaty The treaty of European Union signed in 1992 (see European Union).

Marxism A social, political, and economic theory that interprets international relations as a struggle between states representing ruling elites interested in control over territories, people, and resources.

mastery values The view that individuals may exercise control over and exploit natural resources.

mercantilism The economic view that emphasizes the accumulation of resources and capital by states, as well as state regulation of trade.

microeconomics The field of economics that considers the behavior of individual consumers, companies, and industries.

militarism A tendency to rely on military force in response to foreign threats.

multilateralism Coordination of foreign policy with allies; participation in international coalitions, blocs, and international organizations.

multipolar order A world with multiple centers of power or influence.

mutual assured destruction (MAD) The U.S. doctrine that if two nuclear states have the capacity to destroy each other, they will not use nuclear weapons.

nation A large group of people sharing common cultural, religious, and linguistic features and distinguishing themselves from other large social groups. A nation may also refer to people who have established sovereignty over a territory and have set up international borders recognized by other states.

national purpose In the constructivist view, a major economic goal that political and business elites want to achieve for their country.

national security A state's need to protect its sovereignty, territorial integrity, and vital interests.

nationalism Individual and collective identification with a country or a nation. Nationalism also can become the belief in a nation's special role. Often, it is the belief that an ethnic group has the right to form an independent state.

National-Socialism (Nazism) An extreme form of fascism based on racism, anti-Semitism, and armed aggression.

natural disaster A natural hazard such as an earthquake or a volcano eruption with devastating impact on the ecosystem.

neoliberalism (neoliberal institutionalism) An approach that postulates that states prefer to seek security not through power politics but in the context of complex interdependence among states.

neorealism (structural realism) The theory that each state seeks a secure place in the international system according to the distribution of power.

neutrality Rejection of any formal military or political alliance (see Isolationism).

nongovernmental organization (NGO) Public or private group unaffiliated formally with a government and attempting to influence foreign policy, to raise international concerns about a domestic problem or domestic concerns about a global issue, and to offer solutions.

North (global) In dependency theory, predominantly rich and technology-driven countries that benefit from the raw materials and cheap labor of the (global) South.

North-South gap The wealth gap and other persistent inequalities between the countries in the Northern and Southern hemisphere.

nuclear deterrence Maintaining nuclear weapons with the intention not to use them but to deter others from nuclear attack.

nuclear proliferation The spread of nuclear weapons, material, information, and technologies to create nuclear weapons.

offensive realism The view that some countries choose violence and aggression because of the anarchic nature of the international system.

one-child policy China's policy initiated in 1979 limiting the number of children that a family can have.

outsourcing The practice of moving business and jobs to other countries and regions where labor costs are lower.

overpopulation A high concentration of people within a region, threatening its subsistence, or the minimum conditions to sustain a reasonable quality of life. It can cause serious environmental and social problems.

ozone depletion Steady decline in the amount of ozone in the stratosphere, allowing the sun's damaging ultraviolet radiation to reach the earth.

pacifism A principled opposition to war, and the belief that international disputes should be settled by arbitration and other nonviolent means.

pandemic An international epidemic that spreads across national borders.

parochialism A worldview limited to the small piece of land on which we live or to the narrow experience we have.

peace psychology The study of the ideological and psychological causes of war, in order to develop educational programs to reduce the threat.

peacekeeping Military or nonmilitary intervention to stop violence (peacemaking) and to create the conditions for lasting peace (peace building).

Peace of Westphalia The set of peace treaties signed in 1648 that created the first international system of sovereign states.

Pearl Harbor syndrome Individual attitudes and state policies focused on avoiding sudden and devastating attacks.

periphery In dependency theory, former colonies and underdeveloped, chronically poor states.

policy climate The prevailing sentiment among policy makers and other influential individuals.

political culture A set of values and norms essential to the functioning of international and national political institutions, including the attitudes of states toward each other and individual citizens.

political psychology The study of the interactions between political and psychological factors in individual and group behavior.

political socialization The study of how individuals acquire their political knowledge and beliefs.

postcolonial studies The critique of Western domination in postcolonial Africa, Asia, and Latin America.

power A state's ability to protect its own security and impose its will on other states and actors.

predator state A state conducting policies of systematic disregard for international rules and turning to belligerent actions in the international arena.

preemptive policies Action against terrorists before they strike.

preemptive war Military action launched to destroy the potential threat of an enemy when an attack is believed to be imminent.

preventive war Military action states take to protect themselves if they believe that other states might threaten them in the future.

production The process of creating goods and services with market value.

prospect theory Theory stating that people consistently miscalculate their chances of success and failure.

protectionism Economic restrictions by the state to discourage imports and encourage domestic production, including "import substitution."

proxy wars A war instigated by a major power that does not itself become involved.

rational model In political psychology, the view that politicians act, for the most part, logically, to maximize positive outcomes and to minimize negative outcomes.

realism An approach to international relations that focuses on states and their interests, balance of power, and the structure of international relations.

realpolitik Policy rooted in the belief that the foundation of a nation's security is power and the threat of its use.

refugees Involuntary migrants under threats of political or religious persecution or ethnic and religious violence.

regional trade agreements Mutual commitments that bind several neighboring countries to pursue common economic and financial policies.

rehabilitation Helping someone who has been involved in a radical or terrorist group return to the community.

religious fundamentalism A set of beliefs and behaviors based on strict adherence to religious principles.

republic A type of government in which power rests with citizens, not with an autocratic ruler.

resistance bias In cognitive theories, the rule that leaders resist changing their ideas about international relations.

responsibility to protect (R2P) The principle that if a sovereign country does not protect its own people from identifiable causes of death and acute suffering, then other countries and the international community must take action.

security community A group of countries united by mutual security interests, arrangements, and common liberal values.

security dilemma A situation in which one state's efforts to improve its security cause insecurity in others.

security policy Principles of international behavior to advance a state's fundamental interests and ensure national security.

security regime A region in which a powerful country provides protection to other states in exchange for their cooperation.

separatism The advocacy of or attempt to establish a separate nation within another sovereign state.

socially responsible investing (SRI) A business strategy combining the pursuit of the social good, environmental protection, and profits.

soft power A state's ability to influence other states by example, through economic and social success.

sources of international law Treaties, customs, general principles, the actions of international courts and other organizations, and other processes that regulate international relations.

South (global) Predominantly agricultural countries that are dependent on the rich and technology-driven (global) North.

sovereignty The supremacy of authority exercised by a state over its population and its territory.

state A governed entity with a settled population occupying a permanent area with recognized borders.

state government An institution with the authority to formulate and enforce its decisions within a country's borders.

supranationalism International treaties, international customary law, and general principles of law recognized by civilized nations.

survey The investigative method in which groups of people answer questions on a certain topic.

sustainable development A comprehensive policy that meets the needs of the present without sacrificing the ability of future generations to meet their own needs. This policy is about stimulating economic growth while protecting the environment and natural resources.

tariffs Taxes or financial charges imposed on imported goods.

terrorism Random violence conducted by nonstate actors, such as individuals or groups, against governments or their citizens to achieve political goals.

theory A general concept or scheme that one applies to facts in order to analyze them.

transnational cooperation The interaction of nonstate agencies, networks of states, and groups of citizens.

tribalism A way of thinking and a movement identifying itself not with nation-states but rather with a religious or ethnic group.

two-level game A model in which states react to both domestic and international politics.

tyrant A ruler who uses unlimited power to oppress the people of the ruler's country or its foreign possessions.

unilateralism Reliance on a state's own resources rather than support from others; acting alone in foreign policy.

United Nations An international organization founded in 1945 to preserve peace and protect minorities.

unipolar order A world with only one center of power or influence.

universal jurisdiction The principle that the perpetrators of certain crimes cannot escape justice by moving to another country and invoking its sovereign immunity.

war An organized violent confrontation between states or other social and political entities, such as ethnic or religious groups.

water pollution The byproducts of human activities that are harmful to rivers, lakes, seas, and underground water.

weapons of mass destruction (WMD) Nuclear, chemical, and biological weapons that can quickly and indiscriminately kill tens of millions of people.

xenophobia Fear and contempt of foreign countries and foreigners, helping politicians and regimes to mobilize public opinion, defeat political opposition, win elections, neutralize critics, or justify war.

References

"A Strategic Revolution in HIV and Global Health (Editorial)." 2011. *The Lancet* 377 (9783) June 18: 2055.

Aaronson, Susan Ariel. 2010. "Is China Killing the WTO?" *International Economy*, Winter.

Abadie, Alberto. 2006. "Poverty, Political Freedom, and the Roots of Terrorism." *American Economic Review* (Papers and Proceedings) 96(2): 50–56.

Abdelal, Rawi. 2001. *National Purpose in the World Economy.* Ithaca, NY: Cornell University Press.

Abelson, Rashad. 2015. "Locked Out: The (Un) Constitutionality of Revoking the Passports of Americans Fighting for ISIS." *National Security Law Brief.* January 27. Online at http://www .nationalsecuritylawbrief.com/locked-out-the- unconstitutionality-of-revoking-the-passports- of-americans-fighting-for-isis (accessed April 10, 2015).

Abrams, Irwin. 1957. "The Emergence of the International Law Societies." *Review of Politics* 19(3): 361–380.

Acemoglu, Daron and Robinson, James. 2013. *Why Nations Fail. The Origins of Power, Prosperity, and Poverty.* New York: Random House.

Adamsky, Dima. 2010. *The Culture of Military Innovation: The Impact of Cultural Factors on the Revolution in Military Affairs in Russia, the US, and Israel.* Stanford, CA: Stanford University Press.

Adler, Emanuel. 2008. "The Spread of Security Communities: Communities of Practice, Self-Restraint, and NATO's Post-Cold War Transformation." *European Journal of International Relations* 14(2): 195–230.

Adler, Emanuel, and Michael Barnett, eds. 1998. *Security Communities.* Cambridge: Cambridge University Press.

Agier, Michel. 2010. "Humanity as an Identity and Its Political Effects." *Humanity* (11): 29–46.

Ahmed, Sulman, and Alexander Bick. 2017. "Trump's National Security Strategy: A New Brand of Mercantilism?" *Carnegie Endowment for International Peace.* Online at http:// carnegieendowment.org/2017/08/17/trump- s-national-security-strategy-new-brand-of- mercantilism-pub-72816 (accessed January 9, 2019).

Akçam, Taner. 2007. *A Shameful Act: The Armenian Genocide and the Question of Turkish Responsibility.* New York: Picador.

Al Jazeera. Key Facts About the War in Yemen. 2018 March 25. https://www.aljazeera. com/news/2016/06/key-facts-war- yemen-160607112342462.html

Alamgir, Jalal. 2008. *India's Open-Economy Policy: Globalism, Rivalry, Continuity.* London: Routledge.

Aldous, Richard. 2007. *The Lion and the Unicorn: Gladstone vs. Disraeli.* New York: W. W. Norton.

Allegretti, Aubrey. 2018. *"Russia could kill 'thousands' in UK power station attack, warns Defence Secretary"* Sky News, 26 January Online at https://news.sky.com/story/russia- could-kill-thousands-in-uk-power-station- attack-warns-defence-secretary-11222844 (accessed March 23, 2019).

Allison, Graham. 1971. *Essence of Decision: Explaining the Cuban Missile Crisis.* 1st edition. New York: Little, Brown.

Allison, Graham, and Philip Zelikow. 1999. *Essence of Decision: Explaining the Cuban Missile Crisis.* 2nd edition. New York: Longman.

Almond, Gabriel, and Sidney Verba. 1963. *The Civic Culture.* Boston: Little, Brown.

Almukhtar, Sarah; K. K. Rebecca Lai; Sergio Peçanha; Derek Watkins; and Jeremy White. 2015. "What's Behind the Surge in Refugees Crossing the Mediterranean Sea." *The New York Times.* May 5. Online at http://www. nytimes.com/ interactive/2015/04/20/world/ europe/surge-in-refugees-crossing-the-medi terranean-sea-maps.html (accessed June 22, 2015).

Amadeo, Kimberly. 2017. "War on Terror Facts, Costs and Timeline." *The Balance*. Online at https://www.thebalance.com/war-on-terror-facts-costs-timeline-3306300 (accessed January 9, 2019).

Anderson, Kenneth, and Matthew Waxman. 2013. "Law and Ethics for Autonomous Weapon Systems: Why a Ban Won't Work and How the Laws of War Can." *Stanford University, The Hoover Institution (Jean Perkins Task Force on National Security and Law Essay Series)*. April 14. Online at https://papers.ssrn.com/sol3/papers.cfm?abstract_id=2250126 (accessed January 9, 2019).

Anderson, Kym, ed. 2005. *The World's Wine Markets: Globalization at Work*. London: Edward Elgar.

Anderson, Michael, and Susan Anderson. 2011. *Machine Ethics*. Cambridge, MA: Cambridge University Press.

Angell, Norman. 1910. *The Great Illusion: A Study of the Relation of Military Power in Nations to Their Economic and Social Advantage*. London: Heinemann.

Angus, Ian, and Simon Butler. 2011. *Too Many People?: Population, Immigration, and the Environmental Crisis*. Chicago: Haymarket Books.

Arkin, Ronald. 2009. *Governing Lethal Behavior in Autonomous Robots*. London: Chapman and Hall/CRC.

Arkin, Ronald. 2018. *Ethical Robots in Warfare*. College of Computing. Georgia Tech University. Online at https://www.cc.gatech.edu/ai/robot-lab/online-publications/arkin-rev.pdf (accessed January 13, 2019).

Arrighi, Giovanni. 1994. *The Long Twentieth Century: Money, Power, and the Origins of Our Times*. New York: Verso.

Arrighi, Giovanni. 2010. "The World Economy and the Cold War, 1970–1990." In *The Cambridge History of the Cold War*, Vol. 3, ed. Melvyn P. Leffler and Odd Arne Westad. New York: Cambridge University Press.

Arrighi, Giovanni, and Lu Zhang. 2011. "Beyond the Washington Consensus: A New Bandung?" In *Globalization and Beyond: New Examinations of Global Power and Its Alternatives*, eds. Jon Shefner and Patricia Fernandez-Kelly, 25–57. University Park: Pennsylvania State University Press.

Art, David. 2011. *Inside the Radical Right: The Development of Anti-Immigrant Parties in Western Europe*. Cambridge: Cambridge University Press.

Asal, Victor, and Andrew Blum. 2005. "Holy Terror and Mass Killings? Reexamining the Motivations and Methods of Mass Casualty Terrorists." *International Studies Review* 7(1): 153–155.

Ayittey, George B. N. 2005. *Africa Unchained: The Blueprint for Africa's Future*. New York: Palgrave Macmillan.

Ayman, Roya and Karen Korabik. 2010. "Why Gender and Culture Matter." *American Psychologist* 65(3): 157–170.

Baez, Sandra; Eduar Herrera; Adolfo García; Liane Young; and Agustin Ibanez. 2017. "Outcome-Oriented Moral Evaluation in Terrorists." *Nature Human Behaviour*, volume 1. Online at https://www.nature.com/articles/s41562-017-0118#auth-3 (accessed January 10, 2019).

Baldez, Lisa. 2013. "U.S. Drops the Ball on Women's Rights." CNN. Online at http://www.cnn.com/2013/03/08/opinion/baldez-womens-equality-treaty/ acessed April 25, 2015.

Balding, Christopher. 2018. Why Democracies are turning against Belt and Road. Foreign Affairs. October 24. https://www.foreignaffairs.com/articles/china/2018-10-24/why-democracies-are-turning-against-belt-and-road.

Baldoni, John. 2004. *Great Motivation Secrets of Great Leaders*. New York: McGraw-Hill.

Bales, Kevin, Zoe Trodd, and Alex Williamson. 2009. *Modern Slavery: The Secret World of 27 Million People*. London: Oneworld.

Banerjee, Abhijit, and Ester Duflo. 2011. *Poor Economics: A Radical Rethinking of the Way to Fight Global Poverty*. New York: Public Affairs.

Barner-Barry, Carol, and Robert Rosenwein. 1985. *Psychological Perspectives on Politics*. Prospect Heights, IL: Waveland.

Bass, Gary. 2009. *Freedom's Battle: The Origins of Humanitarian Intervention*. New York: Vintage Books.

Baumgartner, Pete, and Rikard Jozwiak. 2017. "Putin Arrives in Budapest Amid Concerns over EU Unity." Radio Free Europe. Online at https://www.rferl.org/a/putin-russia-hungary-orban-european-union-concerns-trump-sanctions/28273592.html (accessed January 9, 2019).

BBC. 2010. Ethiopia's famine aid 'spent on weapons.' March 3. http://news.bbc.co.uk/1/hi/8535189.stm (accessed January 9, 2019).

BBC. 2017. "Killer Robots: Experts Warn of 'Third Revolution in Warfare.'" August 21. Online at http://www.bbc.com/news/technology-40995835 (accessed January 9, 2019).

BBC Global Survey. 2018. April 22. Online at https://www.ipsos.com/ipsos-mori/en-uk/bbc-global-survey-world-divided (accessed January 9, 2019).

Beck, Barbara. 2011. "All Aboard: Women Will Get a Lift to the Top." *The Economist*. November 17. Special edition: The World in 2012, 99.

Becker, Jasper. 1998. *Hungry Ghosts: Mao's Secret Famine*. New York: Owl Books.

Beech, Hannah. 2013. "The Face of Buddhist Terror." *Time*, July 1. Online at http://ti.me/10zStLO (accessed July 17, 2013).

Bellamy, Alex, and Paul Williams. 2010. *Understanding Peacekeeping*. Cambridge, UK: Polity.

Benvenisti, Eyal, Chaim Gans, and Sari Hanafi, eds. 2007. *Israel and the Palestinian Refugees*. Berlin: Springer.

Beres, Louis R. 2008. "On Assassination, Preemption, and Counterterrorism: The View from International Law." *International Journal of Intelligence and CounterIntelligence* 21(4): 694–725.

Bergman, Ronen. 2008. *The Secret War with Iran: The 30-Year Clandestine Struggle Against the World's Most Dangerous Terrorist Power*. New York: Free Press.

Bergsten, C. Fred. 2005. "Rescuing the Doha Round." *Foreign Affairs* 84(7). Special WTO edition. Online at https://www.foreignaffairs.com/issues/2005/84/7 (accessed August 1, 2015).

Bernstein, Richard. 2009. "Upper Crust Is Often Drawn to Terrorism." *The New York Times*. December 30. Online at http://nyti.ms/6S5b73 (accessed June 25, 2013).

Beschloss, Michael. 2007. *Presidential Courage: Brave Leaders and How They Changed America, 1789– 1989*. New York: Simon & Schuster.

Best, Antony. 2003. "Imperial Japan." In *The Origins of World War Two: The Debate Continues*, ed. Joseph A. Maiolo, 52– 69. New York: Palgrave Macmillan.

Betts, Richard. 2004. *Conflict after the Cold War: Arguments on Causes of War and Peace*. 2nd edition. New York: Longman.

Betts, Richard. 2008. *Conflict after the Cold War: Arguments on Causes of War and Peace*. 3rd edition. New York: Longman.

Betts, Richard. 2011. "Institutional Imperialism." *The National Interest*. May/June: 85–96.

Bhagwati, Jagdish. 2004. *In Defense of Globalization*. New York: Oxford University Press.

Biello, David. 2010. "Where Did the Carter White House's Solar Panels Go?" *Scientific American*. August 6. Online at http://www.scientificamerican.com/article.cfm?id=carter-white-house-solar-panel-array (accessed September 25, 2012).

Birdsall, Nancy, and Francis Fukuyama. 2011. "The Post-Washington Consensus: Development after the Crisis." *Foreign Affairs* 90(2): 45–53.

Black, Richard. 2011. "World's Oceans in 'Shocking' Decline." BBC News. June 20. Online at http://www.bbc.co.uk/news/science-environment-13796479?print=true (accessed September 25, 2012).

Blair, Tony. 2010. *A Journey: My Political Life*. New York: Knopf.

Blake, Andrew 2016. "Islamic State Hacker Sentenced for Assisting Terrorist Group with 'Kill list.'" *The Washington Times*. September 24. Online at https://www.washingtontimes.com/news/2016/sep/24/

ardit-ferizi-hacker-who-aided-islamic-state-senten/ (accessed January 9, 2019).

Blanchard, William. 1996. *Neocolonialism American Style, 1960–2000*. New York: Praeger.

Blewitt, John. 2014. *Understanding Sustainable Development*.

Blight J. G., B. J. Allyn, and D. A. Welch. 1993. *Cuba on the Brink: Castro, the Missile Crisis, and the Soviet Collapse*. New York: Pantheon Books.

Blinken, A. 2015. "Transatlantic Cooperation and the Crisis in Ukraine: Keynote and Discussion with U.S. Deputy Secretary of State Antony J. Blinken." Hertie School of Governance. Online at http://www.hertie-school.org/mediaandevents/events/events-pages/05032015-transatlantic-cooperation-and-the-crisis-in-ukraine/ (accessed April 2, 2015).

Blustein, Paul. 2009. *Misadventures of the Most Favored Nations: Clashing Egos, Inflated Ambitions, and the Great Shambles of the World Trade System*. New York: Public Affairs.

Bodansky, Yossef. 2001. *Bin Laden: The Man Who Declared War on America*. Roseville, CA: Prima Lifestyles.

Boot, Max. 2007. "Another Vietnam?" *Wall Street Journal*. August 24. Online at http://www.cfr.org/publication/14083/another_vietnam.html (accessed July 18, 2013).

Boot, Max. 2009. "Pirates, Then and Now: How Piracy Was Defeated in the Past and Can Be Again." *Foreign Affairs* 88(4): 94–107.

Boot, Max. 2013. "The Guerrilla Myth: Unconventional Wars Are Our Most Pressing National Security Concern." *The Wall Street Journal*. January 18. Online at http://www.wsj.com/articles/SB10001424127887323596204578243702404190338. (accessed April 12, 2015).

Booth, Ken, and Nicholas Wheeler. 2007. *The Security Dilemma: Fear, Cooperation and Trust in World Politics*. New York: Palgrave Macmillan.

Booth, Ken, and Nicholas Wheeler. 2008. *The Security Dilemma: Fear, Cooperation and Trust in World Politics*. New York: Palgrave Macmillan.

Borah, Rupakjyoti. 2011. "BRICS: The New Great Game." *ISN Insights*. June 23. Online at http://bit.ly/12QmLUU (accessed July 19, 2013).

Borch, Fred, and Gary Solis. 2010. *Geneva Conventions*. New York: Kaplan Publishing.

Borgerson, Scott G. 2008. "Arctic Meltdown: The Economic and Security Implications of Global Warming." *Foreign Affairs* 87(2) March/April.

Bortolotti, Dan. 2006. *Hope in Hell: Inside the World of Doctors Without Borders*. Buffalo, NY: Firefly Books.

Boucek, Christopher. 2009. "Saudi Detainee-Rehab Program Mostly Successful." NPR's All Things Considered. December 31. Online at http://bit.ly/12Hel2h (accessed June 30, 2013).

Boucek, Christopher. 2010. "Al Qaeda in 2010." *The Diane Rehm Show*. January 5. Online at http://bit.ly/15QPRqj (accessed July 18, 2013).

Boyce, Robert. 2002. "Economics." In *The Origins of World War Two: The Debate Continues*. eds. Robert Boyce and Joseph Maiolo, 249–267. New York: Palgrave.

Bozo, Frederic. 2009. *Europe and the End of the Cold War*. London: Routledge.

Bozo, Frederic, Marie-Pierre Rey, Berndt Rother, and Ludlow N. Piers, eds. 2012. *Visions of the End of the Cold War in Europe, 1945–1990*. New York: Berghahn Books.

Bozo, Frederic, Andreas Roedder and Mary Elise Sarotte, eds. 2017. German Reunification. A Multinational history. London: Routledge.

"BP Found 'Grossly Negligent' in 2010 Gulf Oil Spill." 2014. *BBC News*. September 4. Online at http://www.bbc.com/news/business-29069184 (accessed March 7, 2015).

Brands, Hal. 2018. *American Grand Strategy in the Age of Trump*. Washington DC: Brookings.

Brandt, Patrick, and Todd Sandler. 2010. "What Do Transnational Terrorists Target? Has It Changed? Are We Safer?" *Journal of Conflict Resolution* 54(2): 214–236.

Bricmont, Jean. 2006. *Humanitarian Imperialism: Using Rights to Sell War*. New York: Monthly Review Press.

Broers, Michael. 2014. *Europe Under Napoleon*. London: I.B.Tauris.

Brown, Paul. 2006. *Notes from a Dying Planet, 2004– 2006: One Scientist's Search for Solutions*. Lincoln, NE: iUniverse, Inc.

Brown, Robert, and Tristan Brown. 2012. *Why Are We Producing Biofuels?* Ames, IA: Brownia LLC.

Bryce, Robert. 2009. *Gusher of Lies: The Dangerous Delusions of "Energy Independence."* New York: Public Affairs.

Buchanan, Allen. 2003. "Reforming the International Law of Humanitarian Intervention." In *Humanitarian Intervention: Ethical, Legal, and Political Dilemmas*, eds. J. L. Holzgrefe and Robert Keohane, 130–174. New York: Cambridge University Press.

Buchanan, Allen. 2010. *Human Rights, Legitimacy, and the Use of Force.* New York: Oxford University Press.

Buchanan, Patrick. 2008. *Churchill, Hitler, and the Unnecessary War: How Britain Lost Its Empire and the West Lost the World.* New York: Crown Publishers.

Buchanan, Patrick. 2009. *Day of Reckoning: How Hubris, Ideology, and Greed Are Tearing America Apart.* New York: St. Martin's Griffin.

Bueno de Mesquita, Ethan. 2005. "Conciliation, Counterterrorism, and Patterns of Terrorist Violence." *International Organization* 59(1): 145–176.

Bull, Hedley. 1977. *The Anarchical Society: A Study of Order in World Politics.* New York: Columbia University Press.

Bull, Hedley, ed. 1988. *Intervention in World Politics.* New York: Oxford University Press.

Burt, Jo-Marie. 2009. "Guilty as Charged: The Trial of Former Peruvian President Alberto Fujimori for Grave Violations of Human Rights." *International Journal of Transitional Justice* 3(3): 384–405.

Burt, Jo-Marie. 2010. *Political Violence and the Authoritarian State in Peru: Silencing Civil Society.* New York: Palgrave Macmillan.

Buzan, Barry, and Lene Hansen. 2009. *The Evolution of International Security Studies.* New York: Cambridge University Press.

Caprioli, Mary, and Mark Boyer. 2001. "Gender, Violence, and International Crisis." *Journal of Conflict Resolution* 45(4): 503–518.

Caro, Robert A. 2012. *The Years of Lyndon Johnson: The Passage of Power.* New York: Alfred A. Knopf Inc.

Carpenter, A. C., and Crendl, A. C. 2018. "Are Eyewitness Accounts Biased? Evaluating False Memories for Crimes Involving In-Group or Out-Group Conflict." *Social Neuroscience* 13(1): 74–93.

Carpenter, Ted. 2006. *America's Coming War with China: A Collision Course over Taiwan.* New York: Palgrave Macmillan.

Carr, Edward H. 1939/1969. *Twenty Years' Crisis, 1919–1939: An Introduction to the Study of International Relations.* 2nd edition. New York: Palgrave Macmillan.

Carr, Edward. 1961/2002. *What Is History?* New York: Palgrave.

Carrière, Erin, Marc O'Reilly, and Richard Vengroff. 2003. "In the Service of Peace: Reflexive Multilateralism and the Canadian Experience in Bosnia." In *International Public Opinion and the Bosnia Crisis*, eds. Richard Sobel and Eric Shiraev. Lanham, MD: Lexington Books, 1–32.

CARSI. 2015. "The Central America Regional Security Initiative." U.S. Department of State. Bureau of Public Affairs. Online at http://www.state.gov/p/wha/rt/carsi/(accessed February 25, 2015).

Carson, Rachel. 1962. *Silent Spring.* New York: Houghton Mifflin.

Catalist. 2018. "Workplaces That Work for Women." Online at http://www.catalyst.org/knowledge/women-corporate-boards-globally (accessed February 25, 2018).

Chakrabarty, Dipesh. 2007. *Provincializing Europe: Postcolonial Thought and Historical Difference.* Princeton, NJ: Princeton University Press.

Chaliand, Gerard, and Arnaud Blin. 2007. *The History of Terrorism: From Antiquity to Al Qaeda.* Berkeley: University of California Press.

Chan, Steve. 1997. "In Search of Democratic Peace: Problems and Promise." *Mershon International Studies Review* 41(1): 59–91.

Chandler, David. 2006. *From Kosovo to Kabul and Beyond: Human Rights and International Intervention.* Ann Arbor, MI: Pluto Press.

Chappel, Louise. 2008. "The International Criminal Court: A New Arena for Transforming Justice." In *Global Governance:*

Feminist Perspectives, eds. Shirin Rai and Georgina Waylen. New York: Palgrave Macmillan.

Checkel, Jeffrey. 1998. "The Constructivist Turn in International Relations Theory." *World Politics* 50(2): 324–348.

Chernyaev, Anatoly. 2000. *My Six Years with Gorbachev*. Translated and edited by Robert D. English and Elizabeth Tucker. University Park: Pennsylvania State University Press.

Cholett, Derek, and James Goldgeier. 1962/2002. "The Scholarship of Decision-Making: Do We Know How We Decide?" In *Foreign Policy Decision-Making*, eds. Richard Snyder, H. W. Bruck, and Burton Sapin. Originally published in 1962, "revisited" by eds. Valerie Hudson, Derek Cholett, and James Goldgeier in 2002. New York: Palgrave Macmillan.

Cholett, Derek, and James Goldgeier. 2008. *America Between the Wars: From 11/9 to 9/11: The Misunderstood Years between the Fall of the Berlin Wall and the Start of the War on Terror*. New York: PublicAffairs.

Christie, D. J. 2012. *The Encyclopedia of Peace Psychology*, ed. Malden, MA: Wiley-Blackwell.

Christison, Bill. 2002. "Former CIA Officer Explains Why the War on Terror Won't Work." *Counter-Punch* (an online magazine) March 4. Online at http://www.counterpunch.org/2002/03/04/former-cia-officer-explains-why-the-war-on-terror-won-t-work/ (accessed June 11, 2015).

Chua, Amy. 2018. *Political Tribes: Group Instinct and the Fate of Nations*. New York: Penguin Press.

CIA. 2018. *The World Factbook*. Online at https://www.cia.gov/library/publications/the-world-factbook/(accessed June 17, 2017).

Clark, Christopher. 2012. *Sleepwalkers. How Europe Went to War in 1914*. New York: Harper Perennial.

Clarke, Peter. 2008. *The Last Thousand Days of the British Empire: Churchill, Roosevelt, and the Birth of the Pax Americana*. New York: Bloomsbury.

Close, Paul. 2000. *The Legacy of Supranationalism*. New York: Palgrave Macmillan.

CNN Library. 2016. "2016 Presidential Campaign Hacking Fast Facts." December 26. Online at https://www.cnn.com/2016/12/26/us/2016-presidential-campaign-hacking-fast-facts/index.html (accessed November 24, 2018).

Cobham, Alex. 2013. "Corrupting Perceptions. Why Transparency International's Flagship Corruption Index Falls Short." *Foreign Policy*, July 22. Online at http://foreignpolicy.com/2013/07/22/corrupting-perceptions/ (accessed February 21, 2015).

Cohen, Joel E. 2005. "Human Population Grows Up." *Scientific American* 293(3): 48–55. Online at http://bit.ly/OUTbgQ (accessed July 15, 2013).

Cohn, Carol. 1987. "Sex and Death in the Rational World of Defense Intellectuals." *Signs* 12(4): 687–718.

Coleman, Loren. 2004. *The Copycat Effect: How the Media and Popular Culture Trigger the Mayhem in Tomorrow's Headlines*. New York: Pocket.

Coll, Steve. 2009. *The Bin Ladens: An Arabian Family in the American Century*. New York: Penguin Press.

Cooper, Barry. 2004. *New Political Religions, or An Analysis of Modern Terrorism*. Columbia: University of Missouri Press.

Copeland, Dale. 1996. "Economic Interdependence and War." *International Security* 20(4): 5–41.

Cordesman, Anthony. 2002. *Terrorism, Asymmetric Warfare, and Weapons of Mass Destruction: Defending the U.S. Homeland*. Westport, CT: Praeger.

Corruption Perception Index. 2015. Online at https://www.transparency.org/cpi2014/results (accessed June 15, 2015).

Costigliola, Frank. 2000. "'I Had Come as a Friend': Emotion, Culture, and Ambiguity in the Formation of the Cold War." *Cold War History* 1(1) August: 103–128.

Cottier, Thomas, and Manfred Elsig, eds. 2011. *Governing the World Trade Organization: Past, Present and Beyond Doha*. New York: Cambridge University Press.

Cowen, Tyler. 2014. *Average Is Over: Powering America Beyond the Age of the Great Stagnation*. New York: Plume.

Crane, George, and Abla Amawi. 1997. *The Theoretical Evolution of International Political Economy: A Reader*. New York: Oxford University Press.

Crawford, Michael, and Jami Miscik. 2010. "The Rise of the Mezzanine Rulers: The New Frontier for International Law." *Foreign Affairs* 89(6) November/ December: 123–132.

Crenshaw, Martha. 2000. "The Psychology of Terrorism: An Agenda for the 21st Century." *Journal of Political Psychology* 21(2): 405–420.

Crenshaw, Martha. 2010. *Explaining Terrorism: Causes, Processes, and Consequences*. New York: Routledge.

Cronin, Audrey. 2002. "Behind the Curve: Globalization and International Terrorism." *International Security* 27(3) Winter: 30–58.

Cronin, Audrey. 2010. "The Evolution of Counterterrorism: Will Tactics Trump Strategy?" *International Affairs* 86(4): 837–856.

Cronin, Bruce. 1999. *Community under Anarchy: Transitional Identity and the Evolution of Cooperation*. New York: Columbia University Press.

Cullen, Heidi. 2010. *The Weather of the Future: Heat Waves, Extreme Storms, and Other Scenes from a Climate-Changed Planet*. New York: Harper.

Cummings, C. L. 2017. "Artificial Intelligence and the Future of Warfare." Research Paper. Chatam House. The Royal Institute of International Affairs. Online at https://www .chathamhouse.org/sites/files/chathamhouse/ publications/research/2017-01-26-artificial-intelligence-future-warfare-cummings-final. pdf (accessed January 9, 2019).

Cutler, Robert. 1981. "Decision Making and International Relations: The Cybernetic Theory Reconsidered." *Michigan Journal of Political Science* 1(2): 57–63. Online at http:// bit.ly/1aqXjeY (accessed July 16, 2013).

D'Silva, Themistocles. 2006. *The Black Box of Bhopal: A Closer Look at the World's Deadliest Industrial Disaster*. Victoria, BC: Trafford Publishing.

D'Souza, Dinesh. 2010. *The Roots of Obama's Rage*. Washington, DC: Regnery Publishing.

Davis, David H. 2007. *Ignoring the Apocalypse: Why Planning to Prevent Environmental Catastrophe Goes Astray*. Westport, CT: Praeger.

Davis, Mike. 2011. "Spring Confronts Winter." *New Left Review*. Online at http:// newleftreview.org/II/72/mike-davis-spring-confronts-winter (accessed July 15, 2013).

de Nevers, Renee. 2003. *Comrades No More. The Seeds of Political Change in Eastern Europe*. Cambridge, MA: MIT Press.

de Rugy, Veronique. 2015. *Wars in the Middle East Have Cost Taxpayers Almost $1.7 Trillion*. Online at http://mercatus.org/publication/wars-middle-east-have-cost-taxpayers-almost-17-trillion (accessed April 11, 2015).

Debs, Alexandre, and H. E. Goemans. 2010. "Regime Type, the Fate of Leaders, and War." *American Political Science Review* 104(3): 430–445.

Dempsey, Gary. 2002. "Old Folly in a New Disguise: Nation Building to Combat Terrorism." Cato Institute. March 21. Online at http://www.cato.org/pub_display.php?pub_id=1288 (accessed September 25, 2012).

Dennis, Anthony. 2002. *Osama bin Laden: A Psychological and Political Portrait*. Lima, OH: Wyndham Hall.

Der Spiegel. 2010. "Beijing's High-Tech Ambitions: The Dangers of Germany's Dependence on China." Online at http://bit.ly/12kRVsf (accessed July 16, 2013).

Desai, Meghnad. 2007. *Rethinking Islamism: The Ideology of the New Terror*. New York: Palgrave Macmillan.

Desertec. 2012. Online at http://www.desertec. org/ (accessed July 19, 2013).

Desertec. 2018. Online at http://www.desertec. org/ (accessed March 4, 2018).

Deutsch, Karl W., Sidney A. Burrell, and Robert A. Kann. 1957. *Political Community and the North Atlantic Area: International Organization in the Light of Historical Experience*. Princeton, NJ: Princeton University Press.

Deutsch, Morton, and Robert Krauss. 1962. "Studies of Interpersonal Bargaining." *Journal of Conflict Resolution* 6(1): 52–76.

Dicker, Rory. 2016. *A History of U.S. Feminisms*. New York: Seal Press.

DiMicco, Dan. 2015. *American Made: Why Making Things Will Return Us to Greatness*. New York: Palgrave Macmillan.

Dobrynin, Anatoly. 2001. *In Confidence: Moscow's Ambassador to Six Cold War President*. Seattle: University of Washington Press.

Donnelly, Jack. 2009. "Realism." In *Theories of International Relations*, eds. Scott Burchill, Andrew Linklater, Richard Devetak, Jack Donnelly, Matthew Patterson, and Christian Reus-Smit. New York: Palgrave Macmillan.

Doremus, Paul N., William W. Keller, Louis W. Pauley, and Simon Reich. 1998. *The Myth of the Global Corporation*. Princeton, NJ: Princeton University Press.

Dower, John. 2000. *Embracing Defeat: Japan in the Wake of World War II*. New York: W. W. Norton.

Doyle, Michael. 1986. "Liberalism and World Politics." *American Political Science Review* 80(4): 1151–1169.

Dreher, Alex and Nathan M. Jensen. Independent Actor or Agent? An Empirical Analysis of the Impact of U.S. Interests on International Monetary Fund Conditions. *The Journal of Law & Economics* 50 (1), 105-124.

Dubik, James. 2010. "Prudence, War and Civil-Military Relations." *Army*, September. Online at http://bit.ly/1ChKNLL (accessed June 20, 2015).

Duchene, Francois. 1994. *Jean Monnet: The First Statesman of Interdependence*. New York: W. W. Norton.

Dueck, Colin. 2010. *Hard Line: The Republican Party and U.S. Foreign Policy Since World War II*. Princeton, NJ: Princeton University Press.

Dutta, Manoranjan. 2005. *China's Industrial Revolution and Economic Presence*. Hackensack, NJ: World Scientific Publishing Company.

Easterly, William. 2001. *The Elusive Quest for Growth: Economists' Adventures and Misadventures in the Tropics*. Cambridge, MA: MIT Press.

Easterly, William. 2006. *The White Man's Burden: Why the West's Efforts to Aid the Rest Have Done So Much Ill and So Little Good*. New York: Penguin Press.

Ebrahim, Alnoor. 2006. *NGOs and Organizational Change*. Cambridge: Cambridge University Press.

Economy, Elizabeth. 2010a. "The Game Changer: Coping with China's Foreign Policy Revolution." *Foreign Affairs* 89(6), November/December: 142–152.

Economy, Elizabeth. 2010b. *The River Runs Black: The Environmental Challenge to China's Future*. Ithaca, NY: Cornell University Press.

Economy, Elizabeth, and Michael Levi. 2014. *By All Means Necessary: How China's Resource Quest Is Changing the World*. New York: Oxford University Press.

EIA (U.S. Energy Information Administration). 2015. Online at http://www.eia.gov/ (accessed January 3, 2019).

Eisenberg, Carolyn. 1996. *Drawing the Line: The American Decision to Divide Germany, 1944–1949*. Cambridge: Cambridge University Press.

Eisenhower, Dwight. 1960. *Public Papers of the Presidents, Dwight D. Eisenhower*, 1035–1040. Online at http://www.h-net.org/~hst306/documents/indust.html (accessed August 1, 2015).

Ekelund, Robert B., Jr., and Robert F. Hébert. 2007. *A History of Economic Theory and Method*. Long Grove, IL: Waveland Press.

Elsea, Jennifer. 2006. "U.S. Policy Regarding the International Criminal Court." CRS Reports for Congress. Online at http://fas.org/sgp/crs/misc/RL31495.pdf (accessed March 3, 2015).

Energy Matters. 2017. *Solar Battery Coast Keep on Getting Lower*. December 21. Online at https://www.energymatters.com.au/renewable-news/solar-batteries-cost-lower-buy-now/ (accessed January 9, 2019).

English, Robert D. 2000. *Russia and the Idea of the West: Gorbachev, Intellectuals and the End of the Cold War*. New York: Columbia University Press.

Enloe, Cynthia. 2000. *Bananas, Beaches, and Bases. Making Feminist Sense of International Politics*. Berkeley: University of California Press.

Enloe, Cynthia. 2007. *Globalization and Militarism*. New York: Rowman & Littlefield.

ENS. 2006. "U.S. Swaps Guatemalan Debt for Forest Conservation." *Environmental News Service*. October 3. http://bit.ly/197W7PT (accessed July 19, 2013).

Erikson, Erik. 1969. *Gandhi's Truth: On the Origins of Militant Nonviolence*. New York: W. W. Norton.

Esty, Daniel, and Andrew Winston. 2006. *Green to Gold: How Smart Companies Use Environmental Strategy to Innovate, Create Value, and Build*

Competitive Advantage. New Haven, CT: Yale University Press.

EU. 2017. "European Commission Press Release." Online at http://europa.eu/rapid/press-release_IP-17-161_en.htm (accessed January 9, 2019).

Eurobarometer. 2011. *Migrant Integration: Aggregate Report*. Conducted by TNS Qual+ at the request of Directorate General Home Affairs. Online at http://bit.ly/noM7CG (accessed June 16, 2013).

Evangelista, Matthew. 1999. *Unarmed Forces: The Transnational Movement to End the Cold War*. Ithaca, NY: Cornell University Press.

Evans, Gareth. 2009. *The Responsibility to Protect: Ending Mass Atrocity Crimes Once and for All*. Washington, DC: Brookings Institution Press.

Evans, Malcolm, ed. 2014. *International Law*. New York: Oxford University Press.

Evans, Peter. 1998. "Transnational Corporations and Third World States: From the Old Internationalization to the New." In *Transnational Corporations and the Global Economy*, eds. Richard Kozul-Wright and Robert Rowthorn, 195–224. New York: St. Martin's Press.

Evans-Pritchard, Ambrose. 2011. "World Power Swings Back to America." *Telegraph*. October 23. Online at http://bit.ly/ptenjk (accessed September 25, 2012).

Fabre, Cécile, and Seth Lazar. 2014. *The Morality of Defensive War*. New York: Oxford University Press.

Fanon, Frantz. 2005. *The Wretched of the Earth*. New York: Grove Press. Originally published in French in 1961.

Farmer, Paul. 2012. *Haiti after the Earthquake*. New York: PublicAffairs.

Fearon, James. 1995. "Rationalist Explanations for War." *International Organization* 49(3): 379–414.

Fearon, James. 1998. "Bargaining, Enforcement, and International Cooperation." *International Organization* 52(2): 269–306.

Fearon, James, and David Laitin. 2003. "Ethnicity, Insurgency, and Civil War." *American Political Science Review* 97(1): 75–90.

Feltman, Jeffrey. 2018. The Only Way to End the War in Yemen. Saudi Arabia Must Move First. *Foreign Affairs. Snapshot*. November 26. https://www.foreignaffairs.com/articles/yemen/2018-11-26/only-way-end-war-yemen

Ferguson, Niall. 2004. *Empire: The Rise and Demise of the British World Order and the Lessons for Global Power*. New York: Basic Books.

Ferguson, Niall. 2010. "The End of Chimerica: Amicable Divorce or Currency War?" Testimony before the Committee on Ways and Means U.S. House of Representatives, March 24. Online at http://belfercenter.ksg.harvard.edu/publication/20029/end_of_chimerica.html (accessed September 22, 2012).

Ferguson, Niall, Maier, Charles, and Manela, Erez, eds. 2011. *The Shock of the Global: The 1970s in Perspective*. Cambridge, MA: Harvard University Press.

Ferree, Myra. 2012. *Varieties of Feminism: German Gender Politics in Global Perspective* Stanford, CA: Stanford University Press.

Festa, Lynn. 2010. "Humanity without Feathers." *Humanity* 1(1): 3–27.

Figes, Orlando. 2012. *The Crimean War: A History*. New York: Picador.

Finnemore, Martha. 1996. *National Interests in International Society*. Ithaca, NY: Cornell University Press.

Finnemore, Martha. 2004. *The Purpose of Intervention: Changing Beliefs about the Use of Force* (Cornell Studies in Security Affairs). Ithaca, NY: Cornell University Press.

Fitzgerald, C. P. 1965. *China: Short Cultural History*. London: Barry & Jenkins.

Fleitz, Fred. 2018. "The Coming North Korea Nuclear Nightmare: What Trump Must Do to Reverse Obama's 'Strategic Patience.'" CreateSpace Independent Publishing Platform.

Fonte, John. 2017. "American Patriotism and Nationalism: One and Indivisible." *National Review* 1, May. Online at https://www.nationalreview.com/2017/05/nationalism-patriotism-american-history-conservatives-progressives (Accessed March 1, 2018).

Foglesong, David. 2007. *The American Mission and the 'Evil Empire.'* New York: Cambridge University Press.

Fong, Vanessa L. 2006. *Only Hope: Coming of Age under China's One-Child Policy*. Palo Alto, CA: Stanford University Press.

Foot, Rosemary. 2010. "The Cold War and Human Rights." *The Cambridge History of the Cold War*, Vol. 3, 445–465. Cambridge: Cambridge University Press.

Forsberg, Tuopmas, and Pursianen, Christor. 2017. "The Psychological Dimension of Russian Foreign Policy: Putin and the Annexation of Crimea." *Global Society* 31(2): 1–25.

Forsythe, David, Roger Coate, and Thomas Weiss. 2004. *The United Nations and Changing World Politics*. Boulder, CO: Westview Press.

Fouskas, Vassilis. 2003. *Zones of Conflict: U.S. Foreign Policy in the Balkans and the Greater Middle East*. Sterling, VA: Pluto Press.

Fredrik, Logevall, and Andrew Preston, eds. 2008. *Nixon in the World: American Foreign Relations, 1969–1977*. New York: Oxford University Press.

French, Hilary. 1994. GEF replenishment. *World Watch* 7(4): 7.

Friedrich, Hans-Peter. 2011. "An Interview of German Interior Minister." *Der Spiegel*, August 9. Online at http://bit.ly/oz01L0 (accessed July 17, 2013).

Friedman, Milton. 1962/2002. Capitalism and Freedom. Chicago: University of Chicago Press.

Fromkin, David. 2009. *The Peace to End All Peace*. New York: Henry Holt.

Fukuyama, Francis. 1993. *The End of History and the Last Man*. New York: Penguin Books.

Fukuyama, Francis. 2011. *The Origins of Political Order: From Prehuman Times to the French Revolution*. New York: Farrar, Straus, and Giroux.

Fukuyama, Francis. 2018. *Identity: The Demand for Dignity and the Politics of Resentment*. New York: Farrar, Straus, and Giroux.

Fulbright, William. 2011. *The Arrogance of Power*. New York: Random House.

Fursenko, Aleksandr, and Timothy Naftali. 1997. *"One Hell of a Gamble": Khrushchev, Castro, and Kennedy, 1958–1964*. New York: W. W. Norton.

Fursenko, Aleksandr, and Timothy Naftali. 2006. *Khrushchev's Cold War: The Inside Story of an American Adversary*. New York: W. W. Norton.

Fusaro, Peter C., and Tom James. 2006. *Energy and Emissions Markets: Collision or Convergence*. Hoboken, NJ: Wiley.

Gaddis, John Lewis. 1982. *Strategies of Containment: A Critical Appraisal of Postwar American National Security Policy*. New York: Oxford University Press.

Gaddis, John Lewis. 2006. *The Cold War: A New History*. New York: Penguin Books.

Gallup Polls. 2016. "Majority of Americans View Cuba Favorably for First Time." Online at https://news.gallup.com/poll/189245/majority-americans-view-cuba-favorably-first-time.aspx (accessed October 2, 2018)

Gallup Polls. 2018. "U.S. Satisfaction with World Standing Hits 13-Year High." Online at *https://bit.ly/2KRdzSO* (accessed July 31, 2018).

Gang, Ding. 2011. "War's Legacy Still Tints Vietnam's View of US." *Global Times*, July 6. Online at http://bit.ly/nH5USI (accessed July 15, 2013).

Gangale, Thomas. 2009. *The Development of Outer Space: Sovereignty and Property Rights in International Space Law*. Westport, CT: Praeger.

Garrett, Laurie. 2005. 'The Next Pandemic?' *Foreign Affairs* 84(4) July/August.

Gartzke, Erik. 2007. "The Capitalist Peace." *American Journal of Political Science* 51(1): 166–191.

Gaston, Kevin, and John Spicer. 2004. *Biodiversity: An Introduction*. Malden, MA: Blackwell Publishing.

Gates, Nathaniel, ed. 1998. *Race and U.S. Foreign Policy During the Cold War*. New York: Routledge.

Gates Foundation. 2019. Online at https://www.gatesfoundation.org (accessed January 3, 2019).

Gause, F. Gregory. 2005. Can Democracy Stop Terrorism? *Foreign Affairs* 84(5): 62–76.

Geiss, Imanuel. 1994. "Great Powers and Empires: Historical Mechanisms of Their Making and Breaking," In *The Fall of Great Powers. Peace, Stability, and Legitimacy*. ed. Geir Lundestad, 23–46. London: Oxford University Press.

Gelb, Leslie, and Richard Betts. 1979. *The Irony of Vietnam: The System Worked*. Washington, DC: Brookings.

Gelpi, Christopher, and Peter Feaver. 2002. "Speak Softly and Carry a Big Stick? Veterans in the Political Elite and the American Use of Force." *American Political Science Review* 96(4): 779–793.

George, Alexander. 1969. "The 'Operational Code': A Neglected Approach to the Study of Political Leaders and Decision-Making." *International Studies Quarterly* 13(2): 190–222.

Gereffi, Gary, and Miguel Korzeniewicz, eds. 1993. *Commodity Chains and Global Capitalism*. New York: Praeger.

German Energy Blog. 2015. Online at http://www .germanenergyblog.de/?p=18231 (accessed March 23, 2015).

Gerrard, Michael, ed. 2007. *Global Climate Change and U.S. Law*. Chicago: American Bar Association.

Gertz, Bill. 2011. "Computer-Based Attacks Emerge as Threat of Future, General Says." *The Washington Times*, September 13. Online at http://bit.ly/mYp915 (accessed July 17, 2013).

Gerwarth, Robert. 2016. *The Vanquished. Why the First World War Failed to End, 1917–1923*. New York: Penguin.

GHA (Global Humanitarian Assistance). 2018. Annual Report. Online at http://devinit. org/wp-content/uploads/2018/06/GHA-Report-2018.pdf (accessed September 3, 2018).

Ghazi, Zabihullah, and Mashal, Mujib. 2018. "Deadly ISIS Attack Hits an Aid Group, Save the Children, in Afghanistan." *The New York Times*, January 24. Online at https://www .nytimes.com/2018/01/24/world/asia/save-the-children-afghanistan.html (accessed January 9, 2019).Gilboy, George. 2004. "The Myth Behind China's Miracle." *Foreign Affairs* 83(4) July/August: 33–48.

Gilpin, Robert. 1981. *War and Change in International Politics*. Cambridge: Cambridge University Press.

Gingrich, Newt. 2017. *Understanding Trump*. New York: Center Street.

Glad, Betty. 2009. *An Outsider in the White House: Jimmy Carter, His Advisors, and the Making of American Foreign Policy*. Ithaca, NY: Cornell University Press.

Glaser, Charles. 2013. "How Oil Influences U.S. National Security." *International Security* 38(2): 112–146.

Gleijeses, Piero. 2003. *Conflicting Missions: Havana, Washington, and Africa, 1959–1976*. Chapel Hill: University of North Carolina Press.

Glejeses, Piero. 2010. "Cuba and the Cold War, 1959–1980." *The Cambridge History of the Cold War*, Vol. 3, 327–348. Cambridge: Cambridge University Press.

Goemans, Henk E., Kristian Skrede Gleditsch, and Giacomo Chiozza. 2009. "Introducing Archigos: A Data Set of Political Leaders, 1975–2003." *Journal of Peace Research* 46(2): 269–283.

Goldfrank, Walter. 2000. "Paradigm Regained? The Rules of Wallerstein's World-System Method." *Journal of World-Systems Research* 6(2): 150–195.

Goldgeier, James. 1999. *Not Whether but When: The U.S. Decision to Enlarge NATO*. Washington, DC: Brookings.

Goldgeier, James, Michael McFaul. 1999. Power and Purpose. US Policy Towards Russia After the Cold War. Washington, DC: Brookings.

Goldgeier, J., and P. Tetlock. 2001. "Psychology and International Relations Theory." *Annual Review of Political Science* 4: 67–92.

Gong, Sasha. 2009. "Those Uppity Peasant Workers: The End of the Era of Cheap Chinese Labor." *The International Economy*, Winter: 10–11, 83.

Goodman, Mel. 2008. *Failure of Intelligence: The Decline and Fall of the CIA*. New York: Rowman & Littlefield.

Gordon, Michael. 2018. "Trump Cites Kim Letter as Sign of Progress with North Korea." *The Wall Street Journal*. Online at https://www.wsj .com/articles/trump-cites-kim-letter-as-sign-of-progress-with-north-korea-1531420438 (accessed July 11, 2018).

Gott, Richard. 2011. *Hugo Chavez and the Bolivarian Revolution*. New York: Verso.

Gottlieb, Gidon. 1994. "Nations without States." *Foreign Affairs* 73(3) May/June.

Gowa, Joanne. 2000. *Ballots and Bullets: The Elusive Democratic Peace*. Princeton, NJ: Princeton University Press.

Graber, Doris. 2010. *Mass Media and American Politics*. 8th edition. Washington, DC: CQ Press.

Graber, Doris, and Johanna Dunaway. 2014. *Mass Media and American Politics*. 9th edition. Washington, DC: CQ Press.

Grandia, Lisa. 2012. *Enclosed: Conservation, Cattle, and Commerce among the Q'eqchi' Maya Lowlanders*. Seattle: University of Washington Press.

Gray, Colin. 1982. *Strategic Studies: A Critical Assessment*. Westport, CT: Greenwood Press.

Greenberg, Adam. 2015. "Akamai Warns of Increased Activity from DDoS Extortion Group. *SC Magazine*. Online at https://www.scmagazine.com/akamai-warns-of-increased-activity-from-ddos-extortion-group/article/533768/ (accessed January 9, 2019).

Greening, Thomas. 1986. "Passion Bearers and Peace Psychology." *Journal of Humanistic Psychology* 26(4): 98–105.

Greenpeace International. 2015. "About Greenpeace." Online at http://www.greenpeace.org/international/en/about (accessed June 17, 2015).

Greer, John Michael. 2005. *How Civilizations Fall: A Theory of Catabolic Collapse*. Online at http://ecoshock.org/transcripts/greer_on_collapse.pdf (accessed June 16, 2015).

Gregory, Derek. 2004. *The Colonial Present: Afghanistan, Palestine*. Malden, MA: Blackwell.

Griffith-Jones, Stephany. 2001. Governance of the World Bank. Paper. http://www.stephanygj.net/papers.html

Grimmett, Richard. 1999. "Foreign Policy Roles of the President and Congress." U.S. Department of State. June 1. Online at http://fpc.state.gov/6172.htm (accessed September 25, 2012).

Grossman, Elizabeth. 2007. *High Tech Trash: Digital Devices, Hidden Toxics, and Human Health*. Washington, DC: Island Press.

Grotius, Hugo. 2016. *On the Law of War and Peace*. Augsburg, Germany: Jazzybee Verlag.

Grotius, Hugo. 2005. *The Freedom of the Seas*. New York: Adamant Media Corporation.

Grover, Velma, ed. 2006. *Water: Global Common and Global Problems*. Enfield, NH: Science Publishers.

Gruber, Lloyd. 2000. *Ruling the World: Power Politics and the Rise of Supranational Institutions*. Princeton, NJ: Princeton University Press.

Guérot, Ulrike, and Mark Leonard. 2011. "The New German Question: How Europe Can Get the Germany It Needs." Online at http://www.ecfr.eu/page/-/ECFR30_GERMANY_AW.pdf (accessed August 1, 2015).

Gunaratna, Rohan. 2002. *Inside Al Qaeda: Global Network of Terror*. New York: Columbia University Press.

Guterres, Anthony. 2015. "Written Text of Speech to the UN Security Council." United Nations High Commissioner for Refugees. February 26. Online at http://www.unhcr.org/print/54ef66796.html (retrieved March 31, 2015).

Haaretz Service. 2010. "Germany's Deutsche Bank Divests from Israel Firm Linked to West Bank Separation Fence." May 30. Online at http://bit.ly/ccUg5s (accessed July 17, 2013).

Haas, Dieter. 2012. *Agricultural Policies in the EU and US: A Comparison of Policy Objectives and Their Realization*. Saarbrücken, Germany: AV Akademikerverlag.

Haas, Ernst B. 1958. *The Uniting of Europe: Political, Social, and Economic Forces, 1950–1957*. Stanford, CA: Stanford University Press.

Haas, Ernst B. 1964. *Beyond the Nation-State: Functionalism and International Organization*. Stanford, CA: Stanford University Press.

Haas, Richard. 2018. *A World in Disarray: American Foreign Policy and the Crisis of the Old Order*. New York: Penguin.

Hathaway, Oona, and Scott Shapiro. 2017. *The Internationalists: How a Radical Plan to Outlaw War Remade the World*. New York: Simon and Schuster

Haberman, Clyde. 1994. "West Bank Massacre: The Overview; Rabin Urges the Palestinians to Put Aside Anger and Talk." *The New York Times*, March 1. Online at http://nyti.ms/15RT6Qw (accessed July 19, 2013).

Haggard, Stephan, and Marcus Noland. 2009. *Famine in North Korea: Markets, Aid, and Reform.* New York: Columbia University Press.

Hahn, Gordon. 2012. "Global Jihadism Comes to Russia's North Caucasus." *Fair Observer,* July 12. Online at http://bit.ly/1LWJwRs (accessed August 1, 2015).

Hainmueller, Jens, and Michael Hiscox. 2007. "Educated Preferences: Explaining Individual Attitudes Toward Immigration in Europe." *International Organization* 61(2): 399–442.

Haltiwanger, John. 2018. "Do Americans Want War with North Korea? Majority of U.S. Public Is Against Military Interventions, Poll Says." *Newsweek,* January 9 , Online at http://www.newsweek.com/war-north-korea-military-interventions-poll-775636 (accessed January 9, 2019).

Hambler, Clive, and Susan Canney. 2013. *Conservation.* New York: Cambridge University Press.

Hamud, Randall, ed. 2005. *Osama Bin Laden: America's Enemy in His Own Words.* San Diego, CA: Nadeem Publishing.

Hanhimaaki, Jussi. 2013. *The Rise and Fall of Détente. American Foreign Policy and the Transformation of the Cold War.* Washington, DC: Potomac Books.

Hanson, Victor. 2001. *Carnage and Culture: Landmark Battles in the Rise of Western Power.* New York: Doubleday.

Hardin, Garrett. 1968. "The Tragedy of the Commons." *Science* 162(3859): 1243–1248.

Harris, Frances. 2004. *Global Environmental Issues.* West Sussex, UK: Wiley.

Harrison, Hope. 2000. "Driving the Soviets up the Wall: A Super-Ally, a Superpower, and the Building of the Berlin Wall, 1958–61." *Cold War History* 1(1): 53–74.

Harrison, Selig, and Clyde Prestowitz, Jr. 1990. "Pacific Agenda: Defense or Economics?" *Foreign Policy* 79(Summer): 60.

Hart, Paul. 1991. "Irving L. Janis' Victims of Group-Think: A Psychological Study of Foreign Policy Decisions and Fiascoes." *Political Psychology* 12(2): 247–278.

Hartman, Laura, and Patricia Werhane. 2009. *The Global Corporation: Sustainable, Effective and Ethical Practices, A Case Book.* New York: Routledge.

Hasegawa, Tsuyoshi. 2005. *Racing the Enemy. Stalin, Truman, and the Surrender of Japan.* Cambridge, MA: Harvard University Press.

Hashimoto, Akiko. 2015. *The Long Defeat: Cultural Trauma, Memory, and Identity in Japan.* New York: Oxford University Press.

Haslam, J. 1984. *The Soviet Union and the Struggle for Collective Security in Europe 1933–1939.* New York: Palgrave Macmillan.

Hayek, Friedrich von. 1944/2007. *The Road to Serfdom.* Chicago: University of Chicago Press.

Heider, Fritz. 1959. *The Psychology of Interpersonal Relations.* New York: Wiley.

Held, David. 2007. *Globalization/Anti-Globalization: Beyond the Great Divide.* Cambridge, UK: Polity.

Helm, Dieter, ed. 2005. *Climate Change Policy.* Oxford: Oxford University Press.

Hemmer, Christopher. 1999. "Historical Analogies and the Definition of Interests: The Iranian Hostage Crisis and Ronald Reagan's Policy toward the Hostages in Lebanon." *Political Psychology* 20(2) June: 267–289.

Henig, Ruth. 2010. *The League of Nations: The Makers of the Modern World.* London: Haus Publishing.

Herrmann, Richard K., and Richard Ned Lebow, eds. 2004. *Ending the Cold War: Interpretations, Causation, and the Study of International Relations.* New York: Palgrave Macmillan.

Herzog, Michael. 2006. "Can Hamas Be Tamed?" *Foreign Affairs* 85(2) March/April: 83–94.

Hilsman, Roger. 1959. "The Foreign-Policy Consensus: An Interim Research Report." *Journal of Conflict Resolution* 3(4): 361–382.

Hinckley, Ronald. 1992. *People, Polls, and Policymakers: American Public Opinion and National Security.* New York: Lexington Books.

Hindmoor, Andrew. 2006. *Rational Choice (Political Analysis).* New York: Palgrave Macmillan.

Hiro, Dilip. 2010. *After Empire: The Birth of a Multipolar World.* New York: Nation Books.

Hirschman, Nancy. 2010. "Choosing Betrayal." *Perspectives on Politics* 8(1) March: 271–278.

Hitchcock, William I. 2008. *The Bitter Road to Freedom. A New History of the Liberation of Europe.* New York: Free Press.

Hitchcock, William I. 2010. "The Marshall Plan and the Creation of the West." In *The Cambridge History of the Cold War*, vol. 1, *Origins*, eds. Melvyn P. Leffler and Odd Arne Westad, 154–174. London: Cambridge University Press.

Hobley, Marcus. 2012. "Public Opinion Can Play a Positive Role in Policy Making." *Guardian*, September 3. Online at http://www.theguardian.com/public-leaders-network/2012/sep/03/public-opinion-influence-policy (accessed June 19, 2015).

Hoekman, Bernard, and Michel Kostecki. 2010. *The Political Economy of the World Trading System.* New York: Oxford University Press.

Hoffman, Bruce. 1998. *Inside Terrorism.* New York: Columbia University Press.

Hoffman, David. 2010. *The Dead Hand: The Untold Story of the Cold War Arms Race and Its Dangerous Legacy.* New York: Anchor.

Hogan, Michael. 1987. *The Marshall Plan: America, Britain, and the Reconstruction of Western Europe, 1947–1952.* Cambridge: Cambridge University Press.

Holsti, Ole. 1992. "Public Opinion and Foreign Policy: Challenges to the Almond-Lippmann Consensus." *International Studies Quarterly* 36(4): 439–466.

Holsti, Ole. 2004. *Public Opinion and American Foreign Policy.* Revised edition. Ann Arbor: University of Michigan Press.

Holzgrefe, J. L., and Robert O. Keohane, eds. 2003. *Humanitarian Intervention: Ethical, Legal, and Political Dilemmas.* Cambridge: Cambridge University Press.

Homer-Dixon, Thomas. 1991. "On the Threshold: Environmental Changes As Causes of Acute Conflict." *International Security* 16(2): 76–116.

Hopewell, Kristen. 2017. *Breaking the WTO: How Emerging Powers Disrupted the Neoliberal Project.* Stanford, CA: Stanford University Press.

Hopkirk, Peter. 1994. *The Great Game: The Struggle for Empire in Central Asia.* New York: Kodansha International.

Horgan, John. 2009. *Walking Away from Terrorism: Accounts of Disengagement from Radical and Extremist Movements.* New York: Routledge.

Horgan, John. 2011. "Interviewing the Terrorists: Reflections on Fieldwork and Implications for Psychological Research." *Behavioral Science of Political Aggression and Terrorism* 4(3): 195–211.

Horgan, John. 2014. *The Psychology of Terrorism.* New York: Routledge.

Horowitz, Juliana. 2009. "Declining Support for bin Laden and Suicide Bombing." Pew Global Attitudes Project, September 10. Online at http://www.pewglobal.org/2009/09/10/rejection-of-extremism/ (accessed June 11, 2015).

Houghton, David. 2008. *Political Psychology: Situations, Individuals, and Cases.* New York: Routledge.

Howard, Russell, and James Forest, eds. 2008. *Weapons of Mass Destruction and Terrorism.* Dubuque, IA: McGraw-Hill.

Hudson, Valerie. 1999. "Cultural Expectations of One's Own and Other Nations' Foreign Policy Templates." *Political Psychology* 20(4): 767–801.

Hufbauer, Gary, and Barbara Oegg. 2003. "Beyond the Nation-State: Privatization of Economic Sanctions." *Middle East Policy* 10(2): 126–34.

Huggan, Graham. 2016. *The Oxford Handbook of Postcolonial Studies.* New York: Oxford University Press.

Hulme, David. 2015. *Global Poverty: Global Governance and Poor People in the Post-2015 Era.* New York: Routledge.

Human Rights Watch. 2015. "Chiba: Draft Counterterrorism Law, A Recipe for Abuses." Online at http://www.hrw.org/news/2015/01/20/china-draft-counterterrorism-law-recipe-abuses (accessed April 11, 2015).

Hunt, Swanee. 2007. "Let Women Rule." *Foreign Affairs* 86(3): 109–120.

Huntington, Samuel. 1993. "The Clash of Civilizations." *Foreign Affairs* 72(3): 22–28.

Husain, Irfan. 2011. *Fatal Faultlines: Pakistan, Islam and the West.* Rockville, MD: Arc Manor.

Husain, Mir Zohair. 2002. *Global Islamic Politics.* New York: Longman.

Husain, Mir Zohair. 2005. *Global Islamic Politics*. New York: Longman.

Huth, Paul, Sarah Croco, and Benjamin Appel. 2011. "Does International Law Promote the Peaceful Settlement of International Disputes? Evidence from the Study of Territorial Conflicts since 1945." *American Political Science Review* 105(2): 415–436.

ICAP. 2015. "Emissions Trading Worldwide." *ICAP Status Report*. Online at https://icapcarbonaction.com/images/StatusReport2015/ICAP_Report_2015_02_10_online_version.pdf (accessed January 9, 2019).

ICJ (International Court of Justice). 2004. *Legal Consequences of the Construction of a Wall in the Occupied Palestinian Territory*. General List No. 131, July 9.

Ignatieff, Michael. 2004. *The Lesser Evil: Political Ethics in an Age of Terrorism*. Princeton, NJ: Princeton University Press.

Ikenberry, G. John. 2010. "The Restructuring of the International System after the Cold War." *The Cambridge History of the Cold War*, Vol. 3, 513–534. Cambridge: Cambridge University Press.

Ikenberry, G. John. 2011a. "The Future of the Liberal World Order." *Foreign Affairs* 90(3) May/June: 56–68.

Ikenberry, G. John. 2011b. *Liberal Leviathan: The Origins, Crisis, and Transformation of the American World Order*. Princeton, NJ: Princeton University Press.

Ikenberry, G. John. 2014. "The Illusion of Geopolitics: The Enduring Power of the Liberal Order." *Foreign Affairs* 93(3) May/June: 80–90.

Ikenberry, G. John, and Joseph M. Grieco. 2002. *State Power and World Markets: The International Political Economy*. New York: W. W. Norton.

Immelman, Aubrey. 2017. "The Leadership Style of U.S. President Donald J. Trump." *Psychology Faculty Publications*. College of Saint Benedict and Saint John University. Online at http://bit.ly/2sV0dfs (accessed March 1, 2018).

"International Health Regulations: The Challenges Ahead (Editorial)." 2007. *The Lancet* 369 (9575) May 26: 1763.

IPU: "Inter-Parliamentary Union." 2018. Online at http:// www.ipu.org/wmn-e/classif.htm (accessed February 24, 2018).

Iriye, Akira. 2002. *Global Community: The Role of International Organizations in the Making of the Contemporary World*. Berkeley: University of California Press.

Ismay, Hastings Lionel. 1960. *The Memoirs of General Lord Ismay*. New York: Viking Adult.

Israel High Court Ruling. 2005. Docket H.C.J. 7957/04 International Legality of the Security Fence and Sections near Alfei Menashe. September 15, 2005. Online at http://www.zionism-israel.com/hdoc/High_Court_Fence.htm (accessed January 9, 2019).

Jackson, Robert. 2005. *Classical and Modern Thought on International Relations: From Anarchy to Cosmopolism* (Palgrave Macmillan History of International Thought). New York: Palgrave Macmillan.

Jacques, Peter. 2009. *Environmental Skepticism* (*Global Environmental Governance*). London: Ashgate.

Janis, Irving, and L. Leon Mann. 1977. *Decision-Making: A Psychological Analysis of Conflict, Choice, and Commitment*. New York: Free Press.

Jarausch, Konrad. 2008. *After Hitler: Recivilizing Germans, 1945–1995*. New York: Oxford University Press.

Jenkins, Willis. 2008. *Ecologies of Grace: Environmental Ethics and Christian Theology*. New York: Oxford University Press.

Jervis, Robert. 1976. *Perceptions and Misperceptions in International Politics*. Princeton, NJ: Princeton University Press.

Jervis, Robert. 1982. "Security Regimes." *International Organization* 36(2): 357–378.

Jervis, Robert. 2002. "Theories of War in an Era of Leading-Power Peace." *American Political Science Review* 96(1): 1–14.

Jervis, Robert. 2003. "The Compulsive Empire." *Foreign Policy* 137: 82–87.

Jisheng, Yang. 2013. *Tombstone: The Great Chinese Famine, 1958–1962*. New York: Farrar, Straus and Giroux

Joffe, Josef. 2009. "The Default Power: The False Prophecy of America's Decline." *Foreign Affairs* 87(5) September/October: 21–35.

Joffe, Josef. 2013. *The Myth of America's Decline: Politics, Economics, and a Half Century of False Prophecies*. New York: Liveright.

Johnson, Pierre M., Karel Mayrand, and Marc Paquin, eds. 2006. *Governing Global Desertification: Linking Environmental Degradation, Poverty, and Participation*. London: Ashgate.

Jones, Jeffrey. 2011. "Americans Increasingly Prioritize Economy over Environment." March 171. Online at http://www.gallup.com/poll/146681/Americans-Increasingly-Prioritize-Economy-Environment.aspx (accessed June 16, 2015).

Jonsson, Christer, and Richard Langhorne. 2004. *Diplomacy*. Thousand Oak, CA: Sage.

Jordan, Darla. 2005. "Spokeswoman of the U.S. State Department." Comments on the U.S. Withdrawal from the International Court of Justice. March 10. AFP.

Jost, John, and Jim Sidanius. 2004. *Political Psychology: Key Readings*. New York: Psychology Press.

Juhasz, Antonina. 2011. *Black Tide: The Devastating Impact of the Gulf Oil Spill*. New York: Wiley.

Kagan, Robert. 2003. *Of Paradise and Power: America and Europe in the New World Order*. New York: Knopf.

Kagan, Robert. 2004a. "America's Crisis of Legitimacy." *Foreign Affairs* 83(2): 65–87.

Kagan, Robert. 2004b. *Of Paradise and Power: America and Europe in the New World Order*. New York: Vintage.

Kagan, Robert. 2012. *The World America Made*. New York: Vintage.

Kahler, Miles, and David Lake, eds. 2003. *Governance in a Global Economy: Political Authority in Transition*. Princeton, NJ: Princeton University Press.

Kahnemen, Daniel, and Jonathan Renshon. 2007. "Why Hawks Win." *Foreign Policy* 158: 34–38.

Kahneman, Daniel, and Amos Tversky. 1972. "Subjective Probability: A Judgment of Representativeness." *Cognitive Psychology* 3: 430–454.

Kahneman, Daniel, and Amos Tversky. 1979. "Prospect Theory: An Analysis of Decisions under Risk." *Econometrica* 47(2): 263–292.

Kalinovsky, Artemy. 2011. A Long Goodbye. The Soviet Withdrawal from Afghanistan. Cambridge, Mass.: Harvard University Press.

Kalyvas, Stathis, and Laia Balcellis. 2010. "International System and Technologies of Rebellion: How the End of the Cold War Shaped Internal Conflict." *American Political Science Review* 104(3): 415–429.

Kamieniecki, Sheldon, and Michael Kraft, eds. 2007. *Business and Environmental Policy: Corporate Interests in the American Political System* (American and Comparative Environmental Policy). Cambridge, MA: MIT Press.

Kane, Thomas. 2006. *Theoretical Roots of U.S. Foreign Policy: Machiavelli and American Unilateralism*. New York: Routledge.

Kant, Immanuel. 1795/2003. *To Perpetual Peace: A Philosophical Sketch*. Indianapolis, IN: Hackett Publishing.

Kaplan, Jeffrey. 2012. *Terrorist Groups and the New Tribalism: Terrorism's Fifth Wave*. New York: Routledge.

Kaplan, Robert. 2012. *The Revenge of Geography: What the Map Tells Us About Coming Conflicts and the Battle Against Fate*. New York: Random House.

Kara, Siddharth. 2017. *Modern Slavery: A Global Perspective*. New York: Columbia University Press.

Karesh, William, and Robert Cook. 2005. "The Human Animal Link." *Foreign Affairs* 84(4) July–August.

Kaufman, Stuart, Richard Little, and William Wohlforth, eds. 2007. *Balance of Power in World History*. New York: Palgrave Macmillan.

Kavaloski, Vincent C. 1990. "Transnational Citizen Peacemaking as Nonviolent Action." *Peace and Change* 15(2) April: 173–194.

Keck, Margaret, and Kathryn Sikkink, eds. 1998. *Activists Beyond Borders: Advocacy Networks in International Politics*. Ithaca, NY: Cornell University Press.

Kello, Lucas. 2013. "The Meaning of the Cyber Revolution." *International Security* 38(2): 7–40.

Kelly, John. 1996. "Chapter 6: Lebanon: 1982–1984." In *U.S. and Russian Policymaking with Respect* to the Use of Force, eds. Jeremy Azrael and Emil Payin. Conference Proceedings. Rand Corporation. Online at http://bit.ly/16P1Fc6 (accessed July 18, 2013).

Kemp, William. 2006. *The Renewable Energy Handbook: A Guide to Rural Energy Independence, Off-Grid and Sustainable Living.* Tamworth, Canada: Aztext Press.

Kennedy, Paul. 1987. *The Rise of the Anglo-German Antagonism, 1860–1914.* St. Anthony, ID Humanity Books.

Kennedy, Paul. 2017. *The Rise and Fall of the Great Powers: Economic Change and Military Conflict from 1500-2000.* London: William Collins.

Kent, John. 2005. "British Policy and the Origins of the Cold War." In *Origins of the Cold War: An International History*, 2nd edition, eds. Melvyn P. Leffler and David S. Painter, 155–167. New York: Routledge.

Keohane, Robert. 1989. *International Institutions and State Power.* London: Westview Press.

Keohane, Robert. 2003. "Political Authority after Intervention: Gradation in Sovereignty." In *Humanitarian Intervention: Ethical, Legal, and Political Dilemmas*, eds. J. L. Holzgrefe and Robert Keohane, 275–298. New York: Cambridge University Press.

Keohane, Robert. 2005. "From International to World Politics." *Perspectives on Politics* 3(2): 316–317.

Keohane, Robert, and Lisa Martin. 1995. "The Promise of Institutionalist Theory." *International Security* 20(1): 39–52.

Keohane, Robert, and Joseph Nye. 1989. *Power and Interdependence.* 2nd edition. New York: HarperCollins.

Kershaw, Ian. 2000. *The Nazi Dictatorship: Problems and Perspectives of Interpretation.* New York: Bloomsbury.

Keynes, John M. 1936/1965. *The General Theory of Employment, Interest and Money.* New York: Harcourt, Brace & World.

Khlevniuk, Oleg. 2008. *Master of the House: Stalin and His Inner Circle.* New Haven, CT: Yale University Press.

Khong, Yuen Foong. 1992. *Analogies at War: Korea, Munich, Dien Bien Phu, and the Vietnam Decisions of 1965.* Princeton, NJ: Princeton University Press.

Kiely, Eugene. 2018. "Manufacturing Jobs 'Roaring Back'?" January 10. *FactCheck.org* Online at https://www.factcheck.org/2018/01/manufacturing-jobs-roaring-back (accessed January 9, 2019).

Kiley, Jocelyn. 2017. "In Polarized Era, Fewer Americans Hold a Mix of Conservative and Liberal Views." Pew Research Center. Online at http://www.pewresearch.org/fact-tank/2017/10/23/in-polarized-era-fewer-americans-hold-a-mix-of-conservative-and-liberal-views (accessed January 9, 2019).

Kimball, Warren. 1997. *Forged by War. Roosevelt, Churchill, and the Second World War.* New York: William Morrow.

Kindleberger, Charles. 1973. *The World in Depression: 1929–1939.* Berkeley: University of California Press.

Kirkpatrick, Jeane. 2002. "Convention on the Elimination of All Forms of Discrimination against Women." Testimony before the Senate Foreign Relations Committee, Washington, DC. June 13.

Kissinger, Henry. 2001. "The Pitfalls of Global Jurisdiction." *Foreign Affairs* 80(4) July/August: 86–96.

Klein, Aaron J. 2005. *Striking Back: The 1972 Munich Olympics Massacre and Israel's Deadly Response.* New York: Random House.

Koseki, Shoichi. 1998. *The Birth of Japan's Postwar Constitution.* Translated by Ray Moore. Boulder, CO: Westview Press.

Kosterman, Rick, and Seymour Feshbach. 1989. "Toward a Measure of Patriotic and Nationalistic Attitudes." *Political Psychology* 10(2): 257–274.

Kotkin, Stephen. 2014. *Stalin.* New York: Penguin.

Kowert, P. 1996. "Where *Does* the Buck Stop?: Assessing the Impact of Presidential Personality." *Political Psychology* 17(3): 421–452.

Krauthammer, Charles. 2008. "Crooked Roads to Democracy." *The Washington Post*, January 4, A21.

Krueger, Alan. 2007. *What Makes a Terrorist: Economics and the Roots of Terrorism.* Princeton, NJ: Princeton University Press.

Krugman, Paul. 2009. "Chinese New Year." *The New York Times*, December 31.

Kuehnast, Kathleen, Chantal de Jonge Oudraat, and Helga Hernes, eds. 2011. *Women and War: Power and Protection in the 21st Century*. Washington, DC: United States Institute of Peace Press.

Kurtz, Howard. 2018. *Media Madness: Donald Trump, the Press, and the War over the Truth*. New York: Regnery Publishing.

Kydd, Andrew. 2005. *Trust and Mistrust in International Relations*. Princeton, NJ: Princeton University Press.

Kydd, Andrew, and Barbara Walter. 2006. "The Strategies of Terrorism." *International Security* 31(1): 49–80.

Lakoff, Andrew. 2010. "Two Regimes of Global Health." *Humanity* 1(1): 59–79.

Larson, Deborah. 1985. *Origins of Containment*. Princeton, NJ: Princeton University Press.

Larson, Deborah. 1997. *Anatomy of Mistrust: U.S.-Soviet Relations During the Cold War*. Ithaca, NY: Cornell University Press.

Lauterpacht, Hersch. 1933/2011. *The Function of Law in the International Community*. New York: Oxford University Press.

Laver, Michael. 1979. *Playing Politics*. London: Penguin.

Laver, Michael. 1997. *Playing Politics: The Nightmare Continues*. New York: Oxford University Press.

Layne, Christopher. 1994. "Kant or Cant: The Myth of the Democratic Peace." *International Security* 19(2): 5–49.

Le Billon, Philippe. 2006. *Fuelling War: Natural Resources and Armed Conflicts*. New York: Routledge.

Leatherman, Janie. 2011. *Sexual Violence and Armed Conflict*. Cambridge, UK: Polity.

Leffler, Melvyn. 2007. *For the Soul of Mankind: The United States, the Soviet Union, and the Cold War*. New York: Farrar, Straus and Giroux.

Lenin, Vladimir. 1916/1996. *Imperialism as the Highest Stage of Capitalism*. New York: Pluto Press.

Levada Center. 2013. Online at http://bit.ly/19M6xlO (accessed August 1, 2015).

Levada Center. 2015. Various polls referring to the United States. Online at http://www.levada.ru (accessed January 9, 2019).

Levada Center. 2017. Various polls referring to foreign threats. Online at: https://www.levada.ru/2017/06/05/vrag-nomer-dva (accessed January 9, 2019).

Lévesque, Jacques. 1997. *The Enigma of 1989: The USSR and the Liberation of Eastern Europe*. Berkeley: University of California Press.

Levey, David, and Stuart Brown. 2005. "The Overstretch Myth." *Foreign Affairs* 84(2) March/April: 2–7.

Levi, Michael. 2009. *On Nuclear Terrorism*. Cambridge, MA: Harvard University Press.

Levi, Michael. 2010a. "Beyond Copenhagen." *Foreign Affairs*. Postscript. February.

Levi, Michael. 2010b. "Reinforcing Climate Promises in Cancun. An Interview." Council on Foreign Relations. November 24. Online at http://www.cfr.org/publication/ 23453/reinforcing_climate_promises_in_cancun.html?cid=rss-analysis-briefbackgrounder sexp-reinforcing_climate_promises_i-112410 (accessed September 25, 2012).

Levi, Michael. 2013. *The Power Surge: Energy, Opportunity, and the Battle for America's Future*. New York: Oxford University Press.

Levi, Michael. 2014. "The Obama-China Climate Deal Can't Save the World. So What?" *Council of Foreign Relations*, November 21. Online at http://www.cfr.org/environmental-policy/obama-china-climate-deal-cant-save-world-so-/p33831 (accessed March 29, 2015).

Levi, Michael, Elizabeth Economy, Shannon O'Neil, and Adam Segal. 2010. "Globalizing the Energy Revolution." *Foreign Affairs* 89(6) November/ December: 111–121.

Levitsky, Steven, and Lucan Way. 2010. *Competitive Authoritarianism: Hybrid Regimes After the Cold War*. New York: Cambridge University Press.

Levy, David. 2009. *Tools of Critical Thinking: Meta-Thoughts for Psychology*. Long Grove, IL: Waveland Press.

Levy, Jack. 1984. "The Offensive/Defensive Balance of Military Technology: A Theoretical and Historical Analysis." *International Studies Quarterly* 28(2) June: 219–238.

Liberman, Peter. 2006. "An Eye for an Eye: Public Support for War against Evildoers." *International Organization* 60(3) July: 687–722.

Lieven, Anatol, and John Hulsman. 2006. *Ethical Realism: A Vision for America's Role in the World.* New York: Pantheon.

Lindkvist, Sven. 2007. *Terra Nullius: A Journey Through No One's Land.* New York: New Press.

Linklater, Andrew. 2009. "The English School." In *Theories of International Relations*, eds. Scott Burchill, Andrew Linklater, Richard Devetak, Jack Donnelly, Matthew Patterson, and Christian Reus-Smit, 86–110. New York: Palgrave Macmillan.

List, Friedrich. 1841/2006. *National System of Political Economy. Volume 1: The History.* New York: Cosimo Classics. Originally published in 1841.

Logevall, Frederik. 2014. *The Embers of War: The Fall of an Empire and the Making of America's Vietnam.* New York: Presidio.

Lomborg, Bjørn, ed. 2004. *Global Crises, Global Solutions.* Cambridge: Cambridge University Press.

Lomborg, Bjørn. 2007. *Cool It: The Skeptical Environmentalist's Guide to Global Warming.* New York: Knopf.

Lomborg, Bjørn. 2010. "An Interview." *Financial Times*, December 9. Online at http://www.lomborg.com/news/financial-times-europe-needs-real-vision-on-climate (accessed August 1, 2015).

Lomborg, Bjørn. 2010a. *Smart Solutions to Climate Change, Comparing Costs and Benefits.* New York: Cambridge University Press.

Lomborg, Bjørn, ed. 2018. *Prioritizing Development: A Cost Benefit Analysis of the United Nations' Sustainable Development Goals.* New York: Cambridge University Press.

Lovelock, James. 2015. *A Rough Ride to the Future.* New York: Overlook Books.

Loyola, Mario. 2010. "Legality over Legitimacy." *Foreign Affairs* 89(4) July–August. Online at http://fam.ag/13TtFQO (accessed July 18, 2013).

Luck, Edward. 2010. "The Responsibility to Protect: Growing Pains or Early Promise?" *Ethics and International Affairs* 24(4): 349–365.

Lukes, Igor, and Erik Goldstein, eds. 1999. *The Munich Crisis, 1938.* New York: Routledge.

Lundestad, Geir. 1986. "Empire by Invitation? The United States and Western Europe, 1945–1952." *Journal of Peace Research* 23(3) September: 263–277.

Lundestad, Geir. 2012. *The Rise and Decline of the American "Empire": Power and Its Limits in Comparative Perspective.* New York: Oxford University Press.

Lüthi, Lorenz. 2008. *The Sino-Soviet Split: Cold War in the Communist World.* Princeton, NJ: Princeton University Press.

Lynn, William J. 2010. "Defending a New Domain. The Pentagon's Cyberstrategy." *Foreign Affairs* 89(5) September/October: 97–108.

MacMillan, Margaret. 2003. *Paris 1919: Six Months That Changed the World.* New York: Random House.

MacMillan, Margaret. 2013. *The War That Ended Peace: The Road to 1914.* New York: Random House.

MacNair, Rachel. 2003. *The Psychology of Peace: An Introduction.* Santa Barbara, CA: Praeger.

Maddox, Bronwen. 2001. "Japan Dips Toe in Military Waters." *Times* (London), November 29: News 1.

Madeley, John. 2009. *Big Business, Poor Peoples: How Transnational Corporations Damage the Global Poor.* London: Zed Books.

Madigan, Janet. 2007. *Truth, Politics, and Universal Human Rights.* New York: Palgrave Macmillan.

Magdoff, Fred, and John B. Foster. 2011. *What Every Environmentalist Needs to Know about Capitalism.* New York: Monthly Review Press.

Magri, Paolo, and Annalisa Perteghnella, eds. 2015. *Iran after the Deal: The Road Ahead.* Milan, Italy: Milan Institute for International Studies.

Mahbubani, Kishore. 2002. *Can Asians Think? Understanding the Divide Between East and West.* South Royalton, VT: Steerforth.

Mahler, Gregory. 2004. *Politics and Government in Israel: The Maturation of a Modern State.* Lanham, MD: Rowman & Littlefield.

Maier, Charles. 1997. *Dissolution: The Crisis of Communism and the End of East Germany.* Princeton, NJ: Princeton University Press.

Mak, Geert. 2008. *In Europe: Travels Through the Twentieth Century*. New York: Vintage.

Malcolm, Andrew. 2010. "War Is Hell on Presidents' Approval Rating." *The Los Angeles Times*, September 4. Online at http://articles.latimes.com/2010/sep/04/nation/la-na-ticket-20100905 (accessed January 9, 2019).

Malloy, Michael, ed. 2015. *Economic Sanctions*. Cheltenham, UK: Elgar Research Collection.

Manela, Erez. 2009. *The Wilsonian Moment: Self-Determination and the International Origins of Anticolonial Nationalism*. New York: Oxford University Press.

Mansfield, Edward D., and Jack Snyder. 2007. *Electing to Fight: Why Emerging Democracies Go to War*. Cambridge, MA: MIT Press.

Maoz, Zeev, and Bruce Russett. 1993. "Normative and Structural Causes of Democratic Peace, 1946–1986." *American Political Science Review* 87(3): 624–638.

Marrar, Khalil. 2008. *The Arab Lobby and U.S. Foreign Policy*. New York: Routledge.

Marsh, Peter. 2012. *The New Industrial Revolution: Consumers, Globalization, and the End of the Mass Production*. New Haven, CT: Yale University Press.

Martin, Terry. 2001. *The Affirmative Action Empire: Nations and Nationalism in the Soviet Union, 1923–1939*. Ithaca, NY: Cornell University Press.

Marx, Karl, and Friedrich Engels. 1848/2011. *The Communist Manifesto*. SoHo Books.

Mastny, Vojtech. 1979. *The Cold War and Soviet Insecurity*. New York: Oxford University Press.

Matlock, Jack. 2004. *Reagan and Gorbachev. How the Cold War Ended*. New York: Random House.

Matthews, Jessica. 1997. "Power Shift." *Foreign Affairs* 76(1): 50–66.

Mazower, Mark. 2000. *Dark Continent: Europe's Twentieth Century*. New York: Vintage.

Mazower, Mark. 2008. *Hitler's Empire. How the Nazis Ruled Europe*. New York: Penguin.

McBee, Thomas P. 2018. *Amateur: A True Story about What Makes a Man*. New York: Scribner.

McCallum, M. L., and G. W. Bury. 2013. "Google Search Patterns Suggest Declining Interest in the Environment." *Biodiversity and Conservation*. Published online March 30. Online at http://link.springer.com/article/10.1007%2Fs10531-013-0476-6#page-1 (accessed March 30, 2015).

McCarthy, Michael. 2011. "Global Warning: Climate Sceptics Are Winning the Battle." *The Independent*, October 11. Online at http://ind.pn/oakpOW (accessed July 18, 2013).

McDonald, Bryan. 2011. *Food Security*. Cambridge, UK: Polity.

McFarlane, Robert. 1998. "An Interview." In *Cold War: The Complete Series*. Episode: Star Wars. Warner Home Video, 2012.

McFaul, Michael. 2009. *Advancing Democracy Abroad: Why We Should and How We Can*. New York: Rowman & Littlefield.

McGovern, Joe. 2006. *The Kyoto Protocol*. Pittsburgh, PA: Dorrance Publishing Co.

McKinnon, Ron. 2010. "A Reply to Krugman." *International Economy*, Winter.

McNamara, Robert. 1996. *In Retrospect: The Tragedy and Lessons of Vietnam*. New York: Vintage.

McNeill, William. 1994. Introductory Historical Commentary. In *The Fall of Great Powers. Peace, Stability, and Legitimacy*, ed. Geir Lundestad, 3–22.. London. Oxford University Press.

McSweeney, Kelly. 2017. *UN to Host Discussion about AI in Warfare*. ZDNet. Online at http://www.zdnet.com/article/un-to-host-discussion-about-ai-in-warfare (accessed January 9, 2019).

Mead, Walter R. 2018. "Environmentalists Need to Get Real." *The Wall Street Journal*, September 4, A15.

Mearsheimer, John. 1990. "Why We Will Soon Miss the Cold War." *The Atlantic Monthly* 266 (2) August: 35–50.

Mearsheimer, John. 1994-95. The False Promise of International Institutions. *International Security* 19 (3), 5–49

Mearsheimer, John. 2003. *The Tragedy of Great Power Politics*. New York: W. W. Norton.

Mearsheimer, John J. 2014. "Why the Ukraine Crisis Is the West's Fault: The Liberal Delusions That Provoked Putin." *Foreign Affairs* 93(5) September/October: 77–89.

Mearsheimer, John, and Stephen Walt. 2007. *The Israel Lobby and U.S. Foreign Policy*. New York: Farrar, Straus and Giroux.

Meyer, William. 2016. *The Progressive Environmental Prometheans: Left-Wing Heralds of a "Good Anthropocene."*.New York: Palgrave Macmillan.

Meyerson, Harold. 2010. "Time to Stand Up to China on Trade." *The Washington Post*, September 15, 23.

Miéville, China. 2006. *Between Equal Rights: A Marxist Theory of International Law*. Chicago: Haymarket Books.

Milani, Abbas. 2011. *The Shakh*. New York: Palgrave.

Milgram, Stanley. 1963. "Behavioral Study of Obedience." *Journal of Abnormal and Social Psychology* 67(4): 371–378.

Miller, Martin. 2013. *The Foundations of Modern Terrorism: State, Society and the Dynamics of Political Violence*. New York: Cambridge University Press.

Mishra, Pankaj. 2018. "The Rise of China and the Fall of the 'Free Trade' Myth." *The New York Times Magazine*. Online at https://www.nytimes.com/2018/02/07/magazine/the-rise-of-china-and-the-fall-of-the-free-trade-myth.html (accessed January 9, 2019).

Mitzen, Jennifer. 2005. "Reading Habermas in Anarchy: Multilateral Diplomacy and Global Public Spheres." *American Political Science Review* 99(3): 401–417.

Mohamoud, Abdullah. 2006. *State Collapse and Post-Conflict Development in Africa: The Case of Somalia 1960–2001*. West Lafayette, IN: Purdue University Press.

Monroe, James. 1823/2015. "Seventh Annual Message to Congress, December 2." Online at http://miller center.org/president/ speeches/detail/3604 (accessed June 15, 2015).

Moore, Scott. 2014. "Pollution Without Revolution." *Foreign Affairs* June 10. Online at http://www.foreignaffairs.com/articles/141559/scott-m-moore/pollution-without-revolution (accessed March 29, 2015).

Moravcsik, Andrew. 1997. "Taking Preferences Seriously: A Liberal Theory of International Relations." *International Organization* 51(4): 513–553.

Moravcsik, Andrew. 2001. "Why Is the U.S. Human Rights Policy So Unilateralist?" In *Multilateralism and U.S. Foreign Policy*, eds. Stewart Patrick and Shepard Forman. Boulder, CO: Lynne Rienner.

Morgenthau, Hans J. 1948/2006. *Politics among Nations: The Struggle for Power and Peace*. 7th edition, revised by Kenneth W. Thompson and W. David Clinton. New York: McGraw-Hill.

Morgenthau, Hans. 1978. *Politics among Nations: The Struggle for Power and Peace*, 5th edition, Revised. New York: Alfred A. Knopf.

Morris, Ian. 2010. *Why the West Rules—For Now: The Patterns of History and What They Reveal about the Future*. New York: Farrar, Straus and Giroux.

Morrison, S. 2017. *America Betrayed: Globalist Elites Destroyed the Economy: Here's How We Fix It*. Independently Published.

Moyne, Samuel. 2011. *The Last Utopia. Human Rights in History*. Cambridge, MA: Harvard University Press.

Moyo, Dambisa. 2010. *Dead Aid: Why Aid is Not Working and How There Is a Better Way for Africa*. Vancouver, BC: Douglas & McIntyre Ltd.

Moyo, Dambisa. 2018. *Edge of Chaos: Why Democracy Is Failing to Deliver Economic Growth and How to Fix It*. New York: Basic Books.

Mral, Bridgitte, Majid Krosravnik, and Ruth Wodak, eds. 2013. *Right-Wing Populism in Europe: Politics and Discourse*. New York: Bloomsbury Academic.

Mueller, John. 1989. *Retreat from Doomsday: The Obsolescence of Major War*. New York: Basic Books.

Muller, Jerry. 2008. "Us and Them: The Enduring Power of Ethnic Nationalism." *Foreign Affairs* 87(22) March/April: 18–35.

Munz, Rainer. 2003. *Diasporas and Ethnic Migrants: Germany, Israel and Russia in Comparative Perspective*. London: Routledge.

Murray, Henry. 1943. "Analysis of the Personality of Adolf Hitler: With Predictions of His Future Behavior and Suggestions for Dealing with Him Now and After Germany's Surrender." October. Cornell University Law Library.

Online at http://library2.lawschool.cornell.edu/donovan/pdf/Batch_15/Vol_XC.pdf (accessed August 1, 2015).

Murray, Iain. 2008. *The Really Inconvenient Truths: Seven Environmental Catastrophes Liberals Don't Want You to Know About—Because They Helped Cause Them.* Washington, DC: Regnery Publishing.

Myers-Lipton, Scott. 2015. *Ending Extreme Inequality: An Economic Bill of Rights to Eliminate Poverty.* Boulder, CO: Paradigm Publishers.

Nacos, Brigitte. 2009. *Terrorism and Counterterrorism. Understanding Threats and Responses in the Post–9/11 World.* 3rd edition. New York: Longman.

Nacos, Brigitte, Robert Shapiro, and Pierangelo Isernia, eds. 2000. *Decision-Making in the Glass House.* Boulder, CO: Rowman & Littlefield.

NAF (New America Foundation). 2019. "Drone Strikes: Yemen". Online at: https://www.newamerica.org/in-depth/americas-counterterrorism-wars/us-targeted-killing-program-yemen (accessed March 22, 2019).

NAF (New America Foundation). 2012. "The Year of the Drone. An Analysis of U.S. Drone Strikes in Pakistan, 2004–2012." Online at http://counter-terrorism.newamerica.net/drones (accessed August 8, 2012).

Naim, Moises and Francisco Toro. 2018. Venezuela's Suicide. Lessons from a Failed State. *Foreign Affairs.* November-December.

Naimark, Norman. 1996. *Russians in Germany: A History of the Soviet Zone of Occupation, 1945-1949.* Cambridge, Mass.: Harvard University Press.

Naimark, Norman. 2002. *Fires of Hatred: Ethnic Cleansing in Twentieth Century Europe.* Cambridge, MA: Harvard University Press.

Naimark, Norman. 2010. "The Sovietization of Eastern Europe, 1944–1953." In *The Cambridge History of the Cold War*, eds. Melvyn P. Leffler and Odd Arne Westad, Vol. 1, 175–197. Cambridge: Cambridge University Press.

Narizny, Kevin. 2003. "Both Guns and Butter, or Neither: Class Interests in the Political Economy of Rearmament." *American Political Science Review* 97(2): 203–220.

Narlikar, Amrita. 2005. *WTO: A Very Short Introduction.* New York: Oxford University Press.

NASA. 2018. "Scientific Consensus: Earth's Climate Is Warming." Online at *https://climate.nasa.gov/scientific-consensus* (accessed January 9, 2019).

National Commission on Terrorist Acts upon the United States. 9-11 Commission Report. November 27, 2002. Online at http://www.9-11commission.gov/report/index.htm (accessed September 25, 2012).

National Security Strategy. 2017. "A New National Security Strategy for a New Era." Online at https://www.whitehouse.gov/articles/new-national-security-strategy-new-era (accessed January 9, 2019).

Nau, Henry. 2002. *At Home Abroad: Identity and Power in American Foreign Policy.* Ithaca, NY: Cornell University Press.

Nebehay, Stephanie. 2018. "Thousands of Women, Men, Children Raped in Syria's War: U.N. Report." *Reuters,* March 15. Online at https://www.reuters.com/article/us-mideast-crisis-syria-warcrimes-sexual/thousands-of-women-men-children-raped-in-syrias-war-u-n-report-idUSKCN1GR1PZ (accessed January 9, 2019).

Nelson, Anna Kasten. 1992. "Review of the American 'Empire': And Other Studies of U.S. Foreign Policy in a Comparative Perspective by Geir Lundestad." *American Historical Review* 97(2): 641–642.

Neumann, Iver. 1996. *Russia and the Idea of Europe: A Study in Identity and International Relations.* London: Routledge.

Newman, Edward, Ramesh Thakur, and John Tirman. 2006. *Multilateralism under Challenge?: Power, International Order, and Structural Change.* Tokyo: United Nations University Press.

Nonini, Donald, ed. 2007. *The Global Idea of "The Commons."* New York: Berghahn Books.

Nordhaus, Richard. 2008. *A Question of Balance: Weighing the Options on Global Warming Policies.* New Haven, CT: Yale University Press.

Nye, Joseph. 1990. *Bound to Lead: The Changing Nature of American Power.* New York: Basic Books.

Nye, Joseph. 2002. *The Paradox of American Power: Why the World's Only Superpower Can't Go It Alone.* Oxford: Oxford University Press.

Nye, Joseph. 2004. *Soft Power: The Means to Success in World Politics.* New York: Public Affairs.

Nye, Joseph. 2011. *The Future of Power.* New York: Public Affairs.

O'Brien, Patrick Karl, and Armand Clesse, eds. 2002. *Two Hegemonies: Britain 1846–1914 and the United States 1941–2001.* Aldershot, UK: Ashgate.

O'Sullivan, Aisling. 2017. *Universal Jurisdiction in International Criminal Law: The Debate and the Battle for Hegemony.* New York: Routledge.

Olson, Mancur. 1971. *The Logic of Collective Action: Public Goods and the Theory of Groups.* Cambridge, MA: Harvard University Press.

Oneal, John R., and Bruce M. Russett. 1997. "Classical Liberals Were Right: Democracy, Interdependence, and Conflict, 1950–1985." *International Studies Quarterly* 42(2) June: 264–294.

Open Letter. 2015. *Autonomous Weapons: an Open Letter from AI & Robotics Researchers.* The Future of Life Institute. Online at https://futureoflife. org/open-letter-autonomous-weapons (accessed January 9, 2019).

Oppenheim, Lassa. 2008. *Oppenheim's International Law.* 9th edition. Eds. Robert Jennings and Arthur Watts. New York: Oxford University Press.

Orbinski, James. 2009. *An Imperfect Offering: Humanitarian Action for the Twenty-First Century.* New York: Walker & Company.

Organski, A. F. K. 1968. *World Politics.* New York: A. Knopf. Originally published 1958.

Osnos, Evan. 2014. "The Biden Agenda." *The New Yorker*, July 28. Online at http://www .newyorker.com/magazine/2014/07/28/biden-agenda (accessed August 1, 2015).

Owen, John M. 2005. "Iraq and the Democratic Peace." *Foreign Affairs* 84(6) November/December.

Page, Benjamin, and Robert Shapiro. 1988. "Foreign Policy and the Rational Public." *Journal of Conflict Resolution* 32: 211–247.

Pai, Tsiao-Hung. 2018. *Bordered Lives: How Europe Fails Refugees and Migrants.* Oxford: New Internationalist.

Pant, Harsh. 2011. "China and Pakistan: A New Balance of Power in South Asia." *ISN: International Relations and Security Network.* June 20. Online at http://bit.ly/1VTGzpE (accessed August 1, 2015).

Pape, Robert. 2003. "The Strategic Logic of Suicide Terrorism." *American Political Science Review* 97(3): 343–361.

Park, Mi. 2018. *The IMF and WTO. How Does Geopolitics Influence Global Finance and International Trade?* Vancouver, Canada: Coal Harbour Publishing.

Parker, Kathleen. 2010. "Obama, Our First Female President." *The Washington Post*, June 30. Online at http://wapo.st/cHTwjC (accessed July 15, 2013).

Parmesan, Camille, and Gary Yohe. 2003. "A Globally Coherent Fingerprint of Climate Change Impacts across Natural Systems." *Nature* 421: 37–42.

Patterson, Amy. 2006. *The Politics of AIDS in Africa.* Boulder, CO: Lynne Rienner.

Payne, Ruby. 2013. *A Framework for Understanding Poverty: A Cognitive Approach.* Highlands, TX: aha! Process.

Pearce, Fred. 2007. *When the Rivers Run Dry: Water— The Defining Crisis of the Twenty-First Century.* Boston, MA: Beacon Press.

Peçanha, Sergio, and Tim Wallace. 2015. "The Flight of Refugees Around the Globe." *The New York Times*, June 20. Online at www .nytimes.com/interactive/2015/06/21/world/ map-flow-desperate-migration-refugee-crisis. html (accessed June 22, 2015).

Pechatnov, Vladimir. 2006. *Stalin, Roosevelt, and Truman. The USSR and USA in the 1940s* (in Russian). Moscow: Terra.

Peerenboom, Randall. 2008. *China Modernizes: Threat to the West or Model for the Rest?* Oxford: Oxford University Press.

Peers, Steve. 2016. *The Brexit: The Legal Framework for Withdrawal from the EU or Renegotiation of EU Membership.* Oxford, UK: Hart Publishing.

Peet, Richard. 2009. *Unholy Trinity: The IMF, World Bank and WTO.* 2nd edition. London: Zed Books.

Pelligrini, Dominick, ed. 2010. *Nuclear Weapons' Role in 21st Century U.S. Policy.* Hauppage, NY: Nova Science.

Peters, Anny; Maja Micevska-Scharf; Francien Van Driel and Willy Jansen. 2010. "Where Does Public Funding for HIV Prevention Go To? The Case of Condoms versus Microbicides and Vaccines." *Globalization and Health* 6(1): 23. Online at http://www.globalizationandhealth.com/content/6/1/23 (accessed September 25, 2012).

Pew Research Center. 2009. "U.S. Seen as Less Important, China as More Powerful." December 3. Online at http://bit.ly/10Op1jG (accessed July 19, 2013).

Pew Research Center. 2010. "Americans Spending More Time Following the News: Ideological News Sources: Who Watches and Why." September 12. Online at http://bit.ly/rlXOQ8 (accessed July 19, 2013).

Pew Research Center. 2011. "Confidence in Osama bin Laden." Online at http://www.pewglobal.org/2011/05/02/osama-bin-laden-largely-discredited-among-muslim-publics-in-recent-years/ (accessed August 1, 2015).

Pew Research Center. 2013. "Climate Change and Financial Instability Seen as Top Global Threats." Online at http://www.pewglobal.org/2013/06/24/climate-change-and-financial-instability-seen-as-top-global-threats (accessed March 30, 2015).

Pew Research Center. 2013a. *Muslim Publics Share Concerns about Extremist* Groups. Online at http://www.pewglobal.org/2013/09/10/muslim-publics-share-concerns-about-extremist-groups (accessed April 12, 2015).

Pew Research Center. 2014a. "Americans: Disengaged, Feeling Less Respected, but Still See U.S. as World's Military Superpower." Online at http://www.pewresearch.org/fact-tank/2014/04/01/americans-disengaged-feeling-less-respected-but-still-see-u-s-as-worlds-military-superpower/

Pew Research Center. 2015. "How Americans View the Top Energy and Environmental Issues." Online at http://www.pewresearch.org/key-data-points/environment-energy-2/ (accessed March 29, 2015).

Pew Research Center. 2016. "International Migration: Key Findings from the U.S., Europe and the World." Online at http://www.pewresearch.org/fact-tank/2016/12/15/international-migration-key-findings-from-the-u-s-europe-and-the-world (accessed January 9, 2019).

Pew Research Center. 2017. "News Use Across Social Media Platforms." Online at http://www.journalism.org/2017/09/07/news-use-across-social-media-platforms-2017 (accessed January 27, 2018).

Pew Research Center. 2017a. "U.S. Image Suffers as Publics Around World Question Trump's Leadership." Online at http://www.pewglobal.org/2017/06/26/u-s-image-suffers-as-publics-around-world-question-trumps-leadership.

Pew Research Center. 2018. "For Earth Day, Here's How Americans View Environmental Issues." http://www.pewresearch.org/fact-tank/2017/04/20/for-earth-day-heres-how-americans-view-environmental-issues (accessed April 22, 2018).

Pew Research Center. 2018a. "Origins and Destinations of the World's Migrants, 1990–2017." Online at http://www.pewglobal.org/2018/02/28/global-migrant-stocks/?country=US&date=2017 (accessed April 22, 2018).

Pew Research Center. 2018b. "U.S. International Relations Scholars, Global Citizens Differ Sharply on Views of Threats to Their Country." Online at http://www.pewresearch.org/fact-tank/2018/05/09/u-s-international-relations-scholars-global-citizens-differ-sharply-on-views-of-threats-to-their-country (accessed July 22, 2018).

Philippides, Marios, ed. 2007. *Mehmed II the Conqueror and the Fall of the Franco-Byzantine Levant to the Ottoman Turks: Some Western Views and Testimonies* (Medieval and Renaissance Texts and Studies). Amherst: University of Massachusetts Press.

Phuong, Catherine. 2010. *The International Protection of Internally Displaced Persons.* New York: Cambridge University Press.

Pielke, Roger. 2010. *The Climate Fix: What Scientists and Politicians Won't Tell You About Global Warming*. New York: Basic Books.

Pillar, Paul. 2001. *Terrorism and U.S. Foreign Policy*. Washington, DC: Brookings Institution Press.

Pin-Lin, Chong. 2010. "Can China Become the World's Engine for Growth?" Symposium contribution. *International Economy*, Winter: 10.

Ping, C. K. 2017. "19th Party Congress: Xi Jinping Affirms China's Commitment on Green Development." *The Straights Times*. Online at http://www.straitstimes.com/asia/east-asia/19th-party-congress-xi-jinping-says-china-must-cooperate-with-other-nations-on (accessed January 9, 2019).

Pitts, F. H. 2017. *Critiquing Capitalism Today: New Ways to Read Marx (Marx, Engels, and Marxisms)*. New York: Palgrave Macmillan.

Plaut, Martin. 2010. "Ethiopia Famine Aid "Spent on Weapons." BBC News. March 3. Online at http:// news.bbc.co.uk/2/hi/8535189.stm (accessed September 25, 2012).

Plokhy, S. M. 2010. *Yalta: The Price of Peace*. New York: Viking Adult.

Pohlman, Edward. 2013. *China's "One Child": Policy, Population, Pollution, Protest*. Albany, New York: Planet Ethics Press.

Politico. 2017. "Trump Now Twitter's Most Followed World Leader." *Politico*. October 4. Online at https://www.politico.com/story/2017/10/04/trump-most-followed-world-leader-twitter-243444 (accessed January 7, 2019).

Polman, Linda. 2011. War Games. The Story of Aid and War in Modern Times. New York: Viking.

Pons, Silvio. 2014. *The Global Revolution. A History of International Communism, 1917–1991*. New York: Oxford University Press.

Post, Jerrold. 1990. "Explaining Saddam Hussein: a Psychological Profile." Presented to the House Armed Services Committee. December 1990. http://www.au.af.mil/au/awc/awcgate/iraq/saddam_post.htm

Post, Jerrold. 2004. *Leaders and Their Followers in a Dangerous World: The Psychology of Political Behavior* (Psychoanalysis and Social Theory). Ithaca, NY: Cornell University Press.

Post, Jerrold. 2005a. "The New Face of Terrorism: Socio-Cultural Foundations of Contemporary Terrorism." *Behavioral Sciences and the Law* 23(4): 451–465.

Post, Jerrold. 2005b. "When Hatred is Bred in the Bone: Psycho-Cultural Foundations of Contemporary Terrorism." *Journal of Political Psychology* 26(4): 615–636.

Post, Jerrold. 2008. *The Mind of the Terrorist. The Psychology of Terrorism from the IRA to al-Qaeda*. New York: Palgrave Macmillan.

Power, Samantha. 2002. *A Problem from Hell: America and the Age of Genocide*. New York: Basic Books.

PPPIRC. 2018. *Carbon Capture and Storage*. Public-Private-Partnership In Infrastructure Resource Center. Online at http://ppp.worldbank.org/public-private-partnership/ppp-sector/clean-technology/carbon-capture-and-storage/carbon-capture-and-storage (accessed January 9, 2019).

Prebisch, Raúl. 1989. *Antología del pensamiento político, social y económico de América Latina* (In Spanish). Buenos Aires: Ediciones de Cultura Hispánica.

Priest, Dana, and William Arkin. 2010a. "A Hidden World, Growing Beyond Control." *The Washington Post*. July 19, A7.

Priest, Dana, and William Arkin. 2010b. "National Security, Inc." *The Washington Post*, July 20, A1.

Priest, Dana, and William Arkin. 2011. *Top Secret America: The Rise of the New American Security State*. Boston: Little, Brown.

Primakov, Evgeny. 2009. *Russia and the Arabs: Behind the Scenes in the Middle East from the Cold War to the Present*. New York: Basic Books.

Protocol of the Modern Diplomat. (2013). Foreign Service Institute, U.S. Department of State. Online at https://www.state.gov/documents/organization/176174.pdf (accessed January 9, 2019).

Putnam, Robert. 1988. "Diplomacy and Domestic Politics: The Logic of Two-Level Games." *International Organization* 42(3): 427–460.

Queenan, Jeri. 2013. "Global NGOs Spend More on Accounting Than Multinationals." *Harvard Business Review*. April 23. Online at https://hbr.org/2013/04/the-efficiency-trap-of-global (accessed March 5, 2015).

Qutb, Sayyid. 1964/2007. *Milestones*. Chicago: Kazi Publications.

Ramet, Sabrina. 2005. *Thinking about Yugoslavia: Scholarly Debates about the Yugoslav Breakup and the Wars in Bosnia and Kosovo*. New York: Cambridge University Press.

Rankin, Jennifer. 2010. "Rules on Unusual Food Heading to Arbitration." *EuropeanVoice.com*. July 1. Online at http://www.europeanvoice.com/article/impor ted/rules-on-unusual-food-heading-to-arbitration/68372.aspx (accessed September 25, 2012).

Rapkin, David P., and Jonathan R. Strand. 2006. "Reforming the IMF's Weighted Voting System." *The World Economy* 29(3): 305–324.

Rapoport, David. 2004. "The Four Waves of Terrorism." In *Attacking Terrorism*, eds. Audrey Cronin and James Ludes. Washington, DC: Germantown University Press.

Rashid, Ahmed. 2008. *Descent into Chaos: The United States and the Failure of Nation Building in Pakistan, Afghanistan, and Central Asia*. New York: Viking Adult.

Rasmussen, Sune Engel. 2018. "Besieged Rouhani Takes Hard Line." *The Wall Street Journal*. July 12. A9.

Reardon, Betty. 1985. *Sexism and the War System*. New York: Teachers College Press.

Rechkemmer, Andreas. 2004. *Postmodern Global Governance: The United Nations Convention to Combat Desertification*. Baden-Baden, Germany: Nomos Verlagsgesellschaft.

Reeves, Richard. 2001. *President Nixon: Alone in the White House*. New York: Simon & Schuster.

Reich, Robert. 2017. "Robert Reich Is Not Impressed by the Corporate Conscience." *Fast Company*. Online at https://www.fastcompany.com/40508754/robert-reich-is-not-impressed-by-the-corporate-conscience (accessed January 11, 2019).

Reicher, Stephen and Alexander Haslam 2016. "Fueling Terror: How Extremists Are Made". *Scientific American*. March 25. Online at: https://www.scientificamerican.com/article/fueling-terror-how-extremists-are-made/ (accessed March 23, 2019).

Renshon, Stanley. 2004. *In His Father's Shadow: The Transformations of George W. Bush*. New York: Palgrave Macmillan.

Renshon, Stanley. 2009. *National Security in the Obama Administration: Reassessing the Bush Doctrine*. New York: Routledge.

Renshon, Stanley. 2011. *Barack Obama and the Politics of Redemption*. New York: Routledge.

Reus-Smit, Christian. 2009. "Constructivism." In *Theories of International Relations*, 4th edition, eds. Scott Burchill, Andrew Linklater, Richard Devetak, Jack Donnelly, Matthew Patterson, and Christian Reus-Smit, 212–236. New York: Palgrave Macmillan.

Rey, Marie-Pierre. 2004. "Europe Is Our Common Home: A Study of Gorbachev's Diplomatic Concept." *Cold War History* 4(2): 33–65.

Rey, Marie-Pierre. 2008. "The USSR and the Helsinki Process, 1969–75: Optimism, Doubt, or Defiance?" In *Origins of the European Security System. The Helsinki Process Revisited, 1965–1975*, eds. Andreas Wenger, Vojtech Mastny, and Christian Nuenlist. New York: Routledge Press.

Reynolds, John. 2012. "Deterring and Responding to Asymmetrical Threats." BiblioScholar.

Rieff, David. 2006. *At the Point of a Gun: Democratic Dreams and Armed Intervention*. New York: Simon & Schuster.

Ritchie, Elspeth Cameron, Patricia Watson, and Mathew Friedman, eds. 2005. *Interventions Following Mass Violence and Disasters: Strategies for Mental Health Practice*. New York: The Guilford Press.

Roan, Sharon. 1989. *Ozone Crisis: The 15-Year Evolution of a Sudden Global Emergency*. Hoboken, NJ: Wiley.

Roberts, Adam. 2000. "The So-Called 'Right' of Humanitarian Intervention." *Yearbook of International Humanitarian Law* 3: 3–51.

Roberts, J. Timmons, and Bradley Parks. 2006. *A Climate of Injustice: Global Inequality, North-South Politics, and Climate Policy*. Cambridge, MA: MIT Press.

Robins, Robert, and Jerrold Post. 1995. *When Illness Strikes the Leader: The Dilemma of the Captive King*. New York: Yale University Press.

Rodin, Judith, and Margot Brandenburg 2014. *The Power of Impact Investing*. Philadelphia: Wharton Digital Press.

Rodnick, Dani. 2017. *Straight Talk on Trade: Ideas for a Sane World Economy*. Princeton, NJ: Princeton University Press.

Rogers, Peter, Kazi F. Jalal, and John Boyd. 2007. *An Introduction to Sustainable Development*. New York: Routledge.

Rogowski, Ronald. 1990. *Commerce and Coalitions: How Trade Affects Domestic Political Alignments*. Princeton, NJ: Princeton University Press.

Rooney, Ben. 2015. "Best and Worst Countries for Women on Corporate Boards." *CNN Money*. Online at http://money.cnn.com/2015/01/13/news/companies/women-corporate-board-global/ (accessed April 17, 2015).

Rosato, Sebastian. 2003. The Flawed Logic of Democratic Peace Theory. *American Political Science Review*. 97 (4), 585-602.

Rose, Gideon, ed. 2013. *The Clash of Civilizations?* New York: Council of Foreign Relations.

Rosenau, James. 1961. *Public Opinion and Foreign Policy: An Operational Formation*. New York: Random House.

Rosenau, James. 1999. "Toward an Ontology for Global Governance." In *Approaches to Global Governance Theory*, eds. Martin Hewson and Timothy J. Sinclair. Albany: State University of New York.

Rosenau, James, Ernst-Ulrich von Weizsäcker, and Ulrich Petschow, eds. 2005. *Governance and Sustainability. Exploring the Roadmap to Sustainability after Johannesburg*. Sheffield, UK: Greenleaf Publishing.

Roth, John, and Carol Rittner, ed. 2012. *Rape: Weapon of War and Genocide*. St. Paul, Minnesota: Paragon House.

Rothfeder, Jeffrey. 2016. Why Donald Trump Is Wrong About Manufacturing Jobs and China. *New Yorker*. March 14.

Rothkoff, David. 2014. "Obama's 'Don't Do Stupid Shit' Foreign Policy." *Foreign Policy*, June 4, Online at https://foreignpolicy.com/2014/06/04/obamas-dont-do-stupid-shit-foreign-policy (accessed January 9, 2019).

Royle, Trevor. 2004. *Crimea: The Great Crimean War, 1854–1856*. New York: Palgrave Macmillan.

Ruggie, John. 2013. *Just Business: Multinational Corporations and Human Rights*. New York: Norton.

Russet, Bruce, and John Oneal. 2001. *Triangulating Peace: Democracy, Interdependence, and International Organizations*. New York: W. W. Norton.

Rynning, Sren, and Jens Ringsmose. 2008. "Why Are Revisionist States Revisionist? Reviving Classical Realism as an Approach to Understanding International Change." *International Politics* 45(1): 19–39.

Sachs, Jeffrey. 2005. *The End of Poverty: Economic Possibilities for Our Time*. New York: Penguin Press.

Sachs, Jeffrey. 2015. *The Age of Sustainable Development*. New York: Columbia University Press.

Sageman, Marc. 2004. *Understanding Terror Networks*. Philadelphia: University of Pennsylvania Press.

Said, Edward. 1994. *Culture and Imperialism*. New York: Vintage.

Samuel, Katja. 2013. *The OIC, the UN, and Counter-Terrorism Law-Making: Conflicting or Cooperative Legal Orders?* Oxford: Hart.

Sanford, George. 2009. *Katyn and the Soviet Massacre of 1940: Truth, Justice, and Memory*. New York: Routledge.

Sakwa, Richard. 2016. Frontline Ukraine. Crisis in the Borderlands. London: I.B.Tauris

Sapolsky, Robert M. 2006. "A Natural History of Peace." *Foreign Affairs* 85(1) January/February: 104–120.

Saradzhyan, Simon. 2010. "Chechnya: Divisions in the Ranks." *ISN: International Relations and Security Network*. August 11. Online at http://www.isn.ethz.ch/isn/Current-Affairs/Security-Watch/Detail/?lng=en&id=120017 (accessed September 20, 2012).

Sarkesian, Sam C., John Allen Williams, and Stephen J. Cimbala. 2007. *U.S. National Security: Policymakers, Processes and Politics*. 4th edition. Boulder, CO: Lynne Rienner.

Sarotte, Mary. 2009. *1989: The Struggle to Create Post-Cold War Europe*. Princeton, NJ: Princeton University Press.

Sathasivam, Kanishkan. 2005. *Uneasy Neighbors: India, Pakistan and U.S. Foreign Policy*. London: Ashgate.

Saunders, Doug. 2018. "Canadians Are Seeing the Whole World Through an Anti-American Lens." *Globe and Mail*. April 14, Online at https://www.theglobeandmail.com/opinion/article-canadians-are-seeing-the-whole-world-through-an-anti-american-lens (accessed January 9, 2019).

Savranskaya, Svetlana and Thomas Blanton. 2018. NATO Expansion. What Yeltsin Heard. https://nsarchive.gwu.edu/briefing-book/russia-programs/2018-03-16/nato-expansion-what-yeltsin-heard.

Scharre, Paul. 2017. "Why We Must Not Build Automated Weapons of War." *Time*, September 25. Online at http://time.com/4948633/robots-artificial-intelligence-war (accessed January 9, 2019).

Schein, Virginia E. 2002. "A Global Look at Psychological Barriers to Women's Progress in Management". *Journal of Social Issues* 57(4): 675–688.

Schellnhuber, Hans-Joachim, Gary Yohe, Wolfgang Cramer, Tom Wigley, and Nebojsa Nakicenovic, eds. 2006. *Avoiding Dangerous Climate Change*. Cambridge: Cambridge University Press.

Schlesinger, Stephen. 2003. *Act of Creation: The Founding of the United Nations: A Story of Superpowers, Secret Agents, Wartime Allies and Enemies and Their Quest for a Peaceful World*. Boulder, CO: Westview Press.

Schmidt, Gustav, ed. 2001. *A History of NATO— The First Fifty Years*. Three-Volume Set. New York: Palgrave Macmillan.

Schulte, Constanze. 2005. *Compliance with Decisions of the International Court of Justice*. New York: Oxford University Press.

Schultz, Richard. 2004. "Showstoppers: Nine Reasons Why We Never Sent Our Special Operation Forces after al Qaeda before 9/11." *Weekly Standard*, January 26, 25–33.

Schultz, William Todd. 2005. *Handbook of Psychobiography*. New York: Oxford University Press.

Schweller, Randall. 1997. "New Realist Research on Alliances: Refining, Not Refuting, Waltz's Balancing Proposition." *American Political Science Review* 91(4): 913–917.

Schweller, Randall. 2008. *Unanswered Threats: Political Constrains on the Balance of Power*. Princeton, NJ: Princeton University Press.

Scott, Bruce. 2001. "The Great Divide in the Global Village." *Foreign Affairs* 80(1) January/February: 160–177.

Scully, Eileen. 2001. *Bargaining with the State from Afar*. New York: Columbia University Press.

Sears, David, Leonie Huddy, and Robert Jervis, eds. 2003. *Oxford Handbook on Political Psychology*. New York: Oxford University Press.

Sen, Amartya. 1981. *Poverty and Famines: An Essay on Entitlement and Deprivation*. Oxford: Oxford University Press.

Sen, Amartya. 2011. *The Idea of Justice*. Cambridge, MA: Harvard University Press.

Seth, Shobhit. 2018. "The Reasons Why China Buys U.S. Treasury Bonds." *The Investopedia*. January 2. Online at https://www.investopedia.com/articles/investing/040115/reasons-why-china-buys-us-treasury-bonds.asp (accessed January 9, 2019).

Shah, Anup. 2014. "Foreign Aid for Development Assistance." September 28. Online at http://www.globalissues.org/article/35/foreign-aid-develop-ment-assistance (accessed March 30, 2015).

Shahan, Cynthia. 2014. "China Puts Billions Into Electric Cars & EV Charging Stations." *Clean Technica*, December 24. Online at http://cleantechnica.com/2014/12/24/china-puts-billions-electric-cars-ev-charging-stations (accessed March 30, 2015).

Shapiro, Judith. 2001. *Mao's War against Nature: Politics and the Environment in Revolutionary China*. New York: Cambridge University Press.

Sharp, Paul. 2009. *Diplomatic Theory of International Relations* (Cambridge Studies in International Relations Series). New York: Cambridge University Press.

Shaw, Malcolm. 2017. *International Law*. New York: Cambridge University Press.

Shear, Michael. 2017. "Trump Will Withdraw U.S. from Paris Climate Agreement." *The New York Times*, June 1. Online at https://www.nytimes.com/2017/06/01/climate/trump-paris-climate-agreement.html (accessed March 3, 2018).

Sheiner, Louise. 2018. "The Long-Term Impact of Aging on Federal Budget." *Brookings*. Online at https://www.brookings.edu/research/the-long-term-impact-of-aging-on-the-federal-budget (accessed April 22, 2018).

Shelley, Louise. 2010. *Human Trafficking: A Global Perspective*. New York: Cambridge University Press.

Shepard, Todd. 2006. *The Invention of Decolonization*. Ithaca, NY: Cornell University Press.

Shiraev, Eric and Vladislav Zubok. *Anti-Americanism in Russia: From Stalin to Putin*. New York: Palgrave Press, 2000.

Shiraev, Eric. 2013. *Russian Government and Politics*. 2nd edition. New York: Palgrave Macmillan.

Shiraev, Eric. 2019. "Looking forward.... Maybe: The 2016 United States' Presidential Elections From Russia's Standpoint." In: Jesus Velasco (Ed). International Reactions to the 2016 Presidential Elections in the USA. New York: Routledge

Shiraev, Eric, and Konstantin Khudoley. 2019. *Russian Foreign Policy*. London: Macmillan.

Shiraev, Eric, and David Levy. 2017. *Cross-Cultural Psychology: Critical Thinking and Contemporary Applications*. 6th edition. New York: Routledge.

Shiraev, Eric, and Richard Sobel. 2006. *People and Their Opinions: Thinking Critically about Public Opinion*. New York: Longman.

Shiraev, Eric, and Konstantin Khudoley. 2019. *Russian Foreign Policy*. London: Macmillan.

Shirer, William. 1990. *The Rise and Fall of the Third Reich: A History of Nazi Germany*. New York: Simon & Schuster.

Shlapentokh, Vladimir, Eric Shiraev, and Eero Carroll. 2008. *The Soviet Union: Internal and External Perspectives on Soviet Society*. New York: Palgrave Macmillan.

Simon, Steven, and Jeff Martini. 2004. "Terrorism: Denying al Qaeda Its Popular Support." *The Washington Quarterly* 28(1) Winter: 131–145.

Simons, Marlise. 2013. U.S. Grows More Helpful to International Criminal Court, a Body It First Scorned. *The New York Times*, April 2. Online at http://nyti.ms/1M8M9ww (accessed March 5, 2015).

Sinclair, Hugh. 2012. *Confessions of a Microfinance Heretic: How Microlending Lost Its Way and Betrayed the Poor*. Crawfordsville, IN: Berrett-Koehler.

Singer, Burt; Awash Teklehaimanot; Andrew Spielman; Al Schapira; and Yesim Tozan, eds.; Jeffrey D. Sachs, series editor. 2005. *Coming to Grips with Malaria in the New Millennium*. London: Earthscan.

Singer, Hans W. 1999. *Growth, Development and Trade: Selected Essays of Hans W. Singer*. Northhampton, MA: Edward Elgar Publishing.

Singer, P. W., and Allan Friedman. 2014. *Cybersecurity and Cyberwar: What Everyone Needs to Know*. Oxford: Oxford University Press.

Singh, Michael. 2010. "Iran Re-Revolution: How the Green Movement Is Repeating Iranian History." *Foreign Affairs*. July 26. Online at http://fam.ag/aQJunk (accessed September 25, 2012). Registration is required. Another version is available online at http://bit.ly/1bwKeUK (accessed July 16, 2013).

Sjoberg, Laura, ed. 2009. *Gender and International Security: Feminist Perspectives*. New York: Routledge.

Sloan, Stanley. 2010. *Permanent Alliance?: NATO and the Transatlantic Bargain from Truman to Obama*. New York: Continuum.

Sloan, Stephen. 2006. *Terrorism: The Present Threat in Context*. London: Berg Publishers.

Smith, Adam. 1776/1977. *An Inquiry into the Nature and Causes of the Wealth of Nations*. Chicago: University of Chicago Press.

Smith, Charles. 2016. *Palestine and the Arab-Israeli Conflict: A History with Documents*. 9th edition. New York: St. Martin's.

Smith, Jeff. 2013. *Cold Peace: China-India Rivalry in the Twenty-First Century*. Plymouth, UK: Lexington Books.

Smith, Peter, and Shalom Schwartz. 1997. "Values." In *Handbook of Cross-Cultural Psychology*, vol. 3, eds. J. Berry, M. Segall, and C. Kagitcibasi, 77–118. Boston: Allyn & Bacon.

Sniderman, Paul, Louk Hagendoorn, and Markus Prior. 2004. "Predisposing Factors and Situational Triggers: Exclusionary Reactions to Immigrant Minorities." *American Political Science Review* 98(1): 35–50.

Snyder, Jack. 2000. *From Voting to Violence. Democratization and Nationalist Violence*. New York: W. W. Norton.

Snyder, Jack. 2005. *Electing to Fight: Why Emerging Democracies Go to War*. Cambridge, MA: MIT Press.

Snyder-Hall, R. Claire. 2010. "Third-Wave Feminism and the Defense of 'Choice.'" *Perspectives on Politics* 8(1): 255–261.

Sobek, David. 2008. *Causes of War*. Cambridge, UK: Polity.

Sobel, Richard. 2001. *The Impact of Public Opinion on U.S. Foreign Policy Since Vietnam*. New York: Oxford University Press.

Sobel, Richard, and Eric Shiraev, eds. 2003. *International Public Opinion and the Bosnia Crisis*. Lanham, MD: Lexington Books.

Soetaert, Wim, and Erik Vandamme, eds. 2009. *Biofuels*. West Sussex, UK: Wiley.

Soeters, Joseph. 2005. *Ethnic Conflict and Terrorism: The Origins and Dynamics of Civil Wars*. New York: Routledge.

Sommerland, Joe. 2018. "World Refugee Day 2018: How Many Displaced People Are There Around the Globe and What Is Being Done to Help?" *The Independent*, June 20. Online at https://ind.pn/2Iai4Sk (accessed September 3, 2018).

Spector, Bertram, ed. 2005. *Fighting Corruption in Developing Countries: Strategies and Analysis*. Bloomfield, CT: Kumarian Press.

Spector, Stephen. 2008. *Evangelicals and Israel: The Story of American Christian Zionism*. New York: Oxford University Press.

Spivak, Gayatri Chakravorty. 1999. *A Critique of Post-Colonial Reason: Toward a History of the Vanishing Present*. Cambridge, MA: Harvard University |Press.

Steinbruner, John D. 1974. *The Cybernetic Theory of Decision: New Dimensions of Political Analysis*. Princeton, NJ: Princeton University Press.

Steiner, Zara. 2013. *The Lights that Failed. European International History 1919-1933*. London: Oxford University Press.

Stern, Jessica. 2010. "Mind over Martyr: How to Deradicalize Islamist Extremists." *Foreign Affairs* 89(1) January/February: 95–108.

Stern, Jessica, and J. M. Berger. 2015. *ISIS: The State of Terror*. New York: Ecco.

Stern, Nicholas. 2007. *The Economics of Climate Change: The Stern Review*. Cambridge: Cambridge University Press.

Stewart, William. 2006. *How to Prepare for a Pandemic and Other Extended Disasters*. Charleston, SC: BookSurge Publishing.

Stiehm, Judith. 2009. "Theses on the Military, Security, War and Women." In *Gender and International Security: Feminist Perspectives*, ed. Laura Sjoberg, 17–23. New York: Routledge.

Stiglitz, Joseph. 2002. *Globalization and Its Discontents*. New York: W. W. Norton.

Stiglitz, Joseph. 2011. "The Price of 9/11." *Economist's View*. September 1. Online at http://economists-view.typepad.com/economistsview/2011/09/stiglitz-the-price-of-911.html (accessed September 24, 2012).

Stiglitz, Joseph. 2017. *Globalization and Its Discontents, Revisited*. New York: W. W. Norton.

Stoddard, Abby. 2006. *Humanitarian Alert: NGO Information and its Impact on U.S. Foreign Policy*. Bloomfield, CT: Kumarian Press.

Stokols, Eli. 2017. "Donald Trump Withdraws from Paris Climate Deal Despite Allies' Opposition." *The New York Times*. Online at https://www.wsj.com/articles/donald-trump-to-exit-paris-climate-deal-officials-say-1496343854 (accessed January 9, 2019).

Strand, Jonathan. 2013. *Regional Development Banks: Lending with a Regional Flavor* (Global Institutions). New York: Routledge.

Stueck, William. 2010. "The Korean War." In *The Cambridge History of the Cold War*, eds. Melvyn P. Leffler and Odd Arne Westad, Vol. 1, 266–287. Cambridge: Cambridge University Press.

Suzuki, Shogo, Zhang, Yongjin.,and Quirk, John, eds. 2016. *International Orders in the Early Modern World: Before the Rise of the West*. London: Routledge.

Sweig, Julia. 2010. "A New Global Player: Brazil's Far-Flung Agenda." *Foreign Affairs* 89(6) November/December: 173–184.

Takiff, Michael. 2010. *A Complicated Man: The Life of Bill Clinton as Told by Those Who Know Him*. New Haven, CT: Yale University Press.

Taubman, William. 2004. *Khrushchev: The Man and His Era*. New York: W. W. Norton.

Taubman, William. 2017. Gorbachev. His Life and Times. New York: Simon and Schuster.

Tavares, Rodrigo. 2009. *Regional Security: The Capacity of International Organizations*. New York: Routledge.

Tetlock, Philip. 2011. "In an interview to the *Washington Post*." Online at http://wapo.st/1MEfbZI (accessed August 1, 2015).

Tetlock, Philip, Richard Lebow, and Geoffrey Parker, eds. 2006. *Unmaking the West: "What If?" Scenarios That Rewrite History*. Ann Arbor: University of Michigan Press.

Theiss-Morse, Elizabeth. 2009. *Who Counts as an American?: The Boundaries of National Identity*. New York: Cambridge University Press.

Thomas, Chris D., Alison Cameron, Rhys E. Green, and Michel B. Akkenes. 2004. "Extinction Risk from Climate Change." *Nature* 427: 145–148.

Thomas, Daniel. 2001. *The Helsinki Effect: International Norms, Human Rights, and the Demise of Communism*. Princeton, NJ: Princeton University Press.

Thompson, Nicholas. 2009. *The Hawk and the Dove: Paul Nitze, George Kennan, and the History of the Cold War*. New York: Henry Holt.

Thu, Huong Le. 2018. "Has China Got Everyone Wrong?" *The National Interest*. Online at https://nationalinterest.org/feature/has-china-got-everyone-wrong-26706 (accessed January 9, 2019).

Thucydides. 2003. *History of the Peloponnesian War*. Translated by Rex Warner. New York: Penguin Classics.

Thurow, Lester. 1992. *Head to Head: The Coming Battle among Japan, Europe, and America*. New York: William Morrow.

Tickner, Ann. 1992. *Gender in International Relations: Feminist Perspectives on Achieving Global Security*. New York: Columbia University Press.

"Time to Call the Sweep?" 2010. *The Economist*. November 18, 2010. Online at http://www.economist.com/node/17519770 (accessed September 25, 2012).

Tomaszewski, Fiona. 2002. *A Great Russia: Russia and the Triple Entente, 1905 to 1914*. Westport, CT: Praeger.

Tomz, Michael, and Jessica Weeks. 2013. "Public Opinion and the Democratic Peace." *American Political Science Review* 107(4) November: 849–865.

Trachtenberg, Mark. 1999. *A Constructed Peace: The Making of the European Settlement 1945–1963*. Princeton, NJ: Princeton University Press.

Tran, Mark. 2015. "Phenomenal Success for New Film That Criticises China's Environmental Policy." March 2. Online at http://bit.ly/1wKtjov (accessed May 7, 2015).

Trinitapoli, Jenny, and Alexander Weinreb. 2012. *Religion and AIDS in Africa*. New York: Oxford University Press.

True, Jacqui. 2009. "Feminism". In *Theories of International Relations*, eds. Scott Burchill, Andrew Linklater, Richard Devetak, Jack Donnelly, Matthew Patterson, and Christian Reus-Smit. 4th edition. New York: Palgrave Macmillan, 237–59.

Tumulty, Karen. 2011. "Will Obama Be Reelected? The Economy Could Hold the Answer." *The Washington Post*, August 5, A1.

Tyson, Alec. 2017. "Americans Are Split on the Principle of Pre-Emptive Military Force." *Pew Research Center*. Online at http://www.pewresearch.org/fact-tank/2017/11/28/americans-are-split-on-the-principle-of-pre-emptive-military-force (accessed January 9, 2019).

UN Climate Change. 2018. The Paris Agreement. Online at http://unfccc.int/paris_agreement/items/9485.php (accessed January 9, 2019).

UN Documents. *Report of the World Commission on Environment and Development: Our Common Future.* 1987. Online at http://www.un-documents.net/wced-ocf.htm (accessed July 15, 2013).

UN High Commissioner for Refugees. 2018. https://www.devex.com/organizations/united-nations-high-commissioner-for-refugees-unhcr-46715 (accessed July 15, 2018).

UN High Commissioner for Refugees. 2018a. "Internally Displaced People." Online at http://www.unhcr.org/en-us/internally-displaced-people.html (accessed September 30, 2018).

UN Peacekeeping. 2018. "Mandates and the Legal Basis for Peacekeeping." https://peacekeeping.un.org/en/mandates-and-legal-basis-peacekeeping.

UN Refugees. 2018. Online at http://www.un.org/en/sections/issues-depth/refugees (accessed September 29, 2018).

UN World Food Programme. 2015. "Hunger Statistics." Online at https://www.wfp.org/hunger/stats (accessed March 31, 2015).

UNAIDS. 2015. "Global AIDS Response Progress Reporting." Online at http://www.unaids.org/en/dataanalysis (accessed April 2, 2015).

UNAIDS. 2018. *Ending the AIDS Epidemics by 2030.* Online at http://www.unaids.org/en (accessed September 27, 2018).

UNEP (United Nations Environment Programme). 2010. *Annual Report.* New York: United Nations.

United Nations. 1981. "The United Nations' Convention on the Elimination of All Forms of Discrimination Against Women" Online at https://bit.ly/2GD8qqZ (accessed March 23, 2019).

United Nations. 2004. "A More Secure World: Our Shared Responsibility." Report of the High-Level Panel on Threats, Challenges and Change. http://www.un.org/en/peacebuilding/pdf/historical/hlp_more_secure_world.pdf (accessed August 1, 2015).

United Nations. 2006. "Translating Principles into Practice: Humanitarian Policies." *Humanitarian Negotiations with Armed Groups: A Manual and Guidelines for Practitioners.* Online at https://docs.unocha.org/sites/dms/Documents/HumanitarianNegotiationswArmedGroups Manual.pdf (accessed March 23, 2015).

United Nations Information Service (UNIS). 2013. Press Releases. Online at http://www.unis.unvienna.org/unis/en/pressrels/2013/unisinf488.html (accessed March 20, 2015).

United Nations Population Division. 2004. *World Population Prospects: The 2004 Revision.* New York: United Nations.

UNRA. 2018. UN Refugee Agency. Syria Regional refugee response. Online at https://data2.unhcr.org/en/situations/syria (accessed January 9, 2019).

U.S. Department of State. 2013. *Protocol of the Modern Diplomat.* Online at https://www.state.gov/documents/organization/176174.pdf (accessed March 11, 2019)

U.S. Department of State. 2017. Office to Monitor and Combat Trafficking in Persons. Online at https://www.state.gov/j/tip/ (accessed January 29, 2018).

U.S. Department of State. 2018. "Trafficking in Persons Report, 2018." Online at https://www.state.gov/j/tip/rls/tiprpt/2018/index.htm (accessed October 1, 2018).

U.S. Department of State. 2018a. U.S. Relations with Vietnam. https://www.state.gov/r/pa/ei/bgn/4130.htm (accessed January 9, 2019).

US EIA 2018. US Energy Information Administration. "Oil: Crude and Petroleum Products." Online at https://www.eia.gov/energyexplained/index.cfm?page=oil_imports (accessed January 9, 2019).

Van Evera, Stephen. 2001. *Causes of War: Power and the Roots of Conflict.* Ithaca, NY: Cornell University Press.

van Loon, Jeremy. 2011. "Canada May Miss $6.7 Billion Carbon Offset Bill by Exiting Kyoto Protocol." *Bloomberg.com.* Online at http://bloom.bg/siU2bD(accessed July 16, 2013).

Vattel, Emerich de. 1758/2001. *Law of Nations or Principles of the Law of Nature, Applied to the Conduct and Affairs of Nations and Sovereigns.* Holmes Beach, FL: Gaunt.

Vattimo, Gianni and Santiago Zabala. 2014. *Hermeneutic Communism: From Heidegger to Marx.* New York: Columbia University Press.

Vernon, Raymond. 1971. *Sovereignty at Bay: The Multinational Spread of U.S. Enterprises*. New York: Basic Books.

Victor, David. 2006. "Recovering Sustainable Development." *Foreign Affairs* 85(1) January/ February.

Victor, David; Granger Morgan; Jay Apt; John Stein-bruner; and Katharine Ricke. 2009. "The Geoengineering Option: A Last Resort against Global Warming?" *Foreign Affairs* 88(2) March/ April: 64–76.

Volkan, Vamik, and Norman Itzkowitz. 1984. *The Immortal Ataturk: A Psychobiography*. Chicago: University of Chicago Press.

von Clausewitz, Carl. 1832/1982. *On War*. New York: Penguin Books.

Walk Free Foundation. 2018. *Understand Modern Slavery*. Online at https://www .walkfreefoundation.org (accessed January 9, 2019).

Walker, Gordon. 2009. "Globalizing Environmental Justice: The Geography and Politics of Frame Contextualization and Evolution." *Global Social Policy* (9) December: 355–382.

Walker, Gordon. 2012. *Environmental Justice: Concepts, Evidence and Politics*. New York: Routledge.

Wallechinsky, David. 2006. *Tyrants: The World's 20 Worst Living Dictators*. New York: Harper Paperbacks.

Wallerstein, Immanuel. 1979. *The Capitalist World-Economy*. Cambridge: Cambridge University Press.

Wallerstein, Immanuel. 2004. *World-System Analysis: An Introduction*. Durham, NC: Duke University Press.

Walley, Noah, and Bradley Whitehead. 1994. "It's Not Easy Being Green." *Harvard Business Review* 72(3) May/June: 46–51.

Walt, Stephen. 1987. *The Origins of Alliances*. Ithaca, NY: Cornell University Press.

Walt, Stephen. 1991. "The Renaissance of Security Studies." *International Studies Quarterly* 35(2): 211–39.

Walt, Stephen. 1998. "One World, Many Theories." *Foreign Policy* 110(Spring): 29–46.

Walt, Stephen. 2005a. "The Relationship between Theory and Policy in International Relations." *Annual Review of Political Science* 8: 23–48.

Walt, Stephen. 2005b. "Taming American Power." *Foreign Affairs* 84(5) September/October: 105–120.

Walt, Stephen. 2018. *The Hell of Good Intentions: America's Foreign Policy Elite and the Decline of U.S. Primacy*. Washington DC: Just World Books.

Waltz, Kenneth. 1958/2001. *Man, the State and War*. New York: Columbia University Press.

Waltz, Kenneth. 2010. *Theory of International Politics*. Long Grove, IL: Waveland Press.

Wapner, Paul. 2002. "Paradise Lost? NGOs and Global Accountability." *Chicago Journal of International Law* 3(155): 155.

Ward, Andrew, and Nathalie Thomas. 2017. "BP Warms to Renewables with $200m Stake in Solar Developer. *The Financial Times*. Online at https://www.ft.com/content/f2ca752e-e0d9-11e7-8f9f-de1c2175f5ce (accessed January 9, 2019).

Ward, Martin. 1999. "Who Are the Many?" *The Ottawa Citizen*. August 2, B6.

Waters, Tony. 2006. *The Persistence of Subsistence Agriculture*. Lanham, MD: Lexington Books.

Waylen, Georgina. 2010. "A Comparative Politics of Gender: Limits and Possibilities." *Perspectives on Politics* 8(1) March: 223–231.

Webb, James. 2014. *The Long Struggle against Malaria in Tropical Africa*. New York: Cambridge University Press.

Webb, Michael, and Steven Krasner. 1989. "Hegemonic Stability Theory: An Empirical Assessment." *Review of International Studies* 15(2): 183–198.

Weinberg, Leonard, and Ami Pedahzur. 2003. *Political Parties and Terrorist Groups*. New York: Routledge.

Weiss, Michael, and Hassan Hassan. 2015. *ISIS: Inside the Army of Terror*. New York: Regan Arts.

Weiss, Thomas. 2004. "The Sunset of Humanitarian Intervention? The Responsibility to Protect in a Unipolar Era." *Security Dialogue* 35(2): 135–153.

Weiss, Thomas. 2007. *Humanitarian Intervention: Ideas in Action*. Cambridge, UK: Polity.

Weiss, Thomas. 2012. *Humanitarian Intervention: Ideas in Action.* Cambridge, UK: Polity.

Welsh, Jennifer M., ed. 2004. *Humanitarian Intervention and International Relations.* New York: Oxford University Press.

Wendt, Alexander. 1992. "Anarchy Is What States Make of It: The Social Construction of Power Politics" *International Organization* 46(2): 391–425.

Wendt, Alexander. 1999. *Social Theory of International Politics.* Cambridge: Cambridge University Press.

Wendt, Alexander. 2003. "Why a World State Is Inevitable." *European Journal of International Relations* 9(4): 491–542.

Westad, Odd Arne. 2007. *The Global Cold War: Third World Interventions and the Making of Our Times.* New York: Cambridge University Press.

Westad, Odd Arne 2012. *Restless Empire. China and the World Since 1760.* London: The Bodley Head.

Westad, Odd Arne. 2017. The Cold War. A World History. London: Allen Lane.

WFP. 2018. *World Food Programme.* Online at http://www1.wfp.org/overview (accessed January 9, 2019).

Whalley, John. 1997. "Why Do Countries Seek Regional Trade Agreements?" In *The Regionalization of the World Economy,* ed. Jeffrey Frankel, 63–86. Chicago: University of Chicago Press.

White, Brian. 2007. *Britain, Détente and Changing East-West Relations.* London: Routledge.

Wibben, Annick. 2011. *Feminist Security Studies. A Narrative Approach.* New York: Routledge.

Wieviorka, Michel. 2007. "From Classical Terrorism to 'Global' Terrorism." *International Journal of Conflict and Violence* 1(2): 92–104.

Wilkinson, Katharine K. 2012. *Between God and Green: How Evangelicals Are Cultivating a Middle Ground on Climate Change.* New York: Oxford University Press.

Willets, Peter. 1983. *The Non-Aligned Movement: The Origins of a Third World Alliance.* London: Pinter Publishing.

Williams, Michael. 2006. *Deforesting the Earth: From Prehistory to Global Crisis, an Abridgment.* Chicago: University of Chicago Press.

Williamson, David G. 1998. *Bismarck and Germany 1862–1890.* 2nd edition. Seminar Studies in History Series. New York: Longman.

Wilson, James. 2014. *The Triumph of Improvisation. Gorbachev's Adaptability, Reagan's Engagement, and the End of the Cold War.* Ithaca, NY: Cornell University Press.

Winter, Charlie. 2017. "War by Suicide: A Statistical Analysis of the Islamic State's Martyrdom Industry." *International Centre for Counter-Terrorism—The Hague.* Online at https://icct.nl/wp-content/uploads/2017/02/ICCT-Winter-War-by-Suicide-Feb2017.pdf (accessed January 9, 2019).

Wittkopf, Eugene. 1990. *Faces of Internationalism: Public Opinion and American Foreign Policy.* Durham, NC: Duke University Press.

Wittkopf, Eugene, and James McCormick, eds. 2004. *The Domestic Sources of American Foreign Policy: Insights and Evidence.* Lanham, MD: Rowman & Littlefield.

Wohlforth, William C. 1999. "The Stability of a Unipolar World." *International Security* 24(1): 5–41.

Wohlforth, William C., ed. 2003. *Cold War Endgame: Oral History, Analysis, Debates.* University Park: Pennsylvania State University Press.

Wolfe, Nathan. 2011. *The Viral Storm: The Dawn of a New Pandemic Age.* New York: Times Books.

Wolff, Michael. 2018. *Fire and Fury: Inside the Trump White House.* New York: Holt.

Woodall, Pam. 2011. "Hey Big Spenders." *The Economist.* Special Edition: The World in 2012, 140.

Woods, Kevin, David Palkki, and Mark Stout, eds. 2011 *The Saddam Tapes: The Inner Workings of a Tyrant's Regime, 1978–2001.* New York: Cambridge University Press.

Woods, Michael, and Mary Woods. 2007. *Droughts (Disasters Up Close).* Minneapolis, MN: Lerner Publications.

Woods, Ngaire. 2007. *The Globalizers: The IMF, the World Bank, and Their Borrowers.* Ithaca, NY: Cornell University Press.

Woodward, Bob. 2007. *State of Denial: Bush at War. Part III.* New York: Simon & Schuster.

World Bank. 2015. "GDP (Gross Domestic Product)." Online at http://data.worldbank.org/indicator/NY.GDP.MKTP.CD (accessed April 12, 2015).

World Bank. 2018. "Fertility Rate, Total (Births per Woman)." Online at https://data.worldbank.org/indicator/SP.DYN.TFRT.IN (accessed April 12, 2018).

World Health Organization. 2017. "Malaria: Key Facts." Online at http://bit.ly/1MRjVqW (accessed February 28, 2018).

World Health Organization. 2018. *2.1 Billion People Lack Safe Drinking Water At Home, More Than Twice As Many Lack Safe Sanitation.* Online at http://www.who.int/news-room/detail/12-07-2017-2-1-billion-people-lack-safe-drinking-water-at-home-more-than-twice-as-many-lack-safe-sanitation (accessed October 3, 2018).

World Health Organization. 2018a. *Ten Facts on Malaria.* Online at http://www.who.int/features/factfiles/malaria/en (accessed January 9, 2019).

World Resources Institute. 2018. Online at http://www.wri.org/our-work/topics/climate. (accessed January 9, 2019).

World Trade Organization. 2018. Online at https://www.wto.org/english/tratop_e/region_e/regfac_e.htm (accessed April 18, 2018).

Wright, Lawrence. 2006. *The Looming Tower: Al Qaeda and the Road to 9/11.* New York: Vintage Books.

Wrong, Michela. 2002. *In the Footsteps of Mr. Kurtz: Living on the Brink of Disaster in Mobutu's Congo.* New York: Harper Perennial.

Wurzel, Rüdiger, and Connelly, James. 2012. *The European Union as a Leader in International Climate Change Politics.* New York: Routledge.

WWF. 2018. "Deforestation." Online at https://www.worldwildlife.org/threats/deforestation. (accessed February 29, 2018).

WWF. 2018a. "Species Threatened by Climate Change." Online at http://wwf.panda.org/about_our_earth/aboutcc/problems/impacts/species/ (accessed February 29, 2018).

Yan, Sophia. 2017. "Made in China" Isn't So Cheap Anymore, and That Could Spell Headache for Beijing. *CNBC.* Online at https://www.cnbc.com/2017/02/27/chinese-wages-rise-made-in-china-isnt-so-cheap-anymore.html (accessed January 9, 2019).

Yankelovich, Daniel. 2005. "Poll Positions." *Foreign Affairs* 84(5) September/October: 2–16.

Yanofsky, David. 2013. "Somali Piracy Was Reduced to Zero This Year." *Quartz.* December 27. Online at https://qz.com/161704/somali-piracy-was-reduced-to-zero-this-year (accessed January 9, 2019).

Yergin, Daniel, and Joseph Stanislaw. 1998. *The Commanding Heights: The Battle Between Government and the Marketplace That Is Remaking the Modern World.* New York: Free Press.

Young, Michael. 2010. "Development at Gunpoint? Why Civilians Must Reclaim Stabilization Aid." *Foreign Affairs.* December 19. Online at http://fam.ag/hqPHpb (accessed July 18, 2013).

Yue, Jianyoung. 2018. *China's Rise in the Age of Globalization: Myth or Reality?* New York: Palgrave.

Zahariadis, Nikolaos. 2008. *State Subsidies in the Global Economy.* New York: Palgrave Macmillan.

Zakaria, Fareed. 2008. *The Post-American World.* New York: W. W. Norton.

Zarin, Khurram. 2018. "Ten Deadliest Natural Disasters of 21st Century." *Scienceve.* Online at http://www.scienceve.com/10-deadliest-natural-disasters-of-21st-century (accessed July 28, 2018).

Zartman, William. 2018. "Kim Jong Un and the Art of the Asian Deal." *The Wall Street Journal.* June 24, Online at https://www.wsj.com/articles/kim-jong-un-and-the-art-of-the-asian-deal-1529862421 (accessed July 8, 2018).

Zaslavsky, Victor. 2004. *Class Cleansing: The Massacre at Katyn.* New York: Telos Press Publishing.

Zelikow, Philip, and Condoleezza Rice. 1995. *Germany Unified and Europe Transformed: A Study in Statecraft.* Cambridge, MA: Harvard University Press.

Zellen, Barry S. 2009. *Arctic Doom, Arctic Boom: The Geopolitics of Climate Change in the Arctic.* Westport, CT: Praeger.

Ziegler, Jean. 1981. *Switzerland Exposed*. New York: Schocken Books.

Zinn, Howard. 2002. *The Power of Nonviolence: Writings by Advocates of Peace*. Boston: Beacon Press.

Zizek, Slavoj. 2009. "Berlusconi in Tehran." *London Review of Books* 31(14), July 23: 3–7.

Zoellick, Robert. 2012. *Robert Zoellick on China 2030 Report: Transcript of Media Questions and Answers*. Beijing, China, February 27. Online at http://bit.ly/zHjAiy (accessed July 19, 2013).

Zubok, Vladislav. 2007. *A Failed Empire. The Soviet Union in the Cold War from Stalin to Gorbachev*. Chapel Hill: University of North Carolina Press.

Zubok, Vladislav. 2014. With His Back Against the Wall: Gorbachev, Soviet Demise, and German Reunification, *Cold War History*. 14 (4), 619–645.

Credits

Chapter 1 p. 1: ironwas / Shutterstock; p. 8: Camillo Cinelli via Shutterstock; p. 12: Abd. Halim Hadi / Shutterstock; p. 15: Evan Vucci / AP / Shutterstock; p. 17: Photo by Mario Tama / Getty Images; p. 22: Gabriel_Ramos; p. 24: Evan Lorne / Shutterstock.

Chapter 2 p. 37: Kyodo via AP Images; p. 42: Everett – Art / Shutterstock; p. 51: Bettmann/Getty Images; p. 53: Photo by Alfred Eisenstaedt / Pix Inc. / The LIFE Picture Collection / Getty Images; p. 56: Jia daitengfei - Imaginechina via AP Images; p. 57: Uncredited / AP / Shutterstock; p. 62: Korean Central News Agency / Korea News Service via AP Images; p. 66: Horst Faas / AP / Shutterstock; p. 69: imageBROKER/Shutterstock.

Chapter 3 p. 78: Greg Baker / Pool / EPA-EFE / Shutterstock; p. 82: bpk, Berlin / The Congress of Berlin (closing session), 1892 / Werner, Anton von (1843-1915) / Art Resource, NY; p. 85: Lee Lockwood / Time Life Pictures / Getty Images; p. 86: AP Photo / Ebrahim Noroozi; p. 91: North Wind Picture Archives via AP Images; p. 94: AP Photo / Bilal Hussein; p. 97: AP Photo / Themba Hadebe; p. 107: Bettmann / Getty Images; p. 112: Brais g Rouco / SOPA Images / Shutterstock.

Chapter 4 p. 116: Youssef Badawi / EPA-EFE / Shutterstock; p. 121: Albert Harlingue / Roger Viollet / Getty Images; p. 125: Bikas Das / AP / Shutterstock; p. 132: AP Photo / Sayyid Azim; p. 133: Christophe Ena / AP / Shutterstock; p. 151: AP Photo / Bill Allen.

Chapter 5 p. 155: AP Photo / RIA Novosti, Alexei Druzhinin, Presidential Press Service; p. 158: AP Photo / Farah Abdi Warsameh; p. 160: AP Photo / Sakchai Lalit; p. 161: SANA via AP, File; p. 170: Hani Mohammed / AP / Shutterstock; p. 173: STR / AFP / Getty Images; p. 176: Photo by Daniel Reinhardt / picture-alliance / dpa / AP Images;

p. 182: Photo By Tom Williams / CQ Roll Call via AP Images; p. 184: Bettman / Getty Images.

Chapter 6 p. 189: JIM HOLLANDER / EPA-EFE / Shutterstock; p. 193: AP Photo / Sakchai Lalit; p. 200: Interpol via AP; p. 207: Leemage / Getty Images; AP Photo / Abd Raouf, file; p. 209: AP Photo / Musa Sadulayev, File; p. 213: Korea Summit Press Pool via AP, File; p. 220: National Archives, courtesy of USHMM Photo Archives.

Chapter 7 p. 223: Jan Woitas / picture-alliance / dpa / AP Images; p. 227: AP Photo / Ahn Young-joon; p. 232: Klaus Ohlenschläger / picture-alliance / dpa / AP Images; p. 236: Bettmann / Getty Images; p. 240: AP Photo / Ben Curtis; p. 250: Photo by Mamunur Rashid / NurPhoto / Sipa USA (Sipa via AP Images); p. 252: CATHERINE HENRIETTE / AFP / Getty Images; p. 255: Qi shancheng – Imaginechina via AP Images.

Chapter 8 p. 258: gary yim / Shutterstock; p. 261: AP Photo / Raad Adayleh; p. 262: © Alexandra Boulat / VII / Redux; p. 268: AP Photo / Lefteris Pitarakis; p. 272: AP Photo / Ng Han Guan; p. 276: Liam Cleary / Shutterstock; p. 282: Terrence Spencer / Time Life Pictures / Getty Images; p. 288: Gorodenkoff / Shutterstock; p. 289: © Viktor Korotayev / Reuters; p. 292: AP Photo / Fernando Vergara.

Chapter 9 p. 298: Ricardo Maldonado Rozo / EPA-EFE / Shutterstock; p. 306: Alejandro Balan / picture-alliance / dpa / AP Images; p. 309: © Lunamarina | Dreamstime.com; p. 313: Danny Lawson / PA Wire URN:19761756 (Press Association via AP Images); p. 317: Kike Calvo via AP Images; p. 322: AP Photo / Keith Srakocic; p. 325: AP Photo / Mahesh Kumar A.; p. 331: Bodo Marks / picture-alliance / dpa / AP Images.

Chapter 10 p. 334: AP Photo / Bilal Hussein; p. 338: AP Photo / Tatan Syuflana, File; p. 339:

Index

Page numbers followed by *f, i, m,* or *t* indicate figures, illustrations, maps, or tables, respectively.